T0259796

Pro J2EE 1.4: From Professional to Expert

SUE SPIELMAN AND MEERAJ KUNNUMPURATH
WITH
NEIL ELLIS AND JAMES L. WEAVER

APress Media, LLC

Pro J2EE 1.4: From Professional to Expert

Originally published by Apress in 2004

ISBN 978-1-59059-340-0 ISBN 978-1-4302-0756-6 (eBook)
DOI 10.1007/978-1-4302-0756-6

Lead Editor: Steve Anglin
Technical Reviewers: Thomas Marrs and Matthew Moodie

Project Manager: Tracy Brown Collins
Copy Edit Manager: Nicole LeClerc
Copy Editor: Kim Wimpsett
Production Manager: Kari Brooks
Production Editor: Kelly Winquist
Compositor: Diana Van Winkle, Van Winkle Design Group
Proofreader: Nancy Sixsmith
Indexer: Bill Johncocks
Artist: Diana Van Winkle, Van Winkle Design Group
Cover Designer: Kurt Krames
Manufacturing Manager: Tom Debolski

The source code for this book is available to readers at `http://www.apress.com` in the Downloads section.

For Liz.

All of our knowledge, by definition, is fragmentary and tainted by our personal bias, filters, and individual prejudices. The known by its very nature is relative and therefore limited. If an absolute truth exists, it must be beyond the scope of knowledge. Become the Seeker of the absolute truth with an open heart.
—Sue Spielman

Contents at a Glance

Contents

Chapter 9 Building the Best Application You Can......459

Chapter 10 Using Session Beans......495

Chapter 15 Introducing Enterprise Java Web Services 695

About the Authors

Sue Spielman is the president and senior consulting engineer of Switchback Software (`http://www.switchbacksoftware.com`), a consulting firm that specializes in the architecture, design, and implementation of business and Web application development using the latest in J2EE and J2ME technologies. She is also the CEO/CTO of Mobilogics (`http://www.mobilogics.com`), a company focused on building software for the mobile data services market that utilizes LBS and geospatial technologies. Based in Denver, Colorado, she is a featured and sought-after speaker at technical conferences domestically and internationally. Sue is an author for Java.net, is a columnist for O'Reilly's OnJava.com, and has frequently been published in industry magazines including *Software Development*, *JavaPro*, *XML & Web Services Magazine*, and DevX.com. She's the author or coauthor of a number of Java-related books, including *The Struts Framework: Practical Guide for Java Programmers* (Morgan Kaufmann, 2002), *JSTL: Practical Guide for JSP Programmers* (Morgan Kaufmann, 2003), and *The Web Conferencing Book* (AMACOM, 2003). In addition to her development experience, Sue serves as a technical expert witness for domestic and international clients involved in multimillion-dollar lawsuits.

Meeraj Kunnumpurath has been using enterprise Java for more than four years. He's a Sun Certified Java Programmer and Web component developer. He also writes for popular Web sites and journals.

He loves football (as it's called outside the United States). He's a big fan of the Chelsea Football Club and hopes they win the premiership this season.

About the Contributing Authors

James L. Weaver is the chief scientist at Learning Assistant Technologies (http://www.lat-inc.com), a company that specializes in developing learner-centric tools. He's also the president of JMentor (http://www.jmentor.com), which is a Java mentoring, training, and consulting practice.

Neil Ellis is an independent J2EE consultant based in the UK.

About the Technical Reviewers

Tom Marrs, a 19-year veteran of the software industry, is the president and senior software architect at Vertical Slice, a consulting firm that designs and implements mission-critical business applications using the latest J2EE and open-source technologies, along with providing architecture evaluation and developer training and mentoring services.

Tom is the coauthor of *Developing J2EE Applications with JBoss* (O'Reilly, 2004), has been published in *Java Developers' Journal*, and has authored and/or coauthored technical training courses. Tom speaks regularly at software conferences and reviews best-selling technical books for major publishers.

An active participant in the local technical community, Tom has served as president and board member of award-winning user groups in the Denver metro area.

Matt Moodie enjoys a life of fun in Glasgow, Scotland. He's a keen novice gardener with a houseful of plants. He'd like to thank Laura for her love and friendship.

Acknowledgments

IT'S HARD TO IMAGINE the journey this book has taken. When I look back on it, I suppose it mimics life in general. It's been a generic roller coaster ride, with excitement, hard work, disappointment, accomplishment, discipline, joy, frustration, and commitment. I could go on, but you get the idea. I've have the great fortune of being able to say that this isn't the first time I've put myself through the publishing roller coaster, so you'd think I'd be prepared for the ride. Sometimes, even with all of our preparations, these preparations don't apply until you meet a new challenge head on and fearlessly. As always, many people behind the scenes take my techno-speak and geek diagrams and turn them into something much more than what they first were. Thanks to the technical reviewers who provided me great feedback: Thomas Marrs and Matthew Moodie. Also thanks to the Apress gang: Gary Cornell for sticking with the project, Steve Anglin for his patience, Tracy Brown Collins for keeping the ball rolling, Kim Wimpsett for her excellent copy editing, and Kelly Winquist for her production assistance.

As I've already said, this book was definitely on its own journey—like the never-ending journey of the lives we all live. I'd like to thank a few people who have come into my journey and moved me in unexpected ways; they may not even have been aware of it. Therein lies the beauty of the journey. You never know where it'll take you—just live moment to moment. These special people include Bill Lowe, Stephanie Perlowski, Sherrie Mitchell, Sally Ball, Robert Wheaton, Cindy Stone, and Mary Ahlbrandt. Thanks for coming into my path and a lotus flower to you all.

Thanks to my mom and dad, of course, who continue to teach me on a daily basis the unconditional love and support that actually defines the word *family*.

Finally, Elizabeth, thanks for your continuous understanding, undivided attention, patience, support, sense of humor, encouragement, and love. This is a person who knows more about Java development than any sane person (who isn't a developer, or even that technical, for that matter) ever should.

—Sue Spielman

I THANK TRACY BROWN COLLINS, Kim Wimpsett, Kelly Winquist, Steve Anglin, and Neil Ellis for helping me with the work I have done for this book.

I thank God for giving me this opportunity. For his pleasure, I would like to present one of his verses, which I believe was part of the divine revelation to the holy prophet (PBUH):

> *Virtue does not mean for you to turn your faces towards the East and West, but virtue means one should believe in God [Alone], the Last Day, angels, the Book and prophets; and no matter how he loves it, to give his wealth away to near relatives, orphans, the needy, the wayfarer and beggars, and towards freeing captives; and to keep up prayer and pay the welfare tax; and those who keep their word whenever they promise anything; and are patient under suffering and hardship and in time of violence. Those are the ones who act loyal and they perform their duty.*
>
> *—Quran (2:177)*

—Meeraj Kunnumpurath

CHAPTER 1

Introducing and Installing J2EE 1.4

SINCE THIS IS A BOOK for developers by developers, you'll get the most from it by running the examples and experimenting. This chapter helps you make sure you've properly installed the Java 2 Enterprise Edition (J2EE) 1.4 software development kit (SDK) and walks you through the steps of setting up the environment and writing a simple application. This is vital to ensuring that you don't encounter needless frustration as you work through the examples. You'll also get a taste of the essential steps of creating a J2EE application, what those steps do, and why you need them.

In this chapter, you'll learn the following:

- What the exact prerequisites for installing the J2EE 1.4 SDK are and how to configure your system to run enterprise Java applications

- How to construct a simple JSP application and how to deploy and run this application

Even if you already have your environment set up, it's probably a good idea to read through the development steps in this chapter, not only to ensure that your environment is set up correctly, but also to give you some essential insight into the fundamentals of building a J2EE application.

All of the installation files are available from the Sun Web site. Both the J2EE SDK and the Java 2 Standard Edition (J2SE) SDK (required to run the J2EE SDK) are freely available at `http://java.sun.com`. The uniform resource locator (URL) for J2EE SDK 1.4 is `http://java.sun.com/j2ee/1.4/`, and the URL for J2SE SDK 1.4 is `http://java.sun.com/j2se/1.4/`.

> **NOTE** *This chapter assumes you're running Windows 2000 Professional or XP Professional. The J2EE 1.4 SDK doesn't support earlier versions of Windows. The Sun Web site (*`http://java.sun.com/j2ee`*) has installation details of other supported operating systems (Solaris SPARC 8 and 9 and Red Hat Linux 7.2).*

Installing the J2EE 1.4 SDK

Installing the J2EE 1.4 SDK couldn't be much easier. The J2EE environment is based on the J2SE platform, so you need to install that before following the steps described in this chapter. You'll need to ensure that you've got the Java development kit (JDK) for J2SE 1.4 (or later) installed. If you've got an earlier JDK, you need to update it. If you're not certain which version of J2SE you have, you can try running the J2EE SDK 1.4 installation anyway. If you don't have the correct version of J2SE installed, you'll see a warning message, and you'll have to abort the installation. You should then install the correct version of the J2SE SDK and run the J2EE SDK installation again.

Alternatively, you can simply go to a command-line prompt and type **java -version** at the command prompt. The Java interpreter should print the version information:

```
> java -version
java version "1.4.0"
Java(TM) 2 Runtime Environment, Standard Edition (build 1.4.0-b92)
Java HotSpot(TM) Client VM (build 1.4.0-b92, mixed mode)
```

The version listed should be at least 1.4.0. If you get something other than what's shown, refer to Table 1-1.

Table 1-1. Troubleshooting Problems When Installing J2EE

PROBLEM	SOLUTION
Java version is earlier than 1.4.0.	Obtain and install the latest version of the J2SE SDK. You may want to uninstall the older version before installing the newer version. (You don't have to, but unless you have some compelling reason to keep it around, it's just dead weight).
`java -version` returns the message "'java' is not recognized as an internal or external command, operable program, or batch file."	The J2SE SDK isn't installed, or the `PATH` environment variable doesn't include the path to the Java executables. Check the `PATH`, and correct the problem, or reinstall the J2SE SDK.

Once you've done that, installing J2EE is a breeze—just run the installation program. The installation program will first check to make sure you've got the right version of the J2SE SDK. Then, make a note of where you're installing the J2EE SDK on your system—you'll need to know this path after the installation is complete in order to update and add some environment variables.

> **TIP** *The Windows operating system uses environment variables as shortcuts to selected directories on your system. You can set either user-specific environment variables or (provided you're logged in as a user with administrative rights) systemwide environment variables. Once you set an environment variable for your Java installation, you'll find it much quicker and easier to compile and run your Java applications from the command line, as you'll see shortly.*

Once the installation is complete, it's time to set up the environment variables you'll need to run the examples in this book. You can check and set these from the System Properties. From the Control Panel, choose the System applet. Select the Advanced tab, and click the Environment Variables button (see Figure 1-1).

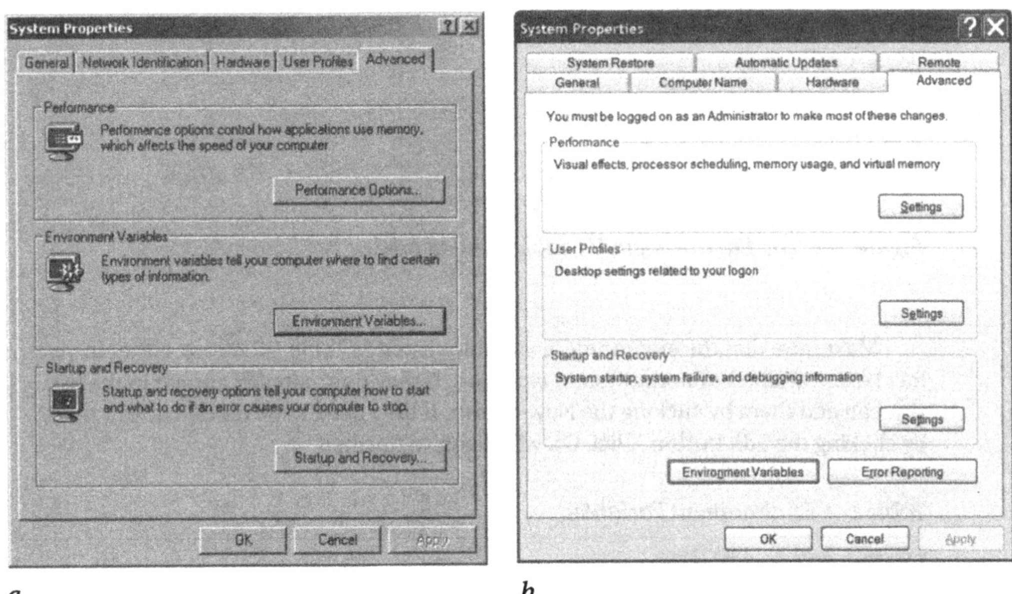

a. *b.*

Figure 1-1. The Advanced tab of System Properties in Windows 2000 (left) and Windows XP (right)

When you click the Environment Variables button, a dialog box will allow you to check and set the values for environment variables (see Figure 1-2).

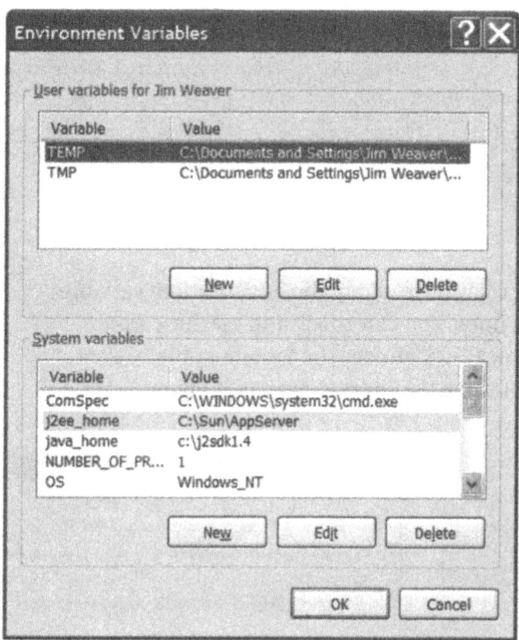

Figure 1-2. The Environment Variables dialog box

Make sure that the environment variables listed in Table 1-2 are set either in your local user variables or in the system variables. If they don't already appear in the list, you can add them by clicking the New button. If they need to be modified, edit them by clicking the Edit button. Click OK when you've finished.

Table 1-2. Environment Variables

VARIABLE NAME	SETTINGS
`JAVA_HOME`	Contains the path to the directory where J2SE is installed (for example, `c:\j2sdk1.4`).
`J2EE_HOME`	Contains the path to the directory where the J2EE SDK is installed (for example, `c:\Sun\AppServer`).
`PATH`	This should include the path to the `bin` directories of the J2SE SDK and the J2EE SDK (for example, `c:\j2sdk1.4\bin;c:\Sun\AppServer\bin;...`). You can alternatively use the `JAVA_HOME` and `J2EE_HOME` environment variables in your path to make things a little simpler (for example, `%JAVA_HOME%\bin;%J2EE_HOME%\bin;...`). Note that the system will search through for executable files using the `PATH` variable, starting with the directories that appear first in the path. To ensure that there aren't other versions of the J2SE or J2EE interfering on this machine, make sure these new entries go at the front of the `PATH` variable.

You'll also want to download the free J2EE SDK 1.4 documentation at `http://java.sun.com/j2ee/1.4/docs/`.

Testing the J2EE 1.4 SDK Installation

If everything went according to plan, your system should be set up and ready to use, so the following sections walk through some quick tests to ensure that you're ready to run the code in this book.

Starting the J2EE Server

The next step to verifying that your installation is working correctly is to start the J2EE server. You launch the server from menus that are automatically created during installation, so choose the following option from the Start menu: All Programs ➤ Sun Microsystems ➤ J2EE 1.4 SDK ➤ Start Default Domain.

A command window will open with messages similar to the following, the last one prompting you to press any key to continue:

```
Starting Domain domain1, please wait.
Log redirected to C:\Sun\AppServer\domains\domain1\logs\server.log.
Domain domain1 started.
Press any key to continue . . .
```

At this point the J2EE server is started. Go ahead and press any key as requested, open a browser, and go to `http://localhost:8080`. The Web browser should display the default J2EE Web page (see Figure 1-3).

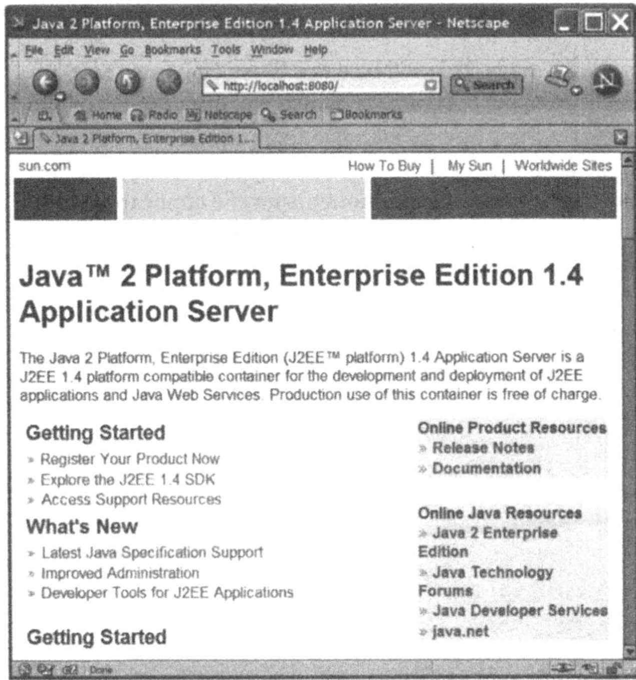

Figure 1-3. The default J2EE Web page

If you have any problems accessing this Web page, refer to Table 1-3.

Table 1-3. Troubleshooting Problems When Running J2EE

PROBLEM	SOLUTION
The Web browser reports "Page cannot be displayed" when trying to open the URL `http://localhost:8080`.	Make certain there weren't any errors reported when starting the J2EE server. If you see messages indicating that the server couldn't start because TCP ports were in use by other processes, you may either have another Web server using port 8080 or have another instance of the J2EE server running. Also, make certain that you've specified the port 8080 in the URL (this is the default port used by the J2EE server).

Pat yourself on the back for a job well done. Now you'll shred a little code for a final test.

Compiling and Deploying "Hello World"

As a final test, you'll walk through the process of creating and deploying a JavaServer Pages (JSP) file. This will make certain that the J2EE server is working properly first and give you your first taste of building, deploying, and testing a J2EE application.

This consists of the following steps:

1. Create a working directory. This will give you a sandbox for creating the application files and editing them.

2. Create a text file for the JSP page. This will be a text file of Hypertext Markup Language (HTML) with snippets of Java code, which will be compiled by the J2EE server into a servlet.

3. Using the Deploytool utility, select the components for the application and package them into a Web archive (WAR). The WAR is a `.jar` file that bundles all the application components into a single file for easy deployment.

4. Verify the contents of the WAR. Deploytool has a utility that will test the contents of the WAR to catch problems before it's distributed.

5. Distribute the WAR to the J2EE server. Once this is done, the application is available and ready to be run.

6. Test the application.

So, you'll now get started!

Creating "Hello World"

To get started building a JSP page, follow these steps:

1. Create a directory on your machine that will be your sandbox for this exercise. For this example, we'll use `C:\3405\Ch01`.

2. Create a new file in that directory called `index.jsp` using your favorite text editor. Here's the code for that file:

```
<%--
    file: index.jsp
    desc: Test installation of J2EE SDK 1.4
--%>
<html>
<head>
  <title>Hello World - test the J2EE SDK installation
  </title>
</head>
<body>
<%
  for (int i = 1; i < 5; i++)
  {
%>
   <h<%=i%>>Hello World</h<%=i%>>
<%
  }
%>
</body>
</html>
```

3. Start the J2EE server if it's not already running by following the instructions given previously.

4. Start the J2EE Deploytool application that comes with the J2EE SDK. This tool is a utility that's used to assemble application components into distributable archives and also to distribute the application to the J2EE server. You can invoke this tool by selecting Start ➤ All Programs ➤ Sun Microsystems ➤ J2EE 1.4 SDK ➤ Deploytool. When Deploytool has finished initializing, you'll see its main window (see Figure 1-4).

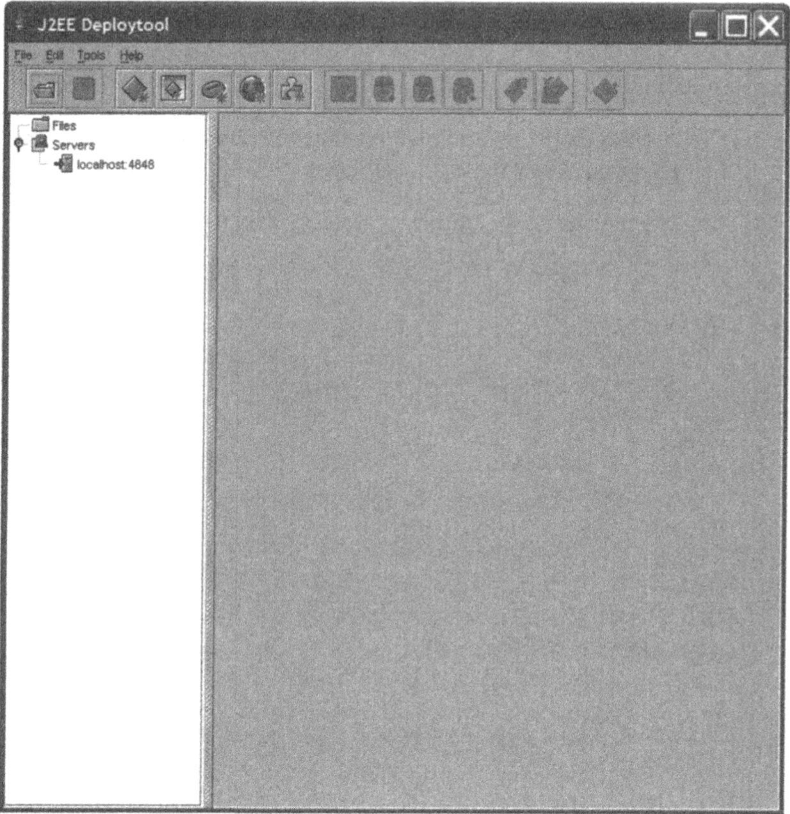

Figure 1-4. Deploytool

5. You need to create a new WAR, which will contain the Web components of the J2EE application, along with a descriptor or "table of contents" that describes what's in the archive. Web applications frequently consist of many more files than this simple application, and the WAR is a convenient means of bundling all of those files into a single file for deployment. Select File ➤ New ➤ Web Component from the menu. This will start the New Web Application Wizard (see Figure 1-5).

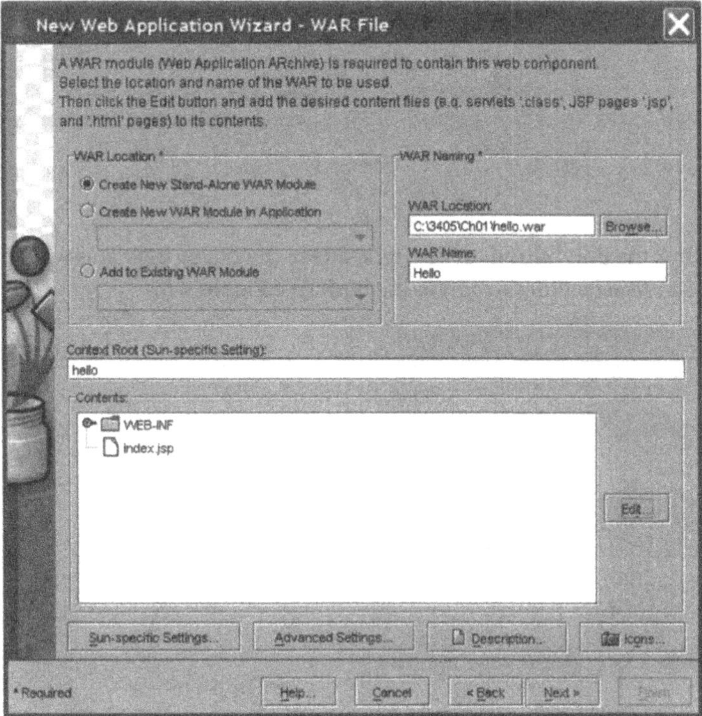

Figure 1-5. New Web Application Wizard

6. On the WAR File page of this wizard, shown in Figure 1-5, do the following:

   - Make certain that the Create New Stand-Alone WAR Module radio button is checked.

   - In the WAR Location text field, enter (or browse to) the path to your working directory, followed by `hello.war` (in our case, `C:\3405\Ch01\hello.war`). This tells Deploytool what to name the WAR file.

   - Enter **Hello** in the WAR Name field, which is the name that will display in Deploytool for this WAR file.

   - Enter **hello** in the Context Root field. This sets what's called the *context root* (which is like a home base) for your WAR file when it's deployed to the server.

> **TIP** *You can think of the context root as a logical directory that's part of the URL. For example, a hypothetical Web application located at* `www.apress.com/codesamples/index.jsp` *has a root context of* `codesamples`. *Note that this doesn't necessarily correspond to a directory on the server called* `codesamples`*—it's a name that the server recognizes and maps to a specific application.*

7. Next, click the Edit button on the right side of the dialog box. This will open a dialog box to select files to add to the WAR (see Figure 1-6).

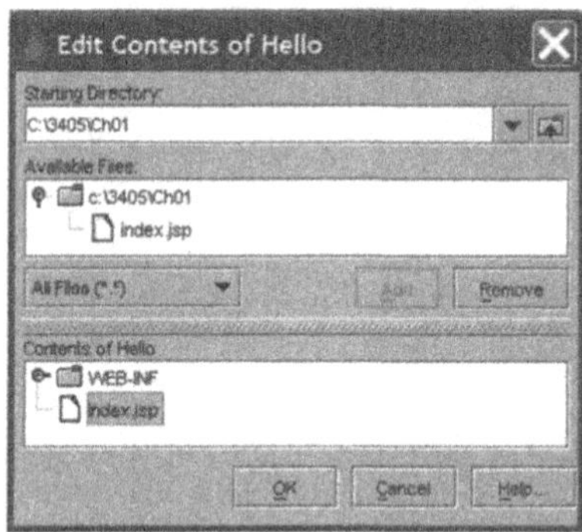

Figure 1-6. Adding files to the WAR

8. In the dialog box shown in Figure 1-6, set the starting directory (using the top textbox) to your working directory. This simply points the dialog box to where your application files are. You should see a folder tree with `index.jsp` appear below your working directory folder. Select `index.jsp`, and click the Add button. You should now see `index.jsp` in the contents tree at the bottom of the dialog box. Click the OK button to close this dialog box. Click the Next button to go to the next page of the wizard (see Figure 1-7).

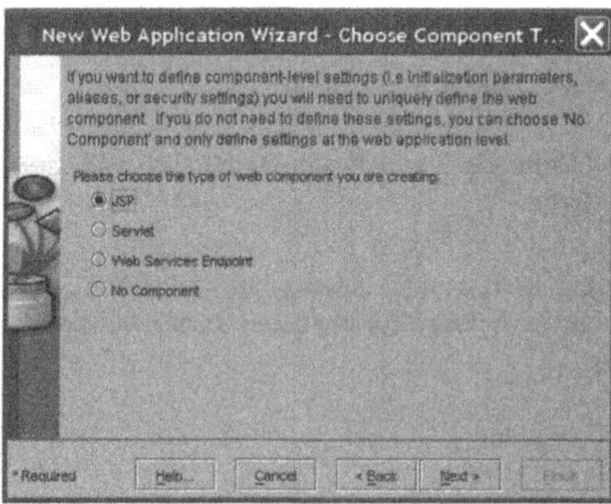

Figure 1-7. Creating components

9. J2EE has several different kinds of components. This particular application includes a JSP component, and this is where you tell Deploytool what kind of component you're building. Select the JSP radio button to indicate that you're creating a JSP component. Click the Next button to go to the next page of the wizard (see Figure 1-8).

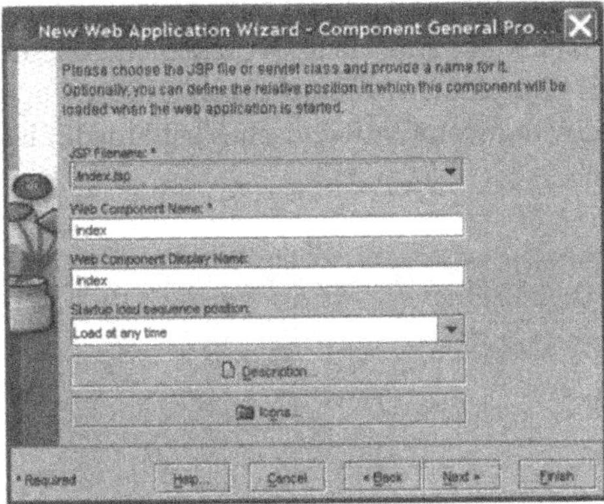

Figure 1-8. Choosing the JSP page

10. Select /index.jsp from the JSP Filename drop-down list. Verify that the other fields appear as shown in Figure 1-8. Click Finish to see the WAR properties (see Figure 1-9).

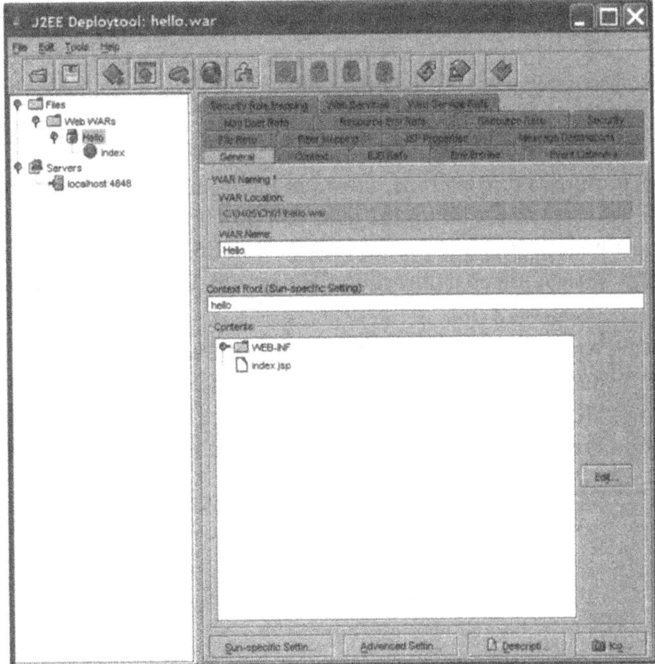

Figure 1-9. WAR properties

11. Deploytool's tree navigator now displays the WAR you just created and its contents. Save your work now. With the Hello WAR highlighted in the tree on the left, select File ➤ Save All.

12. The next step is to verify the WAR. This step will catch problems with bad code in the JSP page and make sure that the WAR doesn't have obvious problems before you deploy it to the server. Make sure Hello WAR is still highlighted, and select Tools ➤ Verify J2EE Compliance from the menu. This will open a window that will help you verify that your WAR complies with the J2EE specification (see Figure 1-10).

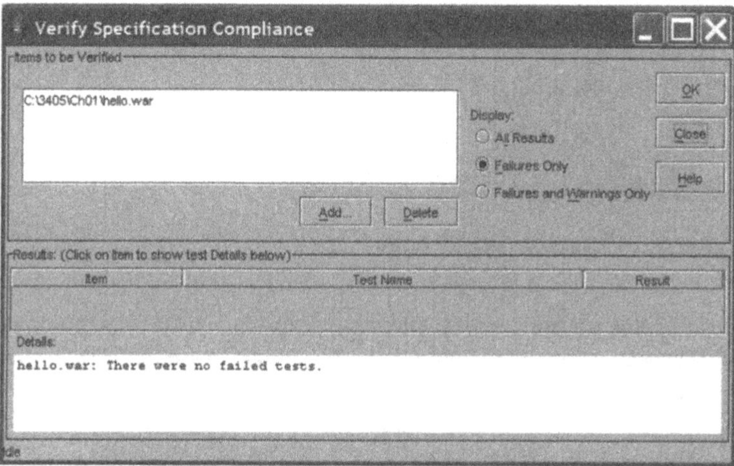

Figure 1-10. Verifying your WAR compliance to the J2EE specification

13. The Display group of radio buttons, shown in Figure 1-10, lets you select how much detail you care to see about the tests you run. If you want to see only messages about failures, select the Failures Only radio button (try not to take it personally—it's not the best phrasing in the world). Click the OK button.

14. If all goes well, you should see a message at the bottom indicating that no tests failed. If your JSP file had problems with its code, you'll get compilation error messages. If you see compilation errors, go back to your JSP file and check it carefully to make sure it matches the code in the book.

15. You're almost done. Next, you need to deploy the WAR to the J2EE server, so click the Close button. With Hello WAR selected in the tree navigator, select Tools ➤ Deploy from the menu. This will open the Deploy Module dialog box (see Figure 1-11).

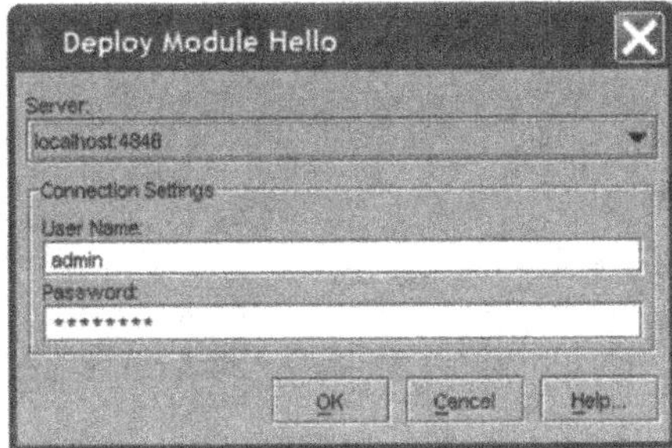

Figure 1-11. The Deploy Module dialog box

16. You'll supply the username and password you specified when installing J2EE SDK 1.4. Click OK, and when the dialog box closes, a window will appear and show the status of the deployment process (see Figure 1-12).

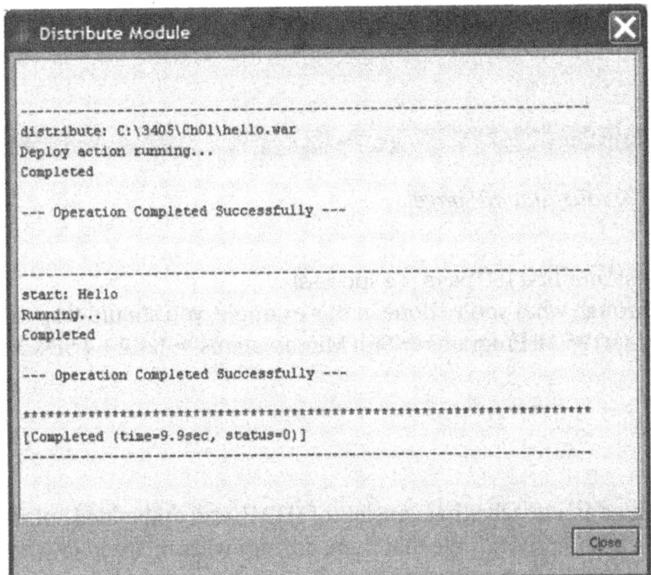

Figure 1-12. Checking the status

17. Wait until you see the "Completed" message, and click Close.

18. It's time to test your first JSP file. Start a Web browser, and go to `http://localhost:8080/hello`. After a couple of seconds, you should see your first JSP page (see Figure 1-13).

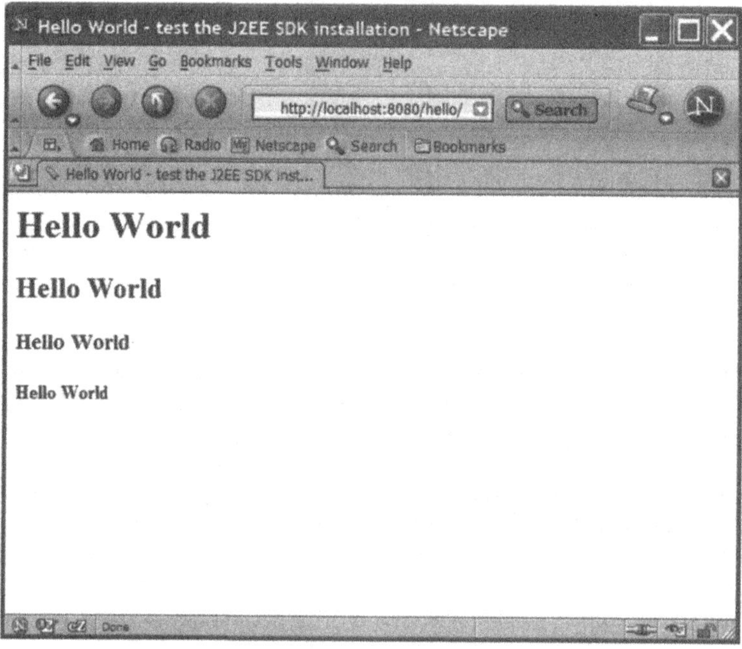

Figure 1-13. Your first JSP page

Congratulations! Your first JSP page is a success!

Before going through what you've done in this example, you should stop the J2EE server by selecting Start ➤ All Programs ➤ Sun Microsystems ➤ J2EE 1.4 SDK ➤ Stop Default Domain.

How It Works

The JSP file you created is a text file that consists of HTML and embedded snippets of code (see Listing 1-1). Notice in this file that there are tags with enclosed Java code.

Listing 1-1. `index.jsp`

```
<%--
    file: index.jsp
    desc: Test installation of J2EE SDK 1.4
--%>
<html>
<head>
  <title>Hello World - test the J2EE SDK installation
  </title>
</head>
<body>
<%
  for (int i = 1; i < 5; i++)
  {
%>
   <h<%=i%>>Hello World</h<%=i%>>
<%
  }
%>
</body>
</html>
```

When the JSP file is compiled into a servlet, that servlet code expands the JSP file's code snippets and HTML into code that writes HTML to an output stream (see Listing 1-2).

Listing 1-2. Generated Servlet Code

```
out.write("\n\n");
out.write("<html>\n");
out.write("<head>\n");
out.write("  <title>Hello World - test the J2EE SDK installation");
out.write("  </title>\n");
out.write("</head>\n");
out.write("<body>\n");
for (int i = 1; i < 5; i++)
{
  out.write("\n   ");
  out.write("<h");
  out.write(String.valueOf(i));
  out.write(">Hello World");
  out.write("</h");
  out.write(String.valueOf(i));
  out.write(">\n");
}
out.write("</body>\n");
out.write("</html>\n");
```

That code, when executed, will write the HTML code in Listing 1-3 to the stream that's sent back to the requesting browser.

Listing 1-3. The "Hello World" HTML

```
<html>
<head>
  <title>Hello Hello World - test the J2EE SDK installation
  </title>
</head>
<body>

   <h1>Hello World</h1>

   <h2>Hello World</h2>

   <h3>Hello World</h3>

   <h4>Hello World</h4>

</body>
</html>
```

That's how the JSP code works. The process of packaging and deploying has a few more steps: To deploy a J2EE application to a server, it has to be bundled into an archive—that's a single file that packages all the requisite files. The WAR has to contain the components that you've created for the application (the JSP file), as well other support files. Those support files include a deployment descriptor that tells the server what's contained in the WAR and how to run it, a manifest for the archive (which is an application's table of contents), and a file containing deployment information specific to the J2EE reference implementation server (see Figure 1-14).

Once you've assembled those contents into a WAR file, you can then deploy that WAR to the J2EE server. That process sends the archive to the server, which then reads the deployment descriptor to determine how to unbundle the contents. In the case of this application, it sees that the WAR contains a JSP file, so it compiles that JSP file into a servlet.

To run the application once it's deployed, you have to request the JSP file by requesting an URL with your Web browser (see Figure 1-15). Notice that the URL consists of the protocol (`http`), the server name (`localhost`), the root context of the application (`hello`), and the requested resource (`index.jsp`).

The server receives the incoming Hypertext Transfer Protocol (HTTP) request and uses the deployment information to invoke the appropriate servlet in a servlet container. The servlet writes HTML to an output stream, which is returned to the Web browser by the server.

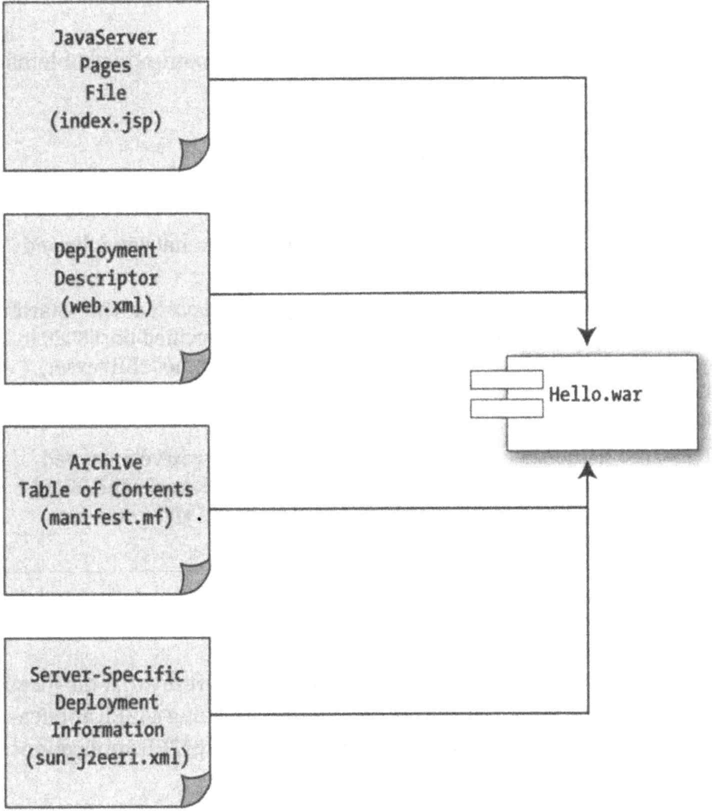

Figure 1-14. Support files

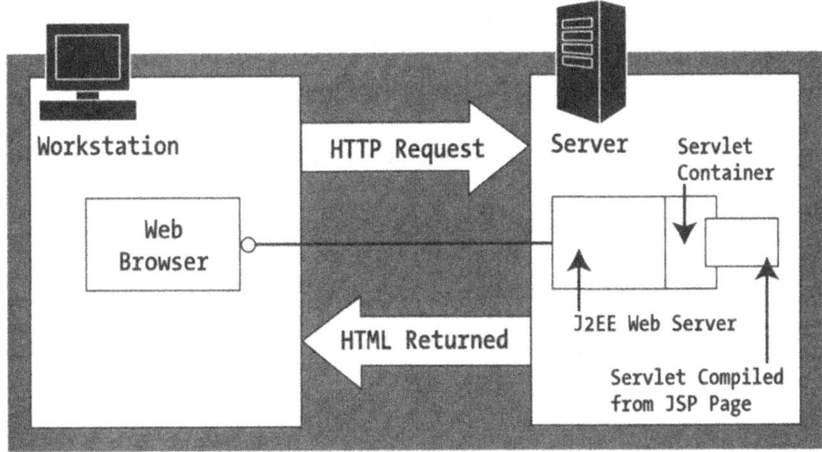

Figure 1-15. The request and response

Problems and Solutions

If you run into any difficulties, refer to Table 1-4, which lists some common problems and how to fix them.

Table 1-4. Troubleshooting Problems When Deploying

PROBLEM	SOLUTION
Verifier reports errors.	Carefully retrace your steps, and ensure that you followed the steps as described.
When testing the JSP file, the Web browser reports "Page cannot be displayed" when trying to open the URL `http://localhost:8080`.	Make certain there weren't any errors reported when starting the J2EE server. Make certain you've specified port 8080 in the URL (this is the default port used by the J2EE server).
When testing the JSP file, it reports a compilation error in the Web browser.	Double-check the code in `index.jsp`. If you've mistyped something, the server won't be able to compile the JSP file. The message in the Web browser should give you a hint where to look.

Summary

This chapter described how to get the J2EE SDK installed and how to verify that the installation was successful. You also got your first taste of creating and running a J2EE application, and you looked at some of the core concepts involved in building J2EE applications:

- JSP pages consist of HTML, with embedded snippets of Java code. The JSP file is compiled into a servlet by the J2EE server, which, when executed, emits HTML back to the requesting client.

- WARs are deployment components that contain the Web components of a J2EE application. The WAR contains the components themselves (such as JSP files) and the deployment descriptor that defines the contents of the WAR. The WAR can also contain server-specific deployment information.

At this point in the book, you should now be familiar with the following procedures:

- How to install and configure the J2EE environment

- How to start and stop the J2EE server

- How to start Deploytool

- The essential steps of building a J2EE application:
  - Creating the application components
  - Bundling the components into an archive
  - Verifying the contents of the archive to catch problems before deploying
  - Distributing the archive to the J2EE server
  - Testing the application

If you've been able to get through this exercise, you're more than ready to dive into more detail. Chapter 3 takes you deeper into the details of JSP pages—you'll learn the essential structure of JSP files and how to enable users to interact with them. Before that, in Chapter 2, you'll look at Web applications, of which JSP pages are a part.

CHAPTER 2

Understanding Web Applications

WEB ARCHITECTURE is a broad term. If you take each of the words at face value, then the words *web* and *architecture* seem to be diametrically opposed to one another. The definition of *web* from the *American Heritage Dictionary* is "something intricately constructed, especially something that ensnarls and entangles"; *architecture* means "a style and method of design and construction." While many a software system has been designed and constructed that can be described only as an entanglement, this chapter will help you understand what *Web architecture* really means.

The complexity of the systems we build to solve problems has been growing dramatically over the last few years. Good architecture takes a problem and tries to express the simplest solution possible to solve it. In case you haven't noticed, it's frequently much harder to architect and design an elegant, simple solution than it is to provide the fastest solution.

In this chapter, you'll examine a number of areas that play a role in creating good Web architectures. They include the following:

- Having a thorough understanding of the technologies that make up Web components
- Applying appropriate design patterns
- Taking containers into consideration
- Dealing with the appropriate protocols
- Defining your application structure
- Employing naming conventions
- Using deployment descriptors
- Interacting with the data source
- Considering portability and performance concerns

You'll explore each of these areas so that you have a solid foundation to approach your Web application development. Keep in mind that some of the components we'll talk about in this chapter are covered in more detail in subsequent chapters. Before getting to all that, though, it's important to have a basic understanding of the tiers that form the Java 2 Enterprise Edition (J2EE) architecture.

Introducing *N*-Tier Structure

As shown in Figure 2-1, you'll typically use a four-tier model when dealing with J2EE applications.

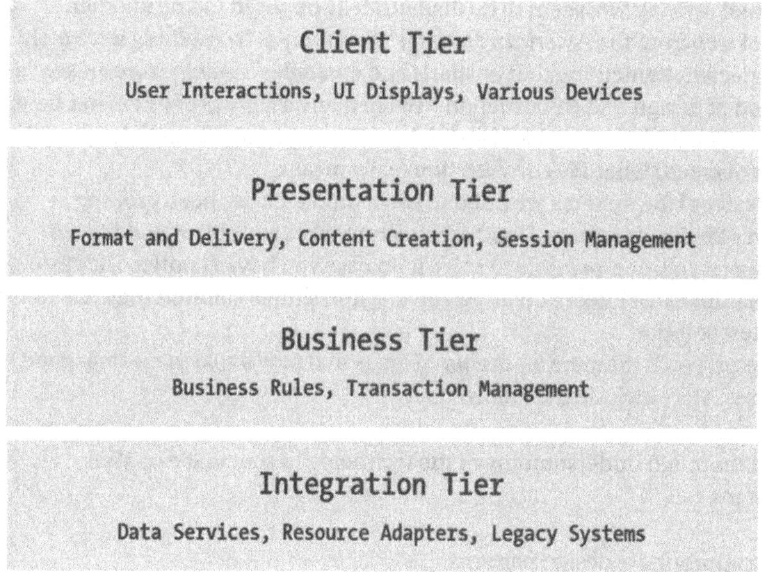

Figure 2-1. Four-tier model for J2EE applications

The *client tier* handles the devices that access the system or the Web application. This is usually where the user interface (UI) takes place and is displayed. Examples of components in this tier are the Web browser, Java applets, and devices such as personal digital assistants (PDAs) and mobile devices.

The *presentation tier* is where the presentation logic is handled; it's the logic that services requests coming from the client tier. Many client service functions can be handled in the presentation tier: managing sessions, providing sign-on capabilities, and providing the access to the business services, as well as preparing and delivering the response to the client tier. You'll learn about the presentation tier components in great detail, but for now, suffice it to say that the components contained in this tier include JavaServer Pages (JSP) and servlets. An important point to drive home early is that JSP pages and servlets aren't UI components. While it's true that JSP pages and servlets produce user interfaces, they're not considered UI elements themselves. This is a subtle but important difference that will come up again when we talk about best practices and applying design patterns.

The *business tier* is where all of the business services that are required, or provided, by the application live. Business logic (and sometimes business data) can be present in this tier. This tier handles the meat and potatoes of your application logic. Business rules and requirements are usually implemented within this tier, as is transaction management. You can use various technologies in the business tier, among them Enterprise JavaBeans (EJBs) and JavaBeans. Refer to Chapters 10–13 for complete details on dealing with EJBs.

The *integration tier* (sometimes also called the *enterprise information system [EIS] tier*) deals with external resources. These may be legacy applications or various data stores that are required by the application. There's usually a relatively tight coupling between the integration tier and the business tier. When data or services are required, the business logic will use the integration tier to access them. This is where you usually see Java Database Connectivity (JDBC) components being used. You can see the tight coupling when using components such as entity or message beans in the business tier that also may have access to the data. We should point out that there are many other backend data sources. These include mainframe, customer relationship management (CRM), enterprise resource planning (ERP) that's accessed with Java Connector Architecture (JCA), messaging systems that can be accessed with Java Message Service (JMS), and CORBA systems that can be accessed with Remote Method Invocation/ Internet Inter-ORB Protocol (RMI/IIOP).

The *resource tier* contains the actual data stores used by an application. This tier also includes external systems and legacy systems that may be required. The difference between the resource tier and the integration tier is that the resource tier is the actual data store, and the integration tier is what has to go on to access that data store. We really won't spend too much time on the resource tier in this book.

With this understanding of how the various tiers fit into place in J2EE applications, you'll continue by looking specifically at some of the components and technologies used within the presentation tier, since this is the tier primarily concerned with Web application components. When dealing with Web applications, you're dealing with two basic kinds of content. The first is dynamic content, and the second is static content. You should make sure you understand the difference.

Dynamic vs. Static Content

While this may be a review for some, we'll explain the difference between dynamic content and static content from the get-go. Dynamic content is content that's generated based on program parameters, Hypertext Transfer Protocol (HTTP) requests and responses, database queries, transformations, and possibly remote procedure calls. In other words, dynamic content changes based on the needs of the current situation.

Static content, on the other hand, is...well...static. Regardless of what else is happening in the application, the output produced for the consumer is the same. This is your typical Hypertext Markup Language (HTML) that contains nothing more than HTML. As you can see, the processing of information to produce dynamic content is where everything interesting in application development lies.

Not all Web sites need dynamic content; many content-based sites don't require user-specific actions or database results. They just display information. However, many other sites—and these days, this may be most sites—need to work with data in some way. *Work with data* could mean something as simple as using a cookie that allows users to customize the pages they see, or it could be something as complex as taking orders and processing payment information in some secure way. Using dynamic content also allows for content to be specific to the consumer of that information, whether a Web browser, a PDA, or some other type of mobile device.

To summarize, using dynamic content does the following:

- Allows for a personalized experience
- Provides content based on user requests
- Provides the right information at the right time
- Allows for display of that content as appropriate for that consumer

Understanding Web Components

J2EE makes a vast array of technologies available; sometimes it becomes difficult to know when to use a technology. From an architectural or application point of view, you want to make sure you pick the appropriate technology for the tier with which you're working. It's very easy (and common) to use a technology past the point of where you should draw the tier line. This is a common situation because, once a development team has used and is comfortable with a technology, they want to drain every last drop out of it that they can. This is understandable since the more familiar you are with a technology, the faster you'll see a result from working with it. This boils down to a matter of productivity. However, this isn't always the best result. It's important, if not critical, to understand from the beginning that Web application architecture clearly defines the tier definitions.

An easy way to put Web components into perspective is to focus on those components that are part of a Web container, as shown in Figure 2-2. As we continue, you'll see where the line between tiers is (or should be correctly drawn). The Web components should be those involved with receiving a request and creating a response to the client, whatever that client may be.

For now, you'll focus on the components managed in the Web containers, starting with JSP and then looking at servlets and some of the components available for use with them. Keep in mind that this is just an introduction to these technologies.

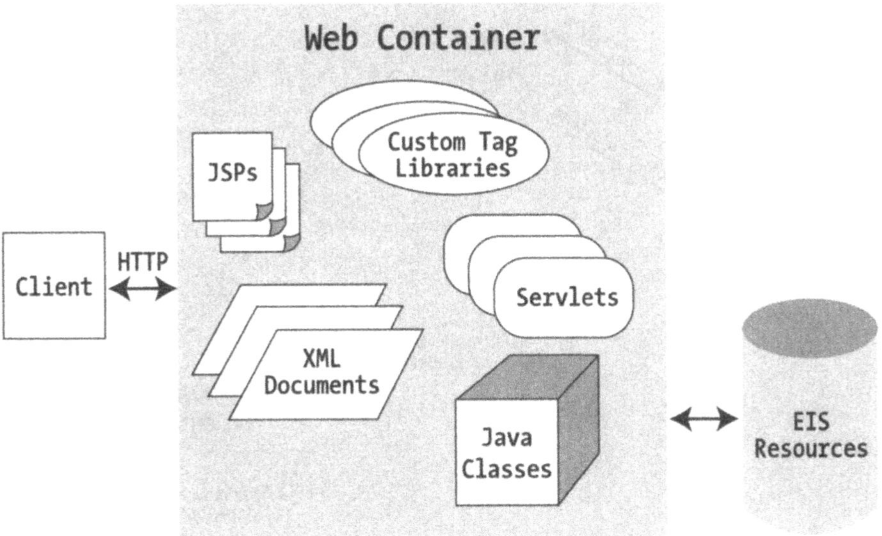

Figure 2-2. Web container boundaries

Servlets

Servlets provide a programmatic way for creating dynamic and structured data. Servlets run inside a Java virtual machine (JVM) and are generic server extensions that can be dynamically loaded when needed by the Web server. Their advantage over earlier server-side technologies, such as Common Gateway Interface (CGI) and FastCGI, is that threads within the Web server handle servlets. This is a much more efficient approach than having separate processes and allows for better scalability in an application. Being written in Java, servlets are portable between operating systems (OSs) as well as between Web servers that support servlets. Servlet technology is part of the `javax` packages.

Many Web servers and add-on servlet engines are available from vendors. You can check your favorite Web server's site and see what's currently available. Since all servlet engines aren't created equal, make sure to investigate what application programming interfaces (APIs) from the Servlet specification are included and that they meet the needs of your application.

Being written in Java, servlets are able to take full advantage of all of the Java APIs. Since there's no process spawning with servlets, servlet invocation is extremely fast—except for the performance hit the first time the servlet is loaded. A servlet will stay in memory once it's loaded, allowing for state management of other resources such as database connections. Figure 2-3 shows the servlet model.

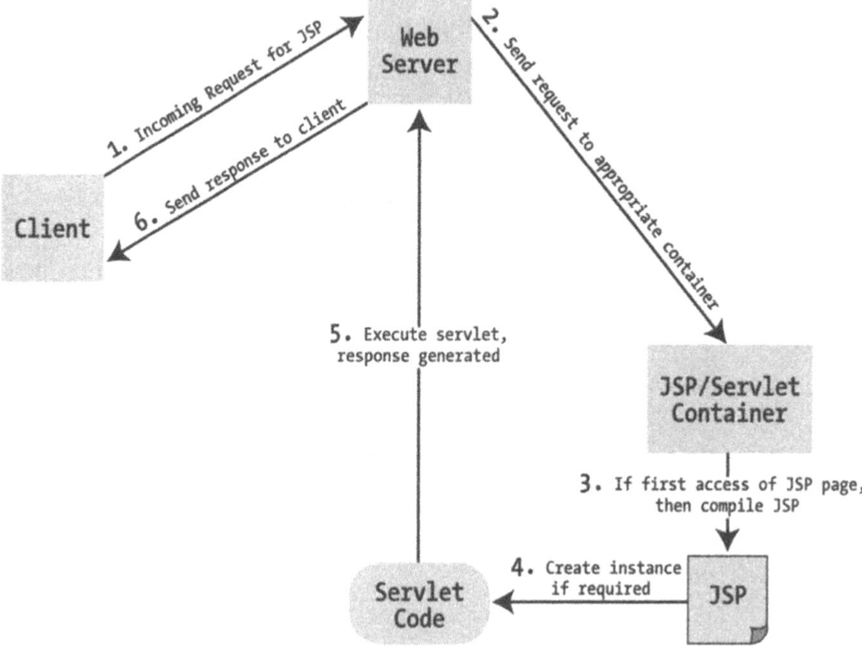

Figure 2-3. Servlet model

The Servlet 2.4 specification includes, among other things, application lifecycle events, a filtering mechanism, internationalization support, extensible deployment descriptors, new APIs for `ServletRequestListener` and `ServletRequestAttributeListener`, and listener exception handling. Chapter 6 covers more on this, but in this chapter you'll take a quick look at some of the key components available when using servlets and when to use them in Web application development. Since JSP technology is based on Servlet technology, we'll answer the obvious question first.

Filters

Filters are a feature of the Java servlet platform that was introduced in the Servlet 2.3 specification. They were designed to make it easy to write components that could be used transparently in a Web application.

> **NOTE** *A* filter *is a mini-servlet. It plugs into the request handling process and executes in addition to the normal page processing.*

A key distinction (which is what makes them more like mini-servlets) is that a filter doesn't generate its own content. Filters may record information about requests, convert content to a different format, or even redirect access to a different page. You can apply filters to any resources served by a servlet engine, so it doesn't matter whether it's static HTML, graphics, a JSP page, or another servlet. One of the key advantages of using a filter is that it can be added to an existing Web application without either the filter or the application being aware of one another. You can use filters for the following purposes:

- Data compression of responses
- Preprocessing of HTTP requests
- Session validation
- Request or response logging

It's certainly possible to do any of these tasks within a servlet; however, the following are a couple of advantages in doing the generic Web application tasks in filters:

- You can use a filter to separate logic from a specific servlet. This allows you to easily reuse the filters. A filter is basically allowing for a reusable component model.
- It's possible to use filters in any Web application that needs the functionality provided in the filter. If there's static content that's generic, you can incorporate the access to that content into a filter.

Filters are defined in the `web.xml` file, similar to the way a servlet is defined. For example, you may define a validation filter to check if a user has a valid session. For example:

```
<filter>
  <filter-name>Session Validation</filter-name>
  <filter-class>apress.SessionValidateFilter</filter-class>
  <description>
    This filter can be used to check if a user has a valid session
  </description>
</filter>
```

Chapter 7 goes into the complete details of defining, building, and configuring a filter, but this should give you an idea of how useful they can be for Web application development.

Web Event Listeners

Web event listeners allow applications to track key events that may take place within the Web application. Tracking events allows Web applications to handle event-driven situations in a concise manner because the code can be written more efficiently for use in the Web application to manage resources. If you write your event listeners generically enough, they can have the same reusability as filters. The following three levels of servlet events are possible in the Servlet 2.4 specification:

- **Servlet context (application-level) event**: This involves resources or state held at the level of the JVM in which the application is running and is therefore associated with the `ServletContext` object.

- **Session-level event**: This involves resources or state associated with the series of requests from a single user session and is therefore associated with the `HttpSession` object.

- **Request-level event**: This involves managing state across servlet requests.

At each of these three levels, the following two event categories exist:

- **Lifecycle changes**: This event level has to do with events such as the creation of `ServletContext`, shutdown of the servlet, session creation and timeouts, and request processing.

- **Attribute changes**: This event level deals with attributes in the particular event level such as an attribute being added, removed, or replaced in the appropriate event object.

Session-level events also include session migration and object binding.

You can create one or more event listener classes for each event category. A single listener class can monitor multiple event categories, or multiple listener classes may be listening to each event type. It's possible to specify the order in which the container invokes the listener for each event type. Chapter 7 covers all of the details on how to create, build, and deploy Web event listeners.

To put how you may use a Web event listener in your Web application into perspective, you'll now look at a quick example. Say you want to be notified when a user's session times out. To do this you could have an `HttpSessionListener` configured in your `web.xml` deployment descriptor like so:

```
<web-app>
  ...
  <listener>
    <listener-class>apress.servlet.listeners.SessionManager</listener-class>
  </listener>
  ...
</web-app>
```

Using the `<listener>` elements under the top-level `<web-app>` element, each listener has its `<listener-class>` subelement that specifies the class name. You should specify event listeners in the order in which you'd like them to be invoked when the application runs.

When a session is invalidated by the Web container making a call to the `invalidate()` method, the `SessionManager` class will be notified, and you can do any appropriate cleanup within your application. The listener would be notified of the following:

- The listener is notified when an `HttpSession` is created and keeps track of all active sessions.
- The listener is notified when the `HttpSession` object times out and the session is removed from the Web application.

The listener may then perform the following action:

- The listener logs a message to the servlet log that the session has timed out.

Servlets and Web Services

Here's a thought for you: If you enter **Java** as a keyword in a Google search, you'll get back roughly 3.9 million hits, give or take a few hundred thousand. Enter **Web services**, and you get back 6.6 million. That makes the term quite the buzzword. Although you should note that before the *Web services* buzzword came into being, it was called a lot of other things and can be dated back to 1975. How retro.

We've had Electronic Data Interchange (EDI), Common Object Request Broker Architecture (CORBA), then Distributed Component Object Model (DCOM), Unix Remote Procedure Call (RPC), and Java Remote Method Invocation (RMI). Each of those technologies failed to gain significant market share or enough momentum to succeed doing basically what Web services are trying to do. There are hundreds of definitions now of what really a Web service is, but the most basic way to explain it is that a Web service is one application that can talk to another application using Simple Object Access Protocol (SOAP).

The standard protocol that has emerged on the Web service front is SOAP, which is the key piece in the Web service interoperability picture. It's the protocol that's used to send messages from one Web service to another. It's basically a presentation-layer protocol for the exchange of Extensible Markup Language (XML) messages built on top of other wire protocols such as HTTP, File Transfer Protocol (FTP), and Simple Mail Transfer Protocol (SMTP).

To understand how SOAP and J2EE work together, you have to understand how J2EE and these other protocols work together. Using Servlet technology, it's possible to receive requests in any of these protocols, so using servlets as the entry point for SOAP messages makes sense. Therefore, servlets are the preferred mechanism for receiving Web service requests in J2EE. The business logic that actually implements the Web service then becomes whatever J2EE technology makes sense for your service. These could include (but are not limited to) JSP pages, other servlets, EJBs, JMS resources, or a plain old Java object (POJO).

SOAP/HTTP Protocol Support

Supporting SOAP in J2EE requires that the relevant servlet knows what to do when receiving a SOAP message. Knowing what to do may result in a number of tasks being required. These tasks can include the following:

- Envelope parsing where the servlet needs to get to the SOAP envelope so that it can pull out the SOAP header and body portions of the envelope.
- Accessing any SOAP attachments that may be part of the payload.
- Validating that the SOAP message format received matches that are defined in the Web Service Description Language (WSDL) file. If the message doesn't conform, then the servlet needs to create a SOAP fault message and send it back to the client.
- Validating XML contained in the SOAP packet against various namespace schemas that may be used.
- Creating XML-to-Java object bindings may be required if there's data contained in the SOAP payload that needs to be passed to other objects, such as an EJB invocation. This is common if the SOAP message is an RPC-style message and the data needs to be pulled out and put into the correct object.
- Converting XML data of message-style invocations for JMS to valid JMS types.

When SOAP comes in over HTTP, it's just part of the HTTP request. You retrieve the SOAP envelope by using the `HttpServletRequest`, `InputStream`, and `getInputStream()` method calls. `InputStream` is then parsed by a SOAP parser (of your choice) used to create a document. This would look similar to the following:

```
org.w3c.dom.Document doc =
    SOAPParser.getDocument(new InputSource(request.getInputStream()));
```

The SOAP message is then retrieved from the document, and you're on your way. You'll find the details on full Web service implementation in Chapter 16. As part of J2EE 1.4, each J2EE-compliant application server must supply a SOAP servlet (this is part of JSR-109). The developer will never see the code snippet that invokes the SOAP parser because the SOAP servlet does this for you. Although the steps for processing SOAP are accurate, you don't need to worry about them because of the vendor-supplied (specification-compliant) SOAP servlet. Your business logic either receives a text message (for message-style Web services) or parameters (for RPC-style Web services)—this is all you need to know.

JSP Pages

JSP pages play an integral role in J2EE Web development. The purpose of the JSP technology is to produce Web pages that deal with dynamic content. Since the data that these pages deal with can change, the business logic that's executed may also change. JSP pages are used as the presentation tier in an *n*-tier system. Therefore, JSP pages commonly represent the View in the Model-View-Controller pattern that we'll talk about later in the "MVC Design Pattern" section.

JSP pages are useful server-side components because even though they're XML documents (although there's more to them than that), JSP pages are usually much more workable for page authors. Let's face it; over the course of the last few years since JSP has been around, it has always been Sun's official opinion that Java programmers shouldn't be the ones writing the JSP files. In reality, and in any production application we've worked on, this isn't the case. Most Java developers have spent some time in the trenches with JSP coding. The good news is you'll learn how JSP 2.0 with the JSP Standard Tag Library (JSTL) adds a number of improvements to the JSP technology to help things along.

This chapter brief introduces JSP. A JSP page is a document that can be broken down into a number of logical pieces. First there's standard markup, usually static HTML, which is used for template text. This template text is delivered in the response as it appears in the JSP. The JSP 2.0 specification defines additional markup that's used for dealing with the more interesting dynamic content. This markup includes embedded logic, executing logic, evaluating expressions, scripting elements, and custom actions.

> **NOTE** Directives *instruct the JSP compiler on how to handle something and are used at page compile time.*

The following is an example of a directive:

```
<%@ taglib uri="http://java.sun.com/jstl/core" prefix="c" %>
```

This directive makes a tag library available on the JSP page so that the actions defined in that library can referenced by the prefix `c`.

Scripting elements are blocks of Java code embedded in the JSP page between the delimiters `<%` and `%>` or by using the `<jsp:scriptlet>` element. Using scriptlet code you can declare variables to use on the JSP page, to instantiate an external class, or to access JavaBeans. You'll see in the "When a JSP, and When a Servlet?" section why using scriptlets isn't really encouraged and how you can avoid doing so with new JSP 2.0 features.

Custom action is another name for a custom tag. We'll use the terms interchangeably, but in our opinion, *custom action* really is a better term. However, note that the libraries are still called *tag libraries*, not *action libraries*. The introduction of the JSTL has made great strides in providing page authors with a complete set of standard actions for use in common situations found when using JSP pages.

What Exactly Is the JSTL?

The JSTL came about under JSR-52 of the Java Community Process (JCP). You can find the specification at `http://jcp.org/jsr/detail/52.jsp`. JSR-52 covers the creation of a standard tag library for JSP pages and allows this library to be available to all compliant JSP containers. These tag libraries provide a wide range of custom action functionality that most JSP authors have found themselves in need of in the past.

Having a defined specification for how the functionality is implemented means that a page author can learn these custom actions once and then use and reuse them on all future products and on all JSP containers that support the specification. Therefore, you can finally take the *custom* out of custom action and replace it with *standard*. No more creating your own iteration action for the tenth time. Additionally, JSP authoring tools now support these standard actions and can assist the JSP page author in rapid development.

To sum up how the JSTL got here, an expert group was set up and given the task of creating custom actions that would be valuable to a range of JSP authors and developers, and that's exactly what the group created. You'll take an in-depth look at the various tag libraries and actions that are available in the JSTL in Chapter 4. For now, the following are the four functional areas provided in the JSTL (though the JSTL is commonly referred to as a *single* tag library, it's actually composed of four tag libraries):

- Core
- XML manipulation
- SQL
- Internationalization and formatting

Using the JSTL in Web Applications

Although custom tags enable tag libraries to be shared across many different user communities and Web applications, engineers and page authors can be derive direct benefits from a standard tag library. These benefits include the following:

- It's easy to learn, and it provides a wide range of functionality.
- JSP authors and JSP authoring tools can easily generate pages on all compliant JSP containers using standard tags.

- Standard tags created by the expert group will meet the needs of a wide variety of communities.
- The tags will already be well tested and ready for use.
- Training costs are lower because you can use targeted training materials.
- It offers simplified portability and maintainability of JSP pages and applications.
- It offers specialized implementations of the library so that containers can provide both portability and higher performance.
- With all the time you save using the JSTL, you'll be able to concentrate on making the core value of your application even greater.
- Aside from the development process benefits that will be realized by using the JSTL, the functionality contained in the JSTL is impressive.

JSP Pages As Servlets

The JSP specification is an extension of the Servlet API. In fact, a JSP page is actually compiled into a servlet by the JSP compiler. The first time an incoming request specifies the JSP page, the JSP container will compile the file into a servlet. Figure 2-4 shows this process.

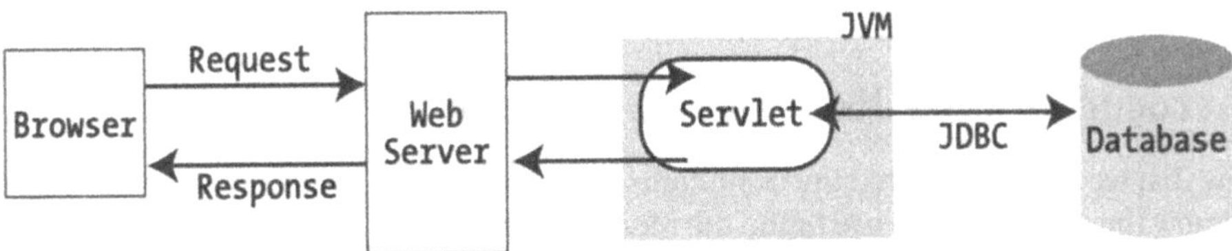

Figure 2-4. Incoming JSP request

The resultant servlet uses the servlet context and allows for defining objects within certain scopes. Scope comes into play when dealing with objects that are used by the JSP page, an example being a JavaBean. Chapter 3 covers the JSP 2.0 specification in detail. For now, know that JSP files are used in the presentation tier for handling dynamic content. Even though a JSP page is compiled into a servlet, JSP pages differ from servlets in their programming model. JSP pages are much easier to create and manage because you're basically dealing with a text file. The compilation step is removed (it's handled by server), and some deployment steps are removed—changes are picked up at run time, so server doesn't need to be restarted. You'll now see how servlets fit into the food chain.

When a JSP, and When a Servlet?

The question becomes this: When does one write a JSP page, and when does one just write a servlet? Did Shakespeare have such difficulties between a play and a sonnet? But we digress. The answer is this: It really depends on the purpose. For most layout concerns, it's wiser to write a JSP page and access the information necessary through scriptlets, custom tags, the JSTL, or JavaBeans. This is usually not the case when using servlets because presentation and logic are commonly used in the infamous `out.println()`.

Using JSP pages, the presentation stays mostly separate from the logic. Make a note of the word *mostly* in the previous sentence. The *mostly* is what JSTL tries to get rid of. JSTL makes the attempt to turn it into *completely*. When dealing with code primarily in terms of logic, it's best to create a servlet to do the work. Having a lot of logic code inside JSP pages makes for some interesting (read: frustrating) debugging sessions. You'll see throughout the course of this book how using JSTL can eliminate including logic code inside your JSP pages.

Additionally, consider the following factors:

- Rapid development is possible when using JSP pages; it's more time consuming to write a servlet.

- JSP pages can be XML documents, and therefore you can use them in transformations.

- Servlets allow for better lifecycle management than a JSP does.

- Servlets allow for better control of thread safety.

Introducing the MVC Design Pattern

Now that we've covered what the basic components of a Web application are, you need to know the proper way to use them: the Model-View-Controller (MVC) design pattern. Sometimes you may also hear this referred to as the Model 2 approach, but these terms refer to the same design pattern. This pattern keeps the code in the presentation tier separate from the code in the business tier.

The pattern itself was originally developed for use in the graphical user interface (GUI) arena, but it's probably the predominate pattern used for Web application development. The main thrust of the MVC pattern is to take application components and break them into three distinct parts: the Model, the View, and the Controller.

An excellent place to review the relevant J2EE design patterns is on Sun's blueprint site (`http://java.sun.com/blueprints`).

The Model

The Model represents, or *encapsulates*, an application's business logic or state. Model components can be one of a number of technologies: a JavaBean, an EJB, a Java Data

Object (JDO), or just a Java class. For those who may be unfamiliar with JDO, it's an API that's a standard interface abstraction that's used for data persistence. As an application programmer, you can use JDO to directly store the Java domain model instances into the persistent store (database). For more information, you can read through JSR-12 or any of the available JDO implementations available. The primary function of the Model components is to hold the application state and data. Model components communicate with the Controller directly. However, there usually needs to be a bridge component so that Model components can get updates from the Controller when data is required for that Model component.

The View

The View components make up the presentation tier. This is how information from the Model is actually displayed to the user. Typical View components include JSP pages and custom tag libraries. The View components work with the Controller, meaning that there's no flow logic or business logic and no Model information contained in the View.

While it isn't required that you use any custom tags in your JSP pages, most situations will benefit from using them. At the least, actions contained in the JSTL should come in quite handy. Chapter 4 covers all of the features available in the JSTL. Usually, some component needs to serve as a bridge between information given to the View, through the Controller, to the Model. For example, if you're submitting an input form from a Web page, sometimes the Controller will pull the values of the request out into another component that's then passed to the Model. This isn't always required, as it's possible for the Model to pull everything it needs out of the request itself. However, having a standard way to do this task sometimes is quite handy.

The Controller

The Controller is the glue in the MVC pattern and is the only component that handles communication between the View and the Model components. By taking this approach, it's possible to provide the Controller with the appropriate configuration for your application so that it knows the application flow and where each incoming requests needs to be sent. Once it knows this information, it can interpret the user's requests and send them to the appropriate part of the Model.

The concept of the Controller is the core of the popular Struts Framework. Struts (`http://jakarta.apache.org/struts/`) is an open-source Jakarta project that implements the MVC design pattern (among other patterns) for use in Web applications. It should be a rare occasion that you need to write your own MVC framework from scratch.

A number of frameworks are available that you can easily incorporate into your development plans—Struts being the most popular. Not only can you take advantage of a well-designed framework, but you'll also save yourself a lot of time coding, testing, and debugging your own framework. As engineers, we'd rather write the core value code in the application we're working on than reinvent the wheel.

General Application Flow Using MVC

Figure 2-5 shows the general flow of an application using MVC.

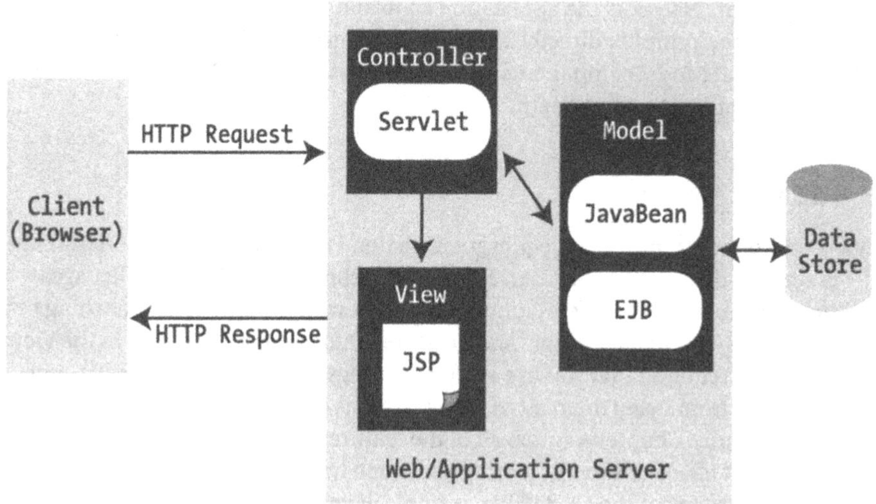

Figure 2-5. MVC model

Using the MVC design pattern, a central Controller mediates the application flow. The first action that happens is usually an HTTP request from the client browser. This event is directed to the appropriate Controller. The Web container is in charge of determining which is the correct Controller to use for any given request. It's fairly standard to configure a servlet in the `web.xml` file with a particular uniform resource locator (URL) mapping pattern so that all requests that conform to that mapping are sent to the correct Controller.

The Controller is usually implemented as a servlet using the Command design pattern. The Controller delegates requests to an appropriate handler. A handler is nothing more than the set of logic that's used to process the request. The handlers are tied to a Model, and each handler acts as an adapter, or bridge, between the request and the Model. The terms actions and handlers are synonymous.

It's good practice to keep your handlers as thin as possible. What we mean by *thin* is that the business logic flow is maintained in the handler, but the actual implementation of the logic is in helper classes. Listing 2-1 shows some pseudocode to demonstrate this because the logic stays pretty much the same, regardless of whether you're using an existing framework such as Struts or you roll your own MVC framework.

Listing 2-1. Pseudocode for a Sample Handler

```
public class myHandler {

  public NextView performBusinessLogic(HttpServletRequest request,
                                       HttpServletResponse response)
                   throws Exception {

    HelperClass myHelper;
    boolean result = false;

    // 1 .Get the various request information required
    someParam1 = request.getParameter("someParam1");
    someParam2 = request.getParameter("someParam2");

    // 2. Decide what to do with the request information
    if (someParam1 != null) and (someParam2 != null){

      // 3. Make the correct method calls to the helper classes
      // These could be JavaBeans, EJBs, JDO, or just Java classes
      if (myHelper == null){
        myHelper = new HelperClass();
        result = myHelper.executeLogic(someParam1,someParam2);
      } else {
        result  = myHelper.executeLogic(someParam1,someParam2);
      }
    }
    // 4. Find the next View for the Controller to forward to
    return(findNextView(result));
  }
}
```

A handler or action typically uses one or more JavaBean or EJB to perform the actual business logic. The action gets any information out of the request necessary to perform the desired business logic and then passes it along to the appropriate helper class. Control is then usually forwarded back through the Controller. The Controller then dispatches to the appropriate View. You can determine the destination of the forwarding by consulting a set of mappings, usually loaded from a database or configuration file. This provides a loose coupling between the View and Model that can make an application significantly easier to create and maintain.

MVC and Separation

The goal of this design is to keep the distinct parts of the MVC architecture cleanly separated. This means that there's no Model-specific processing within the presentation tier. This also means there's no presentation logic in the Model. If you stick by these basic rules of thumb, then you'll improve your component reuse. You'll be able to change implementations in any of the layers with a minimal effect on the others. By designing your Model components carefully, you can actually reuse your business logic in other non-Web clients pretty easily. This is something to keep in mind if you're working on an application that may also require legacy system integration with different types of clients.

Although implementing an entire MVC architecture from scratch isn't all that simple, you should use this pattern in your Web applications for a number of reasons. One reason is to ensure a clean separation between application layers at each tier. You can accomplish this using patterns such as Value Object where you facilitate data exchange between tiers.

For example, you don't want to have a business tier object depend on information in `HttpServletRequest`. If this occurs, create a generic object that contains the information you need and extract the data from `HttpServletRequest`. Then use your generic object in your interfaces. This keeps the tiers from being dependant on one another and also makes for a more portable and secure application.

Sometimes it seems like overkill to implement additional objects to pass information between layers, but in the long run it's well worthwhile. Not only will it keep your tiers in better shape because they won't be cluttered, it'll prevent unnecessary chatty calls to objects on the server to get information.

Having a clean separation also makes it easier for development teams to divide roles and responsibilities in code; you'll also find that your application is much easier to maintain because as changes arise, and they always do, they will be easier to isolate without having to redo objects.

Understanding Containers

The word *container* is used frequently in Web application development. However, it isn't always clear what exactly is meant by it. The term *container* is usually relative to the specific technology involved. A number of different containers work together within a single Web application, and J2EE servers provide different containers for different technologies. For example, there could be a JSP/servlet container or an EJB container. The container handles the life cycle of events related to the technology the container is implementing. Figure 2-6 shows how a Web application may use various containers.

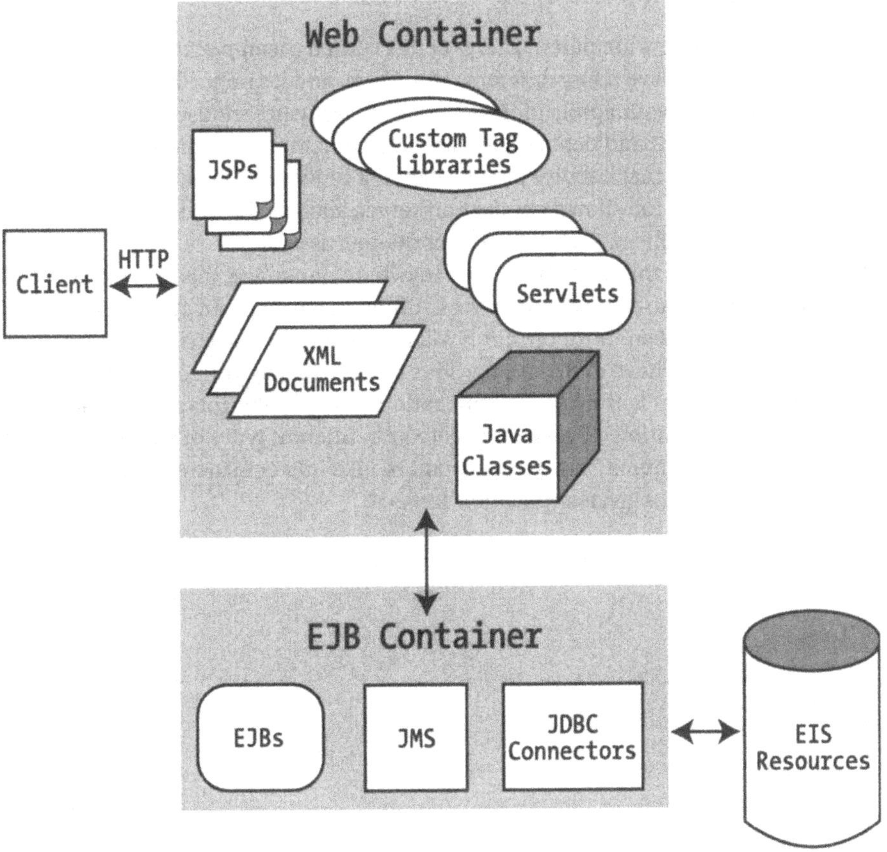

Figure 2-6. Web and EJB containers

Each container provides three functions for the type of application component it supports. These are as follows:

- Deploying the components
- Managing the component
- Executing and handling the lifecycle events of the components

Choosing Your Application Server

Sometimes the containers are part of a larger entity called the *application server*. An application server can have many different containers, and it's important to have a good understanding of your application server because it can seriously affect your Web application development and deployment. Keep in mind that you can have a Web server (such as Tomcat) that handles just the Web tier requests. Tomcat contains a JSP and servlet container. A full-blown application server, such as JBoss, implements all of the required J2EE containers, such as an EJB container, as well.

Even though Java is the "write once, run anywhere" language, this isn't necessarily the case when it comes to application servers. Although you code an application one way in Java, it doesn't mean the application will run with the same characteristics in all application servers. You have to make conscious choices during your application's development about what features of an application server you're going to take advantage of. Different application servers are targeted for different types of applications. The following are some items that are important to take into consideration for rolling out Web applications on a given application server:

- Performance
- Cost
- Development
- Support
- Compliance
- Administration
- Scalability
- Reliability

Many of the items listed are just a start of things to consider; this list could also go on to include such features as usability (how good is the administrative console?), clustering, load balancing, failover support, security, and deployment support. System architects need to consider these types of issues when making system implementation decisions.

While some of these items may play a more important role than others, it's important to understand how they will affect your Web application from the beginning; if you deploy on one specific application server using special features of that server but then you need to move your application to another application server, you'll find that the process can require a fair amount of work. It's also true that issues such as performance and scalability can be dramatically different from one application server to another, depending on the internal algorithms used in the particular application server. This is especially true in the land of EJBs. Some examples of this include the following:

- Use of connection pooling and the types of drivers provided for JDBC support.
- Use of caching features and how configurable the cache is.
- Support of Web servers for request handling performance.
- If you plan on using container-managed persistence (CMP), how is it implemented for the EJB support?

Prioritizing Your Application's Features

Sometimes there's a fair amount of money, time, and training invested in an application server at a given company, so the choice of application server may not be very flexible. Even in this situation, it's still important to know how the application server chosen is going to affect the Web application you're about to develop. The best way to understand the possible effects of a given application server is to prioritize what's important for your Web application and then either find the application server that best meets your needs or, if using an application server that's been specified, figure out how to best implement your Web application.

The following are some suggestions for the types of issues you want to prioritize for your development:

Load: If you run in a large-scale environment (intranet or Internet) and expect to have lots of traffic to your site, performance should be at the top, or near the top, of your list. Not all application servers perform alike. In fact, a wide range of issues can contribute to how well (or not so well) the server can perform under load.

Experience: A good way to gather insight into an application server, both good and bad, is to hit some of the mailing lists for users and developers for that application server. By doing so, you'll see what other developers have experienced.

Version: Make sure you determine ahead of time what version of the specifications your project will be using. Then double-check to make sure that the application server supports that version. Not every application server supports the latest version of the JSP, EJB, JMS, or Servlet specifications. A great place to find out how compliant a server is with a specification is to read the mailing list for the server. You can count on there being a lively discussion in areas where the application server isn't compliant.

Administration: Administration is a key, but sometimes overlooked, issue. You can waste a huge amount of time configuring application servers. We find it's mandatory to have remote administrator capabilities as well as command-line access. The ease of deployment during development is also a rather large hidden cost. If it takes each engineer five minutes to deploy every time they need to test, the cost quickly adds up in terms of lost time. Being able to monitor the server is also important for making corrections to deployment parameters.

While some of these may not seem that important to you as an engineer, they're in fact critical to the success of your development. It can't be stressed enough that it's monumentally important that engineers have an understanding of application servers in a J2EE environment. Not doing so is a sure way to fail on your project.

Packaging Web Applications

The process of packaging J2EE components into an application release is an important step in having your Web application deployed correctly. You would think that packaging something up and deploying it should be a no-brainer, but in fact this isn't the case. If you don't understand how to package and deploy your application correctly, you'll have an application on your hands that doesn't run.

You can deal with packaging in a number of ways. One is to have it done for you automatically, using an assembly tool. A number of integrated development environments (IDEs) generate the deployment descriptor files for you, and Java build tools (such as Ant) produce the appropriate directory structures. Ant is an open-source Jakarta project that has grown in popularity quite dramatically and is now incorporated into many IDEs. You can download Ant at `http://ant.apache.org/`.

You'll inevitably end up making changes and corrections to your application packaging, even if you have an IDE generate it for you. If you don't understand the basics of what's going on, you'll be spending many hours figuring it out. You'll now look at what's involved with packaging and deploying a typical Web application. Figure 2-7 shows the big picture of how components are packaged.

Packaging involves taking all of the components that make up the application and creating the appropriate modules for them. By combining modules, you can create a complete Web application. The following are all part of the packaging:

- Java classes
- Interfaces
- Images and sound files
- JSP files
- Servlets
- Static HTML files
- Resource bundles

- Applets or JavaBeans
- Application clients
- Connectors
- Descriptive metadata of the application

All of these components go into a Web archive (WAR) file as detailed in Figure 2-7 and described in the following sections.

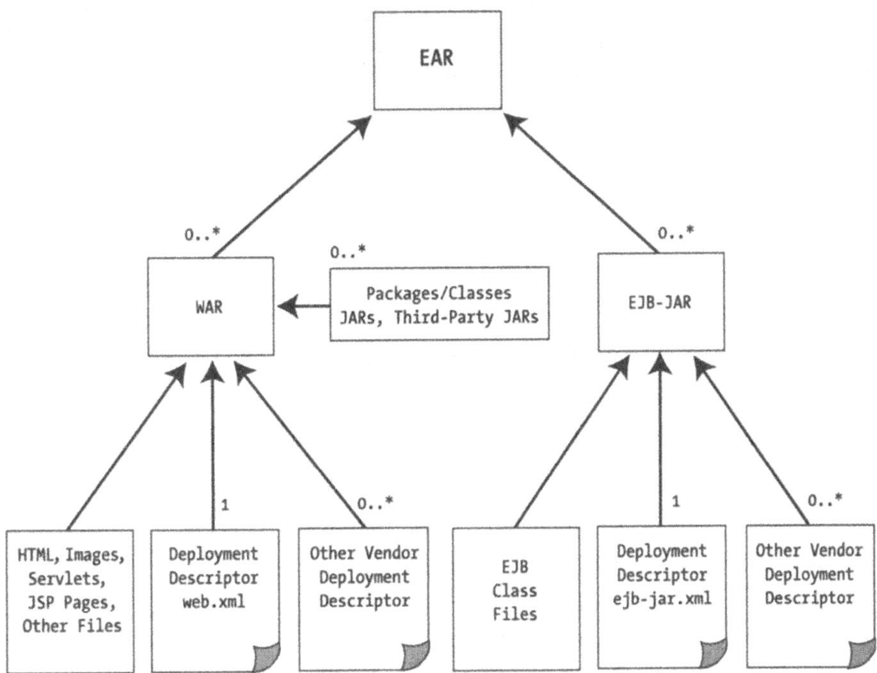

Figure 2-7. Packaging overview

Web Application Structure

While the architecture of Web applications can vary greatly, the structure that's imposed on a J2EE Web application is fairly straightforward. The structure is thoroughly defined so that compliant Web containers know what to expect when an application is deployed, allowing it to be deployed correctly. This arrangement allows for such things as autodeployment of applications. For example, if you drop an application into a deployment directory of a Web container, the next time the container starts, it'll automatically create the necessary directories so that it's available for use when the Web server is running.

The structure of a WAR is defined as a hierarchy of directories, the root of the hierarchy being the *document root*. The document root is a directory where the application context points. Anything located in the document root becomes a public document accessible through the Web application. For example, if `index.html` was in the document root of the `j2ee` context, it could be accessed through `/j2ee/index.html`.

It's important to understand how your application context can affect your Web container. The context path for an application determines the URL namespace for that application. As there are rules applied for matching URLs to context paths, you can't deploy two applications with the same context. Otherwise, the Web container wouldn't be able to determine which application should actually receive the request. Usually the Web container will give an error if you try to deploy an application that already has a context defined or is a substring of an existing context.

Since the document root is public, you need some type of file protection. After all, you don't necessary want someone to have access to your application's class files or other sensitive information. Figure 2-8 shows the structure hierarchy of directories.

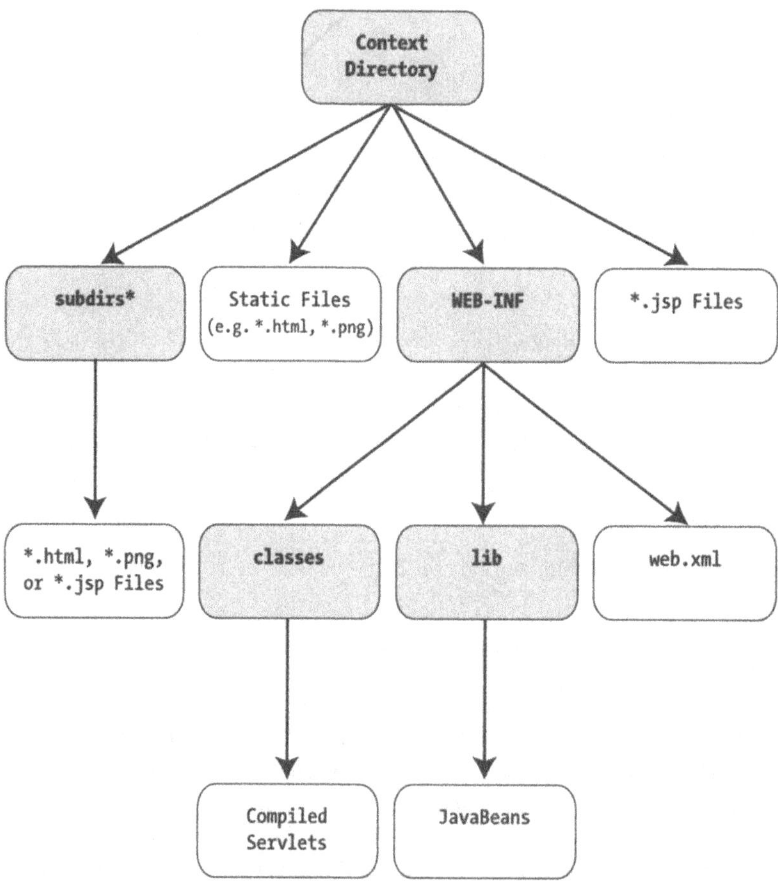

Figure 2-8. Structured hierarchy of directories

Within a WAR file, the `WEB-INF` directory contains all the items that are required by the application but aren't accessible through the document root; it's commonly used as a *safe place* for an application because no file contained in this directory may be served directly to a client by the container. This prevents someone from accessing information that they have no business using. However, the contexts of the `WEB-INF` directory are visible to the servlet container so that your servlet code can use the `getResource()` and `getResourceAsStream()` method calls on the `ServletContext` object to get to those objects. Putting application-specific files in this directory is one way that an application developer can let the container enforce access security without having to do anything other than put the files in the `WEB-INF` directory.

It makes sense to follow the defined file structure in your WAR file. If you take a look at the book's sample application, you'll see that the structure is as follows:

Document root: The document root becomes `apresssample` because that's what your WAR file is called. By default, Web containers will deploy WAR files under the same name as the WAR file. All of your client files and images necessary for the application are under the document root. If this were a more complex application, it may make sense to have a directory structure that's further broken down according to the application's needs. For example, you'd have all JSP pages in one directory, all images in another, and so on.

/WEB-INF/web.xml: The *Web application deployment descriptor* is the XML file describing the servlets, other components, and deployment information that make up the application.

/WEB-INF/classes/: This directory contains any Java class files and resources required for the application. This can include Java archive (JAR) files of both servlet and nonservlet classes. You must maintain the Java package hierarchy structure in the `classes` directory; otherwise you'll get a `ClassNotFoundException`.

/WEB-INF/lib/: This directory contains JAR files that contain the Java class files and resources required by the application, such as third-party class libraries or JDBC drivers.

The files in the `/WEB-INF/classes/` and `/WEB-INF/lib/` directories are automatically visible to your Web application. There's no need to alter the system `CLASSPATH` for classes that may be accessed from other parts of your Web application if they run in the same context.

JAR Files

You have a number of reasons for using JAR files in your Web application packaging. Among those reasons are as follows:

- **Security**: You can digitally sign the contents of a JAR file. Users who recognize your signature can then optionally grant your software security privileges it wouldn't otherwise have.

- **Performance**: If your Web application needs to use an applet, you can bundle the applet in a JAR file. Doing so allows for the applet's class files (and any necessary resources) to be downloaded to a browser in a single HTTP request.

- **Size**: The JAR format uses a zip compression on your files. This allows you to compress your files, making them more efficient for disk space as well as download size.

- **Package sealing**: Using package sealing, it's possible for packages stored in JAR files to be optionally sealed so that the package can enforce version consistency. Sealing a package within a JAR file means that all classes defined in that package must be in the same JAR file.

- **Package versioning**: A JAR file can hold data about the files it contains, such as vendor and version information.

- **Portability**: The mechanism for handling JAR files is a standard part of the Java platform's core API.

To create a JAR file, or to perform various tasks such as listing the table of contents or extracting the data it contains, you use the `jar` tool provided as part of the Java Development Kit (JDK). You invoke this tool using the `jar` command. Table 2-1 shows some of the possible commands for common tasks.

Table 2-1. `jar` Commands

TASK	COMMAND
Creating a JAR	`jar -cvf jar-file input-file(s)`
Viewing contents of a JAR	`jar -tvf jar-file`
Extracting the entire contents of a JAR	`jar -xvf jar-file`
Extracting specific files in a JAR	`jar -xvf jar-file archive-file(s)`

The creation of the JAR files required for your Web application should really be something that's included in a build task since it'll probably happen frequently. Try using an Ant `jar` task. This is a sample of how to do that:

```
<target name="jar-package" depends="prepare.dist">
  <jar jarfile="test.jar"
       basedir="${build.home}" includes="**"/>
</target>
```

This is just a small snippet of a larger build file. In this sample, you're creating a target you can use throughout the build file. The name of this target is `jar-package`, so anyone else who wants to use this target can refer to it as `jar-package`. The `depends` attribute will call another task to make sure that any environment variables or settings are set correctly prior to this task being run. Then you'll create a JAR file called `test.jar` that will include all of the files present in the `build.home` property. Properties are used throughout Ant so that tasks can refer to them when necessary. Since this isn't an Ant book, we won't go into all of the details of how Ant works, but we suggest you take a look at the link provided earlier for complete details.

A Web application can require many different JAR files. These may include EJB JARs, application client JARs, or just JARs that required specific package sealing or versioning that were already mentioned. The point is that you can take all of these JARs and start assembling them into the next component step in your application. This would usually be a WAR file.

WAR Files

A WAR file is a complete Web application. This includes all of the necessary JAR files, presentation files (such as JSP pages), resource and image files, and configuration information. This configuration information is kept in a file called `web.xml`. The `web.xml` file is what's called a *deployment descriptor*. The descriptor contains such information as servlet name and description, servlet class, initialization parameters, and any other startup information that may be required.

EAR Files

An enterprise archive (EAR) file consists of multiple applications. Using modules and EAR files makes it possible to assemble a number of different J2EE applications with some of the same components. So, an EAR is composed of JAR and WAR files. You build the EAR file using the same `jar` tool as JAR files; in fact, an EAR file is a standard JAR file with an `.ear` extension. One of the main advantages of the EAR file structure is that all files contained within that archive are by default in a common classpath—this is useful when deploying EJBs that reference each other. Otherwise, the EJB has to contain the interfaces of another that it wants to reference.

An EAR file structure is as follows:

- A root directory contains WARs, JARs, EJB JARs, and application client JAR files. Basically, any of the other files already mentioned make up a Web application.

- A `META-INF` directory holds the `application.xml` deployment descriptor. The `application.xml` descriptor lists the various components that make up the EAR file.

- Sometimes a container vendor requires that you provide a vendor-specific deployment descriptor.

Understanding Protocols

When designing your Web application, considering the protocols you'll use may affect some of your architecture, design, or implementation decisions. Most standard Web applications that use nothing more than the browser as the client device will probably use HTTP, HTTP proxies, or HTTPS as their protocol. (HTTPS is HTTP over SSL; SSL stands for Secure Socket Layer and is used for protecting data.) Most enterprise environments will include a firewall that limits access from the internal network to the public Internet, and vice versa. It's typical for access using HTTP to pass through such firewalls on port 80.

Even if a proxy server is being used, port 80 is still the norm. Since HTTP is the most popular protocol to allow through a firewall, it's one of the very reasons that SOAP has become so popular for use with Web services. Simply put, nothing extra needs to be configured on the server to allow for Web service traffic because, in fact, it's just HTTP traffic. That's why you need the extra step to pull out the SOAP message from the HTTP request.

However, it isn't typical that general Transmission Control Protocol/Internet Protocol (TCP/IP) traffic, including Remote Method Invocation/Java Remote Method Protocol (RMI/JRMP) and RMI/IIOP, can pass through firewalls. In fact, many times if you have an information technology (IT) department standing by, it'll forbid applications from using these protocols if you need external access. Good luck trying to get IT to change that policy.

These considerations have implications on using various protocols to communicate between application components. Some J2EE application servers may provide support for tunneling, which means that one protocol is contained within another one. This is usually done so that communications can work through firewalls. Not every vendor supports tunneling, so it's best to check your vendor documentation. Figure 2-9 shows the various protocols supported by Web containers in the J2EE environment.

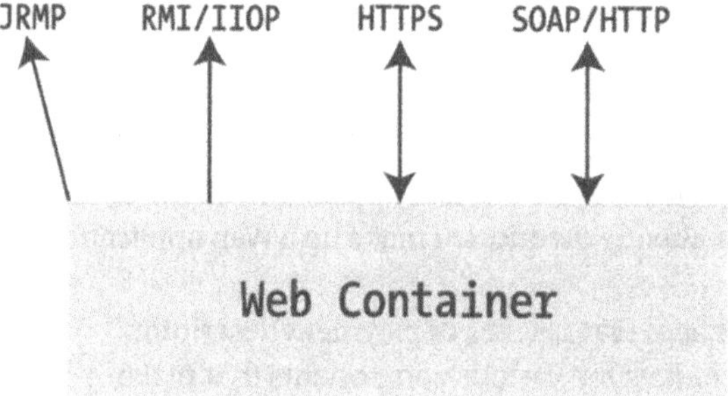

Figure 2-9. Web container picture with protocols

You'll now look at what each protocol can provide so that you have a good understanding for which one may suit your application best.

HTTP

HTTP is the standard protocol used on the Web.

> **NOTE** *HTTP is a request/response, stateless protocol. The client identifies the server by a uniform resource indicator (URI), connects to it using TCP/IP, issues an HTTP request message, and receives an HTTP response message over the same TCP connection.*

A client, usually a Web browser, sends a request to a Web server. The Web server receives the information and initiates specific processing on the server. There are eight different request methods: `GET`, `POST`, `HEAD`, `OPTIONS`, `PUT`, `TRACE`, `DELETE`, and `CONNECT`. However, of these eight, only `GET` and `POST` are commonly used.

GET Request Method

The `GET` request is the most common request method used in HTTP. It's used to access resources, such as documents and images or result sets. You can use `GET` requests to retrieve dynamic information. You accomplish this using query parameters that are encoded in the request URL. When passing parameters in a URL, the resulting string is also referred to as a *query string*. A request parameter is identified by using a `?`, followed by the parameter name and then value. Parameters are separated by the `&` symbol. So, for example, if you wanted to send a request that had a parameter called `student` with a value of `Liz`, the URL would look something like this:

```
http://www.apress.com/j2ee?student=Liz
```

If you added another parameter called `level` with a value of `advanced`, then the URL would look like this:

```
http://www.apress.com/j2ee?student=Liz&level=advanced
```

The Web server receiving this request would then parse the parameters and values and use them to base a response on. One thing to note is that, since `GET` requests shouldn't really need to send large amounts of data, there's sometimes a limit imposed on the size of the `GET` request (although this has for the most part been discarded in browsers). You should check your browser to see if a character limit is enforced. It's typically about 240 characters.

`GET` requests, since they use URL and query strings, allow a user to bookmark the address in their browser or just cut and paste it into an e-mail message. This, of course, has other effects in Web applications. It becomes possible for a user to log into an application and bookmark a page and then later come back to that bookmark when they're no longer logged into the application. It's up to the application to have a mechanism that prevents a user from doing this. For this reason, don't use a `GET` request when you have requests that can cause damage if they execute again. A good example is if you're updating a database or processing a credit card order. You usually don't want activities such as these to execute more than once.

POST Request Method

You use POST requests for sending large amounts of data to the server. Using the POST request allows for all of the data to be passed to the server as part of the HTTP request body, regardless of how much data exists. Besides this size difference in request data, a POST doesn't change the URL at all. In other words, the client Web browser doesn't display anything different to the user or present a query string. As a result, a POST request can't be bookmarked or reloaded. This makes sense if you think about it because if you're using a POST request, the information you're dealing with is supposed to be sent to the server only once. If reloading was allowed, then it could change the state of the server in an undesirable way.

A good example of using a POST request is uploading a file to a Web server.

GET and POST in HTML Form Processing

Since we're talking about GET and POST requests, we may as well touch base on the ever-abused, and confused, HTML form processing. In practical applications, Web application developers haven't exactly followed the intent of GET and POST. It became common practice to use POST for request URLs that got to be too long and unwieldy with parameters; the long URLs couldn't be handled by the limitation on the GET request size.

Even though GET was intended to be used for just "getting" data, it has been used for sending form data that isn't all that big. It's important to note that GET gives no protection against causing a change on the server. So if you really don't want to allow that credit card to be charged twice because the user didn't want to wait and hit reload in the browser window, you need to make sure you're using the correct request.

For example, with METHOD="GET" the form data is encoded into a URL. This means you can achieve an equivalent to a form submission by entering the URL (with the appropriate parameters) onto the location line of the browser. When using a METHOD="POST", the form data is encoded using multipart/form data, and therefore it isn't visible to the location line of the browser. For form submission with METHOD="GET", the browser constructs a URL as described previously, and then it processes it as if following a link (or as if the user had typed the URL directly). The browser divides the URL into parts and recognizes a host, and then it sends to that host an HTTP GET request with the rest of the URL as an argument. It's then up to the server to process it. Submission of a form with METHOD="POST" causes an HTTP POST request to be sent with the data encoded accordingly.

Other Request Methods

Other request methods are also available; however; they're used much less frequently than the `GET` and `POST` methods. It doesn't hurt to at least understand what their purpose is in case you need them in your Web application development. The request methods are as follows:

HEAD: A `HEAD` request is sent from the client when it wants to see only the headers of a response. You can use this to determine such things as the size or type of a document. It's used as a "read-only" request. No document body is returned.

OPTIONS: You can use the `OPTIONS` request to find out which HTTP request methods the server supports.

PUT: You can use the `PUT` request to store a resource on a server under a given URL that may not already exist. This differs from using `POST` in that when using `POST`, the target resource already exists.

TRACE: `TRACE` allows the client to see what's being received at the other end of the request chain and use that data for testing or diagnostic information.

DELETE: You can use the `DELETE` request for removing information corresponding to a given URL. After a successful `DELETE` method, the URL becomes invalid for any future requests.

CONNECT: `CONNECT` is reserved for use with a proxy that can dynamically switch to being a tunnel.

The HTTP Response

HTTP is a request/response protocol: For each request, there's a response. In each response there's a status code and other information contained in the response headers, as well as any document data that was returned as a result of the request. The request headers frequently are set as a result of a status code. Status codes are three-digit numbers, where the first digit defines the general classification of the response. The HTTP specification categorizes responses as follows:

- ***1xx***: Informational. Request received, continuing process.
- ***2xx***: Success. The action was successfully received, understood, and accepted.
- ***3xx***: Redirection. Further action must be taken to complete the request.
- ***4xx***: Client error. The request contains bad syntax or can't be fulfilled.
- ***5xx***: Server error. The server failed to fulfill an apparently valid request.

For example, several of the "document moved" status codes have an accompanying `Location:` header, and a 401 (unauthorized) code must include an accompanying `WWW-Authenticate:` header.

However, specifying headers can play a useful role even when no unusual status code is set. For example, response headers can be used to do the following

- Supply the modification date (for caching).
- Instruct the browser to reload a page.
- Determine content size.

Lots of HTTP response headers are available, but we won't go into all of them here. These are some of the more common response headers used in servlet programming:

Cache-Control: The `Cache-Control:` general header field specifies directives that must be obeyed by all caching mechanisms along the request/response chain. It's used for specifying how a caching system should handle the document. Using this header you can tell the client how to deal with the document: A value of `no-cache` states that the client shouldn't cache the document at all, `no-store` indicates that the cache or proxy server shouldn't store or cache this document, and `max-age=seconds` indicates when a document should be considered stale. Note that HTTP/1.0 caches may not implement `Cache-Control:` and may implement only `Pragma: no-cache`.

Expires: The `Expires:` response header specifies a date/time after which the response is considered stale.

Location: The `Location:` response header field redirects the recipient to a location other than the request URI for completion of the request or identification of a new resource.

Retry-After: The `Retry-After:` response header field can indicate how long the service is expected to be unavailable, or it may be used with any 3*xx* (redirection) response to indicate the minimum time the user-agent is asked to wait before issuing the redirected request.

Specifying headers is useful when returning a response from a servlet. The Servlet specification has a number of ways to set response header information; you'll explore those in Chapter 6.

HTTPS

When a Web application needs to deal with sensitive data, such as passwords, credit cards, or other e-commerce information, you don't want the data going across the wire so that anyone can see it. Unfortunately, when using standard HTTP, this is the case. Data is freely sent for anyone to peruse. To prevent this, you can use HTTPS, which is HTTP over SSL.

You can use HTTPS both for incoming and outgoing data traffic. Encryption is done at the source whether that's the server or the client, and it's decrypted at the destination. There's a public key exchange between the client and server so that each side is able to encrypt and decrypt the data. SSL 3.0 support is required in J2EE 1.4 containers. You can find the specification at `http://wp.netscape.com/eng/ssl3`.

Using SSL is simple enough. All that's required is that you use the `https` URL instead of the `http` URL. For example, the following would use the standard, unsecured HTTP port:

```
http://www.apress.com/j2ee/login.jsp
```

The next example would ensure that data related to this request and response would use SSL for security:

```
https://www.apress.com/j2ee/login.jsp
```

Web containers advertise the HTTPS service on the standard HTTPS port, which is 443, as opposed to the standard HTTP port, which is 80.

HTTP/SOAP

SOAP is a presentation-layer protocol for the exchange of XML messages. Using SOAP makes it easy to put XML and HTTP together. While it's possible to use SOAP over other protocols, you'll look at the protocol binding to HTTP. The container must provide support for SOAP1.1 layered on HTTP.

> **NOTE** *Obviously, the other protocols are FTP and SMTP. However, the reason why there isn't much effort in this area is because HTTP is becoming the de facto wire protocol underneath SOAP. Few people are using FTP or SMTP to transport SOAP.*

You'll want to use SOAP, as it's the protocol of choice, if you're dealing with Web services. It's also important to note that using SOAP allows for applications to communicate over HTTP, thereby not causing headaches when dealing with firewalls. When using SOAP, it's important to make sure you're using the same version on both sides of the wall.

As mentioned, HTTP is a request/response protocol. The client identifies the server by a URI, connects to it using TCP/IP, issues an HTTP request message, and receives an HTTP response message over the same TCP connection. If using SOAP over HTTP, then it's safe to assume that the SOAP message returned in the HTTP reponse is the same as the SOAP message sent in an HTTP request.

Applications can use two message-exchange patterns to exchange SOAP messages via HTTP:

- The first way uses the HTTP `POST` method for conveying SOAP messages in the bodies of HTTP request and response messages.

- The second uses the HTTP `GET` method in an HTTP request to return a SOAP message in the body of an HTTP response.

What you're doing in your application will determine which method you use. If you need to use data within the body of an HTTP `POST` to create or modify the state of a URI resource, then you'd use the first approach. If you're not altering the URI resource, you'd use the second approach. Chapter 16 addresses SOAP in more detail.

> **NOTE** *Chances are you don't need to worry about HTTP issues anymore because you won't use HTTP directly to invoke Web services. Java API for XML Messaging (JAXM) and Java API for XML-Based RPC (JAX-RPC) were designed to hide the complexities of SOAP constructs and the underlying protocol. With these APIs, you don't even see HTTP. In fact, the wire-level protocol binding to HTTP is handled in the WSDL.*

A number of compatibility issues can rear their ugly heads if you're not careful. One example is when data is serialized into objects, which are then translated from the native language of the software application to SOAP. The data is then sent over the wire, where it must be deserialized. It's here where native languages introduce dependencies on the data. For example, the way Java defines date objects is different from the way Microsoft .NET defines date objects. This has the unfortunate effect of allowing SOAP data types with the same name to have different implementations. You'll see these types of issues with such things as dates, floating-point numbers, and big decimals.

You can imagine that there are interoperability problems across platforms. It's important that you thoroughly test your application in all of the environments in which you think it'll be running. JSR-109 (part of the J2EE 1.4 specification) provides for interoperability between .NET and J2EE-based Web services. Once J2EE 1.4 comes out and is fully supported by vendors, most of the compatibility issues should be solved. This will work because each platform will standardize its interpretation of the WSDL files and the bindings between Web services and their respective J2EE components. While SOAP does have some growing up to do, J2EE 1.4 will help greatly in the maturation process.

JRMP

Java Remote Method Protocol (JRMP) is also referred to as the RMI transport protocol. JRMP is supported as an outgoing protocol from the Web container. This means if you have a Java component, such as a servlet, you can invoke methods on other objects, such as an applet, using RMI, and it can allow for callbacks. The RMI protocol uses two other protocols for its on-the-wire format: Java Object Serialization and HTTP.

The Java Object Serialization protocol marshals parameters and returns data. HTTP is used to `POST` a remote method invocation and obtain return data if needed. Using HTTP is also the way to get RMI to work through a firewall.

You can see how the protocols start to become incestuous. Sometimes you may need to use JRMP in your Web application. If you do, the following items are of interest:

- It's possible to get JRMP to work through firewalls, but it's usually not that easy because RMI uses direct socket connections. If the RMI call is being sent to an object behind a firewall, the socket will not be created, and the invocation will fail.

- Using RMI requires that a naming registry be available so that the clients have a way to obtain references to the remote objects.

- Many browsers don't support RMI.

RMI/IIOP

IIOP is how CORBA-compliant environments integrate into the Java environment. Since the distributed object programming models were developed separately, they have trouble talking together. RMI over IIOP combines the features of RMI with the interoperability of CORBA. The real purpose of RMI/IIOP is to make it easy for server objects created using the RMI/IIOP API to be exported as JRMP or IIOP by just changing deployment properties. If you're dealing with objects that access CORBA objects, you should be aware of these issues:

- A CORBA object's IDL can't always be mapped to an RMI-IIOP Java interface. This is because the semantics of CORBA objects defined in interface definition language (IDL) are a superset of those supported by RMI/IIOP objects.

- The difference between a CORBA object and an RMI/IIOP object is only an implementation issue.

- The CORBA 2.3 specification incorporates the interoperability for RMI/IIOP. This includes Objects by Value, as defined in Java as object serialization and Java-to-IDL mapping. Java-to-IDL mapping converts RMI Java interfaces into CORBA IDL definitions.

So, in short, RMI/IIOP is a way to interoperate with CORBA objects if that's required by your Web application.

Introducing Web Application Architecture

Web application architecture has developed over the years. First we had client-server, and then we had three-tier applications. Three-tier architectures introduced dynamic content to the Web; a client, a server, and a backend database all work together to form an application. Then the fourth tier made room for thin-client architectures. When Java applets were introduced, they were thought to be the solution for supporting different client platforms with their own specific code. The deployment of client application code would disappear because now it'd be possible for a client to download applet code on demand. However, many engineers overlooked the unfortunate side effect of applets: They had to be downloaded, a chore that was found to take quite some time. Additionally, the security sandbox requirements of Applets created difficulties for useful applications. The solution, or evolution, was to add another tier.

The fourth tier was the presentation tier. This allowed the server to do all of the work for the client; the server would then "present" it to the client. The real job of the presentation tier became to prepare information for display by a client (usually as HTML) and also to take information from the client and make it available to the application's business rules. Alas, applets started going the way of the mastodon. It's also at this time that the Web server itself actually was just part of the infrastructure, not really part of the application. So what was being called the *server* actually became the business tier. The application architectures looked very similar to Figure 2-10.

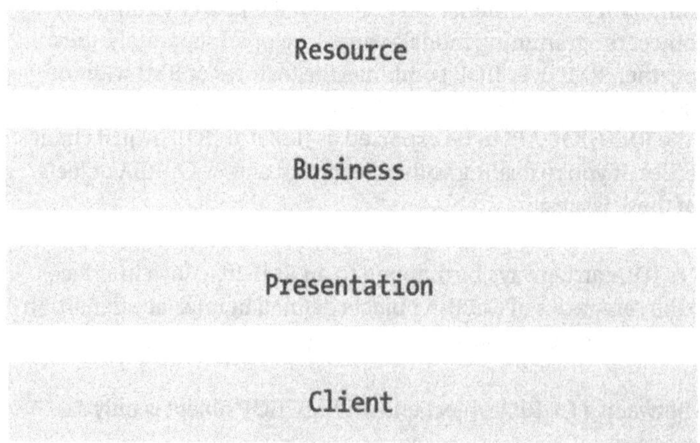

Figure 2-10. Evolving tiers

It's also at this point that you saw the introduction of JSP and Servlet technology and how they fit into Web application architecture. Also note that XML starts playing a role in architecture now in order to represent structured data. Added to all this, the X acronyms start to explode. With data being represented in XML, you also needed a way to transform it; therefore, Extensible Stylesheet Language (XSL) and XSL Transformations (XSLT) emerged. Finally, XPath and XPointer were developed to access the Document Object Model (DOM), used to represent XML documents.

With the presentation and business tiers separated, it's possible for the business rules to be implemented regardless of what the actual end client is. Whether your application is supporting browsers, cell phones, PDAs, handheld devices, or TV-top boxes, the business rules stay the same. The only thing that changes is how the data is presented to the client.

The next step in the evolution of Web application architecture was the incorporation of services into the business tier, allowing logic to be encapsulated so that APIs can be exposed. In turn, this allows applications to be written to an API. So, if the implementation of that API changes, the change doesn't affect the other parts of the application. You'll see in the sample application later in the book how it's possible to write to an API and then change the implementation underneath it. This is exactly how you'll change the sample application from a JavaBean/JDBC implementation to an EJB implementation for use in later chapters.

Application Considerations and Concerns

When architecting an application, you need to consider a number of system properties. Each one can impact your Web application, depending on what's required for that property. These properties are as follows:

Security: This is the system's ability to resist attack, preserve privacy, and guarantee the integrity of the data. Security covers a broad range of topics including single sign-on, authentication, and cryptography.

Capacity: Capacity answers the How much, how fast, and how many? questions. These questions can be asked in reference to transactions, data movement, or documents served. You need to measure the system so that its capacity correlates to the requirements.

System responsiveness: This is an indication of how quickly the system reacts to user inputs. For example, if the user submits a form, how fast does a response need to be presented to the user?

Reliability: Reliability refers to how dependable the system is. If the application needs to be taken down once a day, it isn't very reliable. If the application can continue running for weeks or months at a time, it's highly reliable.

Availability: How probable is it that the system will be available at the times it's required? Availability and reliability are closely related because if your system isn't reliable, then it won't be available.

Scalability: This is determined by how difficult it is to increase the application's capacity. Capacity could be defined in terms of supported simultaneous users or number of documents served in a certain amount of time.

Architecture vs. Configuration

Web application architecture isn't the same as application configuration. This distinction is subtle but important. The logical architecture of your Web application should be separate from its configuration. When designing an application, discussion revolves around how the components are broken down, not necessarily where they live. Even though an application can consist of multiple components in different tiers, there's nothing to say that all of those tiers need to live on different machines. For example, it's standard during development to have an application server running on your development machine, as shown in Figure 2-11.

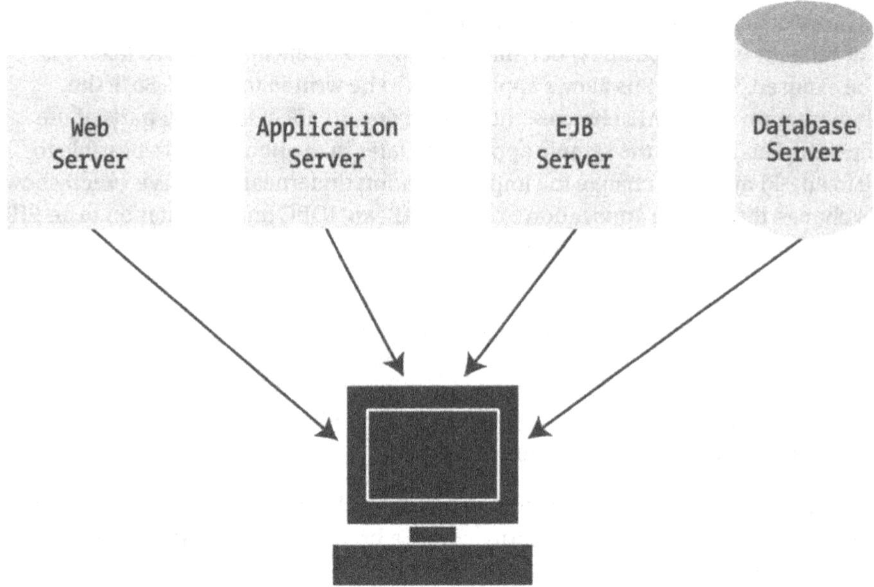

Figure 2-11. Development environment—everything on one machine

This may include a JSP/servlet container, an EJB container, and possibly a completely separate database. All of these components are logically separate, but the fact that they're configured to run on the same machine is just coincidence.

When you deploy the sample application into a production environment, the configuration will probably change. The database server will probably be located on a separate machine. You could also very well set up a demilitarized zone (DMZ) between the Web server and the other containers. In computer networks, a DMZ is a "neutral zone" between a company's private network and the outside public network. It prevents outside users from directly accessing a server that has company data. If someone hacks into your Web server, that doesn't mean that they have access to all of your business-related data and components. Figure 2-12 shows an example configuration.

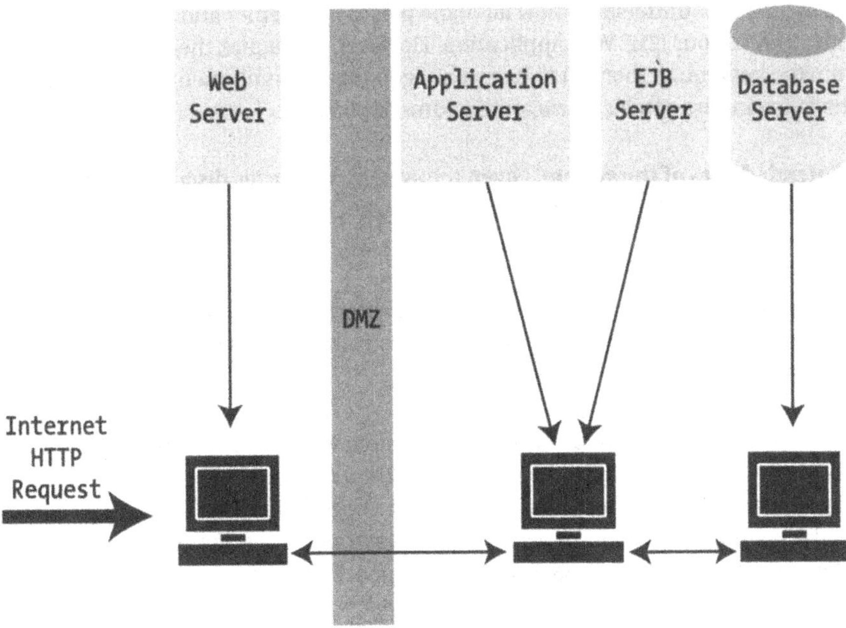

Figure 2-12. Web server/DMZ/containers/database on separate machines

Exploring Application Scenarios

Over and over again developers go with the latest and greatest technology for implementation. This isn't always bad, but if the technology isn't required for the problem you're trying to solve, then, yes, in that instance it's bad. The J2EE programming model is inherently flexible so that developers can pick and choose which technology is best suited for the problem at hand. Each of the technologies has trade-offs, and sometimes getting through the rhetoric of choosing when to use a technology is in and of itself a full-time job.

The very first step in your Web application development should be to determine what your application's scenario is going to be among the smorgasbord of options available. Figure 2-13 shows a sample of the possible combinations that need to be present for your application.

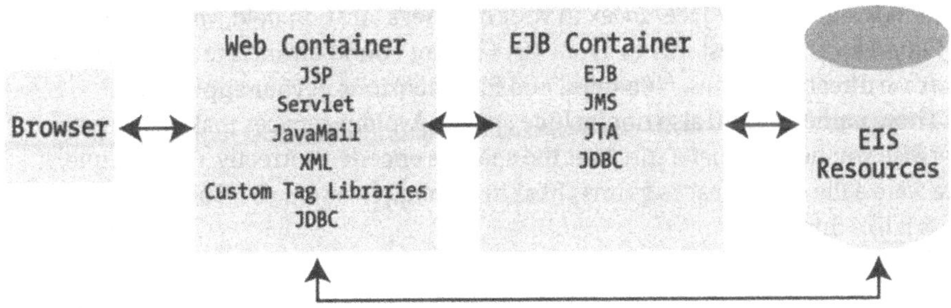

Figure 2-13. Possible application scenarios

You should now understand how all of the pieces fit together and what factors come into play in your J2EE Web application. However, if you pick the wrong architecture from the beginning, then you'll have a hodgepodge of components on your hands.

The following are some criteria and features to consider:

- **Intended uses of the system**: Given the system properties discussed earlier, is it necessary to implement cache mangers, resource managers, or failover capabilities?
- **Platform**: What platform and devices does the system need to support? Is it necessary to build in transformations from the get-go so that you can seamlessly integrate multiple devices?
- **Browsers**: What's the oldest browser the system will support? Support for earlier browsers may be limited to using HTML 3.2/4.0 or Extensible HTML (XHTML) as a transition format and using `User-Agent:` negotiation. You should also consider assumptions about browser features such as frames, JavaScript support, Cascading Style Sheets (CSS), or plug-in support.
- **Transactions**: Do you need transaction management for multiuser support?
- **Open source**: Should you go with open source or license an application or solution that may already solve your problem?
- **Documents**: How will you cover the naming and addressing of documents between systems?
- **Backward compatibility**: What protocols need to be supported for integration with legacy systems?

Using Naming Conventions

The platform that your Web container runs on can affect your Web application. Any *nix (Unix, Linux, Solaris, HP-UX, and so on) environment is case sensitive; if you try and access files from hyperlinks within your pages, they need to match the case on the server. For example, if you have the URL `http://www.apress.com/j2ee/INDEX` instead of `http://www.apress.com/j2ee/index` in your browser's location field, you'll get a 404 File Not Found error. The best way to avoid 404 File Not Found errors is to consistently use lowercase directory names, filenames, and file extensions in your application.

These names should also not include spaces. Avoiding spaces makes life easier; otherwise you need to make sure that the space is encoded correctly. For example, if there were a file called `spaces galore.html` in your application, you'd always have to access it like this:

```
http://www.apress.com/proj2ee/spaces%20galore.html
```

which, as you can imagine, is a pain that you can easily avoid.

NOTE *If you're building a new site, or redesigning an existing site, it's strongly recommended you use lowercase names (with no spaces) for all directories and files.*

Relative vs. Absolute URL Paths

When referring to a URL using the whole URL schema (protocol, domain name of server, path, query parameters), we're talking about an *absolute URL*. Absolute URLs identify a resource *independently of any context*. This means that no matter where you are on the Web, you can always, absolutely, resolve that URL because you have all of the information necessary to do so. For example, you can find the following absolute URL regardless of where you're accessing it from:

```
http://www.apress.com/j2ee/index.html
```

A *relative URL* identifies a resource relative to its context: It isn't always necessary to give the full address of a URL. A relative URL is eventually turned into an absolute URL by the Web container and then fetched accordingly. For example, if there's a link referenced in your application, you can render the following HTML:

```
<a href="/training/module/modinfo.html">Training Module Information</a>
```

This shows the path to the file from the root of the Web context directory. This is designated by the leading forward slash in the path. The next example is relative to where the current page is located. This is specifying a URL that's one directory level up from the current page's directory:

```
<a href="../modinfo.html">Training Module Information</a>
```

Why does it matter how you reference your URLs from your Web application? Glad you asked. If you use absolute path references throughout your applications, you'll be unable to move your site to another Web server and have internal links function properly. Going back through your application and updating URLs is the last thing you want to be doing the day before an application goes live, simply because the physical servers have been changed—not to mention that relative URLs represent less typing.

NOTE *Using relative URLs in Web applications is preferable to using absolute URL paths.*

However, even doing this can cause problems. For example, if the internal directory structure of the application changes, all internal links could break. In general, though, you have more control over the structure of your directories than you do over an application moving to a different server location.

Using Deployment Descriptors

Deployment descriptors describe a J2EE Web application so that the container knows how to manage the application once it's deployed. The deployment descriptor is nothing more than an XML file that declaratively describes how to deploy the various modules that make up the Web application. Having this information in a deployment descriptor allows you to change system settings without having to actually change code in your application.

The deployment descriptor for Web applications is a file called `web.xml` located in the `/WEB-INF` directory of the Web application. The various XML elements used in the deployment descriptor are defined in terms of an XML schema document. In the Servlet 2.4 specification, it's now possible to extend deployment descriptors. This allows application developers to inject application- or framework-specific configuration information directly into the deployment descriptor. Chapter 17 goes into the details of how this works.

These are the types of information contained within the deployment descriptor:

- `ServletContext` initialization parameters
- Session configuration
- Servlet declaration
- Servlet mappings
- Application lifecycle listener classes
- Filter definitions and filter mappings
- Multipurpose Internet Mail Extensions (MIME) type mappings
- Welcome file list
- Error pages
- Possibly security information
- Declaration of custom tag libraries
- Syntax for looking up Java Naming and Directory Interface (JNDI) objects

Listing 2-2 shows a sample `web.xml` file. Chapter 17 covers the details of all of the elements, but this should give you an idea of what the deployment descriptor looks like.

Listing 2-2. Sample web.xml File

```
<?xml version="1.0" encoding="ISO-8859-1"?>

<web-app xmlns="http://java.sun.com/xml/ns/j2ee"
        xmlns:xsi="http://www.w3.org/2001/XMLSchema-instance"
        xsi:schemaLocation="http://java.sun.com/xml/ns/j2ee web-app_2_4.xsd"
        version="2.4">

  <!-- Define servlet-mapped example filters -->
  <filter>
    <filter-name>Servlet Mapped Filter</filter-name>
    <filter-class>filters.ExampleFilter</filter-class>
    <init-param>
      <param-name>attribute</param-name>
      <param-value>filters.ExampleFilter.SERVLET_MAPPED</param-value>
    </init-param>
  </filter>

  <!-- Define filter mappings for the defined filters -->
  <filter-mapping>
    <filter-name>Servlet Mapped Filter</filter-name>
    <servlet-name>invoker</servlet-name>
  </filter-mapping>

  <!-- Define example application event listeners -->
  <listener>
    <listener-class>listeners.ContextListener</listener-class>
  </listener>
  <listener>
    <listener-class>listeners.SessionListener</listener-class>
  </listener>

  <!-- Define servlets that are included in the example application -->
  <servlet>
    <servlet-name>J2EEServlet</servlet-name>
    <servlet-class>apress.j2ee.servlets.J2EEServlet</servlet-class>
  </servlet>

  <servlet-mapping>
    <servlet-name>
      J2EEServlet
    </servlet-name>
    <url-pattern>
      /j2ee
    </url-pattern>
  </servlet-mapping>

</web-app>
```

Understanding Data Store Interaction with Web Components

Somewhere along the line you're more than likely going to be dealing with some kind of data store. Usually this data store is a database, such as a relational database management system (RDBS). However, the data you're dealing with could also be part of an object-oriented database, hierarchical file, or some other legacy system. Whatever the data store, the format of the data should be in as neutral a format as possible. Granted, this isn't always possible because you may be dealing with a complex database schema that's being used by more than just the application you're writing, but it's something for which to strive.

Web applications typically interact with data stores in the following two ways:

Entity and session beans: Use the EJB programming model by using entity beans and stateful and stateless session beans. The entity EJBs are then mapped to the database schema, and data interaction is handled however the EJBs are being persisted, whether through bean-managed persistence (BMP) or CMP. For more details on this, refer to Chapters 10 and 11.

DAO: Use data access objects (DAOs) that represent the underlying data store. The DAOs are then used to abstract the data so that it can be accessed by the Web application. DAOs can be as simple as a Java class written to deal with a particular schema. Note that if you're writing DAOs, you probably want to have some utility classes that actually get and release database connections as well as manage connection pools. This should be generic to your DAOs, but you'll have to deal with the JDBC aspects of the data store somewhere.

It's possible, and you'll see how in the sample application, to write to DAOs with a specified API so that the Web application isn't aware of the underlying implementation used to access the data store. If desired, you can then change the implementation to use EJBs later. The data store interactions with the Web components will remain the same as defined by the API. However, when possible, if you can store your data so that it can easily be represented in XML documents, then you'll have the flexibility of keeping your data store separate from your data structure.

> **NOTE** *Use XML for structuring the data and then use transformations to target various sources.*

By using transformations you can target the data for the appropriate presentation or use by another system. Examples of using data for transformation targets include the following:

- Business-to-business (B2B) formats
- XHTML

- Wireless Markup Language (WML)
- Portable Document Format (PDF)
- HTML

These should be regarded as output formats, not data formats.

Addressing Portability Concerns

Java is the "write once, run anywhere" language, right? Well, maybe it's really "write once, run sometimes." OK, that may be a little cynical, but the reality of deploying a Java application across application servers is far from headache free. It's not that the potential for portability across applications isn't there; it's just that if you're truly planning on making your application portable, then there are some basic ideas you should keep in mind. Also, don't confuse portability with reuse; you can reuse components across applications if the applications all run on the same application server. *Portability* is the ability to run on different application servers without modification.

You probably need to be concerned about different levels of portability, depending on your development situation. If you're building an application that's very specific to your company or client, and this application is going to run on only one specific application server (or so the client says), then you probably don't need to be as nervous about tying your application to that particular application server. However, if you're building an application that has the potential to be deployed on many different application servers, you should continue reading this chapter.

Supported JDKs

You need to make sure you're using a JDK that's supported on the application servers on which your application will run. This is true whether you're using an older JDK or a newly released one. Many times it may not be possible to be on the latest and greatest version of the JDK, or the application server just doesn't support that version yet. The support for the JDK can also cause classloader issues within your application.

Different Application Vendors

How the application vendor interprets a specification can also play a role in whether your application runs correctly in different containers. The version of the XML parser is another area that seems to be a source of concern for many applications. It's sometimes necessary to replace the server's version of the XML parser with one required by your application. Note, however, this isn't always possible and sometimes needs to be investigated.

When dealing with EJBs, it's possible to use CMP. EJBs using CMP perform better than those that don't, but at the expense of portability. Sometimes this is necessary as it's faster to implement an EJB using CMP because you don't have to worry about writing all of the code behind EJB persistence. When dealing with CMP, you're tying your application to the application server's implementation of object persistence. This is true even though CMP is well defined in the J2EE specification, so J2EE applications servers must all function in the same way regarding life cycle and run time. Because of this, your CMP EJB code will remain the same across application servers. The only thing that changes is the application server–specific EJB deployment descriptor. You can mitigate this by using XDoclet, a popular open-source project (`http://www.xdoclet.org`), to generate the EJB-CMP XML deployment descriptor for many vendors.

If you want to keep your applications portable, you should also avoid using special features that some application servers provide. For example, many servers provide their own custom tag libraries that are optimized for their containers. If you build your JSP files using proprietary custom tag libraries, it may be rather difficult to run them in other application servers. This is also true of deployment descriptor information that may be specific to a vendor. A typical example of this is setting caching parameters that are used by the container. How one vendor describes their attributes is usually not the same as how another one does.

Tips for Maintainability Concerns

By following some simple rules of thumb, you can make the difference between a well-designed J2EE application and a maintenance nightmare. The number requirements of your specific application will determine the number of tiers. A typical scenario may include the following tiers: a client tier that handles user interaction for multiple devices; a presentation tier handling user requests; a business tier that contains the business rules and logic; an application tier that uses other services (such as messaging); and an information systems tier that connects to backend data storage, other systems, or legacy applications.

When designing an *n*-tier application, consider the following issues that can affect your application's maintainability:

Did you identify the functionality clearly enough so that it lives within one tier? If you find that functionality must cross a tier, then you need to reevaluate your model and break down your objects and interfaces further.

Did you define your objects and interfaces so that a specific object doesn't need to be passed between tiers? If you find you need to pass an object between tiers, make it a generic object. For example, you don't want to have an application tier object depend on information in `HttpServletRequest`. If this occurs, create a generic object that contains the information you need and extract the data from `HttpServletRequest`, and then use your generic object in your interfaces. This keeps the tiers from being dependant on each other and also makes for a more portable and secure application.

Given your business requirements, can you apply a specific pattern that addresses a specific tier? As you become more familiar with J2EE development, you'll be able to identify scenarios where a specific pattern is appropriate. Using such patterns makes your tier separation cleaner and eliminates the reinvent-the-wheel syndrome, allowing you to gain valuable experience from others who have used the pattern successfully. The J2EE patterns catalog is well worth the time to investigate and understand. You can find it at `http://java.sun.com/blueprints/patterns/j2ee_patterns/index.html`.

If you answer all of these questions correctly, then you're on your way to a design that encompasses the "ity" words: flexibility, scalability, security, and maintainability.

Tips for Performance Concerns

Performance issues in applications are the subjects of many books. We won't go into how to analyze an application for performance. Instead, there are a couple of basic areas to look at so that when you're building your applications, you can make correct design and implementation decisions for these areas. We'll start with some basic ways to increase Java performance, and then we'll touch on some of the issues more specific to J2EE Web applications.

The following sections are the starting points for improving your Web application performance. These are general items to consider. You should spend some time with your application vendor documentation to see how you can set the appropriate values for the application server. Each vendor has different options available to accomplish these tasks.

Choice of JVM and JIT Options

The JVM runs the Java bytecode. It's possible to specify just-in-time (JIT) options that can be used to optimize performance. When using JIT, the first time a method of a class is called, the JIT compiler will compile the method to native machine code and execute it. Once the code is compiled, it's stored in the JVM's cache so that the next call to that method executes just the compiled code. The compiled code is valid only for the duration of the JVM. Once the program completes, all of the compiled code is thrown away.

Keep in mind that upgrading or moving to a different vendor's JVM will require you to do some benchmark testing. What works well in one JVM might not have the same results in another.

Java Heap Size and Garbage Collection

The JVM process of cleaning up unused objects in the heap is called *garbage collection*. The heap is where the objects of a Java program, regardless of whether they're actively being used, and the free memory available to an application live. When an object can no longer be reached from anywhere in the running program, the object is considered garbage and collected so that it can increase the free memory available to the application.

The JVM heap size determines how often and how long the JVM spends collecting garbage. Applications can benefit from adjustments in both the frequency of and the amount of time spent in garbage collection. If the heap size is large, chances are that garbage collection will be slower because there will be more objects to collect. At the same time, however, this should occur less frequently because there will be more room to store objects in the first place. If you set your heap size in accordance with your memory needs, full garbage collection is faster but occurs more frequently.

> **NOTE** *The goal of tuning the heap size for a Web application is to minimize the time you spend doing garbage collection while maximizing the number of clients that can be handled at a given time.*

Garbage collection time can vary and usually takes 5–20 percent of the application's execution time. You can use the `verbosegc` flag on the JVM to collect basic garbage collection statistics. Statistics that help you decide how to best tune your application include the following:

- Total time spent in garbage collection. A target of less than 15 percent of execution time is good.
- Average time spent per garbage collection.
- Average amount of memory collected per garbage collection.
- Average number of objects collected per garbage collection.
- Pools.

Various areas of Web application performance can benefit from object pooling. These include bean pools, connection pools, and object pools. The algorithm used within a pool can make the difference between a well-performing application and one that's crawling. When possible, cache as much as possible so that you can reuse objects instead of re-creating them, which increases the need for garbage collection. If your application is dealing directly with the resource tier, then using connection pools and cached prepared statements for database access can prove to be very effective in terms of increasing performance.

Sessions

You've already seen that HTTP is a request/response protocol. In other words, it's a stateless protocol. However, many situations that Web applications have to deal with are based on a user's session and require some way to maintain state across multiple requests. This is where session management comes into play and is usually handled by JSP or servlet code. The following are some rules of thumb to keep in mind when performing session management:

- Don't store large objects in the `HttpSession` object because serialization may be needed; keep the amount of data stored in the session as small as possible. When serialization is on a request-by-request basis, it can cause performance slowdowns, especially if your application needs to handle many clients simultaneously.

- When you're finished with a session, release the `HttpSession` instead of waiting for the JVM to garbage collect it.

- If dealing with session creation from a JSP, use the following to turn off automatic session creation to make sure that the container doesn't update the session:

```
<%@ page session="false" %>
```

- It's also a good idea to use the following to get the already existing session:

```
<%
HttpSession session = javax.servlet.http. ↵
HttpServletRequest.getSession(false);
%>
```

- In fact, to avoid having scriplet code scattered throughout your JSP pages, it's a good idea to have a custom tag that can be used for this type of functionality.

- Memory-based session mechanisms are the fastest if you can avoid serializing the session data.

- Cookie-based session mechanisms are efficient when you don't need to store large amounts of data in the session; however, it's common that cookies aren't enabled in a browser. If this is the only mechanism you're relying on, then you need to make sure that cookies will always be available.

- Database-based session mechanisms are slow but provide the most reliable way to persist a session.

- File persistence is the slowest mechanism for managing sessions.

For other performance tuning tips, visit `http://www.javaperformancetuning.com/`.

Handling Data Transfer

Obviously, the more data that's transferred between the client and the Web server, the more of a performance hit will be taken in the Web application. Using cookies for session management causes a lot of data to be transferred back and forth. You should always avoid doing unnecessary server round-trips on requests. This is especially crucial when dealing with remote objects, such as EJBs. Overuse of network calls can severely cripple an application's performance. You can mitigate round-tripping issues by using proper J2EE patterns such as Session Façade, Service Locator, and Value Objects, to name a few.

Forwarding

An easy way to avoid extra client-server round-trips is to use *forwarding* instead of *redirecting* in your JSP pages. When you use forwarding, the JSP container invokes the target page through an internal method call on the server. Therefore, the same request is used for processing on the new page, and the browser doesn't realize it. For example, you still see the original URL on the address line in the browser.

When doing a redirect, the page doing the redirect tells the browser to make a new request to the target page. The URL shown in the browser therefore changes to the URL of the new page. When doing a redirect, any request scope objects are no longer available to the new page because the browser creates a new request. If you need the information from the request, you can either pass it as a request parameter or save the data in a session or application scope object.

Security

In terms of security and data transfer, the encryption/decryption process comes at a performance price. Data throughput for a Web server transmitting via HTTPS can be as little as one-tenth that of data transmission when using standard HTTP. For this reason, you shouldn't deploy an entire Web application that uses SSL.

> **NOTE** *For the fastest performance, deploy a Web application that uses HTTP and employ HTTPS only for those pages and processes that transmit sensitive data.*

Summary

This chapter has covered the major factors in building J2EE Web applications. The goal was to introduce all of the components so that you have a good understanding of where they fit into the big picture, what factors play a role in architecture and design decisions, and an overall view of how to build robust applications.

We covered the main J2EE components of Web applications: JSP pages, servlets, and some of the main features used in each of these technologies. These features include custom actions and the JSTL in JSP technology, as well as filters and Web event listeners in the Servlet technology.

Understanding these features is just as important as knowing where and when to apply them. You examined the role that the MVC design pattern plays in the architecture of J2EE Web applications. As you looked at each component in the pattern, you saw how an application's flow of execution typically works.

Next you looked at the critical role that containers play in the success of Web applications. We broke a container down into its constituent parts and described the purpose of each one. Then we talked about some of the key issues to be aware of when dealing with Web containers so that you have a good understanding of how they can affect your Web application. This includes the structure of a Web application and the various ways applications are packaged and deployed in containers.

It's necessary to understand the protocols available to your Web application so you can choose the most appropriate protocol for your Web application's needs. You examined HTTP, HTTPS, SOAP, JRMP, and RMI/IIOP.

You then looked at the various architectural issues of building Web applications. These include understanding the different scenarios encountered when writing Web applications and identifying the important design issues in your applications. Understanding some basics about how naming conventions, URL access, and deployment descriptors work gives you a solid foundation on which to build your Web applications.

Last, we touched on how Web applications interact with data stores and on the importance of understanding the various concerns of all Web applications. These concerns include how to deal with portability, maintainability, and performance. We talked about various ways to deal with these concerns by providing tips to keep in mind when building your Web applications.

With this chapter under your belt, you'll begin looking at the nitty-gritty of the technologies you've learned about, and you'll see how to apply them when building J2EE Web applications.

CHAPTER 3

Working with JSP 2.0

THE JAVASERVER PAGES (JSP) technology has been a key part of the Java 2 Enterprise Edition (J2EE) platform for quite some time. The goal of the JSP technology is to simplify dealing with presentation and dynamic data on Web pages. JSP technology is based on Servlet technology; in fact, all JSP pages are eventually compiled into servlet code. However, writing a JSP page is far less involved than writing servlet code. In fact, page authors who don't have Java experience often write JSP pages. A JSP page is a markup document that can be in either JSP syntax or Extensible Markup Language (XML) format.

This chapter covers the basic mechanisms used in a JSP page. This includes the following:

- Introducing JSP technology
- Understanding the page life cycle
- Understanding directives, actions, scripting, implicit objects, and scoping
- Examining the new expression language in detail
- Introducing localization and handling content
- Addressing debugging and performance concerns
- Using best practices

Introducing JSP Technology

If the purpose of JSP technology were to be summed up in one sentence, it would be this: JSP provides a flexible mechanism to produce dynamic content.

That one sentence will be the focus of the next two chapters. JSP works with the concepts of template and dynamic data; *template data* is fixed content, such as text or XML data, and *dynamic data* changes according to some request. You can combine dynamic data with template data. This provides a flexible mechanism for creating Web pages.

It's also possible to have functionality that's used throughout a Web application and to encapsulate that functionality for use on JSP pages. JSP offers two mechanisms for encapsulated functionality: JavaBeans and custom actions. JavaBeans are just Java classes that follow the JavaBean specification, and custom actions provide a mechanism for building libraries, listeners, and functions and for performing validations. Custom actions are so powerful and feature rich that Chapter 5 is just about using custom actions in JSP 2.0.

JSP has always been focused on the presentation aspects of Web applications, but Java programmers have gotten their coding hands into the logic processing and have mistakenly included logic in JSP pages. Over time, this has led to some unfortunate, and unreadable, pages. *Scriptlets*, small sections of Java code that are embedded into the markup of a JSP page, is the true culprit here.

However, the JSP 2.0 specification will allow you to say "goodbye" to scriptlet coding in JSP files. While the mechanism remains available for use, using scriptlets in JSP files is just plain poor engineering.

Introducing JSP 2.0

JSP technology has been the presentation layer of the J2EE platform since the platform was introduced in 1999. If you're working with the J2EE platform, then at some point you'll probably need to use JSP technology to build Web applications. Previous versions of the JSP specification introduced such features as custom tag extensions, XML representations of JSP pages, and a validation mechanism.

In JSP 2.0, first you'll notice that the new major revision number is warranted. Since JSP 1.2, there has been some significant functionality added. This includes the following:

- The incorporation of the expression language (EL) introduced in the JSP Standard Tag Library (JSTL)
- JSP fragments that allow for a portion of JSP syntax to be encapsulated into a Java object
- Tag files that are a much simpler way to write custom actions using JSP syntax
- Simple tag handlers that represent a new interface with a much simpler life cycle than previous custom action interfaces and that can be integrated with JSP fragments
- The addition of new standard actions to support JSP fragments and tag files

The pages that follow in this chapter and the next two provide a detailed look at JSP and all of these new features.

Understanding the Page Life Cycle

When a JSP page is created, it's considered to be a Web component. Web components run in their appropriate containers. For example, a JSP file runs within a JSP container. The container provides the services that support the component; in a sense, the container enforces the contract between itself and its component. As you saw in Chapter 2, the container is responsible for translating the JSP from a text-based document into runnable servlet code.

A JSP page and the container actually deal with two phases: *translation time* and *run time*. Translation time is where a number of tasks are performed: The container takes a JSP file, performs various tasks such as validation, generates the appropriate servlet code, and compiles and loads the servlet. This stage is where translation errors occur if you have syntax errors on your JSP page or custom actions that can't be resolved.

The container translates a JSP page the first time the JSP page is requested, which sometimes slows performance the first time you request a JSP page (see the "Performance" section later in this chapter for some specific performance enhancements for JSP pages). After the JSP page has been translated, it's just a matter of executing the servlet code. If the JSP page changes, the next time you request the JSP page, it'll be retranslated so that new servlet code can be generated.

The execution of a JSP page—or, more precisely, the servlet code that represents the page—occurs at run time. When a request for a certain JSP page comes into the container, the implementation class of the JSP page that was created at translation time is instantiated. This is analogous to what you know about running Java classes; the container executes the servlet code and takes the appropriate actions. Understanding the two phases of JSP technology is important because different tasks happen in each phase. Figure 3-1 shows the entire process.

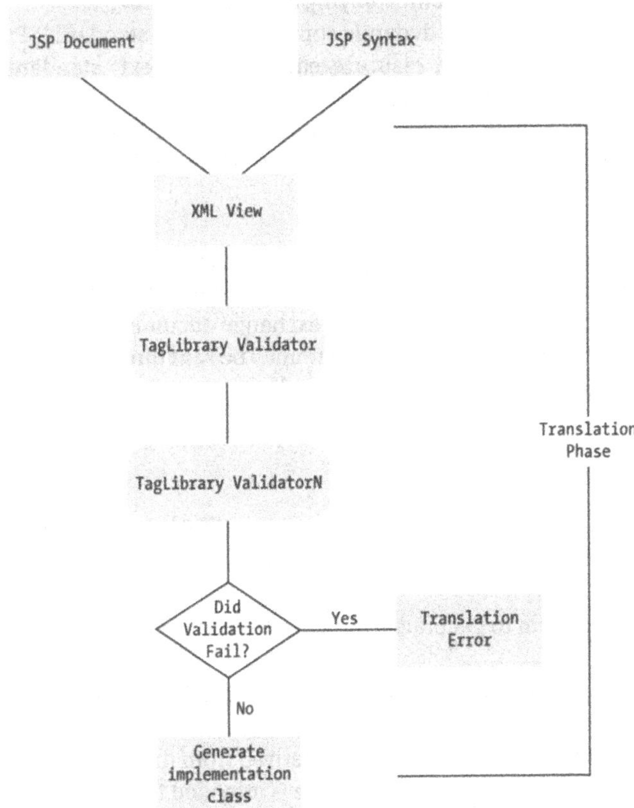

Figure 3-1. JSP phases

When the JSP container generates the servlet class that corresponds to the JSP, there's a well-defined contract that's established between the container and the JSP. The overall job of the JSP container can be summed up as follows: The JSP container delivers requests from a client to a JSP page implementation object, and responses from the JSP page implementation object to the client.

JSP Documents

It's possible to represent JSP content in XML syntax. A compliant XML document that represents a JSP page is called a *JSP document.*

> **NOTE** *A JSP document is a JSP page that's a namespace-aware XML document. It's identified as a JSP document to the JSP container so that it can be translated into an implementation class.*

A JSP document needs to be identified, either implicitly or explicitly, to the JSP container so it can be processed as an XML document. This includes such activities as checking for a well-formed file and, if present, applying any requests (such as entity declarations). JSP documents generate dynamic content using the standard JSP semantics. You'll see how you can use the new `<jsp:element>` and `<jsp:text>` standard actions in JSP documents later in the "<jsp:element>" section.

The main purpose of JSP documents is in the generation of dynamic XML content, but they can also generate any dynamic content. You may want to create a JSP document vs. a JSP page for the following reasons:

- You can pass JSP documents directly to the JSP container. As more and more content is written in XML, XML-based languages such as Extensible HTML (XHTML) and Scalable Vector Graphics (SVG) can exchange documents in applications such as Web services; the generated content may be sent directly to a client, or it may be part of some XML processing pipeline.

- XML-aware tools can manipulate JSP documents.

- You can apply transformation to a textual representation, using languages such as XSL Transformation (XSLT), to generate a JSP document.

- You can use object serialization to generate a JSP document automatically.

You can also author tag files using XML syntax. The rules are similar to that of JSP documents. But we'll make the distinction between the *XML view* of a JSP page and a JSP document. The XML view is an XML document that's derived from the JSP page and produced by the container. The XML view of a JSP page is intended for use in validating the JSP page against some description of the set of valid pages.

Using the TagLibraryValidator class associated with a tag library, it's possible to validate a JSP page.

It's important to understand the distinction between the XML view and the JSP documents for this discussion of the new standard actions `<jsp:element>` and `<jsp:text>`. Figure 3-2 shows the relationship between the JSP document, JSP syntax, and XML view of a page.

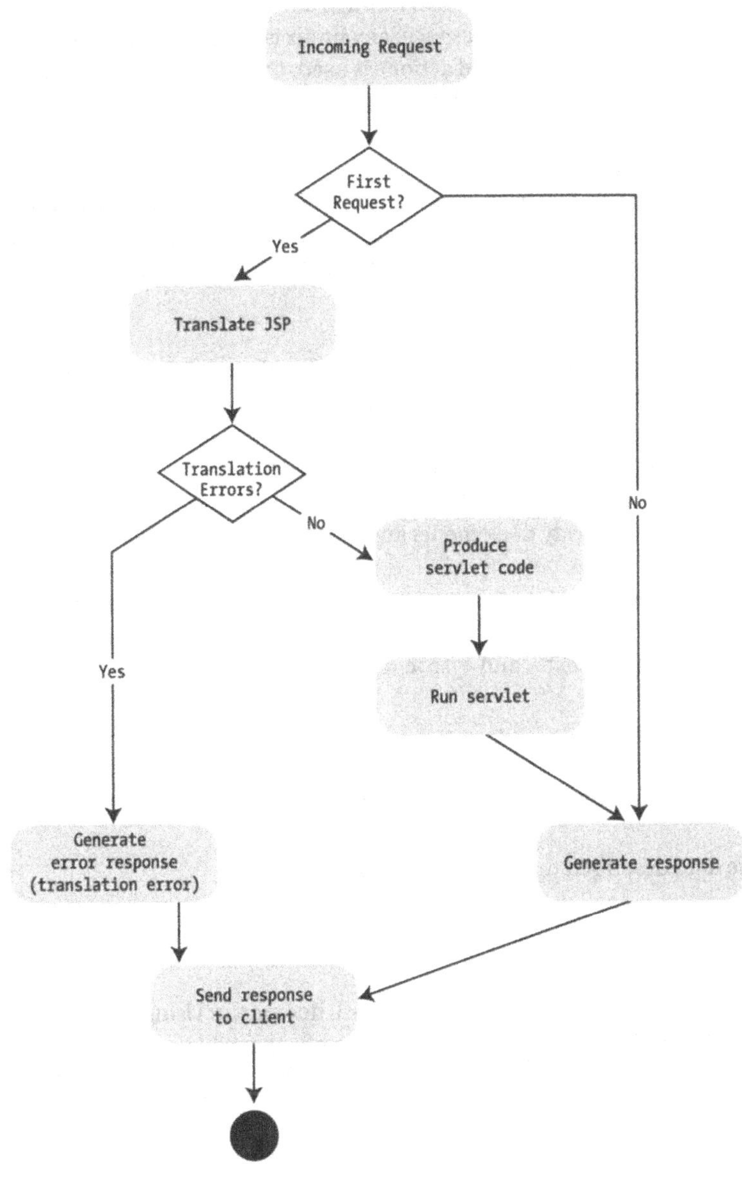

Figure 3-2. Translation phase of documents

JSP Document Syntax

The following describes the syntax elements of a JSP document:

- A JSP document may not have a `<jsp:root>` as its top element. While `<jsp:root>` was mandatory in JSP 1.2, most JSP documents in JSP 2.0 probably won't use it since JSP now has a namespace.

- JSP documents identify standard actions through a well-defined uniform resource indicator (URI) in its namespace; any prefix is valid as long as the correct URI identifying JSP 2.0 standard actions is used. Custom actions are identified using the URI that identifies their tag library; `taglib` directives aren't required and can't appear in a JSP document.

- A JSP document can use XML elements as template data. These template data elements may have qualified names because they're in a namespace, or they can be unqualified. You can use the `<jsp:text>` element to define some template data verbatim.

- A JSP document must be a valid XML document. Therefore, you can't use some JSP features in a JSP document. The elements you can use are as follows:

  - JSP directives and scripting elements in XML syntax
  - EL expressions in the body of elements and in attribute values
  - All JSP standard actions
  - The `<jsp:root>`, `<jsp:text>`, and `<jsp:output>` elements
  - Custom action elements
  - Template data described using `<jsp:text>` elements
  - Template data described through XML fragments

A Simple JSP Document

In the simplest sense, a JSP document looks like an XML document. Using the URI namespace of both JSP and the JSTL, you can define a prefix that will be used for accessing those actions. It's customary to use `fmt` as the prefix for the formatting tag library, but it's possible to specify whatever prefix you want to use in your documents.

The custom action element `<fmt:formatDate>` is one of JSTL actions in the formatting library. We're showing the action here so that you can get a feel for how you can use JSP and JSTL syntax within a JSP document. We'll cover the JSTL in much greater detail in the next chapter. The JSP document doesn't have an XML declaration; therefore, the encoding will default to UTF-8. However, the output will include an XML declaration because of the defaulting rules and the absence of a `<jsp:output>` element that would direct the container to do otherwise (see Listing 3-1).

Listing 3-1. JPSX Sample

```
<html  xmlns:jsp="http://java.sun.com/JSP/Page"
          xmlns:fmt="http://java.sun.com/jsp/jstl/fmt" >

          <jsp:directive.page contentType="text/html"/>
          <head>
                    <title>JSPX Example</title>
          </head>
          <body>
                   <h1>JSPX Example</h1>
                    <hr/>
   <p>This example shows how it is now possible to write JSP files as XML
 documents. Note that you no longer have to use &lt;jsp:root&gt; because it
 is now defined as a namespace. You can see how to use JSP directives,
 JSP actions, and JSTL actions.</p>
      <jsp:useBean id="now" class="java.util.Date"/>
         <fmt:formatDate value="${now}" pattern="MMMM d, yyyy, H:mm:ss"/>
         </body>
</html>
```

HTTP

While you're probably familiar with HTTP, you should make sure you understand the relationship between the Hypertext Transfer Protocol (HTTP) and JSP pages. While it isn't a requirement that JSP be based on HTTP, it's by far the most common protocol in JSP development. This means that the same characteristics of HTTP present themselves as implementation issues for page authors over and over again. For example, HTTP is a stateless protocol, which means that the server doesn't store any information about requests. Each request is a separate entity, and the server doesn't recognize multiple requests from the same client as being related. When using a JSP page, it may be necessary to remember the client's state so that you can run the appropriate business logic and create the appropriate response.

The point to understand is that when working with JSP pages, you'll typically be dealing with the semantics and characteristics of HTTP. The `HttpJspPage` interface is what's used to interact with this protocol.

HttpJspPage Interface

Aside from creating the appropriate response from a request for a given protocol, a JSP page may also indicate how some events are to be handled. In JSP 2.0, the JSP author can affect only the `init` and `destroy` events. The `javax.servlet.jsp` package contains a number of classes and interfaces that describe and define the contracts between a JSP page implementation class and the runtime environment provided for an instance of the class by the container.

Two interfaces, `JspPage` and `HttpJspPage`, define the main contract between the implementation and the container. Neither of these classes is actually used by the page author, but rather the container uses them to generate the appropriate servlet code for the JSP page. `HttpJspPage` extends `JspPage` and is used by most pages that use HTTP. The `HttpJspPage` interface has three methods (which can all be found in the generated servlet code of a JSP page):

public void jspInit(): This method is invoked when the JSP page is initialized. It allows page authors to provide initialization to the JSP page. This method will redefine the `init()` method defined in the `Servlet` class. When this method is called, all the methods in `Servlet`, including `getServletConfig()`, are available.

public void jspDestroy(): The `jspDestroy()` method is invoked when the JSP page is about to be destroyed. A JSP page can override this method by including a declaration element and use it to clean up any resources that the JSP page may have. This method redefines the `destroy()` method defined in the `Servlet` class.

public void _jspService(javax.servlet.http.HttpServletRequest request, javax.servlet.http.HttpServletResponse response): The `_jspService()` method corresponds to the body of the JSP page and contains the Java code that represents the JSP syntax from the original page. This method is defined automatically by the JSP container and is never defined by the JSP page author.

In most circumstances, it isn't necessary or required for the page author to provide the `jspInit()` and `jspDestroy()` methods. Page authors never define the `_jspService()` method. The container handles defining and implementing this method.

To summarize, the following three major events take place in the page life cycle:

1. The container invoking the `jspInit()` method initializes the page. The `jspInit()` method may be defined by the page author. This method is called only once to initialize the JSP page on the first request. An example of this is as follows:

```
<%!
public void jspInit(){
    String rootPath =  getServletConfig().getServletContext(). ➥
                                 getRealPath("/") ;
//Do other interesting things ...
}
%>
```

2. The `_jspService()` method is generated by the container and called to handle each request. The response is produced from within this method and then returned to the container so that it can be passed back to the client.

3. The `jspDestroy()` method is primarily invoked when the JSP page is destroyed; however, a JSP container implementation can call this method at any time to reclaim resources. The page author can define this method if any cleanup is required.

```
<%!
public void jspDestroy(){
    // Do any cleanup in this method that is called
    // by the Servlet container
}
%>
```

Introducing JSP Syntax and Usage

The entire purpose of a JSP page is to take a request and create a response for it. Simple enough. However, to do so, there's just a little bit more to know. The following sections will introduce the syntax and usage of JSP 2.0 files.

Because JSP pages contain a fair amount of HTML, they're very XML-like. By definition, a JSP page is a well-formed, structured document. During the translation phase, the JSP page is exposed as an XML document, called the *XML view*. When this is done, the JSP container will use the XML view as input to an XML parser that can then take advantage of entity declarations and validation.

In the previous versions of the JSP 1.2 specification, there were some standard actions that were available only in JSP syntax, not in XML. In JSP 2.0, these discrepancies have been addressed so that it's possible to compose a JSP page in XML. The advantage of being able to define a JSP page in XML format is that you're now able to reliably use a JSP page anywhere you can use an XML document, such as in a transformation to support various presentation devices. It also makes it easier to use JSP in many of the common XML editing tools. We use the term *JSP document* because the XML file is using the JSP namespace throughout the XML document.

General Rules of Syntax

The following general rules apply to creating well-formed JSP files:

- JSP tags are case sensitive.

- It's possible to use JSP syntax or the XML version for directives and scripting elements.

- Tags can be based on XML syntax.
- Attribute values are always quoted. Similar to XML, either single or double quotes can be used. If you're using XML entity references, you can also use `&apos` and `"`.
- JSP pages are typically named with the `.jsp` extension. However, with JSP 2.0 it's possible to have JSP fragments that may not compile into full JSP pages. `.jspf` or `.jsf` are suggested as extensions for those files. JSP files that are delivered as XML documents usually have the `.jspx` extension.
- The `<jsp-property-group>` element of `web.xml` can indicate that some group of files, perhaps not using any of the previous extensions, contains JSP pages. You can also use this property to indicate which ones are delivered as XML documents.
- Whitespace is preserved within the body text of a JSP document when the document is translated into a servlet.
- Uniform resource locators (URLs) that start with a slash (/) are considered context-relative to the Web application, and the `ServletContext` provides the base URL. Page-relative URLs that don't start with / are considered relative to the current JSP page. This follows the conventions defined in the Servlet 2.4 specification.

JSP Elements

A JSP page has two parts: elements and template data. The elements are the part that the JSP container understands and translates. Anything else contained on a JSP page that the container doesn't translate is considered template data. The following are three types of element categories:

Directives: These configure how the container, when creating the servlet, generates the Java code. Directives are typically used to set global values within a particular JSP page; therefore, they affect the entire page.

Actions: These can be either standard or custom. Standard actions are those well-known tags that affect the runtime behavior of the JSP page, and therefore the response generation. Standard actions are available by default to all JSP pages without declaring the tag library. Custom actions are those created by the page author or a third party. You'll spend Chapter 5 learning how to create custom actions in JSP 2.0.

Scripting elements: These provide the logic that joins the template data and actions together. In JSP 2.0, you can now use the EL to simplify data access from a variety of sources. You can use EL in JSP standard actions, custom actions, and template data.

You'll now look at each one in more detail.

Directives

Directives pass information to the JSP container; therefore, a directive doesn't produce any output to the current output stream of the JSP page. The directives have the following common syntax:

```
<%@ directive { attr="value" }* %>
```

While this syntax is both easy to type and concise, you'll note that it isn't compatible with XML. There are equivalent ways to represent a directive in XML formant, but it's slightly different for each directive. We'll show each one as we discuss it.

You can use the following three directives in JSP 2.0:

- The `page` directive
- The `include` directive
- The `taglib` directive

Page Directive

The `page` directive provides a mechanism to define the attributes for the JSP page. In the following example, you're using the `page` directive to set the content type of the page as well as the language that will be used for scripting:

```
<%@ page contentType="text/html;charset=UTF-8" language="java" %>
```

When using the `language` attribute, it applies to the body of the entire translation unit.

> **NOTE** *The* translation unit *is defined as the JSP page and any files included using the* `include` *directive.*

Table 3-1 defines the page directive attributes.

Table 3-1. The page *Directive*

ATTRIBUTE	DESCRIPTION	POSSIBLE VALUES	DEFAULT VALUE
`language`	Defines the scripting language to be used in scriptlets, expression scriptlets, and declarations.	`scriptingLanguage`	`java`.
`extends`	Provides a mechanism to define a fully qualified class name of the superclass that the container will extend to generate the translated page. It's important to note that using this attribute can eliminate the benefit and some functionality you gain from the container. Using this attribute will restrict your container.	`className`	Not used.
`import`	Same meaning as the `import` statement in Java classes.	`ImportList`; comma-separated list	Not used.
`session`	Specifies whether this page participates in the HTTP session. If set to `true`, then the implicit object `session` is available for access. This object is of type `javax.servlet.http.HttpSession`. If set to `false`, the object isn't available, and attempted access to it will cause an error.	`true|false`	`true`.
`buffer`	Specifies the buffering model for writing content to the output stream. The value of `none` indicates to write directly through to the `ServletResponse using its PrintWriter`. When specifying a buffer size, it must be in kilobytes (KB). Output is buffered with a buffer size that's not smaller than the size specified.	`none|sizekb`	Container implementation dependant. Usually at least 8KB.
`autoFlush`	When set to `true`, the output buffer is automatically flushed when the buffer is full. Set to `false`, this will raise an exception when the buffer is full.	`true|false`	`true`.
`isThreadSafe`	Tells the container whether the page is thread safe with proper synchronization implemented on the page. A value of `true` indicates that the container may send multiple requests to the page. If the value is `false`, requests will be queued and sent one at a time.	`true|false`	`true`.
`info`	Used to set an informational string that's incorporated into the page and accessible using the `Servlet.getServletInfo()` method.	`info_text`	Not used.

(continued)

Table 3-1. The page *Directive (continued)*

ATTRIBUTE	DESCRIPTION	POSSIBLE VALUES	DEFAULT VALUE
errorPage	Defines a URL to a resource to which any java.lang.Throwable object thrown but not caught by the current page is forwarded for error processing.	error_url	Not used.
isErrorPage	Indicates if this JSP page is intended to be the URL target of another JSP page's errorPage. If set to true, then the implicit script language variable exception is available and references the Throwable object from the offending JSP page. If this value is false, then the exception variable isn't available and will cause a translation error if it's referenced.	true|false	false.
contentType	Defines the character encoding for the JSP page and the Multipurpose Internet Mail Extensions (MIME) type for the response of the JSP page. Values are of the form MIMETYPE or MIMETYPE;charset=CHARSET with optional whitespace after the semicolon (;).	ctinfo	The default value for MIMETYPE is text/html for JSP pages in standard syntax or text/xml for JSP documents in XML syntax. If neither CHARSET nor pageEncoding is specified, the default value for CHARSET is ISO-8859-1 for JSP pages in standard syntax or UTF-8 for JSP pages in XML syntax.
pageEncoding	Defines the character encoding for the JSP page. Value is of the form CHARSET, which must be the Internet Assigned Numbers Authority (IANA) value for a character encoding.	peinfo	The CHARSET value of contentType is used as default if present, or ISO-8859-1 otherwise.
isELIgnored	Defines whether EL expressions are evaluated for this translation unit. If true, EL expressions (of the form ${...}) are evaluated when they appear in template text or action attributes. If false, the container ignores EL expressions.	true|false	For backward compatibility with older JSP containers, if the web.xml is in Servlet 2.3 format, the default is false. If the web.xml is in Servlet 2.4 format, the default is true.

As you can see, the page directive offers the page author a wide range of attributes to use. If you use an undefined attribute, you'll get a translation error from the container. Listing 3-2 shows a JSP page, called pageDirective.jsp, which uses many of the page directive attributes.

Listing 3-2. pageDirective.jsp

```
<%@ page contentType="text/html; charset=UTF-8"
         session="true" buffer="16kb" autoFlush="true"
         isErrorPage="false" isThreadSafe="true"
         info="Page directive sample usage"
         import="java.util.Date"%>

<html>
  <head>
    <title>Page directive sample usage</title>
  </head>
  <body>
    This is a sample of using an imported class from the page directive:
    <br/>
    <%= "The current date is: " + new Date() %>
  </body>
</html>
```

Include Directive

The `include` directive tells the container to substitute the defined resource content inline to the JSP page. This can be template text or code. This substitution will occur wherever you specify the `include` directive. The resource specified in the `include` directive must be a relative URL that's accessible by the container. The syntax of the `include` directive is as follows:

```
<%@ include file="relativeURL" %>
```

If the included file changes, it doesn't necessarily trigger a recompilation of the JSP file. While some JSP containers may have their own algorithm for notification, if an included file changes, recompilation isn't required in the JSP 2.0 specification. If the container supports this type of functionality, then when an included file is changed, it'll force a recompile of the JSP page and save you the trouble of making sure an older compiled version isn't lying around.

Any elements present in the included resource will also be processed. So, for example, you can include the previous page directive sample in a JSP page using the following syntax:

```
<%@ include file="pageDirective.jsp" %>
```

The page directive and execution of the `Date()` will be present and processed in the current JSP page.

It isn't a requirement that the `file` attribute be the URL of a JSP page. It can be any resource file that's relative to the current Web application. Using an `include` directive is a common way to template your JSP files. If you have a simple layout, there may be areas that don't change frequently, such as a header or footer that contains a copyright statement. A convenient way to make sure you have to make updates to only one file is to use the `include` directive. For example:

```
<%@ include file="copyright.html" %>
```

The content that's included using the `include` directive is parsed at translation time of the JSP page. You use the `include` action to include resources at run time.

Taglib Directive

The `taglib` directive allows a JSP page to work with custom tag libraries (*taglibs*). The `taglib` directive in a JSP page declares that the page uses a tag library, uniquely identifies the tag library using a URI, and associates a tag prefix with the actions in the library. In JSP 2.0, it's also possible to have tag files in a directory called `/WEB-INF/tags`. You can specify this directory in the `tagdir` attribute to indicate to the container that it should evaluate any tag files that may be present and possibly generate implicit tag library descriptor (TLD) files for them. Chapter 5 covers using tag libraries, creating your own custom actions, using tag files and JSP fragments, using TLDs, and using the libraries within your JSP pages.

The syntax of the `taglib` directive is as follows:

```
<%@ taglib (uri="tagLibraryURI" | tagdir="tagExtensionDir") prefix="tagPrefix" %>
```

Table 3-2 describes the attributes for the `taglib` directive.

Table 3-2. The `taglib` *Directive*

ATTRIBUTE	DESCRIPTION
`uri`	Either an absolute URI or a relative URI specification that uniquely identifies the TLD associated with this prefix.
`tagdir`	Indicates this prefix is to be used to identify tag file extensions installed in the `/WEB-INF/tags` directory or a subdirectory. If a TLD is present in the specified directory, it's used. Otherwise, an implicit tag library is used. Only one of `uri` or `tagdir` may be specified. Otherwise a translation error will occur.
`prefix`	Defines the prefix string that's used to access tags (or actions) defined in the tag library. Empty prefixes are illegal. The following prefixes are reserved: `jsp`, `jspx`, `java`, `javax`, `servlet`, `sun`, and `sunw`.

If the container can't locate a tag library description that's specified in the `uri` attribute, a translation error will be generated. The `taglib` directive needs to appear prior to any actions from that library being used with the defined prefix.

In the following example, you define a taglib with a prefix called `proj2ee`. Any tag files that are found in the `/WEB-INF/tags` directory will be available to you in your JSP page. You can see that there's an action defined called `simpletag`:

```
<%@ taglib prefix="proj2ee" tagdir="/WEB-INF/tags" %>
<proj2ee:simpletag />
```

In the next example, you're accessing a defined tag library using a URI:

```
<%@ taglib prefix="proj2ee" uri="/apress-taglib" %>
<proj2ee:classic />
```

Standard Actions

Actions may affect the current `out` stream and use, modify, and create objects. Standard actions make it easier for the page author to accomplish common tasks. They affect how a JSP page behaves at run time and may act upon the incoming request. A standard action is one that compliant JSP containers will support vs. a custom action that's created by a page author or other party. JSP 2.0 introduces a number of new standard actions, bringing the total number of standard actions to 15. The following sections walk through each one.

<jsp:useBean>

One of the powerful features of JSP pages is that they have access to the Java programming environment. The standard action `<jsp:useBean>` can make a Java object available for use. It's then possible to get and set the properties on the object (a JavaBean). The bean is defined within a given *scope* and is given an ID with a newly declared scripting variable.

It's now possible to disable scripting on JSP pages using the `isScriptingEnabled` page directive attribute. When a `<jsp:useBean>` element is used in a scriptless page, no Java scripting variables are created; instead, an EL variable is created.

The flexibility of the `<jsp:useBean>` action is in the ways that a bean can be described. It's possible to use a variety of attributes, including the class `name`, class and type, bean name and type, or just a type. The exact semantics depend on the attributes given. The `<jsp:useBean>` will try to find an existing object using the `id` and `scope` attributes. If the object isn't found, it'll attempt to create the object using the other attributes. Table 3-3 describes the attributes.

Table 3-3. `<jsp:useBean>` *Attributes*

ATTRIBUTE	DESCRIPTION	POSSIBLE VALUES	DEFAULT VALUE
`id`	The case-sensitive name used to identify the object instance in the specified scope's namespace. The `id` is also the scripting variable name declared and initialized with that object reference.	The `id` name conforms to the current scripting language variable naming conventions.	None
`scope`	The scope in which the reference to the bean is available.	`page`, `request`, `session`, or `application`	`page`
`class`	Case-sensitive fully qualified class name. If the `class` name or `beanName` aren't specified, then the object must be available in the given scope.	Any valid class name	No default value
`beanName`	The name of a bean, as provided to the `instantiate()` method of the `java.beans.Beans` class. This attribute can take a request-time attribute expression as a value. It's possible to supply a `beanName` and `type`, and not include a `class` attribute.	Valid bean name	No default value
`type`	Optional attribute that defines the type of the scripting variable defined. The Java type casting rules are followed for class and superclasses. If the `type` isn't the object class, superclass, or interface implemented by the class, a `java.lang.ClassCastException` is thrown at request time.	Java class	Value of the `class` attribute

We'll now present a `<jsp:useBean>` example, but it makes sense to first cover the `<jsp:getProperty>` and `<jsp:setProperty>` standard actions because it's common to use all three actions together.

<jsp:getProperty>

This action accesses a defined property of a bean. The bean that you're interested in getting the property from must be declared on the JSP page (for example, using `<jsp:useBean>`) prior to using `<jsp:getProperty>`. This action makes the value of the property available so that it can be written to the current `JspWriter`. For example:

```
<p>The course id is
  <jsp:getProperty name="courseBean" property="courseId" />
</p>
```

The property value is converted to a String within the <jsp:getProperty> action in one of two ways depending on the type of the property. If the property is an object, then the toString() method is called. If the property is a primitive, then the valueOf() method of the wrapper class is called.

The syntax of <jsp:getProperty> is as follows:

```
<jsp:getProperty name="name" property="propertyName" />
```

Table 3-4 describes the attributes available to <jsp:getProperty>.

Table 3-4. <jsp:getProperty> *Attributes*

ATTRIBUTE	DESCRIPTION	POSSIBLE VALUES	DEFAULT VALUE
name	The name of the object instance from which the property is obtained	Valid JavaBean class	None given
property	Name of the property to get	Valid defined property	None given

<jsp:setProperty>

This property sets a bean property value. The bean must have been previously defined using the <jsp:useBean> standard action. It's possible to set both simple or indexed properties. You can set a bean's property in the following ways using <jsp:setProperty>:

- Using a parameter in the request object
- Using a String constant value
- Using a value from a request-time attribute

If <jsp:setProperty> is being used to set an indexed property, the value must be an array. As a convenient way to set all of the properties in a bean at once, you can use a wildcard. For example:

```
<jsp:setProperty name="courseBean" property="*" />
```

This would take all of the parameters in a request, match their names and types to the defined properties in the bean, and then assign the values to those properties that match. In the previous sample, the appropriate values would be set into the bean properties contained in the courseBean. If a parameter in the request has a value of "", the corresponding property isn't modified.

Another approach is to set specific values in a bean. Specifying the name of the bean, the property you're interested in setting, and the name of the parameter to use from the request will accomplish this:

```
<jsp:setProperty name="courseBean" property="courseName" param="title" />
```

Under the covers, the `<jsp:setProperty>` standard action uses Java introspection to determine the properties, their types, if they're simple or indexed, and the getter/setter methods.

The syntax of `<jsp:setProperty>` is as follows:

```
<jsp:setProperty name="beanName" property_expression />
```

Here the `property_expression` takes the form of one of the following:

- `property="*"`
- `property="propertyName"`
- `property="propertyName" param="parameterName"`
- `property="propertyName" value="propertyValue"`

Table 3-5 describes the available attributes.

Table 3-5. `<jsp:setProperty>` *Attributes*

ATTRIBUTE	DESCRIPTION	POSSIBLE VALUES	DEFAULT VALUE
`name`	The name of the bean instance.	This value must match the `id` attribute value used in `<jsp:useBean>` prior to using a `<jsp:setProperty>`.	None given
`property`	Name of the bean property that's being set.	Valid defined property in the bean specified by the `name` attribute.	None given
`param`	The name of the request parameter whose value you want to give to a bean property. If you omit `param`, the request parameter name is assumed to be the same as the bean property name. If the `param` isn't set in the request object, or if it has the value of `""`, the `<jsp:setProperty>` element has no effect.	The name of the request parameter usually comes from a Web form.	None given
`value`	The value to assign to the given property.	This attribute can accept a request-time attribute expression as a value. An action may not have both `param` and `value` attributes.	None given

<jsp:useBean>, <jsp:setProperty>, and <jsp:getProperty> Interaction

You'll now look at a sample interaction between `<jsp:useBean>` and `<jsp:setProperty>`. You define a bean called `courseBean` that holds information about a selected course. You'll notice that you have a setter/getter for only the `courseName` property, not the `courseId` property. `courseName` is the only property you want to have set from the JSP page. The `courseId` will be set by a private method called `setCourseId()`, but will be available for getting.

The important point here is that you can determine what you want to make public to your JSP pages and what you want to handle in your bean code. The `getCourse-Description()` method returns a value to a `<jsp:getProperty>` even though there isn't a property called `courseDescription`. So all in all, this little bean shows a lot of variations of how `<jsp:getProperty>` and `<jsp:setProperty>` interact with a bean. Listing 3-3 shows the code for `courseBean`.

Listing 3-3. `courseBean`

```
package com.apress.proj2ee.chapter03.beans;

public final class CourseBean {
  private String courseName;
  private int courseId;

  public CourseBean(){}

  public String getCourseName() {
    return courseName;
  }

  public void setCourseName(String courseName) {
    this.courseName = courseName;
    setCourseId(courseName);
  }

  public String getCourseDescription(){
     switch (courseId) {
     case 1:
       return("This is an introduction course to J2EE 1.4");
     case 2:
       return("This is an intermediate course on J2EE 1.4");
     case 3:
       return("You'd better be a Java pro for this course");
     default:
       return("Sorry, but I'm not sure what course you are interested in.");
    }
  }
```

```
  public String getCourseId(){
    return(Integer.toString(courseId));
  }

  private void setCourseId(String courseName){
    if (courseName.equalsIgnoreCase("Intro")) {
      courseId=1;
    } else if (courseName.equalsIgnoreCase("Intermediate")) {
      courseId=2;
    } else if (courseName.equalsIgnoreCase("Pro")) {
      courseId=3;
    } else {
      courseId=0;
    }
  }
}
```

You can make this bean (and its functionality) available to your JSP page by using the `<jsp:useBean>` action. You'll notice that you have an embedded `<jsp:setProperty>`. This is because you can instantiate the bean and then have any appropriate values set from the incoming request. The following code demonstrates this (all the code for this page is in `bean.jsp`):

```
<jsp:useBean id="courseBean" scope="page"
             class="com.apress.proj2ee.beans.CourseBean" >
  <jsp:setProperty name="courseBean" property="*" />
</jsp:useBean>
```

Once the bean has been declared on the page, you can access any of the properties you need to get at by using `<jsp:getProperty>`:

```
<h1>Your course selection information is: </h1>
<p>The name of the course is
  <jsp:getProperty name="courseBean" property="courseName" />
</p>
<p>The course id is
  <jsp:getProperty name="courseBean" property="courseId" />
</p>
<p>The description of this course is:
  <jsp:getProperty name="courseBean" property="courseDescription" />
</p>
```

You saw earlier that values for bean properties can come from the request, usually through a form. The parameters of the form need to match the name of the property for the values to be set correctly using this:

```
<jsp:setProperty name="courseBean" property="*" />
```

In this sample, the JSP page that has the form submit is called `selectcourse.jsp`:

```
<html>
  <head>
    <title>Working with JavaBeans in a JSP Page</title>
  </head>
  <body>
    <form method="post" action="bean.jsp" >
      <p>Select the course you are interested in:
        <select name="courseName">
          <option value="Intro">Introduction to J2EE 1.4
          <option value="Intermediate">Intermediate J2EE 1.4
          <option value="Pro">Advanced J2EE 1.4
        </select>
      </p>
      <p><input type="submit" value="Select a course">
    </form>
  </body>
</html>
```

<jsp:param>

You use the `<jsp:param>` action to pass parameter values to other actions. This is done using a name/value pair. Actions that work with the `<jsp:param>` action include `<jsp:include>`, `<jsp:forward>`, and `<jsp:plugin>`. If `<jsp:param>` is used within any other action besides the ones just mentioned, a translation error will occur.

When being used with either `<jsp:include>` or `<jsp:forward>`, the page will see the original request object, with the original parameters as well as the new parameters, but the new values take precedence over any existing values. For example, if the request has a parameter `courseName=Intro`, and a parameter `courseName=Pro` is specified for `<jsp:forward>`, the forwarded request shall have `courseName=Pro,Intro`. Note that the new parameter has precedence. The scope of the new parameters is only that of the `<jsp:include>` or `<jsp:forward>` call.

The syntax of `<jsp:param>` is as follows:

```
<jsp:param name="parameterName" value="parameterValue" />
```

Table 3-6 describes the attribute descriptions.

Table 3-6. `<jsp:param>` *Attributes*

ATTRIBUTE	DESCRIPTION	POSSIBLE VALUES	DEFAULT VALUE
`name`	Name of the parameter	Anything	None given
`value`	Value of the parameter	Any value including a request-time expression	None given

<jsp:include>

This element provides a mechanism for including both static and dynamic resources on a JSP page. The resource must be in the same context as the current page and must be written to the current `JspWriter` (or `out` variable). Since the included page has only access to the output stream, it can't set anything in the response; this includes headers or cookies. If an included page tries to use methods such as `setCookie()`, it will be ignored. This is a similar constraint as imposed by the `include()` method of the servlet `RequestDispatcher` class.

When using the `<jsp:include>` action, it may be necessary to use the `<jsp:param>` action as this is how parameter values are passed to the included page. There's also an attribute called `flush` that determines whether the page buffer is flushed prior to the inclusion. Once the buffer has been flushed, it's no longer possible to forward to another resource in the Web application, so use this with caution. This includes using the error page.

The syntax of `<jsp:include>` without using a parameter is as follows:

```
<jsp:include page="url" flush="true|false"/>
```

If parameters are specified, then each parameter value is defined in one or more `<jsp:param>` actions like so:

```
<jsp:include page="url" flush="true|false">
  { <jsp:param .... /> }*
</jsp:include>
```

Table 3-7 describes the attribute descriptions for this action.

Table 3-7. `<jsp:include>` *Attributes*

ATTRIBUTE	DESCRIPTION	POSSIBLE VALUES	DEFAULT VALUE
`page`	Defines the resource that will be included. The URL is interpreted relative to the current JSP page.	Accepts a request-time attribute value (which must evaluate to a `String` hat's a relative URL specification).	None given
`flush`	Optional Boolean attribute. If `true`, the buffer is flushed prior to the inclusion.	`true|false`	`false`

Since we're talking about including content, you may recall that we've already talked about the `include` directive. Just to refresh your memory, the `include` directive looks like this:

```
<%@ include file="filename" %>
```

So what's the difference between the two? There are a few actually, so we'll go through them now.

You use the include directive at compilation time to include static content. The container parses the content; typically a resource included with the include directive will be included on multiple JSP pages. This may be something such as a header or footer file. However, if the resource changes, then the including page needs to be recompiled. This is typically a function of how smart your JSP container is and whether it knows time stamps have changed and files need to be recompiled.

When using the <jsp:include> action, you can include both static and dynamic content at request time. The content isn't parsed, but it's included inline to the JSP page. The resulting JSP page is then translated.

To summarize when you may want to use the include directive vs. <jsp:include>, consider the following:

- Use the include directive when you have resources you don't think are going to change often.

- Use <jsp:include> when the resources require dynamic data or change frequently.

<jsp:expression>, <jsp:scriptlet> , and <jsp:declaration>

You can use three scripting elements in JSP documents. They are <jsp:expression>, <jsp:scriptlet>, and <jsp:declaration>. When used in a JSP document, these elements are valid only in the XML syntaxes. You use the jsp:declaration element to declare scripting language constructs that are available to all other scripting elements. There are no attributes associated with the jsp:declaration element. The body is the declaration itself. Declarations don't produce any output into the current out stream.

Declarations are initialized when the JSP page is initialized and are made available to other declarations, scriptlets, and expressions. An example of a declaration is as follows:

```
<jsp:declaration> Int i </jsp:declaration>
```

The < jsp:scriptlet> element describes actions to be performed in response to some request. These actions are defined as *scriptlets*, which are program fragments. A <jsp:scriptlet> element has no attributes and its body is the scriptlet itself:

```
<jsp:scriptlet> if (Calendar.getInstance().get(Calendar.AM_PM)
                          == Calendar.AM) {</jsp:scriptlet>
Good Morning
<jsp:scriptlet> } else {</jsp:scriptlet>
Good Afternoon
<jsp:scriptlet> } </jsp:scriptlet>
```

The `<jsp:expression>` element describes complete expressions in the scripting language that get evaluated at response time. A `<jsp:expression>` element has no attributes, and its body is the expression. For example:

```
<jsp:expression> application.getAttribute("port") </jsp:expression>
```

<jsp:forward>

A `<jsp:forward>` allows the runtime dispatch of the current request to a static resource, a JSP page, or a servlet. The URL that's defined must be in the same context as the current page. A `<jsp:forward>` effectively stops the execution of the current page, making this a server-side redirect. Therefore, the response buffer is cleared, and any changes that are needed are made to the request parameters. The parameters follow the same logic covered in the "<jsp:param>" section.

If anything was written to the output stream that wasn't buffered prior to the `<jsp:forward>`, a `java.lang.IllegalStateException` will be thrown. This is similar to the `forward()` method call of a servlet `RequestDispatcher`.

`<jsp:forward>` has a single attribute, page, which is a relative URL. This could be a static value, or it could be computed at request time, as in these two examples:

```
<jsp:forward page="/common/termsofuse.jsp" />
<jsp:forward page="<%= nextPage %>" />
```

<jsp:plugin>

If you have Java applets that are part of your application, using the `<jsp:plugin>` action provides the support for including a Java applet in a JSP page. While it's possible to have the appropriate HTML code embedded in your JSP page, using `<jsp:plugin>` allows the functionality to be browser neutral. In other words, you don't have to worry about browser differences. The action will generate the appropriate `<object>` and `<embed>` tags with the appropriate attributes based on the configuration defined in the `<jsp:plugin>` attributes. The JSP container will use the `user-agent` string to determine what version of the browser is being used.

Also, the following two optional support tags work with `<jsp:plugin>`:

- `<jsp:params>` passes any additional parameters to the applet or bean.

- `<jsp:fallback>` specifies any content that should be displayed in the browser if the plug-in couldn't be started; this could be because the generated `<object>` and `<embed>` tags aren't supported or because of some other runtime issue. If the plug-in can start but the applet or JavaBeans component can't be found or started, a plug-in specific message will be presented to the user, most likely a pop-up window, giving a `ClassNotFoundException`.

If either one of the previously mentioned support tags are used in any other context, other than as a child of `<jsp:plugin>`, a translation error will occur.

As you may imagine if you've worked with applets before, a whole slew of attributes are available in this action to handle to configuration settings. The syntax of the <jsp:plugin> action is as follows:

```
<jsp:plugin type="bean|applet"
            code="objectCode"
            codebase="objectCodebase"
          { align="alignment"}
          { archive="archiveList"}
          { height="height"}
          { hspace="hspace"}
          { jreversion="jreversion"}
          { name="componentName"}
          { vspace="vspace"}
          {title="title"}
          { width="width"}
          { nspluginurl="url"}
          { iepluginurl="url"}
          { mayscript="true|false" }>
 { <jsp:params>
   { <jsp:param name="paramName" value="paramValue" /> }+
   </jsp:params> }
 { <jsp:fallback> arbitrary_text </jsp:fallback> }
</jsp:plugin>
```

Table 3-8 describes the attributes.

Table 3-8. <jsp:plugin> *Attributes*

ATTRIBUTE	DESCRIPTION	REQUIRED
type	Identifies component type, either Java bean or applet.	Yes
code	Same as the HTML syntax defined in the HTML specification.	Yes
codebase	Same as the HTML syntax.	Yes
align	Same as the HTML syntax.	No
archive	Same as the HTML syntax.	No
height	Same as the HTML syntax, possible to use a runtime expression value.	No
hspace	Same as the HTML syntax.	No
jversion	Identifies the version number of the JRE the component requires to operate. Default to "1.2".	No
name	Same as the HTML syntax.	No
vspace	Same as the HTML syntax.	No
title	Same as the HTML syntax.	No
width	Same as the HTML syntax.	No
nspluginurl	URL where JRE plug-in can be downloaded for Netscape Navigator. The default is implementation defined.	No
iepluginurl	URL where JRE plug-in can be downloaded for IE. The default is implementation defined.	No
mayscript	As defined by HTML specification.	No

Because of the security concern of having a plug-in execute without a user being aware of it, some browsers don't allow an object's height or width to be zero. You'll need to check your browser to see if this is a restriction. If so, even though these attributes aren't required, you'll need to include them to generate code that will work correctly.

<jsp:attribute>

The `<jsp:attribute>` action is new in JSP 2.0 and fits in with the new JSP fragment mechanism. Prior to JSP 2.0, you could pass input to tag handlers in two ways, either through attribute values or through the element body. Attribute values were always evaluated once (if they were specified as an expression), and the result was passed to the tag handler. The body could contain scripting elements and action elements and be evaluated zero or more times on demand by the tag handler.

Using `<jsp:attribute>`, based on the configuration of the action being invoked, the body of the element specifies a value that's evaluated once, or it specifies a JSP fragment, which is in a form that makes it possible for a tag handler to evaluate it as many times as needed.

The `<jsp:attribute>` action allows the page author to define the value of an action's attribute in the body of an XML element. The `<jsp:attribute>` must appear only as a subelement of a standard or custom action. If you try to use it otherwise, a translation error will occur. When being used for custom action invocations, `<jsp:attribute>` can be used for both classic and simple tag handlers.

To get an idea of what we're talking about, you'll now see a simple use of `<jsp:attribute>`. In the following sample, you have a custom action called `text`. This action is using `<jsp:attribute>` to define an attribute called `headingType` with the value of `H1`:

```
<apress:text>
  <jsp:attribute name="headingType">
    H1
  </jsp:attribute>
</apress:text>
```

You can use `<jsp:attribute>` in a number of ways. Each option has different expected behavior. These are the various ways to use `<jsp:attribute>`:

For custom action attributes of type `javax.servlet.jsp.tagext.JspFragment`, the container will create a `JspFragment` out of the body of the `<jsp:attribute>` action and pass it to the tag handler. This applies for both classic and simple tag handlers. A translation error will result if the body of the `<jsp:attribute>` action isn't scriptless in this case.

If the custom action using `<jsp:attribute>` accepts dynamic attributes (which we'll discuss in detail in Chapter 5) and the name of the attribute isn't one explicitly indicated for the tag, then the container will evaluate the body of `<jsp:attribute>` and assign the computed value to the attribute using the dynamic attribute algorithm. Since the type of the attribute is unknown and the body of `<jsp:attribute>` evaluates to a `String`, the container will pass in an instance of `String` to the action.

For standard or custom action attributes that accept a request-time expression value, the container will evaluate the body of the `<jsp:attribute>` action and use the result of this evaluation as the value of the attribute. The body of the attribute action can be any JSP content in this case. If the type of the attribute isn't `String`, the standard type conversion rules will be applied.

For standard or custom action attributes that *do not* accept a request-time expression value, the container must use the body of the `<jsp:attribute>` action as the value of the attribute. A translation error will result if the body of the `<jsp:attribute>` action contains anything but template text.

If the enclosing action is `<jsp:element>`, the values of the name attribute and the body of the of the attribute will be used to construct the element dynamically.

If the body of the `<jsp:attribute>` action is empty, it's the equivalent of specifying `""` as the value of the attribute. Note that after being trimmed, nonempty bodies can also result in a value of `""`. The `<jsp:attribute>` action accepts a `name` attribute and a `trim` attribute.

Table 3-9 describes the attributes.

Table 3-9. `<jsp:attribute>` *Attributes*

ATTRIBUTE	DESCRIPTION	REQUIRED	DEFAULTS
`name`	Associates the action with one of the attributes the tag handler is declared to accept.	Yes	None given
`trim`	Determines whether the whitespace appearing at the beginning and at the end of the element body should be discarded. Whitespace includes spaces, carriage returns, line feeds, and tabs.	No	`true`

The container will trim at translation time only, not at run time. This means that if you have a custom action that produces whitespace, it won't be affected by the `trim` attribute, regardless of what the value of `trim` is.

<jsp:body>

Most page authors are probably used to the body of a standard or custom action invocation being defined implicitly as the body of the XML element of the invocation. You can also define the body of a standard or custom action explicitly using the `<jsp:body>` standard action. Using `<jsp:body>` is required if one or more `<jsp:attribute>` elements appear in the body of the tag. If one or more `<jsp:attribute>` elements appear in the body of a tag invocation but no `<jsp:body>` element appears or an empty `<jsp:body>` element appears, it's the equivalent of the tag having an empty body.

It's also legal to use the `<jsp:body>` standard action to supply bodies to standard actions for any standard action that accepts a body (except for `<jsp:body>` and `<jsp:attribute>`).

For example, in the following code, you have a custom action that includes defining an attribute called `nonfragment`. You then use the `<jsp:body>` to indicate the body of the custom action:

```
<proj2ee:simpletag x="10" y="20" z="test">
  <jsp:attribute name="nonfragment">
    Nonfragment Template Text
  </jsp:attribute>
  <jsp:body>
    In body: <br/>
  </jsp:body>
</proj2ee:simpletag>
```

The body standard action accepts no attributes.

<jsp:invoke>

While `<jsp:invoke>` is defined as a standard action, it's specifically for use in tag files. We'll talk about tag files extensively in Chapter 5, so we won't go into all the details of a tag file here. However, the main point is that a tag file is actually a JSP file used to describe custom actions and uses JSP syntax. If `<jsp:invoke>` is used in a JSP file that isn't a tag file, a translation error will occur. `<jsp:invoke>` takes the name of an attribute that's a fragment and invokes the fragment, sending the output of the result to the `JspWriter` or to a page scope variable that can be used later in the page. If the fragment identified by the given name is `null`, `<jsp:invoke>` will behave as though a fragment was passed in that produces no output.

You'll now look at some different ways to use `<jsp:invoke>` to get a better idea of how it works. The most basic command is to invoke a JSP fragment with the given name specified in the `fragment` attribute, with no parameters. The fragment will be invoked using the `JspFragment.invoke()` method. Remember that each JSP fragment is represented as a `JspFragment` object in the container. Passing in `null` for the `writer` parameter means that the results will be sent to the `JspWriter` of the `JspContext` associated with the `JspFragment`. The following is an example of this type of invocation:

```
<jsp:invoke fragment="frag"/>
```

It's also possible to give a fragment access to variables that it may need for its evaluation. JSP fragments have access to the same page scope variables as the page or tag file in which they were defined, as well as to variables in the request, session, and application scopes. Tag files have access to a local page scope, separate from the page scope of the calling page.

When a tag file invokes a fragment that appears in the calling page, the JSP container provides a way to synchronize variables between the local page scope in the tag file and the page scope of the calling page. We'll talk about the way synchronization is handled for variables in tag files in detail in Chapter 5. For now, for each variable that's to be synchronized, the tag file author must declare the variable with a scope of either `AT_BEGIN` or `NESTED`. The container will then generate code to synchronize the page scope values for the variable in the tag file with the page scope equivalent in the calling page or tag file.

The following is an example of a tag file providing a fragment access to a variable:

```
<%@ variable name-given="var1" scope="AT_BEGIN" %>
...
<c:set var="var1" value="1"/>
<jsp:invoke fragment="anotherFragment"/>
```

The `<jsp:invoke>` action also provides a way to store output of a fragment. Using the `var` or `varReader` attribute, it's possible to send output to a scoped attribute. To accomplish this, the `JspFragment.invoke()` method uses a custom `java.io.Writer` that's passed in instead of using `null`.

If `var` is specified, a `java.lang.String` object is made available in a scoped attribute with the name specified by `var`. If `varReader` is specified, a `java.io.Reader` object is made available in a scoped attribute with the name specified by `varReader`. Choosing whether you need a `String` or a `Reader` object will depend on what you plan on doing with the output of the fragment.

A `Reader` object can be passed to another custom action for further processing and allows for the action to perform a reset on the `Reader` by calling the `reset()` method. This can be useful if you want the result of the invoked fragment to be read again without reexecuting the fragment. The optional `scope` attribute indicates the scope of the variable specified in `var` or `varReader`. The default is page scope. The following is an example of using `var` or `varReader` and the `scope` attribute:

```
<jsp:invoke fragment="frag2" var="resultString" scope="session"/>
<jsp:invoke fragment="frag3" varReader="resultReader" scope="page"/>
```

Table 3-10 describes the attributes available for the `<jsp:invoke>` action.

<jsp:doBody>

Like `<jsp:invoke>`, the `<jsp:doBody>` action can be used only in tag files. A translation error will occur if the action is used in a JSP page. The `<jsp:doBody>` standard action behaves exactly like `<jsp:invoke>`, except that it operates on the body of the tag instead of on a specific fragment passed as an attribute.

`<jsp:doBody>` invokes the body of the tag, sending the output of the result to a `JspWriter` or to a defined scoped attribute. There's no need for the `fragment` attribute to specify the name for this standard action because it always acts on the tag body. The `var`, `varReader`, and `scope` attributes are all supported with the same semantics as defined for the `<jsp:invoke>` action. Fragments are given access to variables in the same way for `<jsp:doBody>` as they are for `<jsp:invoke>`. If no body was passed to the tag, `<jsp:doBody>` will behave as though a body was passed in that produces no output. The body of a tag is passed to the simple tag handler as a `JspFragment` object. A translation error shall result if the `<jsp:doBody>` action contains a nonempty body. This is an example of using `<jsp:doBody>`:

```
<jsp:body>
bdy of tag that defines an AT_BEGIN scripting variable ${var1}.
</jsp:body>
```

Table 3-11 describes the attributes for `<jsp:doBody>`.

Table 3-10. `<jsp:invoke>` *Attributes*

ATTRIBUTE	DESCRIPTION	REQUIRED	DEFAULTS
`fragment`	The name used to identify the fragment during this tag invocation.	Yes	None given
`var`	The name of a scoped attribute to store the result of the fragment invocation. The result will be stored as a `java.lang.String` object. A translation error will occur if both `var` and `varReader` are specified. If neither `var` nor `varReader` are specified, the result of the fragment goes directly to the `JspWriter`.	No	None given
`varReader`	The name of a scoped attribute to store the result of the fragment invocation. The result will be stored as a `java.io.Reader` object. See the previous `var` description restrictions.	No	None given
`scope`	A valid JSP scope in which to store the resulting variable. A translation error will result if this attribute appears without specifying either the `var` or the `varReader` attribute. A scope of `session` should be used with caution since not all calling pages may be participating in a session. A container must throw an `IllegalStateException` at run time if scope is `session` and the calling page doesn't participate in a session.	No	`page`

Table 3-11. `<jsp:doBody>` *Attributes*

ATTRIBUTE	DESCRIPTION	REQUIRED	DEFAULTS
`var`	The name of a scoped attribute to store the result of the fragment invocation. The result will be stored as a `java.lang.String` object. A translation error will occur if both `var` and `varReader` are specified. If neither `var` nor `varReader` are specified, the result of the fragment goes directly to the `JspWriter`.	No	None given
`varReader`	The name of a scoped attribute to store the result of the fragment invocation. The result will be stored as a `java.io.Reader` object. See the previous `var` description for restrictions.	No	None given
`scope`	A valid JSP scope in which to store the resulting variable. A translation error will result if this attribute appears without specifying either the `var` or `varReader` attribute. A scope of `session` should be used with caution since not all calling pages may be participating in a session. A container must throw an `IllegalStateException` at run time if scope is `session` and the calling page doesn't participate in a session.	No	`page`

<jsp:element>

You use the `<jsp:element>` action to dynamically define the value of the tag of an XML element. If you want to have a standard, flexible way to do so, `<jsp:element>` is your action. You can use this action in JSP pages, tag files, and JSP documents. This action has an optional body that can use the `<jsp:attribute>` and `<jsp:body>` actions to generate any element. The only mandatory attribute is `name`, which is a `String`. The value of the `name` attribute determines the tag of the XML element that's generated. Custom actions can generate any content, both structured and unstructured.

The syntax of the `<jsp:element>` action may have a body. Two forms of this action are valid, depending on whether the element has any attributes. In the first form, no attributes are present:

```
<jsp:element name="name">
  optional body
</jsp:element>
```

In the second form, zero or more attributes are requested, using `<jsp:attribute>` and `<jsp:body>`, as appropriate:

```
<jsp:element name="name">
  optional_subelement*
</jsp:element>

optional_sublement ::=
<jsp:body>
<jsp:attribute>
```

Table 3-12 describes the only mandatory attribute.

Table 3-12. `<jsp:element>` *Attribute*

ATTRIBUTE	DESCRIPTION	REQUIRED	DEFAULTS
name	The value of name is that of the element generated. The name can be a QName. There are no constraints on this value, and it's accepted as is.	Yes	None given

The following sample shows how to use `<jsp:element>` with the optional `<jsp:attribute>` and `<jsp:body>` elements. You're accessing some dynamic content from the HTTP request using the `param` variable:

```
<jsp:element name="course" >
<jsp:attribute name="title">${param.title}</jsp:attribute>
<jsp:body>Testing jsp element body using an EL variable
                ${param.testValue}</jsp:body>
</jsp:element>
```

The `<jsp:text>` action generates template text in either a JSP page or a JSP document. `<jsp:text>` is similar to the XSLT `xsl:text` element in that it will preserve whitespace as opposed to using an HTML `<p>`. While this is usually fixed content, it can also generate dynamic content. This is where you need to be careful. The following example is a fragment that could be in either a JSP page or a JSP document:

```
<jsp:text>
  This is some template text without using any expressions
</jsp:text>
```

The next sample shows how an expression may be used within the `<jsp:text>`:

```
<jsp:text>
  This is content that will display the value of the incoming userId:
  ${request.userId}
</jsp:text>
```

When using this action, some of the functionality may be slightly different depending on whether you're using it in a JSP page or a JSP document. When being used in a JSP document, the content needs to conform to being a well-formed XML document. So if you're using expressions in your content, you need to make sure you use the correct entity reference. For example, using the following:

```
<jsp:text>
  This is illegal in a JSP document: ${request.lastLoginAttempt < 5}
</jsp:text>
```

would cause a translation error, but the following example wouldn't because of the entity reference:

```
<jsp:text>
  This is legal in a JSP document: ${request.lastLoginAttempt lt 5}
</jsp:text>
```

When a `<jsp:text>` is encountered, the content in the body of the element is passed through to the current `out` variable. The `<jsp:text>` action may seem familiar to those who work with XSLT, as it's similar to the `<xslt:text>` element.

There are no attributes defined for `<jsp:text>`, but the action can have an optional body, as you've seen in the examples. This action can appear anywhere that template data can appear and may have EL expressions within the body.

<jsp:output>

You can use the `<jsp:output>` element only in JSP documents and in tag files that are in XML syntax. It's used to modify the XML declaration property of the output of a JSP document or tag file. In JSP 2.0, the XML declaration is the only property that can be modified.

Most of the time you won't need to use `<jsp:output>` because the default value of the property is defined. Using the `omit-xml-declaration` attribute, it's possible to prevent the declaration from being generated. The valid values are yes, no, `true`, and `false` and will indicate whether an XML declaration is to be inserted at the beginning of the output. The generated XML declaration is of the following form:

```
<? xml version="1.0" encoding="encodingValue" ?>
```

The `encodingValue` is the character encoding as set by the JSP page.

Table 3-13 describes the attribute available with `<jsp:output>`.

Table 3-13. `<jsp:output>` *Attributes*

ATTRIBUTE	DESCRIPTION	REQUIRED	DEFAULTS
`omit-xml-declaration`	Indicates whether to omit the generation of an XML declaration. Acceptable values are `true`, yes, `false`, and no.	No	The default value for a JSP document that has a `<jsp:root>` element is yes. The default value for JSP documents without a `<jsp:root>` element is no. The default value for a tag file in XML syntax is always yes.
`doctype-root-element`	Must be specified if and only if `doctype-system` is specified, or a translation error must occur. Indicates the name that's to be output in the generated DOCTYPE declaration.	No	—
`doctype-system`	Specifies that a DOCTYPE declaration is to be generated and gives the value for the system literal.	No	—
`doctype-public`	Must not be specified unless `doctype-system` is specified. Gives the value for the public ID for the generated DOCTYPE	No	`<!DOCTYPE nameOfRootElement SYSTEM "doctypeSystem">`

<jsp:root>

The `<jsp:root>` element can appear only as the root element in a JSP document or in a tag file in XML syntax. If it's used in a JSP page, a translation error will occur. The `<jsp:root>` element isn't required by JSP documents and tag files. `<jsp:root>` has two purposes:

- The first is to indicate that the JSP file is in XML syntax, without having to use configuration group elements or by using the `.jspx` extension.

- The other use of the `<jsp:root>` element is to accommodate the generation of content that isn't a single XML document: either a sequence of XML documents or some non-XML content.

You can use a `<jsp:root>` element to provide zero or more `xmlns` attributes that correspond to namespaces for the standard actions, for custom actions, or for generated template text. Unlike in JSP 1.2, not all tag libraries used within the JSP document need to be introduced on the root; tag libraries can be incorporated as needed inside the document using additional `xmlns` attributes:

```
<jsp:root xmlns:jsp="http://java.sun.com/JSP/Page"
          xmlns:c="http://java.sun.com/jstl/core_rt"
          version="2.0">
```

The `<jsp:root>` element has one mandatory attribute, the version of the JSP specification that the page is using. When `<jsp:root>` is used, the container will, by default, not insert an XML declaration. It's possible to change the default by using the `<jsp:output>` element.

Table 3-14 describes the attribute description for `<jsp:root>`.

Table 3-14. `<jsp:root>` *Attribute*

ATTRIBUTE	DESCRIPTION	REQUIRED	DEFAULTS
`version`	The version of the JSP specification used in this page. Valid values are `1.2` and `2.0`. It's a translation error if the container doesn't support the required version.	Yes	None defined

Available Object Scope

One of the most powerful features of the JSP architecture is that a JSP page can access, create, and modify server-side objects. These objects can then be made visible to actions, EL expressions, and scripting elements. When an object is created, it defines or defaults to a given scope. Some objects are created implicitly by the container, and others can be created explicitly through actions, EL, or scripting.

The scope describes what entities can access the object. For example, if an object is defined to have page scope, then it's visible only for the duration of the current request on that page. Actions can access objects using a name in the `pageContext` object. An object exposed through a scripting variable has a scope within the page. Scripting elements can access some objects directly via a scripting variable. Some implicit objects are visible via scripting variables and EL expressions in any JSP page.

The following are the available object scopes.

Page Scope

Objects with page scope are accessible only within the page where they're created. The object is valid only during the processing of the response, and once the response is sent back to the client or the request is forwarded, the reference is no longer valid. References to objects with page scope are stored in the `pageContext` object and can be accessed using the `getAttribute()` method of the `pageContext` object. This is the default scope given when objects are created with the `<jsp:useBean>` standard action.

Request Scope

Objects with request scope are accessible from pages processing the same request where they were created. Once the request is processed, all references to the object are released. As long as the `HttpRequest` object still exists, even if the request is forwarded to another page, the object is still available. References to objects with request scope are stored in the request object and made available using the `setAttribute()` method of the request implicit object, as shown in the following sample:

```
request.setAttribute(USER_NAME, userId);
```

Session Scope

Objects with session scope are accessible from pages processing requests that are in the same session as the one in which they were created. For an object to be defined in session scope, the page itself must be session aware as defined by its `page` directive. An object is no longer valid once the session becomes invalidated. References to objects with session scope are stored in the session object, as follows:

```
session.setAttribute(USER_NAME, userId);
```

Application Scope

Objects with application scope are accessible from JSP pages that reside in the same application. This creates a global object that's available to pages that are session aware as well as those that aren't. References to objects with application scope are stored in the application object associated with page activation. The application object is an instance of `javax.servlet.ServletContext` that's obtained from the servlet configuration object. When the `ServletContext` is released, application scope variables are no longer accessible.

Note that application scope variables use a single namespace. Therefore, you need to take care that your code is thread safe when accessing objects in application scope. Application scope variables are typically created and populated at application startup and then used in a read-only mode for the remainder of the application.

Implicit Objects

A number of interfaces are provided in the Servlet application programming interface (API). Since a JSP page eventually becomes a servlet, it makes sense that you should have access to some of these objects through the JSP page. Certain classes encapsulate the functionality in which you're interested. Among the classes are `HttpServletRequest`, `HttpServletResponse`, and `HttpSession`. There's no need for the page author to do any extra coding to access these objects. They're made available as standard variables to scripting languages, as well as the expression language, and are automatically available.

Implicit objects are available through the `pageContext` object. The `pageContext` is an object that provides a context to store references to objects used by the page, encapsulates implementation-dependant features, and provides convenience methods. A JSP page implementation class can use a `pageContext` to run unmodified in any compliant JSP container while taking advantage of implementation-specific improvements such as a high-performance `JspWriter`.

Table 3-15 defines the available implicit objects.

Table 3-15. Implicit Objects

VARIABLE NAME	TYPE	SEMANTICS	SCOPE
`request`	Protocol-dependant subtype of `javax.servlet.ServletRequest` (for example, `javax.servlet.http.HttpServletRequest`	The request triggering the service invocation.	`request`
`response`	Protocol-dependant subtype of `javax.servlet.ServletResponse` (for example, `javax.servlet.http.HttpServletResponse`)	The response to the request.	`page`
`pageContext`	`javax.servlet.jsp.PageContext`	The page context for this JSP page.	`page`
`session`	`javax.servlet.http.HttpSession`	The session object created for the requesting client (if any). This variable is valid only for HTTP-based protocols.	`session`
`application`	`javax.servlet.ServletContext`	The servlet context obtained from the servlet configuration object using the `getServletConfig().getContext()` method.	`application`
`out`	`javax.servlet.jsp.JspWriter`	An object that writes into the output stream.	`page`
`config`	`javax.servlet.ServletConfig`	The `ServletConfig` for this JSP page.	`page`
`page`	`java.lang.Object`	The instance of this page's implementation class processing the current request.	`page`

In addition to all of the implicit objects mentioned in Table 3-15, the variable described in Table 3-16 is available to JSP error pages.

Table 3-16. The `exception` *Variable*

VARIABLE NAME	TYPE	SEMANTICS	SCOPE
`exception`	`java.lang.Throwable`	The uncaught `Throwable` that resulted in the error page being invoked	page

Scripting Elements

You use scripting elements to insert code, usually Java code, into a JSP page. Scripting elements are commonly used to manipulate objects and perform some computation on an object or runtime value. Scripting elements have been the cause of many a mangled design; Java code is usually needed because the separation of presentation and business logic isn't defined well enough in the application. Therefore, you end up with a big mess of code interlaced with presentation when, in fact, this shouldn't be the case. JSP 2.0 adds the much cleaner and readable EL expressions as an alternative to scripting elements. We'll talk about the EL in detail in "The JSP 2.0 Expression Language."

The following scripting element sections are intentionally short because scripting elements should go the way of the dinosaurs in JSP pages. A good design and skillful page author shouldn't be using scripting elements in code any longer. It's possible to disable scripting elements through the use of the `<scripting-invalid>` element in the `web.xml` deployment descriptor. That way, if any scriptlets are found in a JSP page at translation time, they will cause a translation error. This section is only here because if you're looking at JSP pages that already contain scripting elements, at least you'll understand what you're seeing.

There are three scripting element types: declarations, scriptlets, and expressions. The syntax starts with a `<%` as follows:

```
<%! this is a declaration %>
<% this is a scriptlet %>
<%= this is an expression %>
```

Declarations

Declarations declare variables and methods in the scripting language used in a JSP page. A declaration must be a complete declarative statement according to the syntax of the scripting language being used. It's used to define variables and methods of instance scope. Variables defined in declarations may be accessed from multiple threads, so they must be thread safe. When using a declaration, no output is sent to the current `out` variable. Declarations are initialized when the JSP page is initialized and are made available to other declarations, scriptlets, and expressions.

Scriptlets

A *scriptlet* is a chunk of Java code that's executed at run time. Scripting can do just about anything you can do in Java and therefore can affect the current `out` variable. It's typical that scriptlets are intermingled with template text. This causes a JSP page to be quite difficult to read since each section of scriptlet has to be contained between the `<% scriptlet code %>` syntax. Scriptlets don't have the same thread-safety issue as declarations because the variables and code are local to the `_jspService()` method.

Expressions

An *expression* is a way to send a value of a Java expression to the `out` variable. The expression is evaluated at request-processing time, and the result is converted to a `String`. If the result of the expression is an object, the `toString()` method is called. If the value can't be coerced into a `String` at translation time, then a `ClassCastException` will be raised.

Comments

Before we move on to the JSP 2.0 expression language, we'll talk about how to comment your JSP pages. Two types of comments are available in JSP page.

The first is for the page author to comment upon what the JSP page is doing. In this case, you don't want those comments showing up in the output to the client. A JSP comment is of the following form:

```
<%-- this is a JSP comment that would not show up in the client output --%>
```

The second way provides a mechanism for comments that are intended to be included in the output sent to the client. To generate comments that appear in the response output stream to the requesting client, you use the HTML and XML comment syntax as follows:

```
<!-- comment that the user will see  -->
```

The JSP container treats these comments as uninterpreted template text. If you desire, the generated comment can also have dynamic data by using this expression syntax:

```
<!-- comments <%= some expression %> more comments ... -->
```

The body of the content is completely ignored by the container. Comments are useful for documentation but also are used to comment out some portions of a JSP page. Note that JSP comments don't nest. An alternative way to place a comment in JSP is to use the comment mechanism of the scripting language. For example:

```
<% /** this is another comment ... **/ %>
```

The JSP 2.0 Expression Language

The EL is a powerful feature added into JSP 2.0. Initially it was introduced in the JSTL 1.0 specification, but the expert groups of JSTL 1.0 and JSP 2.0 have been working closely together from the start on the EL features. The goal has always been to incorporate the EL into the JSP specification. More than likely, various J2EE expert groups will use the EL. The upcoming technology of JavaServer Faces is expected to use the same EL. The language semantics are exposed through an API described in the `javax.servlet.jsp.el` package.

The EL gives the page author a much simpler syntax for doing data manipulation. The EL is invoked by using the construct `${expr}`, where `expr` represents some EL expression. It's possible to use the EL in template text as well as attribute values for both standard and custom actions in JSP 2.0. This is slightly different from what was introduced in the JSTL, as only attribute values were supported. The following example shows the EL being used in an attribute:

```
<c:if test="${course.studentsEnrolled > course.maxStudents}">
  The course <c:out value="${course.title}"/> is currently full.
</c:if>
```

Using the `<c:if>` conditional tag (which we'll talk about in Chapter 4; you can use the EL in the `test` attribute to determine if you can still sign up for a course. If the course is full, you can access the `course` object by using the EL and assigning that to the `value` attribute. Anyone who has worked with JSP pages before can certainly appreciate the ease of use and coding simplification possible with the EL.

When using an identifier (such as `course`, for example) with the EL, it's the same as if you had used `PageContext.findAttribute(identifier)`. The identifier itself can reside in any of the known JSP scopes. If the identifier isn't found in any scope, then a `null` value is returned.

The EL was intentionally kept simple. It provides the following:

- Access to variables in the available namespace (which is the `pageContext`)
- Nested properties and accessors to collections
- Relational, logical, and arithmetic operators
- Extensible functions mapping into static methods in Java classes
- A set of implicit objects

The EL makes JSP pages much cleaner and easier to read and (we hope) scriptlet free. The EL provides the encouragement to lose any of those nasty bad scriptlet habits you may have picked up along the way. It also eliminates the need to know Java to write expressions within your pages. By setting the `isScriptingEnabled` attribute used in the page directive to `false` as follows, you'll prevent a JSP page from compiling if it contains any scriptlet code. In this case, JSP pages can use EL expressions but are prevented from using Java scriptlets, Java expressions, or Java declaration elements:

```
<%@ page contentType="text/html; charset=UTF-8" isELIgnored="false" %>
```

It's also possible to disable scripting through the `<scripting-enabled>` JSP configuration element. This provides a way to define a group of pages all at once instead of using the page directive in every page. The `web.xml` file snippet containing the JSP configuration element is as follows:

```
<jsp-property-group>
  <url-pattern>*.jsp</url-pattern>
  <el-ignored>false</el-ignored>
</jsp-property-group>
```

For the EL evaluations to be carried out by the container, the Web application needs to be packaged with a Servlet 2.4 deployment descriptor. This is defined in the `web.xml` as follows:

```
<web-app xmlns="http://java.sun.com/xml/ns/j2ee"
        xmlns:xsi="http://www.w3.org/2001/XMLSchema-instance"
        xsi:schemaLocation="http://java.sun.com/xml/ns/j2ee web-app_2_4.xsd"
        version="2.4">
  ...
</web-app>
```

If your pages are packaged with a Servlet 2.3 deployment descriptor, the JSP 2.0 container will not perform any EL evaluation. A Servlet 2.3 deployment descriptor is as follows:

```
<!DOCTYPE webapp
  PUBLIC "-//Sun Microsystems, Inc.//DTD Web Application 2.3//EN"
        "http://java.sun.com/j2ee/dtds/web-app_2_3.dtd">
<web-app>
  ...
</web-app>
```

> **NOTE** *If you're expecting EL evaluations to take place and they're being written to the output stream as template text, chances are you need to change your deployment descriptor to be in Servlet 2.4 format.*

You'll now look further at each area of the EL.

Accessing Variables

When a page author accesses data in a JSP, they work with objects and the values they hold. For the most part these objects have been JavaBeans or collections. The EL has two ways to access data structures. The operators are . (also called the *dot* operator) and [ ]. Using these operators makes it possible to easily access encapsulated data from objects. You've already seen this access in the previous example by accessing `course.studentsEnrolled`. Using the dot operator is a shortcut for accessing an object's property.

Take a brief look at the previous sample:

```
The course ${course.title} is currently full.
```

You access the value of `title`, which is a property of the `course` object. You use the [ ] `operator` for accessing collections, which includes lists, maps, and arrays. So, for example, you can access the following `Map` object like so:

```
Course Description: <c:out value="${courseDesc[course.courseId]}"/>
```

Being able to index by a value or by a `String` is convenient, depending on what type of collection is being referenced.

Using Accessors and Nested Properties

The EL follows ECMAScript, better known as *JavaScript*, in its use of the . and [ ] operators. You can access properties of both ordered and unordered collections using the [ ] syntax. However, you can use numbers only with ordered collections. When working with an unordered collection, you use a string. For instance, the following expression:

```
${course["title"]}
```

is equivalent to this:

```
${course.title}
```

A situation that might require the bracket notion is where a special character that's legal in a property name such as a period (.) or hyphen (-) is used in the variable name. In this case, you can't use the dot notation and must use [ ]. For example, if the property was instead called `course-title`, you'd access it with [ ] notation using quotes as follows:

```
${course["course-title"]}
```

Relational, Logical, and Arithmetic Operators

The EL provides support for any type of relational, logical, or arithmetic operation you need to perform. All results are Boolean values.

The relational operators include: ==, !=, <, >, <=, >=, eq, ne, lt, gt, le, and ge. The last six operators are made available to avoid having to use entity references in XML syntax. Entity references are sometimes required because if you place a character such as < inside an XML element, the parser will throw an error because it thinks this is the start of a new element. All illegal XML characters have to be replaced by entity references. Table 3-17 shows an example of each of the logical, relational, and arithmetic operators, using either the operator or the entity reference.

Logical operators include those you'd expect: AND, NOT, and OR. They're used to perform Boolean operations of expressions. You can use parentheses within the expression to order the evaluation. For example, the following:

```
${ (7==7 and 6 == 6) && 5 < 6}
```

would evaluate to ${true && true}; therefore, the resulting expression would be true. The && needs to be expressed using the & entity reference for each & in an XML document. Personally, we just prefer to use and since we're always up for the least amount of typing.

You can also use arithmetic and prefix operators with the EL. Arithmetic operators consisting of addition (+), subtraction (-), multiplication (*), division (/ or div), and remainder/modulo (% or mod). The empty prefix operator is also provided for testing whether a value is null or empty. For example:

```
<c:if test="${empty course}">
  A course must be selected.
</c:if>
```

Table 3-17 shows how to use each of the operators.

Table 3-17. Operators

<table>
<tr><th>OPERATOR</th><th>DESCRIPTION</th><th>EXAMPLE</th><th>EL RESULT</th></tr>
<tr><td>== (eq)</td><td>Equals</td><td>${7 == 7}</td><td>True</td></tr>
<tr><td>!= (ne)</td><td>Not equals</td><td>${7 ne 7}</td><td>False</td></tr>
<tr><td>< (lt)</td><td>Less than</td><td>${6 lt 7}</td><td>True</td></tr>
<tr><td>> (gt)</td><td>Greater than</td><td>${6 > 7}</td><td>False</td></tr>
<tr><td><= (le)</td><td>Less than or equal to</td><td>${6 <= 7}</td><td>True</td></tr>
<tr><td>>= (ge)</td><td>Greater than or equal to</td><td>${6 ge 7}</td><td>False</td></tr>
<tr><td>and (&&)</td><td>Logical AND operation</td><td>${7 == 7 and 6 == 6}</td><td>True</td></tr>
<tr><td>not (!)</td><td>Logical NOT operation</td><td>${not 6 == 6}</td><td>False</td></tr>
<tr><td>or (||)</td><td>Logical OR operation</td><td>${7== 7 || 6 == 6}</td><td>True</td></tr>
</table>

Functions

The EL has the notion of *qualified functions*. This notion reuses the notion of qualification from XML namespaces (and attributes), XSL functions, and JSP custom actions. Functions are mapped to `public static` methods in Java classes that are specified in the TLD. Each tag library may include zero or more static functions that are listed in the TLD. The name given to the function in the TLD is what's exposed to the EL.

A `public static` method in the specified `public` class will implement the function. The function name must be unique in the tag library. If the function isn't declared correctly, or there are multiple functions with the same name, a translation-time error will be generated. You'll now take a look at a sample.

Define a class called `Functions.java` that can contain a `public static` method called `currentDate()`:

```
package com.apress.proj2ee.chapter03;

import java.util.Date;

/**
 * Defines the functions used in the Pro J2EE 1.4 sample tag library.
 *
 * <p>Each function is defined as a static method.</p>
 */
public class Functions {
  public static Date currentDate() {
    return new Date();
  }
}
```

You then add the function definition to the TLD file like so:

```
<taglib xmlns="http://java.sun.com/xml/ns/j2ee"
        xmlns:xsi="http://www.w3.org/2001/XMLSchema-instance"
        xsi:schemaLocation="http://java.sun.com/xml/ns/ ↵
j2ee web-jsptaglibrary_2_0.xsd"
        version="2.0" >
  ...
  <function>
    <description>Get the current date</description>
    <name>currentDate</name>
    <function-class>com.apress.proj2ee.chapter03.Functions</function-class>
    <function-signature>java.util.Date currentDate()</function-signature>
  </function>
  ...
</taglib>
```

You can then access this function on a JSP page as shown in the following example:

```
<%@ taglib prefix="proj2ee" uri="/apress-taglib"%>

<html>
  <head>
    <title>Pro J2EE 1.4 - Using Functions</title>
  </head>
  <body>
    Evaluate the current date by calling the currentDate function:
     ${proj2ee:currentDate()}
  </body>
</html>
```

The value is returned by the method evaluation, in this case, the current date. If the Java method is declared to return `void`, a `null` is returned. If an exception is thrown during the method evaluation, the exception must be wrapped in an `ELException`, and the `ELException` must be thrown. The EL, for any exception that may occur during parsing or expression evaluation, uses an `ELException` exception.

Implicit Objects Available in the EL

Quite a few implicit objects are exposed through the EL. These objects allow for access to any variables that are held in the particular JSP scopes. Objects include `pageScope`, `requestScope`, `sessionScope`, and `applicationScope`. All of these *x*`Scope` objects are `Maps` that map the respective scope attribute names to their values. Using the implicit objects `param` and `paramValues`, it's also possible to access HTTP request parameters. This holds true for request header information as well as for using the implicit objects `header` and `headerValues`.

The `param` and `header` objects are `Maps` that map the parameter or header name to a `String`. This is similar to doing a `ServletRequest.getParameter(String name)` or `ServletRequest.getHeader(String name)`. The `paramValues` and `headerValues` are `Maps` that map parameter and header names to a `String[]` of all values for that parameter or header. Again, this is as if you had made `ServletRequest.getParameterValues(String name)` or `HttpServletRequest.getHeaders(String)` calls.

`initParam` gives access to context initialization parameters, and `cookie` exposes cookies received in the request. The implicit object `pageContext` gives access to all properties associated with the `PageContext` of a JSP page such as the `HttpServletRequest`, `ServletContext`, and `HttpSession` objects and their properties.

You'll now look at a couple of samples of how to use the implicit objects:

- `${pageContext.request.servletPath}` will return the servlet path obtained from the `HttpServletRequest`.

- `${sessionScope.loginId}` will return the session-scoped attribute named `loginId` or `null` if the attribute isn't found.

- `${param.courseId}` will return the `String` value of the `courseId` parameter or `null` if it's not found.

- `${paramValues.courseId}` will return the `String[]` containing all values of the `courseId` parameter or `null` if it's not found.

Table 3-18 summarizes the available implicit objects.

Table 3-18. Implicit Objects

OBJECT NAME	DESCRIPTION
`pageContext`	The `PageContext` object.
`pageScope`	A `Map` that maps page-scoped attribute names to their values.
`requestScope`	A `Map` that maps request-scoped attribute names to their values.
`sessionScope`	A `Map` that maps session-scoped attribute names to their values.
`applicationScope`	A `Map` that maps application-scoped attribute names to their values.
`param`	A `Map` that maps parameter names to a single `String` parameter value (obtained by calling `ServletRequest.getParameter(String name)`).
`paramValues`	A `Map` that maps parameter names to a `String[]` of all values for that parameter (obtained by calling `ServletRequest.getParameterValues(String name)`).
`header`	A `Map` that maps header names to a single `String` header value (obtained by calling `ServletRequest.getHeader(String name)`).
`headerValues`	A `Map` that maps header names to a `String[]` of all values for that header (obtained by calling `HttpServletRequest.getHeaders(String name)`).
`cookie`	A `Map` that maps cookie names to a single `Cookie` object. Cookies are retrieved according to the semantics of `HttpServletRequest.getCookies()`. If the same name is shared by multiple cookies, an implementation must use the first one encountered in the array of `Cookie` objects returned by the `getCookies()` method. Note that the ordering of cookies is currently unspecified in the Servlet specification.
`initParam`	A `Map` that maps context initialization parameter names to their `String` parameter value (obtained by calling `ServletContext.getInitParameter(String name)`).

Automatic Type Conversion

A convenient feature of the EL is its automatic type conversion. A full set of coercion between various object and primitive types is supported; *coercion* means that the page author isn't responsible for converting parameters into the appropriate objects or primitives.

JSP 2.0 defines appropriate conversions and default values that are used by the EL. For example, a `String` parameter from a request will be coerced to the appropriate object or primitive. If you're dealing with item (or object) `A`, the coercion rules apply for each given type. These rules are available in JSP 2.0 specification in the various sections of JSP.2.8. The container implementation does these coercions for you, but it's always a good idea to understand how, and in what order, the rules are being applied.

Default Values

Another valuable feature of the EL is that it supports default values for expressions. This is handy for allowing JSP pages to handle simple errors gracefully instead of throwing a NullPointerException. Using default values allows the page author to handle the logic flow better and therefore allows the user to have a better experience. In most cases, you can avoid common error situations. It becomes possible to allow the users to continue without having an error page displayed. The default values are type correct according to what the EL indicates, and they allow the JSP page to recover from what would have been an error.

We'll now provide an example. The expression ${course.title} evaluates to null if there's no title associated with the course object. By evaluating to null, the specified default value is used without creating a worry about a NullPointerException being thrown by the JSP page. The full expression would look like this:

```
<c:set var="title" value="${course.title}" default="No Title Available"/>
Course Title: <c:out value="${title}"/>
```

When doing iterations, if a value isn't found, it'll default to zero. So, for example, when using the <c:forEach> tag, you can specify a begin, end, and step attribute. If the value of begin uses a parameter that isn't defined, it'll default to zero. So, in the following sample, if the start parameter wasn't defined, then you'd start iterating at zero and end after ten iterations:

```
<c:forEach items="${courseCatalog}"
          begin="${param.start}"
          end="{$param.start + 10}">
  ...
</c:forEach>
```

Handling Errors

An error in a JSP page may occur at either translation or request time. The first time a JSP page is accessed in a client request (unless it has been precompiled) the JSP container will translate and compile the target JSP page. If an error occurs during this translation, you'll see an error that's probably familiar to many page authors: error status code 500 Server Error. Usually a stack trace and some error message describes what might be causing the problem. A welcome addition to the JSP 2.0 specification is the mandatory use of the jsp:id attribute. This helps identify exactly where an error might have occurred on the page instead of you having to look at the generated Java code and figure out the line number that might correspond to the problem area.

During the processing of client requests, errors can occur in either the body of the JSP page implementation class or in some other code, such as a JavaBean class. Runtime errors that occur follow the Java exception mechanism. Exceptions can be caught and handled in the body of the JSP page if the page author chooses. The <c:catch> action discussed in Chapter 4 is just for this purpose.

If an exception isn't caught, the request will be forwarded, along with the exception, to the error page URL. The error page is specified by using the `errorPage` attribute of the page directive and specifying a URL. The `errorPage` itself is identified by using the `isErrorPage` attribute of the page directive. The exception is accessible by using the implicit object `exception`. In addition to `exception`, an `errorPage` also has the following request attributes available:

- `javax.servlet.error.status_code`
- `javax.servlet.error.request_uri`
- `javax.servlet.error.servlet_name`

By using the `PageContext.getErrorData()` method, it's possible to get an instance of the `javax.servlet.jsp.Error-Data` class. This provides a simple way to access the attributes mentioned previously through the EL. For example, an error page can access the status code using this syntax:

```
${pageContext.errorData.statusCode}
```

The following code shows an error page:

```
<%@ page isErrorPage="true" %>

<h3>The following error occurred in your application:</h3>
<br/>
<hr/>
<p><font color="red" size="4">
  Exception = ${pageContext.exception.message}"</p>
<p>
  The request URI is: ${pageContext.errorData.requestURI}"
</p>
<p>
  The status code is: ${pageContext.errorData.statusCode}"</p>
<p>
  The servlet name is : ${pageContext.errorData.servletName}"
</font>
<br/>
</p>
```

This is a simple JSP that forces an exception to be thrown. The `errorPage` attribute of the page directive defines the URI of the error page:

```
<%@ page errorPage="/errorpage.jsp" %>

<%
throw new Exception("Force an exception to be thrown");
%>
```

Internationalization of JSP Pages

If you've been building Web applications, chances are by now you've probably been asked to internationalize your application. If not, then surely in the near future you'll be asked to do so. JSP pages on their own don't provide the platform to internationalize an application. It's a combination of J2SE classes, Servlet APIs, and actions provided in tag libraries such as the JSTL that have an entire collection of locale and formatting actions. We'll discuss the international features of the JSTL in Chapter 4. Here we'll talk about what you can address in the JSP specification, which basically is the character encodings.

What Is Character Encoding?

Character encoding is the organization of numeric codes that represent all the meaningful characters of a script system. Each character is stored as a number. When a user enters characters, the user's key presses are converted to character numeric codes; when the characters are displayed on the screen, the character codes are converted to the glyphs of whatever font is being used.

> **NOTE** Character encoding *is matching the binary representation of a character with the printed character based on a table.*

Java has made it much easier to deal with character encoding because, internally, all characters are represented in Unicode. Unicode provides support for every language there is. As of J2SE 1.4, the Unicode 3.0 character set is supported. The problem lies in the character encodings used across the Web. A number of Unicode transformations exist, including UTF-8, UTF-16BE, UTF-16LE, and the familiar ISO-8859, which is better known as Latin-1, an extension of ASCII containing many European characters. If you need to look up a support character encoding, you can find it at `http://www.iana.org/assignments/character-sets/`.

> **NOTE** *The page character encoding is the character encoding in which the JSP page or tag file itself is encoded.*

You can specify page encoding in a couple of different ways:

- Using the JSP configuration element `<page-encoding>` whose URL pattern matches the page.
- With the `pageEncoding` attribute of the `page` directive of the page.

- Using the `charset` value of the `contentType` attribute of the `page` directive. This determines the page character encoding if neither the `<page-encoding>` element nor the `pageEncoding` attribute is provided.
- If none of the previous list is provided, ISO-8859-1 is used as the default character encoding.

For tag files in standard syntax, the page character encoding is determined from the `pageEncoding` attribute of the `<tag>` directive of the tag file or is ISO-8859-1 if the `pageEncoding` attribute isn't specified.

The JSP page also has to worry about the response character encoding if that response is in the form of text. This is managed primarily by the `javax.servlet.ServletResponse` object's `characterEncoding` property. The JSP container determines an initial response character encoding along with the initial content type for a JSP page and calls `ServletResponse.setContentType()` with this information before processing the page.

If you want to explicitly set the initial content type and initial response character encoding, you can use the `contentType` attribute of the page directive. The initial response content type is set to the `TYPE` value of the `contentType` attribute of the `page` directive. If the page doesn't provide this attribute, the initial content type is `text/html` for JSP pages in standard syntax and `text/xml` for JSP documents in XML syntax.

Localization vs. Internationalization

Localization is the process of translating the text that's displayed to the user into their native language. This is slightly different from *internationalization*, which is the act of making sure your application can support multiple locales. A locale represents local customary formatting such as time and date displays, decimal representations, and monetary displays.

When an application is internationalized, it'll display the correct formatting for whichever locale is being used by the client. When an application is localized, it'll display all of the text in that local language. Localization is typically handled through J2SE mechanisms such as property or resource files. It's possible to have all of the internationalization issues as well as property file message lookups based on the appropriate locale handled by custom actions such as those provided in the JSTL. You'll explore those in more detail in Chapter 4.

Debugging

JSP has never been the easiest technology to debug. Primarily this is the case because, as you now know, JSP pages are translated into servlet source code and then compiled. So they become `.java` files. The problem is that what you see in your JSP page and the error that gets generated from the `.java` code rarely (if ever) correspond line for line. This makes for some frustrating guessing at the line number given, the actual JSP source code, and the sometimes cryptic error message that's displayed in your browser.

It gets even worse when we're talking about runtime errors that might include an exception that's thrown from some compiled servlet code or JavaBean. Most of us have resorted to printing a slew of statements to the output to see what's going on and then carefully removing (or commenting) them from the JSP code. Fun, huh? Well, here are a couple of tips that can assist you in not turning your hair gray when having to debug JSP pages.

If you're debugging a translation-time problem, locate the generated `.java` file that's created by the container. In Tomcat, these files are located in the `work` directory. Depending on how your Tomcat installation is set up, you'll need to navigate the directory structure until you reach the directory for your Web application. It'll be called the same name as your `.war` file. There you'll find all of the `.java` and `.class` files of the JSP pages that have been accessed. Usually you can open the `.java` file in an editor and go to the line number that's displayed in the stack trace in the browser.

In JSP 2.0, the mandatory support of the `jsp:id` attribute makes it much easier to identify where a translation error is coming from without actually going into the `.java` source. If you're working with tag library validator (TLV) files, then you can add a nicely formatted message that indicates the `jsp:id`. The `jsp:id` can be printed along with the error message, and you can look directly at your JSP source to identify the problem. Chapter 5 contains a complete TLV example.

When dealing with runtime debugging, it gets a little trickier. Your best bet is to investigate the various JSP integrated development environment (IDE) debugging tools available. Rather than endorse one product over another, we'll let you evaluate the various features of each one, and the price tag, to see what best fits your needs. Typically you can have a full debugger with call stacks, breakpoints, and watchpoints. Some are free, such as Eclipse (`http://www.eclipse.org/`), and others cost something. However, if you're going to be doing any heavy-duty JSP work, it probably makes sense to see what IDE best suits your needs for debugging. One way or another, you'll probably need one.

Performance

There's a never-ending quest on the part of Web developers to get Web applications to load and execute faster. Performance, in general, is affected by so many variables that sometimes it becomes extremely difficult to qualify what exactly can be used to acquire "faster" performance or, for that matter, what *performance* really means. Many forests have been toppled for the books available on this very subject.

While many issues concerning the Web container affect the performance of Web applications, each vendor's documentation is the best place to find what parameters to use to fine-tune the performance of the container. And it's up to you to make sure you spend some quality time with that documentation. It could very well make the difference between the so-so performance of your application and having it scream.

That said, we'll present a couple of generic items for optimizing JSP performance: buffering and precompiling JSP files.

Buffering

The JSP container buffers data as it's sent from the server to the client. It's up to the page author how this is accomplished so that you can take the needs of your application into consideration. You can use the following two attributes of the page directive to determine how buffering is done for the JSP output:

- The `buffer` attribute defines the buffer size.
- The `autoFlush` attribute determines how the container should handle flushing the buffer.

They're both shown in the following page directive:

```
<%@ page contentType="text/html; charset=UTF-8"
        session="true" buffer="16kb" autoFlush="true" %>
```

The `out` variable writes all content and is an instance of a `PrintWriter`. The initial `JspWriter` object is associated with the `PrintWriter` object of the `ServletResponse` in a way that depends on whether the page is or isn't buffered. If the page isn't buffered, output written to this `JspWriter` object will be written through to the `PrintWriter` directly. But if the page is buffered, the `PrintWriter` object will not be created until the buffer is flushed and operations such as `setContentType()` are legal.

Since this flexibility simplifies programming substantially, buffering is the default for JSP pages. If you're managing your buffers, you have to pay a bit more attention to the state of the buffer. If the buffer size you define using the `buffer` attribute is exceeded, you can flush the buffer or have an exception raised.

Both approaches are valid, and thus both are supported in the JSP technology. The behavior of a page is controlled by the `autoFlush` attribute, which defaults to `true`. In general, JSP pages that need to be sure that correct and complete data has been sent to their client may want to set `autoFlush` to `false`. On the other hand, JSP pages that send data that's meaningful even when partially constructed may want to set `autoFlush` to `true`, such as when the data is sent for immediate display through a browser. Each application will require that you consider their specific needs to determine what's the correct buffering approach.

Headers aren't sent to the client until the first flush method is invoked. Therefore, it's possible to call methods that modify the response header, such as `setContentType()`, `sendRedirect()`, or error methods up until the flush method is executed and the headers are sent. After that point, these methods become invalid, as per the Servlet specification, and you'll get a runtime error.

Precompiling

The major performance hit taken by a JSP page happens the first time it's accessed by the container for a client request. At this point, the container will translate the JSP page into its servlet `.java` file, and then if there are no translation errors, compile that file into a `.class` file. While this happens the first time the page is accessed, it can still cause performance issues on large sites. One way to avoid this is to precompile the JSP pages and include them in a `.war` file. The servlet class files of the corresponding JSP are then made available to the container as JSP files by defining them in the `web.xml` file:

```
<webapp>
  ...
  <servlet>
    <servlet-name>hello</servlet-name>
    <servlet-class>hello_jsp.class</servlet-class>
  </servlet>
  <servlet-mapping>
    <servlet-name>hello</servlet-name>
    <url-pattern>/hello.jsp</url-pattern>
  </servlet-mapping>
  ...
</webapp>
```

New for JSP 2.0 is a precompilation protocol that's used with an HTTP request. Also, the new version introduces some basic reserved parameter names. The precompilation protocol is related to—but not the same as—the notion of compiling a JSP page into a servlet class. All request parameter names that start with the prefix `jsp_` are reserved by the JSP 2.0 specification and shouldn't be used by an application as a parameter. This may make for some unhappy campers if you have an application that by some unfortunate chance uses `jsp_` for the prefix of some of its HTTP parameters.

A request to a JSP page that has a request parameter with the name `jsp_precompile` is a *precompilation request*. The `jsp_precompile` parameter may have no value or may have the value `true` or `false`. In all cases, the request will not be delivered to the JSP page but will suggest to the container to precompile the JSP page into its implementation class. This will be a container optimization as to whether it pays attention to the request.

Using JSP Best Practices

JSP pages have been around long enough now that most of use have a handle on what we should be doing with them and what we shouldn't. However, sometimes just knowing isn't enough to stop bad habits. The following is a list of best practices that you can keep in mind when working with JSP pages. At least if you go against any of them, you'll have that annoying voice in the back of your head saying that you know better! If you follow most (if not all) of the following best practices, you'll find you have much better JSP pages:

- Eliminate using scriptlets.
- Use the Model-View-Controller (MVC) pattern and frameworks.
- Place business logic in JavaBeans.
- Use existing custom tag libraries.
- Use custom actions.

- Use templates as much as possible.
- Use the correct inclusion mechanism.
- Use common configuration settings when possible.
- Be user-friendly, and use the JSP exception mechanism.
- Be page author–friendly, and use JSP comments.
- Take advantage of validation.
- Make your pages readable.

We'll cover each of these best practices in the following sections.

Eliminate Using Scriptlets

Admit it: At one point or another you've written Java code into your JSP pages. Well, put it behind you now, and move forward. While the temptation might still occur, avoid writing scriptlet code into your JSP pages. Although it might seem like a good idea at the time (kind of like that tattoo you got that Saturday at 3 a.m.), it'll end up being much more work than just doing it correctly from the start. You'll find that as the application grows more complex and more developers become involved, it's much harder to maintain—not to mention that it's a pain to read. No matter how much you try to "pretty up" the format, you'll still have your co-workers cursing you out one day.

Another advantage of not having Java code embedded in the JSP page is that finally it'll become possible for Joe Page Author, who doesn't know a lick of Java, to maintain the presentation page. This, after all, was the intent of JSP in the first place. This will let the Java developers focus on business logic as they implement the behavior behind the custom tags and allow the presentation page authors to use the custom tags just as they use ordinary HTML tags.

Use the MVC Pattern and Frameworks

MVC enables the development of applications that are easier to create, test, maintain, and enhance. Applications with the tiers properly separated are more reusable because the Java components aren't tied to a Web browser and can be used by other parts of the application. This is even more important if you have an application that will be deployed to different devices, not just to Web browsers. If this is the case, then you'll be able to reuse all of your model code and will just have to deal with the appropriate view target.

Quite a few frameworks implement MVC and allow you to plug and play the portions of your application that provide your value-add. Probably the most popular is the Jakarta Struts Framework. You can find out more about Struts at `http://jakarta.apache.org/struts/index.html`. Struts works well with JSP, Velocity Templates, XSLT, and other presentation frameworks. Other popular frameworks that incorporate best practices that might be worth your while investigating are J2EE Blueprints, JavaServer Faces, and Apache Turbine.

Place Business Logic in JavaBeans

A best practice for programming in general is eliminating redundancy. The more places you have something repeated, the better the chance of having a bug in it. Java code included directly inside a JSP page isn't as readily accessible to other JSP pages. By putting any business logic within a JavaBean, common behavior not only can be used by other JSP pages but also by other portions of the application. For all intents and purposes, a JavaBean is just a Java class that follows a couple of special rules. They're also easily accessible from any JSP page.

Use Existing Custom Tag Libraries

With the introduction of the JSTL, it just doesn't make sense to reinvent the same date format custom tag over and over again. Extremely valuable actions are available within the JSTL that all JSP page authors should use. The JSTL isn't the only tag library available, but it probably will be the only tag library that's optimized by container vendors—well, except for any tag libraries that they provide exclusively for their container.

If you're not concerned with vendor portability, then there probably is a whole set of custom tag libraries that come with your container. There are also custom tag libraries available with the Struts Framework, as well as on the Jakarta Taglibs project located at `http://jakarta.apache.org/taglibs/index.html`. Before deciding to write your own custom actions, check out what's already available. It'll save you time coding and debugging, and it'll allow you to spend more time focusing on your business application.

Use Custom Actions

JSP 2.0 has introduced a number of new features such as tag files and simple tag handlers that make it easy and compelling to create your own custom actions. If you have logic that's specific to your application, sometimes it's necessary to write your own custom actions.

Keep in mind that when writing custom actions they're reusable within JSP files, but not necessary outside of the JSP pages. This is where you need to determine if it makes sense to create a custom action or a JavaBean that can potentially be reused in different areas of your model. A compromise is to try and extract common behaviors or business logic. Utilize JavaBeans or EJBs that perform those common behaviors and call them from the custom action. That way you can take advantage of the best of both worlds.

Template As Much As Possible

Large-scale Web sites frequently have a common look and feel to them. This is a perfect situation to consolidate common layout features and then create a template mechanism for their use. This allows for a common file to control the layout of the application. When it's time to make changes to the layout, you'll have to modify only the one control file. The rest of the pages will automatically reflect the layout change. This is a much quicker way to make changes in your Web application and to enhance the maintainability of your code. A number of template custom tag libraries are specifically for this purpose and are included with such frameworks as Struts. If you're interested in a more advanced and powerful templating framework available in open-source projects, take a further look into Tiles at `http://www.lifl.fr/~dumoulin/tiles/`.

Another variation on this theme is the use of stylesheets. Stylesheets allow for a single file to dictate the appearance of your pages. For example, Cascading Style Sheets (CSS) are commonly used to control such display characteristics as fonts, font sizes, and table layouts. As with templates, stylesheets allow for a one-stop shop for making display control changes. These changes will then be picked up by all of the JSP pages at once and increase the maintainability of your code.

Use the Correct Inclusion Mechanism

The process of templating your layout is usually a good time to identify code that might be common between templates. It's best to eliminate code and layout duplication. If you come across JSP syntax or template text that's used in a number of places, refactor the common portion out of multiple pages and into a single file. Again, having one place to make changes is always better than having to do it in multiple places.

You can use two JSP *include* mechanisms. When refactoring common code, make sure you're using the correct include mechanism to bring that common piece of functionality onto the page. The general rule is that if the content changes frequently, use the `include` action. If the file is primarily static (HTML or template text), use the `include` directive.

Use Common Configuration Settings When Possible

Try to make it a general rule to combine your common configuration settings into one JSP file and then include that file in each of your JSP pages. This is useful for a number of reasons. It makes sure that the page directives are set correctly for common items such as content type and for disabling scripting. It also provides a single point of contact for all of the custom tag library prefixes.

There's nothing more annoying (OK, there are probably a few things more annoying, but this is right up there) than having different prefixes defined within a JSP page for the same custom tag library. Usually this is the case because there was more than one page author working on different pages. It's much more consistent to just define all custom tag libraries in one file and then have everyone access the same prefixes throughout the application.

If it's necessary on a particular page to redefine a configuration setting, it's not the end of the world. This should be the exception, though, not the rule.

Be User-Friendly, and Use the JSP Exception Mechanism

How many developers know users who become overwhelmingly happy when they have an exception stack displayed in their browser when they were expecting to see the quarterly profit results from accounting? Not many, probably. Exception stacks provide helpful and useful information for developers but rarely are considered as helpful to users.

With the introduction of the `<c:catch>` action in the JSTL it's possible to catch exceptions that might not be devastating to the user. The page author can determine what the best or appropriate action to take is. Sometimes the user is none the wiser that an exception occurred. This mechanism isn't meant to replace the JSP error page mechanism but instead provide a way for the page author to shield the user from exceptions that aren't really all that bad.

When something really bad happens, you should use the JSP error page mechanism. When using an error page, it's possible to give a more user-friendly message and point the user in a direction that will allow them to continue with their work or contact the appropriate person. You can use error pages to capture the same stack information that would've been displayed to the user in such a way that it's sent directly to the developer or stored in some persistent format. You can use the error page to log any information that would be useful for the developer without the unsightly exception stack being displayed to the user.

Be Page Author-Friendly, and Use JSP Comments

While your stroke of genius might be obvious to you, it's rarely obvious to others. What better way for your co-workers to appreciate your skill than to explain to them exactly what you're doing in your code? To some, adding comments to files seems to be akin to having your teeth pulled. However, it doesn't take that much extra time. If we can do the extra typing, so can you.

Sometimes it helps to have a comment template defined so that at least pages will have a consistent description. It's equally important to comment within JSP code so that it's easy to follow. Since there are multiple ways to comment a JSP page, you should consider which type of comment to use in the page. HTML comments, which are in the form `<!-- comments ... -->`, will be viewable in the compiled JSP page's HTML source code. This means that any user can go to a View ➤ Source from their favorite browser and view your comments, which may not be what you want.

Using JSP comments in the form `<%-- JSP comment --%>` means they can't be viewed as part of the page's source through the browser. Java comments can also occur in JSP pages inside Java scriptlet sections; however, you know you'll never need to use Java comments because you won't be defining scriptlet sections in your pages any longer, correct? If you do, however, they won't be viewable in the browser. Most of the time, you'll want to use JSP comments.

Take Advantage of Validation

In JSP 2.0 it has become much easier to create JSP documents that use well-formed XML syntax. By having your JSP pages in XML format, it makes it easier to perform XML validation on your pages. You can use XML tools to validate the JSP against a specified document type definition (DTD). In addition, using TLV classes is important. By taking advantage of this JSP facility, it makes it much easier for page authors to create pages using custom actions knowing that they're using the actions correctly. Using a TLV prevents the misuse of an action in the translation stage, instead of at run time.

Make Your Pages Readable

We debated whether to include this best practice, thinking that readers might say, "Do you really need to tell me that?" We concluded that the answer is "yes," primarily because of the hundreds (maybe thousands) of JSP pages we've seen that make us think, "Obviously people don't think this is important." We'll be the first to admit that part of this problem might be because of the overuse of scriptlet code in JSP pages. The constant `<% %>` all over the place gets to be quite annoying. However, even if you take that out of the equation, there are still a couple of general rules that, when followed, can make for an easier read.

For one, make sure you include line spacing between logical sections. Comments preceding the JSP code can also help explain what the reader is about to see. Make sure you close your tags, primarily HTML tags. Raise your hand if you've ever forgotten the `</table>` and had to track it down. It also helps to use some standard indenting so that it's easier to read the structure. By using some common sense or establishing style guidelines for your project, you can save yourself and your fellow developers wasted time trying to read through files that are "glommed" together.

Summary

This chapter has covered a lot of ground. The release of the JSP 2.0 specification has incorporated many useful and exciting features for page authors. This chapter introduced some of these features, including JSP fragments and tag files. We talked about how JSP fits into the MVC model. We then went into details about understanding the page life cycle. You spent much of this chapter getting up to speed on the various JSP directives and actions. You should understand all of the available objects that are at your disposal in the JSP environment and how to use them within JSP pages.

The introduction of the EL is a major improvement toward simplifying JSP pages. We went into detail on the available features in the EL as well as how to use it in your pages. We then covered international issues, debugging, and performance concerns when dealing with JSP. Last, the chapter ended with some best practices so that you can write some excellent JSP pages.

CHAPTER 4

Using the JSTL

The JSP Standard Tag Library (JSTL) came about under JSR-52 of the Java Community Process (JCP). You can find the specification at `http://jcp.org/jsr/detail/52.jsp`. JSR-52 covers the creation of a standard tag library for JavaServer Pages (JSP) and allows this library to be available to all compliant JSP containers. The JSTL is a comprehensive set of standard actions that most (if not all) JSP developers can use. The real value of the JSTL is that it provides a way to dramatically increase the productivity of JSP authors. The standard actions are delivered in a simple, flexible fashion that can reduce the learning curve of creating JSPs. While the JSTL is meant to be used with JSP technology, it's actually a separate set of functionality.

The JSTL provides a wide range of custom action functionality that most JSP authors have found themselves in need of in the past. Having a defined specification for how the functionality is implemented means that a page author can learn these custom actions once and then use and reuse them on all future products on all application containers that support the specification. Therefore, you can finally take the *custom* out of *custom action* and replace it with *standard*. No more creating your own iteration action for the tenth time.

Additionally, JSP authoring tools now support these standard actions and can assist the JSP page author in rapid development. So, to sum up how the JSTL got here, an expert group created a set of custom actions that's valuable to a range of JSP authors and developers.

Why a JSP Standard Tag Library?

We've answered the question, what is the JSTL? We'll now answer the why question. Why a JSP standard tag library, and for that matter, why now? The answer to both is quite simple: because writing your own custom actions is a time-consuming pain.

With the introduction of JSP 1.1, a standard mechanism existed for the creation of tag libraries. Initially, we all referred to this mechanism as *custom tags*; now we refer to it as *custom actions*. This terminology change came about in the current release of JSP 2.0 and the JSTL. That's why you still see the collection of actions called *tag libraries* as opposed to *action libraries*. Otherwise, we'd be referring to the JSAL instead of the JSTL. Both terms, *custom tags* and *custom actions*, refer to the same technology.

Why Now?

While custom tags were a big improvement in functionality over the JSP 1.0 specification, it still left room for the reinventing-the-wheel syndrome. How many times is it necessary to create a custom tag for formatting a date for different customers? Apparently, the answer was "a lot." JSP page authors saw the same custom tag functionality being required over and over again.

Out of this need grew the start of open-source projects to provide numerous tag libraries. Granted, the Jakarta Taglibs project provides hundreds of custom tags within the various libraries. However, there still was no standard—no way to just learn the tag once and be done with it. The lack of a standard tag library helped fuel the fire for the JSTL.

Although the creation of a standard tag library could have been folded into the JSP 2.0 specification, having a separate expert group ensures that the basic mechanisms in JSP 1.2 are applicable to any tag library. It also allows for the possibility of supporting both JSP 1.2 and JSP 1.1 containers.

Why You Really Want to Use the JSTL

Although the mechanism of custom tags enabled the creation of libraries to be shared across many different user communities, engineers and page authors gain direct benefits by using a standard tag library:

- It's easy to learn and provides a wide range of functionality.
- JSP authors and JSP authoring tools can easily generate pages on all compliant JSP containers using standard tags.
- Standard tags created by the expert group will meet the needs of a wide variety of communities.
- The tags will already be well tested and ready for use.
- The library reduces training costs by providing targeted training materials and simplified portability and maintainability of JSP pages and applications.
- You'll find specialized implementations of the library so that containers can provide both portability and higher performance.
- With all the time you save using the JSTL, you'll be able to concentrate on making the core value of your application even greater.
- You can identify better separation of roles for Java developers and page authors.

Aside from the development process benefits that will be realized by using the JSTL, the functionality contained in the JSTL is impressive.

Understanding the Need for Encapsulation

Most JSP 1.1 (or higher) containers already provide a tag library for use by their customers. It has been clear in the JSP authoring community that there was a need for encapsulation of functionality. The reasons are quite simple: if functionality is encapsulated, JSP authors can use the custom tags without much knowledge of Java or by making any other coding effort.

Encapsulation also allows for reuse of common functionality within an application and across applications. With each custom tag written, the testing and debugging of that tag has to take place only once. Once it has been tested, debugged, and used, the return on investment for the developer as well as the source code greatly increases.

Getting the JSTL

Before you can use the JSTL, you need to have an environment set up correctly. You can do this easily (and quickly) by following the download and installation directions that are on the Jakarta site at `http://jakarta.apache.org/taglibs/doc/standard-doc/intro.html`. The Jakarta site hosts the reference implementation of JSTL 1.1. If you're in need of a container to use, Tomcat 5.0 supports for JSP 2.0 as well as the Servlet 2.4 specification. You can download and install Tomcat from `http://jakarta.apache.org/tomcat/`.

Making Life Easier: JSTL in Action

You've seen the evolutionary process that has taken place in the servlet-JSP arena. You've seen how you can write your own servlet that does the same thing that a JSP page can do, assuming you're a Java programmer, and then abstract and encapsulate some of that required functionality into custom actions. Using the JSTL takes away the development requirement of writing your own tag library descriptor (TLD) files, writing your own tag handlers, and creating your own tag libraries. To put it simply, JSTL provides the functionality, and you provide the purpose.

You'll now create a JSP page using actions from the JSTL Core tag library. Listing 4-1 shows how to say "hello" to a friend in JSTL style.

Listing 4-1. "Hello, My Friend" Program

```
<%@ page contentType="text/html; charset=UTF-8" %>
<%@ taglib uri="http://java.sun.com/jstl/ea/core" prefix="c" %>
<html>
  <head>
    <title>Hello Sample</title>
  </head>
  <body>
    <h1>
      Hello <c:out value="${param.name}" default="my friend" />
    </h1>
  </body>
</html>
```

Using the `out` tag provided in the Core tag library, you've pulled a value out of a parameter called `name` from your Hypertext Transfer Protocol (HTTP) request to display. If this value is `null`, then the default *my friend* will automatically be used instead. If you were to replicate this functionality by writing your own custom tag, you'd have to code a TLD and tag handler for doing so. Using the JSTL, you have the functionality with no more than one line's worth of effort.

If you really wanted to get crazy, you could utilize one more JSTL tag and turn the simple JSP page into a completely internationalized page ready for any language that your clients might be using (and you have translated strings for). Listing 4-2 shows the internationalized version of "Hello, My Friend."

Listing 4-2. "Hello, My Friend" Program, Internationalized

```
<%@ page contentType="text/html; charset=UTF-8" %>
<%@ taglib uri="http://java.sun.com/jstl/core" prefix="c" %>
<%@ taglib uri="http://java.sun.com/jstl/fmt" prefix="fmt" %>
<html>
  <head>
    <title><fmt:message key="hellotitle"/></title>
  </head>
  <body>
    <h1>
      <fmt:message key="hello"/>
      <c:out value="${param.name}" default="<fmt:message key='myfriend'/>" />
    </h1>
  </body>
</html>
```

Using the `<fmt:message>` action, you're able to specify a key to use for a resource bundle. This ensures that the string that will be displayed will correspond to the correct locale of the user. We'll go through the details of how you do this later in the "Using Internationalization Actions" section, but for now you can see that this is quite easy to accomplish.

This is just the beginning of the power of the JSTL actions. If you take out the Hypertext Markup Language (HTML), you've accomplished quite a bit in just a handful of lines. You've declared use of the JSTL tag libraries, accessed data from a resource bundle, pulled out a parameter from the HTTP request, and determined the correct message to display to your output stream.

You might have noticed that you're using the `${}` syntax from the JSP specification. The JSTL takes advantage of using the expression language (EL) to make it easy to reference objects. You learned about the EL in the previous chapter, and you'll use it extensively in the upcoming examples.

Getting a JSTL Functional Overview

The JSTL encapsulates common functionality that a typical JSP author would encounter. This set of common functionality has come about through the input of the various members who are in the expert group. Since this expert group has a good cross-section of

JSP authors and users, the actions provided in the JSTL should suit a wide audience. The JSTL is a set of custom actions that's based on the JSP 1.2 and Servlet 2.3 specifications. While the JSTL is commonly referred to as a single tag library, it's actually composed of the following four tag libraries:

- The Core library
- The XML library
- The Internationalization and Formatting library
- The SQL library

Core

The Core library provides general-purpose actions that get and set scoped variables, write to the `JspWriter`, and handle catching exceptions. The actions in Core library also take advantage of the EL features. Also included in the Core library are those actions related to using conditional processing, handling iterations, and dealing with uniform resource locator (URL) resources. Writing a message to the `JspWriter` is as simple as this:

```
<c:out value="Hello my friend" />
```

XML

The XML library addresses the basic needs of a page author when using XML in their pages. The actions in this library handle parsing and writing Extensible Markup Language (XML) content, handling flow control, and performing transformations. The following example shows how you can import an XML document, parse it, set the Document Object Model (DOM) object in a variable called `doc`, access information from that document using XPath, and then set an additional variable based on data for further use (not bad for four lines of JSP code):

```
<%@ page contentType="text/html; charset=UTF-8" %>
<%@ taglib uri="/WEB-INF/c-rt.tld" prefix="c" %>
<%@ taglib uri="/WEB-INF/x-rt.tld" prefix="x" %>

<!-- parse an XML document -->
<c:import url="courselist.xml" var="xml"/>

<x:parse doc="${xml}" var="parsedDoc"/>
<!-- access XML data via XPath expressions -->
<x:out select="$parsedDoc/catalog/course/title"/>

<!-- set a scoped variable -->
<x:set var="courseTitle" scope="request"
       select="$parsedDoc/catalog/course/title"/>
```

You'll notice that you aren't using the EL `${}` syntax to access the `parsedDoc` variable. We'll go into more details on this in the "Using XML Transformation Actions" section, but the short reason is that you're actually using XPath in the `select` attribute, not the EL.

Internationalization and Formatting

The Internationalization and Formatting library is concerned with actions that assist the page author in internationalizing their application. This includes actions related to locales and resource bundles, date, time, and time zone issues. In the following example, you're using a default locale and doing a key lookup on the default `ResourceBundle` for that application. Also shown is how easy it is to provide parametric content to your message resources:

```
<fmt:message key="welcome">
  <fmt:param value="${visitCount}" />
<fmt:message/>
```

This is just the tip of the iceberg as far as the international and formatting features are concerned.

SQL

The SQL library provides the capabilities to interact with databases. This includes dealing with data sources and doing queries, updates, and transactions. Using the SQL actions in combination with iteration actions makes it very easy to loop through result sets, as shown in the following example:

```
<sql:query var="courseList" dataSource="${datasource}">
  SELECT * FROM course WHERE title = 'JSTL' ORDER BY instructor
</sql:query>
<table>
  <c:forEach var="course" items="${courseList.row}">
    <tr>
      <td><c:out value="${course.title}" /></td>
      <td><c:out value="${course.author}" /></td>
    </tr>
  </c:forEach>
</table>
```

> **NOTE** *Accessing a database from your JSP files isn't a good idea because you break the standard Model-View-Controller (MVC) design pattern. While the SQL actions make it easy to get information directly from the database, it's discouraged in application development that will be used for production applications.*

JSTL Descriptor Files

The TLD files define these libraries. By using separate TLDs to expose the tags, the functionality for each set of actions is apparent and makes more sense. Using separate TLDs also allows each library to have its own namespace.

To sum up, the layout of the JSTL is straightforward. The overriding theme throughout the JSTL is simplifying the life of the page author. There has always been a need (although not a requirement) that the page authors have some understanding of a programming language (usually Java) to create complex pages. This dilemma is what has hampered the true role separation between the JSP page author and the Java programmer. Using the tags provided in the JSTL, you're closer to reaching that clean division of labor. The functional areas in the JSTL help a page author identify what type of functionality is needed and where to find it.

Understanding JSTL Basics

Many of the JSTL actions use some common elements. It's helpful to first go through what these common elements are so that we don't have to repeat ourselves throughout all of the actions. The common elements are as follows:

- Scoped variables
- The `var` and `scope` attributes
- Variable visibility
- Dynamic vs. static attributes
- How errors and exceptions are handled
- How action body content is handled

The following sections go through each one and show how you apply it to the JSTL actions.

Scoped Variables

Actions usually collaborate with their environment in implicit ways, in explicit ways, or in both ways. Implicit collaboration often happens via a well-defined interface that allows nested tags to work seamlessly with the ancestor tag exposing that interface. The JSTL iterator tags support this mode of collaboration.

Explicit collaboration happens when a tag explicitly exposes information to its environment. Traditionally, this is by exposing a scripting variable with a value assigned from a JSP scoped attribute (which was saved by the tag handler). Because the JSTL supports an EL, the need for scripting variables is significantly reduced. This is why all the JSTL tags expose information only as JSP scoped attributes (no scripting variable exposed). These exported JSP scoped attributes are referred to as *scoped variables* in the JSTL specification; this helps to prevent too much overloading of the term *attribute*.

var and scope Attributes

Now that you understand JSP variables and scopes in general, you'll learn how they all apply to the JSTL. Many actions provided in the JSTL allow variables to be exported. The convention is to use the name var for attributes that export information.

You can look at <c:set> (one of the actions available in the Core tag library that sets the value of a scoped variable). In the following sample, you're setting a variable called course to the value jstl and allowing that variable to be visible in session scope:

```
<c:set value="jstl" var="course" scope="session" />
```

If you didn't specify a value for scope, page scope is the default. It's also important to note, as per the JSP specification, that specifying session scope is allowed only if the page has sessions enabled. If an action exposes more than one scoped variable, the main one uses attribute names var and scope, and secondary ones have a suffix added for unique identification. For example, in the <c:forEach> action there's both a main and a secondary variable that can be defined. The var attribute is the main variable and exposes the current item of the iteration, and the varStatus attribute is the secondary variable and exposes the current status of the iteration.

Variable Visibility

Another point to understand is how the scope attribute defines the visibility of a variable. Scoped variables exported by JSTL actions are categorized as either *nested* or *at-end*. Nested scoped variables are visible only within the body of the action and are stored in page scope. Since nested scoped variables are always saved in page scope, no scope attribute is associated with them. In the JSTL 1.0 specification, scoped variables exposed by actions are considered at-end by default. If a scoped variable is nested, providing a scope attribute in the action allows the scope to be explicitly stated. At-end scoped variables are visible only at the end of an action's execution.

Dynamic and Static Attributes

You can almost always specify attribute values of JSTL actions dynamically by using a request-time expression value, such as the scripting language of the page, or by using an expression value. We said *almost always* because the following two exceptions apply when you specify JSTL actions dynamically via a request-time expression value:

- The first exception to this convention is for the select attribute of XML actions. The select attribute is defined to specify a String literal that represents an expression in the XPath language.
- The second exception is for attributes that define the name and scope of scoped variables exported by JSTL actions.

Handling Errors and Exceptions

When dealing with dynamic data, you must have a mechanism in place for handling errors and exceptions. When using JSTL actions, the syntax varies from action to action. We'll discuss the specific syntax of each action as you encounter it. If a syntax error in an action is found, then it's reported at translation time. Any constraints on the action, such as required attributes or conflicts when using certain attributes, are also reported at translation time.

The exception is if the attribute value is dynamic, such as an expression. Since there's no way to validate whether the value is correct until run time, these types of errors are reported at run time. When using the runtime-based libraries, the conversion from a `String` value to the expected type of an attribute is handled according to the rules defined in the JSP specification, section 2.4. The runtime-based libraries are the runtime versions of the JSTL actions. They're used if you're using an earlier JSP container and don't have access to the EL.

In general, handling exceptions on a JSP page has been, well, to be polite about it, a pain. The JSTL tries to make it easier from this point forward. The JSTL doesn't try to replace the `errorpage` mechanism, but it instead tries to improve when and how errors are thrown and handled. A number of conventions are in place to try to avoid having runtime exceptions constantly being thrown. Table 4-1 describes these conventions

Table 4-1. Exception Conventions

ERROR OR EXCEPTION	HOW IT'S HANDLED
Invalid value on `scope` attribute	Translation-time validation error.
Empty `var` attribute	Translation-time validation error.
Dynamic attributes *with* a fixed set of valid `String` values containing a `null` value	Use the default value.
Dynamic attributes *with* a fixed set of valid `String` values containing an invalid value	Throw an exception.
Dynamic attributes *without* a fixed set of valid values with a `null` value	Behavior specific to the action.
Dynamic attributes *without* a fixed set of valid values with an invalid type	Throw an exception.
Dynamic attributes *without* a fixed set of valid values with an invalid value	Throw an exception.
Exceptions caused by the body content	Always propagate, possibly after handling them.
Exceptions caused by the action itself	Always propagate, possibly after handling them.
Exceptions caused by the EL	Always propagate.
Exceptions caused by XPath	Always propagate.

The <c:catch> action enables page authors to catch exceptions. <c:catch> exposes the exception through its var attribute. The var is removed if no exception has occurred. We'll go into more detail on the <c:catch> action later in the "Working with the Core Actions" section.

When a JSTL action throws an exception, it's an instance of javax.servlet.jsp.JspException or a subclass. Sometimes it may be the case where the action catches an exception that occurred in its body. In that case, its tag handler will provide the caught exception as the root cause of the JspException it rethrows. By default, JSTL actions don't catch or otherwise handle exceptions that occur during evaluation of their body content. However, you can access the exception with the method getRootCause() of the JspException class, which was added in JSP 1.2.

Action Body Content

When we talk about the body content of an action, what we're speaking of is the content between the start and end tags of the action. You can rewrite the <c:set> example like so:

```
<c:set var="course" scope="session >
  jstl
</c:set>
```

In this example, jstl becomes the body content of the action.

You define how an action handles the body content by using the <body-content> element in the TLD file. An action has three choices for defining body content. You can define it as empty, as JSP, or as tagdependent. For example, the body content is defined in the <c:set> action as being taken from the c.tld file as follows:

```
<tag>
  <name>set</name>
  <tag-class>org.apache.taglibs.standard.tag.el.core.SetTag</tag-class>
  <body-content>JSP</body-content>
  <description>
    Sets the result of an expression evaluation in a 'scope'
  </description>
  ...
</tag>
```

The <body-content> element is optional in the TLD file, so if it's not defined, the default value is JSP. If the body content is defined as empty, this means there can be no body content for the action. Having an empty body also allows for the tag to be written using either the long format or the short format, like this:

```
<apress:tag></apress:tag>
```

or like this:

```
<apress:tag/>
```

Defining the body content as `JSP` means that the body of the tag may contain standard JSP elements. This could include markup, content, scriptlets, and expressions. Using the body content type `JSP` also means that the body content can be empty. When the body content is defined as `JSP`, the content such as scriptlets, expressions, and escape characters are all processed or evaluated as usual. This also means that tags can be nested within each other, and they'll still be evaluated correctly. Many of the JSTL actions are of body content type `JSP`.

The third type that body content is `tagdependent`. This means that the JSP container won't process the content in any way. It'll be left to the tag to handle how it wants to process or evaluate the content.

If a JSTL action accepts body content, an empty body is always valid unless it's explicitly stated otherwise. If there's nothing in the body content, it's considered empty. If the body content is used to set the value of an attribute, then an empty body content sets the attribute value to an empty string. So, the following example would set the `var` name to an empty string:

```
<c:set var="course" scope="session >
</c:set>
```

Understanding Configuration Settings

Most Web applications require some type of configuration. Typically, you accomplish this in the deployment descriptor file. As originally defined in the Servlet 2.3 specification, this file is the `web.xml` file, and it describes necessary context initialization parameters.

You can define a number of initialization parameters for the JSTL. The JSTL provides what are called *configuration variables*. These variables allow data to be overridden dynamically for a particular JSP scope (page, request, session, application) by using a scoped variable. This is extremely useful because the JSTL tag libraries can use default values for attributes that aren't explicitly defined in the particular action. An example of this is a default locale used for internationalization actions.

The term *configuration setting* is used for data that can set by using a context initialization in a descriptor file or dynamically with a configuration variable. If you were setting one of these configuration settings through a context parameter so that there was an appropriate default for your application, you could reference it like so:

```
<web-app>
  ...
  <context-param>
    <param-name>
      javax.servlet.jsp.jstl.fmt.locale
    </param-name>
    <param-value>
      en_US
    </param-value>
  </context-param>
  ...
</web-app>
```

In the JSTL, there's configuration data associated with international, formatting, and SQL actions. Tables 4-2 through 4-7 contain a full description of all of the available configuration settings that are related to the internationalization and configuration settings of SQL settings.

Table 4-2. Locale Configuration Settings

DESCRIPTION	USED, SET, OR SPECIFIED BY
Variable name	`javax.servlet.jsp.jstl.fmt.locale`
Description	Specifies the locale to be used by the internationalization and formatting actions, thereby disabling browser-based locales.
Java constant	`Config.FMT_LOCALE`
Type	`String` or `java.util.Locale`
Set by action	`<fmt:setLocale>`
Used by actions	`<fmt:bundle>`, `<fmt:setBundle>`, `<fmt:message>`, `<fmt:formatNumber>`, `<fmt:parseNumber>`, `<fmt:formatDate>`, `<fmt:parseDate>`

Table 4-3. Fallback Locale Configuration Settings

DESCRIPTION	USED, SET, OR SPECIFIED BY
Variable name	`javax.servlet.jsp.jstl.fmt.fallbackLocale`
Description	Specifies the fallback locale to be used by the internationalization and formatting actions if none of the browser's preferred locales match any of the available locales
Java constant	`Config.FMT_FALLBACK_LOCALE`
Set by action	None
Used by actions	`<fmt:bundle>`, `<fmt:setBundle>`, `<fmt:message>`, `<fmt:formatNumber>`, `<fmt:parseNumber>`, `<fmt:formatDate>`, `<fmt:parseDate>`

Table 4-4. Localization Context Settings

DESCRIPTION	USED, SET, OR SPECIFIED BY
Variable name	`javax.servlet.jsp.jstl.fmt.localizationContext`
Description	Specifies the default internationalization and localization context to be used by the internationalization-capable formatting actions.
Java constant	`Config.FMT_LOCALIZATION_CONTEXT`
Type	`String` or `javax.servlet.jsp.jstl.fmt.LocalizationContext`
Set by action	`<fmt:setBundle>`
Used by actions	`<fmt:message>`, `<fmt:formatNumber>`, `<fmt:parseNumber>`, `<fmt:formatDate>`, `<fmt:parseDate>`

Table 4-5. Time Zone Settings

DESCRIPTION	USED, SET, OR SPECIFIED BY
Variable name	`javax.servlet.jsp.jstl.fmt.timeZone`
Description	Specifies the application's default time zone.
Java constant	`Config.FMT_TIMEZONE`
Type	`String` or `java.util.TimeZone`
Set by action	`<fmt:setTimeZone>`
Used by actions	`<fmt:formatDate>`, `<fmt:parseDate>`

Table 4-6. SQL Data Source Settings

DESCRIPTION	USED, SET, OR SPECIFIED BY
Variable name	`javax.servlet.jsp.jstl.sql.dataSource`
Description	The data source to be accessed by the SQL actions
Java constant	`Config.SQL_DATA_SOURCE`
Type	`String` or `javax.sql.DataSource`
Set by	`<sql:setDataSource>`, deployment descriptor, `Config` class
Used by actions	`<sql:query>`, `<sql:update>`, `<sql:transaction>`

Table 4-7. SQL `MaxRows` Settings

DESCRIPTION	USED, SET, OR SPECIFIED BY
Variable Name	`javax.servlet.jsp.jstl.sql.maxRows`
Description	The maximum number of rows to be included in a query result. If the maximum number of rows isn't specified, or is `-1`, no limit is enforced on the maximum number of rows. Value must be greater than or equal to `-1`.
Java constant	`Config.SQL_MAX_ROWS`
Type	`Integer`
Set by	Deployment descriptor, `Config` class
Used by actions	`<sql:query>`

Configuration Variables

The configuration variables are considered to be scoped variables and, because of this, fall under the definition of how scoped variables names work according to the JSP specification. The JSP specification states, "A scoped variable name should refer to a unique object at all points in the execution." This means all the different scopes (page, request, session, and application) that exist within a `PageContext` really should behave as a single namespace.

So, what does this mean for your JSTL configuration settings? If you allowed for the standard JSP scoping implementation to work, setting a scoped variable in any one scope overrides it in any of the other scopes. Since it's possible to specify the scope of a variable during an action, this becomes problematic because the value of the configuration setting may be overwritten for a scope you didn't intend.

The Config Class

To prevent the type of scope problem we just talked about from happening when actions set the configuration variables, the JSTL provides a class called `javax.servlet.jsp.jstl.core.Config`. You can use this class to manage the configuration variables as if scopes had their own private namespace. This allows actions to set variables for any scope they need. The `Config` class provides a number of constants that can be conveniently used to refer to the various configuration settings:

```
public static final String FMT_LOCALE =
  "javax.servlet.jsp.jstl.fmt.locale";
public static final String FMT_FALLBACK_LOCALE =
  "javax.servlet.jsp.jstl.fmt.fallbackLocale";
public static final String FMT_LOCALIZATION_CONTEXT =
  "javax.servlet.jsp.jstl.fmt.localizationContext";
public static final String FMT_TIME_ZONE =
  "javax.servlet.jsp.jstl.fmt.timeZone";
public static final String SQL_DATA_SOURCE =
  "javax.servlet.jsp.jstl.sql.dataSource";
public static final String SQL_MAX_ROWS =
  "javax.servlet.jsp.jstl.sql.maxRows";
```

The `Config` class also provides a number of methods that manage the various configuration settings. These include various flavors of `get`, `set`, and `remove` to handle setting configuration settings in each of the scopes. There's also a `find()` method provided so that you can locate a particular configuration setting as defined by its context initialization name. The `find()` method will search each of the scopes in the order defined in the JSP scope rules and return the first occurrence it finds as an `Object`. If nothing is found, then it returns a `null`. The order that the scopes are evaluated is page, request, session, and then application.

Now that we've covered the basics of working with the JSTL, we'll describe the actions available in each of the tag libraries, starting with the Core tag library.

Using the Core Tag Library

The Core area comprises the following four distinct functional sections:

- General-purpose actions used to manipulate the scoped variables found within a JSP page. These general-purpose actions also encompass error handling.
- Conditional actions used for doing conditional processing within a JSP page.

- Iterator actions that make it easy to iterate of collections of objects.
- URL-related actions for dealing with URL resources in a JSP page.

You'll now look at each functional section in the Core tag library a bit more closely.

General-Purpose Actions

Four general-purpose tags exist. The `<c:out>` tag provides a way to write a value to the `JspWriter`. This is similar to using the following JSP expression to write dynamic data to the client:

```
<%= scripting language expression %>
```

The value to be written to the `JspWriter` is specified as a `value` attribute. For example:

```
<c:out value="${sessionScope.courseInfo.title}"/>.
```

You can use the EL to accomplish this. It should be obvious that the following:

```
The title of the course you just purchased is
<c:out value="${sessionScope.courseInfo.title}">
```

is much easier to read (and write) than this:

```
<%@ page import="com.apress.proj2ee.jstl.courseInfo" %>
<% CourseInfo courseInfo = (CourseInfo)pageContext.getAttribute("courseInfo",
PageContext.SessionScope);
%>
The title of the course you just purchased is <%= courseInfo.getTitle() %>
```

You can use the `<c:set>` tag to set the value of a scoped variable in any JSP scope or to set a property of a specified target object. It's possible to set the value using the EL or to set the value by using the body content of the tag. If using a target object, the target must evaluate to a JavaBean or `java.util.Map` object.

If the target is a JavaBean, it must contain the appropriate getter/setter methods. If the target is `null` and the object is other than a `Map` or JavaBean, or the JavaBean doesn't have the property getter/setter methods, then an exception will be thrown.

The `<c:remove>` removes an object from scope. This functionality is similar to doing the following:

```
PageContext.removeAttribute(varName);
```

`<c:catch>` is another way to handle exceptions. It can handle errors from any action as well as from multiple actions at once. It's not meant to be a replacement for the JSP error page but rather a way to fine-tune how your exceptions are handled. If you have an exception that's germane to the JSP page, then it's best to let it propagate to the error page specified for the JSP page.

You can catch exceptions that aren't really critical with the <c:catch> tag and handle them better for the user. When an exception is thrown, it's stored in a page-scoped variable that's identified by the var attribute of the tag. If there's no exception, the scoped variable is removed if it already existed. Specifying a var isn't mandatory, and if one isn't specified, the exception is caught—but not saved. In the following example, you're forcing an exception because a URL is required on the import. An exception will be thrown, and you can then test the variable urlError to display a more useful error message to the user. The getMessage() method is called by default when printing the value of the exception:

```
<c:catch var="urlError">
    <c:import url="" />
</c:catch>
<c:if test="${not empty urlError}">
     <b>Your file was not found</b>
     </br>
     Here's more information on the error:
    </br>
     <c:out value="${urlError}" />
</c:if>
```

Conditional Actions

The JSTL supports both simple and mutually exclusive conditional actions. This means it's possible to support if constructs as well as if/then/else constructs. It's common to have dynamic data that determines what needs to happen on the JSP page. Using scriptlets has been the most common way to accomplish this, but using scriptlet code takes you back to the "page author who needs to know scripting language" syndrome—not to mention that the JSP pages start to quickly look like a mess and become difficult to read. The JSTL conditional actions make it easy (and cleaner) to do conditional processing in a JSP page.

Simple Conditional

The <c:if> action provides a simple conditional action. If the test condition specified evaluates to true, then the body content is evaluated, and the result is written to the current JspWriter. It's possible to save the results of the test condition into an exported scoped variable by specifying the var and scope attribute. In the following example, a simple conditional is shown by defining an EL expression to evaluate. If it evaluates to true, then the <c:if> action will evaluate the body content:

```
<c:if test="${user.previousOrders == 0}">
  Welcome to the ProJ2EE course catalog. We hope you find something you like.
</c:if>
```

If you wanted to provide some shopping incentives for a new user, you could use the var attribute and add some additional features. In the following example, you're defining the EL to evaluate, test, store the result of the test in `firstTimeBuyer` (which is given session scope), and conditionally evaluate the content of the tag. Then, in the subsequent `<c:if>`, you're testing the scoped variable `firstTimeBuyer` again, and you act accordingly:

```
<c:if test="${user.previousOrders == 0}"
      var="firstTimeBuyer"
      scope="session">
  Welcome to the ProJ2EE course catalog. We hope you find something you like.
</c:if>
...other procesing logic in another JSP page

<%-- If a first time buyer, let's give them a 10% discount on the order --%>
<c:if test ="${firstTimeBuyer}">
  Congratulations! You get a 10% discount on your first order.
</c:if>
```

Mutually Exclusive Conditionals

When using a mutually exclusive conditional action, only one of the possible alternative actions gets its body content evaluated. This is the familiar `if/else` or `if/then/else` programming structure. You use the JSTL actions `<c:choose>`, `<c:when>`, and `<c:otherwise>` to construct mutually exclusive conditional statements. Note that the `<c:if>` and `<c:when>` actions are different. A `<c:if>` action always processes its body content if its test condition evaluates to `true`. Only the first `<c:when>` action whose test condition evaluates to `true` will have its body content processed. It doesn't matter how many `<c:when>` actions are nested in the `<c:choose>` action.

The `<c:choose>` action has no attributes and primarily sets the context for a mutually exclusive conditional. The `<c:choose>` action can contain the `<c:when>` and `<c:otherwise>` nested subtags. When using these actions, just one of the nested actions will be processed at most. The test conditional of `<c:when>` that evaluates to `true` will have its body content evaluated and written to the current `JspWriter`. There can be as many `<c:when>` actions as desired. The `<c:otherwise>` action must be the last action nested within the `<c:choose>`. It isn't required to use a `<c:otherwise>`, but if it's used, there can be only one.

The body content of the `<c:otherwise>` is evaluated only if none of the test conditions for the `<c:when>` actions evaluated to `true`. For example, the following sample code shows how the text rendered depends on a user's buying habits. Using the EL in the test conditions, you can direct your sales strategy to the appropriate purchasing habit of the user:

```
<c:choose>
  <c:when test="${user.lastPurchaseAmount > 100}">
    Welcome big spender, check out all the new courses you can buy!
  </c:when>
  <c:when test="${user.lastPurchaseAmount > 30}">
```

```
    Welcome, we've got some new courses that you might be interested in!
  </c:when>
  <c:when test="${user.lastPurchaseAmount > 1} &&
              ${user.lastPurchaseAmount <= 30} ">
    Welcome, let us help you find some great courses!
  </c:when>
  <c:otherwise>
    Come on, there has to be something that interests you!
  </c:otherwise>
</c:choose>
```

Creating Custom Logic Actions

While the simple and mutually exclusive tags provided by the JSTL should provide most of the functionality anyone might require, it's possible to create your own custom logic actions if necessary. You can also use these custom logic actions with the JSTL actions to create a robust, relatively straightforward, simple way to do all kinds of conditional processing. You can expose variables from your custom logic actions the same way that the `<c:if>` exports its `var` attribute. Other actions can then use the exposed variable.

An abstract class, `ConditionalTagSupport`, extends `javax.servlet.jsp.tagext.TagSupport`. `ConditionalTagSupport` resides in the `javax.servlet.jsp.jstl.core` package and allows a developer to create a custom implementation of conditional actions. Using this class, it's possible for a Boolean result to be exposed as a JSP scoped variable. You can then use the Boolean result as the test condition in a `<c:when>` action in much the same way that you used the `var` attribute in the earlier sample. `ConditionalTagSupport` provides support for the following:

- Conditional processing of the action's body based on the returned value of the abstract method `condition()`
- Storing the result of `condition()` as a Boolean object into a JSP scoped variable identified by the attributes `var` and `scope`

The JSTL is extensible and can easily morph to fit an exact need.

Iterator Actions

There has always been a strong requirement to iterate through collections. In fact, this is probably one of the most common tasks you need to perform. One can only venture a guess at how many JSP pages have implemented their own versions of iterating through something. You can certainly accomplish iterating using scriptlet code in a JSP page, but, face it, there's got to be a better way. Coding iterations and handling different types of collections can get cumbersome. The iterator actions in the JSTL focus on making iterating as easily as possible over a variety of collection types.

Two iteration actions exist: `<c:forEach>` and `<c:forTokens>`. All of the standard Java 2 Standard Edition (J2SE) `java.util.Collection` and `java.util.Map` types are supported in the `<c:forEach>` action. These include the following:

- `List`
- `LinkedList`
- `ArrayList`
- `Vector`
- `Stack`
- `Set`
- `HashMap`
- `Hashtable`
- `Properties`
- `Provider`
- `Attributes`

You'll now look at the iteration actions in more detail.

<c:forEach>

The `<c:forEach>` action uses the `items` attribute to specify a collection of objects. The action then repeats its nested body content over the `items`. If `items` is `null`, then no iteration is performed since it's treated as an empty collection. The current item in the iteration is exported as a variable. The variable has nested scope visibility. For most collections, this is an object in the collection. However, if it's an array of primitive types or a `Map` object, the current item is handled slightly differently. If the collection is of type `java.util.Map`, then the current item will be of type `java.util.Map.Entry`. The following two properties are exposed:

- **key**: The key under which this item is stored in the underlying `Map`
- **value**: The value that corresponds to this key

Also, an object is exported that holds the status information of the iteration. The status is exposed using the `public interface LoopTagStatus` contained in the `javax.servlet.jsp.jstl.core` package. A number of interfaces are exposed with the iteration actions; among them are `LoopTag` and `LoopTagSupport`.

Another nice feature of the iteration actions is their ability to specify ranges for the iteration. This makes it possible to iterate through a specified portion of a collection. The begin and end attributes are the indices used to determine the range. If begin is specified, it must be greater than or equal to 0. If end is specified, it must be greater than or equal to begin.

The items attribute isn't required when using the <c:forEach> action. If the items attribute isn't specified, then the value of the current item is set to the integer value of the current index. This makes it easy to do a for loop if needed.

A step attribute allows the iteration to take place in the specified step amount. If step is specified, it must be greater than or equal to 1. Note though that if you're using a Map collection, you obtain the Set view of the mappings from the Map by using the entrySet() method. You obtain an Iterator object from the Set by using the iterator() method. The items of the collection are processed in the order returned by that Iterator object. Therefore, the begin and end attributes really depend on the order of the Map. The difference between the begin, end, and step attributes is that begin tells where to start in the collection, end specifies where to stop, and step indicates how to increment through the collection.

Keep in mind that when an object is exported, it's also available for other tags. It becomes possible for tags to collaborate with each other quite easily. It's a common requirement that when iterating over collections, you want to display one item in one way and another item in a different way. Of course, it's usually not possible to determine this until run time when you can examine the dynamic data being provided by the model in the collections. It becomes much easier to implement these types of requirements using the iteration and conditional actions.

For example, you're looping through a collection of courses in the following iteration:

```
<table>
  <c:forEach var="course" items="${courses}" varStatus="status">
    <tr>
      <td><c:out value="${course.title}"/></td>
    </tr>
  </c:forEach>
</table>
```

Now suppose you decide you want to display only the first ten courses in your collection. You do this by adding the range attributes, begin and end:

```
<table>
  <c:forEach var="course" items="${courses}" varStatus="status"
             begin="0" end="9">
    <tr>
      <td><c:out value="${course.title}"/></td>
    </tr>
  </c:forEach>
</table>
```

Now say that when you print the first ten courses, you want to highlight the first five. You do this by adding in a collaboration with the conditional `<c:choose>` action:

```
<table>
  <c:forEach var="course" items="${courses}" varStatus="status"
             begin="0" end="9">
    <tr>
      <c:choose>
        <c:when test="${status.count < 4}">
          <td bgcolor="#FFFF00">
            <c:out value="${course.title}"/>
          </td>
        </c:when>
        <c:otherwise>
          <td><c:out value="${course.title}"/></td>
        </c:otherwise>
      </c:choose>
    </tr>
  </c:forEach>
</table>
```

<c:forTokens>

We've talked about the `<c:forEach>` action, but there's also the `<c:forTokens>` action. `<c:forTokens>` has the same basic attributes as `<c:forEach>`, but with two important differences. First, the `items` attribute is a `String` of tokens to iterate over. When iterating over tokenized `Strings`, it's necessary to define a delimiter to determine the characters that separate the tokens in the `String`. Therefore, `<c:forTokens>` also has a `delims` attribute. This `String` contains the set of delimiters to use to iterate through the tokens. If `delims` is `null`, then the items are treated as one contiguous `String`.

If `<c:forTokens>` reminds you of `java.util.StringTokenizer`, that's a good thing. The tokens of the string are retrieved using an instance of `StringTokenizer` with the attributes `items` and `delims` as arguments.

While it's still possible to specify a `step` attribute value, you use the step to indicate that the iteration should process only those tokens defined by the step value. For example, say you have a `String` called `courseList` that's populated with tokens as a result of some business logic. The contents of `courseList` is `Using the JSTL,Learning J2EE 1.4,EJBs to the Max`. You specify the delimiter as `","` and use the actions as follows:

```
You have ordered the following courses:<br>
<c:forTokens var="currentToken" items="${courseList}"
             delims=",">
  [<c:out value="${currentToken}"/>]
</c:forTokens>
```

The body content written to the JspWriter looks like this:

```
You have ordered the following courses:
[Using the JSTL][Learning J2EE 1.4][EJBs to the Max]
```

URL-Related Actions

The last actions to be covered as part of the Core tag library are the URL-related actions. All of the URL-related tags relate to linking, importing, and redirecting. Dealing with URLs and handling links and redirects are common tasks in JSP pages. You'll now look at these URL-related actions and see what they can provide.

First, we should talk about the types of resources that can be imported. Using <jsp:include> has been the way to include both static and dynamic content into JSP pages. <jsp:include> had some limitations as to the types of files that could be included. Then there's the fact that anything included with this standard action had to reside in the same context as the page itself. This is fine for simple Web applications, but as Web applications grow and cooperate with each other, it's a much better idea to allow content to come from anywhere. The limitations of <jsp:include> has been overcome with the <c:import> action.

<c:import>

You use <c:import> to import, or include, the content of a URL-based resource. The resource itself can be relative, absolute, within the same context, or in a foreign context from the requesting JSP page. You have a number of ways to use the <c:import> action. The only required attribute is url, which is the URL of the resource to import. You'll look at a simple example using a relative URL in the same context, and then you'll build upon it by adding some of the other attributes supported in the action. The first sample looks like this:

```
<c:import url="/hotoffthepress.html"/>
```

It's possible to specify the scope of the URL resource by adding the scope attribute (the default scope is set to page):

```
<c:import url="/hotoffthepress.html"
          scope="session" />
```

If the latest course releases were being handled by a separate application contained in the context newreleases, but you still wanted to access the hotoffthepress.html file, you'd add a foreign context so the correct file would be imported:

```
<c:import url="/hotoffthepress.html"
          scope="session"
          context="/newreleases" />
```

You'll now see the difference between scope and context. The scope is the JSP scope in which this URL resource will be available. The context is from where the resource actually comes. The flexibility that's provided for the types of content using the <c:import> action is important. Just as important are the performance gains attained with the <c:import> action.

Using <jsp:include> falls short in efficiency in a number of ways. First, when the content of the imported resource is used as the source for another action, unnecessary buffering occurs. <jsp:include> reads the content of the response and writes it to the body content of the enclosing action. The enclosing action must then reread the same content. This isn't the most efficient way to do things, but it's typical of the way that custom actions work that do transformations where the content is included and then transformed within a different custom action.

A better approach, and one provided with <c:import>, is to access the input source directly and avoid the buffering involved in the body content of the nested action. By default, any imported content is included inline to the JSP page. However, when using the var and varReader attributes, it becomes possible to expose the content through String and java.io.Reader objects. By doing so, you avoid the performance issue of the <jsp:include> action. Using the String or Reader object allows other tags to have direct access to the specified resource content. The following is an example:

```
<c:import url="/hotoffthepress.html" var="newReleases"/>
<apress:newcourses in="${newReleases}"/>
```

In this example, you're importing a resource and exposing a String object. The custom action <apress:newcourses> can then use this object to perform whatever tasks are necessary. By using the varReader attribute, you could've also exposed the content as a Reader object, like so:

```
<c:import url="/hotoffthepress.html" varReader="newReleases">
  <apress:newcourses in="${newReleases}"/>
</c:import>
```

Notice that using a varReader has nested visibility. You must enclose the custom action accessing the Reader object because it takes the responsibility away from the consumer tag to prevent resource leaks. If the consumer tag accidentally left the resource open, then memory leaks could occur until garbage collection is performed. The <c:import> tag takes care of closing the appropriate resource. In doing so, after the end_tag method of <c:import> is called, you no longer have access to the Reader object. <c:import> is one of the most valuable and useful actions provided in the JSTL.

<c:url>

When using <c:url>, you can build a URL with the correct encoding and rewriting rules applied. Only a relative URL is rewritten. This is the case because, for absolute URLs, you want to prevent a situation where an external URL could be rewritten that exposes the session ID. With this limitation, if the page author wants to use session tracking, they must use only relative URLs with <c:url> to link to local resources.

You can use <c:url> with or without body content. You can use the body content to specify query string parameters. There is the URL specified using the value attribute. You can specify context if necessary. By default, the result of the URL processing is written to the current JspWriter. As with <c:import>, it's possible to export the result as a JSP-scoped variable defined via the attributes var and scope. The var is a String object:

```
<c:url value="/apress/order" var="orderUrl"/>
<a href='<c:out value="${orderUrl}"/>'>Place an order</a>
```

You can also specify <c:param> subtags within the body of <c:url> for adding to the URL query string parameters. If necessary, they'll be properly encoded. The next section discusses <c:param> a bit.

<c:param>

You use the <c:param> action to add request parameters to a URL. It can be a nested action of <c:import>, <c:url>, and <c:redirect>. The name and value are correctly encoded if necessary. You can specify the value of the parameter as an attribute or in the body content. This is an example of both utilizations:

```
<c:url value="/apress/order" var="orderUrl">
  <c:param name="title" value="${course.title}"/>
  <c:param name="courseId"/>
    ${course.courseId}
  </c:param>
</c:url>
```

If there's no name specified or the name is null, it isn't necessarily an error, although nothing will be processed. A null value is just processed as an empty value. The ordering of the query parameter rules work the same way they do with <jsp:include>. This means that new parameters are added to, or replace, the original parameters. The new parameters, with new values, take precedence over existing values.

The scope of the new parameters is the parent actions, either <c:import> or <c:url>. The new parameters (and values) will not apply after the end_tag method is called. So, in the following example:

```
<c:url value="/apress/order?title=ProJ2EE">
  <c:param name="title" value="JSTL"/>
</c:url>
```

the value of the title parameter would be JSTL, overriding the title ProJ2EE in the <c:url> action. The value is defined in the <c:param> body content.

<c:redirect>

This action sends an HTTP redirect response to the client and aborts the processing of the page. The action implementation that returns `SKIP_PAGE` from the `doEndTag` method call does this. `<c:redirect>` has two attributes: the `url` that will be used to redirect to and an optional `context`. The URL (relative or absolute) follows the same URL rewriting rules as `<c:url>`.

There are reasons why you'd want to use a redirect. If you've finished processing a JSP page and then go forward to the next page, you may notice that the URL displayed in the Web browser is the path to the previous JSP page. The way to avoid this and have the correct URL displayed is to redirect.

> **NOTE** *When doing a redirect, the page doing the redirect informs the browser to make a new request to the target page. The URL shown in the browser therefore changes to the URL of the new page.*

When doing a redirect, any request scope objects are no longer available to the new page because the browser creates a new request. Redirecting to a resource in a foreign context is possible by using the `context` attribute. The URL specified must start with a / because it's a context-relative URL, and as defined, the context name must start with a /.

Using `<c:redirect>` is simple enough. The following sample would redirect to the `courselist.html` file in the `newreleases` context:

```
<c:redirect url="/courselist.html" context="/newrelease" />
```

Working with the XML Core Actions

The XML tag library contains actions that deal with XML manipulations. We can't think of any application we've developed in the last few years that didn't use XML to represent the data in the Web tier. XML is the data format of choice for exchanging information. You'll find a strong similarity between the XML core actions and the actions provided in the Core tag library. However, there's a difference; the XML core actions use XPath for their expression language. You can find the URI to access the XML core actions at `http://java.sun.com/jstl/xml`.

Getting to Know XPath

XPath, one of the major elements of XSL Tranformations (XSLT) and a World Wide Web Consortium (W3C) recommendation, is a set of syntax rules for defining parts of an XML document. While not written in XML, XPath uses path expressions to make it possible to locate specific nodes within an XML document. These expressions look a lot like how you access traditional file paths. For example, if you had the following simple XML document:

```
<?xml version="1.0" encoding="ISO-8859-1"?>
<catalog>
  <course edition="1">
    <title>Using the JSTL</title>
    <instructor>Sue Spielman</instructor>
  </course>
</catalog>
```

you could access the title by using the XPath expression `/catalog/course/title`. If you want to reference the attribute edition of the `course` element, you do this by using the standard `@` syntax of XPath, so it might look like `<x:out select="@edition" />`.

Library Functions

A library of standard functions are available in XPath for working with strings, numbers, and Booleans. XPath supports numerical, equality, relational, and Boolean expressions. You can use expressions to access nodes, sets of nodes, and attributes. A default function library comes with the XPath engine provided with the JSTL. Some engines provide extension functions or allow customization to add new functions, but the XPath function library in JSTL is limited to the core function library of the XPath specification. Table 4-8 describes the supported XPath functions.

Table 4-8. XPath Functions

METHOD NAME	DESCRIPTION
`count`	Returns the number of selected elements
`id`	Selects elements by their unique ID
`last`	Returns a number equal to the context size from the expression evaluation context
`local-name`	Returns the local part of the expanded name of the node in the argument nodeset that's first in document order
`name`	Returns the name of an element
`namespace-uri`	Returns the namespace URI of the expanded name of the node in the argument nodeset that's first in document order
`position`	Returns a number equal to the context position from the expression evaluation context

Table 4-9 describes the XPath `String` functions.

Table 4-9. XPath `String` *Functions*

METHOD NAME	DESCRIPTION
`concat`	Returns the concatenation of its arguments
`contains`	Returns `true` if the first string contains the second string; otherwise returns `false`
`normalize-space`	Removes leading and trailing spaces from a string
`starts-with`	Returns `true` if the first string starts with the second string; otherwise returns `false`
`string`	Converts an object to a string
`string-length`	Returns the number of characters in a string
`substring`	Returns a substring
`substring-after`	Returns a substring after a substring
`substring-before`	Returns a substring before a substring
`translate`	Translates letters in a string

Table 4-10 describes the XPath number functions.

Table 4-10. XPath Number Functions

METHOD NAME	DESCRIPTION
`ceiling`	Returns the smallest integer that's not less than the argument
`floor`	Returns the largest integer that's not greater than the argument
`number`	Converts its argument to a number
`round`	Returns the integer that is closest to the argument
`sum`	Returns the sum, for each node in the argument nodeset, of the result of converting the string values of the node to a number

Finally, Table 4-11 describes the available XPath Boolean functions.

Table 4-11. XPath Boolean Functions

METHOD NAME	DESCRIPTION
`boolean`	Converts its argument to Boolean
`false`	Returns `false`
`lang`	Returns `true` or `false` depending on whether the language of the context node as specified by `xml:lang` attributes is the same as or is a sublanguage of the language specified by the argument string
`not`	Returns `true` if its argument is `false` and returns `false` otherwise
`true`	Returns `true`

Variable Mappings

To make it as easy as possible to access data from within a JSP page in specific scopes, the XPath engine provides variable mappings. The scopes are defined in the same way as those implicit objects you're familiar with in the EL. Table 4-12 shows the available XPath variable mappings.

Table 4-12. XPath Mappings

EXPRESSION	VARIABLE MAPPING
`$foo`	`pageContext.findAttribute("foo")`
`$param:foo`	`request.getParameter("foo")`
`$header:foo`	`request.getHeader("foo")`
`$cookie:foo`	The cookie's value for name `foo`
`$initParam:foo`	`application.getInitParameter("foo")`
`$pageScope:foo`	`pageContext.getAttribute("foo", PageContext.PAGE_SCOPE)`
`$requestScope:foo`	`pageContext.getAttribute("foo", PageContext.REQUEST_SCOPE)`
`$sessionScope:foo`	`pageContext.getAttribute("foo", PageContext.SESSION_SCOPE)`
`$applicationScope:foo`	`pageContext.getAttribute("foo", PageContext.APPLICATION_SCOPE)`

Through these mappings, you can use JSP-scoped variables, request parameters, headers, cookies, and context initialization parameters inside XPath expressions. For example, using some more XPath syntax, you'll see that it's possible to access an XML element's attributes by using the @ symbol. The following code snippet:

```
/catalog/course[@edition=$param:current]
```

would find the `<course>` element with an attribute `edition` equal to the value of the HTTP request parameter `current`.

Accessing Resources

When using XML actions, obviously one of the first things you want to do is access some type of resource such as an existing XML document. You do this by importing resources using the Core URL action `<c:import>` already mentioned. XML actions such as `<x:parse>` and `<x:transform>` can then use the resource. For example, you can import a URL resource and then export it into a variable named `xml`. This variable is then used as the XML document to the parse action:

```
<c:import url="http://apress.proj2ee/course?id=12345" var="xml"/>
<x:parse xml="${xml}" var="doc"/>
```

You'll see how it's possible to resolve references to external entities using various attributes when you get to the `<x:parse>` and `<x:transform>` actions.

Using the select Attribute

All of the XML actions of JSTL allow a way to specify XPath expressions. You accomplish this by using the `select` attribute. The `select` attribute is always specified as a string literal that's evaluated by the XPath engine. A dedicated attribute for XPath expressions avoids confusion; since some of the XML actions have similar functions to the Core actions, it's important to not get the XPath expression confused with the JSP EL.

The `select` attribute is shown in this simple sample where the XPath expression specifies the title to be selected from the XML document and output to the `JspWriter`:

```
<x:out select="$doc/catalog/course/title"/>
```

`<x:out>` is comparable to `<c:out>`, as you'll see next.

<x:out> Action

The `<x:out>` action provides the same functionality as the Core `<c:out>` action. It allows an XPath expression to be evaluated and then outputs the result of the evaluation to the current `JspWriter` object.

As previously mentioned, the `select` attribute holds the XPath expression to be evaluated. Once the expression is evaluated, the result is converted to a `String` and written to the current `JspWriter`. Using `<x:out>` is the same as if you had used either the standard JSP syntax `<%=...%>` to display the result of an expression or `<c:out>` to display the result of an expression in the EL syntax.

`<x:out>` also has an optional Boolean attribute called `escapeXml`. This attribute determines whether the characters `<`, `>`, `&`, `'`, and `"` should be converted to their corresponding character entity codes, as shown in Table 4-13. This attribute defaults to `true`.

Table 4-13. Character Entities

CHARACTER	ENTITY CODE
<	<
>	>
&	&
'	'
"	"

As an example, using the XML document you previously viewed, the following statement would output the course title:

```
<x:out select="$doc/catalog/course/title"/>
```

You might wonder, since you're referencing the XML document using the $doc in the XPath expression, how you actually got the XML document into scope. You do this using the `<x:parse>` action that you'll learn about now.

`<x:set>` Action

You also have a `<x:set>` action corresponding to the `<c:set>` action. This action evaluates an XPath expression and then saves the result into a scoped variable as defined by the `var` attribute. In addition to the `var` and `scope` attributes you've seen in other actions, `<x:set>` also has the `select` attribute for defining the XPath expression.

In the following example, using the same XML document as the source, you can see how you'd use `<x:set>` to access an element in an XML document and then save the value into a request scoped variable named `title`. The contents of the variable `courseTitle` would be the JSTL:

```
<x:set var="courseTitle" scope="request" select="$doc/catalog/course/title"/>
```

`<x:parse>` Action

You use the `<x:parse>` action to parse an XML document. The resulting object is then saved into a scoped variable as defined by either the `var` attribute or the `varDom` attribute. The `varDom` attribute is a `String` that holds the name of the scoped variable. The type of the scoped variable is `org.w3c.dom.Document`. The type of the `var` attribute depends on the implementation of the `<x:parse>` action, so you'll need to consult the vendor documentation for whichever implementation of the JSTL you end up using. In the reference implementation, the type of the scoped variable as defined by `var` is also of type `org.w3c.dom.Document`.

The `<x:parse>` action performs the parse on the document; it doesn't perform any validation against document type definitions (DTDs) or schemas. You can specify the XML document to be used for the parse with the `xml` attribute or inline by including it the action's body content.

varDom Attribute

The `varDom` attribute exposes a DOM document, making it possible to use the variable for collaboration with other custom actions you may have created. You can use objects exposed by `var` and `varDom` to set the context of an XPath expression. This is exactly what you saw in the `<x:set>` and `<x:out>` example when you referenced the `$doc` in the `select` attribute.

In the following sample, you import a document using the `<c:import>` action. Then you use that XML document for the parse. The results are stored in the `var` attribute of the `parse` action. You then use `$doc` as the context for your other XML actions:

```
<c:import url="catalog.xml" var="xml"/>
<x:parse doc"${xml}" var="doc"/>
<x:out select="$doc/catalog/course/title"/>
```

If your source XML document is null or empty, a JspException will be thrown.

You can also use a systemId attribute as the system identifier URI for parsing the XML document.

Using Filtering

You can use the filter attribute to apply an object that implements the org.xml.sax.XMLFilter interface to the source document. You can use this if the implementation of the XML tagset being used is based on DOM-like structure. If you've dealt with large DOM objects before, you're aware of the performance issues associated with it. Using a filter can help reduce the performance impact, but frankly, to go into how to set up and build a filter is beyond the scope of this book.

You can use the filter attribute to allow filtering of the input data prior to having it parsed by the implementation. This filtering will produce a smaller (and, we hope, more manageable) DOM-like structure. If your filter is null, then no filtering is performed.

Using filtering is a good example of when you might want to create your own custom tag that implements setting up and creating a filter. This allows you to expose the configuration of a filter through a custom tag so that a page author can perform whatever filtering is appropriate in a given situation. The filter object is then used in the <x:parse> action. The XMLFilter object, which is part of the Simple API for XML (SAX) 2, isn't the focus of this book.

XML Flow Control Actions

While the XML core actions provide the basic functionality to parse and access XML data, the XML flow control actions perform conditional processing and iterations.

Using XPath expressions, the XML control flow actions determine whether to process JSP code. These actions act in much the same way as the Core tag library flow control actions already mentioned, except for the utilization of XPath instead of the EL. Therefore, to avoid redundant information, you'll see only the differences between the XML and the Core actions (<c:if>, <c:choose>, and <c:forEach>), where appropriate.

<x:if> Action

The <x:if> action uses the select attribute to specify the XPath expression. The expression is evaluated, and the resulting object is converted to a Boolean. The result is determined according to the semantics of the XPath boolean() function. These semantics are as follows:

- A number is true if, and only if, it's not positive, negative, zero, or not a number.
- A nodeset is true if, and only if, it's nonempty.
- A string is true if, and only if, its length is nonzero.

If the result is true, then <x:if> will render its body. So, for example, if you want to see if you have the XML data for a selected course, you could do so by evaluating the XPath expression shown in the select attribute:

```
<x:if select="$doc/catalog/course/title='Using the JSTL'">
  You've made a fine choice!
</x:if>
```

You can use the familiar var and scope attribute when using the <x:if> action to save the Boolean result.

<x:choose>, <x:when>, and <x:otherwise> Actions

We'll cover these actions together since they're related to each other. These tags are analogous to a Java switch statement; the <x:choose> action selects one of any number of possible alternatives. The alternatives consist of a sequence of <x:when> elements followed by an optional <x:otherwise>.

Each <x:when> element has a single select attribute. When an <x:choose> element is processed, each of the <x:when> elements has its expression evaluated in turn. The result is converted to a Boolean following the same rules as <x:if>. Only the body of the first <x:when> whose result is true is rendered. If none of the test conditions of nested <x:when> tags evaluates to true, then if an <x:otherwise> tag is present, its body is evaluated.

The following are constraints on <x:choose>. The body of the <x:choose> action can contain only the following:

- Whitespaces may appear anywhere around the <x:when> and <x:otherwise> subtags.

- One or more <x:when> actions must all appear before <x:otherwise>.

- Zero or one <x:otherwise> action must be the last action nested within the <x:choose>.

The following are constraints on <x:when> and <x:otherwise>:

- Both must have <x:choose> as an immediate parent.

- <x:when> must appear before an <x:otherwise> action that has the same immediate parent.

- <x:otherwise> must be the last action in the nested <x:choose>.

To put all of these tags together, we'll go through an example. In this example, you're checking to see if there's a <title> element contained in an XML resource. If so, then you print a message to the current JspWriter; otherwise you'll print a not-as-nice message to the current JspWriter to let the user know they haven't selected anything yet:

```
<x:choose>
  <x:when select="$doc/catalog/course/title">
    Thank you for purchasing <x:out select="$doc/catalog/course/title"/>
  </x:when>
  <x:otherwise>
    There are no titles selected.
  </x:otherwise>
</x:choose>
```

<x:forEach> Action

The <x:forEach> action evaluates the given XPath expression in the select attribute and iterates over the result, thereby setting the context node to each element in the iteration. When using <x:forEach>, if the select attribute is null, then a JspException is thrown. As long as there are items to iterate over, the body content is processed by the JSP container and written to the current JspWriter. To demonstrate, the following sample will evaluate all of the nodes that have a course element and then print the edition attribute:

```
<x:forEach select="$doc//course">
  This course is edition <x:out select="@edition"/>.
</x:forEach>
```

Using XML Transformation Actions

The XML transformation actions provide a mechanism for page authors to use XSLT stylesheets. Extensible Stylesheet Language (XSL) is used for expressing stylesheets. It consists of three parts: XSLT, XPath, and XSL Formatting Objects. XSLT is the part of XSL that's used to do transformations.

Typically, transformations take an XML document and turn it into another XML document or into another type of document that's recognized by a browser or device. This is the mechanism used to turn XML into, say, Extensible HTML (XHTML) or Wireless Markup Language (WML). Using XSLT stylesheets is a common way to support multiple client devices from a Web application. Each device—PC, mobile device, personal digital assistant (PDA)—may have its own XSLT stylesheet associated with the client type. The data can then be formatted correctly and specifically for that targeted device.

XSLT is quite powerful and can add new elements into an output file, remove elements, and rearrange and sort elements. It can also perform evaluations to determine which elements to display from a given XML document. XSLT is a whole beast unto itself and is beyond the scope of this book. If you're planning on using XSLT and haven't yet, it probably makes sense to spend some time getting up to speed on it.

It's frequently a requirement that the same stylesheet is used to transform different source XML documents. The overhead of constantly loading the stylesheet can become a burden on the application. JSTL allows the stylesheet to be processed once and then saved into what's called a *transformer object*. This transformer object can then be cached and used for future transformations so you improve performance.

The following sections show how the transformations are handled.

<x:transform> Action

The `<x:transform>` action applies an XSLT stylesheet to an XML document. If either the XML document or the source XSLT document supplied to the action is `null`, then a `JspException` will be thrown. You can provide the XML document in the `xml` attribute or as the body content of the action. The XSLT stylesheet is provided in the `xslt` attribute. Like the other XML actions, `<x:transform>` doesn't provide any DTD or schema validation.

The result of the transformation is written to the current `JspWriter` by default; however, it's possible to capture the result of the transformation in two other ways. First, you can specify a `javax.xml.transform.Result` object by using `result` attribute. Second, you can save an `org.w3c.dom.Document` object in the scoped variable specified by the (you guessed it!) `var` and `scope` attributes.

It's also possible to specify the `xmlSystemId` and `xsltSystemId` attributes that identify a system identifier URI for either an XML document or an XSLT stylesheet, respectively. The following code completes a transformation, given XML and XSLT documents:

```
<c:import url="courselist.xml" var="xml"/>
<c:import url="catalogList.xsl" var="xslt"/>
<x:transform xml="${xml}" xslt="${xslt}"/>
```

<x:param> Action

Using the `<x:param>` action, it's possible to set transformation parameters for the `<x:transform>` action. You can nest the `<x:param>` action only within a `<x:transform>` action. Using the `name` and `value` attributes can provide a parameter name and value. It's also possible to specify the value within the body content of `<x:param>`.

If you look at the previous example, you can add a parameter to it by simply doing the following:

```
<x:transform xml="${xml}" xslt="${xslt}">
  <x:param name="displayAll" value="true"/>
</x:transform>
```

Using Internationalization Actions

Various pieces play a role when working with internationalization in an application, and it's time to look at the various actions available to you in the JSTL. The internationalization of applications is commonly referred to as I18N, for the 18 letters between *I* and *N* in the word *internationalization*. We mentioned at the beginning of this chapter that there are two functional areas related to I18N. These are the following:

- Locale and resource bundles
- Formatting for numbers, dates, and currency

You'll now look at the actions related to locales and resource bundles. First you need to get a bearing on how resource bundles and locales operate since they play a critical role in the I18N actions.

Using the <fmt:message> Action

Before we start talking about the various actions available in the I18N, we'll introduce the `<fmt:message>` action. If you really want to do the least work necessary to build an internationalized application, `<fmt:message>` really is the only action you need to consider. The `<fmt:message>` action takes advantage of the localization context (which we'll talk about in the next section). By using `<fmt:message>`, you can output values from your resource bundles as simply as follows:

```
<fmt:message key="welcome"/>
```

The appropriate resource bundle will look up the key `welcome`, and the translated string will be provided. This is about as easy as it gets to incorporate international support into your application.

The `<fmt:message>` action also supports parameterized content, also called *parametric replacement*. For example, you can provide variables that will be used within the string used by the `key` attribute. Say you want to personalize your welcome page and pass the name of a user so you can welcome them. To do this, you use the `<fmt:param>` subtag. The "Using <fmt:param> Action" section covers this in more detail, but as a quick example so you're familiar with the format, the action might look like this:

```
<fmt:message key="welcome" >
  <fmt:param value="${userNameString}"/>
</fmt:message>
```

In this example, you'd be accessing a variable called `userNameString` that would then be used as a parameter to the message. If you were accessing the English version of the resource bundle, *Welcome Sue* would appear in the `JspWriter`.

Now, with the basics of <fmt:message> under your belt, you'll take a more in-depth look at how the I18N actions work.

Working with Localization Context

All of the I18N actions work with a localization context. This context is used when determining how to localize the data provided to the action. The class LocalizationContext is found in the javax.servlet.jsp.jstl.fmt package. Quite a few of the JSTL I18N actions use this class. They include <fmt:message>, <fmt:formatNumber>, <fmt:parseNumber>, <fmt:formatDate>, and <fmt:parseDate>.

The following are the two main pieces of data used by the context:

- The resource bundle that's typically included in your Web application in the Java archive (JAR) or Web archive (WAR) file
- The locale for which the resource bundle was found

The context uses an order of precedence to determine what the correct resource bundle should be. It determines the order of precedence as follows:

- First the bundle attribute of the <fmt:message> actions is used if it's specified. The I18N localization context associated with it is used for localization specific to that message action.
- If no bundle attribute was specified, then the next place to check is the <fmt:bundle> action.

You can nest <fmt:message> actions inside a <fmt:bundle> action. If this is the case, then the I18N localization context of the enclosing <fmt:bundle> action is used for localization. When we go into the details on the <fmt:bundle> action, we'll talk about how the resource bundle is actually determined and what the algorithm looks like when using the basename attribute. The basename is the bundle's fully qualified resource name. The basename is represented in a similar way to that of a fully qualified class name using the dot notation. However, there's no defined suffix for a basename. This is an example of a basename:

```
com.apress.proj2ee.sample.Resources
```

You'd then use this basename as the base for creating the appropriate named resource bundle. So, if you were using an English resource bundle, you could set the locale and country code to en_US. You'd create the complete name of the resource bundle using the basename and the appropriate locale information like so:

```
com.apress.proj2ee.sample.Resourcesen_US
```

If neither the bundle attribute nor the <fmt:bundle> action is specified, then the default localization context is used. You do this by using the configuration setting variable javax.servlet.jsp.jstl.fmt.localizationContext. If the configuration setting is of type Config.FMT_LOCALIZATION_CONTEXT, its resource bundle component javax.servlet.jsp.jstl.fmt.LocalizationContext is used for localization. Otherwise, the configuration setting is of type String. When the type is String, the value is interpreted as a resource bundle basename.

We'll now walk you through a couple of examples to show the various ways to set the localization context when used on a JSP page. These samples are probably extreme cases of when you want to change the resource bundles. Usually you have a locale that's used throughout the page; however, these will give you an idea of how the various precedence levels work if the following actions appeared on the same page:

```
<%-- This action would use the configuration setting --%>
<fmt:message key="welcome" />

<%-- Use the bundle with the specified base name --%>
<fmt:bundle basename="com.apress.proj2ee.sample.Resource">

  <%-- Localization context established by parent <fmt:bundle> tag --%>
  <fmt:message key="welcome" />

  <%-- Localization context established by attribute bundle --%>
  <fmt:message key="welcome" bundle="com.apress.proj2ee.sample.NewResource " />

</fmt:bundle>
```

Setting Preferred Locales

We've been talking about the localization context and locales so far, but we haven't really gone into the details of how to set and change the preferred locale. Doing so is useful since you may have different locales being used by different users of the same application at the same time. You can retrieve the resource bundle of the localization context in a couple of ways, and the following sections address those processes. The algorithm used to retrieve the resource bundle requires the following two pieces of information:

- The basename of the resource bundle
- The preferred locales

Setting the Preferred Locales

You have two ways to set the preferred locales. You can do it in the application itself, or you can use the browser to determine the correct locale. If you use both ways, the application-based locale setting will take precedence.

Application-Based Method

When implementing the application-based method, you set the locale by using the configuration setting variable `javax.servlet.jsp.jstl.fmt.locale`. Using this variable will disable the browser-based locales. You can set this variable to the `String` constant `Config.FMT_LOCALE` if you wanted to set it programmatically. If you use a `String` value, it's interpreted as the printable representation of a locale. This must contain a two-letter (lowercase) language code (as defined by ISO-639) and optionally a two-letter (uppercase) country code (as defined by ISO-3166). You must separate language and country codes with a hyphen (-) or underscore (_).

> **NOTE** *It's useful to set the locale using the application-based method in situations where you want your users to be able to pick their preferred locale.*

After you select the appropriate locale, you can set a scoped variable accordingly. Another case where this may be useful is where a client's preferred locale is retrieved from a database and installed for the page using the `<fmt:setLocale>` action. You can use the `<fmt:setLocale>` action to set the `javax.servlet.jsp.jstl.fmt.locale` configuration variable as follows:

```
<fmt:setLocale value="en_US" />
```

Browser-Based Method

In the browser-based locale setting, the client determines which locale(s) should be used by the Web application by using its browser. The action retrieves the client's locale preferences by calling `ServletRequest.getLocales()` (or `pageContext.getRequest().getLocales()`) on the incoming request. This returns an enumeration of the locales (in order of preference) that the client wants to use. If client's request doesn't provide an `Accept-Language:` header, which is what specifies the supported languages for the response of this request, the returned locale enumeration contains the run time's default locale so there will always be at least one element in the enumeration.

It doesn't really matter which method you use to determine the locale setting. In both cases, the algorithm defined to determine which resource bundle to use for the localization context uses an enumeration of the preferred locales.

Formatting Locales

The formatting actions also need to use information from the localization context. If, for some reason, a formatting action can't leverage the locale from the localization context—maybe because the context doesn't have a locale set or the formatting action can't establish a reference to the existing localization context—it must establish the formatting locale on its own. To do so, an algorithm similar to that just discussed is used.

The algorithm compares preferred locales against the set of locales that are available for a specific formatting action. The available locales are found in two different ways depending on whether you're talking about number or date actions. The locales available for actions `<fmt:formatNumber>` and `<fmt:parseNumber>` are determined by using the available Java class method calls. For numbers, this is `java.text.NumberFormat.getAvailableLocales()`. The locales available for `<fmt:formatDate>` and `<fmt:parseDate>` are determined by a call to `java.text.DateFormat.getAvailableLocales()`.

Once you have the available locales, you can do a lookup. The locale lookup is similar to the resource bundle lookup, as described in the next section, except that instead of trying to match a resource bundle, the locale lookup tries to find a match in a list of available locales. A match of the specified locale against an available locale is attempted in the following order:

- Language, country, and variant are the same.
- Language and country are the same.
- Language is the same, and the available locale doesn't have a country.

So, there's a two-step process to find the formatting locale. First, when there are multiple preferred locales, they're processed in the order they were returned by a call to `ServletRequest.getLocales()`. If a match wasn't found, a locale lookup is done for the fallback locale as specified in the `javax.servlet.jsp.jstl.fmt.fallbackLocale` configuration setting. If this match is found, then that's what is used as the formatting locale. Otherwise, it's up to the action to take some type of corrective steps to remedy the problem.

How Resource Bundle Are Decided

Once you have the basename and the ordered set of preferred locales, the resource bundle for the localization context is determined according to a mechanism similar to that already found in the J2SE platform. By using similar semantics, the JSTL takes advantage of the `getBundle()` method in the `java.util.ResourceBundle`. This is how to use this method:

```
ResourceBundle myResources =
     getBundle(baseName, locale, this.getClass().getClassLoader());
```

This is how the bundle lookup is usually done in the J2SE; you'll also see what the differences are in the JSTL. `getBundle()` then iterates over the candidate bundle names to find the first one for which it can instantiate an actual resource bundle. For each candidate bundle name, it attempts to create a resource bundle:

> First, it attempts to load a class using the candidate bundle name. If such a class can be found and loaded using the specified class loader, if it's assignment compatible with `ResourceBundle`, if it's accessible from `ResourceBundle`, and if it can be

instantiated, then getBundle() creates a new instance of this class and uses it as the result resource bundle.

Otherwise, getBundle() attempts to locate a property resource file from within the containers classpath. It generates a path name from the candidate bundle name by replacing all . characters with / and appending the string .properties. It attempts to find a resource with this name using ClassLoader.getResource(). If it finds a resource, it attempts to create a new PropertyResourceBundle instance from its contents. If successful, this instance becomes the result resource bundle.

If no result resource bundle is found, a MissingResourceException is thrown.

JSTL omits doing lookups on the current default locale as returned by Locale.getDefault() as well as omits doing lookups on the root resource bundle, which is the basename. The reason for these omissions is so that other locales may be considered before applying the JSTL fallback mechanism. The lookup on the fallback locale is performed for using the javax.servlet.jsp.jstl.fmt.fallbackLocale configuration setting. If a match is found, the fallback locale and the matched resource bundle are stored in the I18N localization context.

The root resource bundle is considered only if there's no fallback mechanism or the fallback mechanism fails to determine a resource bundle. If such a resource bundle exists, it's used as the resource bundle of the localization context but doesn't have any locale. If the resource bundle doesn't exist, then the localization content won't contain a resource bundle (obviously) or a locale. What happens in this case is that the I18N action is required to take the appropriate steps to make sure that the action can still function correctly.

Once a resource bundle has been found and selected for the localization context, the searching stops. The order for the lookup is determined by the enumeration from the getLocales() call. This is an important point to be clear about because if you have browser-based locale settings that contain both English and Spanish, in that order, and English is defined by just the language code for English (en), but the language and country code for Spanish (es_ES) is used, the resource bundle for en will be used if it's found and the search stops.

When using resource bundles for a specific language and country, it's preferable that there be a language resource available. If you're expecting the language/country resource to be used for the lookup, you need to specify both the language and the country code so that the exact match will be found. For example, Resources_fr_FR should be backed by a resource bundle covering just the language in a resource bundle called Resources_fr. You typically create a country specific bundle if the country differences are too great for just the single language reference—for example, Resources_en_US and Resources_en_GB.

Now that you've made it through the entire explanation for how you accomplish the resource bundle lookups, the simplified version of the search order is as follows:

- Basename + _ + language + _ + country + _ + variant
- Basename + _ + language + _ + country
- Basename + _ + language

- Fallback locale
- Basename

Resource Bundle Lookup Samples

You'll now take a look at a few sample situations. You'll define the basename, the order of the preferred locales that would be returned in the enumeration, the fallback locale, and the available resource bundles. By following the logic of the resource bundle lookup algorithm, you'll see which resource is selected and then set in the resulting localization context. Table 4-14 describes these samples.

Table 4-14. Resource Bundle Lookup Samples

SETTINGS	AVAILABLE RESOURCE(S)	RESULTING LOCALIZATION CONTEXT SETTINGS
Basename: `MyResources` Ordered preferred locales: `en_US`, `fr_CA` Fallback locale: `fr_CA`	`MyResources_en`, `MyResources_fr_CA`	Resource bundle: `MyResources_en` Locale: `en`
Basename: `MyResources` Ordered preferred locales: `de`, `fr` Fallback locale: `en`	`MyResources_en` `MyResources_en`	Resource bundle: Locale: `en`
Basename: `MyResources` Ordered preferred locales: `ja`, `en_GB`, `en_US`, `en_CA`, `fr` Fallback locale: `en`	`MyResources_en`, `MyResources_fr`, `MyResources_en_US`	Resource bundle: `MyResources_en` Locale: `en`
Basename: MyResources Ordered preferred locales: `fr`, `ja` Fallback locale: `en`	`MyResources_fr_CA`, `MyResources_ja`, `MyResources_en`	Resource bundle: `MyResources_ja` Locale: `ja`

Using the LocaleSupport Class

The logic just discussed for doing resource bundle lookups is exposed as the general convenience method `getLocalizedMessage()` in the `javax.servlet.jsp.jstl.fmt.LocaleSupport` class. Using this class is helpful if you have a tag handler implementation that needs to do message lookups. You may take advantage of this method so that the tag handler can produce localized messages easily. If you're producing exception messages or application-specific errors that will be used on error pages, using the `getLocalizedMessage()` with a provided message key will make it simple to find the resource. You can specify a basename, or you can use the default resource bundle in the localization context for doing the lookups. You locate the default resource bundle from the localization context by retrieving it from the javax.servlet.jsp.jstl.fmt.localizationContext configuration setting. It's also possible to take advantage of using parametric replacement in the messages. You accomplish this by using the args parameter, as shown in the following available method signatures:

```
public static String getLocalizedMessage(PageContext pc, String key)
public static String getLocalizedMessage(PageContext pc, String key,
                                         String basename)
public static String getLocalizedMessage(PageContext pc, String key,
                                         Object[] args)
public static String getLocalizedMessage(PageContext pc, String key,
                                         Object[] args, String basename)
```

Encoding the Client Response

The last item to consider when doing I18N actions is how the response is returned to the client. The response needs to be encoded with the correct locale setting so that the browser correctly renders it. The responsibility of setting the response's locale lies with the I18N action. The only exception to this is if the localization context didn't have a locale set.

The way the action sets the locale is by calling the ServletResponse.setLocale() and SerlvetResponse.setContentType() methods with the locale that's currently set in the localization context. These must be called before the ServletResponse.getWriter() is called because the value of the locale and charset affects the construction of the JspWriter.

A number of actions can call the setLocale() method. When using the <fmt:setLocale> action, the setLocale() method is always called. Some of the other actions that may call it are as follows:

- <fmt:bundle>
- <fmt:setBundle>
- A <fmt:message> that establishes an I18N localization context
- Any formatting action that establishes a formatting locale on its own

Once sessions are enabled, and after an action has called ServletResponse.setLocale(), the action must determine the character encoding associated with the response locale (by calling ServletResponse.getCharacterEncoding()) and store it in the session-scoped JSTL variable javax.servlet.jsp.jstl.fmt.request.charset. This attribute sets the response encoding to be the same as the request encoding. It's used by the <fmt:requestEncoding> action, which is discussed shortly.

Locale and Resource Bundle Actions

The following six actions relate to this functional area:

- `<fmt:setLocale>`
- `<fmt:bundle>`
- `<fmt:setBundle>`
- `<fmt:message>`
- `<fmt:param>`
- `<fmt:requestEncoding>`

<fmt:setLocale> Action

The `<fmt:setLocale>` action stores the locale specified by the `value` attribute in the `javax.servlet.jsp.jstl.fmt.locale` configuration variable. This action has three attributes defined: the `value` that's either a `String` or a `java.util.Locale`, a `variant` that's vendor- or browser-specific (for example, `WIN` for Windows or `MAC` for Macintosh), and a `scope` that specifics the scope of the locale configuration variable.

The scope can be any of the standard JSP scopes: page, request, session, or application. If `value` is of type `java.util.Locale`, the `variant` attribute is ignored. If this action is used, it has the effect of disabling browser-based locale capabilities. Therefore, if you're going to use this action, make sure you do so at the beginning of the JSP prior to using other I18N actions. While the `value` attribute is required, if it's `null` or empty, the runtime default locale is used.

<fmt:bundle> Action

The `<fmt:bundle>` action creates the localization content and loads a resource bundle into that context. You use this action when you want a bundle to be specific to the body content of this action.

The `basename` attribute specifies the fully qualified resource name to use for the resource bundle. This looks a lot like a class name reference using the `.` notation you've already used. However, keep in mind that there's no file type suffix. If the `basename` attribute is `null` or empty, or a resource bundle can't be found, the `null` resource bundle is stored in the I18N localization context.

The resource bundle algorithm we discussed to determine which bundle is actually loaded then uses this name to do the resource bundle lookup. The scope of the I18N localization context is limited to the action's body content. The `prefix` attribute is provided as a convenience for very long message key names. If the prefix is specified, it's used by any nested <fmt:message> actions. The prefix is prepended to the key attribute of the nested action. For example, the following:

```
<fmt:bundle basename="Resources">
  <fmt:message key="com.apress.proj2ee.sample.title"/>
</fmt:bundle>
```

and the following:

```
<fmt:bundle basename="Resources" prefix="com.apress.proj2ee.sample.">
  <fmt:message key="title"/>
</fmt:bundle>
```

are equivalent references to the key attribute used in the <fmt:message> action.

<fmt:setBundle> Action

<fmt:setBundle> may appear similar to <fmt:bundle>, but there are significant differences. <fmt:setBundle> provides a way to create an I18N localization context and then provides a way to store it in a defined scoped variable. If the var attribute isn't defined, then the javax.servlet.jsp.jstl.fmt.localizationContext configuration variable stores the context. When this configuration variable is used, it becomes the new default localization context in the defined scope attribute. If the var attribute is used, then the class type is javax.servlet.jsp.jstl.fmt.LocalizationContext.

Like in the <fmt:bundle> action, if the basename is null or empty, or a resource bundle can't be found, the null resource bundle is stored in the localization context.

A quick sample of using the <fmt:setBundle> actions looks like this:

```
<fmt:setBundle basename="com.apress.proj2ee.sample.Resources"
               var="enBundle"
               scope="page"/>
```

This sample is defining a page-scoped variable called enBundle (for English bundle) that can be found using the basename defined. As you'll see in a moment, you can then use this variable in other actions.

<fmt:message> Action

If you're a true minimalist, the only I18N action you really need to know is the <fmt:message> action that we briefly talked about at the beginning of this chapter. Defaults can take care of everything else related to resource bundles and locales.

> **NOTE** *The <fmt:message> action is what provides the actual mechanism for looking up a message from the localized string messages provided in a resource bundle.*

String messages appear on your JSP pages by using the current `JspWriter`. You can use `<fmt:message>` without any body content, or it can contain the `<fmt:param>` action that allows for parametric replacements. The following samples show how you'd use different resources bundles:

```
<html>
<body>
  <fmt:message key="welcome" >
        <fmt:param value="${userNameString}"/>
  </fmt:message>


  <%-- This action would use the configuration setting --%>
  <fmt:message key="welcome" />

  <%-- Use the bundle with the specified base name --%>
  <fmt:bundle basename="com.apress.proj2ee.examples.Resource">

  <%-- Localization context established by parent <fmt:bundle> tag --%>
  <fmt:message key="welcome" />

  <%-- Localization context established by attribute bundle --%>
  <fmt:message key="welcome" bundle="com.apress.proj2ee.examples.NewResource " />

  </fmt:bundle>

</body>
</html>
```

`<fmt:message>` must have a key attribute that defines the message key to use in the resource bundle as well as a number of optional attributes. These include a `bundle` attribute that contains a specific localization context to use for the message key lookup, a `var` that's the name of an exported scoped variable that holds the localized message, and a `scope` attribute that defines the scope of the `var` if one was defined. There's no default on the scope of the `var`, so if you specify the `var` attribute, you must also define the `scope` for it. When using the `var` attribute, the result is stored in the named `var` attribute and isn't written to the current `JspWriter` object.

In the case when a key specified can't be found, or it's `null` or empty, the message is processed as if undefined. In this case, a message is returned that contains ??????. If the localization context that this action is using doesn't have any resource bundles associated with it, an error message of the form ???<key>??? is produced. The <key> portion would be replaced with the name of the given key.

Keep in mind that when the key specifies the message by using the key attribute, if the action is nested inside a `<fmt:bundle>` action and the parent `<fmt:bundle>` action contains a `prefix` attribute, then the specified `prefix` is prepended to the message key.

<fmt:param> Action

It's possible to accomplish parametric replacement in messages by using the <fmt:param> subtag. You can use one <fmt:param> subtag for each parameter value required. The parametric replacement happens in the order of the <fmt:param> subtags.

Using parameters within messages takes advantage of the functionality already provided in the Java Development Kit (JDK) by using the `java.text.MessageFormat`. If there's more than one <fmt:param> subtag, the message is supplied to the method `MessageFormat.applyPattern()`, the values of the <fmt:param> tags are collected in an array of objects, and this is supplied to the method `MessageFormat.format()`.

The locale of the `MessageFormat` is set to the appropriate localization context locale before `MessageFormat.applyPattern()` is called. If the message is compound (has more than one parameter) and no <fmt:param> subtags are specified, then `MessageFormat` isn't used.

When using <fmt:param>, you're able to specify the parameter value by using the `value` attribute or by including the value in the body content of the tag. <fmt:param> tags must always be nested inside a <fmt:message> action.

<fmt:requestEncoding> Action

The <fmt:requestEncoding> action sets the request encoding to be the same as the encoding used for the response. You may use this action to set the request's character encoding to be able to correctly decode request parameter values whose encoding is different from ISO-8859-1, which is the default value.

This action is primarily needed because most browsers fail to follow the HTTP specification that includes a `Content-Type:` header in their requests. For example, if you have parameters coming in using UTF-8 encoding, you'd use the following code on the JSP page before trying to access any of the parameters:

```
<fmt:requestEncoding value="UTF-8"/>
```

Otherwise, the parameters wouldn't be decoded correctly and would be displayed as garbage characters.

If the character encoding of the request parameters isn't known in advance, the `value` attribute must not be specified. This will give the action a chance to resolve the charset in the following manner. In this case, the <fmt:requestEncoding> action first checks if there's a charset defined in the request `Content-Type:` header. If not, it uses the character encoding from the `javax.servlet.jsp.jstl.fmt.request.charset`-scoped variable. This variable appears in session scope. If this scoped variable isn't found, the default character encoding (ISO-8859-1) is used.

Formatting Actions

Formatting actions are the second major group of actions that falls under the I18N umbrella. These actions are for data that contains numbers, dates, and times to be formatted and parsed correctly according to the current locale settings. The formatting actions handle such pieces of data as percentages, currency, or numbers. The available formatting actions are as follows:

- `<fmt:timeZone>`
- `<fmt:setTimeZone>`
- `<fmt:formatNumber>`
- `<fmt:parseNumber>`
- `<fmt:formatDate>`
- `<fmt:parseDate>`

It's possible to define specific patterns to use so that you can customize how the formatting appears for certain actions. You'll look at a few samples of this when we talk about the `<fmt:formatNumber>` action. The same pattern options, as well as style options, are available in terms of doing date and time formatting. You can tailor time information on a page to the preferred time zone of a client by using `<fmt:timeZone>`. This is useful if the server hosting the page and its clients reside in different time zones.

While the formatting actions can be defined as a group of actions, a subset of these actions actually works in concert with the I18N resource bundle and locale actions by using the locale settings found in the localization context. This subset is as follows:

- `<fmt:formatNumber>`
- `<fmt:parseNumber>`
- `<fmt:formatDate>`
- `<fmt:parseDate>`

These actions follow similar rules to the resource bundle and locale actions in terms of determining which localization context to use. If a formatting action is nested inside a `<fmt:bundle>` action, the locale of the localization context using in the enclosing `<fmt:bundle>` is used. If there's no locale defined in that localization context, then the default localization context as specified in the `javax.servlet.jsp.jstl.fmt.localizationContext` configuration setting is used if it exists and if the value is of type `LocalizationContext`.

Remember, it's possible for the value of that configuration setting to be either a type or a `String`. If the value is a `String`, then the formatting action will establish its own localization context and use its locale as the formatting locale. The resource bundle of this newly established localization context is determined in the same manner already mentioned in the "How Resource Bundles Are Decided" section of this chapter. If you still don't have a locale defined in the localization context, then a formatting locale lookup establishes the preferred locale to use. Refer to the "Formatting Locales" section in this chapter to see again how you accomplish that.

Determining the Time Zone

The date formatting actions also take advantage of the time zone setting. The appropriate time zone setting to use is determined in the following order:

- Use the time zone from the action's `timeZone` attribute.
- If the `timeZone` attribute isn't specified and the action is nested inside a `<fmt:timeZone>` action, use the time zone from the enclosing `<fmt:timeZone>` action.
- Use the time zone given by the `javax.servlet.jsp.jstl.fmt.timeZone` configuration setting.
- Use the JSP container's time zone.

The following sections cover the available formatting actions and show what they provide.

<fmt:timeZone> Action

The `<fmt:timeZone>` action specifies the time zone in which time information is to be formatted or parsed for any nested actions it contains. It takes a `value` attribute that can be either a `String` or a `java.util.TimeZone`. If `value` is a `String`, then it's interpreted as one of the time zone IDs that are supported by the Java platform or a custom time zone ID. You do this by using the `java.util.TimeZone.getTimeZone()` method call. If no `value` is specified, then the default is the Greenwich mean time (GMT) time zone.

If you need more information on the types of supported time zone formats, refer to the Javadocs for the `java.util.TimeZone` class.

<fmt:setTimeZone> Action

The `<fmt:setTimeZone>` action stores a specified time zone into a variable that's scope defined or into the time zone configuration variable. The `value` attribute follows the same rules as those applied in the `<fmt:timeZone>` action.

The `var` attribute is a `String` that's used to export a variable that stores an instance of a time zone of type `java.util.TimeZone`. If no `var` is specified, then the time zone configuration variable `javax.servlet.jsp.jstl.fmt.timeZone` is used. The scope of this `var`, or time zone configuration variable, is determined by the setting of the `scope` attribute, which can be any of the standard JSP scopes.

<fmt:formatNumber> Action

You use the `<fmt:formatNumber>` action so that all numbers, currency, and percentages are represented correctly according to the current locale. You can use the `<fmt:formatNumber>` action without a body content by specifying the number in the `value` attribute. Alternatively, you can specify the value within the body content as the numeric value to be formatted. A whole host of attributes are associated with this action, as defined in Table 4-15.

Table 4-15. `<fmt:formatNumber>` *Attributes*

ATTRIBUTE	PURPOSE
`value`	Numeric value if not defining value in body content.
`type`	`number|currency|percent` (defaults to number).
`pattern`	A custom formatting pattern. Empty or null patterns are ignored.
`currencyCode`	ISO-4217 currency code, used only when `type` is equal to currency.
`currencySymbol`	Currency symbol used only if `type` is equal to currency.
`groupingUsed`	`true|false` (defaults to `true`) to indicate whether output should contain grouping separators.
`maxIntegerDigits`	Maximum number of digits to show in the integer portion of formatted output.
`minIntegerDigits`	Minimum number digits to show in the integer portion of formatted output.
`maxFractionDigits`	Maximum number of digits to show in a fractional portion of formatted output.
`minFractionDigits`	Minimal number of digits to show in a fractional portion of formatted output.
`var`	Exported scoped variable name that holds the formatted result as a `String`.
`scope`	`page|request|session|application` (defaults to page scope). If `scope` is specified, `var` must also be specified.

When using this action, if it fails to determine a formatting locale, it uses `Number.toString()` as the output format. Also, in the case of an exception occurring during the parsing of the value, the exception is caught and rethrown as a `JspException`. The message of the exception will contain the `String` value. The caught exception will provide the root cause of the exception.

When using the `pattern` attribute, the pattern symbols that can be used are those that are supported by the class `java.text.DecimalFormat`. For a complete list of these symbols, refer to the Javadocs for that class.

If the numeric `value` is given as a `String` literal, it's first parsed into a `java.lang.Number`. If the `String` doesn't contain any decimal point, it's parsed using `java.lang.Long.valueOf()`. If there's a decimal point, `java.lang.Double.valueOf()` is used. The formatted result is output to the current `JspWriter` object. However, if the `var` attribute was specified, then the output is stored in the named scoped variable.

A number of attributes are specific to formatting options; the `groupingUsed` attribute specifies whether the formatted output will contain any grouping separators. The same is true for how many digits or portions of a fractional should be displayed by using the various `min/max` attributes described Table 4-15. When dealing with currency, the currency symbol of the formatting locale is used by default. However, you can override this default by using the `currencySymbol` or `currencyCode` attributes.

<fmt:parseNumber> Action

The `<fmt:parseNumber>` action takes a string representation of numbers, currencies, or percentages that have been formatted in a locale-specific or custom manner and parses the string correctly. Like the `<fmt:formatNumber>` action, `<fmt:parseNumber>` can have its value specified in the `value` attribute or as the body content. Also like the `<fmt:formatNumber>` action, quite a few attributes can be specified. Table 4-16 defines the available attributes.

Table 4-16. `<fmt:parseNumber>` *Attributes*

ATTRIBUTE	DESCRIPTION
`value`	String to be parsed.
`type`	Specifies the type to use to parse the value attribute. Can be `number|currency|percent`. It defaults to number.
`pattern`	Custom formatting pattern used when parsing the string held in `value`.
`parseLocale`	A `String` or `java.util.Locale` that's to be used as the default formatting when parsing the string contained in value or to which the `pattern` attribute (if specified) is applied.
`integerOnly`	Specifies whether just the integer portion of a value should be parsed.
`var`	An exported scoped variable that contains a parsed `java.util.Number`.
`scope`	Scope of `var`.

You can specify the numeric value to be parsed by using the `value` attribute. If `value` isn't specified, it's read from the action's body content. You can specify the parse pattern to use with the `pattern` attribute. If the `pattern` attribute isn't specified, then the appropriate pattern is looked up in the current locale.

If a pattern string is specified using the `pattern` attribute, the syntax specified must be consistent with that defined by `java.text.DecimalFormat`. If looked up in a locale-dependent fashion, the parse pattern is determined via a combination of the `type` and `parseLocale` attributes. If the attribute `pattern` is `null` or empty, it's ignored. Depending on the value of the `type` attribute, the given numeric value is parsed as a number, a currency, or a percentage.

The way that the parse pattern for numbers, currencies, or percentages is determined is by calling the appropriate method: `getNumberInstance()`, `getCurrencyInstance()`, or `getPercentInstance()` in the `java.text.NumberFormat` class using the locale specified in the `parseLocale` attribute. If `parseLocale` is `null` or empty, it's treated as if it was missing. If `parseLocale` is missing, the current formatting locale is used as the parse locale.

When specifying a pattern, the formatting symbols in the pattern (such as decimal separator and grouping separator) are given by the parse locale. The `integerOnly` attribute specifies whether just the integer portion of the given value should be parsed.

As with the `<fmt:formatNumber>` action, if the `var` attribute is given, the parse result (of type `java.lang.Number`) is stored in the named scoped variable. Otherwise, it's output to the current `JspWriter` object using `java.lang.Number.toString()`. If the numeric string, whether defined in the `value` attribute or the body content, is `null` or empty, the scoped variable defined by attributes `var` and `scope` is removed. The reason for doing this is that it allows "empty" input to be distinguished from "invalid" input, which causes an exception.

<fmt:formatDate> Action

`<fmt:formatDate>` formats dates and times in such a way that they're locale-sensitive or formatted according to a custom pattern. This action handles both date and time styles so that it's possible to format just a date, just a time, or both date and time from a given value. The attributes available in this action reflect this (see Table 4-17).

Table 4-17. `<fmt:formatDate>` *Attributes*

ATTRIBUTE	DESCRIPTION
`value`	A date or time to be formatted.
`type`	Specifies whether the date, time, or both should be formatted. Defined using `time|date|both`. Defaults to `date`.
`dateStyle`	Predefined formatting style for dates. Used if `type` is missing, or set to `date` or `both`. Otherwise, it's ignored. Can be `default|short|medium|long|full`. Defaults to `default`.
`timeStyle`	Predefined formatting style for times. Used if `type` set to time or both. Otherwise, it's ignored. Can be `default|short|medium|long|full`. Defaults to `default`.
`pattern`	Custom formatting for dates and times.
`timeZone`	Either a `String` or a `java.util.TimeZone` to determine which time zone to use when representing time.
`var`	Exported scoped variable containing a `String` of the formatted result.
`scope`	Scope of `var`.

You can specify the date/time value to be parsed by using the `value` attribute. If `value` isn't specified, it's read from the action's body content. Depending on the value of the `type` attribute, only the time, the date, or both the time and date components of the date specified are formatted. The format used will depend on what formatting style was specified in the `dateStyle` attribute and/or `timeStyle` attribute.

It's also possible to apply a customized formatting style to the times and dates by specifying the `pattern` attribute. If a pattern is specified, the `type`, `dateStyle`, and `timeStyle` attributes are all ignored. The specified formatting pattern must use the pattern syntax specified by `java.text.SimpleDateFormat`.

If the string representation of a date or time needs to be formatted, the string must first be parsed into a java.util.Date using the <fmt:parseDate> action. You can then supply this parsed result to the <fmt:formatDate> action using a variable. For example:

```
<fmt:parseDate value="9/7/02" var="parsed" />
<fmt:formatDate value="${parsed}" />
```

As with the other actions that have a var attribute, the result is output to the current JspWriter object. However, if the var attribute is specified, it's stored in the named scoped variable and will be available for the scope specified in the scope attribute.

<fmt:parseDate> Action

As with <fmt:parseNumber>, <fmt:parseDate> is the string representation of dates and times that have been formatted in a locale-specific or custom manner are then parsed correctly. You may specify the date string to be parsed either by using the value attribute or by including the string in the tag's body content. The string specified must conform to the parsing format that's going to be used. Otherwise, the parse will fail.

The type attribute indicates whether the string specified is supposed to contain only a time, only a date, or both. You specify the predefined formatting styles by using the dateStyle and timeStyle attributes. These styles will use the locale specified by the parseLocale attribute. If the parseLocale attribute is missing, the formatting locale, covered previously, is used as the parse locale.

If you want to use a different format for the date string, it's possible to do so by using a pattern. You must specify the pattern that's to be used to parse the string in the pattern attribute. If you define the pattern attribute, it must use the pattern syntax specified by java.text.SimpleDateFormat. You can find the complete description of all of the available syntaxes in the Javadocs for that class. If the pattern attribute is defined, the type, dateStyle, and timeStyle attributes are all ignored.

When dealing with time, if the given time information doesn't specify a time zone, it's interpreted in the time zone determined by the algorithm we talked about in the "Determining the Time Zone" section of this chapter.

Like all of the other actions that allow for a var, a value is stored in it. The var stores the result of the parse as a java.util.Date. If no var attribute is specified, the output is sent to the current JspWriter using java.util.Date.toString().

Using the SQL Actions

The JSTL includes a number of actions that provide a mechanism for interacting with databases. The previous sentence should, at a minimum, send up a red flag in your architectural visions. One might ask, Do I really want to be able to perform SQL actions such as queries, updates, and transactions from my JSP page? Isn't that business logic that belongs in the model? The answer is "yes." Yes, yes, yes.

To follow a MVC architecture, which is the predominate design pattern used in building Web applications today, you definitely want to keep your model information in your business logic. This means you don't want it in your JSP pages. Why, then, are these actions even provided in the JSTL? Good question; it's one that has been discussed with various members of the JSR-52 expert group. The reason is the *C* for *community* in JCP. The community has asked for it, so the community has gotten it.

Many think that for prototyping, for small-scale applications, or for very simple applications, or if you just don't have the engineering staff to implement a full MVC model, then the SQL actions may prove useful. While we can (barely) see the point being made to use the SQL actions for prototyping or small-scale applications, we can't ever validate the argument that you just won't have the time to implement an MVC model correctly. If that's the only reason you're choosing to use the SQL actions, then we suggest you investigate such frameworks as Struts, which is part of the Jakarta projects; you can find it at `http://jakarta.apache.org/struts/index.html`. Struts is an MVC framework that you can learn quickly and will provide a much cleaner architecture than having Model information located throughout your JSP pages.

With that said, we don't consider it an architectural flaw to have the SQL actions included in the JSTL. However, we do consider it an architectural flaw to use them in your application development. It's up to the page author and application architect to make sure that the design patterns are being adhered to correctly, if not for the maintenance issue of the application, then for the practice of good engineering. However, since these actions are included in the JSTL, we must make sure you understand them and their features so you can make an informed decision for yourself.

The JSTL SQL actions provide functionality that allows for the following:

- Making database queries
- Accessing query results
- Performing database modifications
- Database transactions

What all of the SQL actions have in common is that they work against a specific data source. You'll now examine how you set up and configure the data source. You'll then go through the other configuration settings as well as the available interfaces. Then you'll walk through each of the actions provided in the SQL tag library.

Working with the Data Source

SQL actions operate on a data source. A *data source* is an implementation of the `javax.sql.DataSource` interface and allows for the retrieval of a connection, or connections, to a specific database or data source. Most Java Database Connectivity (JDBC) functionality is accomplished by implementation various interfaces; the database driver does this. Each driver vendor implements the core features of the JDBC functionality. This includes objects in the `java.sql` package such as `Connection`, `Statement`, and `ResultSet`. Other interfaces in the `javax.sql` package might also be implemented, but it's up to the driver vendor to do so.

The Connection object acts as a factory for Statement objects. Statement objects allow you to submit a SQL command to the database. Using the DataSource object, within the context of a java.sql.Connection object, SQL statements execute against the data source using the connection, and the appropriate result set or return value is returned. While most of this is handled behind the scenes for you in the SQL action implementation, it's good to see a bit of what's actually happening. If you want more details on how the innards of JDBC implementations work, many resources are available.

Configuring a Data Source

You can configure a data source in two ways: through an attribute and through a configuration setting. Using the dataSource attribute of the SQL actions, it's possible to explicitly configure the data source for the action. For example, you can set a data source using the setDataSource action (which we'll talk about in a minute) like so:

```
<sql:setDataSource var="myDataSource"
                   driver="org.gjt.mm.mysql.driver"
                   url="jdbc:mysql://localhost/db" />
```

and then use that data source in a query by specifying the variable to the datasource attribute like so:

```
<sql:query datasource="${myDataSource}" ... />
```

If all SQL actions are going to use the same data source, it's more convenient to set the data source by using the configuration setting javax.servlet.jsp.jstl.sql.dataSource. You can use the constant Config.SQL_DATA_SOURCE to refer to this configuration setting. You can specify the dataSource as either a String or a javax.sql.DataSource. When using the configuration setting, you can specify a data source as a string in the following two ways:

JNDI relative path: The first way is through a Java Naming and Directory Interface (JNDI) relative path, assuming a container supporting JNDI. For example, you can specify it with the absolute JNDI resource path:

```
java:comp/env/jdbc/myDatabase
```

The JNDI relative path to the data source resource would simply be jdbc/myDatabase, given that java:comp/env is the standard JNDI root for a J2EE application. It's also important to note that doing a lookup without caching the InitialContext or the DataSource is expensive because it can cause excessive network calls to be made.

JDBC parameters: The second way is by specifying the parameters needed by the JDBC DriverManager class, using the following syntax:

```
url[,[driver][,[user][,password]]]
```

For example: you'd use jdbc:mysql://localhost/,org.gjt.mm.mysql.Driver.

In the latter case, the database doesn't require a username or password. This is probably not the way you'd want a production database, but to keep the sample simple, it's fine. If the `,` or `\` character occurs in any of the JDBC parameters, it can be escaped by a preceding `\`.

The JDBC `java.sql.DriverManager` class provides a way to manage all drivers, but it isn't very efficient. It's best to use the `DriverManager` during prototyping—which, come to think of it, is really the only time you should be using the SQL actions anyway. Remember that you're better off using a `DataSource` object that provides connection management or connection pooling features because connection management is one of the most expensive areas of performance when dealing with the database.

Using a Data Source

Now that you've seen how to configure a data source, you'll look at how you actually use it with the various SQL actions. The actions that use the data source to access a database are `<sql:query>`, `<sql:update>`, and `<sql:transaction>`.

You obtain a reference to the data source according to the following algorithm. The application vendor supporting the JSTL will implement this algorithm. However, it's important to understand how it works so that you know what you can expect when dealing with data sources settings. The steps are as follows:

1. First, if the `datasource` attribute is specified in the action itself, then use that.

2. Otherwise, get the configuration setting associated with `javax.servlet.jsp.jstl.sql.dataSource` using the `find()` method in the `Config` class. If the value found isn't `null`, then use it. Keep in mind that you can define the value of the configuration setting as either a `DataSource` object or a `String`.

3. If it's a `DataSource` object, then this is the data source used by the action.

4. Otherwise, there's still some work to be done. For a `String` value, it's assumed that it's a JNDI relative path. The data source is retrieved from the container's JNDI naming context by the concatenation of the specified relative path to the J2EE defined root. The J2EE defined root is `java:comp/env/`.

5. If the JNDI lookup fails, then it's assumed that the string specifies JDBC parameters. This is the syntax you looked at in the previous section that defines the URL, driver, username, and password.

6. If a driver is specified, then make sure the driver is loaded.

7. The data source is then accessed by the named URL through the `DriverManager` class. Empty strings are used if no user or password is specified.

8. If you get to this point and still don't have a data source, then you're out of luck, and an exception is thrown.

9. If a data source isn't specified in either the attribute or the configuration variable, then an exception is thrown. You can't say you didn't try.

You should gain a performance advantage when dealing with data sources from the application vendor's implementations. An implementation doesn't need to create new objects each time a SQL action is called. It may reuse objects that it previously created for identical arguments.

Using the maxRows Configuration Setting

Working with result sets can be time consuming. If you have a large result set being returned from a query, it's possible that your users can be sitting at their browsers twiddling their thumbs. Therefore, it's common to limit the number of rows returned on a query. This prevents using unnecessary resources on the server, but more important, it allows you to tune your application more efficiently so that your users don't surf to another site.

You specify the maximum number of rows to be included in a query result by the variable named `javax.servlet.jsp.jstl.sql.maxRows`. You can reference this variable by using the constant `Config.SQL_MAX_ROWS`. The value of this variable is an `Integer` that must be greater than `-1`. You can set `maxRows` from the `Config` class or from the deployment descriptor.

If the maximum number of rows isn't specified or is `-1`, it means there's no limit on the result set. If you're not using the maximum rows, you should know for sure that you're not going to be returning thousands of records. Having runaway queries definitely leads to some unhappy users.

Using Interfaces and Classes

The JSTL provides two interfaces (`Result` and `SQLExecutionTag`) and one class (`ResultSupport`) for the SQL actions. You use these in the implementation of various actions found in the SQL tag library. If you're writing your own custom actions, you might be interested in them. The following sections show what each has to offer.

Result Interface

You can find the `Result` interface in the `javax.servlet.jsp.jstl.sql` package. This interface represents the result of a `<sql:query>` action. It provides access to the following information in the query results:

- The result rows
- The column names
- The number of rows in the result

- An indication whether the returned rows represent the complete result or just a subset that's limited by a maximum row setting

Table 4-18 describes the available methods and the return value for each one.

Table 4-18. `Result` *Interface*

METHOD	DESCRIPTION	RETURN VALUE
`getRows()`	Returns the result of the query as an array of `SortedMap` objects. Each item of the array represents a specific row in the query result.	`java.util.SortedMap[]`
`getRowsByIndex()`	Returns the result of the query as an array of arrays. The first array dimension represents a specific row in the query result. The array elements for each row are object instances of the Java type corresponding to the mapping between column types and Java types defined by the JDBC specification when the `ResultSet.getObject()` method is used.	`Object[][]`
`getColumnNames()`	The names of the columns in the result. The order of the names in the array matches the order in which columns are returned in method `getRowsByIndex()`.	`String[]`
`getRowCount()`	The number of rows in the result.	`int`
`isLimitedByMaxRows()`	True if the query was limited by a maximum row setting.	`boolean`

SQLExecutionTag Interface

This interface allows the tag handlers implementing it to receive values for parameter markers (?) in their SQL statements. You'll find this interface in the `javax.servlet.jsp.jstl.sql` package. The `SQLExecutionTag` interface is exposed so that new custom parameter actions you may write can retrieve their parameters from any source and process them before substituting them for a parameter marker in the SQL statement of the enclosing `SQLExecutionTag` action. This interface is implemented by both `<sql:query>` and `<sql:update>`.

The `addSQLParameter()` method of this interface is called by nested parameter actions (such as `<sql:param>`) to substitute `PreparedStatement` parameter values for ? parameter markers in the SQL statement of the enclosing `SQLExecutionTag` action. When implementing this interface, you must keep track of the index of the parameter values being added. Table 4-19 describes the `SQLExecutionTag` interface method.

Table 4-19. SQLExecutionTag *Interface Method*

METHOD	DESCRIPTION	RETURN VALUE
addSQLParameter(Object value)	Adds a PreparedStatement parameter value	void

ResultSupport Class

You'll find the ResultSupport class in the javax.servlet.jsp.jstl.sql package. This support class allows for the creation of javax.servlet.jsp.jstl.sql.Result objects from source java.sql.ResultSet objects. Working with a Result objects is much easier for a page author because it allows for access and manipulation of data from a SQL query. The following are the two possible ways to call the toResult() method:

```
public static Result toResult(java.sql.ResultSet rs)
public static Result toResult(java.sql.ResultSet rs, int maxRows)
```

The first takes a ResultSet and converts it to a Result; the second converts maxRows of a ResultSet to a Result.

Using the SQL Actions

This tag library provides the following six actions:

- <sql:setDataSource> for exporting a variable that defines a data source
- <sql:query> for querying to database
- <sql:update> for updating the database
- <sql:transaction> for establishing a transaction context for doing queries and updates
- <sql:param> for setting parameter markers (?) used in SQL statements
- <sql:dataParam> for setting parameter markers (?) of type java.util.Date in SQL statements

You'll now look at each action in more detail.

<sql:setDataSource> Action

<sql:setDataSource> exports a data source as a scoped variable or as the javax.servlet.jsp.jstl.sql.dataSource data source configuration variable. Using the var and scope attributes, the data source specified is exported. If no var is specified, the data source is exported in the javax.servlet.jsp.jstl.sql.dataSource configuration variable.

You can specify the data source by using the dataSource attribute. You can specify this as a DataSource object, as a JNDI relative path, or as using a JDBC parameter string. If you don't want to use the dataSource attribute, it's also possible to specify the data source by using the four JDBC parameters as attributes. All four of the parameters are just String types. These attributes are driver, url, user, and password. Using the JDBC attributes is just an easier way to configure the data source than specifying the values in the string syntax for the dataSource attribute.

In the following example, you'll see how to specify a data source using the JDBC parameters. You're making this data source available as an exported variable called datasource. This can then be used by other actions if they want to use this particular data source, as shown by the <sql:query> action:

```
<sql:setDataSource var="datasource"
                   driver="org.gjt.mm.mysql.driver"
                   url="jdbc:mysql://localhost/db"
                   user="guest"
                   password="guest"/>
<sql:query dataSource="${datasource}" ... />
```

<sql:query> Action

No mystery here—the <sql:query> action queries a database, and there are a number of attributes used with this action. It's possible to specify a data source by using the datasource attribute. If present, it will override the default data source using the algorithm discussed in the "Configuring a Data Source" section. If the datasource is null after the algorithm, then a JspException is thrown. If a datasource is specified, then the <sql:query> action must be specified inside of a <sql:transaction> action. We'll talk about <sql:transaction> in a minute.

A single result set is returned from a query. If the query produces no results, an empty Result object (of size zero) is returned. This would be the case for a SQL statement that contained an INSERT, DELETE, UPDATE, or a SQL statement that returns nothing, such as a SQL DDL statement. Returning an object of size zero is consistent with the way return values are handled by the executeUpdate() method of the JDBC Statement class. This result set contains rows of data if there are results. The data is then stored in a scoped variable that's defined by the var and scope attributes. The default scope is page.

There must be a way to specify the SQL query to be used. You can do this by using the sql attribute or by including the SQL statement in the action's body content. The code in the next two examples does the same thing. The first example defines the SQL in an attribute, and the second example defines the SQL in the body content:

```
<sql:query sql="SELECT * FROM courses WHERE title = 'JSTL' ORDER BY instructor"
           var="titles" dataSource="${datasource}"
</sql:query>

<sql:query var="titles" dataSource="${datasource}" >
  SELECT * FROM courses WHERE title = 'JSTL' ORDER BY instructor
</sql:query>
```

A query can contain parameter markers. These markers are indicated by using ? in the query. Using parameter markers identifies JDBC PreparedStatement parameters. The way to supply parameters is by using a nested <sql:param> parameter action: One parameter action is required for each parameter in the SQL statement. The actual mechanism used for this parametric replacement is the implementation of the SQLExectionTag interface. If you wanted to have the title as a parameter to the query, you could do so as shown in this example:

```
<sql:query sql="SELECT * FROM courses WHERE title = ? ORDER BY instructor"
           var="titles" datasource="${datasource}"
  <sql:param value="${titleSelected}"/>
</sql:query>
```

We've already talked about the max rows configuration setting. You'll now see how it's used in the <sql:query> action along with the maxRows attribute. If the maxRows attribute is specified, then that value takes precedence over the value specified in the configuration setting. It's commonplace that the maxRows and startRow attribute are used together. The startRow specifies the index of the first row to be included in the Result object returned by the action. You then specify maxRows of 5 and a startRow of 7, as in this example:

```
<sql:query sql="SELECT * FROM courses WHERE title = 'JSTL' ORDER BY instructor"
           var="titles" datasource="${datasource}"
           maxRows="5"
           startRow="7" />
```

The returned Result object (which is actually the result set) will start with the row at index 7. The rows 0 through 6 that were contained in the result set by the original query will be skipped. All remaining rows of the original query will be included, up to the number specified by the maxRows value. Note that if maxRows isn't specified as an attribute or as a configuration setting configured, or it's equal to -1, then all rows are returned from the database. The Result object would contain the rows startRow + maxRows.

If you're using startRow, keep in mind that you probably want to make sure that the order of rows remains consistent. The best way to do this is to use an ORDER BY clause in your SQL statement. Otherwise, not all relational database management system (RDBMS) implementations are the same, and you might get different results on different databases. You can use startRow and maxRows to page through large query results by manipulating the values, so they can be quite useful.

The Connection object that's used for a <sql:query> is the one that either was obtained from the parent <sql:transaction> or was previously obtained when the data source was looked up. If <sql:query> isn't nested in a <sql:transaction>, then the Connection object is released when the <sql:query> tag has completed.

<sql:update> Action

The <sql:update> action executes SQL INSERT, UPDATE, and DELETE statements. It's also possible to perform a SQL statement that returns nothing, such as a Data Definition Language (DDL) statement. You can specify the SQL statement either by using the sql attribute or by providing the statement in the action's body content. Like <sql:query>, <sql:update> can have parameter markers within the SQL statement. The parameter values are then provided with the <sql:param> action. The connection to the database is handled the same way that it's handled for <sql:query>. If the datasource attribute is specified for the action, then <sql:update> can't be nested within a <sql:transaction>.

Using the var attribute you're familiar with by now, you can specify a scoped variable to store the result of the <sql:update> action. The scope attribute is used only when a var attribute is specified. The result is an Integer and will be the number of rows that were affected by the update. Zero is returned if no rows were affected and for any SQL statement that returns nothing (such as SQL DDL statements). This is the same behavior you'd expect if you used the executeUpdate() method of the JDBC class Statement.

You'll now see how you'd the <sql:update> action. In the following example, you specify a datasource as well as request scoped variable called updateResult. The value of updateResult will be how many rows were affected on the execution of this update. In this case, the value of updateResult will be 1:

```
<sql:update dataSource="$(datasource)" var="updateResult" scope="request">
  UPDATE course SET Title = 'Using the JSTL'WHERE instructor = 'Spielman'
</sql:update>
```

<sql:transaction> Action

The <sql:transaction> action groups nested <sql:query> and <sql:update> actions so that they're all performed as a single transaction. The isolation level of the transaction is defined by using the isolation attribute. The attribute values are those defined by java.sql.Connection. The transaction isolation levels prevent events from happening between concurrent transactions. We'll briefly describe the various events that can occur and then correlate what each isolation level allows.

The three types of events are as follows:

Dirty reads: A *dirty read* occurs when a transaction reads data written by a concurrent uncommitted transaction—for example, one transaction is writing some data to the database. The second is then reading that data, but the first rolls the transaction back. The second transaction has read data that doesn't exist.

Nonrepeatable reads: A *nonrepeatable read* occurs when a transaction rereads data it has previously read and finds that the data has been modified by another transaction that was committed since the initial read.

Phantom reads: A *phantom read* occurs when a transaction reexecutes a query with the same search criteria and a different result set is returned. This can happen because another transaction may have already done a commit that changed the result set.

Table 4-20 describes the four isolation levels and the corresponding behaviors. You need to evaluate what your application is doing to determine which is the correct isolation level to use.

Table 4-20. Isolation Levels

VALUE	DIRTY READ	NONREPEATABLE READ	PHANTOM READ
`read_committed`	Prevented	Prevented	Allowed
`read_uncommitted`	Allowed	Allowed	Allowed
`repeatable_read`	Allowed	Allowed	Allowed
`serializable`	Prevented	Prevented	Prevented

When using the `<sql:transaction>` action, if the database management system (DBMS) set as the data source doesn't support transactions, then an exception will be thrown. The DBMS support for transactions is determined by the tag handler for `<sql:transaction>` by making a `Connection.getTransactionIsolation()` method call against the data source in the `doStartTag()` of the action. For this particular action, it's important to understand how the tag handler implementation happens. The reason being is that when dealing with transactions, rollbacks might be necessary.

The `doEndTag()` method will call `Connection.commit()` on the transaction, and `doCatch()` will cause a `Connection.rollback()` to happen. If all goes well with the completed transaction, then the `doFinally()` method is called. This will restore the transaction level if it was changed from the DBMS default, restore the autocommit mode, and close the connection.

> **NOTE** *If you're using Java Transaction API (JTA) user transactions with a* `<sql:transaction>`, *beware. The behavior of the action is undefined within that context.*

You'll now walk through the following transaction sample:

```
<sql:transaction isolation="read_uncommitted"
                 dataSource="${dataSource}">
  <sql:update>
    UPDATE course SET title = 'Working with JSTL' WHERE instructor = 'Spielman'
  </sql:update>
  <sql:update>
    UPDATE course SET courseId = '007' WHERE instructor = 'Spielman'
  </sql:update>

</sql:transaction>
```

In this sample, you define all `<sql:update>` actions to be part of one transaction. The data source to use is defined by a variable that has already been set to a particular database. If one of the updates fails, then the transaction will be rolled back and neither update will appear in the database.

<sql:param> and <sql:dateParam> Actions

Both of these actions are subtags to the `<sql:query>` or `<sql:update>` actions. Actually, any custom action that you build that implements the `SQLExecutionTag` interface will be able to use `<sql:param>` and `<sql:dateParam>`. These actions set the values of parameter markers in a SQL statement. These are the ? that appear in the statements, as you saw in a previous example.

When using `<sql:param>`, you can specify the value either by using the `value` attribute, which is of type `Object`, or by using the action's body content. If the value is `null`, then it's set to the SQL value `NULL`. The parameters must be in the order as specified in the SQL statement. If you're using body content to specify the parameter, keep in mind that a `String` needs to map to a column value that's `CHAR`, `VARCHAR`, or `LONGVARCHAR`.

You use `<sql:dateParam>` for parameters that are of type `java.util.Date`. The value must be specified using the `value` attribute. There's also a `type` attribute to indicate whether this is a `timestamp`, `date`, or `time` value. The default value for the `type` attribute is `timestamp`. The action will convert the provided `java.util.Date` instance to the correct instance depending on the `type` attribute value. This would be a `java.sql.Date`, `java.sql.Time`, or `java.sql.Timestamp`.

When to Use JSTL Actions

You've seen throughout this chapter that a number of useful actions are available in the JSTL. It should certainly eliminate the need for many custom actions to be written (or rewritten), as many of the custom actions that you see in Web applications today have some flavor of what's being provided in the JSTL.

It's our opinion that it will be more beneficial in the long run to use the JSTL custom actions in Web applications vs. going with custom actions that might be provided and are vendor-specific. For one thing, it will make your application more portable to other containers. For another, all compliant containers will support the JSTL, so there should certainly be performance benefits that you'll see as containers roll out with their JSTL implementation.

The question remains, when should you write your own custom actions? The answer is, when you really need to do so. When possible, use the functionality that's provided in the JSTL. However, if you need to write your own custom actions for something specific to your Web application, you should first examine the available classes and interfaces that we spoke about as provided by the JSTL. If you extend classes or implement interfaces from the JSTL, your custom actions will at least have the same look and feel to your JSP authors who might be working with the actions. Doing so also makes it possible to have actions cooperate if they're based on the same classes and/or interfaces.

If you carefully look at the JSTL and see if you can extend the classes provided, and you really don't think it's possible, then it will be necessary for you to write your own custom actions.

Summary

The JSTL provides a standard mechanism for page authors to use custom actions. The JSTL provides encapsulation for the following functional areas:

- Core actions
- XML actions
- Internationalization actions
- Database-related actions

The JSTL uses an EL that's defined in both the JSTL specification as well as in the JSP 2.0 specification. Using the EL makes it much easier and cleaner to reference objects and perform expressions within the custom actions.

CHAPTER 5

Using Custom Actions in JSP 2.0

THE JAVASERVER PAGES (JSP) 1.1 specification introduced custom actions (or *custom tags* as they're frequently called). You can use custom actions for encapsulating the Java functionality you may frequently need on a JSP page; they allow you to use this functionality as markup. A custom action is really nothing more than a Java class that implements some specific interfaces. You can think of custom actions as view helper classes. You'll see as you progress through this chapter that in JSP 2.0, it's now possible to write custom actions completely in JSP syntax if you choose. You use custom actions so that your JSP pages can remain free of Java code. By creating a custom action and defining a descriptor file for it, you can take advantage of code reuse, debug functionality once, and provide a consistent mechanism for access across your JSP files.

Using custom actions allows the JSP author to take advantage of the following features:

- Customizing actions by using attributes passed from the calling page
- Accessing all the objects available to JSP pages
- Modifying the response generated by the calling page
- Communicating with other actions by creating cooperating actions
- Allowing nested actions

The JSP Standard Tag Library (JSTL) has provided a mechanism so common functionality has a standard implementation and standard attributes (you saw this in Chapter 4). Your first stop for functionality you may need should be the JSTL because you'll probably find the action you need there. However, it sometimes may be necessary to build your own custom actions that are specific to your application. This may include application-specific functionality that you're using repeatedly.

In this chapter, you'll learn how to write and use your own custom actions. This includes the following:

- Writing classic and simple tag handler classes. When you use a custom tag in your JSP page, the tag handler class executes the functionality of the tag.

- Writing and using JSP fragments and `.tag` files.
- Creating the tag library descriptor (TLD). The TLD defines the tag library and provides additional information about each tag, such as the name of the tag handler class, attributes, and other information. It also provides a validation mechanism for tag libraries.
- Referencing the TLD in the Web application deployment descriptor (`web.xml`).
- Using the tag library in your JSP source using the JSP `<taglib>` directive. A *tag library* is a collection of JSP tags.
- Writing validator classes to validate your custom action libraries.

So, if you've been suffering from a custom action phobia, you'll be over it by the time you get through this chapter.

Deciding When a Custom Action Is Needed

Frequently in Web application development, the same tasks happen repeatedly within a Web page. Typically, these tasks deal with presentation logic. When you come across this type of situation, a lightbulb should illuminate, and you should consider making the task a custom action. Of course, you should first check the JSTL before reinventing the wheel. Once you've created a custom action, you can then take advantage of the encapsulated functionality easily by just referencing the custom actions using Extensible Markup Language (XML).

It's possible to encapsulate functionality in JavaBeans, and many page authors do this. So when should you use a custom action instead? The answer is rather simple. If you need access to the JSP object environment in a reusable piece of code, then use a custom action.

This is another easy rule of thumb to follow:

- JavaBeans are usually named as nouns.
- Custom actions are usually named as verbs.

For example, you could have a `courseCatalog` JavaBean and a `displayCourseCatalog` custom action. The advantage of building a custom action is that you'll be able to reuse logic—and you'll need to debug the code only once. It'll also be easy to deploy custom actions in reusable libraries.

Depending on the type of custom action you're building, you may be dealing with a variety of components. First, we'll talk about action components for a classic custom action. Second, we'll discuss new facilities available in JSP 2.0 called *tag files* and *JSP fragments*. Finally, we'll cover simple tag extensions.

Using Classic Custom Actions

Custom actions have been in the JSP specification for quite some time. JSP 2.0 has two flavors of custom actions: classic and simple. It's important to understand how the classic custom actions work so you have a vocabulary available to talk about the other types of actions.

The *tag handler* is a Java class that implements the functionality of the custom action. A classic tag handler is a Java class that implements the `Tag`, `IterationTag`, or `BodyTag` interface, and it's the runtime representation of a custom action. You'll find these interfaces in the `javax.servlet.jsp.tagext` package. The `JspTag` interface introduced in JSP 2.0 serves as a base class for `Tag` and `SimpleTag`. This interface doesn't actually define anything and therefore mostly exists for organizational and type-safety purposes.

Although it may seem that classic custom actions are being replaced with the simple tag, this isn't necessarily the case. If you have existing custom actions, then you won't have to change a thing. You can simply migrate the custom actions and libraries to JSP 2.0, and they should work.

The Tag Interface

The `Tag` interface defines the basic methods needed in all tag handlers (except simple tags, which we'll talk about in the "SimpleTag Interface" section). These methods include setter methods, which initialize a tag handler with context data and attribute values, and the `doStartTag()` and `doEndTag()` methods. Listing 5-1 shows the `Tag` interface definition.

Listing 5-1. `Tag` *Interface*

```
package javax.servlet.jsp.tagext;
import javax.servlet.jsp.*;

public interface Tag extends JspTag {

    public final static int SKIP_BODY = 0;
    public final static int EVAL_BODY_INCLUDE = 1;
    public final static int SKIP_PAGE = 5;
    public final static int EVAL_PAGE = 6;

    void setPageContext(PageContext pc);
    void setParent(Tag t);
    Tag getParent();
    int doStartTag() throws JspException;
    int doEndTag() throws JspException;
    void release();

}
```

Other Interfaces

The IterationTag interface is an extension to Tag that provides the additional method doAfterBody(), which is invoked for the reevaluation of the tag's body.

The BodyTag interface is an extension of IterationTag with two new methods for when the tag handler wants to manipulate the tag body: setBodyContent() passes a buffer (the BodyContent object), and doInitBody() provides an opportunity to process the buffer before the first evaluation of the body in the buffer.

In addition to the Tag, InteractionTag, and BodyTag interfaces, an auxiliary interface is commonly implemented by classes that implement Tag, IterationTag, or BodyTag: the TryCatchFinally interface, which was introduced in JSP 1.2 to help deal with catching exceptions. The interface provides two methods.

The doCatch() method is invoked if a Throwable occurs while evaluating the body inside a tag or in any of the following methods:

- Tag.doStartTag()
- Tag.doEndTag()
- IterationTag.doAfterBody()
- BodyTag.doInitBody()

The other method, doFinally(), is invoked in all cases after doEndTag() for any class implementing Tag, IterationTag, or BodyTag.

The JSP page implementation class instantiates a tag handler object or, in the case of a classic handler, reuses an existing tag handler object for each action in the JSP page. The handler object is responsible for the interaction between the JSP page and other server-side objects, such as JavaBeans. Two support classes are convenient to use as base classes:

TagSupport: TagSupport is a utility class intended to be used as the base class for new tag handlers that implement Tag. The TagSupport class implements the Tag and IterationTag interfaces and adds additional convenience methods including getter methods for the properties in Tag. TagSupport has one static method, findAncestorWithClass(), that's included to help with the coordination among cooperating tags.It's common for a tag handler to extend TagSupport and just override a couple of the methods.

BodyTagSupport: BodyTagSupport is a utility class intended to be used as the base class for defining tag handlers implementing BodyTag. The BodyTagSupport class implements the BodyTag interface and adds additional convenience methods including getter methods for the bodyContent property and the getPreviousOut() method to get the previous out JspWriter. Like TagSupport, tag handlers that need to get at the body content will extend BodyTagSupport and redefine only a few methods.

The next sections walk through the tag life cycle first so you can see the interaction between the custom action and the JSP container. Then you'll put it all together with a sample custom action.

Understanding Custom Action Life Cycles

Custom actions have a defined life cycle that depends on the interface implemented by the custom action. When an action is encountered in a JSP page, the container performs a number of tasks. The following sections first show the `Tag` lifecycle and then show the other methods available to the `IterationTag` and `BodyTag` interfaces.

When a JSP page containing a custom action is translated into a servlet, the action is converted to various method calls on the tag handler object. The container then invokes those methods when the JSP page's servlet executes because the custom action actually becomes part of the servlet code. The life cycle is defined as part of the JSP specification.

Tag Life Cycle

Figure 5-1 shows the life cycle of a custom action implementing the `Tag` interface.

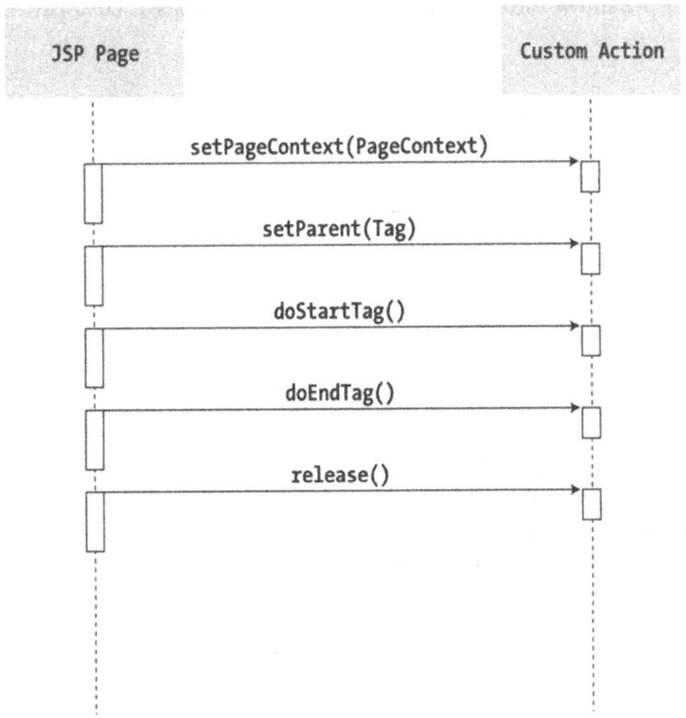

Figure 5-1. Tag lifecycle sequence diagram

When an action is encountered on a JSP page, the first step is to make the action aware of its current environment by calling the setPageContext() method of the tag handler. An instance of javax.servlet.jsp.PageContext is passed as a parameter to the method. The PageContext instance allows the tag handler to access any object that can be used from that JSP page such as variables and request, response, and session objects. This is the same instance as the implicit variable pageContext, which we talked about in Chapter 3.

The next step is to make sure that the action knows about its parent tag since it's possible to have cooperating tags that can be nested within each other. You do this by passing an instance of the closest enclosing tag handler to the setParent(Tag t) method of the tag handler with which you're dealing. If there's no enclosing tag handler, then a null is passed to setParent().

Now that all the context information is set so that the tag handler knows about the environment it's running in and also its parent, the next step is to call the doStartTag(). This method is called when the JSP page encounters the start of the tag. The method signature looks like this:

```
int doStartTag() throws JspException
```

Therefore, it's possible that the doStartTag() method can encounter and throw an exception. The integer that's returned determines what happens after the start tag has been processed. Listing 5-2 shows the code for the tag handler for a classic custom action.

Listing 5-2. Tag Handler for a Classic Custom Action

```
package com.apress.proj2ee.chapter05;

import javax.servlet.jsp.tagext.TagSupport;
import javax.servlet.jsp.*;

public final class Classic extends TagSupport {

  public int doStartTag() throws JspException{
    // Do nothing more, then write something to the JspWriter
    try {
      pageContext.getOut().write("Simple example of a classic ⏎
 tag that skips over the body content");
    } catch (java.io.IOException ioe) {
      throw new JspTagException(ioe.getMessage());
    }
    // skip over any body that might be present for this tag
    return(SKIP_BODY);
  }
}
```

Since you're extending `TagSupport`, you're just overriding the `doStartTag()` method here to see how to do so. For example, it's possible to return `SKIP_BODY` as defined in the `Tag` interface to indicate that the JSP container should skip over or ignore the body of the tag if anything is present. You may want to use `SKIP_BODY` if you have a tag that's basing functionality on roles. If a request is being checked for a specific user role, then the tag can determine whether it should evaluate the body. For example, if you returned `SKIP_BODY` from the tag handler for `<proj2ee:classic>`, like so:

```
<proj2ee:classic>
  This body would not be evaluated!
</proj2ee:classic>
```

the body wouldn't be evaluated.

After the action has been evaluated, when the end tag is encountered in the JSP page, the `doEndTag()` method will be called on the tag handler. The `doEndTag()` signature looks just like the `doStartTag()`:

```
int doEndTag() throws JspException
```

Usually the `doEndTag()` will return `EVAL_PAGE` instead of `SKIP_BODY` to indicate that the JSP container should continue evaluating the rest of the JSP page.

As the last step in the tag life cycle, the `release()` method is called. The `release()` method makes sure any resources that the tag may have used during its life cycle are freed. For example, if a database connection were being used, the tag handler would make sure the connection was released or returned to a connection pool. It's important to note that the JSP container may pool tag handler instances.

> **NOTE** *The* `release()` *method isn't called after every* `doEndTag()` *but is called when the JSP container finishes with the tag handler instance. Therefore, it's possible there could be several invocations of* `doStartTag()` *and* `doEndTag()` *before* `release()` *is actually called.*

The implication of `release()` not being called is that you need to make sure any state stored for instance variables is reset correctly. One place to do this is in the `doStartTag()` method, since this method is guaranteed to be called each time the tag is encountered.

Doing cleanup in the `doEndTag()`, which at first glance may seem like the obvious place to reset variables, isn't the best place, either. If the `TryCatchFinally` interface is implemented in the tag handler, the `doEndTag()` may not be called if an exception was thrown. A better place to do tag handler cleanup is in the `doFinally()` method of the `TryCatchFinally` interface implementation. In this example, you know for sure that the method will be called on all occasions.

Attributes

Currently you have a custom action that implements the `Tag` interface by using the `TagSupport` utility class. You'll build upon this action by introducing attributes. You set attributes after the `setParent()` method is called but before the `doStartTag()` in the tag life cycle, as shown in Figure 5-2.

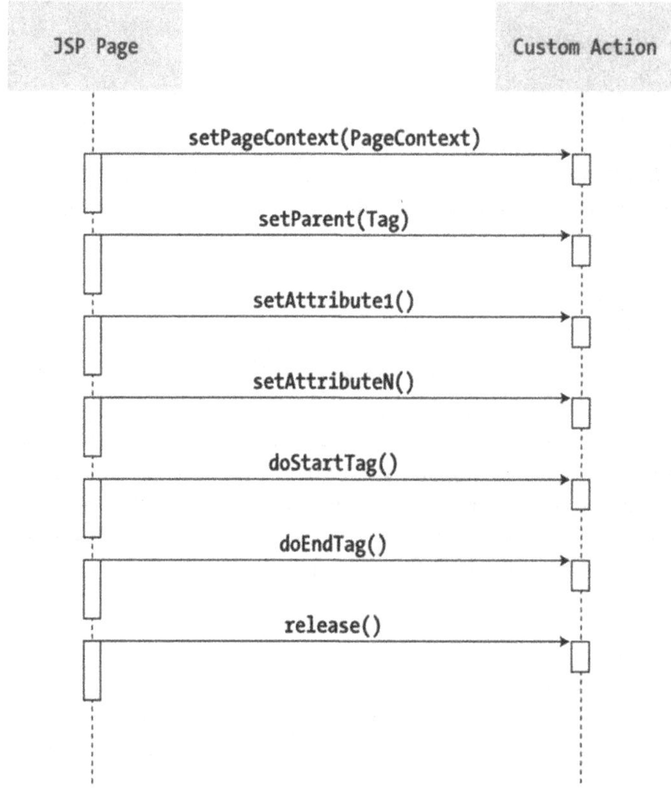

Figure 5-2. Tag life cycle

A `setAttribute()` method call will be made on each of the attributes defined in the action.

For example, the following tag currently prints a message to the `JspWriter` with the line of code from the tag handler:

```
pageContext.getOut().write("Simple example of a classic tag ↩
   that skips over the body content");
```

Maybe you want to specify a color for the text. You can do this by adding an attribute definition to the TLD file (see Listing 5-3).

Listing 5-3. Adding an Attribute Definition

```
<?xml version="1.0" encoding="UTF-8" ?>

<taglib xmlns="http://java.sun.com/xml/ns/j2ee"
    xmlns:xsi="http://www.w3.org/2001/XMLSchema-instance"
    xsi:schemaLocation="http://java.sun.com/xml/ns/j2ee web-jsptaglibrary_2_0.xsd"
    version="2.0" >

  <tlib-version>1.0</tlib-version>
  <jsp-version>2.0</jsp-version>
  <short-name>simple</short-name>
  <uri>/apress-taglib</uri>
  <description>
    A simple tab library for the Pro J2EE custom tag examples
  </description>

  <tag>
    <name>classic</name>
    <tag-class>com.apress.proj2ee.chapter05.Classic</tag-class>
    <description> Demonstrate a classic custom tag </description>

    <attribute>
      <name>color</name>
      <required>false</required>
      <rtexprvalue>false</rtexprvalue>
    </attribute>

  </tag>
</taglib>
```

Note the following about this code:

The `<name>` is the name that the attribute will be referred to in the custom action. In this case, you're calling the attribute `color`.

The `<required>` element is a Boolean value that determines whether this attribute is required. Since this is an optional attribute, you set the value to `false`. It's also possible to set the value to `no`. If you wanted to make this attribute required, you could've set the value to `true` or yes. When defining an attribute, if the `<required>` element isn't specified, then the attribute is optional for the action.

The `<rtexprevalue>` is also a Boolean value that indicates whether the value of the attribute is the result of a request-time expression or a translation-time value. Since you'll specify the color in your JSP page, you set the value to `false`. Like the `<required>` element, this element also defaults to `false`.

You add a setter method to your tag handler so that the JSP container sets the attribute correctly and then uses the attribute value by slightly changing the way you write to the `JspWriter`. Listing 5-4 shows the updated tag handler.

Listing 5-4. The Updated Tag Handler

```
package com.apress.proj2ee.chapter05;

import javax.servlet.jsp.tagext.TagSupport;
import javax.servlet.jsp.*;

public final class Classic extends TagSupport {

  private String color="black";

  public int doStartTag() throws JspException{
    // Do nothing more, then write something to the JspWriter
    try {
      pageContext.getOut().write("<font color=\"" + color +
                             "\">" +
 "Simple example of a classic tag that skips over the body content"
                             + "</font>");
    } catch (java.io.IOException ioe) {
      throw new JspTagException(ioe.getMessage());
    }
    // skip over any body that might be present for this tag
    return(SKIP_BODY);
  }

  public void setColor(String color){
    this.color = color;
  }
}
```

You can now use the custom action in your JSP with the `color` attribute like so:

```
<proj2ee:classic color="red">
  This body would not be evaluated!
</proj2ee:classic>
```

Working with attributes allows you to reuse custom actions quite easily. For a more complicated example, you may want to do some special formatting based on the various attributes that you could set. You wouldn't have to code this information into your JSP files, but instead would use the runtime environment to determine formatting.

IterationTag Interface

You can use the `javax.servlet.jsp.tagext.IterationTag` interface to loop through an action's body content to iteratively evaluate the body. Again, the tag handler can also derive from `TagSupport` if it needs to iteratively evaluate the body. You introduce the method `doAfterBody()` with the following signature:

```
int doAfterBody() throws JspException
```

Each time an action's body is processed, this method is called. The action determines whether to evaluate the body again by returning one of two values: `EVAL_BODY_AGAIN` from the `IterationTag` interface or `SKIP_BODY` from the `Tag` interface. If `EVAL_BODY_AGAIN` is returned, the JSP container will evaluate the tag's body again. This will guarantee at least one more call to the `doAfterBody()` method. `SKIP_BODY` indicates that the body content shouldn't be evaluated again.

For the `doAfterBody()` method to be called, the `doStartTag()` method must return `EVAL_BODY_INCLUDE`. Otherwise, the `doAfterBody()` method will never be called. The `IterationTag` interface is useful when you have to loop through body content without manipulating it.

> **NOTE** *JSP 1.2 introduced* `IterationTag` *in JSP 1.2 and is the preferred way to accomplish iterations in your classic custom actions. It's possible to do this with* `BodyTag`*, but this technique requires performance overhead that's no longer necessary.*

If you look at the lifecycle sequence diagram in Figure 5-3, you can see that the `doAfterBody()` method call is made until the `SKIP_BODY` is returned.

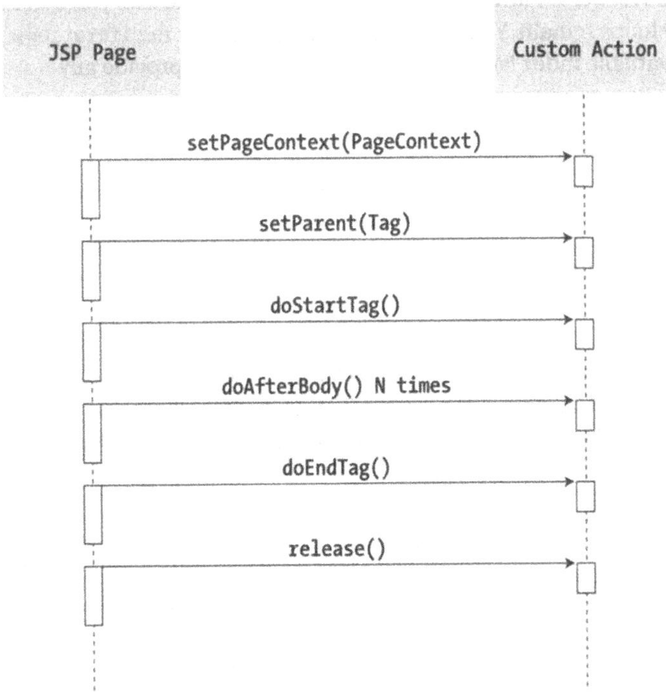

Figure 5-3. `IterationTag` *life cycle*

You'll now see a sample that shows what changes are necessary to use a custom action that iterates through body content. The sample will be a loop action that takes an iterations attribute. This attribute will indicate how many times to iterate over the provided body content.

IterationTag Example

This section first walks through the tag handler and then shows the changes required in the TLD file. Then, you'll see how to use the action from a JSP page.

You'll notice that the iteration action also extends TagSupport. This is because the TagSupport utility class also implements the IterationTag interface, so there's a default implementation of doAfterBody(). However, you'll override that method in the custom action:

```
package com.apress.proj2ee.chapter05;

import javax.servlet.jsp.tagext.TagSupport;
import javax.servlet.jsp.*;

public final class Loop extends TagSupport {
```

Next, you define the iterations attribute, as well as a local variable that you'll use to determine how many loops remain. You provide a setter method for the iterations attribute, but since the variable index isn't exposed, you don't need to provide any mutator methods for it:

```
private int iterations=1;
private int index=0;

public void setIterations(int i){
  iterations = i;
}
```

The doStartTag() sets the initial values for the iteration. You first set the number of iterations as the current index, and then you return EVAL_BODY_INCLUDE so that the body content will be evaluated at least once. If you returned SKIP_BODY, then the doAfterBody() method wouldn't be called:

```
public int doStartTag() throws JspException{
  index = iterations;
  // evaluate the body that might be present for this tag
  return(EVAL_BODY_INCLUDE);
}
```

Each time the body content is evaluated, the doAfterBody() method is called by the container. Here you determine if you want to keep looping and evaluate the body content again. If you've already iterated the number of times specified by the iterations attribute, then you simply return SKIP_BODY:

```
  public int doAfterBody() throws JspException {
    index--;
    if (index > 0){
      return(EVAL_BODY_AGAIN);
    } else {
      // we're done iterating
      return(SKIP_BODY);
    }
  }
}
```

Difference in Tag Description

The main difference for the tag description in the TLD is that you're now specifying a body content type by using the `<body-content>` element. The `<body-content>` element doesn't affect the interpretation of the body by the tag handler; it affects what the JSP container does with the body. `<body-content>` is an optional element that lets the JSP container know what to expect for the tag's body content. `<body-content>` can specify the following three values:

empty: `empty` indicates that the body of the tag must be empty.

JSP: `JSP` means that the tag can contain regular JSP elements, including markup, content, scriptlets, expressions, or any other valid JSP code. When JSP is specified, it's possible that the body content can also be empty.

tagdependent: `tagdependent` means that the JSP container won't process the content. It's up to the tag to process and evaluate the body content. This is typically used if there's body content that needs to be interpreted "as is" by the action (for example, if there was a SQL statement in the body content).

With the addition of the `<body-content>` element, the tag definition from the TLD file looks like Listing 5-5.

Listing 5-5. The Updated Tag Definition

```
<tag>
  <name>loop</name>
  <tag-class>com.apress.proj2ee.chapter05.Loop</tag-class>
  <description>
    Demonstrate a classic custom tag using IterationTag
  </description>
  <body-content>JSP</body-content>
  <attribute>
    <name>iterations</name>
    <required>false</required>
    <rtexprvalue>false</rtexprvalue>
  </attribute>
</tag>
```

Last, you can use the action on the JSP by including the following code:

```
<proj2ee:loop iterations="3">
  <br/>
  Print the body content the number of times specified by the iterations attribute
</proj2ee:loop>
```

BodyTag Interface

The BodyTag interface extends IterationTag. Using the BodyTag interface, tag handlers can implement methods so that the custom action can use body information. Prior to JSP 1.2, BodyTag was the only way to do iterations. However, as you've seen, it's possible (and easier) to use IterationTag to do so now. The question becomes, when do you want to use BodyTag instead of IterationTag? You'll find out now.

The BodyTag interface extends IterationTag by adding another constant, EVAL_BODY_BUFFERED, as well as the following two methods:

- setBodyContent(BodyContent b), which takes a BodyContent object that contains the body text and sets a reference to it

- doInitBody(), which initializes or processes the BodyContent object before the first evaluation of the body. Note that this is called after the body content is set but before it's evaluated.Listing 5-6 shows the entire BodyTag interface.

Listing 5-6. BodyTag *Interface*

```
package javax.servlet.jsp.tagext;
import javax.servlet.jsp.JspException;

public interface BodyTag extends IterationTag {

  public final static int EVAL_BODY_BUFFERED = 2;

  void setBodyContent(BodyContent b);
  void doInitBody() throws JspException;
}
```

You should implement BodyTag if the result of an iteration interpretation is to be further manipulated. You do this by creating a BodyContent object.

BodyContent Object

The BodyContent is a subclass of JspWriter. Recall from Chapter 3 that the JspWriter object is referenced by the implicit variable out as well as through the PageContext object by using the getOut() method. Custom actions can get a reference to the JspWriter and add information to the content in this manner.

> **NOTE** *While* BodyContent *is a subclass of* JspWriter, *what's written to it isn't automatically written into the current* JspWriter *for the page.*

The content of BodyContent is the result of evaluation. You can think of BodyContent as a temporary holding place for content. As the content isn't written back to the JspWriter for the page, it's possible to manipulate the content contained in the BodyContent. You'll notice in the following code that BodyContent contains an enclosing JspWriter instance. This JspWriter instance is assigned when the tag is used on the page. It represents the output stream to which the content of the BodyContent instance will be written when the tag is finished.

Listing 5-7 shows the code for BodyContent (as implemented in Tomcat under the Apache software license).

Listing 5-7. BodyContent

```
package javax.servlet.jsp.tagext;

import java.io.Reader;
import java.io.Writer;
import java.io.IOException;
import javax.servlet.jsp.*;

public abstract class BodyContent extends JspWriter {

  protected BodyContent(JspWriter e) {
    super(UNBOUNDED_BUFFER , false);
    this.enclosingWriter = e;
  }

  public void flush() throws IOException {
    throw new IOException("Illegal to flush within a custom tag");
  }

public void clearBody() {
    try {
      this.clear();
    } catch (IOException ex) {
      // TODO -- clean this one up.
      throw new Error("internal error!;");
    }
  }

  public abstract Reader getReader();

  public abstract String getString();
  public abstract void writeOut(Writer out) throws IOException;
```

```
  public JspWriter getEnclosingWriter() {
    return enclosingWriter;
  }

  private JspWriter enclosingWriter;
}
```

The next step is to see how and when the BodyContent object is created and used in the BodyTag life cycle.

With the addition of the two new methods mentioned, new activities can take place in the life cycle of the tag. If you look at Figure 5-4, you can see where the interaction takes place.

If doStartTag() returns an EVAL_BODY_BUFFERED, indicating that a BodyContent object will be used, setBodyContent() is invoked, and then doInitBody() is called before the first body evaluation. This provides an opportunity to interact with the body. Note that EVAL_BODY_INCLUDE and SKIP_BODY can still be returned, just like in the IterateTag life cycle. If EVAL_BODY_BUFFERED is returned, then a BodyContent object will be created to capture the body evaluation.

The following summarizes what happens depending on the return value from doStartTag():

- If the TLD file specifies that the action must always have an empty action, as indicated by the value of <body-content> being empty, then the doStartTag() method must return SKIP_BODY. Otherwise, the doStartTag() method may return SKIP_BODY, EVAL_BODY_INCLUDE, or EVAL_BODY_BUFFERED.

- If SKIP_BODY is returned, the body isn't evaluated, and doEndTag() is invoked.

- If EVAL_BODY_INCLUDE is returned, setBodyContent() isn't invoked, doInitBody() isn't invoked, the body is evaluated and sent directly to the current out, doAfterBody() is invoked, and then, after zero or more iterations, doEndTag() is invoked.

- If EVAL_BODY_BUFFERED is returned, setBodyContent() is invoked, doInitBody() is invoked, the body is evaluated and written to the BodyContent, doAfterBody() is invoked, and then, after zero or more iterations, doEndTag() is invoked. Note that doAfterBody() is called after the body is evaluated, and it's mandatory for the method to return an indication of whether the body evaluation should continue.

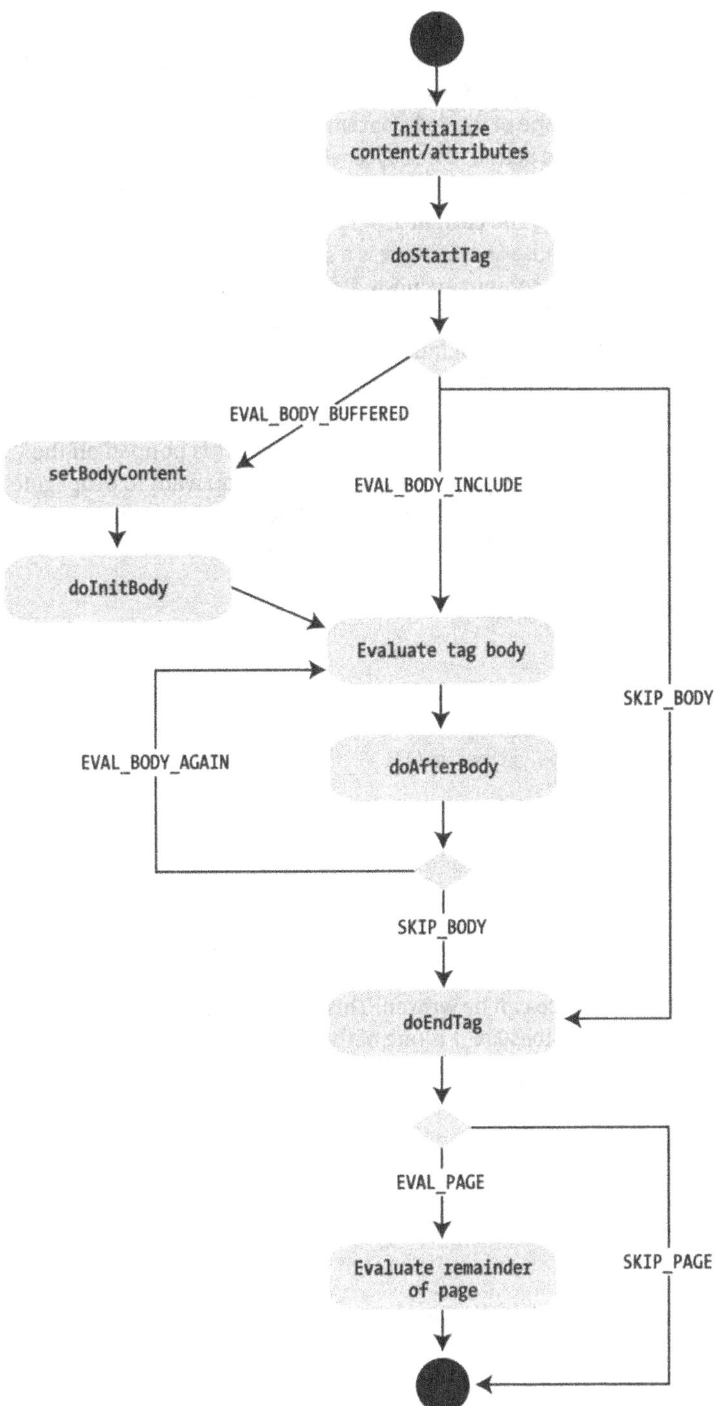

Figure 5-4. BodyTag *activity diagram*

Manipulating BodyContent

The BodyContent object holds the body text. The JSP container creates a new BodyContent object and passes it to the BodyTag via setBodyContent() so that the tag handler can manipulate body content. The scope of the BodyContent is only until the end of the custom action. For the duration of the action, the BodyContent becomes the out variable. Therefore, everything that's written between the start and end of the action is sent to the BodyContent and *not* the JspWriter. The current JspWriter becomes the enclosing writer for the BodyContent instance. Because BodyContent is a subclass of JspWriter, when custom actions that manipulate body content are nested, the BodyContent of the current action becomes the enclosing JspWriter of the nested action.

The JSP container handles the manipulation of the implicit out variable so the page author never needs to worry about writing to out. Under the covers, however, the current output may really be going into a BodyContent object. The container will maintain a stack of enclosing writers. When a nested BodyContent is popped off the stack, the content it maintains is then gone. Because of this, if you want to propagate the BodyContent content, it needs to be explicitly written back to the page using the enclosing writer. You typically do this in the doEndTag() as follows:

```
public int doEndTag() throws JspException {
  if (bodyContent != null) {
    try {
      bodyContent.writeOut(getPreviousOut());
    } catch {IOException ioe) {
      throw new JspTagException(ioe.getMessage());
    }
  }
  return(EVAL_PAGE);
}
```

You'll note that this code uses a convenience method in the BodyTagSupport class called getPreviousOut(). This method gets the enclosing JspWriter so that the contents of the current BodyContent instance can be written. This ensures that your content isn't lost. Forgetting to call the getPreviousOut() is one of the most common programming errors when coding custom actions.

> **NOTE** *If you don't write the current* BodyContent *content to the previous* JspWriter, *you'll lose the content contained in the* BodyContent.

Depending on what you need to do in your action, you have a couple of ways to get the contents of the BodyContent. The options include the following:

- Getting the content into a String by using bodyContent.getString()

- Getting the content into a `JspWriter` by using `bodyContent.getEnclosingWriter()`
- Taking the body content and writing into its `JspWriter` using `bodyContent.writeOut(Writer out)`

Using Classic Custom Actions

Classic custom actions have two required components: the tag handler and the TLD file. The tag handler is a Java file that's written to implement one of the custom action interfaces: `Tag`, `IterateTag`, and `BodyTag`. We'll talk about each of these interfaces and their accompanying life cycles. To use the custom action you create, you'll want to have a JSP file to access it. You'll start with the tag handler and the TLD file so you have a basis for the following discussion.

The *tag handler* is the Java code that actually performs the logic of the action. It's a JavaBean that implements one of three defined interfaces. The following three interfaces are defined in the `javax.servlet.jsp.tagext` package:

- `Tag`
- `IterationTag`
- `BodyTag`

The tag handler is a container-managed object that's used to evaluate custom actions. This occurs at run time when the JSP page executes. Depending on the interface implemented for the tag handler, it must support certain lifecycle events that can happen over the course of the custom action. The implementation of these lifecycle events in the handler provides the custom actions with the opportunity to integrate other server-side actions that may be required. Note that the methods that are inherited from either `Tag` or `BodyTag` are actually points in the life cycle of the tag execution. The methods are called in a particular order according to the lifecycle rules.

Even though a tag handler is a JavaBean, it's initially created using a zero-argument constructor, not with the method `java.beans.Beans.instantiate()`. The attributes within a custom action are typically defined in the TLD file, but those attributes are exposed through the tag handler. The setter methods are provided in the tag handler and are called by the JSP container when required. Introspection is done on the JavaBean by the container to determine the appropriate setter method to call.

One of the key features that a custom action has over a JavaBean is that the tag handler has access to the objects available on the JSP page. This includes all of the JSP context information as well as parameters that may be passed in. It's also possible for tag handlers to have scripting variables associated with it. These scripting variables are defined at translation time and include the type and scope of the variables. The container handles keeping the page context synced up with changes made to scripting variables so they can be accessed.

Tag Handler Properties

All tag handlers have access to two properties. The properties are as follows:

- `pageContext`, which is the JSP page where the tag is located
- `parent`, which points to the tag handler of the closest enclosing action

If you extend the `TagSupport` or `BodyTagSupport` base classes, you don't need to implement the accessor methods, as they're already provided for you. Of course, tag handlers may have other properties that are specific to the custom action. If an attribute is exposed in a custom action, then a JavaBean component holds the property. So, if you have an attribute defined in a TLD, then you'd better have a setter method for it in your tag handler. If the mutator method isn't found, the JSP container will throw an exception.

The container initializes the properties of a tag handler instance that are exposed as attributes in a custom action. The container calls the setter method before the instance is used. Once the property is set, it's considered persistent so that the tag handler code can access the property and use it as it wishes from the time `doStartTag()` is called until `doEndTag()` is called. If the tag handler is implementing the `TryCatchFinally` interface, this may be the `doFinally()` call. The `doStartTag()` and `doEndTag()` are all methods that are defined in the `Tag` interface. Note that a tag handler shouldn't keep any properties that maintain references to other tag handlers beyond the lifecycle events `doStartTag()`, `doEndTag()`, and `doFinally()` if applicable. Since the tag handlers are container managed, an instance of a tag handler can't know whether a reference is still valid.

> **NOTE** *It's best to avoid maintaining any references at all to other tag handlers because the handlers are container managed, and an instance of a tag handler can't know whether a reference is still valid.*

How Tag Handlers Deal with Empty and Nonempty Actions

A tag handler implements one of the three defined interfaces for custom actions. However, it's possible that an action can have no body for the tag handler to process. If an action is empty, meaning that it has no body to process, then it's possible for the action to be used in the following long or short form:

- `<proj2ee:myTag/>` is the short form.
- `<proj2ee:myTag></proj2ee:myTag>` is the long form.

How does this affect the tag handler? If an action is empty, the methods that are related to body manipulation aren't invoked. It's possible to indicate in the TLD file that a tag can be empty. You do this using the `<body-content>` element, as you'll see in the next section. If the tag has a nonempty body, and then no body is provided, a translation error will be thrown. Therefore, the actions must indicate at translation time whether it's possible to have an empty body. This indicates whether the tag handler methods that deal with body evaluation and processing will be called.

The tag handler and the TLD files are closely related to each other, so you'll now look at the TLD file in more detail.

Defining a TLD

The TLD contains the information that describes custom actions in a tag library (and must be valid XML). The JSP container uses this information so that the container has an understanding of the requirements of the action. The JSP container must enforce all constraints that are described in a TLD. So if you use an action that doesn't conform to its specification—for example, not specifying a required attribute—a translation error is thrown.

A tag library usually consists of more than one custom tag, so it's typical to have a TLD file that contains the description of many custom actions. A JSP page then accesses these actions using a prefix that's defined for that library. For example, you can reference a TLD file from a JSP page as follows:

```
<%@ taglib prefix="proj2ee" uri="/WEB-INF/tld/apress.tld" %>
```

Any custom actions that you wanted to access from this tag library would include the prefix defined in the `taglib` directive. The JSP container actually uses the TLD to interpret pages that include `taglib` directives. For example, the following code shows a tag called `someTag` that's defined in the TLD specified in the `apress.tld`:

```
<proj2ee:someTag/>
```

As of JSP 2.0, the format for the TLD is represented in an Extensible Markup Language (XML) schema definition. An XML schema file is also called an Extensible Schema Definition (XSD) file. Using an XSD, instead of a document type definition (DTD) file, allows for a more extensible TLD that can be used as a true single-source document that contains all of the information required about the tags it contains. The XML schema for a TLD document is `http://java.sun.com/xml/ns/j2ee/web-jsptaglibrary_2_0.xsd`.

You define this information in the tag library description of the TLD like so:

```
<?xml version="1.0" encoding="UTF-8" ?>

<taglib xmlns="http://java.sun.com/xml/ns/j2ee"
        xmlns:xsi="http://www.w3.org/2001/XMLSchema-instance"
        xsi:schemaLocation="http://java.sun.com/xml/ns/j2ee ↵
                            web-jsptaglibrary_2_0.xsd"
        version="2.0">
  ...
</taglib>
```

The <taglib> element is the document root. All tag library deployment descriptors must indicate the tag library schema and the version. The tag library namespace is `http://java.sun.com/xml/ns/j2ee`, and you indicate the version of the schema by using the `version` attribute. The instance documents can indicate the published version of the schema using the `xsi:schemaLocation` attribute for the Java 2 Enterprise Edition (J2EE) namespace with the following location: `http://java.sun.com/xml/ns/j2ee/web-jsptaglibrary_2_0.xsd`.

Using the <taglib> Element

The <taglib> element contains any number of <tag> elements. Each <tag> element must have a unique name in the <name> subelement; if you used a custom action in a JSP page, the JSP container needs to know which specific tag it needs to validate against. The following are the available subelements of <taglib>, as defined in the JSP 2.0 specification:

- **description**: A string describing how to use this taglib.
- **display-name**: The <display-name> element contains a short name that's intended to be displayed by tools.
- **icon**: Optional icon that can be used by tools.
- **tlib-version**: The version of the tag library implementation.
- **short-name**: A simple default short name that could be used by a JSP authoring tool to create names with a mnemonic value; for example, you can use it as the preferred prefix value in the `taglib` directives.
- **uri**: A uniform resource indicator (URI) uniquely identifying this taglib.
- **validator**: Optional `TagLibraryValidator` information.
- **listener**: Optional event listener specification.
- **tag**: One or more tags in the tag library.
- **tag-file**: One or more tag files in the tag library.
- **function**: Zero or more expression language (EL) functions defined in this tag library.
- **taglib-extension**: Zero or more extensions that provide extra information about this taglib that's meant for tools to use.

As an example, you'll now add some of these subelements to your TLD file. In the following code, you define this tag library to be version 1.0 using the JSP 2.0 specification. Tools to create the preferred prefix can use the short name for this library. Listing 5-8 shows how you define a unique URI for the library and, finally, how you include a brief description of this library.

Listing 5-8. Defining a Unique URI

```
<?xml version="1.0" encoding="UTF-8" ?>

<taglib xmlns="http://java.sun.com/xml/ns/j2ee"
        xmlns:xsi="http://www.w3.org/2001/XMLSchema-instance"
        xsi:schemaLocation="http://java.sun.com/xml/ns/j2ee ⏎
                            web-jsptaglibrary_2_0.xsd"
        version="2.0">

  <tlib-version>1.0</tlib-version>
  <short-name>proj2ee</short-name>
  <uri>/apress-taglib</uri>
  <description>
    A tab library for the Pro J2EE custom tag examples
  </description>
```

Place the TLD file in the location specified in the URI element in relation to your current application. This is how the container knows where to find it. Now you'll make your tag library definition file useful by defining a custom action.

Using the <tag> Element

You use the <tag> subelement to define a unique custom action. The JSP container will use this information to find the appropriate classes for this action, as well as determine how it should interpret the action. The <tag> element has a number of subelements that it can contain. The JSP 2.0 specification defines these as the following:

- **description**: Optional tag-specific information.
- **display-name**: A short name that's intended to be displayed by tools.
- **icon**: Optional icon element that can be used by tools.
- **name**: The unique action name.
- **tag-class**: The tag handler class implementing `javax.servlet.jsp.tagext.JspTag`.
- **tei-class**: An optional subclass of `javax.servlet.jsp.tagext.TagExtraInfo`.
- **body-content**: The body content type.

- **variable**: Optional scripting variable information.
- **attribute**: All attributes of this action that are evaluated prior to invocation.
- **dynamic-attributes**: Whether this tag supports additional attributes with dynamic names. If `true`, the `<tag-class>` must implement the `javax.servlet.jsp.tagext.DynamicAttributes` interface; it defaults to `false`.
- **example**: Optional informal description of an example of how to use this tag.
- **tag-extension**: Zero or more extensions that provide extra information about this tag used by tools.

You'll look at how to use each of the subelements of `<tag>`, but first we'll clarify what the `<body-content>` subelement does. It's usually up to the JSP container how to handle certain subelements, but for the most part, they're meant to be hints to the container so that you can optimize as much as possible and so they assist developer tools in providing support for custom actions. The `<body-content>` subelement indicates the primary intended use for this tag and what its content should be. The following are the four values for `<body-content>`:

- **tagdependent**: The body of the tag is interpreted by the tag implementation itself and is most likely in a different language. For example, it may be SQL that's embedded in the tag that the tag will evaluate within its tag handler.
- **JSP**: JSP is a category that has body content containing custom and core tags, scripting elements, and Hypertext Markup Language (HTML) text.
- **empty**: The body must be empty.
- **scriptless**: The body accepts only template text, EL expressions, and JSP action elements. No scripting elements are allowed.

If the `<body-content>` isn't defined, then it defaults to JSP. The XSD defines both uppercase and lowercase for the four values, so you can use either one. For example, `EMPTY` and `empty` will both be evaluated correctly.

Defining a Tag

To define a tag, at the least you need to provide a value for the `<name>` and `<tag-class>` elements, as shown in the following code snippet from the TLD:

```
<tag>
  <name>classic</name>
  <tag-class>com.apress.proj2ee.chapter05.Classic</tag-class>
</tag>
```

Here you're defining a custom action called classic. When this action is encountered on a JSP page, the container uses the tag handler defined by <tag-class> to process the tag. The classic tag in this state isn't too interesting, so you'll add more information to the tag definition. In the following code, you'll add a description, body content type, and an optional attribute that will be used by the action.

The <attribute> subelement has a number of subelements of its own. This includes a required <name>, an optional <required> (which defines whether this attribute is mandatory), and an optional <rtexprvalue>. The <rtexprvalue> determines whether the value of the attribute can be specified by a request-time expression. If the <rtexprvalue> element is true (or yes), then the <type> element defines the return type expected from any expression specified as the value of the attribute. The <required> and <rtexprvalue> elements both default to false:

```
<tag>
  <name>classic</name>
  <tag-class>com.apress.proj2ee.chapter05.Classic</tag-class>
  <description> Demonstrate a classic custom tag </description>
  <body-content>JSP</body-content>
  <attribute>
    <name>color</name>
    <required>false</required>
    <rtexprvalue>false</rtexprvalue>
  </attribute>
</tag>
```

The <function> Element

Functions are new in JSP 2.0. The <function> element provides information about each function in the tag library that'll be exposed to the EL. As with the <tag> element, the <function> element can have several subelements, including the following:

- **description**: Optional tag-specific information
- **display-name**: A short name that's intended to be displayed by tools
- **icon**: Optional icon that can be used by tools
- **name**: A unique name for this function
- **function-class**: Provides the fully qualified class name of the Java class containing the static method that implements the function
- **function-signature**: Provides the Java signature of the static Java method that's to be used to implement the function
- **example**: Optional informal description of an example using this function
- **function-extension**: Zero or more extensions that provide extra information about this function for tool consumption

A function class can hold any number of function signatures. If you have a number of functions that you'll be using in an application, it makes sense to logically group them into appropriate classes. To define a function called `currentDate`, you define it in the TLD file as follows:

```
<function>
  <description>Get the current date</description>
  <name>currentDate</name>
  <function-class>com.apress.proj2ee.chapter05.Functions</function-class>
  <function-signature>java.util.Date currentDate()</function-signature>
</function>
```

With the function defined in the TLD file, you could then access it from a JSP file. It becomes possible to have EL expressions—as well as function results—used as parameters to functions. To use the function is as simple as using the `taglib` directive to gain access to the TLD and then calling the function as part of an expression. This is shown in the following bold line of code:

```
  <%@ taglib prefix="proj2ee" uri="/apress-taglib"%>

<html>
  <head>
    <title>Pro J2EE 1.4 - Using Functions</title>
  </head>
  <body>
Evaluate the current date by calling the
currentDate function:
${proj2ee:currentDate()}
  </body>
</html>
```

Listing 5-9 shows the code in `Functions.java`.

Listing 5-9. `Functions.java`

```
package com.apress.proj2ee.chapter05;

import java.util.*;

/**
 * Defines the functions for the JSP 2.0 chapter samples
 *
 * <p>Each function is defined as a static method.</p>
 */
public class Functions {
    public static java.util.Date currentDate() {
        return new java.util.Date();
    } }
```

The <listener> Element

The `<listener>` element defines an event listener object that's instantiated and registered automatically by the JSP container. Using the `<listener-class>` subelement of `<listener>` specifies the listener class that's instantiated. This listener class must be registered as a Web application listener bean.

The order that listeners are registered is undefined, but they're all registered before an application starts. It's up to the container to locate all the TLD files, read the `<listener>` elements, and treat them the same way as if they're an extension of those event listeners defined in the `web.xml` file. Listener objects are defined in the Servlet 2.4 specification, and you'll take a closer look at how to create and use listener objects in Chapter 7.

The <tag-file> Element

With the introduction of tag files in the JSP 2.0, a new element called `<tag-file>` defines an action in the tag library that's implemented as a `.tag` file.

The `<tag-file>` element exists for the following two reasons:

- **Transparency**: The tag library developer may not want page authors to know whether the tag was developed using a tag file or using a Java tag handler. Sometimes, the tag handler may be more easily implemented as a tag file first and then rewritten in Java later for performance reasons.

- **Heterogeneity**: A tag library developer may want to combine tag files and Java tag handlers in the same tag library and allow page authors to import them using the same URI.

The `<tag-file>` element has the following two required subelements:

- **name**: The unique action name.

- **path**: Where to find the `.tag` file implementing this action, relative to the root of the Web application or the root of the Java archive (JAR) file for a tag library packaged in a JAR. When the path specifies a root of a JAR file, it must always begin with `/META-INF/tags`.

Having a `<tag-file>` element is just part of the flexibility of using `.tag` files. The `tagdir` attribute of the `taglib` directive is a somewhat informal mechanism that allows rapid development of tag files without going through the pain or formality of writing a TLD.

It's possible to have no TLD file defined at all when using `.tag` files, but if you want to keep your `taglib` directive consistent in a large application, it makes sense to include the tag files within your TLD. Using the `<tag-file>` and `<tag>` elements, it's possible to combine both classic tag handlers and tag handlers implemented using tag files in the same tag library. This way, the client really doesn't have to care how the tag was implemented. Given that <tag> and <tag-file> share a namespace, a tag library is considered invalid if <tag-file> and <tag> elements have the same <name> defined.

You define a .tag file in your TLD as follows:

```
<tag-file>
  <name>simpletag</name>
  <path>/WEB-INF/tags/simpletag.tag</path>
<tag-file>
```

Tag files, which collectively form tag libraries, may not have an explicitly defined TLD. In the case where they don't, the container generates an implicit TLD that can be referenced using the tagdir attribute of the taglib directive. So, if you explicitly defined your <tag-file>, you'd change the taglib directive in the JSP page from using the following for implicit creation of the action definition by the container:

```
<%@ taglib prefix="proj2ee" tagdir="/WEB-INF/tags" %>
```

to using an explicit TLD, as follows:

```
<%@ taglib prefix="proj2ee" uri="/apress-taglib"%>
```

The <taglib-extension> and <tag-extension> Elements

The JSP 2.0 TLD supports the notion of tag extension elements and tag library extension elements. These are elements added to the TLD by the tag library developer that provide additional information about the tag using a schema defined outside of the JSP specification. This facility is similar to the new extensibility facility introduced in the Servlet 2.4 specification that we'll cover in more detail in the next chapter.

The information contained in these extensions is intended for tool use only and isn't accessible at run time. In addition, JSP containers must consider invalid any tag library that specifies mustUnderstand="true" for any tag or tag library extension element. This is to preserve application compatibility across containers.

Tag library extension elements provide extension information at the tag library level and are specified by adding a <taglib-extension> element as a child of <taglib>. Tag extension elements provide extension information at the tag level and are specified by adding a <tag-extension> element as a child of <tag>. To use these elements, you must first define an XML namespace and import it into the TLD.

This mechanism should prove useful to those who are packaging their custom action libraries. It will make it possible for additional features, such as sound or video, to be used within tools that deal with the library.

Understanding Tag Files

JSP 2.0 introduces a way for page authors to create tag extensions using only JSP syntax. This is known as a *simple tag extension*. Tag files have been introduced so that it's no longer a requirement that you know Java to create a custom action. While the official party line has always been that page authors are primarily presentation focused, the reality is that Java programmers have always gotten their hands dirty in the JSP code. This is one of the reasons why you see so many JSP files littered throughout scriptlet code, rivaling some of the finest graffiti. At the least, the introduction of tag files provides page authors who are truly presentation folks with the tools to get further along with their job.

Tag Files

A *tag file* is a source file that provides a way for a page author to abstract a fragment of JSP code and make it reusable via a custom action without too much work. Tag files have a `.tag` extension and can contain nothing more than template text, or they can contain JSP and markup code.

In the following code, the `attribute` directive defines attributes that will be used by a JSP fragment. You're also using the new EL to access those attributes, as well as the new standard action `<jsp:body>` to invoke the body of the defined fragment. JSP fragments provide a lot of flexibility to the page author. You'll take a closer look at how the fragments work in the next section. The point here is that you have a reusable piece of code in familiar JSP syntax:

```
<%@ attribute name="color" %>
<%@ attribute name="courseName" %>
<table border="1" bgcolor="${color}">
  <tr>
    <td><b>${courseName}</b></td>
  </tr>
  <tr>
    <td>
      <jsp:doBody/>
    </td>
  </tr>
</table>
```

The following are a number of reasons for using tag files when doing JSP development:

Tag files make a great reuse mechanism for page authors. Previously, page authors had only `<jsp:include>` and `<%@ include %>` at their disposal. Tag files are a much more flexible and efficient reuse mechanism. They allow for better customization of the included content as well as the nesting of tags.

Tag files are a great way to hide ugly scriptlets. They make a great tool for moving your JSP pages from scripting-based code to much cleaner JSTL-style code with no scriptlets and with EL expressions instead of scripting expressions. Page authors can easily abstract scriptlets into tag files and then invoke the tags. Over time, you can convert the scriptlet-based tag files to JSTL-style code, or you can encapsulate them in Java tag handlers where applicable.

Just as JSP pages are well suited for replacing servlets that primarily output HTML content, tag files are well suited for tag handlers that primarily output HTML content.

The directory `/WEB-INF/tags` is now a standard directory that will be recognized by compliant containers. The JSP container will process any file with the `.tag` extension that's present in this directory or a subdirectory of tags. The container will create an implicit TLD file as well as a simple tag handler. This eliminates the need to write your own TLD file.

You can package tag files in one of three ways. Where you locate your files, and which files you provide, will determine which packaging the JSP container will use. The three ways are as follows:

- In `/WEB-INF/tags` with no TLD. The custom actions are then imported into the JSP using `<%@ taglib prefix="..." tagdir="/WEB-INF/tags" %>`.

- In `/WEB-INF/tags` with a supplementary TLD. This allows for greater customization of the tag file and makes it transparent to the caller that the tag was implemented as a tag file. You'd import the TLD using `<%@ taglib prefix="..." uri="..." %>`.

- In `/META-INF/tags` in a JAR file with a TLD. This is ideal for tag files that are part of a tag library in a JAR file that can simply be dropped into your Web application.

Tag files are helpful for rapid development. Some containers, such as Tomcat 5.0, support dynamic recompilation of tag files. Simply deploy your tag file in `/WEB-INF/tags` or a subdirectory, and tweak it until it works. You don't have to recompile and redeploy for every change during development.

We'll cover the details contained in this `.tag` file in detail in the "Tag File Sample" section with a simple sample. It'll be easier to understand once you're familiar with both the tag file and the JSP fragment to explain the details.

> **NOTE** *Use tag files to create tag libraries using just JSP syntax. This eliminates the need for tag handlers and TLD files.*

JSP Fragments

Another new feature of JSP 2.0 is JSP fragments. Page authors can now create custom action fragments that can be invoked to produce customized content. Fragments are different from simple attributes in that they're evaluated by tag handlers during a tag's invocation. This is different from simple attributes, which are evaluated by the container. Using the `<jsp:attribute>` standard action element, you can describe a body as a fragment or just as template text. The JSP fragment *is* the body of the `<jsp:attribute>`. The body then specifies the value of an attribute that's declared as a fragment. Depending on the configuration of the action being invoked, the body of the element specifies a value that's evaluated only once, or it specifies the body as a JSP fragment. For example, you can define an attribute named y and assign a value of `test2` to it using the following code:

```
<jsp:attribute name="y">
  test2
</jsp:attribute>
```

This fragment may be invoked only once, but the following fragment may be invoked many times for evaluation:

```
<jsp:attribute name="stringFrag">
  This is the output of concatenating two defined strings: ${result}
</jsp:attribute>
```

While a JSP fragment is coded in JSP syntax, the fragments themselves are represented by the JSP container in Java by an instance of the `javax.servlet.jsp.tagext.JspFragment` interface. Pieces of JSP code are translated into JSP fragments in the context of a tag invocation.

You can create a JSP fragment in two ways. The first is when providing the body of a `<jsp:attribute>` for an attribute that's defined as a fragment or of type `JspFragment` in a tag file. You do this by specifying `fragment="true"` in the `attribute` directive like so:

```
<%@ attribute name="stringFrag" fragment="true" %>
```

The second way a JSP fragment is created is when providing the body of a tag invocation handled by a simple tag handler (which we'll talk about in the next section). Before being passed to a tag handler, the `JspFragment` instance is associated with the `JspContext` of the surrounding page.

> **NOTE** *The* `JspContext` *serves as the base class for the* `PageContext` *class and abstracts all information that isn't specific to servlets.*

You do this because, theoretically, fragments can work with other technologies, not just JSP pages. By having a `JSPContext`, it allows access in an implementation-dependent manner. In addition, the fragment is associated with the parent `Tag` or `SimpleTag` instance for collaboration purposes, so if a custom action is invoked from within the fragment, `setParent()` on the enclosing tag can be called with the appropriate value. The associations of the fragment and the `JSPContext` (and handler) are maintained for the duration of the tag invocation in which it's used.

With a familiarity of tag files and JSP fragments, you'll now work your way through the various approaches to building custom actions. You'll start with the classic actions, and then you'll look at the simple actions and fragments in action.

Exploring Tag Files in Detail

We discussed `.tag` files earlier in this chapter to get you familiar with the components available to custom actions. You'll now revisit `.tag` files in a bit more detail. Using `.tag` files, you can create custom actions using only JSP syntax.

You use tag files in conjunction with JSP fragments and simple tag handlers. By using tag files, it's as easy to write a custom action as it is to write a JSP page. This is a rather large improvement over previous versions of the JSP specification. Tag files, and the way they're packaged, have been designed to provide just as much power as classic tag handlers, yet they remain simple and easy to use.

> **NOTE** *A* tag file *is a source file that provides a way for a page author to abstract a fragment of JSP code and make it reusable via a custom action.*

Tag files play an important role in providing a more convenient way to develop custom actions that are focused on template text. Tag files should have a `.tag` extension and can include other files that are either a complete tag or a fragment of a tag file. Since it's all just JSP code anyway, this works in a similar fashion to including other JSP files. If you have a fragment of a tag file, it's recommended that the extension is `.tagf`.

For each tag file in the Web application, the container makes a tag handler available to JSP pages and other tag files. The details of how this is actually implemented are container specific. For example, some containers may choose to compile tag files into Java simple tag handlers, and others may decide to interpret the tag handlers. You'll need to check your documentation to see how it's being handled for the container you're using.

Syntax

Basically, a tag file is a JSP file, with a couple of differences. Some directives aren't available or have limited availability, and some tag file–specific directives are available. Table 5-1 shows the directives available to tag files. For all the attributes available to each directive, refer to Chapter 3, where they're discussed in detail.

It's legal for a tag file to forward to a page via the `<jsp:forward>` standard action. The forward is handled through the request dispatcher, just as it is for JSP page. When `RequestDispatcher.forward()` returns, it's up to the container to stop processing the tag file and throw a `javax.servlet.jsp.SkipPageException`.

Table 5-1. Tag File Directives

DIRECTIVE	AVAILABLE?	INTERPRETATION/RESTRICTIONS
page	No	A tag file isn't considered a page. You must use the tag directive instead. If this directive is used in a tag file, a translation error will occur.
taglib	Yes	Identical to JSP pages.
include	Yes	Identical to JSP pages. If you're going to use include, then the included file must also comply with valid syntax for a tag file. Otherwise, a translation error will occur.
tag	Yes	Only applicable to tag files. Using this directive in a JSP will cause a translation error.
attribute	Yes	Only applicable to tag files. Using this directive in a JSP will cause a translation error.
variable	Yes	Only applicable to tag files. Using this directive in a JSP will cause a translation error.

You should take care when a classic tag handler that implements the Tag interface is invoked from a tag file. Keep in mind that you can use SimpleTag extensions in environments other than servlets. The Tag interface relies on PageContext, which is servlet-centric.

> **NOTE** *Using classic tag handlers indirectly from a tag file binds using the tag file to servlet environments.*

Also, you can use only two standard actions in tag files: <jsp:invoke> and <jsp:doBody>.

<jsp:invoke>

You can use the <jsp:invoke> standard action only in tag files, which will result in a translation error if used in a JSP page. You use it to invoke a fragment and send the output of the result to the JspWriter. The fragment is determined by the name attribute. You can specify other optional parameters. It's also possible to send the output to a page-scoped variable that can be used later on the page for other manipulations.

When this standard action is used, the fragment is invoked using the JspFragment.invoke() method. null is passed as the Writer parameter to this method to indicate that the results should be sent to the JspWriter of the JspContent associated with the JspFragment object. In simpler terms, null will force the write to the current JspWriter. The following is an example of using invoke:

```
<jsp:invoke fragment="stringFrag" />
```

If you want to save the results of the invoke on a fragment into a scoped attribute, you can use the var or varReader attribute. The var attribute is a String, and the varReader attribute is a Reader object. When using either of these attributes, a custom Writer is passed instead of null. Depending on the type of further manipulation you may be doing with the Writer, you'll have to decide whether you want a String or a Reader.

String objects will contain the content sent by the fragment to the Writer, and the Reader object can actually produce the content sent by the fragment to the Writer. The Reader can be reset, which means if the reset() method is called, the result of the invoked fragment can be reread without reexecuting the fragment.

You can use the scope attribute to set the resulting scoped variable. You can set scope to the standard JSP scopes: page, request, session, or application.

The following two examples show how to use the var, varReader, and scope attributes:

```
<jsp:invoke fragment="stringFrag" var="resultString" scope="request"/>
<jsp:invoke fragment="intFrag" varReader="resultReader" scope="session"/>
```

<jsp:doBody>

The standard action <jsp:doBody> is similar to <jsp:invoke>, with one difference. When using <jsp:doBody>, the body of the tag is processed instead of a specific fragment passed as an attribute. It invokes the body of the tag, sending the output of the result to the JspWriter or to a scoped attribute.

You can use <jsp:doBody> only in a tag, and it'll result in a translation error if used in a JSP page. Since <jsp:doBody> operates only on the body of the tag, there's no name attribute for this standard action. The var, varReader, and scope attributes are all supported with the same semantics as for <jsp:invoke>.

The body of a tag is passed to the simple tag handler as a JspFragment object.

Tag File Sample

It's possible to have a tag file that doesn't do anything except have text in it that can be written to a JspWriter. You'll look at something a bit more interesting to see how you can put the features to work. You'll start with a simple tag file that takes two strings, concatenates them into a result variable, and then invokes the body of a JSP fragment. You'll see immediately that you can use JSP syntax by having a comment that describes your file:

```
<%-- stringtag.tag sample to demonstrate using tag files--%>
```

Next, you'll define the core taglib from the JSTL so that you can use the <c:set> action to set a variable into scope. Standard practice is to define the core taglib with the prefix c when using the JSTL:

```
<%@ taglib prefix="c" uri="http://java.sun.com/jstl/core_rt" %>
```

Next, you'll define two attributes that this tag will use (the attribute directive is valid to use only in tag files). In the following code, you're defining an attribute named x and an attribute named y. Both are defined as the default type of String. You'll be able to access these variables in your tag file:

```
<%@ attribute name="x" %>
<%@ attribute name="y" %>
```

The next attribute defines a JSP fragment called stringFrag. By setting the fragment attribute equal to true, the type of this object will be JspFragment. The container will handle populating the attribute correctly for you with whatever content is specified on the calling page:

```
<%@ attribute name="stringFrag" fragment="true" %>
```

You then define a variable called result that will be accessible to the JSP fragment. You can see here the relationship between the JSP fragment and the tag file. They work closely together; the tag file is analogous to the tag handler file, and the JSP fragment is the actual action used:

```
<%@ variable name-given="result" variable-class="java.lang.String" %>
```

Next, you have some template text that will be written to the JspWriter that includes some standard HTML, as well as access to the variables you defined. The values of the attributes are set from the JSP fragment, and the tag file sets the result. At this point, because you haven't assigned a value to result, it's empty:

```
<h1>Working with string attributes</h1>
In Tag file x = ${x}<br>
In Tag file y = ${y}<br>
In Tag file result = ${result}<br>
<h1>About to invoke stringFrag </h1>
```

The value of result is set by concatenating the two strings using the <c:set> action as well as the EL:

```
<c:set var="result" value="${x} + ${y}"/>
```

Finally, you invoke the body of the stringFrag fragment by using the <jsp:invoke> standard action:

```
<jsp:invoke fragment="stringFrag" />
```

Since you're working with tag files, you don't have to explicitly define a TLD for the custom action. The container will build one for you implicitly as long as the tag file is in the /WEB-INF/tags directory, or a subdirectory of tags, and has the .tag or .tagf extension. In this example, it will be stringtag.tag.

simpletag.jsp

You'll see the JSP file that defines the fragment you're using in the tag file. In the JSP file, you first must use the taglib directive to specify where the custom action definition is. If you're instructing the container to create the implicit TLD for you, then you use the tagdir attribute as follows. You can then access the defined custom actions from the tag files using the proj2ee prefix:

```
<%@ taglib prefix="proj2ee" tagdir="/WEB-INF/tags" %>
```

Next, you access the previous custom action, called stringtag. You'll see two different ways, for example purposes only, of specifying an attribute value. The first is by having the attribute value defined in the action element. Here you're setting the custom action attribute x equal to the string test1. The second is using the <jsp:attribute> standard action. The body of the <jsp:attribute> defines<$I~attribute values, JSP; defining, using the value for the attribute named by name. In this case, you're setting an attribute called y equal to the value test2:

```
<proj2ee:stringtag x="test1" >

  <jsp:attribute name="y" >
    test2
  </jsp:attribute>
```

Next, you have an attribute that's defined as a fragment. The value of stringFrag becomes the evaluation of the body. In this case, you have some template text that also includes an EL variable. Therefore, you have a custom action that can pass parameters to its body content and then have that body content evaluated as a JSP fragment:

```
  <jsp:attribute name="stringFrag">
    This is the output of concatenating two defined strings: ${result}
  </jsp:attribute>

</proj2ee:stringtag>
```

If you execute this JSP file, your browser output looks like Figure 5-5.

Keep in mind that you created this simple custom action just using JSP syntax. You didn't even have to create a TLD file. The container generated the code required to execute the actions for you. This will prove to be a valuable JSP 2.0 feature. In fact, the basic change in the way that you can now write custom actions was the reason behind the specification having a major revision change.

If you're really motivated and want to see the code that's generated from your JSP container based on your .tag file, you can find it in the $CATALINA_HOME\work\Catalina\localhost\<webapp_name>\org\apache\jsp\tag\web directory. This will give you an appreciation for the tag handler Java code you don't have to write to create a custom action in JSP 2.0. Note that the class extends SimpleTagSupport. You'll explore how to write your own SimpleTag classes later in the "Using Simple Tags" section. This is the code:

```
package org.apache.jsp.tag.web;
import javax.servlet.*;
import javax.servlet.http.*;
import javax.servlet.jsp.*;

public final class stringtag_tag extends javax.servlet.jsp.tagext.SimpleTagSupport
    implements  org.apache.jasper.runtime.JspSourceDependent {
  ...
```

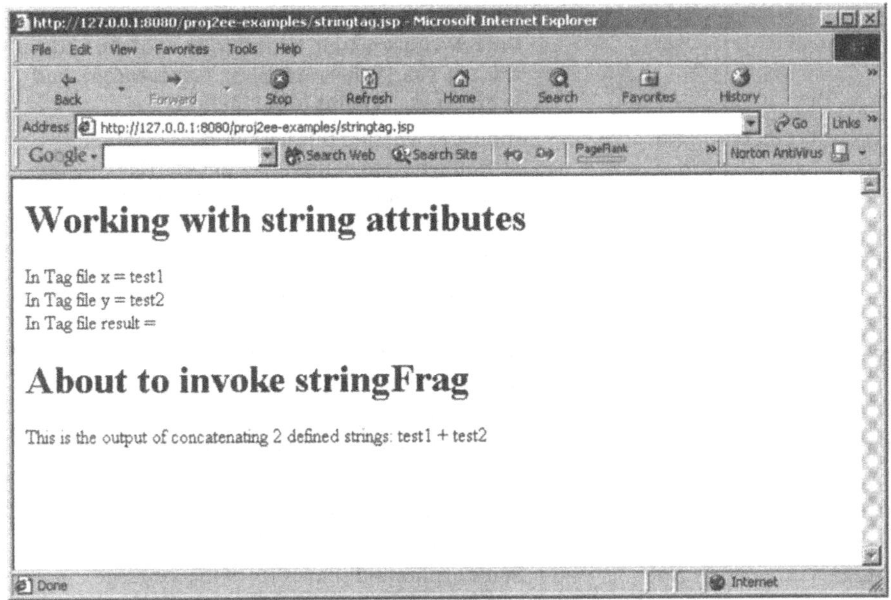

Figure 5-5. Browser output

XML Syntax of a Tag File

Like JSP files, a tag file has an equivalent XML document. You can use files written as XML documents as input to other XML transformations. The XML view of a tag file is exposed from the JSP compiler to the tag library validators (TLVs). The purpose of the XML view is to expose it in a consistent format to TLVs so they can make sure their particular tag library is being used correctly.

If you didn't have the XML view, then TLVs would have to be able to parse both standard and XML syntax. The XML view of a tag file is identical to the XML view of a JSP page, except that there are additional XML elements defined to handle tag file-specific features. While in general you won't see the XML view of the tag file, it's good to understand some of the additional elements you may need to be aware of if you were doing Document Object Model (DOM) or Simple API for XML (SAX) parsing in a TLV for a library.

<jsp:directive.tag>

This element is a child of the root element and appears at the beginning of the tag file. The tag directive attribute list available to the element is the same as that available to the tag directive (see Table 5-2).

Table 5-2. Attributes for `<jsp:directive.tag>`

ATTRIBUTE	REQUIRED?	DESCRIPTION
display-name	No	A short name displayed by tools. Defaults to the name of the tag file, without the .tag extension.
body-content	No	Provides information on the content of the body of this tag. Valid values are empty, tagdependent, and scriptless. Defaults to scriptless.
dynamic-attributes	No	Indicates whether this tag supports dynamic attribute names. If this is set to true, then the tag handler must implement the DynamicAttributes interface. Defaults to false.
small-icon	No	Relative path from the tag source file of an image file containing a small icon. This is used by tools. Defaults to no small icon.
large-icon	No	Relative path from the tag source file of an image file containing a large icon. This is used by tools. Defaults to no large icon.
description	No	String that describes this tag. Defaults to no description.
example	No	String that presents an example of a use of this action. Defaults to no example.
language	No	Same syntax and semantics of the language attribute of the page directive.
import	No	Same syntax and semantics of the import attribute of the page directive.
pageEncoding	No	Same syntax and semantics of the pageEncoding attribute in the page directive. There's no corresponding global configuration element in web.xml.
isELIgnored	No	Same syntax and semantics of the isELIgnored attribute of the page directive. There's no corresponding global configuration element in web.xml.

The syntax of the element is as follows:

```
<jsp:directive.tag list_of_available_attributes />
```

<jsp:directive.attribute>

Zero or more of these elements may be present, and they'll appear in succession. Each is a child of the root element, and they must appear in the beginning of the tag file, after the `<jsp:directive.tag>` (see Table 5-3).

Table 5-3. Attributes for `<jsp:directive.attribute>`

ATTRIBUTE	REQUIRED?	DESCRIPTION
`name`	Yes	The unique name of the attribute being declared.
`required`	No	Whether this attribute is required (`true`) or optional (`false`). Defaults to `false` if not specified.
`fragment`	No	Whether this attribute should be considered a JSP fragment (`true`). If this attribute is `true`, the type attribute is fixed at `javax.servlet.jsp.tagext.JspFragment`, and a translation error will result if the type attribute is specified. If this attribute is `true`, the `rtexprvalue` attribute is fixed at `true`. Defaults to `false`.
`rtexprvalue`	No	Whether the attribute's value may be dynamically calculated at run time by a scriptlet expression. Defaults to `false`.
`type`	No	The runtime type of the attribute's value. Defaults to `java.lang.String` if not specified.
`description`	No	Description of the attribute. Defaults to no description.

The syntax of this element is as follows:

```
<jsp:directive.attribute list_of_available_attributes />
```

<jsp:directive.variable>

Zero or more of these elements may be present, and they must appear in succession. Each must be a child of the root element and must appear in the beginning of the tag file, after the last `<jsp:directive.attribute>` (see Table 5-4).

The syntax of this element is as follows:

```
<jsp:directive.variable list_of_available_attributes />
```

Table 5-4. Attributes for `<jsp:directive.variable>`

ATTRIBUTE	REQUIRED?	DESCRIPTION
`name-given`	Yes	Defines a scripting variable to be defined in the page invoking this tag. Either the `name-given` attribute or the `name-from-attribute` attribute must be specified. Specifying neither or both attributes, or if two variable directives have the same `name-given`, will result in a fatal translation error.
`name-from-attribute`	Yes (if `name-given` not specified)	Defines a scripting variable to be defined in the page invoking this tag. The specified name is the name of an attribute whose (translation-time) value will give the name of the variable. Specifying neither or both attributes, or if two variable directives have the same `name-from-attribute`, will result in a fatal translation error.
`description`	No	Description of the attribute. Defaults to no description.
`variable-class`	No	The name of the class of the variable. The default is `java.lang.String`.
`scope`	No	The scope of the scripting variable defined. Can be either `AT_BEGIN`, `AT_END`, or `NESTED`. Defaults to `NESTED`. A translation occurs if both `scope` and `fragment` are specified.
`declare`	No	Whether the variable is declared or not. Defaults to `true`. A translation error occurs if both `declare` and `fragment` are specified.
`alias`	No (unless `name-from-attributes` is specified)	Defines a locally scoped attribute to hold the value of this variable. The container will synchronize this value with the variable whose name is given in `name-from-attribute`. Required when `name-from-attribute` is specified. A translation error must occur if used without `name-from` attribute. A translation error must occur if the value of `alias` is the same as the value of a `name` attribute of an `attribute` directive or the `name-given` attribute of a variable directive in the same translation unit.

Sample XML Tag File

If you want to express the example tag file in its XML file representation, you do the following (note that the JSP comments in the form of `<%-- --%>` must be removed because they aren't passed to the XML view of the page). You declare the tag using the `<jsp:directive.tag>` element. This is followed by a conversion of each `<%@ attribute %>` to its corresponding `<jsp:directive.attribute>` element:

```
<?xml version="1.0"?>

<jsp:directive.tag display-name="stringtagXML"
                  description="Simple tag file that concatenates strings"
                 dynamic-attributes="false" />
<jsp:directive.attribute name="x" type="java.lang.String" />
<jsp:directive.attribute name="y" type="java.lang.String" />

<jsp:directive.attribute name="stringFrag" fragment="true" />
```

After the attributes are complete, you define each `<%@ variable %>` to the appropriate `<jsp:directive.variable>`:

```
<jsp:directive.variable name-given="result" variable-class="java.lang.String" />
```

The `<html>` element defines the various namespaces you're interested in, using the `xmlns` attribute. The prefix used in the `<%@ taglib %>` follows the colon of the `xmlns`, and then the appropriate URI is set:

```
<html
   xmlns:jsp="http://java.sun.com/JSP/Page"
   xmlns:c="http://java.sun.com/jstl/core_rt">
```

You'll notice that your template text remains the same. However, since you're using expressions within your template text, you surround the appropriate text with a `<jsp:text>` element. The other actions `<c:set>` and `<jsp:invoke>` work just as they did in the JSP file (see Listing 5-10).

Listing 5-10. XML Tag File Example

```
  <title>XML Example of a Tag File</title>
  <body>
    <h1>Working with string attributes</h1>
    <jsp:text>In Tag file x = ${x}</jsp:text>
    <br/>
    <jsp:text>In Tag file y = ${y}</jsp:text>
    <br/>
    <jsp:text>In Tag file result = ${result}</jsp:text>
    <br/>

    <h1>About to invoke stringFrag </h1>

    <c:set var="result" value="${x} + ${y}"/>

    <jsp:invoke fragment="stringFrag" />
  </body>
</html>
```

Packaging Tag Files

Tag files have the flexibility of being located and packaged in a number of ways. You can place tag files in one of two locations of a Web application:

The first possibility is in the /META-INF/tags directory in a JAR file. The JAR file is then installed in the /WEB-INF/lib directory of the Web application. Tags placed here are typically part of a reusable library of tags that can then be used in any Web application.

The second possibility is in a subdirectory of the /WEB-INF/tags directory of the Web application. Tags placed here are usually used by a specific application and require little packaging.

> **NOTE** *Tag files that appear in any other location aren't considered tag extensions and will be ignored by the JSP container. They're just treated as content file to be served.*

It's also possible to describe the tags within a TLD, as already mentioned. The <tag-file> element specifies the location of the tag file defining a tag in the tag library. Two additional TLD elements describe tag files: <tag-file> and <path>. The <tag-file> element describes the location of a tag file defining a tag in this tag library. You must use the <name> and <path> subelements to define the tag name and location of the tag file relative to the TLD. The following is an example:

```
<tag-file>
  <name>simpletag</name>
  <path>/WEB-INF/tags/simpletag.tag</path>
</tag-file>
```

Tag Files in a JAR

If you have a set of tag files you'd like to bundle so that other Web applications can use them, it makes sense to build a JAR file. To use tag files that are bundled in a JAR, you must define them in a TLD. If you have tag files that appear in the JAR but aren't defined in a TLD, the JSP container will ignore them. If you try to use the tag, you'll get an error that it isn't defined.

When used in a JAR file, the <tag-file> element specifies the full path of the tag file from the root of the JAR. Therefore, it must always begin with /META-INF/tags.

Tag Files Directly in a Web Application

If you have tag files that are deployed just for a Web application, you can place the tag files in the `/WEB-INF/tags` directory of the Web application. It's also possible to put the tag files in a subdirectory of that directory. If you put tag files in these directories, then the tag files are made accessible to JSP pages without the need to explicitly write a TLD.

The JSP 2.0 container interprets the `/WEB-INF/tags` directory and each subdirectory under it to determine what tag files appear. In doing so, the container implicitly defines a tag library containing tag handlers that are defined by the tag files that appear in that directory. The directory structure doesn't relate the tag files in any way just because they're in the same directory.

This makes it convenient for page authors to quickly abstract reusable JSP code by simply creating a new file and placing the code inside it. Some containers will actually compile the tag files as soon as they're placed in the directory. This should prove helpful for increasing the speed of development instead of having to recompile, repackage, and deploy new tag libraries for a simple change. For example, the following Web application contains three tag libraries: tags, courses, and student-info:

```
/WEB-INF/tags/
/WEB-INF/tags/simpletag.tag
/WEB-INF/tags/stringtag.tag
/WEB-INF/tags/courses/
/WEB-INF/tags/courses/coursefull.tag
/WEB-INF/tags/courses/course-tags.tld
/WEB-INF/tags/student/info/
/WEB-INF/tags/student/info/displayinfo.tag
```

The JSP container will generate an implicit tag library for each directory under and including `/WEB-INF/tags`. You can import the tag library only via the `tagdir` attribute of the `taglib` directive. The TLD will have the following values created by the container:

<tlib-version>: `<tlib-version>` for the tag library defaults to 1.0.

<short-name>: `<short-name>` is derived from the directory name. If the directory is `/WEB-INF/tags`, the short name is simply `tags`. Otherwise, the full directory path (relative to the Web application) is taken, minus the `/WEB-INF/tags` prefix. Then, all / characters are replaced with -, which yields the short name. Note that short names aren't guaranteed to be unique.

<tag-file>: A `<tag-file>` element is considered to exist for each tag file in this directory, with the following subelements:

- The `<name>` for each is the filename of the tag file, minus the `.tag` extension
- The `<path>` for each is the path of the tag file, relative to the root of the Web application

For example, the implicit TLD that would be created for the /WEB-INF/tags/student/info directory would look like Listing 5-11.

Listing 5-11. Implicit TLD

```
<?xml version="1.0" encoding="UTF-8" ?>

<taglib xmlns="http://java.sun.com/xml/ns/j2ee"
    xmlns:xsi="http://www.w3.org/2001/XMLSchema-instance"
    xsi:schemaLocation="http://java.sun.com/xml/ns/j2ee web-jsptaglibrary_2_0.xsd"
    version="2.0">
  <tlib-version>1.0</tlib-version>
  <short-name>student-info</short-name>
  <tag-file>
    <name>displayinfo</name>
    <path>/WEB-INF/tags/student/info/displayinfo.tag</path>
  </tag-file>
</taglib>
```

When the Web application is deployed, the JSP container searches for all tag files present in the /WEB-INF/tags directory and subdirectories. When the tag file is processed, it becomes available for use in JSP pages.

> **NOTE** *Even though the container creates an implicit tag library, a TLD that may exist in the Web application can still create additional tags from the same tag files using the* <tag-file> *element.*

Precompiled Tag Handlers

It's possible to compile tag files into Java classes and then bundle them as a tag library. You may consider doing this if you want to distribute your tag files in binary form without the source code. If you're planning on precompiling your tag files into tag handlers (using whatever tool you decide that will produce the portable code), you can put the tag handlers in a JAR file.

It's also possible to compile .tag files into tag handlers and place the resulting classes in WEB-INF/classes. If you were using a JAR, this implies that you need to create the TLD and make sure you've included the correct information. In the case of precompiled tag files, you'd no longer be able to use <tag-file>. You'd refer to the precompiled tag handler like you would any other SimpleTag handler—by pointing to the generated class using the subelement of <tag> and <tag-class>.

You need the explicit TLD so that the container knows where to locate the files. It won't be able to implicitly create the TLD for you, since it recognizes `.tag` extensions only in the `/WEB-INF/tags` directory (or subdirectories).

If you decide to not JAR the tag handlers, you can include the class files in the Web application's `classes` directory and just point to the path in the TLD. There's no restriction about where the tag handlers need to be placed, but the drop-and-run functionality of the `/WEB-INF/tags` directory isn't going to buy you anything here because, since the tag implementation is a Java class, the container will no longer automatically recognize the tag file.

Using Simple Tag Extensions

So far, we've been talking about custom actions as they relate to what's now referred to as *classic actions*. As you can tell, classic can also translate into complex. The various interfaces and life cycles for classic tag handlers are necessarily somewhat complex because of the interaction of scriptlets and scriptlet expressions in tag bodies. These scriptlets can rely on surrounding context that may be defined using scriptlets in the enclosing page. Therefore, there needs to be a way to handle such interaction, which is why we've already talked about three interfaces.

The EL and JSTL made it possible to author JSP pages that can remain scriptlet free. Many of the requirements that the classic tag handlers needed to take into consideration are no longer relevant in many cases. This allows for a definition of a tag invocation protocol that's easier to use in many cases. Enter the simple tag extension introduced in JSP 2.0. Simple tag extensions are just that: an easier way to implement custom actions with a life cycle that's easy to use.

In addition to being simpler to work with, simple tag extensions don't directly rely on any Servlet APIs. Not being tied to the Servlet technology leaves room for future integration with other technologies. This is because `PageContent` now extends `JspContext`. `JspContext` provides generic services such as storing the `JspWriter` and keeping track of scoped attributes whereas `PageContext` has functionality specific to serving JSP pages in the context of servlets. The `Tag` interface relies on `PageContext`; `SimpleTag` relies only on `JspContext`.

You can write simple tag extensions in one of the following two ways:

In Java, by defining a class that implements the `javax.servlet.jsp.tagext.SimpleTag` interface.

In JSP syntax, using tag files. Having the ability to write custom actions in JSP syntax means that custom actions now come into reach for those page authors who don't know Java. Advanced page authors can also use this syntax as can tag library developers who know Java but are producing tag libraries that are primarily template-based presentation or who want to take advantage of existing tag libraries.

SimpleTag Interface

Simple tag handlers are those that implement the SimpleTag interface. The invocation protocol used by SimpleTag is simplified from the one used for classic tag handlers. The javax.servlet.jsp.tagext.SimpleTagSupport class provides a default implementation for all methods in SimpleTag. The complete interface definition is as follows:

```
public interface SimpleTag extends JspTag {
  public void doTag()throws JspException, java.io.IOException;
  public void setParent(JspTag parent);
  public JspTag getParent();
  public void setJspContext(JspContext pc);
  public void setJspBody(JspFragment jspBody);
}
```

First, you'll notice SimpleTag interface doesn't extend Tag; rather, it extends directly from JspTag. What this means is that SimpleTag doesn't have any inherent JSP/servlet knowledge embedded within it. The second noticeable difference is that SimpleTag has only one lifecycle method, doTag(), defined as the following:

```
public void doTag()throws JspException, java.io.IOException
```

The doTag() method is called only once for any given tag invocation. Therefore, all code related to this tag is contained in one nice, neat method. This includes tag logic, iteration, and body evaluations. Thus, it's considerably easier to get the job done than with the IterationTag interface you've already seen.

It's possible to support body content using the setJspBody() method. The container invokes the setJspBody() method with a JspFragment object encapsulating the body of the tag. The tag handler implementation can call invoke() on that fragment to evaluate the body as many times as it needs.

A SimpleTag handler must have a public no-arguments constructor, and most SimpleTag handlers should extend javax.servlet.jsp.tagext.SimpleTagSupport. This is the convenience class, similar to TagSupport or BodyTagSupport. Some helpful methods included in this class are as follows:

```
public JspFragment getJspBody()
public static final JspTag findAncestorWithClass(JspTag from,
                                                  java.lang.Class klass)
```

getJspBody()

getJspBody() returns the body passed in by the container via setJspBody(). The JspFragment encapsulates the body of the tag. If the JspFragment is null, it indicates that tag has a body content type of empty.

findAncestorWithClass()

`findAncestorWithClass()` finds the instance of a given class type that's closest to a given instance. This method uses the `getParent()` method from the interface and is used for coordination among cooperating tags. For every instance of `TagAdapter` encountered while traversing the ancestors, the tag handler returned by `TagAdapter.getAdaptee()` is compared to `klass`. If the tag handler matches this class, and not its `TagAdapter`, then an instance of the closest ancestor is returned.We'll talk about `TagAdapters` in the "Do You Need a TagAdapter?" section.

Simple Tag Handler Life Cycle

The life cycle of a `SimpleTag` handler is easier to understand than the other tag handler interface life cycles you've already seen. When a simple tag handler is required on a JSP page, it's instantiated by the container, executed, and then discarded. There are no complicated caching semantics when using this interface since nothing is cached or reused. The expert group decided that performance gains that may be made using caching mechanisms dramatically increased the difficulty in writing portable tag handlers and made the handlers error prone.

> **NOTE** *If performance concerns are critical, implement your tag handler as a simple tag and then take some performance metrics to see if your criteria are met before embarking on the more complicated and time-consuming path of writing a classic handler.*

The following lifecycle events take place for the simple tag handler:

- A new tag handler instance is created each time the tag is encountered by the container. You do this by calling the zero-argument constructor.
- The container calls the `setJspContext()` and `setParent()` methods.
- The container calls the setters for each attribute defined for this tag in the order in which they appear in the JSP page or tag file. If the attribute value is a runtime expression or an EL expression, it's evaluated first and then passed to the setter; if the attribute is a dynamic attribute, then `setDynamicAttribute()` is called.
- The container calls `setJspBody()` method to set the body of this tag, as a `JspFragment`. If the tag is declared to have a `<body-content>` of `empty`, then `null` is passed to `setJspBody()`.

- The container calls the doTag() method, which contains all of the logic for the handler. This includes body evaluations, iterations, and basically anything that would have been in the various other methods used in a classic tag.
- The doTag() method returns, and all variables are synchronized.

Figure 5-6 shows this process.

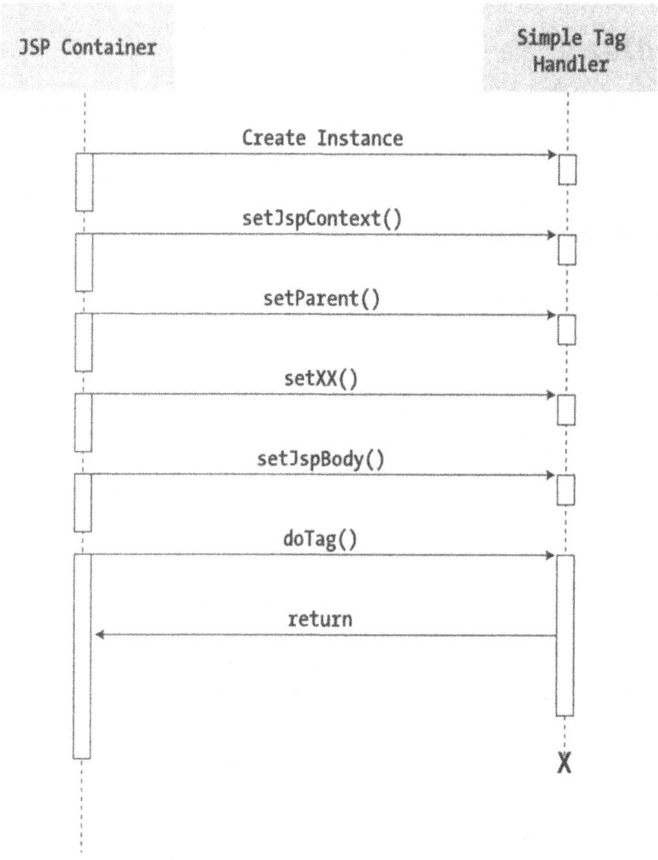

Figure 5-6. Simple tag handler

If the body of a SimpleTag is present, then it's translated into a JSP fragment. For example, in the following code, the template text cell 3 will be contained in a JspFragment object and passed to the setJspBody() of the tag handler:

```
<proj2ee:dynamicTableCell align="center" >
  cell 3
</proj2ee:dynamicTableCell>
```

Once the `JspFragment` object is set, the tag handler can access it and execute that fragment as many times as required using the `invoke()` method. You can accomplish this using the `getJspBody()` method of the `SimpleTagSupport` class and passing a `JspWriter` or parameter to the fragment. In this case, you're using the current `JspWriter` and not passing any parameters:

```
getJspBody().invoke(null, null);
```

In a moment, you'll see an example of how to build a `SimpleTag`, but first you'll learn about dynamic attributes. This will complete the picture and give you the opportunity to go through the `SimpleTag` handler with a purposeful sample.

Working with Dynamic Attributes

Introduced in JSP 2.0, dynamic attributes allow attributes to be declared on the fly. This allows runtime information to be used in the actual naming of the attribute. Any tag handler can optionally extend the `DynamicAttribute` interface to indicate that it supports dynamic attributes. If you're using a TLD file, you also have to indicate that dynamic attributes are accepted. The `DynamicAttribute` is a public interface that has one method:

```
public void setDynamicAttribute(java.lang.String uri, java.lang.String localName,
                                java.lang.Object value)
```

This method is called when a tag declared to accept dynamic attributes is passed to an attribute that isn't declared in the TLD. The `uri` parameter is the namespace of the attribute or just `null` if the default namespace should be used. The `localName` parameter is the name of the attribute being set, and the `value` parameter is the actual value of the attribute. This method can throw `JspException` if it doesn't accept the attribute. If the exception is thrown, then the container won't call `doStartTag()` or `doTag()`. Which of those methods is being used depends on the interface being implemented, either `Tag` or `SimpleTag`.

Tag handlers that implement `DynamicAttribute` must also have an entry for the tag in the TLD to indicate that dynamic attributes are accepted. You do this by including the `<dynamic-attributes>` element and setting it to `true` within a tag definition as follows:

```
<tag>
  ...
  <dynamic-attributes>true</dynamic-attributes>
  ...
</tag>
```

For any attribute that isn't declared in the TLD for this tag, instead of getting an error at translation time, the `setDynamicAttribute()` method is called with the name and value of the attribute. It's the responsibility of the tag handler to remember the names and values of the dynamic attributes.

> **NOTE** *If a tag handler is declared in the TLD as supporting dynamic attributes but it doesn't implement the* `DynamicAttributes` *interface, the tag handler will be considered invalid by the container.*

A tag handler can keep track of its dynamic attributes by using a `HashMap` as follows:

```
private HashMap attributes = new HashMap();
...
public void setDynamicAttribute(String uri, String localName, Object value)
  throws JspException {

  attributes.put(localName, value);
}
```

The call to `setDynamicAttribute()` will be made for each dynamic attribute in the tag invocation. The attributes are set in the order that they appear on the JSP page. A valuable feature of dynamic attributes is that they can accept runtime expression values. Therefore, you can now use the EL to determine a value that's going to be used for a dynamic attribute. It's possible to mix defined attributes and dynamic attributes in a single tag invocation.

In the following sample, `width` and `style` are dynamic attributes and aren't defined in the tag handler, and `evenCell` is a declared attribute:

```
<proj2ee:dynamicTableCell width="50%" style="font-weight: bold" evenCell="false"/>
```

Building a SimpleTag Handler with Dynamic Attributes

A number of tag libraries try to emulate HTML or XML tags but do some extra processing for some of the attributes. This is true in the popular Struts Framework `struts-html` tag library. Some attributes are specific to the tag handlers, and others are just passed through; that is, the tag handler doesn't really care if they're present or not, but they may play a role in the output that's generated.

Rather than trying to come up with an exhaustive list of every possible attribute a page author may need to pass to an HTML `<td>` element, the tag handler could be implemented to care only about a few of them and just pass the rest along. This is an improvement over what library developers face today. What happens today is that the tag library developer forgets a couple of attributes, and then users of the library complain until it's fixed. Dynamic attributes make it possible to avoid some of those types of inconvenient bugs.

You'll now see how to build a tag handler that deals with dynamic attributes and how the attributes are actually used. As shown in the following code, `DynamicTableCellTag` extends the `SimpleTagSupport` convenience class and implements the `DynamicAttributes` interface:

```
package com.apress.proj2ee.chapter05;

import javax.servlet.jsp.JspException;
import javax.servlet.jsp.JspWriter;
import javax.servlet.jsp.tagext.SimpleTagSupport;
import javax.servlet.jsp.tagext.DynamicAttributes;
import java.util.HashMap;
import java.util.Iterator;
import java.io.IOException;

public class DynamicTableCellTag extends SimpleTagSupport
    implements DynamicAttributes {
```

When using SimpleTag, there's only one lifecycle method to implement: doTag(). In your handler, you first define a HashMap that will be used to store the dynamic attributes that will be set by the container. The attrValue object is a generic attribute value that a dynamic attribute holds. The evenCell is a defined attribute so you can see how dynamic and declared attributes interact. The evenCell attribute determines whether the cell being generated is an even or odd cell. This handler will set the background color of the cell depending on the value of this attribute:

```
private HashMap attributes = new HashMap();
private Object attrValue = null;
private boolean evenCell = false;
```

The doTag() method is the meat of the tag handler. The first thing you do is to get the current JspWriter from the JspContext. Simple tags have the flexibility to run in other environments besides the servlet environment, so you're explicitly getting the value from the JspContext:

```
public void doTag() throws JspException, IOException {
  JspWriter out = getJspContext().getOut();
```

Next, you'll iterate through all of the attributes that have been set. The attribute name and value are a result of the JSP container making calls to setDynamicAttribute(), which is in the implementation of the interface.

For each attribute, you'll get the value and then format it correctly according to an HTML table cell element. As an example, you can use a private method called validate-Value() if there's any type of validation you may want to do. You can decide whether you want to continue with the processing by throwing an Exception if the validation fails.

Next, you check your defined attribute to see if you have a value set for it. If so, then you'll present the appropriate background color for the cell. Note that it's perfectly logical that you may have just made evenCell a dynamic attribute called bgcolor and passed the appropriate value when you wanted to use it:

```
Iterator i = attributes.keySet().iterator();
out.println("<td ");
while( i.hasNext() ) {
  String key = (String)i.next();
  attrValue = attributes.get( key );
  if (!validateValue(attrValue)) {
    throw new JspException();
  }

out.println(  key + " = \"" + attrValue + "\" " );

  if (evenCell) {
    out.println(" bgcolor=\"#00FF00\"");
  } else {
    out.println(" bgcolor=\"#008000\"");
  }
}
```

Once you've completed forming your `<td>` element, you close out the tag:

```
out.println(" >");
```

Now comes another interesting part: When using `SimpleTagSupport`, it's still possible to get the tag's body content. Make a note of how easy this is so you can look back to the code to get the body content with a classic implementation and then appreciate the simplicity. Here, the JSP container will set the body content value in a `JspFragment` object by calling `setJspBody()`, which is part of the `SimpleTag` interface. The `SimpleTagSupport` class provides the convenience method `getJspBody()`, and you use it to get the `JspFragment` object. You can then simply use the `invoke()` method on the fragment to run the contents of that fragment.

You're passing two `null` values here. The first one indicates that you just want to write to the current `JspWriter`. The second parameter would be a `HashMap` of parameters if the fragment required any. In this case, you just have template text included for your body content, so you don't require any parameters:

```
getJspBody().invoke(null);
```

Then to finish it off, you close the `<td>` element with the appropriate `</td>`:

```
    out.println(" </td>");
  }
```

Each time this tag is invoked from a JSP page, the `doTag()` method will be executed.

The following code shows the rest of the tag handler for completeness. The `setEvenCell()` is the required setter for the attribute you explicitly declared for this tag. We've already talked about the implementation of the `setDynamicAttribute()` method. The `validateValue()` method just shows how you can have your own custom code within your tag handlers that still interacts within the `doTag()`:

```
  public void setEvenCell(boolean evenCell){
    this.evenCell = evenCell;
  }

  public void setDynamicAttribute( String uri, String localName, Object value )
  throws JspException {
    attributes.put( localName, value );
  }

  private boolean validateValue(Object attrValue){
    return true;
  }
}
```

Before continuing, you'll now briefly look at the TLD file entry to describe this tag and the JSP file that actually uses the tag. The TLD file entry looks just like any other tag entry discussed, with one exception. The `<dynamic-attributes>` element is set to `true` for the tag:

```
<tag>
  <description>
    Demonstrate using dynamic attributes to build an HTML table cell
  </description>
  <name>dynamicTableCell</name>
  <tag-class>com.apress.proj2ee.chapter05.DynamicTableCellTag</tag-class>
  <dynamic-attributes>true</dynamic-attributes>
  <body-content>scriptless</body-content>
  <attribute>
    <name>evenCell</name>
    <required>false</required>
  </attribute>
</tag>
```

Setting `<dynamic-attributes>` to `true` will indicate to the JSP container that the `<tag-class>` defined implements the `DynamicAttributes` interface. If this attribute is set and the tag class doesn't implement the interface, an error will occur.

The JSP file shows the true power of using dynamic attributes. You first define the taglib you'll use:

```
<%@ taglib prefix="proj2ee" uri="/apress-taglib"%>
```

In this example, the sole purpose is to see the flexibility in using the dynamic attributes. You define an HTML table and then create each cell based on some criteria. Granted, if you were implementing this for a more robust environment, you may want to make the table itself a custom action with dynamic attributes as well as introduce some runtime values or EL evaluations into the attribute values.

For now, you'll stick with the basics so you can see how the mechanism works. Then it'll be up to you to create dynamic attributes to your heart's content:

```
Demonstrate using dynamic attributes to build an HTML table
<html>
  <body>
    <table border="2" cellpadding="0" cellspacing="0" width="100%">
      <tr>
```

The first use of the custom action shows both a dynamic attribute `width` and the defined attribute `evenCell`. There's also a body content value of `cell 1`:

```
<proj2ee:dynamicTableCell width="50%" evenCell="true" >
  cell 1
</proj2ee:dynamicTableCell>
```

The attributes are set in the order they appear, regardless of whether it's a dynamic or declared attribute. The container calls the appropriate method. In this example, you'd get calls in the following order:

- `setDynamicAttribute` that would look like this:

  ```
  setDynamicAttribute(null, "width", "50%")
  setEvenCell(true)
  ```

- The container would set the body content using the `setJspBody()` method call.

The next evaluation of the tag has two different dynamic attributes and another call to your declared attribute. The `evenCell` attribute is being set here to a different value so that it's clear that each invocation of the tag handler is a new invocation:

```
<proj2ee:dynamicTableCell width="50%" style="font-weight: bold"
                          evenCell="false" >
  cell 2
</proj2ee:dynamicTableCell>
```

The third call to the custom action has another dynamic attribute, without the declared attribute. The `evenCell` value will be that of the default defined in the tag handler. You then close out the rest of your table elements to finish your table:

```
      </tr>
      <tr>
        <proj2ee:dynamicTableCell align="center" >
          cell 3
        </proj2ee:dynamicTableCell>
      </tr>
    </table>
  </body>
</html>
```

From this brief sample, it should be clear that using `SimpleTagSupport` as well as dynamic attributes provides a lot of flexibility within your tag handlers. It makes it easier to implement custom actions that are based on some well-known set of attributes without putting the burden on the tag developer to implement every attribute.

Do You Need a TagAdapter?

The `javax.servlet.jsp.tagext.TagAdapter` class encapsulates any `SimpleTag` and exposes it using a `Tag` interface. Recall that `SimpleTag` doesn't extend from `Tag`, and this causes a problem because `Tag.setParent()` accepts only a `Tag` instance. Therefore, a classic tag handler can't have a `SimpleTag` as its parent. This becomes an issue if you have collaboration going on between actions.

To alleviate this dilemma, `TagAdapter` wraps a `SimpleTag` so that it can be set as the parent of a classic tag using `setParent()`. If you need to retrieve the encapsulated instance of the `SimpleTag`, you do so using the `getAdaptee()` method of the instance.

The `TagAdapter` class methods look just like those of classic handlers. The methods include the following:

```
int doEndTag()
int doStartTag()
void release()
void setPageContent(PageContext pc)
void setParent(Tag parentTag)
```

However, none of these methods is permitted to be called. Calling them throws a `java.lang.UnsupportedOperationException` exception.

The methods of interest are as follows:

`JspTag getAdaptee()`, which gets the tag that's being adapted to the `Tag` interface. This is usually a `SimpleTag`, but using a `JspTag` instance allows this method to support other tag types should they become available.

`Tag getParent()` that returns the parent of this tag, which is always `getAdaptee().getParent()`. This can be either the enclosing `Tag` if `getAdaptee().getParent()` implements `Tag` or an adapter to the enclosing `Tag`. An adapter would be returned if `getAdaptee().getParent()` doesn't implement `Tag`.

Using a Tag Library Validator Class

As you've seen, custom actions can provide a lot of functionality to the page author. Along with that comes flexibility; but be warned, sometimes *too much* flexibility is allowed. The JSP container provides some validation implicitly. For example, the TLD makes sure that an action has all of the required attributes, that runtime expressions are used where appropriate, or that the correct body content type is being used with the action.

It's also possible for the action to do validation within the tag handler to make sure the information it's receiving is valid. These types of validation are fine, but what about if you want to validate page structure? Case in point: you want to make sure that one tag is always nested within another specific tag or that tags are used in a certain order on the page.

When a page author wants to restrict how an action is used or validate that an action is being used correctly, it's possible to use a validator class. A `TagLibraryValidator` class, or just a TLV, may be listed in the TLD for a tag library.

During translation of a JSP page, but prior to the Java code being generated, the JSP page is transformed to its XML representation. This is the XML view mentioned earlier. This view is handy for validation purposes. This view is exposed to a `validate()` method in the validator class as a `javax.servlet.jsp.tagext.PageData` object. Using the `getInputStream()` method of `PageData`, it's possible to access the entire page. The TLV is used on a library level, not on a page level. This means that whenever the tag library is imported onto a page using the `taglib` directive, the TLV is used to validate the page.

The method signature of `validate()` is as follows:

```
public ValidationMessage[] validate(java.lang.String prefix,
                                    java.lang.String uri,
                                    PageData page)
```

The `prefix` and `uri` parameters are passed in so that the TLV can concern itself only with those tags of the library it's trying to validate. The values are set from the `taglib` directive on the page. The `PageData` contains the XML view of the JSP page that's being validated. The return value of `ValidationMessage[]` is an array of `ValidationMessage` objects. If the return value is `null`, or the array length is zero, then the page is considered valid.

As of JSP 2.0, JSP containers must support the `jsp:id` attribute. This helps provide higher-quality validation errors. The container will track the JSP pages as passed to the container and will assign a unique ID to each element. This ID is then passed as the value of the `jsp:id` attribute; each XML element in the XML view available will be extended with this attribute.

The `TagLibraryValidator` can then use the attribute in one or more `ValidationMessage` objects. The container, in turn, can use these values to provide the location of the error. The mandatory support of `jsp:id` is something that's a more than welcome addition if you've ever tried to locate JSP errors. The `ValidationMessage` object has the following methods of interest:

- `getId()` for getting `jsp:id` value
- `getMessage()` for getting the localized validation message

The validator class is specified in the TLD by using the `<validator>` element. This allows the container to know which class to use when the tag library is to be validated.

You'll now see a complete sample to see how this all fits together. It doesn't really matter what order you accomplish these tasks; as long as they're all completed correctly, your validation will take place. Note that to code a validator class, you need to be somewhat familiar with either the DOM or SAX processing. This familiarity is necessary because you'll parse an XML file to determine if the custom action is specified correctly.

We won't go into detail about how the DOM or SAX processing works. If you're going to be coding complex validators, you should spend some time getting familiar with the processing APIs. With that said, you'll now look at a validator class implementation.

Defining the Validator Class

In this section, you'll define a validator class. This class will be called when the `taglib` directive is found in a JSP page. Set up the Java file so that your class extends from `TagLibraryValidator` (see Listing 5-12).

Listing 5-12. Validator Class

```
package com.apress.proj2ee.chapter05.tlv;

import java.io.*;
import java.util.*;
import javax.servlet.jsp.*;
import javax.servlet.jsp.tagext.*;
import javax.xml.parsers.*;
import org.xml.sax.*;
import org.w3c.dom.*;
import org.xml.sax.helpers.*;

public class APressTLV extends TagLibraryValidator {
```

For simplicity's sake, you'll define some constant variables that you can use within your validator for checking well-known IDs or attributes. Typically, you want to have your error messages in a resource file so that they can be localized if that's required. You'll also define some specific HTML formatting information so that when the errors are displayed, it's immediately obvious what the problem is by the fact that each error will be larger than other type and will be displayed in red (see Listing 5-13).

Listing 5-13. HTML Formatting

```
private static String JSP_ID = "jsp:id";
// List of actions you are interested in
private static String COURSE = "course";
/* List of error messages
 * These messages could (should) go into a resource file for localization
 * purposes.
 * For simplicity, we are defining them here.
 */
private static String REQUIRED_ATTRIBUTE = " is a required attribute.";
// Attributes
```

```
private static String COURSE_NAME = "courseName";

// Validation Formatting
private static String FORMAT_ERROR_OPEN="<h2><font color=\"#FF0000\">";
private static String FORMAT_ERROR_CLOSE="</font></h2>";
// Print XML View of JSP
private static boolean xmlView = true;
```

Next you have some of the TLV lifecycle event methods: First is a zero-argument constructor, followed by the `release()` method (see Listing 5-14). In the constructor, you'll create a document builder so that you have a reference to an XML parser. Since the JSP container can reuse TLVs, creating an XML parser through a factory allows you to create it once, store it, and then use it whenever it's required. This allows for some performance improvement. If there are any resources that your validator requires, you can free them in the `release()` method.

Listing 5-14. TLV Lifecycle Event Methods

```
private DocumentBuilder docBuilder;

public APressTLV() {
  super();
  try {
    DocumentBuilderFactory factory = DocumentBuilderFactory.newInstance();
    this.docBuilder = factory.newDocumentBuilder();
  } catch (ParserConfigurationException pce){
    pce.printStackTrace();
  }
}

public void release() {
  super.release();
}
```

The real method of interest in the validator is the `validate()` method. This method is called to do the actual validation that's required for the tag library. `validate()` takes three parameters. The first is the `prefix` of the taglib that's used on the JSP page. This is defined in the `taglib` directive using the `prefix` attribute. The next parameter is the `uri`, also from the `taglib` directive.

The third parameter is the page data itself. This is the XML view of the JSP page and is the XML file that will be parsed to determine which elements are of interest to the validator. You get a DOM view of the XML document using the `docBuilder.parse()` method. Then you do the actual validation in the private `validateNode()` method. `validate()` returns any error messages related to the tag library found on the JSP page. However, the real workhorse here is the `validateNode()` method (see Listing 5-15).

Listing 5-15. `validateNode()` *Method*

```
public synchronized ValidationMessage[] validate(
  String prefix, String uri, PageData page) {

  List messages = new ArrayList();

  try {
    if (xmlView) {
      printXMLView(page);
    }
    Document doc = docBuilder.parse(page.getInputStream());
    Node node = doc.getDocumentElement();
    validateNode(prefix, node, messages);
  } catch (IOException ioe){
    ioe.printStackTrace();
  } catch (SAXException saxe) {
    saxe.printStackTrace();
  }

  return(ValidationMessage[])messages.toArray(new ValidationMessage[] {});
}
```

The `validateNode()` method takes the current XML node and checks to see if it's an item of interest. You're examining only those elements in the JSP page that are related to the tag library actions defined for this library. This is where the defined validation happens according to how the library author decides.

In the sample shown in Listing 5-16, you're simply checking to make sure that an attribute called `courseName` is used in the tag. If it isn't, then you add the appropriate error message to the messages list so that the JSP container can display it. You're using the `jsp:id` so that you can give more information to the JSP author about where the error occurred.

The `validateNode()` method is called recursively until the entire XML document has been processed. Each error message will be added to the list correctly with the appropriate `jsp:id`. This allows all of the errors found on the page related to the tag library to be displayed at once, instead of by piecemeal. This makes it easier for the page author to fix all of the errors before trying to redeploy.

Listing 5-16. `validateNode` *Method Example*

```
private void validateNode(String prefix, Node node, List messages){

  if (node.getNodeName().equals(prefix + ":" + COURSE)){
    if (!node.hasAttributes()){
      messages.add(formatError(null, COURSE_NAME + REQUIRED_ATTRIBUTE));
    } else {
      NamedNodeMap attributes = node.getAttributes();
      Node courseName = attributes.getNamedItem(COURSE_NAME);
```

```
        if (courseName == null) {
          String jspId = null;
          Node jspIdAttribute = attributes.getNamedItem(JSP_ID);
          if (jspIdAttribute != null){
            jspId = jspIdAttribute.getNodeValue();
          }
          messages.add(formatError(jspId, COURSE_NAME + REQUIRED_ATTRIBUTE));
        }
      }
    }

    if (node.hasChildNodes()) {
      NodeList children = node.getChildNodes();
      for (int i = 0;i < children.getLength(); i++){
        validateNode(prefix, children.item(i), messages);
      }
    }
  }
```

A couple of utility routines format the validation error messages and print the XML view of the JSP page (see Listing 5-17). This view can be useful since it makes it a lot easier to find the `jsp:id` attribute being reported.

Listing 5-17. Utility Routines

```
  private ValidationMessage formatError(String jspId, String error){
    return (new ValidationMessage(FORMAT_ERROR_OPEN + JSP_ID + "=" + jspId,
                                  error + FORMAT_ERROR_CLOSE));
  }

  private void printXMLView(PageData page){
    InputStream in = page.getInputStream();
    int aChar;
    try {
      while ((aChar = in.read()) >= 0){
        System.out.print((char)aChar);
      }

    } catch (Exception e){
      System.out.println("Exception thrown while ⏎
                          printing XML View " + e.getMessage());
    }
  }
}
```

The <validator> TLD Entry

Before being able to use the validator class, you need to associate it with a tag library. You do this in the TLD file using the `<validator>` element and defining the validator class. The code to do so is as follows:

```
<validator>
  <validator-class>com.apress.proj2ee.chapter05.tlv.APressTLV</validator-class>
</validator>
```

Validating a JSP Page

Lastly, you'll look at the JSP page that has the action declared on it. The `proj2ee` prefix and the `/apress-tablib` URI are passed as the `prefix` and `uri` parameters in the `validate()` method of the validator:

```
<%@ taglib prefix="proj2ee" uri="/apress-taglib" %>
<html>
  <body>
    This page will demonstrate how a TLV works
    <br><hr>
      <proj2ee:course/>
      <proj2ee:course/>
  </body>
</html>
```

In this sample, you have the `course` action used in two elements, neither of which have the appropriate `courseName` attribute that you're validating. The reason why we're showing two elements here is so that you can see that there's a unique `jsp:id` returned for each element in Figure 5-7.

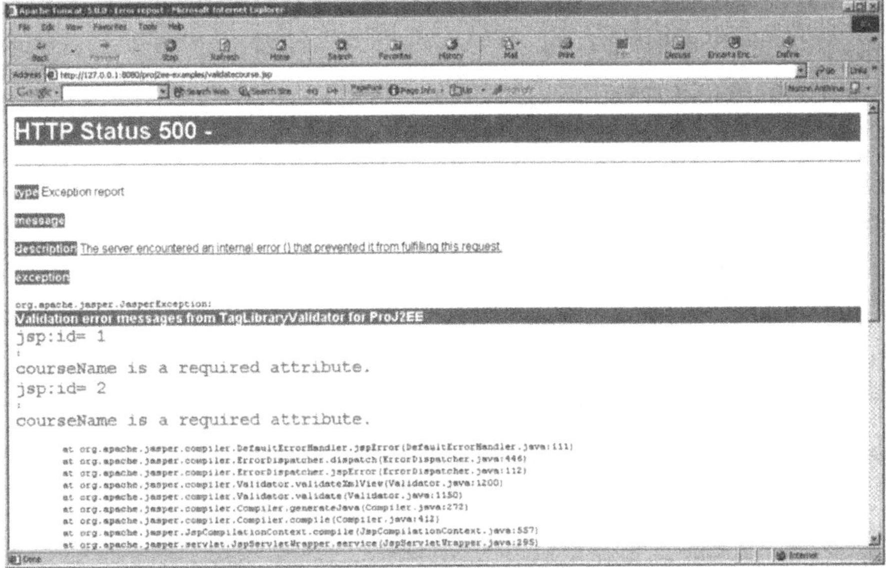

Figure 5-7. Unique `jsp:id`

It's then trivial to look at the output from your utility method that prints the XML view and see exactly where the error is located. If you look at the XML view of this JSP page, you can quickly locate the `jsp:id` that matches the ones displayed in your error message (see Listing 5-18).

Listing 5-18. XML View

```
<jsp:root
  jsp:id="0"
  xmlns:jsp="http://java.sun.com/JSP/Page"
  version="1.2"
  xmlns:proj2ee="/apress-taglib"
>
<jsp:text><![CDATA[

]]>
</jsp:text><jsp:text><![CDATA[

]]>
</jsp:text><jsp:text><![CDATA[
<html>

]]>
</jsp:text><jsp:text><![CDATA[
<body>
This page will demonstrate how a TLV works
]]>
</jsp:text><jsp:text><![CDATA[
<br>]]>
</jsp:text><jsp:text><![CDATA[
<hr>
]]>
</jsp:text><proj2ee:course
  jsp:id="1"
/>
<jsp:text><![CDATA[

]]>
</jsp:text><proj2ee:course
  jsp:id="2"
/>
<jsp:text><![CDATA[


]]>
</jsp:text><jsp:text><![CDATA[
</body>
]]>
</jsp:text><jsp:text><![CDATA[
</html>]]>
</jsp:text></jsp:root>
```

Summary

This chapter has covered a lot of ground. After reading it, you should have a thorough understanding of the new features available in the JSP 2.0 specification. We covered what you need to know to write your own custom actions, regardless of which implementation you choose. Custom actions are useful for creating reusable JSP components.

New in the JSP 2.0 specification are the notions of tag files and JSP fragments. These are simple ways to create custom actions without having to know how to write Java. They provide a mechanism for page authors to create their own custom tag libraries without the worry of having to write complicated Java code. Using tag files provides a mechanism for eliminating writing TLD files since the JSP container generates implicit TLD files for them. There's also a flexible mechanism in place for packaging and deploying tag libraries in JSP 2.0.

It's also possible to write classic actions using the various interfaces available. These include the following:

- `Tag`
- `BodyTag`
- `IterationTag`

Another feature introduced in this chapter was the new JSP 2.0 `SimpleTag` interface, which has a much simpler life cycle defined than the classic tag interfaces. `SimpleTag` allows for all of the power of cooperating and iteration tags with less hassle in the coding. Other new features include using dynamic attributes in actions that allow tag handlers to accept attributes that haven't been declared in a TLD.

In addition, you learned how to build and configure validators for tag libraries. This is a powerful mechanism for providing detailed validation on custom action usage within a tag library. It allows the library implementer the ability to ensure that the actions are being used as intended on the JSP page. It also allows for a much more detailed mechanism for providing the page author with error messages, not only as to what the problem is, but also the `jsp:id` for locating the exact location of the problem.

Anyone who is working with JSP technology should have an understanding of the power of using custom actions within JSP pages and take advantage of the many features provided.

CHAPTER 6

Working with Servlets

Servlets form the basis for much of the Web application architecture in the Java 2 Enterprise Edition (J2EE) platform. Since being introduced back in 1996, they've become the de facto standard for how you deal with various elements of your server-side code. This chapter covers how to incorporate features now available within the Servlet 2.4 specification. During the course of this chapter, you'll do the following:

- You'll examine the classes and interfaces of the Servlet application programming interface (API), focusing particularly on the `javax.servlet` package.
- You'll also consider the classes and interfaces related to the life cycle of a servlet.
- You'll look at the request/response cycle and the interfaces and classes associated with it.
- You'll look at document type definitions (DTDs) and Extensible Markup Language (XML) schemas; the deployment descriptor is now defined in terms of an XML schema document.
- You'll learn about lifecycle, attribute, request, and response event listeners, which are mechanisms for listening to events that may be of interest to an application.
- You'll learn about filters that give you the ability to configure filters to be invoked under the request dispatcher.
- You'll see best practices when dealing with servlets.
- You'll develop an application using the servlet classes and interfaces discussed in this chapter.

Introducing Servlet 2.4

Servlets are one of the most popular technologies of the J2EE environment. They're the basic building blocks for the Web-based applications discussed in this book. For example, each JavaServer Pages (JSP) page is translated and compiled into a servlet class, as you saw in Chapter 3. In its most basic sense, a servlet is just a Java class used to extend the capabilities of Web servers. Well, OK, maybe there's a little more to it, but, really, it all boils down to that. Servlet technology is the basis for a number of J2EE 1.4 technologies, including the following:

- Java API for XML-Based RPC (JAX-RPC)
- Java portlet technology
- Java API for XML Messaging (JAXM)
- Frameworks such as Struts, JavaServer Faces, and the Sun ONE application framework

You access the servlet via a request/response programming model. This model is usually Hypertext Transfer Protocol (HTTP), which is what you'll focus on in this chapter.

The Servlet API consists of the following two packages:

- The `javax.servlet` package contains nine classes and fourteen interfaces that describe and support generic, protocol-independent servlets.
- The `javax.servlet.http` package contains seven classes and eight interfaces that describe and define the servlet running under HTTP, along with support for dealing with the runtime environment provided by a servlet container.

The prevalence of interfaces in the Servlet API allows you to customize and optimize servlet implementations to the requirements of a specific servlet container. For example, the API specifies servlet request and response interfaces, but the container provides the underlying class implementations for them. From the container vendor's point of view, this allows the container to determine the optimal implementation, given the container's characteristics and requirements and the client's requirements for the Web application. These could include an objective such as optimization for HTTP access.

Introducing Servlets and the MVC Pattern

Before diving into the details of writing servlets, this section takes a step back and shows where servlets fit into the scheme of things. While you can use servlets for many tasks that are required when generating dynamic content, they fit nicely into the Controller role in the Model-View-Controller (MVC) pattern. The Controller object knows about how components are wired together. Usually this happens by means of some type of configuration file specific to your application or framework. The term *wired* in this case[1] means that the Controller knows what to do when users manipulate data within the model.

A Controller translates interactions with the View into actions to be performed by the Model. In a Web application, this interaction usually appears as HTTP `GET` and `POST` requests. The actions performed by the Model include activating business processes and changing the state of the model. The Controller responds by selecting an appropriate View, based on the user interactions and the outcome of the Model actions.

If you're working with an existing framework, chances are that there's already a Controller servlet in place for you. This is the case with the Struts Framework where you find the `ActionServlet` class. This class implements the Front Controller pattern. The Front Controller pattern is an example of a pattern within a pattern, since it's frequently used within the MVC pattern.

All the requests for an application go through the Controller. The advantage of this setup is that you can keep common functionality in one place. Items such as security, application initialization state, or any workflow that's required by all requests in the application can reside in one place. This may include applying filters or listeners, which we'll talk about later in this chapter in the "Filter Definitions and Filter Mappings" section.

Introducing the javax.servlet Package

The `javax.servlet` package provides the contract between the Web application and the Web container. It allows the servlet container vendor to focus on developing the container in the manner most suited to their requirements (or those of their customers), as long as they provide the specified implementations of the servlet interfaces for the Web application. From a developer's perspective, the package provides a standard library to process client requests and develop servlet-based Web applications.

Figure 6-1 shows the classes and interfaces present in the `javax.servlet` package.

At the heart of the `javax.servlet` package is the `Servlet` interface that defines the core structure of a servlet. This is the basis for all servlet implementations, but for most servlet implementations, you subclass from a defined implementation of this interface that provides the basis for your Web applications.

The additional interfaces and classes provide additional services to the developer. An example of such a service is the servlet container that provides the servlet with access to the client request through a standard interface. The `javax.servlet` package therefore provides the basis for developing a cross-platform, cross-servlet container Web application, allowing the programmers to focus on developing a Web application.

Developers sometimes tend to focus on the `javax.servlet.http` package, but understanding the `javax.servlet` package will help you use both packages optimally. Additionally, should you need to, you can use this package to build your own servlet

---

1. This is as opposed to the case of the software engineer who is wired on their daily dose of caffeine.

implementation that uses a protocol that isn't HTTP. For example, you could extend from the `javax.servlet` package to implement a Simple Mail Transfer Protocol (SMTP) servlet that provides e-mail services to clients.

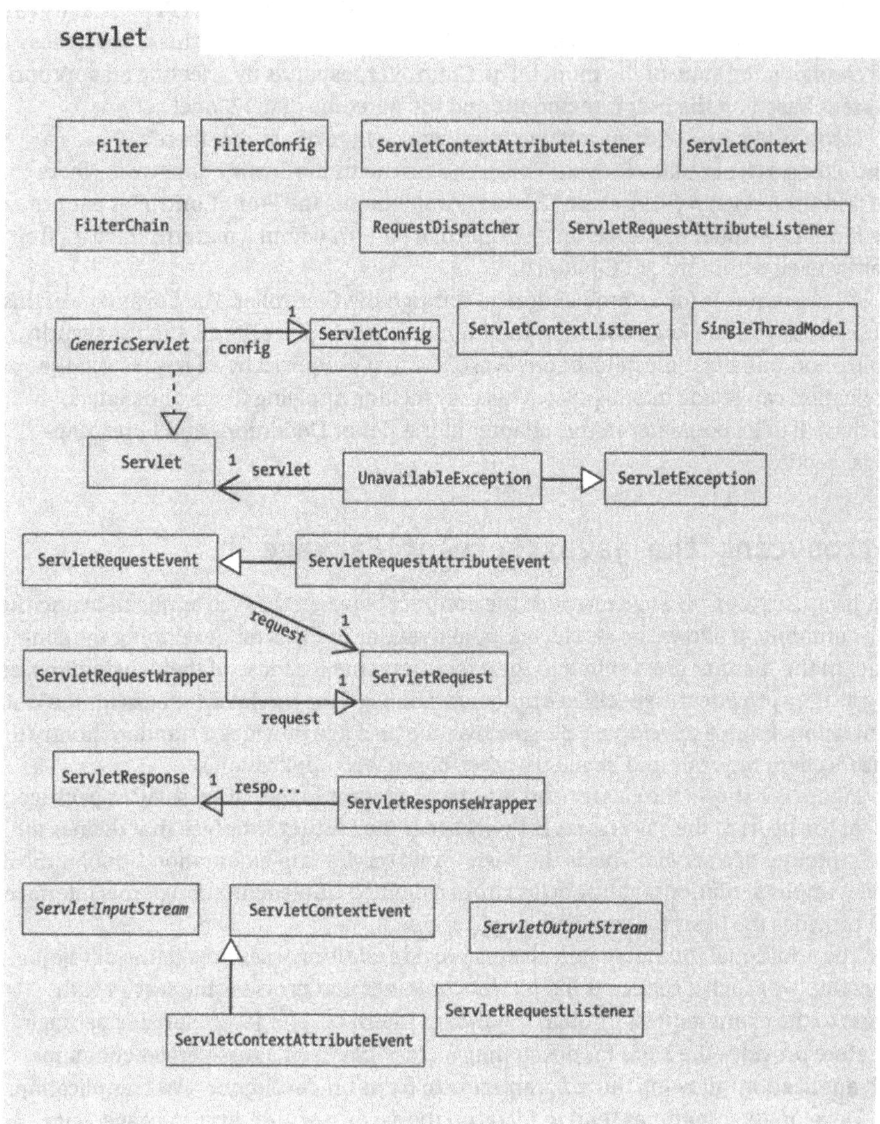

Figure 6-1. `javax.servlet` *classes and interfaces*

The following sections cover the interfaces, classes, and exception classes of the `javax.servlet` package.

The javax.servlet Interfaces

The `javax.servlet` package comprises 14 interfaces. The servlet container provides the implementation of the following seven interfaces:

- `ServletConfig`
- `ServletContext`
- `ServletRequest`
- `ServletResponse`
- `RequestDispatcher`
- `FilterChain`
- `FilterConfig`

The container must provide these objects to the servlet. It provides them as interfaces so that the vendor can decide the most suitable implementation for their container.

Probably the most important method of the `ServletConfig` interface is the `getServletContext()` method. This method returns the `ServletContext` object. The `ServletContext` object communicates with the servlet container when you want to perform actions such as writing to a log file or dispatching requests. There's only one `ServletContext` object per Web application (per Java virtual machine [JVM]). This is initialized when the Web application starts and destroyed only when the Web application shuts down. One useful application of the `ServletContext` object is as a persistence mechanism. A programmer may store attributes in the `ServletContext` so that they're available throughout a user's visit, not just for the duration of their request.

The servlet container provides classes that implement the `ServletRequest` and `ServletResponse` interfaces. These classes provide the client request information to the servlet and the object used to send a response to the client.

`RequestDispatcher` defines an object that manages client requests by directing them to the appropriate resource on the server.

`FilterChain`, `FilterConfig`, and `Filter` (which you'll see in the following list of interfaces) make up the filtering functionality now available to developers. You can use a `Filter` to filter both requests and responses to and from a servlet. You can also combine them into chains; the request comes in at one end and goes through each filter in turn, before being processed by the container. The response then goes down the chain in reverse.

> **TIP** *Filtering has a wide range of uses including authentication, logging, and localization. We'll cover it in detail in Chapter 8.*

The programmer building the Web application implements the remaining seven interfaces:

- `Servlet`
- `ServletRequestListener`
- `ServletRequestAttributeListener`
- `ServletContextListener`
- `ServletContextAttributeListener`
- `SingleThreadModel`
- `Filter`

These programmer interfaces are defined so that the container can invoke the implementations using the methods defined in the interface. Hence, the servlet container needs to know about only the methods defined in the interface while the details of the implementation are up to the developer.

The `Servlet` interface defines the lifecycle methods that cover the main events in the life of the basic servlet: initialization, service, and destruction. The interface also includes the `getServletConfig()` method, which the servlet can use to access the `ServletConfig` object. The servlet container uses a `ServletConfig` object to pass initialization information to the servlet.

The `ServletRequestListener` interface can be implemented by objects that need to be notified of requests coming in and out of scope in a Web component. A request is defined as coming into scope when it's about to enter the first filter in the filter chain that will process it and as going out of scope when it exits the first filter in its filter chain. The `ServletRequestAttributeListener` interface is implemented when an object needs to be notified of attribute changes in a request. This could be when an attribute is added, removed, or replaced in the servlet request.

The `ServletContextListener` interface is a lifecycle interface that programmers implement to listen for changes to the `ServletContext` object. This means that lifecycle events such as the initialization and destruction of the `ServletContext` object trigger a `ServletContextListener` implementation listening to this Web application. A `ServletContextAttributeListener` object performs a similar function, but it listens for changes to the attribute list on the `ServletContext` object.

> **TIP** *The* `SingleThreadModel` *interface has no methods and, when implemented, ensures that a servlet can handle only one request at a time. This interface should rarely, if ever, be implemented by your servlet. Your servlets should strive to be thread safe so they don't take a tremendous performance hit when being used by multiple clients.*

The javax.servlet Classes

This package contains the following nine classes (plus two exception classes that we'll cover in a moment):

- `GenericServlet`
- `ServletContextEvent`
- `ServletContextAttributeEvent`
- `ServletRequestEvent`
- `ServletRequestAttributeEvent`
- `ServletInputStream`
- `ServletOutputStream`
- `ServletRequestWrapper`
- `ServletResponseWrapper`

You can use the `GenericServlet` abstract class to develop protocol-independent servlets; it requires only that you implement the `service()` method. Although it's more common to use the `HttpServlet` class (from the `javax.servlet.http` package), it's relatively straightforward to extend from `GenericServlet` and implement your own protocol-based servlet. The biggest headache is ensuring that you fully and accurately implement the protocol.

`ServletContextEvent` and `ServletContextAttributeEvent` are the event classes used for notification about changes to the `ServletContext` object and to the attributes of it, respectively.

The two new classes in Servlet 2.4, `ServletRequestEvent` and `ServletRequestAttributeEvent`, are the event classes used to indicate lifecycle events and attribute events for a `ServletRequest`. The source of the event is the `ServletContext` of this Web application.

The `ServletInputStream` and `ServletOutputStream` classes provide input and output streams for reading or sending binary data to and from the client, respectively.

Finally, the wrapper classes (`ServletRequestWrapper` and `ServletResponseWrapper`) provide useful implementations of the `ServletRequest` and `ServletResponse` interfaces, respectively. You can then subclass this implementation to allow programmers to adapt or enhance the functionality of the wrapped object for their own Web application. You may do this to implement a basic protocol agreed upon between the client and server or to transparently adapt requests or responses to a specific format required by the Web application.

The javax.servlet Exception Classes

The `javax.servlet` package contains the following two exceptions:

- `ServletException`
- `UnavailableException`

`ServletException` is a general exception that a servlet can throw if it hits problems and has to give up. This may be thrown to indicate a problem with the user's request, with processing the request, or with sending the response.

This exception is thrown to the servlet container, and the application loses control of the request being processed. The servlet container then has the responsibility of cleaning up the request and returning a response to the client. Depending upon the container's implementation and configuration, the container may return an error page to the user indicating a server problem.

It's best to throw a `ServletException` only as a last resort. The preferred mechanism for dealing with an insurmountable problem is to handle the problem and then return an indication of the problem to the client.

The application should throw the `UnavailableException` when a filter or servlet is temporarily or permanently unavailable. This could apply to resources required by the servlet to process requests (such as a database, a domain name server, or another servlet) not available, or it may simply be that the servlet load factor is too high.

Introducing the Servlet Interface

All servlets must implement the `Servlet` interface, but most will extend from a class that has already implemented `Servlet`.

The Servlet API provides the abstract class `GenericServlet` that implements the `Servlet` interface. It provides concrete implementations of all but the `service()` method defined in the `Servlet` interface, so when you extend `GenericServlet`, you must at least implement this method. However, it also means that when you're developing a servlet, you can leave much of the standard work to the methods inherited from `GenericServlet`. You need to override the other methods only if you specifically want to alter the default implementation. You'll look more closely at `GenericServlet` in the "Introducing the GenericServlet Class" section.

The Life Cycle of a Servlet

The `Servlet` interface defines the following lifecycle methods, called by the servlet container:

```
public void init(ServletConfig config) throws ServletException
public void service(ServletRequest req, ServletResponse res)
                                     throws ServletException, IOException
public void destroy()
```

When we talk about the servlet's life cycle, we're talking about the period of time that a servlet instance is created, lives, and dies. The servlet container will create instances of the servlet according to its design and how often the servlet is called. The container has a lot of freedom in managing the servlet's life cycle, in that it can keep a single instance of a servlet around for a long time to process requests, pool a number of instances of the servlet to process requests, or instantiate a new servlet for each request. It makes sense for the container to manage servlet instances according to some optimal pattern of usage so as not to waste resources on the server.

The servlet life cycle is clearly defined. A client makes a request to the Web server, which redirects the request (as necessary) to the servlet container. The process is as follows:

1. The loading and instantiation of the servlet is the responsibility of the servlet container. The container must locate the servlet classes, load the servlet using normal class loading procedures, and instantiate it so it's ready for use.

2. The container initializes the servlet by calling the servlet's `init()` method. The container passes an object implementing the `ServletConfig` interface via the `init()` method. This object provides the servlet with access to the object that implements the `ServletContext` interface (which describes the servlet's run-time environment). The `init()` method is also responsible for performing any other initialization required by the servlet, which can include setting up resources that the servlet will require to process requests, such as database connections.

3. In the event that the servlet is unsuccessfully initialized, an `UnavailableException` or `ServletException` is thrown, the servlet is released, and attempts are made to instantiate and initialize a new servlet.

4. The servlet is now ready to handle client requests. The request and response information is wrapped in `ServletRequest` and `ServletResponse` objects, respectively, which are then passed to the servlet's `service()` method. This method is then responsible for processing the request and returning the response.

5. Instances of both ServletException and UnavailableException can occur during request handling. If an exception is thrown, the container is forced to clean up the request, possibly unloading the instance and calling the servlet's destroy() method.

6. Once the servlet container decides to remove the servlet from service, the container must allow any service() method calls to terminate (or time out). Then it will call the servlet's destroy() method. Once the destroy() method has completed, the container will release the servlet instance for garbage collection. If it needs another instance of the servlet to process requests, it must start the process again.

Obtaining Initialization Parameters

The Servlet interface defines another method that servlets must implement:

```
public ServletConfig getServletConfig()
```

The getServletConfig() method is designed to return a reference to the ServletConfig object, which contains initialization and startup parameters for the servlet. This object is passed to the servlet during initialization and can be stored for future use by the servlet, but how the servlet will treat the ServletConfig object isn't specified in the Servlet specification. Normally it's expected that a reference to it is stored in the servlet so that it can be accessed in the getServletConfig() method.

Servlet Threading Issues

It's important to understand that the container may receive many requests, and often these will occur simultaneously or virtually simultaneously, so your container will be responsible for establishing separate threads to process each request. The service() method may be called simultaneously by the container in different threads to process many different requests.

While the container has the responsibility for handling the requests in separate threads, this can have implications for your servlets. You need to code your servlets to be thread safe. For example, consider a class variable count. If this was accessed and updated from a service() method more than once, its value on the second and subsequent accesses could be altered by another thread servicing another request. Since the value can be altered in another thread, its value may become meaningless unless you *synchronize* access to it. Servlets provide an alternative to this with the SingleThreadModel interface. Don't use this interface for the reason you already saw.

Efficient Servlet Lifecycle Management

When the servlet instance is unloaded from memory by the servlet container, the servlet container will call the `destroy()` method on the servlet. This is called only after all calls to the `service()` method have completed or timed out. The servlet container may unload servlet instances at any time according to the container's policies. The container has to have sensible policies regarding the loading and unloading of servlet instances, as there's a performance cost to inefficient or excessive object creation and destruction. For example, it wouldn't usually make sense to instantiate a new servlet for every request, so containers usually reuse instances.

The purpose of the `destroy()` method is to make sure that any data is finalized and resources are released before the servlet instance is lost. This is one of the reasons why a server should always be shut down gracefully, using the appropriate shutdown command, rather than just closing the server window. Shutting down a server gracefully allows the server to complete any requests that are under way and to call the `destroy()` methods on any remaining servlet instances, ensuring no data is lost and resources are released properly.

Obtaining Information About a Servlet

The final method from the `Servlet` interface that servlets must implement is `getServletInfo()`:

```
public String getServletInfo() throws ServletException, IOException
```

The `getServletInfo()` method returns a `String` object containing information about the servlet. This is expected to contain information such as the servlet's author, version, and copyright information. This method is designed to allow Web server administration tools to display information about the servlet. What it actually returns is up to the programmer. The default implementations return an empty string.

Introducing the GenericServlet Class

The `GenericServlet` class is an abstract class implementation of the `Servlet` interface. It implements the methods as defined by the `Servlet` interface, and servlets normally extend from this class. In addition to those methods defined in the `Servlet` interface, `GenericServlet` defines several other methods. You'll now take a tour of the methods of this class, which are grouped by functionality.

Lifecycle Methods

Servlet initialization is carried out by an init() method:

```
public void init(ServletConfig config)

public void init()
```

You should recognize the first form; it's required by the Servlet interface. When called by the container, the GenericServlet implementation of the init(ServletConfig) method stores a reference to the ServletConfig object in the servlet, and it then calls the second init() method. This version of the init() method is provided as a convenience to eliminate the need to call the superclass method (via super.init(config)) in your code.

> **NOTE** *If you choose to override the* init(ServletConfig) *method, it's up to you to make sure it calls the superclass method; otherwise the reference to the* ServletConfig *object will be lost.*

As you saw in the previous section, the following method processes the client requests and is called by the servlet container:

```
public abstract void service(ServletRequest req, ServletResponse res)
```

It's declared abstract because subclasses must implement a service() method to process their request (this is the purpose of the servlet).

Called by the servlet container, the destroy() method is overridden if there's any persistence of data required or if resources must be released:

```
public void destroy()
```

Servlet Environment Methods

Aside from getServletConfig() and getServletName(), the GenericServlet class provides a number of additional methods relating to the servlet and its environment.

With the ServletContext object that's contained in the ServletConfig object, you can access information about the servlet container in which the servlet is running. Calling the following method returns this ServletContext object:

```
public ServletContext getServletContext()
```

The getInitParameterNames() method returns an Enumeration of the names of the initialization parameters for the servlet:

```
public java.util.Enumeration getInitParameterNames()
```

This allows the servlet to access all initialization parameters without having to know their names in advance. When you've retrieved these names, you can use the following method to access their values:

```
public String getInitParameter(String name)
```

If the named parameter doesn't exist, `null` is returned.

Every servlet is known to the servlet container by a name. The unique servlet name is defined in the `web.xml` deployment descriptor (under the `<servlet>` element) and is the value referenced in the `<servlet-name>` element:

```
<servlet>
  <servlet-name>Servlet1</servlet-name>
  ...
</servlet>
```

Calling the following method will retrieve the name of this servlet's instance:

```
public String getServletName()
```

Utility Methods

`GenericServlet` also provides two logging methods to allow the servlet to write to the Web application's log file:

```
public void log(String message)
public void log(String message, java.lang.Throwable t)
```

This is for debugging and development information mainly, but you can write anything to this file if required; it's also preferable to writing to the console. Programmers are frequently required to support production applications where they have limited access to the server on which the application runs. Access may be limited to shared directories, such as log files, so it's good practice to use the log files rather than the console.

You usually specify the location and name of the log file on the application configuration, but the exact method depends on the container implementation.

A word of warning: While in test and preproduction environments, verbose logging may be useful; in practice, there can be performance implications for frequent logging for active, high-load applications. In production environments, you should be logging only important information such as Web application errors, security information, and other critical information.

If you use the log files excessively in busy production environments, not only do you suffer the input/output (I/O) costs of writing to the file excessively (with the overall implications for the server performance), but also you can lose sight of the important and useful information in the logs. Logging limited to the entry and exit of methods (and parameters/return values) is useful to identify the source of a problem, but you should restrict this to only important methods and points in the process.

Introducing HTTP and Servlets

The `javax.servlet` package provides generic interfaces and classes to service client requests in a protocol-independent manner. This means you can make all compatible requests using the members of this package, but you're limited to generic servlet methods to process your request. Any protocol-specific functionality has to be incorporated into the application by the developer.

You can extend the `javax.servlet` package API to create protocol-specific servlet classes that not only process requests but that also include any protocol-specific logic as required. The `javax.servlet.http` package is just such an extension. It adds support for HTTP-specific functions including the HTTP `GET` and `POST` methods.

You should view the `javax.servlet.http` package in relation to the standard Servlet API. For example, the `javax.servlet.http.HttpServlet` class extends from `javax.servlet.GenericServlet`, adding a number of specific methods to process different types of HTTP requests.

Figure 6-2 shows the classes and interfaces in the `javax.servlet.http` package.

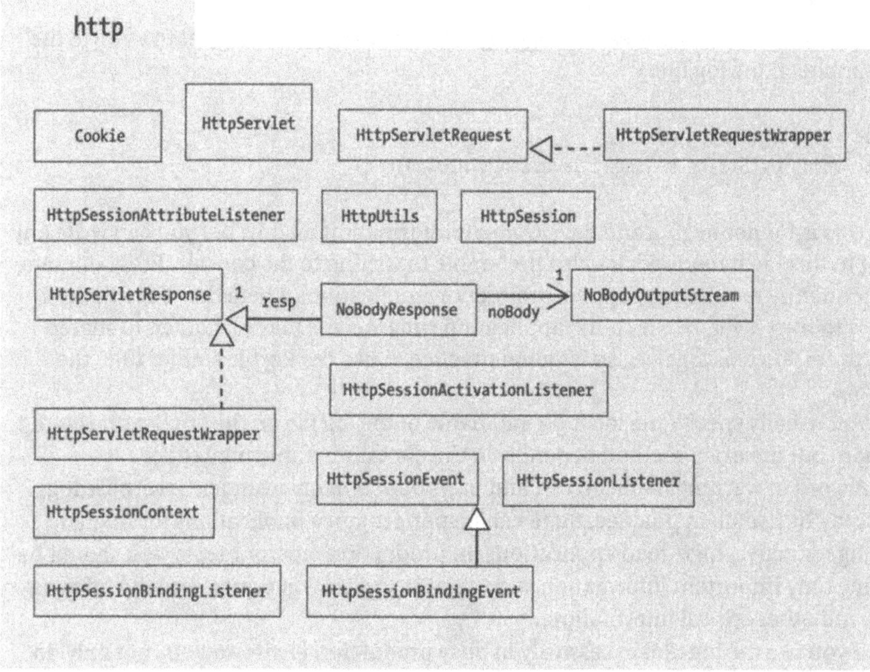

Figure 6-2. `javax.servlet.http` *classes and interfaces*

Of course, many classes and interfaces in the `javax.http.HttpServlet` package continue to use classes and interfaces from the `javax.servlet` package (for example, the streaming and exception classes).

The HttpServlet Class

Many of the servlets you'll develop will extend from `HttpServlet`, rather than `GenericServlet`, because most communication over the Web is carried over HTTP, which `HttpServlet` is designed to handle. When you extend from `HttpServlet`, you gain HTTP functionality. For example, `HttpServlet` uses HTTP versions of the `Request` and `Response` objects. `HttpServlet` overrides the `service()` method of `GenericServlet` and forwards requests to methods designed to process different types of HTTP requests.

Of course, if you use `HttpServlet`, then client requests must be sent using HTTP if they're to be understood. If the clients your application is expected to handle use a protocol other than HTTP, you'll need to use a servlet extended from `GenericServlet`.

Lifecycle Methods

`HttpServlet` inherits two important lifecycle methods from the `GenericServlet` class: `init()` and `destroy()`. The container calls the `init(ServletConfig config)` method after the servlet instance is constructed; it's always called before the servlet handles its first request. As the name implies, the `init()` method performs servlet initialization. This may include creating or loading any objects that the servlet may use during processing.

The `ServletConfig` object provides the servlet with information about any initialization parameters. The `ServletConfig` object also holds a reference to the `ServletContext` object that may be used to find out about the environment in which the servlet is running.

The `destroy()` method is called when the servlet is about to be unloaded. It's here that any resources should be freed and any information is saved that's needed the next time the servlet is loaded.

You can override one of the following two `init()` methods:

```
public void init(ServletConfig config) throws ServletException
public void init() throws ServletException
```

If you override the first one, you must first call `super.init(config)` to ensure that the reference to the `ServletConfig` object passed in by the servlet container is stored in the servlet instance for later use. If you override the second `init()` method, there's no need to call `super.init(config)`; it will be called by the `init(config)` method once the `ServletConfig` object reference is stored.

> **NOTE** *You should usually override only one version of the* `init()` *method because you need to initialize the servlet in only one place. The second method is provided as a convenient alternative, but it doesn't make sense for your servlets to override both and spread the initialization logic.*

Service Methods

The `HttpServlet` class defines two `service()` methods to process requests. The first of these overrides the `service()` method inherited from `GenericServlet`:

```
void service(ServletRequest req, ServletResponse resp)
```

As an HTTP servlet developer, you should never have reason to override this method. This method simply casts the `ServletRequest` and `ServletResponse` objects into their corresponding HTTP objects (`HttpServletRequest` and `HttpServletResponse`) and forwards the request to the second `service()` method:

```
protected void service(HttpServletRequest req, HttpServletResponse resp)
```

In contrast to `GenericServlet`, when you use `HttpServlet` you usually don't override the `service()` method, but instead you override the `doGet()` and `doPost()` methods. The `service()` method in `HttpServlet` typically handles initialization and setup and the dispatching to all the various `doXXX()` methods. This is why you rarely need to override this method, because most of the work is being done in the `doXXX()` methods.

This method should also not be overridden, as it's the responsibility of this method to determine the type of the HTTP request and forward it to the appropriate method to be processed.

> **TIP** *A developer may want to override the* `service()` *method for a few reasons. One reason is if the developer is working with a custom extended version of HTTP—but before doing this you should consider alternate ways of achieving your objective, because one of the biggest benefits of HTTP is its interoperability. It's also important to note that if you do override the* `service()` *method, then you must call the* `doGet()` *and* `doPost()` *methods yourself, since this is what* `service()` *does.*

Handling HTTP Requests

We discussed in earlier chapters that the most common HTTP requests are the `GET` and `POST` methods. You must implement methods to handle these different types of requests. The servlet container will recognize the type of HTTP request that has been made and will pass the request to the correct servlet method. Accordingly, you don't override the `service()` methods as you do for servlets that extend `GenericServlet`, but rather you override the appropriate request methods, like so:

```
protected void doGet(HttpServletRequest req, HttpServletResponse resp)
  throws ServletException, IOException
protected void doPost(HttpServletRequest req, HttpServletResponse resp)
  throws ServletException, IOException
protected void doHead(HttpServletRequest req, HttpServletResponse resp)
  throws ServletException, IOException
protected void doPut(HttpServletRequest req, HttpServletResponse resp)
  throws ServletException, IOException
```

The Servlet 2.4 specification requires support for HTTP/1.1. Not all clients or servers implement the HTTP specification fully; it's up to the developer to choose the appropriate way to handle the request and the appropriate method to be used in a Web application. Whenever possible, this choice should be consistent with the normal use of the request type (for example, `POST` for posting data).

The programmer shouldn't override the `doHead()` method, because the `HttpServlet` implementation correctly returns the `HEAD` request information. The `HEAD` request returns the header information, but not the body of the `GET` request.

With mandatory support of HTTP/1.1 in the Servlet 2.4 specification, it's possible to use some of the HTTP methods that you previously had to be careful about because the client may not support them. The corresponding servlet methods are as follows:

```
protected void doOptions(HttpServletRequest req, HttpServletResponse resp)
  throws ServletException, IOException
protected void doTrace(HttpServletRequest req, HttpServletResponse resp)
  throws ServletException, IOException
```

Clients use `OPTIONS` requests to determine the types of HTTP requests that the server will handle. You'll rarely need to override this method, unless your application needs to "hide" a supported request type from a client. You may want to hide methods from client scans to prevent hacking where hidden methods perform sensitive or administrator tasks.

`TRACE` requests are usually used for debugging. They allow a request from a client to be sent to a server, and the server then returns the request (as received by it) in the body of the response. This is useful to determine whether the client is sending the correct request and whether the request data is being altered in any way midroute.

The default implementation of the `doTrace()` method shouldn't usually be overridden because the default implementation is the same for all servlets. The default implementation will return the header information received by the server back to the client. For applications with custom clients, requests made to the servlet can be examined (to determine if the request is being correctly made) if the request method is modified to an HTTP `TRACE` request and directed at the servlet.

The following `getLastModified()` method allows servlets that can easily determine the last update time of their `GET` request data to do so and then include this in the `doHead()` and `doGet()` responses:

```
protected long getLastModified(HttpServletRequest req)
  throws ServletException, IOException
```

This has the effect of improving caching of output, thereby reducing the load on the server and network.

The ServletRequest Interface

The ServletRequest interface wraps the client request and provides methods that make the request information available to the servlet.

Obtaining Request Parameter Names and Values

Often the first information you want to extract from a client request is the request parameters. This usually tells the servlet what the client is requesting.

To add flexibility to the request, you don't need to know the names of the parameters that will be submitted at the development stage. Instead, you call methods that return the names of the parameters contained in the request and methods that return the values of these parameters.

For example, you can call the getParameterNames() method to receive an Enumeration of String objects corresponding to the names of all the parameters supplied with the request. The method returns an empty Enumeration object if the request didn't contain any parameters, like so:

```
public java.util.Enumeration getParameterNames()
```

To find the value of a specific parameter, you call the following getParameter() method:

```
public String getParameter(String name)
```

This method returns null if the parameter wasn't included in the request. If more than one value may be returned for the parameter, you should use the following getParameterValues() method instead:

```
public String[] getParameterValues(String name)
```

This method returns a String array of values for the specified parameter; you can then iterate through the array to process all the values. The String array is empty if no parameters matching the name are included in the request.

You can also get a Map object, which has a mapping of all the request parameters' names to their values, using the getParameterMap() method:

```
public java.util.Map getParameterMap()
```

The names of the parameters are the keys of the Map object, and the values of the Map object are String arrays.

Retrieving Request Parameter Values in getRequestTable()

You start your getRequestTable() method by creating the HTMLTable object you'll use to create the HTML table:

```
private StringBuffer getRequestTable(ServletRequest request) {

  HTMLTable table = new HTMLTable();
  table.appendTitleRow("Parameters");
```

After adding the title row, you use getParameterNames() to get an Enumeration of the parameter names so you can process the parameters. You use a loop to iterate through the Enumeration:

```
Enumeration e = request.getParameterNames();
while (e.hasMoreElements()) {
  String paramName = (String)e.nextElement();
```

Once you've extracted the current parameter name, you call the getParameter-Values() method on the request object with the name of the parameter for which you're looking. This method returns a String array. Then you loop through the array to add each value associated with the parameter to the table:

```
  String[] paramValues = request.getParameterValues(paramName);
  if (paramValues != null) {
    for (int i = 0; i < paramValues.length; i++) {
      table.appendRow("Parameter: <code>" + paramName +
                      "</code>", paramValues[i]);
    }
  }
}
```

Accessing Request Header Information

Three methods allow the servlet to access information provided in the header of the request. To get the size of the request (useful if a file or other large object is attached), you can use the following getContentLength() method, which returns the length in bytes or returns -1 if it's unknown:

```
public int getContentLength()
```

The following getContentType() method is useful if you want to determine the data type of the data in the request body:

```
public String getContentType()
```

This method returns the Multipurpose Internet Mail Extensions (MIME) type of the request (if known) or null (if unknown). For example, if the client submitted serialized Java objects to the servlet, the MIME type would probably be application/x-java-serialized-object, which is the standard MIME type for serialized Java objects.

The last method, getProtocol(), will provide the name and version of the protocol that was used in making the request (for example, HTTP/1.1):

```
public String getProtocol()
```

Accessing Header Information in getRequestTable()

In the example servlet, you append the title to the table and extract the content-length: header from the request. If the client supplied this value, it'll be some positive integer value. Otherwise, if the client didn't supply it, it'll be -1. In the case that it isn't supplied, you indicate this fact; otherwise, you print the request content size, like so:

```
table.appendTitleRow("Headers");
int requestLength = request.getContentLength();
if (requestLength == -1) {
  table.appendRow("Request Length", "(Not Specified)");
} else {
   table.appendRow("Request Length", requestLength);
}
```

Then you find the content type and protocol used in the request, like so:

```
table.appendRow("Content Type", request.getContentType());
table.appendRow("Request Protocol", request.getProtocol());
```

Using Attributes in the Request

Attributes are the objects (if any) associated with the request. Attributes are similar to request parameters, but instead of being set by the client, they're set by the servlet container, or they may be set by a previous servlet that used the javax.servlet.RequestDispatcher to forward the request and attached information (Java objects) as attributes to the request. Also, instead of just Strings for values, attribute values can be any Java objects.

The getAttributeNames() method returns an Enumeration object of the names of the attributes for this request:

```
public java.util.Enumeration getAttributeNames()
```

The following method returns the specified attribute or `null` if the attribute doesn't exist:

```
public Object getAttribute(String name)
```

The attribute returned is of type `Object`, so to use it as any other type of object, you'll have to cast it into its specific class type.

The `setAttribute()` method stores the specified `Object` with the name in the request object. It's usually used when the request will be forwarded to another servlet (or filter) for processing:

```
public void setAttribute(String name, Object o)
```

Conversely, the `removeAttribute()` method allows you to remove the specified attribute from the request. This is usually used when the request will be forwarded to another servlet (or filter) for processing:

```
public void removeAttribute(String name)
```

Setting and Accessing Request Attributes in getRequestTable()

Since there are no attributes already set, you'll first set two attributes so you can access them. Of course, you wouldn't normally need to set them in the same method that you'd use them in, but the following demonstrates both:

```
table.appendTitleRow("Attributes");
request.setAttribute("My Attribute", "My Attribute Value");
request.setAttribute("Another Attribute", "123");
```

The code to output the attributes is similar to that used for the request parameters. You retrieve an `Enumeration` of attribute names and loop through it, printing the attribute name and the object stored:

```
Enumeration enum = request.getAttributeNames();
while (enum.hasMoreElements()) {
  String attributeName = (String)enum.nextElement();
  Object attributeValue = request.getAttribute(attributeName);
  if (attributeValue != null) {
    table.appendRow("Attribute: <code>" + attributeName + "</code>",
                    attributeValue.toString());
  }
}
```

Obtaining Request Path Information

You use path information from the request to interpret the request and gather additional information useful to processing the request. The `ServletRequest` interface provides a number of useful methods.

This method returns the protocol *scheme* used in making the request (for example `http`, `https`, or `ftp`):

```
public String getScheme()
```

For a servlet that may be configured to receive requests on more than one protocol, the scheme is important for the servlet to be able to extract additional information about the request. Different schemes may have different rules for constructing a uniform resource locator (URL), so the servlet needs to know the scheme so the URL can be properly interpreted. Not all the information needs to be included in the URL (for example, if not included, the port is assumed to be the default for that scheme).

An example is a servlet that's configured to process e-mail Post Office Protocol (POP) requests and Web HTTP requests, where in the first case it serves as a mail server, and in the second it could provide Web access to the e-mail.

> **TIP** *For further information about addressing schemes, see* `http://www.w3.org/Addressing/schemes.html`.

The `getServerName()` method finds out the host server name that received this request:

```
public String getServerName()
```

This is the name by which the client addressed the server. A Web application may have more than one server name by which it can be addressed. This method will return the Internet Protocol (IP) address if the server is addressed by its IP address instead of a name.

The following method returns the port number on which the server received the request:

```
public int getServerPort()
```

Various protocols have default ports that requests are made on; for instance, HTTP has port 80 by default. Tomcat defaults to 8080. However, servers can listen on any free valid port for requests.

Retrieving Request Path Information in getRequestTable()

You can use the previous methods to access the request path information in your `getRequestTable()` method as follows:

```
table.appendTitleRow("Path Information");
table.appendRow("Request Scheme", request.getScheme());
table.appendRow("Request Server", request.getServerName());
table.appendRow("Request Port", request.getServerPort());
```

Checking for Secure Connections

The following method is available to allow the servlet to determine if the request being served was made over a secure connection (for example, over HTTPS):

```
public boolean isSecure()
```

For instance, a servlet may check this before allowing the user to enter confidential information such as credit card or other confidential data.

This method is particularly appropriate to filter or gateway servlets that may be set up to intercept and redirect requests made to resources requiring a secure connection. Web applications transferring personal, payment, or other (moderately) sensitive data may require this.

> **TIP** *You can find more information about security in Chapter 8.*

Checking Security in getRequestTable()

In this example, you'll output only whether the request was made over a secure connection, but you could, based on the result, modify the code to redirect to a secure connection if you wanted:

```
table.appendTitleRow("Security");
table.appendRow("Secure Request", request.isSecure());
```

Using Internationalization in the Request

A few useful methods are available to developers of Web applications that have international content or an international audience. These request methods are useful if you need servlets and filters to process and adapt request processing to different international locales and character sets.

A client may send, as part of its request, information about its preferred locales. Providing a selection of locales is useful because the servlet may not support the client's first choice, but it may support the second or third choice. The order of the locales supplied is the client's order of preference.

The getLocale() method will return the client's first choice of locale. The getLocales() method returns an Enumeration of Locale objects. By default, if no locale is specified by the client, these methods return the default locale for the server (for the getLocales() method, this is an Enumeration of a single Locale object):

```
public java.util.Locale getLocale()
public java.util.Enumeration getLocales()
```

The getCharacterEncoding() method will return the name of the character encoding (null if not specified) used in the request. You may need this method to ensure that the request data is interpreted correctly, using the correct character encoding:

```
public String getCharacterEncoding()
```

The setCharacterEncoding() method can override the character encoding used in the body of the request. You must call it before reading the request parameters or reading input using the getReader() or getInputStream() method. The default character encoding is ISO-8859-1 (Latin-1):

```
public void setCharacterEncoding(String env)
```

> **TIP** *For more information on character sets, see* http://www.iana.org/assignments/character-sets.

Using Internationalization in getRequestTable()

To find the locale used in the request (or the server's default if none was specified), you call the getLocale() method on the request object:

```
table.appendTitleRow("Internationalization");
Locale locale = request.getLocale();
```

You can extract information that you could use to customize your response to the client from the Locale object (see the Java documentation for more information about using the Locale class:
http://java.sun.com/j2se/1.4/docs/api/java/util/Locale.html):

```
table.appendRow("Preferred Locale", locale.toString());
table.appendRow("Country (ISO Code)", locale.getCountry());
table.appendRow("Country", locale.getDisplayCountry());
```

```
table.appendRow("Language", locale.getDisplayLanguage());
table.appendRow("Locale Name", locale.getDisplayName());
table.appendRow("Character Encoding", request.getCharacterEncoding());
```

Reading from the Request

The Servlet API provides two I/O stream wrapper classes for the request input stream and the response output stream. The request object allows you to read information from the request, such as included files or serialized Java objects. You can interpret the stream as binary or character data according to the method you call.

You use the `getInputStream()` method to get a `ServletInputStream` object if you need to read in a file or serialized Java objects or to get similar information from the client's request. You can use the returned object as an `InputStream` object, if required, which you can wrap in any valid input class (for example `ObjectInputStream`) to read in the data:

```
public ServletInputStream getInputStream()
```

Alternatively, you can call the `getReader()` method to get a `java.io.BufferedReader` object to read the body of the request. You can read in character data using this method and wrap the returned object in a suitable input class to read the data (for example, you could use a `FileReader` to read in a file of character data):

```
public java.io.BufferedReader getReader()
```

It's important to note that you can call only one of these methods, not both of them. If you try to call one of these methods, after already having called the other one, the method will throw an `IllegalStateException` to indicate that the other method was called to read the data. You can call the same method a second time, if necessary, to read more data if the original reference to the input object isn't available (such as in a method that's passed the request object, but not the input object). However, you must ensure that the stream isn't previously closed or that the end of the supplied data hasn't been reached.

Obtaining Client Information

The following methods return information contained in the request about the client:

```
public String getRemoteAddr()
public String getRemoteHost()
```

The `getRemoteAddr()` method will return the client's IP address. The server directs the response to this address. You can also access this, but while it may be useful for identifying clients in general terms, on its own, it has limitations because the IP address of a request can be that of a proxy server.

The getRemoteHost() method returns the client's fully qualified name. Across the Web, you use names instead of IP addresses to access Web sites normally; the mappings of IP addresses to names are stored on Domain Name System (DNS) servers. For example, www.apress.com is the remote host that this method will return if the Apress Web server made the request. Note that this also assumes that a DNS server is available to the container. If it can't determine the fully qualified name (either no DNS is available or the IP address wasn't recognized), it returns the IP address.

Retrieving Client Information in getRequestTable()

To round off the getRequestTable() method, you'll add the client's IP address and name to the table. In this example, both methods may output the IP address (using localhost as the Web address) although it depends on your network setup:

```
table.appendTitleRow("Client Information");
table.appendRow("Client IP Address", request.getRemoteAddr());
table.appendRow("Client Name", request.getRemoteHost());
```

You've also finished the method, so you return the table created in the following StringBuffer object:

```
  return table.toStringBuffer();
}
```

You've now completed the method; Figure 6-3 shows the table it generates.

Creating a RequestDispatcher

Calling the getRequestDispatcher() method from the ServletRequest interface returns a RequestDispatcher object that wraps the resource specified in the path parameter:

```
public RequestDispatcher getRequestDispatcher(String path)
```

This allows the servlet to forward the request or to include the requested resource's output in its own output. This method will return null if the container can't return a dispatcher for the requested resource. The path parameter may map to another servlet or a static resource, such as an HTML file.

The ServletResponse Interface

The ServletResponse object sends the servlet's response back to the client. It wraps the response (output stream, header information, data, and so on) in a single interface, allowing access to the methods that prepare and add content to the response.

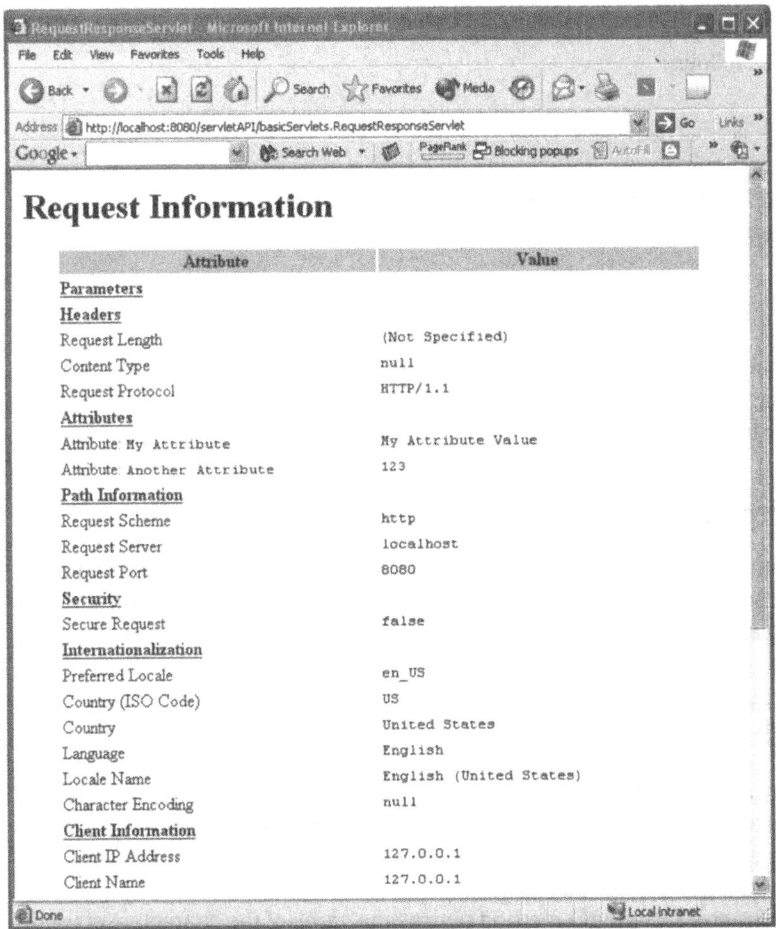

Figure 6-3. The generated table

Setting Content Length and MIME Types

The `ServletResponse` class determines two methods that can set the content length and type of the response.

The `setContentLength()` method sets a header indicating the length of the response:

```
public void setContentLength(int len)
```

Setting this value too low will normally stop the server sending the excess data after the length specified, and most clients will stop reading the response after the specified length. Therefore, it's often better to let the server set this header (if it can buffer the full response before sending) or perhaps to leave it unset.

The second method is the `setContentType()` method. This sets the MIME type of the response. Many protocols other than HTTP use MIME types to indicate the type of output or file as follows:

```
public void setContentType(String type)
```

This method should be called before any output is written to the output stream object. For example:

```
response.setContentType("text/html");
```

For standard Web pages, you always use `text/html`, indicating text data in HTML format. If you were returning serialized Java objects, you'd use `application/x-java-serialized-object`.

Using Internationalization in the Response

You can customize the response to the specific audience and specify technical information on the locale and character set used in the response. The `getLocale()` and `setLocale()` methods allow you to access and reset the `Locale` of the response:

```
public java.util.Locale getLocale()
public void setLocale(java.util.Locale loc)
```

The `setLocale()` method must be called before a call to `getWriter()`, as calling this method sets the character set to that appropriate for the current locale. Calling the `setLocale()` method after calling `getWriter()` has no effect, as the character set of the `PrintWriter` object already has been set.

The `getCharacterEncoding()` method returns the name of the character set used for the MIME body sent in the response. The default is `ISO-8859-1` (`Latin-1`):

```
public String getCharacterEncoding()
```

Using Internationalization in getResponseTable()

You'll now use what you've learned about the `ServletResponse` interface so far to begin constructing the `getResponseTable()` from the example `RequestResponseServlet`. Similar to the `getRequestTable()` method, `getResponseTable()` takes the `ServletResponse` object as a parameter and uses this object to extract information about the response to place it in an HTML table:

```
private StringBuffer getResponseTable(ServletRequest request,
                                      ServletResponse response) {
  HTMLTable table = new HTMLTable();
```

As you did from the request object, you extract the `Locale` from the response object and then print information about the `Locale` for the response:

```
table.appendTitleRow("Internationalization");
Locale locale = response.getLocale();
table.appendRow("Response Locale", locale.toString());
table.appendRow("Country (ISO Code)", locale.getCountry());
table.appendRow("Country", locale.getDisplayCountry());
table.appendRow("Language", locale.getDisplayLanguage());
table.appendRow("Locale Name", locale.getDisplayName());
```

You can also set the `Locale` for the response (before the `getWriter()` method has been called), and in this case you're resetting it to its current value. You do this here because, with an international audience, you don't want to upset the responses for any reader. If you want to try setting the locale specifically, you can substitute the `locale` parameter with `Locale.ENGLISH`, replacing the `ENGLISH` constant with that relevant to your location. Check the API for the list of constants available or construct a new `Locale` object for a location not specified:

```
response.setLocale(locale);
table.appendRow("Character Encoding", response.getCharacterEncoding());
```

When the `locale` of the response is set, basically it's setting the `Content-Language` header. This will happen only if the response hasn't been committed yet. It also sets the response's character encoding appropriately for the locale, if the character encoding hasn't been explicitly set using `setContentType(String)` or `setCharacterEncoding(String)`. If the deployment descriptor contains a `locale-encoding-mapping-list` element, and that element provides a mapping for the given locale, that mapping is used. If nothing is specified, then the mapping from locale to character encoding is container dependent.

Returning Data in the Response

To return data in the body of your servlet's response, you need to access the output object from the response object. You do this by calling one of the following methods:

```
public ServletOutputStream getOutputStream()
public java.io.PrintWriter getWriter()
```

You can use a `ServletOutputStream` object, which can be used directly or wrapped in a suitable I/O object (for example, `ObjectOutputStream` for serialized Java objects) to output a response. Calling the `getWriter()` method instead returns a `PrintWriter` object that can be used to send text back to the client.

Only one of these methods should be called to send the response back to the client. Calling either constructs the corresponding output object, and you can't construct a second object to write to the same stream. So, you need to decide what type of data you'll be sending back to the client (for character data, use `getWriter()`). If it'll be a mixture of types, such as a serialized object first (to pass information about the following data) followed by other data (for example, a file), use the `getOutputStream()` method and wrap the `OutputStream` in appropriate classes for sending the data back.

Output Buffering

Buffering strategies for different servlet containers vary and are implemented in different ways. The container isn't required to implement output buffering, and the choice of strategy used is for the vendor to decide, based on their implementation and their optimum performance objectives. A number of methods are available to servlets to improve or adapt the buffering strategy for their output.

The `getBufferSize()` method returns the size of the underlying buffer used (returns 0 if no buffering is used):

```
public int getBufferSize()
```

The `setBufferSize()` method allows the servlet to suggest a buffer size to the container:

```
public void setBufferSize(int size)
```

The container may choose not to implement the exact size specified by the servlet, but it must implement the size to be at least the size specified. The `setBufferSize()` method *must* be called before any content is returned to the client, or the method will throw a `java.lang.IllegalStateException`.

The `isCommitted()` method allows the servlet to find out if the client has begun to set the response:

```
public boolean isCommitted()
```

The `reset()` method will clear any data in the buffer and the headers and status code if the response isn't yet committed. If the response has been committed, it'll throw an `IllegalStateException`:

```
public void reset()
```

Similarly, the `resetBuffer()` method will reset the data in the buffer (but not the headers or status code) and will throw the `IllegalStateException` if the response has been committed:

```
public void resetBuffer()
```

The `flushBuffer()` method will immediately flush the contents of the buffer to the client. This method will commit the response, which means that the status code and headers will be written to the client:

```
public void flushBuffer()
```

Once a buffer is full, the container will instantly flush its contents to the client, which will commit the response.

Output Buffering in getResponseTable()

You'll call a few of the buffering methods of the response object and add the results to the table in your `getResponseTable()` method. You access the buffer size and then append it to the table:

```
table.appendTitleRow("Buffering");
int buffer = response.getBufferSize();
table.appendRow("Buffer Size", buffer);
```

You extract an attribute that may or may not be set. At this point, it isn't set, but in the `RequestDispatcherServlet` that you'll see later, this may be set. This indicates if the response may be committed without the servlet knowing. The other servlet knows and sets that attribute as an indicator. This indicator prevents you from resetting the buffer size after it has been committed:

```
String written = (String) request.getAttribute("buffer");
```

Next, you increment the buffer size by one each time this is called, but only if it hasn't been committed:

```
if (!response.isCommitted() && !"written".equalsIgnoreCase(written)) {
  response.setBufferSize(buffer + 1);
}
table.appendRow("Is Response Committed",
                new Boolean(response.isCommitted()).toString());
```

It's important to understand that each container request is altering the buffer size, so they have a cumulative effect. If you were to decrease the buffer size, the container may decide to keep a larger buffer size. However, the container must implement at least the size you suggest (bigger if it chooses), so increasing the buffer size without careful consideration can cause the servlet to throw an exception because of the excessive memory allocated to the buffer.

> **CAUTION** *If you increase the buffer size excessively (to the point where an exception is thrown), you'll have to reset the buffer size to a sensible value (by recompiling with a new value or restarting the server) before you can continue with this servlet.*

To see the effects of this, try changing the argument to the `setBufferSize()` method to `buffer * 2`. Each time you execute the servlet, you're doubling the buffer size. Depending on your memory allocation, fairly soon your servlet will throw an exception. When you do this, you have to reset the buffer size to something sensible by recompiling (and not with `buffer + 1` but with something such as `1024`) or restarting the server.

At the end of the method, you return the table in a `StringBuffer` object:

```
    return table.toStringBuffer();
  }
}
```

Finally, Figure 6-4 shows you what the table produced by the `getResponseTable()` method looks like.

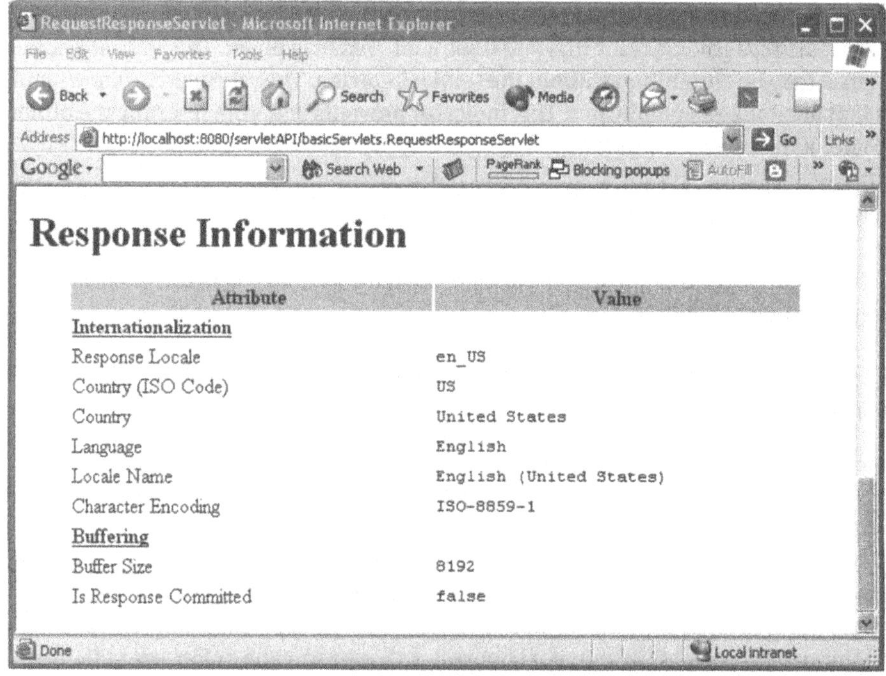

Figure 6-4. The `getResponseTable()` *table*

HTTP Requests and Responses

The `HttpServletRequest` and `HttpServletResponse` interfaces extend the `Servlet-Request` and `ServletResponse` interfaces, respectively, to add methods that are specific to HTTP. The Servlet API provides two generic wrappers for `ServletRequest` and `ServletResponse`: `ServletRequestWrapper` and `ServletResponseWrapper`. These wrappers are extended further to provide convenience wrappers for the HTTP interfaces: `HttpServletRequestWrapper` and `HttpServletResponseWrapper`.

The HttpServletRequest Interface

You can use the methods defined in the HttpServletRequest interface to learn a great deal about a request.

Header Information

Objects implementing the HttpServletRequest interface contain the header information for the HTTP request. The interface defines methods that are designed to extract this information.

The getMethod() method returns the name of the HTTP request method used to make the request (for example, GET or POST):

```
public String getMethod()
```

The getHeaderNames() method returns a java.util.Enumeration of the names of all the headers supplied with the request:

```
public Enumeration getHeaderNames()
```

You can use the getHeader(String) method to return the value of the header, assuming it exists:

```
public String getHeader(String name)
```

The argument to this method could be any header name (for instance, one of the elements of the Enumeration returned by the previous method). For example, calling the method with the user-agent parameter would return information about the client software generating the request (such as Mozilla/4.0 (compatible; MSIE 6.0; Windows NT 5.0)).

You can also use the getHeaders() method, which returns an Enumeration of Strings that contains all the values of the header specified by the supplied name. You use the getHeaders() method where you expect more than one header value of the same name to be included in the header of the request:

```
public Enumeration getHeaders(String name)
```

However, you may not always want the value of a header to be stored in a String. If you know that the value of a header is representing a date, or an integer, you can use the getDateHeader() and getIntHeader() methods instead. The getDateHeader() method returns the value of the header specified by the supplied name as a long value that represents a Date object, which is specified by the number of milliseconds since January 1, 1970, Greenwich mean time (GMT):

```
public long getDateHeader(String name)
```

If you know a header is in an `int`, you can use the `getIntHeader()` method to retrieve it from the request header:

```
public int getIntHeader(String name)
```

Putting it all together, you could use the following code (from `HeaderServlet.java`) to find and print all the headers and corresponding values of the request:

```
public void doGet(HttpServletRequest request, HttpServletResponse response)
  throws IOException {

  PrintWriter out = response.getWriter();

  Enumeration e = request.getHeaderNames();

  while(e.hasMoreElements()) {
    String headerName = (String)e.nextElement();
    String headerValue = request.getHeader(headerName);
    out.println("<html><body>");
    out.println("Header: <code>" + headerName + "</code>");
    out.println(" Value: " + headerValue + "<br/>");
    out.println("</body></html>");
  }
}
```

Here you see how to return text to the client. A `java.io.PrintWriter` is obtained and used to return the text its the `println()` method. The client supplied the headers shown in Table 6-1.

Table 6-1. Headers

HEADER	VALUE
accept	image/gif, image/x-xbitmap, image/jpeg, image/pjpeg, application/vnd.ms-powerpoint, application/vnd.ms-excel, application/msword, */*
referer	http://localhost:8080/httpServlet/index.html
accept-language	en-ie
accept-encoding	gzip, deflate
user-agent	Mozilla/4.0 (compatible; MSIE 6.0; Windows NT 5.0)
host	localhost:8080
connection	Keep-Alive

Only the `host` header is essential, as many Web servers house multiple Web sites on one IP address, so specifying the requested Web host is important.

Path Information

You can extract information about the path used in the request and the query string (for example, `http://localhost:8080/javaserver/chapter06/PathServlet?firstname=Zuni`). The `getQueryString()` method returns the query string of the request or `null` if there was no query string associated with the request URL. For the URL given previously, the method returns `"firstname=Zuni"`:

```
public String getQueryString()
```

The `getContextPath()` method returns the URL context path of the request. This is the first part of the uniform resource indicator (URI), starting with / and not ending in a / character. For servlets in the root or default context, this returns `""`. In the previous URL example, this returns `"/javaserver"`:

```
public String getContextPath()
```

The `getServletPath()` method will return the part of the URL that's used to call the servlet or another file/resource. In the previous example URL, this equates to `"/chapter06/PathServlet"`:

```
public String getServletPath()
```

The `getPathInfo()` method will return any additional path information sent by the client in the request URL:

```
public String getPathInfo()
```

This is any additional path information between the servlet path and the query string. In the previous example, this returns `null` because there's no such additional information. You may use additional information to identify a client (for example, session tracking) or to include a key or ID.

The `getPathTranslated()` method is similar to the previous `getPathInfo()` method in that it refers to the same additional path information, but this method translates this information into a real path:

```
public String getPathTranslated()
```

Mostly, servlets don't need the support of `getPathTranslated()`, but a Common Gateway Interface (CGI) program can't interact with its server and doesn't receive the path parameter. To overcome this deficiency, there's a need to support extra path information, which is encoded in the URL. A servlet can access this information and can translate it into the real path using the methods `getPathlnfo()` and `getPathTranslated()`.

The `getRequestURI()` method specifies the full URI for the request. In the example it'd return `"/javaserver/chapter06/PathServlet"`:

```
public String getRequestURI()
```

The getRequestURL() method constructs the URL that the client used to make the request and returns it. This includes the full URL except for the query parameters, and it returns http://localhost:8080/javaserver/chapter06/PathServlet for the previous example:

```
public StringBuffer getRequestURL()
```

You'll now look at some code that calls these methods on the request object and outputs the result:

```
public void doGet(HttpServletRequest request, HttpServletResponse response)
  throws IOException {

  PrintWriter out = response.getWriter();

  //Request Path Elements
  out.println("<br><b>Request Context Path:</b> " + request.getContextPath());
  out.println("<br><b>Request Servlet Path:</b> " + request.getServletPath());
  out.println("<br><b>Request Path Info:</b> " + request.getPathInfo());
  out.println("<br><b>Request Path Translated:</b> " +
request.getPathTranslated ());
  out.println("<br><b>Request Request URI:</b> " + request.getRequestURI());
  out.println("<br><b>Request Request URL:</b> " + request.getRequestURL());
  out.println("<br><b>Query String:</b> " + request.getQueryString());
}
```

Figure 6-5 shows the result of this block of code.

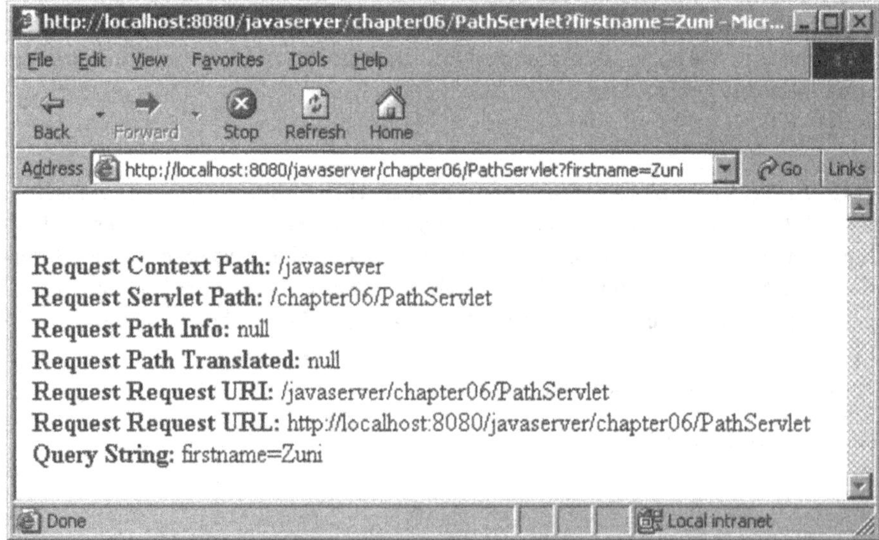

Figure 6-5. The output

Authentication Information

A number of methods exist to help improve security and authentication by allowing the servlet to identify the user (if possible), which enables the servlet to determine what the user has access to or what actions users can perform. You can use authentication schemes such as Basic or Digest authentication to secure the servlet.

The `getAuthType()` method will return the `String` name of the scheme being used:

```
public String getAuthType()
```

The `getRemoteUser()` method will determine the login name of the client making the request if the user is already authenticated to the servlet. If the user hasn't already been authenticated to the servlet, this method will return `null`:

```
public String getRemoteUser()
```

The `getUserPrincipal()` method is similar to the previous method except that it returns a `Principal` object containing the name of the authenticated user (or `null` if the user isn't authenticated):

```
public java.security.Principal getUserPrincipal()
```

The `Principal` object represents the concept of a user entity, which could be an individual, a corporation, or a login ID. You can use the `getUserPrincipal()` method when applications use the `java.security` packages to manage access and security for the application.

You can use the following method to find out if the user who has been authenticated to the server has been designated with the specified role when using the Web application:

```
public boolean isUserInRole(String role)
```

You can use this method to grant or deny access to a user, based on their role.

The HttpServletResponse Interface

The `HttpServletResponse` interface extends from the `ServletResponse` interface and sends the servlet's HTTP-based response back to the client. It includes additional HTTP-specific methods for setting data in the response, such as HTTP headers, sessions and cookies, and status codes.

Headers and MIME Types

The `HttpServletResponse` interface inherits two methods from the `ServletResponse` class related to setting the headers of a response.

The `setContentLength()` method sets the header indicating the length of the response. Setting this value too low will normally stop the server from sending the excess data after the length specified, and most clients will stop reading the response after the specified length. Conversely, setting the size too high may leave the client hanging, waiting for more data once the response has been completed, until it times out. Therefore, it's often better to let the server set this header (if it can buffer the full response before sending) or perhaps leave it unset, unless the content can be easily determined in advance.

The second method inherited from the `ServletResponse` interface is the `setContentType()` method. This sets the MIME (RFC 2045 and 2046) type of the response. Many protocols use MIME types other than HTTP to indicate the type of output or file being sent:

```
response.setContentType("text/html");
```

Here you set the content type to `text/html`. For servlets sending back HTML-based Web pages, this is the MIME type you always use, and it's the most common type that servlets will return to the client. You change this to the appropriate MIME type if you're sending a different data type back to the client.

The most common way to set the headers of an HTTP response is to use the `setHeader()` method to reset an existing header or the `addHeader()` method to add a new header to the response:

```
public void setHeader(String name, String value)
public void addHeader(String name, String value)
```

A number of other convenience header methods exist that allow for the inclusion of data not in `String` format in headers. To set a date header, you could use one of the previous methods, with the date value in `String` format. However, to set the date header directly, you can use the `setDateHeader()` method to set or reset the specified header field. Using the `addDateHeader()` method, you can add a header field with date information:

```
public void setDateHeader(String name, long date)
public void addDateHeader(String name, long date)
```

The `addIntHeader()` and `setIntHeader()` methods allow you to set `int` values in headers in a similar way:

```
public void addIntHeader(String name, int value)
public void setIntHeader(String name, int value)
```

You can check if a header has already been set using the `containsHeader()` method:

```
boolean containsHeader(String name)
```

This will return `true` if the specified header has already been set in the response object. Otherwise, it will return `false`.

Redirecting Requests

To redirect a request to another resource on the server (or anywhere else), you can use the `sendRedirect()` method with the relative or absolute address, as appropriate. If the server is using URL rewriting to maintain sessions, you must call the `encodeRedirectURL()` method (on the response object, as well) with the URL that the client is being redirected to so that the server can add the session information to the URL:

```
void sendRedirect(String location)
```

To use the `sendRedirect()` method, the response must still be buffered on the server (or not started at all) and not committed. You can check if the response has been committed with the `isCommitted()` method, inherited from `ServletResponse`. If you try to redirect the request after the response has been committed, an `IllegalStateException` is thrown. Using `sendRedirect()` effectively commits the response, so you shouldn't write any further to the response.

Using the `sendRedirect()` method is different from using a `RequestDispatcher` object to forward (or include a response); it redirects the entire request to another location for processing. Using a `RequestDispatcher` object, you can either include the content of the resource that the `RequestDispatcher` object represents or forward the request to this resource. If you forward the request using the `RequestDispatcher` object, you may have already sent some data back to the client, and the resource being forwarded to will append to the output already sent (if any).

Status Codes and Errors

The `HttpServletResponse` class has 41 `static int` fields, corresponding to HTTP status codes that can be returned in a response to a client. The most common status code in browsers is the 404 File Not Found error reported when a page or resource has been removed.

You can set the status code to a request using the `setStatus()` method. This is much better than just returning an error to the client, and it can be much more informational because you can specify that a resource is temporarily unavailable (status code 503) or that it's forbidden (status code 403):

```
public void setStatus(int sc)
```

When an error occurs, you can use either of the following `sendError()` methods (taking a status code or taking a code and message):

```
public void sendError(int sc)
public void sendError(int sc, String msg)
```

These also set the status code, but unlike `setStatus()` they also clear the buffer and commit the response, meaning that the servlet can't send any further output to the client in response to this request. Most servers will present a default error page (specific to this error code or all error codes) with information for the client.

Understanding the Request/Response Cycle

Servlets are designed to receive client requests and to develop a response to return to the client. The client's request is mapped to a servlet by the container. You can specify which client requests are mapped to which servlets by configuring the Web application correctly; we'll talk about that issue in Chapter 8. The container also has the responsibility of processing the request into an object-oriented format that the servlet can process, which it does by wrapping the request in a `ServletRequest` object.

Request/Response Interfaces and Wrapper Classes

The `ServletRequest` interface defines the request object that will wrap the client request, which is then passed to the servlet for processing. Similarly, the `ServletResponse` interface defines an object that's passed to the servlet to give the servlet access to the container's response-sending mechanism.

These interfaces define the methods that are made available to the servlet for interpreting the request and returning a response. The Servlet API also provides two convenience wrapper classes to wrap the request and response objects (`javax.servlet.ServletRequestWrapper` and `javax.servlet.ServletResponseWrapper`). They make it easier to implement the `ServletRequest` and `ServletResponse` interfaces and extend their functionality. By default, their methods call the methods of the wrapped object.

You'll take a close look at the servlet request/response interfaces. You'll also build an example servlet called `RequestResponseServlet` that demonstrates using the request and response objects and that returns the data to the client in HTML format.

Implementing the RequestResponseServlet

The `RequestResponseServlet` class extends the `HttpServlet` class. The purpose of the servlet is to generate a page containing two tables, one containing information about the request and the other containing information about the response from the servlet. Figure 6-6 shows what the request table looks like.

Scrolling down the page brings you to the response table (see Figure 6-7).

As you can see, each table simply consists of parameter/value pairs. You'll see the meaning of each parameter during the course of this chapter.

The `RequestResponseServlet` uses a simple `HTMLTable` utility class. This class simplifies the process of creating an HTML table of data so you can concentrate on understanding the methods you're calling in the request and response objects. You'll look at this utility class first, and then you'll learn about the servlet itself.

To run the example, you'll need to add the two Java source code files to the `basicServlets` package source directory. Compile the source code, move the classes into the `classes\basicServlets` directory, and then restart Tomcat. You can then access the servlet with the following URL:

```
http://localhost:8080/servletAPI/servlet/basicServlets.RequestResponseServlet
```

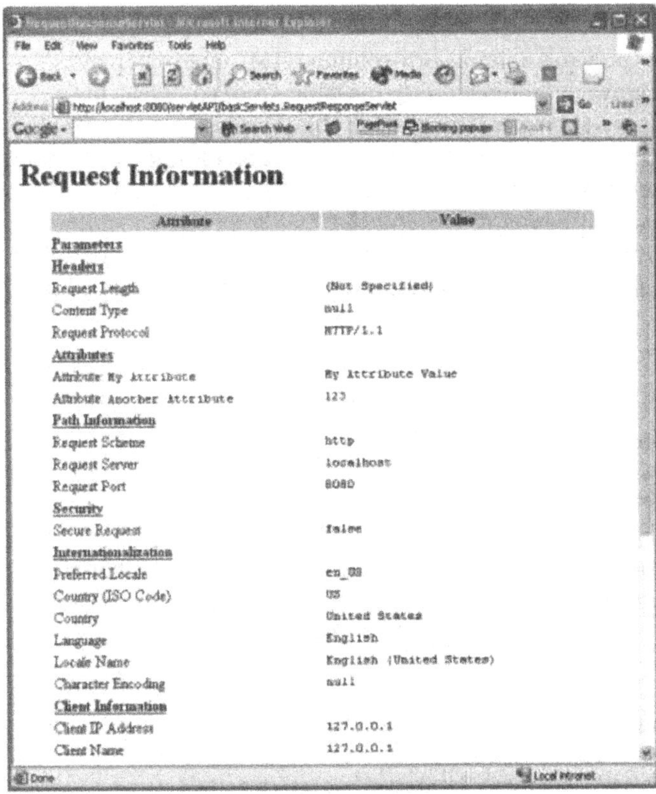

Figure 6-6. The request table

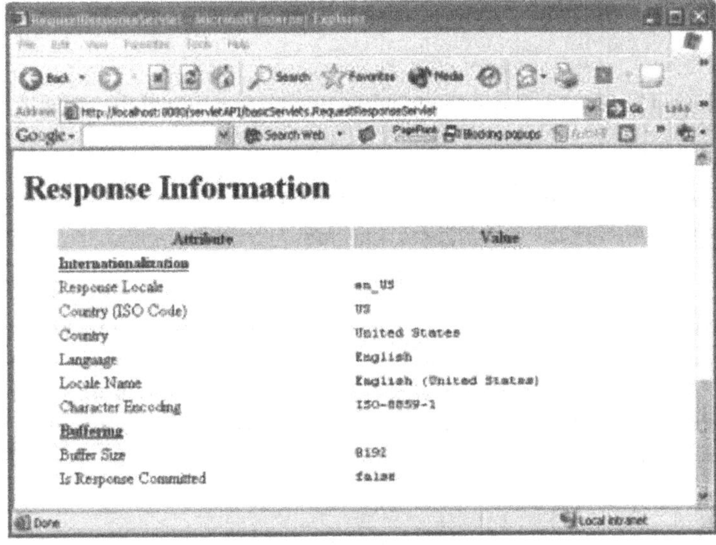

Figure 6-7. The response table

The HTMLTable Utility Class

The `HTMLTable` utility class provides a simple two-column HTML table that may be dynamically created and grown by adding rows to the table. Once complete, the `HTMLTable` object will output a `String` or `StringBuffer` object representing the HTML table. The point of this class is to abstract some of the HTML process into this class so you can reuse the code and so you can move some of the HTML away from the servlet code. (You'll reuse this class in Chapter 7.)

You begin the class by creating the following three `StringBuffer` class variables to hold the table `head` code, the `foot` code, and a `rows` variable to store all the added rows:

```
package com.apress.proj2ee.chapter06;

public class HTMLTable {
  private StringBuffer head;
  private StringBuffer rows;
  private StringBuffer foot;
```

In the `HTMLTable()` constructor method, you initialize and create the table `head` and `foot` objects, and then you initialize the `rows` object to be ready to store row data:

```
public HTMLTable() {
  head = new StringBuffer();
  head.append("<table width=\"90%\" align=\"center\">");
  head.append("<tr><th width=\"50%\" bgcolor=\"lightgrey\">Attribute</th>");
  head.append("<th width=\"50%\" bgcolor=\"lightgrey\">Value</th></tr>");

  rows = new StringBuffer();

  foot = new StringBuffer();
  foot.append("</table>");
}
```

The `appendTitleRow()` method allows you to add a title to a section of the table:

```
public void appendTitleRow(String attribute) {
  rows.append("<tr><td colspan=2><b><u>").append(attribute);
  rows.append("</u></b></td></tr>");
}
```

You provide an `appendRow()` method to add rows to the table, or strictly speaking, to add data to the `rows` `StringBuffer` object. You have three versions of this method, so you can have two `String` parameters and also allow the second variable to be an `int` or `boolean`. The last two overloaded methods convert the parameter into a `String` and forward to the first method. This allows easy maintenance or update of the HTML code, if required:

```
public void appendRow(String attribute, String value) {
  rows.append("<tr><td>").append(attribute);
  rows.append("</td><td><code>").append(value);
  rows.append("</code></td></tr>");
}

public void appendRow(String attribute, int value) {
  appendRow(attribute, new Integer(value).toString());
}

public void appendRow(String attribute, boolean value) {
  appendRow(attribute, new Boolean(value).toString());
}
```

Finally, you have a `toString()` method that overrides the `Object.toString()` method, so printing an `HTMLTable` object will automatically call the overridden `toString()` method and output a well-formatted HTML table. You do this by appending the `rows` and `foot` to the `head` `StringBuffer` object. You also provide a `toStringBuffer()` method, similar to the `toString()` method, that returns the same appended HTML table in `StringBuffer` format:

```
  public String toString() {
    return head.append(rows).append(foot).toString();
  }

  public StringBuffer toStringBuffer() {
    return head.append(rows).append(foot);
  }
}
```

The RequestResponseServlet

The servlet extends the `HttpServlet` class and implements the `doGet()` method to build two tables of information about the request and response objects:

```
import javax.servlet.*;
import javax.servlet.http.*;

import java.io.PrintWriter;
import java.io.IOException;

import java.util.Locale;
import java.util.Enumeration;

public class RequestResponseServlet extends HttpServlet {
```

The doGet() method calls the getRequestTable() and getResponseTable() methods to build HTML tables of request and response information. These are the real content of the page, and you'll implement these methods later in this section, as you come to understand the ServletRequest and ServletResponse interfaces in more depth:

```
public void doGet(ServletRequest request, ServletResponse response)
                                throws ServletException, IOException {
  StringBuffer requestTable = getRequestTable(request);
  StringBuffer responseTable = getResponseTable(request, response);
```

Then you display a simple HTML page with the two tables included. This completes the request processing:

```
  response.setContentType("text/html");
  PrintWriter out = response.getWriter();

  //HTML page
  out.println("<html><head><title>RequestResponseServlet</title>");
  out.println("</head><body>");
  out.println("<h1>Request Information</h1>" + requestTable + "<hr>");
  out.println("<h1>Response Information</h1>" + responseTable);
  out.println("</body></html>");
  out.close();
}
```

So, the most interesting part of the processing of the request and response objects takes place in the getRequestTable() and getResponseTable() methods. These methods take their corresponding ServletRequest or ServletResponse objects as parameters. They then use these objects to extract information about the request/response and construct an HTML table. As we discuss the methods of the ServletRequest and ServletResponse interfaces, you'll develop these methods.

Input and Output Streams

In the previous section, you saw the following two stream classes for reading in the request and writing back the response:

- ServletInputStream
- ServletOutputStream

These classes are abstract classes that the servlet container is responsible for implementing. The ServletInputStream class extends from the abstract java.io.InputStream class. This is the base class for input streams of bytes, and extending from it allows you to construct any necessary input reader objects that take the InputStream class in the constructor. This allows you much greater flexibility in terms of the data you can read in from the client. You can read any data that you can read from an InputStream. You can use the java.io.ObjectInputStream to read in Java serialized objects from a Java applet or application client. You can also use a java.io.BufferedInputStream to read from the input stream and buffer the input.

Similarly, the ServletOutputStream class extends from the abstract java.io.OutputStream class. This is the base class for outputting streams of bytes. This allows you to send response data back with any I/O class that wraps the OutputStream class and enhances its functionality. Therefore, you can serialize Java objects back to the client using the java.io.ObjectOutputStream class, or you can use a PrintWriter to write text to the stream.

These streams provide servlets with the flexibility to support almost any type of client application, including browsers, Java applets, Java applications, and other applications. You use the streams to receive client data and return your response back to the client. You rarely use the ServletInputStream and ServletOutputStream directly. Normally, you wrap these objects in more suitable classes from the java.io package.

The ServletInputStream Class

The ServletInputStream is wrapped in a suitable InputStream class from the java.io package. You can use it wherever you'd use an InputStream to construct an input class, such as a DataInputStream for reading primitive types (and Strings) or an ObjectInputStream for reading serialized Java objects.

For example, you could read in a number of Java objects as follows:

```
ServletInputStream input = request.getInputStream();
ObjectInputStream ois = new ObjectInputStream(input);

String someEvent = (String) ois.readObject();
Date eventDate = (Date) ois.readObject();

input.close();
```

As you can see, the three steps involved are as follows:

1. Access the request's InputStream, and wrap it in an ObjectInputStream.
2. Read in the objects. If you know which objects are being received, you can cast them into their subtype. Alternatively, you could perform a check (using the instanceof operator) before casting. If you try an invalid cast, you'll get a runtime error.
3. Finally, you close the stream.

The ServletInputStream class defines the following method, which reads from the input stream, a line at a time:

```
public readLine(byte[] b, int off, int len)
```

The method returns -1 if the end of the stream is reached before the line has been read.

ServletOutputStream Class

The ServletOutputStream is similar to the ServletInputStream class, in that this class is wrapped in a suitable OutputStream class from the java.io package. You can use it wherever you'd use an OutputStream to construct an output class.

For example, you could serialize a number of Java objects to a Java client, wrapping in the ObjectOutputStream class as follows:

```
ServletOutputStream output = response.getOutputStream();
ObjectOutputStream oos = new ObjectOutputStream(output);

oos.writeObject("a String");
oos.writeObject(new Date());

output.close();
```

Here, the three steps involved are as follows:

1. Access the response's OutputStream, and wrap it in an ObjectOutputStream.
2. Write out the objects to the ObjectOutputStream.
3. Close the stream.

The ServletOutputStream class provides 15 overloaded variants of the print() and println() methods.

The basic print() methods take the full range of primitive types (boolean, char, double, float, int, long) or a String object as parameters, and they print them to the stream. For example:

```
public void print(boolean b)
```

The following variant of the println() method writes a carriage return line feed (CRLF) to the stream:

```
public void println()
```

The println() methods print the full range of primitive types (boolean, char, double, float, int, long) or a String object to the stream, followed by a CRLF. For example:

```
public void println(float f)
```

You can also use the java.io.PrintWriter class for output. If you were returning character-based (text) data to the client, you'd usually use a PrintWriter object to write to the stream. The process is similar to that shown for outputting with ServletOutputStream. The main methods used are the println() or print() methods, similar to those of ServletOutputStream. These are overloaded to take any primitive type or a String as a parameter (see the Javadocs for more information at http://java.sun.com/j2se/1.4/docs/api/java/io/PrintWriter.html). For example:

```
PrintWriter out = response.getWriter();

out.println("<html><head><title>The Page</title></head>");
out.println("<body>Some text</body></html>");

out.close();
```

Introducing Servlet/Container Communication

The servlet container is responsible for managing, creating, and destroying servlets in a Web application. Therefore, the container needs a way to communicate with the servlet, and vice versa.

The servlet container uses objects that implement specific interfaces to pass information into the servlet, such as initialization parameters and information about the container or context in which the servlet is being executed.

These are implemented as interfaces because the interface defines the contract between the objects passed to the servlet and the servlet itself. However, the specific implementation of the interface is the responsibility of the servlet container, and the container may incorporate other features customized to the container. The servlet is given access to the specific methods defined by the interfaces.

The servlet container uses the ServletConfig interface to create an object that contains information that may be required to configure the servlet. It contains any servlet initialization parameters, the servlet's name (as known to the container), and a ServletContext object. The ServletConfig object is passed to the init() method of the servlet, which then stores a reference to this object and, if required, extracts information required to initialize the servlet.

The container constructs the ServletContext interface object to hold information about the servlet and container environment (such as the server name and version, attributes, and so on). The ServletConfig object contains methods to access the ServletContext object, and vice versa.

ServletContext lifecycle events, such as changes to the ServletContext object or the ServletContext attributes, generate ServletContextEvent and ServletContextAttributeEvent objects. You can develop listener classes to listen for these events, implementing the ServletContextListener interface and the ServletContextAttributeListener interface, respectively.

Implementing ContainerServlet

As we discuss the ServletConfig and ServletContext interfaces, you'll implement an example ContainerServlet that will use many of the methods discussed.

The ContainerServlet class extends the HttpServlet class to provide a basic servlet that demonstrates using the ServletConfig and ServletContext objects and returns the data to the client in HTML format. The servlet outputs a table of Servlet-Config and ServletContext parameters, using the simple HTMLTable utility class you developed in the previous example (see Figure 6-8).

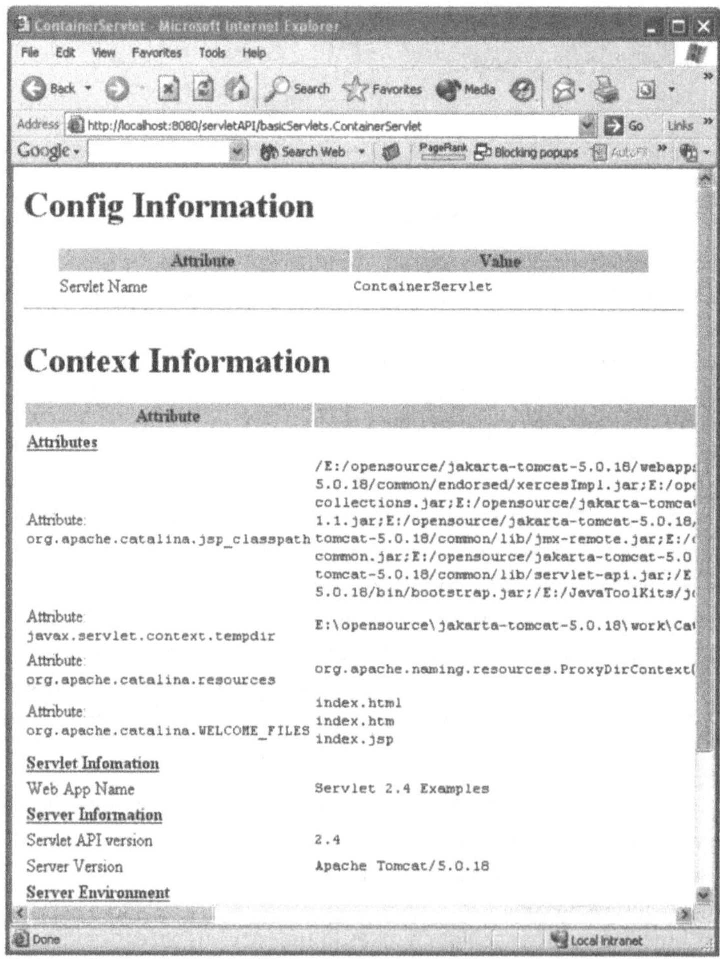

Figure 6-8. ServletConfig *and* ServletContext *parameter table*

As with the previous example, if you want to run the example yourself, you'll need to place the source code files in the basicServlets directory, compile them from the src directory, and then move the Java class files created to the classes\basicServlets directory.

You can access the servlet with the following URL:

```
http://localhost:8080/servletAPI/servlet/basicServlets.ContainerServlet
```

The ContainerServlet

The ContainerServlet example shows how you can retrieve information from the ServletConfig and ServletContext objects provided by the servlet container. Listing 6-1 shows the source code.

Listing 6-1. ContainerServlet

```
package com.apress.proj2ee.chapter06;

import javax.servlet.*;import javax.servlet.http.*;

import java.io.PrintWriter;
import java.io.IOException;
import java.util.Enumeration;
import java.util.Set;

import java.net.URL;
import java.net.MalformedURLException;

public class ContainerServlet extends HttpServlet {
```

The ContainerServlet class is similar to the previous RequestResponseServlet class. You've implemented the goGet() method to process requests. You have two methods to build HTML tables, but in this case the tables contain information about the ServletConfig and ServletContext objects created by the servlet container (see Listing 6-2).

Listing 6-2. ServletConfig *and* ServletContext *Objects*

```
public void doGet(ServletRequest request, ServletResponse response)
  throws ServletException, IOException {

  StringBuffer configTable = getConfigTable(getServletConfig());
  StringBuffer contextTable = getContextTable(getServletContext());

  response.setContentType("text/html");
  PrintWriter out = response.getWriter();

  //HTML page
  out.println("<html><head><title>ContainerServlet</title></head><body>");
  out.println("<h1>Config Information</h1>" + configTable + "<hr>");
  out.println("<h1>Context Information</h1>" + contextTable);
  out.println("</body></html>");
  out.close();
}
```

As you learn about the methods available in the ServletConfig and ServletContext interfaces, you'll build up the getConfigTable() and getContextTable() methods that provide examples of how to use the interface methods.

The ServletConfig Interface

The GenericServlet class implements the ServletConfig interface, so you shouldn't be surprised to find that every method in this interface is implemented (with others) in the GenericServlet class. In fact, when you call a method on the GenericServlet class that's specified by the interface, the GenericServlet class calls the same method on the ServletConfig object passed to it (by the servlet container) in the init() method. The GenericServlet class implements this interface as a convenience, so you don't have to directly reference the ServletConfig object every time you call the method. This means that the method calls in your example should be relatively straightforward and analogous to some of the methods called on the BasicServlet example.

Retrieving Information from ServletConfig

You don't necessarily need to know the servlet initialization parameter names at development time (although usually you would). You can use the getInitParameterNames() method to return an Enumeration of the parameter names that you can iterate though to extract the corresponding values:

```
public java.util.Enumeration getInitParameterNames()
```

The getInitParameter() method extracts the initialization parameter values set for the servlet:

```
public String getInitParameter(String name)
```

The following method returns a reference to the ServletContext object:

```
public ServletContext getServletContext()
```

The following section details the methods you can use on objects of this type. The servlet container knows each servlet by a specific name that's set in the deployment descriptor file. You can retrieve this name using the getServletName() method (essentially the same as the GenericServlet.getServletName() method):

```
public String getServletName()
```

Using ServletConfig in getConfigTable()

The getConfigTable() method takes a reference to the ServletConfig object and returns an HTML table with information from the ServletConfig object. Strictly speaking, since this method is declared within the servlet, you don't have to pass the ServletConfig object in as a parameter because you could just call the getServletConfig() method to get a reference to it. However, this is included as a parameter because you could then refactor this method (and any additional methods) into a separate class without modification:

```
private StringBuffer getConfigTable(ServletConfig config) {
  HTMLTable table = new HTMLTable();
```

You add the servlet name to the table, followed by the initialization parameters (if any). In this case, you haven't configured any for this servlet:

```
  table.appendRow("Servlet Name", config.getServletName());
  Enumeration e = config.getInitParameterNames();
  while (e.hasMoreElements()) {
    String paramName = (String)e.nextElement();
    String paramValue = config.getInitParameter(paramName);
    table.appendRow("Parameter: <code>" + paramName +
                    "</code>", paramValue);
  }
  return table.toStringBuffer();
}
```

Since you haven't added any initialization parameters, the configuration information table shows only the servlet name (see Figure 6-9).

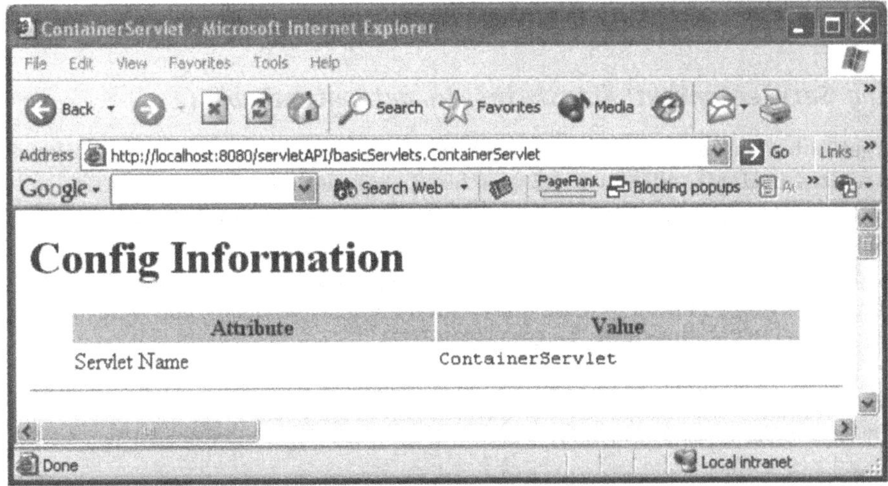

Figure 6-9. Configuration information table

The ServletContext Interface

The `ServletContext` object contains information about the servlet and container environment. The servlet container can give the servlet additional information not already provided by this interface by adding an `attribute` object to the `ServletContext`.

Accessing ServletContext Attributes

Four methods exist to access attributes attached to the ServletContext. This method returns an Enumeration of the attribute names:

```
public java.util.Enumeration getAttributeNames()
```

Calling the getAttribute() method with a specified attribute name returns a reference to the requested attribute (or null if the attribute doesn't exist):

```
public Object getAttribute(String name)
```

Calling the removeAttribute() method will remove the specified attribute (if it exists) from the ServletContext:

```
public void removeAttribute(String name)
```

Calling the setAttribute() method with a name and Object stores the Object (as an attribute), bound to the specified name:

```
public void setAttribute(String name, Object object)
```

Using ServletContext Attributes in getContextTable()

The getContextTable() method takes a reference to the servlet's ServletContext object and returns an HTML table (in a StringBuffer object) with information from the ServletContext object. Similar to the previous method, you could access the servlet's ServletContext object using the getServletContext() method of the GenericServlet (you don't necessarily need to pass it as a parameter). However, you've included it as a parameter in case you want to reuse this method for other servlets. If you were to do so, you'd abstract the method into a separate class:

```
private StringBuffer getContextTable(ServletContext context) {
  HTMLTable table = new HTMLTable();

  table.appendTitleRow("Attributes");
```

Here, you'll iterate through the attributes set by the servlet container. Since the attributes may be any type derived from Object, you check their type, printing the Object.toString() value if they're not String or String arrays:

```
Enumeration e = context.getAttributeNames();
while (e.hasMoreElements()) {
  String paramName = (String)e.nextElement();
  Object paramObject = context.getAttribute(paramName);
  String paramValue = "";
```

```
  if (paramObject instanceof String) {
    paramValue = (String)context.getAttribute(paramName);
  } else if (paramObject instanceof String[]) {
    String[] paramArray = (String[])context.getAttribute(paramName);
    for (int i = 0; i < paramArray.length; i++) {
      paramValue = paramValue + paramArray[i] + "<br>";
    }
  }
  else {
    paramValue = context.getAttribute(paramName).toString();
  }
  table.appendRow("Attribute: <code>" + paramName +
                  "</code>", paramValue);
}
```

Obtaining General Servlet Information

The following methods return information about the servlet and its initialization parameters. The first method returns an `Enumeration` of the parameter names, and the second returns the requested parameter (or `null` if it doesn't exist):

```
public java.util.Enumeration getInitParameterNames()
public String getInitParameter(String name)
```

The `getServletContextName()` method will return the name of this Web application as known to the servlet container:

```
public String getServletContextName()
```

Retrieving General Servlet Information in getContextTable()

To extract information about the servlet, you begin with the Web application's name, as it's known to the servlet container. You then add any initialization parameters to the table:

```
table.appendTitleRow("Servlet Information");
table.appendRow("Web App Name", context.getServletContextName());
Enumeration enum = context.getInitParameterNames();
while (enum.hasMoreElements()) {
  String paramName = (String)enum.nextElement();
  String paramValue = context.getInitParameter(paramName);
  table.appendRow("Parameter: <code>" + paramName + "</code>",
                  paramValue);
}
```

However, since you haven't configured any initialization parameters, they won't be displayed. We'll talk more about how to set up initialization parameters for a servlet in the next chapter.

Getting Server Information

Three methods also exist to access information about the server on which the servlet is running. These two methods return the major and minor versions of the Servlet API, respectively:

```
public int getMajorVersion()
public int getMinorVersion()
```

The following method returns the name and version of the servlet container in which the servlet is running:

```
public String getServerInfo()
```

Getting Server Information in getContextTable()

You can access the version of the Servlet API supported as shown, as well as the server's information and version. This is useful for servlets and Web applications that may be deployed on different servers and need a particular version of the Servlet API, such as 2.4 or later, to function:

```
table.appendTitleRow("Server Information");
table.appendRow("Servlet API version",
        context.getMajorVersion() + "." + context.getMinorVersion());
table.appendRow("Server Version", context.getServerInfo());
```

Getting Information About the Server Environment

Additional methods exist to interact locally with the servlet environment. Calling the `getContext()` method will return a reference to the `ServletContext` object for that relative path (`null` if it doesn't exist):

```
public ServletContext getContext(String uripath)
```

Two methods exist to access a `RequestDispatcher` object that acts as a wrapper for a servlet or specified resource:

```
public RequestDispatcher getNamedDispatcher(String name)
public RequestDispatcher getRequestDispatcher(String path)
```

You use the first method to access a specific `RequestDispatcher` object for a specified servlet name. The second method accesses a specific `RequestDispatcher` object for a specified resource (at the given path). This second method can take the path to a servlet or file, and you can use it to include, or forward, a request to a servlet or static file.

Passing the getRealPath() method a virtual path returns a real file path to this resource on the current server:

```
public String getRealPath(String path)
```

This is the local file location, such as c:\jarkarta-tomcat-5.0\webapps\javaserver\index.html or /apps/tomcat/webapps/javaserver/index.html, that's represented by the virtual path supplied, such as /index.html.

The getResourcePaths() method will return a Set, analogous to a directory listing, of all the paths to resources within the Web application, whose longest subpath matched the parameter:

```
public java.util.Set getResourcePaths(String path)
```

The getResource() method returns a URL object that maps to the specified path. This must be a valid path within the current application context, such as /index.html:

```
public java.net.URL getResource(String path)
```

Calling the getResourceAsStream() method returns an InputStream object that you can use to read the specified resource. You can wrap this InputStream object in a suitable input object to interpret the resource (for instance, text, serialized Java objects, or a binary or other file):

```
public java.io.InputStream getResourceAsStream(String path)
```

Finally, with the getMimeType() method, you can (attempt to) identify the MIME type of the specified file. This method returns null if the MIME type of this file isn't recognized:

```
public String getMimeType(String file)
```

Getting Server Environment Information in getContextTable()

To complete the getContextTable() method, you'll now look at how you can begin to access the server environment, such as local files:

```
table.appendTitleRow("Server Environment");
table.appendRow("Real Path (<code>\"/\"</code>)",
                context.getRealPath("/"));
```

First, you add the real path (file location) corresponding to a location in your application. Second, you retrieve a Set of resource paths for the relative location specified. Here you're looking for the listing of your root directory. You'll then append the paths to a StringBuffer and add this row to the table:

```
Set setPaths = context.getResourcePaths("/");
Object[] arrayPaths = setPaths.toArray();
StringBuffer bufferPaths = new StringBuffer();
for (int i = 0; i < arrayPaths.length; i++) {
  bufferPaths.append((String)arrayPaths[i]).append("<br>");
}
table.appendRow("Paths", bufferPaths.toString());
```

Next, you retrieve a `URL` object for the specified `index.html` page. You could use this `URL` object to retrieve the object, if required, but here you add its location to the table. If there's a problem, you output an indication that this returned a `null` `URL`:

```
try {
  URL url = context.getResource("/index.html");
  if (url != null) {
    table.appendRow("URL (<code>\"/index.html\"</code>)",
                    url.toString());
  } else {
    table.appendRow("URL (<code>\"/index.html\"</code>)", "null");
  }
} catch (MalformedURLException mfe) {
  table.appendRow("MalformedURLException (<code>\"/index.html\"</code>)",
                  mfe.getMessage() );
}
```

Finally, you determine the MIME type for the `index.html` page. In Tomcat, this maps the extension to its MIME type, if known. It doesn't validate that the file exists:

```
    table.appendRow("Mime Type (<code>\"index.html\"</code>)",
                    context.getMimeType("index.html"));
    return table.toStringBuffer();
  }
}
```

Finally, the method returns the table. Figure 6-10 shows a reminder of what it looks like in the browser.

Utility Methods

You have a couple of `log()` methods (similar to those in `GenericServlet`) that write to the Web application's log file, too:

```
public void log(String msg)
public void log(String message, java.lang.Throwable throwable)
```

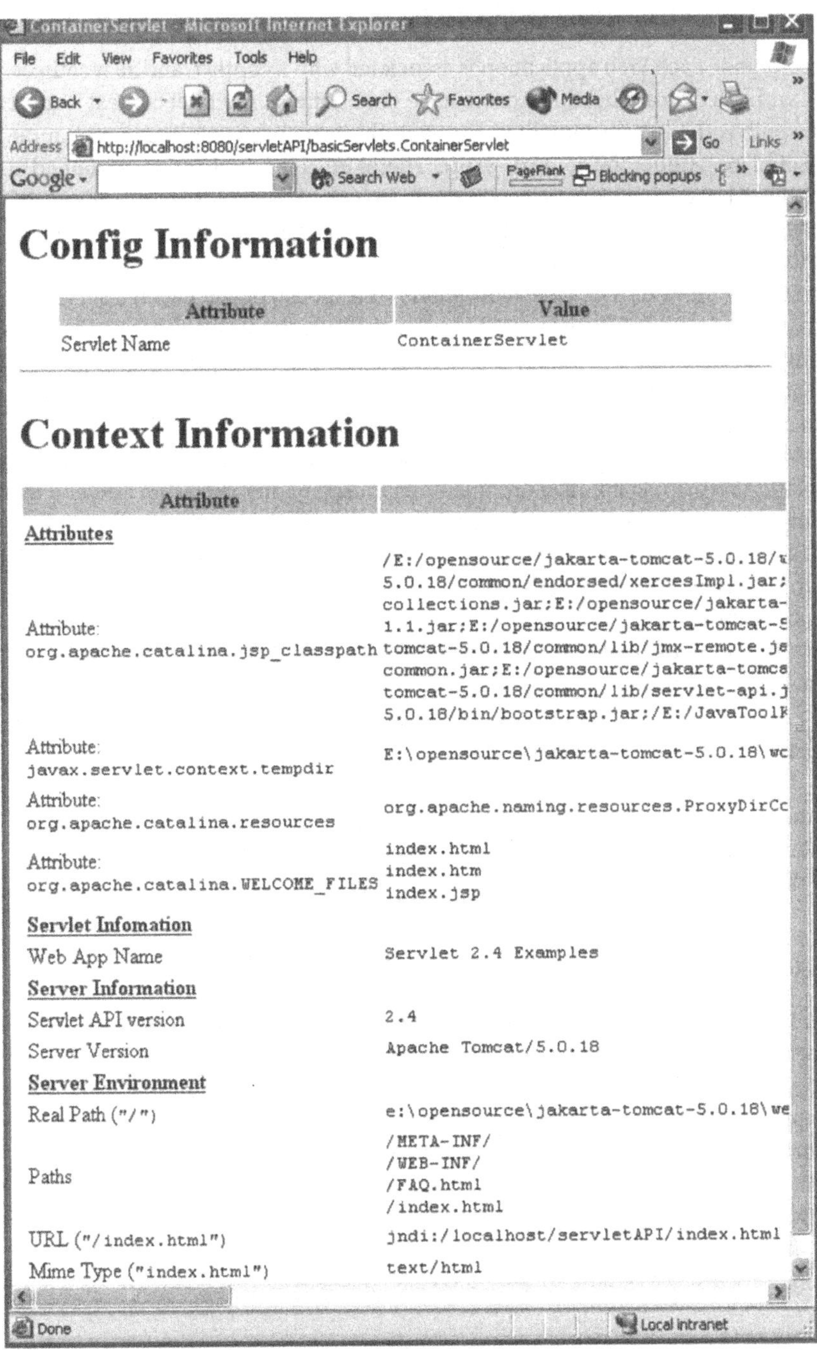

Figure 6-10. The context information table

Introducing the ServletContext

In a Web container, each Web application is associated with a context, and all resources contained within a Web application exist relative to its context. A servlet context is rooted at a known path within a Web container. For example, if you have an e-commerce application, it could exist under the context `/store`. Therefore, if the application contained an HTML file called `home.html`, it'd be accessible at `http://localhost:8080/store/home.html`. All requests that begin with the `/store` request path, known as the *context path*, are routed to the Web application associated with the servlet context.

Each context that exists in a Web container has a special object called a `ServletContext` associated with it. The `ServletContext` represents the Web application's view on the container in which it's deployed. Everything that the Web application is allowed to know about its container can be accessed via the `ServletContext`, and it allows servlets to access resources available to them in the container. You can think of the `ServletContext` as a sandbox for a Web application. This sandbox gives you all the benefits of isolating Web applications mentioned previously (no name clashes and efficient classloading without having to set a classpath).

To create a context for your completed Web application in Tomcat, you have to do only one thing (and you don't always have to do that).

You can examine some of the contexts that exist within a freshly installed version of Tomcat 5.0 by looking in the file `%CATALINA_HOME%/conf/server.xml`. If you look toward the bottom of this file, you'll see a line like this:

```
<Context path="" docBase="ROOT" debug="0">
```

This defines the context for the default application provided with Tomcat 5.0. The next section, which is about deploying your example application to Tomcat, discusses the many parameters you can provide when defining contexts.

Understanding the Deployment Descriptor

We've briefly described the deployment descriptor as a configuration file for the Web application. In this section, you'll take a closer look at it.

The deployment descriptor conveys the elements and configuration information of a Web application between its developers, assemblers, and deployers. The deployment descriptor defines all types of information, from information about the Web application itself to information about its constituent parts, and most important, it contains how those parts are assembled into a complete Web application. This section discusses the elements of the deployment descriptor that are important for most Web applications.

The way in which you write a deployment descriptor is often the key to how well a Web application fits its purpose. It's simple to write the components of a Web application, but considering how it should be assembled is an often-neglected task and not allocated the appropriate development time.

The areas of the deployment descriptor you'll focus on are as follows:

- Servlet definitions and mappings
- Servlet context initialization parameters
- Application lifecyle listener classes
- Filter definitions and filter mappings
- Error pages
- Welcome pages
- Simple file-based security

To illustrate the parts of the deployment descriptor, you'll see a simple example descriptor file and then proceed to an explanation of its constituent parts. For Servlet 2.4, the deployment descriptor is defined in terms of an XML schema document, not a DTD as in previous versions of the specification.

However, you should note the following important rules about the deployment descriptor, which should be adhered to so that the deployment descriptor is valid for Web applications using the Servlet 2.4 specification:

- The deployment descriptor must reside in the `WEB-INF` directory of your Web application.
- It must be a well-formed XML file named `web.xml`.
- This XML file must conform to the XML schema document located at `http://java.sun.com/xml/ns/j2ee/web-app_2_4.xsd`.

The next section shows an example `web.xml` file.

An Example Deployment Descriptor

Listing 6-3 shows the example deployment descriptor. Once you understand the relevant parts of the deployment descriptor, you'll then validate it against the XML schema document.

Listing 6-3. Same Deployment Descriptor

```
<web-app xmlns="http://java.sun.com/xml/ns/j2ee"
        xmlns:xsi="http://www.w3.org/2001/XMLSchema-instance"
        xsi:schemaLocation="http://java.sun.com/xml/ns/j2ee web-app_2_4.xsd"
        version="2.4">
```

At the start of the file, you need to declare the namespace and location of the XML schema document for the file. All servlet deployment descriptors must indicate the Web application schema by using the J2EE namespace `http://java.sun.com/xml/ns/j2ee/` and by indicating the version of the schema using the `version` attribute.

You can publish the version of the schema using the `xsi:schemaLocation` attribute for the J2EE namespace with the following location: `http://java.sun.com/xml/ns/j2ee/web-app_2_4.xsd`. This is different from the way it was done in Servlet 2.3 using the `<!DOCTYPE>` tag.

The subelements of the `<web-app>` element are where you can find all the information for the Web application. These include several elements that give information about the entire Web application. While you won't use every available element defined in the schema in this sample, you can see all the available elements in the schema in Figure 6-11.

The `<display-name>` element allows you to specify a short name for the Web application. This element allows the name of the Web application to be displayed by tools that include the graphical user interface (GUI) deployment utilities supplied with many of the mainstream application servers. It has an optional attribute `xml:lang` to indicate which language is used in the description. The default value of this attribute is English (`en`).

The `<description>` element allows you to provide a short textual description of the purpose of this Web application. This is a simple form of documentation for the overall Web application. This element has an optional attribute called `xml:lang` to specify the language:

```
<display-name>Test Web Application</display-name>
<description>A test web application</description>
```

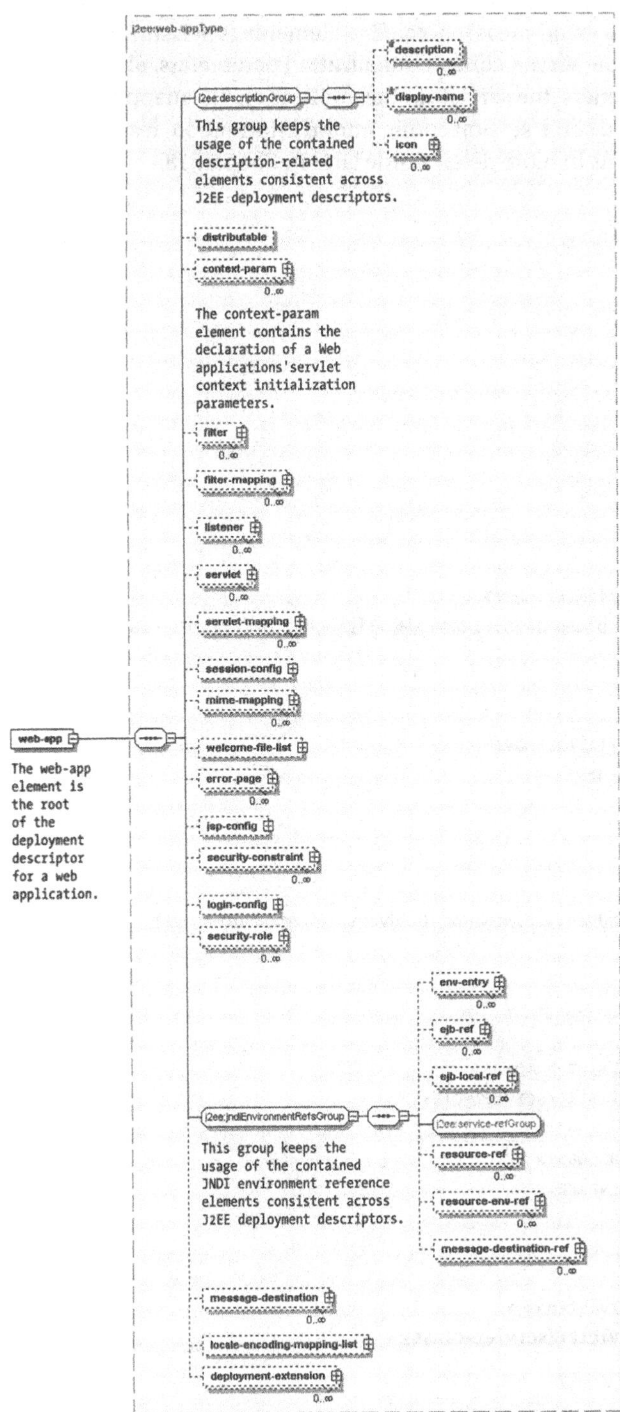

Figure 6-11. The `<web-app>` *element*

Next you have the <context-param>, <filter>, <filter-mapping>, <listener>, <servlet>, <servlet-mapping>, and <session-config> elements (see Listing 6-4). These contain information about the servlet context initialization parameters, filter configurations, any application listeners, the servlets in the application, the mapping of the servlets to specific URLs, and some session configuration information, respectively. You'll examine these elements in more detail a little later in Chapter 18.

Listing 6-4. Other Elements

```
<context-param>
  <param-name>
    adminEmail
  </param-name>
  <param-value>
    admin@apress.com
  </param-value>
</context-param>

<filter>
  <filter-name>SignOnFilter</filter-name>
  <filter-class>com.sun.j2ee.blueprints.signon.web.SignOnFilter</filter-class>
</filter>

<filter-mapping>
  <filter-name>SignOnFilter</filter-name>
  <url-pattern>/*</url-pattern>
</filter-mapping>

<listener>
  <listener-class>
    com.sun.j2ee.blueprints.adventure.web.model.AdventureComponentManager
  </listener-class>
</listener>

<servlet>
  <servlet-name>Servlet1</servlet-name>
  <servlet-class>example.Servlet1</servlet-class>
  <init-param>
    <param-name>version</param-name>
    <param-value>0.1b</param-value>
  </init-param>
</servlet>
<servlet>
  <servlet-name>Servlet2</servlet-name>
  <servlet-class>example.Servlet2</servlet-class>
</servlet>

<servlet-mapping>
  <servlet-name>Servlet1</servlet-name>
  <url-pattern>/home.html</url-pattern>
```

```
</servlet-mapping>
<servlet-mapping>
  <servlet-name>Servlet2</servlet-name>
  <url-pattern>/AnotherServlet</url-pattern>
</servlet-mapping>

<session-config>
  <session-timeout>30</session-timeout>
</session-config>
```

Then you encounter the `<welcome-file-list>` and `<error-page>` elements (see Listing 6-5). Here you define the files to use as the welcome and error pages for the application.

Listing 6-5. The `<welcome-file-list>` *and* `<error-page>` *Elements*

```
<welcome-file-list>
  <welcome-file>
    /index.html
  </welcome-file>
</welcome-file-list>

<error-page>
  <exception-type>
    java.lang.ArithmeticException
  </exception-type>
  <location>
    /chapter06/error.html
  </location>
</error-page>
<error-page>
  <error-code>
    404
  </error-code>
  <location>
    /404.html
  </location>
</error-page>
```

The final set of elements, shown in Listing 6-6, deals with Web application security. Again, we'll explain these tags in more detail later in the "HTTP Authentication" section.

Listing 6-6. Other Elements

```
  <security-constraint>
    <web-resource-collection>
      <web-resource-name>SecureResource</web-resource-name>
      <url-pattern>/admin/*</url-pattern>
      <http-method>GET</http-method>
```

```
      <http-method>POST</http-method>
    </web-resource-collection>

    <auth-constraint>
      <role-name>admin</role-name>
    </auth-constraint>

  </security-constraint>

  <login-config>
    <auth-method>BASIC</auth-method>
    <realm-name>Secure Realm</realm-name>
  </login-config>

</web-app>
```

Although the previous deployment descriptor looks daunting because of its size and use of different, perhaps unfamiliar, elements, you'll soon see that it's simple.

Servlet Context Initialization Parameters

The first section of the deployment descriptor we'll discuss is the section concerning application (or servlet context) initialization parameters. This defines initialization parameters for the whole Web application. You'll see in a moment how to define initialization parameters for a specific servlet.

To achieve this, you use the `ServletContext` object. We discussed the `ServletContext` earlier in the chapter and said that it's a servlet's view into the Web application that contains it. As such, if a parameter is set in the `ServletContext`, it's accessible from all servlets in the Web application.

Through the deployment descriptor you can provide the `ServletContext` with any number of initialization parameters. For example, you could use such parameters to convey application information such as an administrator's e-mail address. These parameters are available to the servlets in the Web application via two abstract methods of the `ServletContext`. These are as follows:

- `getInitParameter(String name)`
- `getInitParameterNames()`

The first method returns a `String` containing the value of the parameter, and the second returns an `Enumeration` containing the names of the parameters in the `ServletContext`.

Since these methods are abstract (like all methods on the `ServletContext` interface), the Web container must provide their implementations. In the example, you define one initialization parameter for your Web application. This is as follows:

```
<context-param>
  <param-name>
    adminEmail
  </param-name>
  <param-value>
    admin@apress.com
  </param-value>
</context-param>
```

This parameter represents the e-mail of the application's administrator. You can pull this into any servlet in the application so that the e-mail used is consistent throughout the system and any modifications to it need to be made in only a single place. To obtain this parameter in any particular servlet, you can use the following code:

```
String adminEmail = getServletContext().getInitParameter("adminEmail");
```

You'll now look at the parts of the example deployment descriptor that relate directly to servlet deployment.

Servlet Definitions and Mappings

Looking at the deployment descriptor, you can see that it defines two servlets in the Web application. You can see this by looking at the number of unique `<servlet>` elements. You can define as many servlets as you need in your application. The first of your two servlets is defined as follows:

```
<servlet>
  <servlet-name>Servlet1</servlet-name>
  <servlet-class>example.Servlet1</servlet-class>
  <init-param>
    <param-name>version</param-name>
    <param-value>0.1b</param-value>
  </init-param>
</servlet>
```

The `<servlet>` element contains several child elements that give information about the servlet. This information includes the unique name that the servlet is registered with in this Web application and the full name of the class that implements the servlet's functionality. The `<servlet-name>` element gives the servlet a unique name within the Web application. In the case of your first servlet, you can see that it's called `Servlet1`.

The `<servlet-class>` element gives the fully qualified class name of the class that implements the functionality of this servlet. In the case of your first servlet, you can see that `Servlet1` is implemented in the class `example.Servlet1`.

In this example, you're defining a servlet class, but it's also possible to specify a JSP file using the `<jsp-file>` element. You can specify one or the other, not both. If a `<jsp-file>` is specified and the `<load-on-startup>` element is present, then the JSP page should be precompiled and loaded.

The element `<load-on-startup>` indicates that this servlet should be loaded (instantiated and have its `init()` method called) on the startup of the Web application. The content of this element is an integer that indicates the order in which the servlet should be loaded. If the value is a negative integer, or the element isn't present, the container is free to load the servlet whenever it chooses. If the value is a positive integer or zero, the container must load and initialize the servlet as the application is deployed. The container must guarantee that servlets marked with lower integers are loaded before servlets marked with higher integers. This element is usually present if you have a dependency on a servlet, such as a logging servlet, that's used by your application.

Looking at the `<servlet>` element for your first servlet, you can see that it contains more than just the name and class of the servlet. It also contains an `<init-param>` element. This element allows you to specify initialization parameters for your servlet. You can use these parameters for many purposes—for example, for setting the language of an application or for defining the location of a configuration file for the application. As you can see, your servlet has one parameter set. The `<param-name>` child element gives the name that the parameter can be accessed by, and `<param-value>` gives the starting value for the parameter.

You can access the parameter from your first servlet using the `getInitParameter()` method on the `ServletConfig` object. Therefore, to get access to the parameter defined for your first servlet, you can use the following code within the servlet's class:

```
String version = getServletConfig().getInitParameter("version");
```

Note that you don't need to get the `ServletConfig` object explicitly, as the `GenericServlet` class implements the `ServletConfig` interface, so the method is available to you.

Servlet Mappings

Once you've defined your servlet through the `<servlet>` element, you need to map it to a particular URL pattern. This is necessary so that the Web container knows which requests to send to a particular servlet.

So, why can you not just pass all requests to the servlet with the same name as the end of the URL? For example, `http://localhost:8080/mywebapp/Servlet1`, would be routed to the servlet defined with the name `Servlet1`. This would seem like a logical approach, and it's in fact the most common way of implementing the mappings between servlets and URLs. However, the approach isn't very flexible. Imagine if you wanted to map more than one URL to the same servlet, which could check, for example, that a user is logged in. This is where the `<servlet-mapping>` element illustrates its power. An example of the power of this mapping is to hide the implementation of your application from the user. As far as the user is concerned, they can't tell if your application is based on servlets, CGI, or any other technology. This can minimize the risk of hacking.

In your example deployment descriptor, your first servlet is invoked every time `http://localhost:8080/javaserver/home.html` (assuming the Web application is called `javaserver`) is encountered. The unique servlet name you defined in `<servlet-name>` is mapped to a URL pattern, which is referenced here as `<url-pattern>`:

```
<servlet-mapping>
  <servlet-name>Servlet1</servlet-name>
  <url-pattern>home.html</url-pattern>
</servlet-mapping>
```

It's worth mentioning at this stage that servlets can be mapped to more than one URL through the use of wildcards in the `<url-pattern>` child of the `<servlet-mapping>` element. For example, the following example maps every URL to the same servlet:

```
<servlet-mapping>
  <servlet-name>ValidatorServlet</servlet-name>
  <url-pattern>/*</url-pattern>
</servlet-mapping>
```

You can also have more than one `<servlet-mapping>` tag per defined servlet. This allows you to map disparate URLs to the same target.

Session Configuration

The `<session-config>` element defines the session timeout interval for all sessions created in this Web application. The `<session-timeout>` subelement specifies the timeout value and is expressed in a whole number of minutes. If the timeout is zero or less, the container ensures that sessions never time out.

If this element isn't specified, the container must set its default timeout period. This setting is typically used if an application wants to provide a forced timeout. For example, if a session is idle for a certain period, you may want to allow the session to be timed out so you can free resources that may be associated with it. Frequently, you'll see a 30-minute timeout on a session, as follows:

```
<session-config>
  <session-timeout>30</session-timeout>
</session-config>
```

Filter Definitions and Filter Mappings

A *filter* is a reusable piece of code that can transform the content of HTTP requests, responses, and header information. Filters don't generally create a response or respond to a request as servlets do; rather, they modify or adapt the requests for a resource, and they modify or adapt responses from a resource. You can chain filters together, and you'll go through some examples in the next chapter.

The <filter> element declares a filter in the Web application. The filter is mapped to either a servlet or a URL pattern in the <filter-mapping> element, using the <filter-name> value as a reference.

Filters can access the initialization parameters declared in the deployment descriptor at run time via the FilterConfig interface. The <filter-name> element is the logical name of the filter. It must be unique within the Web application and can't be empty. The <filter-class> is the fully qualified class name of the filter. The <init-param> element specifies a name/value pair if any initialization parameters are required for the filter.

The container uses the <filter-mapping> element to decide which filters to apply to a request in what order.

> **NOTE** *You need to pay attention to the order that you define filters, as that's the order they'll be applied when processing a request.*

The value of the <filter-name> element must be one of the filter declarations in the deployment descriptor. You can specify the matching request in either <url-pattern> or <servlet-name>:

```
<filter>
  <filter-name>SignOnFilter</filter-name>
  <filter-class>com.sun.j2ee.blueprints.signon.web.SignOnFilter</filter-class>
</filter>
<filter-mapping>
  <filter-name>SignOnFilter</filter-name>
  <url-pattern>/*</url-pattern>
</filter-mapping>
```

If you wanted the filter to be invoked only when a request comes for a specific servlet, you'd use the <servlet-name> element:

```
<filter>
  <filter-name>SignOnFilter</filter-name>
  <filter-class>com.sun.j2ee.blueprints.signon.web.SignOnFilter</filter-class>
</filter>
<filter-mapping>
  <filter-name>SignOnFilter</filter-name>
  <servlet-name>SecurityServlet</servlet-name>
</filter-mapping>
```

Listeners

The <listener> element indicates the deployment properties for an application listener. The subelement <listener-class> declares that a class in the application must be registered as a Web application listener. The value is the fully qualified class name of the listener class:

```
<listener>
  <listener-class>
    com.sun.j2ee.blueprints.adventure.web.model.AdventureComponentManager
  </listener-class>
</listener>
```

The order that the classes are listed is the order in which the listeners will be invoked. The Web container creates an instance of each listener class and registers it for event notifications prior to the processing of the first request by the application.

Listeners can be based on lifecycle or attribute events that happen in the `ServletContext`, `HTTPSession`, and `ServletRequest` objects. It's entirely possible that there are multiple listener classes listening to each event type.

Using Error Pages

In the early days of Web development, if an error occurred in an application, you'd see the familiar HTTP Error 500 or, worse still, a nasty stack trace in the browser window. For example, if your servlet performed an operation that results in an exception, it's quite common to see the output in the client browser, as shown in Figure 6-12.

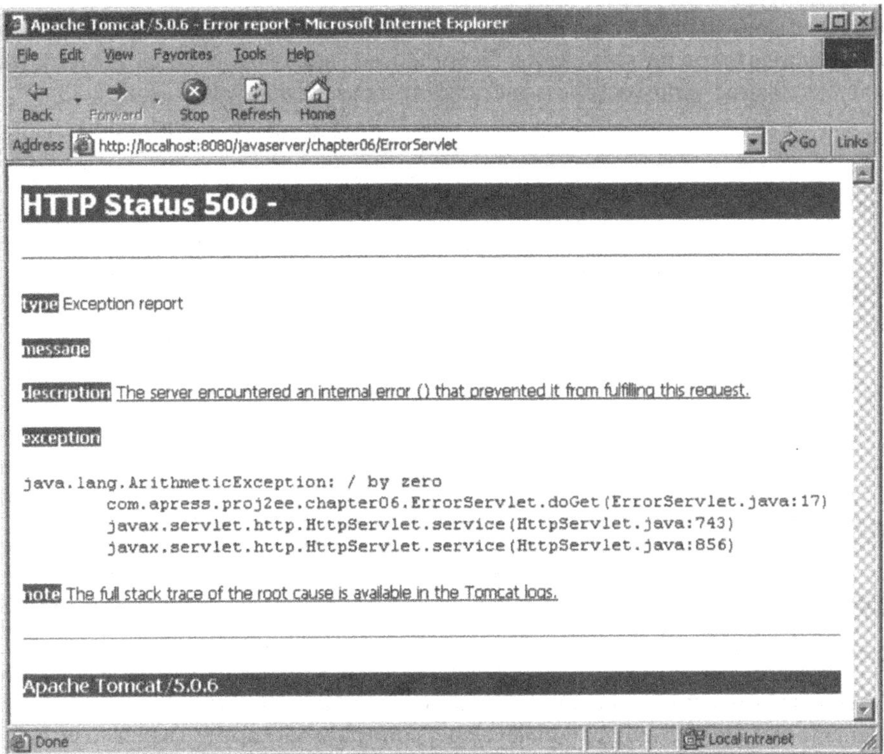

Figure 6-12. HTTP Status 500 error

In a production system, the output of a stack trace such as this doesn't inspire much confidence in the application for the end user. However, you can control how exceptions or errors are displayed to the user with *error pages*. Error pages allow you to specify pages to be shown when particular errors occur; these errors can include Java exceptions, as well as HTTP errors (such as when a page can't be found).

The sample deployment descriptor defines two error pages. The first error page is shown whenever the server encounters a `java.lang.ArithmeticException` (as in Figure 6-12). Listing 6-7 shows the elements to define this.

Listing 6-7. `java.lang.ArithmeticException`

```
<error-page>
  <exception-type>
    java.lang.ArithmeticException
  </exception-type>
  <location>
    /chapter06/error.html
  </location>
</error-page>
```

As you can see, the `<error-page>` element has two children. In this case, these are `<exception-type>`, which defines the exception to catch, and `<location>`, which defines the page to show when the error occurs.

If you were to run the same servlet that produced Figure 6-12, you'd see the resource `error.html` instead of the nasty Java stack trace you saw previously (see Figure 6-13).

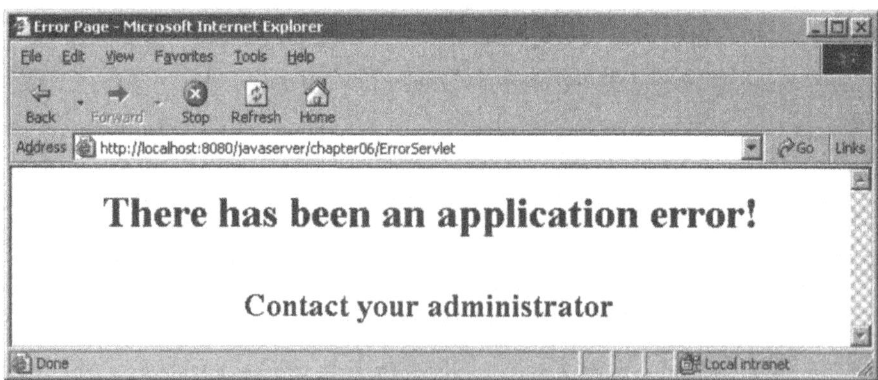

Figure 6-13. `error.html`

This is obviously a lot more user-friendly and readable, and it has the added advantage that the Web application developer controls what happens when an error occurs. However, there are two sides to this coin. Hiding the error information from the user also means hiding it from the people expected to deal with the error. It'd be useful, for example, to log the real error to a file or display it in a collapsible area of the screen. This would isolate the user from a messy stack trace but still allow the programmers to identify the root of the problem.

The sample deployment descriptor also contains an error page definition for an HTTP error. This is defined using the tags shown in Listing 6-8.

Listing 6-8. An HTTP Error

```
<error-page>
  <error-code>
    404
  </error-code>
  <location>
    /404.html
  </location>
</error-page>
```

This looks similar to the previous example, but note the use of the `<error-code>` child element instead of the `<exception-type>` child. This `<error-code>` child defines the HTTP error under which the error page defined will be shown. In this example, whenever the Web container can't find a file requested in the Web application, it will show `404.html` rather than its default error page.

Welcome Pages

If you've developed static Web sites, you'll be familiar with the concept of welcome pages. A welcome page is just a default page for a Web application. Just as a Web site can have a default page (typically `index.html` or `home.html`), a Web application can have a page or resource that's displayed if no specific page within the application is requested.

To define a welcome page for a Web application, you use the elements shown in Listing 6-9.

Listing 6-9. A Welcome Page

```
<welcome-file-list>
  <welcome-file>
    index.html
  </welcome-file>
</welcome-file-list>
```

Note that the file specified in the `<welcome-file>` element may not exist. All this element does is tell the container which files to look for if a request occurs for a directory, rather than a servlet. In this case, the element instructs the container to look for the file `index.html` if no other resource is specified. You can have more than one

`<welcome-file>` element, and the container will look for each resource in order, displaying the first resource found. This is useful, as you can define several common welcome file names (such as `index.html`, `home.html`, `index.htm`, `home.htm`), freeing the developers from having to name their welcome files consistently across the application. In Servlet 2.4, it's possible to have a servlet act as one of the welcome files.

Introducing File-Based Security

So far, your servlets have existed in a vacuum where there's no hacking or distrust. Sadly, this isn't the case in the real world. In reality, you must secure your applications from the dubious characters who exist around the Internet. If you can provide security in your applications, then you can do a whole host of things that would be unadvisable otherwise, such as accepting payments, storing credit card information, and so on.

The issue of security splits into four major areas:

- **Authentication**: Verifying a user is who they say they are
- **Authorization**: Restricting access to resources within an application
- **Confidentiality**: Hiding information from all but authorized parties
- **Integrity**: Ensuring that communications are received unmodified

In the following sections, you'll consider authentication.

HTTP Authentication

Fortunately, HTTP comes with a built-in authentication mechanism. This mechanism is called *Basic authentication*. Basic authentication uses a simple challenge/response system, based on a username and password. The Web container maintains a list of usernames and passwords, and it authenticates the user's details based on this information. The user's details are conveyed to the Web container via a username/password box popped up by the Web browser.

> **TIP** *RFC 2617 details HTTP-based authentication at* `http://www.ietf.org/rfc/rfc2617.txt`.

Basic file-based authentication is easy to configure. In this section, you'll see how to do this for the Tomcat Web container.

The first step in setting up file-based Basic authentication is to decide which resources in your application you want to protect. Once you've done this, you can prepare your deployment descriptor.

The root of the elements defining security is the `<security-constraint>` element. Within this element, you define the resources to secure using the `<web-resource-collection>` element:

```
<web-resource-collection>
  <web-resource-name>SecureResource</web-resource-name>
  <url-pattern>/admin/*</url-pattern>
  <http-method>GET</http-method>
  <http-method>POST</http-method>
</web-resource-collection>
```

You give the collection of resources to secure a name via `<web-resource-name>`. The `<url-pattern>` element defines the URL pattern that represents the resources to secure. In the previous case, everything in the `admin` directory is secured. The `<http-method>` elements define the HTTP methods on the secured resources to which the security applies. In this case, the security is applied to both the `GET` and `POST` methods. If no `<http-method>` elements are present, then the security constraint applies to all HTTP methods.

Once you've described the resources to secure, you must decide which users or groups of users will be able to see the secured resources. You do this using the `<auth-constraint>` element:

```
<auth-constraint>
  <role-name>admin</role-name>
</auth-constraint>
```

The `<role-name>` element gives the role name (user or group) that's able to access this collection of resources.

Having defined the resources to secure and the roles that are able to see the resources, you have to tell your Web application that you want to use Basic authentication. You do this using the `<login-config>` element:

```
<login-config>
  <auth-method>BASIC</auth-method>
  <realm-name>Secure Realm</realm-name>
</login-config>
```

The `<auth-method>` element indicates that you want to use Basic authentication, and the `<realm-name>` tag gives a textual name to show to the user in the pop-up login box. The setup used in this example would show a pop-up to the user like the one shown in Figure 6-14.

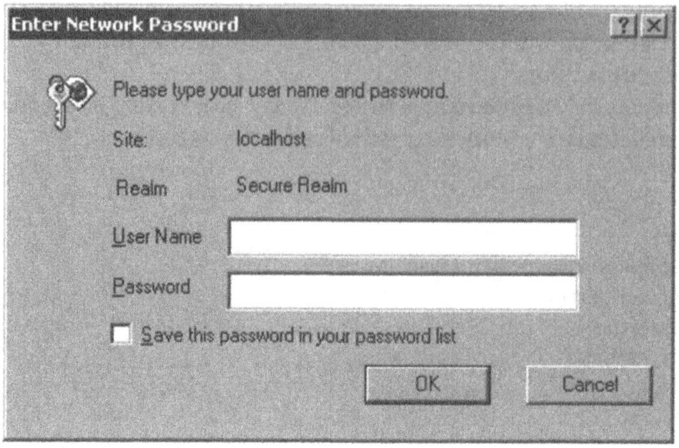

Figure 6-14. Login box

Defining Users in Tomcat

To use security, you also need to set up some users. For file-based security in Tomcat, this is a simple process. The users and groups you want to add can be added to the `tomcat-users.xml` file in the `%CATALINA_HOME%/conf` directory. The following shows a sample setup of this file:

```
<tomcat-users>
  <user name="tomcat" password="tomcat" roles="tomcat" />
  <user name="role1"  password="tomcat" roles="role1"  />
  <user name="george" password="washington" roles="admin" />
</tomcat-users>
```

This defines three users, one of which has a role called `admin`, and as such will be able to access the resources defined previously.

> **TIP** *You'll learn about securing Web applications in more detail in Chapter 9.*

Introducing the ServletContext Lifecycle Classes

Modifications to the `ServletContext` object, such as the initialization or destruction of it by the servlet container, trigger `ServletContextEvent` objects. If your application needs to monitor updates to the context in which the servlet is running, you create a class that implements the `ServletContextListener` interface, and you register it with the servlet container in the application's `web.xml` deployment descriptor configuration file. A listener class method executes when a `ServletContextEvent` event occurs.

Similarly, modifications to `ServletContext` attributes trigger `ServletContext-AttributeEvent` objects. You can also create classes that implement the `Servlet-ContextAttributeListener` interface to listen for these events.

The servlet container notifies the registered classes about the events for which they're listening. It's the container's responsibility to then call the relevant method, defined in the listener interface implemented, to process the event. If the events being listened for never occur, then the servlet container doesn't call the listener methods.

The ServletContextEvent Class

The `ServletContextEvent` object is passed to the relevant listeners for this event. This has a single method. Calling the `getServletContext()` method returns the `Servlet-Context` object that was modified:

```
public ServletContext getServletContext()
```

The ServletContextAttributeEvent Class

The servlet container generates the `ServletContextAttributeEvent` object when the attributes of a particular `ServletContext` are altered. This class has two methods. The first returns the name of the attribute changed, and the second returns the value of the attribute that was altered:

```
public String getName()
public Object getValue()
```

The returned `Object` from the `getValue()` method depends upon the triggering event. If the attribute was added or removed, the added or removed attribute is returned. Alternately, if the attribute was replaced, then the old value of the attribute is returned, allowing it to be saved if required.

The ServletContextListener Interface

You implement the `ServletContextListener` interface to listen for lifecycle events (initialization or destruction) of the servlet context. You implement the following methods to allow your application to react appropriately to these events:

```
public void contextInitialized(ServletContextEvent sce)
public void contextDestroyed(ServletContextEvent sce)
```

The servlet container, in response, calls these methods for the initialization or the pre-shutdown of the `ServletContext`.

The ServletContextAttributeListener Interface

Classes implement the ServletContextAttributeListener interface to listen for changes to attributes in the ServletContext object. Three methods are provided, corresponding to the three types of action that may trigger the ServletContextAttributeEvent. It's the servlet container's responsibility to call these methods once the event trigger occurs:

```
public void attributeAdded(ServletContextAttributeEvent scab)
public void attributeRemoved(ServletContextAttributeEvent scab)
public void attributeReplaced(ServletContextAttributeEvent scab)
```

You implement these methods to process the addition, removal, and replacement of attributes, respectively.

The ServletRequestEvent Class

The ServletRequestEvent object is passed to the relevant listeners for this event. Events of this kind indicate lifecycle events for a ServletRequest. The source of the event is the ServletContext of this Web application. Two methods are available in this object; the getServletRequest() method will return the ServletRequest that's changing:

```
public ServletRequest getRequest()
```

The getServletContext() method returns the ServletContext object that was modified:

```
public ServletContext getServletContext()
```

The ServletRequestListener Interface

The ServletRequestListener interface is implemented to listen for lifecycle events (initialization or destruction) of requests. The following methods are implemented to allow your application to react appropriately to the events when requests are about to come in or go out of scope:

```
public void requestInitialized(ServletRequestEvent sre)
public void requestDestroyed(ServletRequestEvent sre)
```

The ServletRequestAttributeEvent Class

The ServletRequestAttributeEvent class is the event class for notifications of changes to the attributes of ServletRequest. ServletRequestAttributeEvent extends the ServletRequestEvent class:

```
public class ServletRequestAttributeEvent extends ServletRequestEvent
```

The constructor of this class takes the ServletContext, the ServletRequest, and a name/value pair indicating the attributes that are being affected:

```
public ServletRequestAttributeEvent(ServletContext sc,
                                    ServletRequest request,
                                    java.lang.String name,
                                    java.lang.Object value)
```

Two methods are also available in this class. One gets the name of the attribute:

```
public java.lang.String getName()
```

The other gets the value of the attribute:

```
public java.lang.Object getValue()
```

The getValue() method returns the value of the attribute that has been added, removed, or replaced. If the attribute was added, this is the value of the attribute. If the attribute was removed, this is the value of the removed attribute. If the attribute was replaced, this is the old value of the attribute.

The ServletRequestAttributeListener Interface

You can implement a ServletRequestAttributeListener interface in applications interested in being notified of attribute changes in requests. This includes having attributes added, removed, or replaced. If you implemented a ServletRequestAttributeListener interface, a notification when a new attribute was added to the servlet request will invoke the attributeAdded() method. It will be called after the attribute is added:

```
public void attributeAdded(ServletRequestAttributeEvent srae)
```

A notification that an attribute was removed from the servlet request will be sent to attributeRemoved(), which is called after the attribute is removed:

```
public void attributeRemoved(ServletRequestAttributeEvent srae)
```

Notification that an attribute was replaced in the request will cause a call to attributeReplaced() after the attribute is replaced:

```
public void attributeReplaced(ServletRequestAttributeEvent srae)
```

Introducing Additional Interfaces

Finally, the Servlet API provides two interfaces involving servlet threading and request dispatching.

Threading and the SingleThreadModel Interface

Usually, many different client requests may cause the `service()` method of a servlet to execute simultaneously (or virtually simultaneously) in different threads for each request. If the servlet has class-level variables, then if any of the threads update a class variable, another thread could end up with inconsistent values for this class variable.

You have a number of ways to get around this, such as synchronizing access to the variables concerned or moving the variables (if suitable). However, synchronization or locking an object has performance implications because any other threads trying to access the synchronized resource will be blocked from execution until the synchronization lock is removed.

An alternative technique is to implement the `SingleThreadModel` interface in the servlet. This interface defines no methods, so no additional code is required. It's solely used to tag the servlet because the servlet container treats servlets that implement this interface differently.

The container guarantees that only one thread will execute concurrently in the servlet's `service()` method, by synchronizing access to each instance of the servlet. The container may instantiate one or more instances of a servlet implementing this interface and may maintain a pool of servlet instances to process requests.

Most servlets you write need to cope with concurrent requests from remote clients. You'd like those requests to be handled with no side effects resulting from multiple users trying to do the same thing at the same time. It's usually preferred to have a servlet that's thread safe and can handle multiple threads. Threading improves scalability and throughput; however, it requires synchronization to ensure data integrity.

The RequestDispatcher Interface

The servlet container provides the implementation of the `RequestDispatcher` interface. You can use the `RequestDispatcher` in a servlet to forward a request to another resource (servlet, JSP page, Web page, and so on) once you've inspected, and possibly performed some processing on, the request object.

The interface provides two methods: `forward()` and `include()`. Using the `forward()` method means that you forward the request to another resource, and any output in the buffer made before the method call is discarded:

```
public void forward(ServletRequest request, ServletResponse response)
```

You can use the `include()` method almost like a server-side include (SSI), where the servlet can process the request and include the resource (the servlet or HTML Web page output) as part of the page:

```
public void include(ServletRequest request, ServletResponse response)
```

Now you'll see an example of how you could use the `RequestDispatcher` interface.

Implementing the RequestDispatcherServlet

This servlet demonstrates how you can use the `RequestDispatcher` interface. The purpose of this servlet is to present a listbox with a list of resources (servlets and HTML files) available within the Web application and to return information on the requested resource beneath this. The servlet uses a `Dispatching` interface that declares constants corresponding to your previously developed servlets. Any class that implements this interface has access to the constants as if they were declared in that class.

To use the servlet, you'll need to add the source code for the servlet and the interface to the `\src\basicServlets` directory, compile them, and move the classes to the `\classes\basicServlet` directory, as with previous examples. Figure 6-15 shows the servlet at work, displaying the output of the `BasicServlet` included within the Web page. You can access the servlet at the following URL:

```
http://localhost:8080/servletAPI/servlet/basicServlets. ➥
RequestDispatcherServlet?servlet=/basicServlets.BasicServlet
```

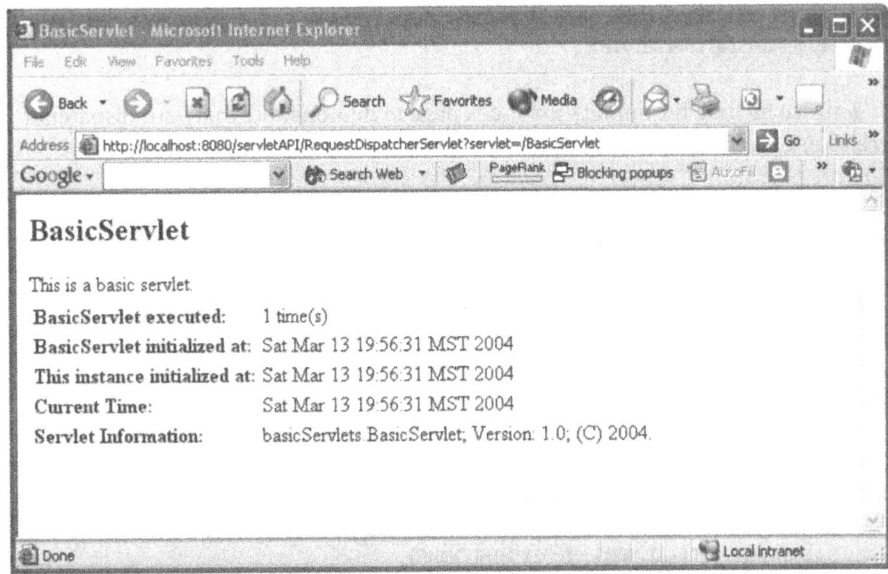

Figure 6-15. `BasicServlet`

The Dispatching Interface

First, the `Dispatching` interface has no methods and simply declares constants that represent your previous servlets:

```
package com.apress.proj2ee.chapter06;

public interface Dispatching {
```

Second, for each servlet you previously developed, you have two constants. The first is the mapping for the servlet resource, and the second is the name of the servlet:

```
public static final String BASIC_SERVLET =
      "servlet/basicServlets.BasicServlet";
public static final String BASIC_SERVLET_NAME = "BasicServlet";

public static final String REQUEST_RESPONSE_SERVLET =
      "servlet/basicServlets.RequestResponseServlet";
public static final String REQUEST_RESPONSE_SERVLET_NAME =
      "RequestResponseServlet";

public static final String CONTAINER_SERVLET =
      "servlet/basicServlets.ContainerServlet";
public static final String CONTAINER_SERVLET_NAME =
      "ContainerServlet";

public static final String REQUEST_DISPATCHER_SERVLET_PACKAGE =
      "basicServlets.RequestDispatcherServlet";
public static final String REQUEST_DISPATCHER_SERVLET_NAME =
      "RequestDispatcherServlet";
```

You also include the application index page to demonstrate that your dispatcher can also use static HTML files as well as servlets:

```
public static final String INDEX_HTML = "index.html";
public static final String INDEX_HTML_NAME = "Index Page";
```

Finally, you create two `String` arrays of the servlet/resource paths and names for use in your `RequestDispatcherServlet`:

```
  public static final String[] RESOURCES =
       {BASIC_SERVLET, REQUEST_RESPONSE_SERVLET, CONTAINER_SERVLET, INDEX_HTML};

  public static final String[] RESOURCES_NAMES =
       {BASIC_SERVLET_NAME, REQUEST_RESPONSE_SERVLET_NAME,
        CONTAINER_SERVLET_NAME, INDEX_HTML_NAME};
}
```

The RequestDispatcherServlet Class

The RequestDispatcherServlet class implements your Dispatching interface so you can access the constants defined previously:

```
package basicServlets;

import java.io.IOException;
import java.io.PrintWriter;
import java.util.Enumeration;
import javax.servlet.*;import javax.servlet.http.*;

public class RequestDispatcherServlet
                          extends GenericServlet implements Dispatching {

  private static StringBuffer form = new StringBuffer();

  public void service(ServletRequest request, ServletResponse response)
                                   throws ServletException, IOException {
```

The start of the servlet code is fairly standard; you access the PrintWriter object and retrieve the servlet parameter indicating which servlet is required:

```
ServletContext servletContext = getServletContext();
ServletConfig config = getServletConfig();
PrintWriter out = response.getWriter();
String servletRequested = request.getParameter("servlet");
```

Next, you access the RequestDispatcher object for the desired servlet. This enables you to use the include() method to access its content on your servlet page. You're using the relative path, and this may include other servlets, JSP pages, and HTML files:

```
RequestDispatcher requestDispatcher =
  servletContext.getRequestDispatcher("/" + servletRequested);

response.setContentType("text/html");
out.println(getPageTitle(servletRequested));
```

You then include the requested resource in your page. This means that the output from the servlet or Web page is included as part of your Web page.

Before you do this, you also attach an attribute to the request. In the Request-ResponseServlet, you check at one point if the response was committed. Since you already have output from this servlet, the response.isCommitted() method may return an incorrect result as it's unaware that it's included in this servlet's output. Therefore, you attach an attribute to the request that serves as an indicator to the RequestResponse-Servlet that you've already started output, and the response.isCommitted() method may return an incorrect result. This is why, in the RequestResponseServlet, you checked for an attribute set:

```
    if (requestDispatcher != null) {
      request.setAttribute("buffer", "written");
      requestDispatcher.include(request, response);
    } else if (servletRequested == null) {
      out.println("Please chose a servlet");
    } else {
      out.println(servletRequested + " isn't recognised by the server");
    }
    out.println("</body></html>");
    out.flush();
  }
```

The `init()` method initializes the form `StringBuffer` object that, because it's unchanging, need be initialized only once:

```
public void init() throws ServletException {
  form.append(getForm());
}
```

The `getPageTitle()` method builds the head of the HTML page that appears before the included resource, as shown in Listing 6-10.

Listing 6-10. The HTML Head

```
private StringBuffer getPageTitle(String servletRequested) {

  StringBuffer sb = new StringBuffer();
  sb.append("<html><head><title>");
  if (servletRequested == null) {
    sb.append("[no servlet requested]");
  } else {
    sb.append(servletRequested);
  }
  sb.append("</title></head><body><h1><code>");
  if (servletRequested == null) {
    sb.append("[no servlet was requested]</code>");
  } else {
      sb.append(servletRequested).append("</code> is shown below");
  }
  sb.append("</h1><p>");
  sb.append(form);
  sb.append("<hr width=100%>");
  return sb;}
```

The `getForm()` method sets up the HTML form. It accesses the constants from the `Dispatching` interface that contain the resources to which the dispatcher object may be directed (see Listing 6-11).

Listing 6-11. The `getForm()` *Method*

```
  private StringBuffer getForm() {
    StringBuffer sb = new StringBuffer();
    ServletConfig config = getServletConfig();

    sb.append("<form method=get action=\"" +
              REQUEST_DISPATCHER_SERVLET_PACKAGE + "\">");
    sb.append("<table><tr><td>Please choose servlet ");
    sb.append("(or other resource) to view:</td>");
    sb.append("<td><select name=\"servlet\">");

    for (int i = 0; i < RESOURCES.length ; i++) {
      sb.append("<option value=\"" + RESOURCES[i] + "\" >" +
                RESOURCES_NAMES[i]);
    }

    sb.append("</select></td></tr><tr><td colspan=2 align=\"center\">");
    sb.append("<input type=\"submit\" ");
    sb.append("value=\"View Servlet/Resource\"></td></tr>");
    sb.append("</table></form> ");
    return sb;
  }
}
```

Using Filters and the Request Dispatcher

Prior to Servlet 2.4, when using and configuring filters, the `<filter-mapping>` in the deployment descriptor was the only mechanism for defining when a filter should be invoked. New in 2.4 is the ability to configure filters to be invoked under request dispatcher `forward()` and `include()` calls. You accomplish this by using the new `<dispatcher>` element in the deployment descriptor. It allows the Web application developer to indicate for a `<filter-mapping>` whether the filter should be applied to requests in a number of way.

A filter will be applied to requests if the subelement `<dispatcher>` is specified in the `<filter-mapping>`. The possible values for the `<dispatcher>` element are as follows:

- `REQUEST`
- `FORWARD`
- `INCLUDE`
- `ERROR`

A value of `REQUEST`, or the absence of any `<dispatcher>` elements, means the filter will be applied under ordinary client calls to the path or servlet, and the `<filter-mapping>` will be used alone.

A value of FORWARD or INCLUDE means the filter will be applied under RequestDispatcher.forward() and RequestDispatcher.include() calls, respectively. The filter will be applied only when the request being processed under a request dispatcher represents the Web component matching the <url-pattern> or <servlet-name>. A value of ERROR means the filter will be applied under the error page mechanism. It's possible to define any combination in the <filter-mapping> element.

You'll now see a couple of examples of how to use filters with the RequestDispatcher.

First, say you have a filter that would be invoked by any client request that starts with /proj2ee1.4 but not underneath a request dispatcher call where the request dispatcher has a path that ends with /proj2ee1.4/.... *Underneath a request dispatcher* means that either a forward or a redirect was done to a URL from a RequestDispatcher object. For example:

```
<filter-mapping>
  <filter-name>Logging Filter</filter-name>
  <url-pattern>/proj2ee1.4/*</url-pattern>
</filter-mapping>
```

Second, say you have a filter that would be invoked only on a request dispatcher include call that ends with a proj2ee1.4. For example:

```
<filter-mapping>
  <filter-name>Logging Filter</filter-name>
  <servlet-name>proj2ee1.4</servlet-name>
  <dispatcher>INCLUDE</dispatcher>
</filter-mapping>
```

Next, you have a filter that would be invoked by any client request that starts with a /proj2ee1.4/... as well as under a request dispatcher forward call where the path ends in /proj2ee1.4/.... For example:

```
<filter-mapping>
  <filter-name>Logging Filter</filter-name>
  <url-pattern>/proj2ee1.4/*</url-pattern>
  <dispatcher>FORWARD</dispatcher>
  <dispatcher>REQUEST</dispatcher>
</filter-mapping>
```

Introducing Servlet Exception Classes

The servlet container normally manages exceptions that occur in servlets. Many exceptions, such as ServletException and IOException (or subclasses of these), are caught and handled by the servlet container, but it's still important to understand the exception-handling process and why they may be thrown. Often, if a client closes a connection before the servlet has finished handling the request, an IOException will be thrown and caught by the servlet container.

Occasionally, when a server is under a heavy load, it may be unable to fulfill requests and may throw an `UnavailableException` (which is a subclass of `ServletException`). The servlet container will then return an error to the client indicating whether this problem is permanent or temporary. Reasons for a permanent `UnavailableException` may include that the resource is configured incorrectly, and a temporary `UnavailableException` may occur if resources (for example, database connections or disk space) are unavailable.

While you're unlikely to throw a `ServletException` directly, you may want to throw an `UnavailableException` when your servlet is unable to access a resource needed to complete the request. You then can indicate how long the client should wait before retrying their request.

You may also create custom exception classes extending from the standard `java.lang.Exception` or `ServletException` classes (as appropriate), which you can use in your Web application.

The ServletException Class

The `ServletException` class provides the following four constructors to instantiate a `ServletException`:

```
public ServletException()
public ServletException(String message)
public ServletException(String message, java.lang.Throwable rootCause)
public ServletException(java.lang.Throwable rootCause)
```

It also provides a `getRootCause()` method to determine the cause of the `Servlet-Exception`:

```
public java.lang.Throwable getRootCause()
```

The UnavailableException Class

The `UnavailableException` class provides two useful constructors. The first specifies the reason for the error and signals permanently unavailable status. The second is used for a temporary problem and takes a second parameter indicating the time (in seconds) that the servlet is expected to be unavailable:

```
public UnavailableException(String msg)
public UnavailableException(String msg, int seconds)
```

The following method returns the expected time that the resource will be unavailable. The number will be negative if there's no estimate or if it's expected to be permanently unavailable:

```
public int getUnavailableSeconds()
```

Finally, the `isPermanent()` method indicates if the problem causing the `UnavailableException` is a permanent or temporary condition:

```
public boolean isPermanent()
```

Handling Listener Exceptions

The various listeners we've already talked about can throw exceptions. However, you need to handle these slightly differently than you handle application exceptions. It's possible for a listener that's being notified of an event to be under the call stack of a different component in the application. For example, this happens if a servlet sets a session attribute and the session listener throws an exception that isn't handled in the code. The container needs to propagate this exception back to the application code, which then handles it. If the exception isn't handled in the application correctly, then the error page mechanism will kick in, so there's some fallback. When the container allows the exception to propagate back to the application, the listener of that event will no longer be called for any further events.

Some exceptions will occur under the same call stack as the application. An example of this is a `SessionListener` that receives notification that a session has timed out and throws an unhandled exception. Another example is a `ServletContextListener` that throws an unhandled exception during a notification of servlet context initialization. In this case, the application implementation has no opportunity to handle the exception. The downside here is that the container may respond to all subsequent requests to the Web application with an HTTP status code 500 to indicate an application error. The way around this is to handle all the exceptions within the notification method implementation.

Introducing Servlet Best Practices

Servlets have been around for some time now, which means there has been plenty of time to find out what works and what doesn't in terms of implementations. The following sections make some suggestions for best practices when writing servlet code for the topics covered so far (you'll look at a couple of other best practices for advanced features in the next chapter):

- Take advantage of `contextInitialized()` and `init()`.
- Pick a framework that implements a Controller.
- Cache static and dynamic data.
- Optimize the `service()` method.
- Consider using a thread pool.

Take Advantage of contextInitialized() and init()

When writing your servlets, take advantage of methods that are guaranteed to be called once, such as the `contextInitialized()` method of the class implementing the `ServletContextListener` interface. This method will be notified when the Web application is ready to process requests. All `ServletContextListener` objects are notified of context initialization before any servlet in the Web application is initialized. Therefore, you can cache information in the `ServletContext` using this method and then let all of the servlets in the Web application have access to it.

The servlet's `init()` method is called only once in the servlet's lifetime, so it's another great place to do initialization. For example, the common approach is to do both static variable allocation and dynamic data processing in the `service()` method. However, taking advantage of `init()` can save you some wasted cycles instead of having to continually allocate static data for each request. You can improve a servlet's performance using `init()` by caching any static data. You can then access this data from the `service()` method.

Pick a Framework That Implements a Controller

If you're planning on writing a servlet that will act as a Controller in the MVC pattern, don't. Why bother reinventing the wheel? Plenty of wheels already exist, are debugged, and are ready for use. Concentrate on writing functionality that's added value for your application. If you're considering using a framework, a number of them use Servlet technology. Struts (`http://jakarta.apache.org/struts/`) is one such framework that already has a class, `ActionServlet`, implemented as a Controller. If you don't want to use the entire framework, at least you can use the `ActionServlet` and tailor it to your needs.

Cache Static and Dynamic Data

Using caching in different areas of your application can significantly improve performance. If there's data that's considered static, such as read-only tables, there's no need to perform a request to access this information each time you need it. You can read the data once, create a variable or data structure, and store the data in memory.

You can use caching for various types of data, whether it's static data, semidynamic data, or dynamic data. *Static* data is data that never changes; *semidynamic* data means that the data changes, but not often. An example of semidynamic data is data that's updated every day or every hour. Semidynamic data changes, but not during every request, and dynamic data changes during every request. While there can be specific performance improvements on semidynamic data, you should consider semidynamic and dynamic data the same in terms of the following best practices:

Browser caching: As you saw previously, caching in the `init()` method is useful for caching static data, and it reduces the creation time of static data for every request; however, remember that you're still passing the data to the client on every request. This type of caching is useful when you want to pass both static data and dynamic data to the client. One more caching technique is using the browser cache and a cache on the server. You can do this by avoiding a call to `service()` if the output content isn't changed. You achieve this technique by implementing the `getLastModified()` method of the `HttpServlet` class.

Caching dynamic data at the server: Web servers send the response with a `Last-Modified:` header that tells the client when the page was last changed. The Web browser sends a request with an `If-Modified-Since:` header, which tells Web server when it last downloaded the page. The server then decides whether the file has changed; if not, it sends a response with the Not Modified 304 status code so that the browser uses its cache page instead of downloading a fresh page. To take advantage of this technique, a servlet should implement the `getLastModified()` method to tell the servlet engine about the last modified time. This method returns time in milliseconds since January 1, 1970.

Application server caching facilities: The third technique is to use your server's caching facility for dynamic data, though not all servers have such functionality. Usually you need to configure the caching properties file. Each server is different, so it's best to check out your server's documentation. Typically, you can specify which servlets you want cached and a session timeout value after which cached content is removed.

The Servlet API's built-in facility: The fourth technique is using the Servlet API's `HttpSession` and `ServletContext` objects for caching. `HttpSession` is available for a user session across multiple requests, and `ServletContext` is available for all the users using the application. You can add cacheable objects into these objects and get those objects whenever you require within their scope. The methods that support caching are as follows:

```
ServletContext.setAttribute(String name, Object cacheableObject);
ServletContext.getAttribute(String name);
HttpSession.setAttribute(String name, Object cacheableObject);
HttpSession.getAttribute(String name);
```

Use listener objects: As already mentioned, implement objects that listen for events such as session events or changes in attribute values. Doing so gives you an opportunity to make data changes to the cache so that information remains current, without having the overhead of constantly changing it.

Optimize service()

When you code the `service()` method for your servlet, typically you'll be doing a lot of writing to output streams. This involves some basic Java performance improvements but is worth mentioning here. You can see some dramatic improvements in performance by following these basic practices:

StringBuffer: Always use `StringBuffer` rather than the + operator when you concatenate multiple strings at run time.

print(): Use the `print()` method instead of `println()`, since `println()` internally calls `print()` anyway. You don't really care about the newline for generating HTML pages, so save yourself an extra method call.

ServletOutputStream: Use the `ServletOutputStream` instead of `PrintWriter` because there's overhead involved in `PrintWriter`. `PrintWriter` is meant for use as a character output stream, and it encodes data to bytes. If you're sending binary data, just use `ServletOutputStream`.

Partial flushes: Do partial flushes on the output buffer to allow the headers and some data to be sent to the client. If you're passing a large amount of data to the client from your servlet, the user may have to wait until the `ServletOutputStream` or `PrintWriter` flushes the data before the display starts to render. This can make your application appear slow to the user. If you want to get the browser to start rendering, start flushing the data using the `flush()` method rather than waiting until the data is completed:

```
ServletOutputStream out = res.getOutputStream();
out.write(header);
out.flush();
// process and write dynamic data here
out.flush(); // flush the dynamic data
out.write(footer);
out.flush();
```

Minimize synchronization: Minimize the amount of code that needs synchronization. Since the `service()` method needs to be thread safe (assuming that you aren't using the `SingleThreadModel`), you should carefully place synchronization blocks around code that absolutely needs it.

Minimize necessary connections: Set the content length to minimize necessary connections. Whenever a browser requests a page, it establishes a socket connection with the Web server to get the requested content. Setting the content length allows for more data to be sent over a single connection, thereby increasing your performance and reducing network traffic. Use the `setContentLength()` method of the response to adjust your content length appropriately. The following will set the `Content-Length:` header:

```
response.setContentLength(size);
```

Control Thread Pool

The servlet container creates a separate thread for every request and assigns that thread to the `service()` method for a multithreaded servlet. When the `service()` method is completed, the thread is removed. Usually, by default, this happens for every request. As you may imagine, this can get expensive with all of this thread creation. There's a better way: use a thread pool.

Most servlet container implementations will have a way to configure a thread pool. Configuration will consist of the number of threads in the pool and the minimum and maximum number of threads to maintain given application characteristics. There's a limit on the number of threads, though this is usually a hardware resource limit. By setting thread pool size correctly, the performance of a servlet improves significantly.

Summary

This chapter introduced the Servlet 2.4 API and focused upon the `javax.servlet` and `javax.servlet.http` packages.

You examined the API structure and design and then looked at the classes and interfaces of the `javax.servlet` package in detail, building some example servlets that used them along the way. You learned about the `Servlet` interface and the `GenericServlet` class that implements this interface, as well as the servlet life cycle.

The chapter then covered the request/response cycle, and it discussed the relevant `ServletRequest` and `ServletResponse` interfaces. The chapter also reviewed their wrapper classes: the `ServletRequestWrapper` and the `ServletResponseWrapper`.

You examined the design and use of the servlet input and output classes `ServletInputStream` and `ServletOutputStream`, followed by a look at servlet container communication through the `ServletConfig` and `ServletContext` interfaces.

Then you learned about the `SingleThreadModel` and the `RequestDispatcher` interfaces. You then looked at the `javax.servlet` package by examining the two servlet exception classes, `ServletException` and `UnavailableException`.

Finally, the chapter wrapped up with some appropriate best practices to try when writing servlets. The next chapter covers some of the more advanced features of the Servlet API.

CHAPTER 7

Using Advanced Servlet Features

Chapter 6 covered the features that are available when writing servlets. In this chapter, you'll explore some of the more advanced features you can use to build robust Web applications. You'll learn about the following:

- Tracking client identity and state
- Working with and maintaining sessions
- Working with lifecycle events
- Using advanced session features
- Creating, configuring, and using filters

Previous chapters noted that Hypertext Transfer Protocol (HTTP) is the protocol most commonly used to communicate with Web applications. Unfortunately, HTTP offers no mechanism for data to be retained between requests; in other words, it can't track the activities of a user across requests.

Why is this important? Well, consider the ubiquitous shopping cart application. A client using this will make several requests to the application; each request may be to add/remove a product to/from the cart, to checkout, and so on. For the application to know what the client has bought upon checking out, it needs to keep track of whatever the user has selected across requests. This means not only uniquely identifying the user on each request, but probably also storing data (state) across requests and associating it with the user. Associating requests with a particular user in this way is often known as maintaining a *session*, and many Web applications use sessions.

You often need to maintain sessions, but HTTP is stateless, so various mechanisms have been devised to enable you to do so. They include the following:

- Rewriting uniform resource locators (URLs)
- Creating cookies
- Using hidden form fields

This chapter discusses these mechanisms, and it shows how they can help maintain state between requests in your Web applications. You'll also see how you can use a selection of interfaces and classes from the Java Servlet application programming interface (API) to create, destroy, and manipulate Java objects that represent sessions in your servlets. The chapter also discusses event listener interfaces that you can use to create classes that listen for changes to the `Session` object.

Over the course of the chapter, you'll build a Web application (based upon servlets) that allows the user to create and modify notes, so you'll also learn how to use these interfaces and classes.

Understanding the Stateless Nature of HTTP

HTTP is by far the most common protocol used to communicate with Web applications.

Consider this communication process: The client sends an HTTP request to a Web server. The server receives the request, applies the necessary processing logic, creates a response, and sends it back to the client. This request/response process happens across a single network connection. At the end of the process, the server closes the connection. In addition, any failure on the server side or any network failure could terminate the request. The client may also terminate the connection before receiving the response from the server. This means that, when the client sends another request, all the request/response cycle happens again, but you must establish a new network connection.

Now, an optional feature in HTTP 1.1 called *keep-alive* allows the client to use the same connection across multiple requests. However, browsers use this feature only when the server supports it and only when the requests happen in rapid succession.

At this point, you may be asking, why do HTTP-based connections exist only for the length of a single request/response cycle? Web servers cater to a potentially large number of users. For a server, accepting a network connection means listening to incoming requests over a socket. This consumes operating system–level resources, including threads and memory. To be able to serve a large number of users, HTTP uses new connections for every request; this means connections aren't held beyond the duration of a request and a response, which minimizes the waste of system resources.

Given this stateless nature of HTTP, basic servlet programming is also stateless. Consider the `javax.servlet.Servlet` interface or the abstract `javax.servlet.http.HttpServlet` class that you use to write your own servlets. Within a service method (such as `doGet()` or `doPost()`), each servlet extracts request parameters, processes some application logic, and then generates the response. After writing the response to the HTTP request, the servlet loses its attachment to the request. For all practical purposes, you may even consider that the servlet instance doesn't even exist. Since an instance may not exist beyond a single request, you can't store any data in the instance variables of a servlet.

From the servlet developer's point of view, this statelessness is a constraint. However, from the server/container's point of view, it's required to offer better performance and scalability by not spawning a new servlet instance for each new HTTP request. This constant spawning is how Common Gateway Interface (CGI) programs work, which is why you see such an improvement when using servlets over CGI scripts. You improve Web container performance because you avoid object allocation for each new request, and you improve scalability because the container will have more resources left to serve more requests.

Why Track Client Identity and State?

The fact that HTTP is a stateless protocol has important consequences when you communicate with Web applications via HTTP. In the introduction to this chapter, we discussed one scenario where you need to maintain state, the shopping cart application. Consider another scenario: Typical online banking can involve one or more banking transactions. Most such transactions may spawn across several pages. To maintain the transactions, you need a mechanism to uniquely identify the user, to track the activity of the user within the site, and to relate the transactions to the account/transaction data stored in backend systems.

Both of these scenarios have the following two important activities:

- **Tracking the identity of a user**: Because the user makes multiple requests to the same Web application over a period of time, you need a mechanism that links these requests. Effectively, this means you need to associate each request with a client identifier so you can identify requests from the same user.

- **Maintaining user state**: Since there's often data associated with each request, you'll need a way to associate the request data with the user who made the request, as well as a way to preserve that data across requests.

The ability to associate a request with the client that made the request is known as maintaining a *session*. However, the obvious next question to ask is, what mechanisms can you use to maintain sessions?

How Do You Maintain Sessions?

In the previous section, you saw that you need to keep track of state in a number of situations. Essentially this means you must preserve the identity of the client and the data associated with the client across requests. Since HTTP is a stateless protocol, just how do Web applications manage to keep track of users?

In the following sections, we'll discuss the various mechanisms you can use to maintain state across requests. You'll consider the following approaches:

- URL rewriting
- Cookies
- Hidden form fields

These techniques maintain sessions in not only Java-based applications but also Web applications written in many other languages. Out of these three, the most common approach is to use cookies.

The Java Servlet API provides a way of maintaining sessions via two of these techniques: cookies and URL rewriting. You'll examine the session-related interfaces and classes from the API in the "Session Management Using the Servlet API" section.

Session handling is based on a simple idea that two entities can identify each other by exchanging some token (a unique identifier that both entities recognize) with each message. For instance, if your name is Bob, and the name Bob is unique as far as the server is concerned, you may send the token `Bob` with each request to the server to uniquely identify you. Of course, this token doesn't need to be your name; it can be any piece of data that uniquely identifies you. The idea behind all session-handling techniques is the same; they all rely on exchanging a server-generated unique ID with each request.

The next section discusses the URL rewriting approach to session tracking.

Session Tracking Using URL Rewriting

URL rewriting is based on the idea of embedding a unique ID (generated by the server) in each URL of the response from the server. That is, while generating the response to the first request, the server embeds this ID in each URL. When the client submits a request to that URL, the browser sends this ID back to the server. The server can therefore identify the ID with all requests. This section shows this approach with the aid of a simple servlet named `TokenServlet` (see Listing 7-1). This servlet does the following:

- Checks to see if the client sent any token with its request.
- If no token was sent, a new one is created.
- Provides two links back to the servlet—one including the token and one not.

Listing 7-1. TokenServlet

```
package sessions;

import java.io.*;
import java.util.Random;
import javax.servlet.http.*;
import javax.servlet.ServletException;

public class TokenServlet extends HttpServlet {

  protected void doGet(HttpServletRequest request, HttpServletResponse response)
      throws ServletException, IOException {
```

First, you get the token from the request:

```
String tokenID = request.getParameter("tokenID");
```

Second, you prepare the response:

```
response.setContentType("text/html");
PrintWriter writer = response.getWriter();
writer.println("<html><head><title>Tokens</title></head><body ");
writer.println("style=\"font-family:verdana;font-size:10pt\">");
```

If the client didn't send any token, you create a new one:

```
if(tokenID == null) {
  Random rand = new Random();
  tokenID = Long.toString(rand.nextLong());
  writer.println("<p>Welcome. A new token " +
                 tokenID + " is now established</p>");
} else {
```

If the client sent a token, then you acknowledge the client:

```
  writer.println("<p>Welcome back. Your token is " + tokenID + ".</p>");
}
```

Then, you prepare the links for sending requests back:

```
String requestURLSame = request.getRequestURL().toString() +
                        "?token=" + tokenID;
String requestURLNew = request.getRequestURL().toString();
```

Finally, you write the response and close the connection:

```
    writer.println("<p>Click <a href=" + requestURLSame +
                   ">here</a> again to continue browsing with the " +
                   "same identity.</p>");
    writer.println("<p>Otherwise, click <a href=" + requestURLNew +
                   ">here</a> again to start browsing with a new identity.</p>");
    writer.close();
  }
}
```

Create a Web application called `token`, compile the previous source code, and add the class to the `WEB-INF/class/sessions` directory. Then create the simple deployment descriptor shown in Listing 7-2 for the Web application.

Listing 7-2. Deployment Descriptor

```
<?xml version="1.0"?>

<web-app xmlns="http://java.sun.com/xml/ns/j2ee"
xmlns:xsi="http://www.w3.org/2001/XMLSchema-instance"
xsi:schemaLocation=http://java.sun.com/xml/ns/j2ee web-app_2_4.xsd
version="2.4">
  <servlet>
    <servlet-name>track</servlet-name>
    <servlet-class>sessions.TokenServlet</servlet-class>
  </servlet>

  <servlet-mapping>
    <servlet-name>track</servlet-name>
    <url-pattern>/track/*</url-pattern>
  </servlet-mapping>
</web-app>
```

Deploy the Web application, restart Tomcat, and navigate to `http://localhost:8080/token/track`. You should see something like the page shown in Figure 7-1.

The initial request `http://localhost:8080/token/track` doesn't include the query parameter `tokenID`. The servlet creates a new token and generates two links. The first link includes a query string, but the second link doesn't. If you click the first link, you'll see the page shown in Figure 7-2.

Since there's a query parameter in the request, the servlet recognizes the user from this parameter and displays the *Welcome back* message. If you click the second link instead, the browser displays a page with a different token, as shown in Figure 7-3.

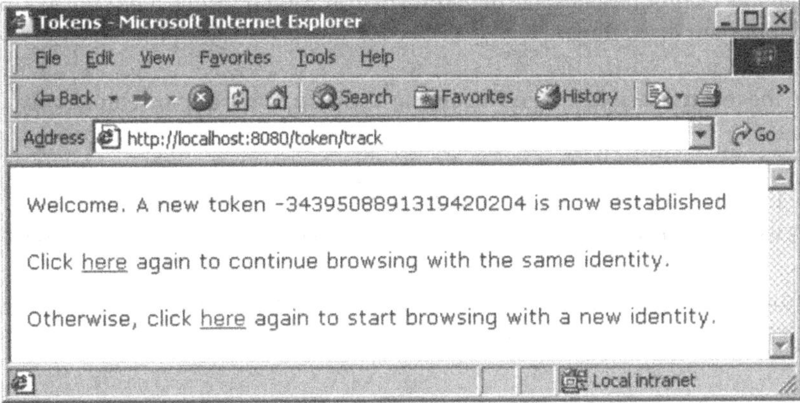

Figure 7-1. Creating a token

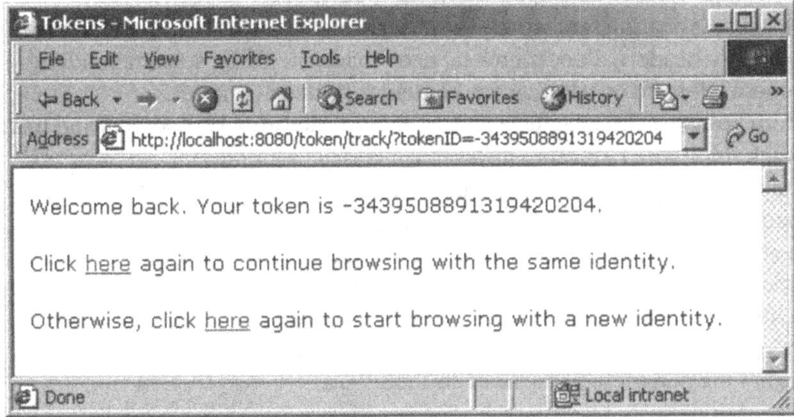

Figure 7-2. Recognizing the user

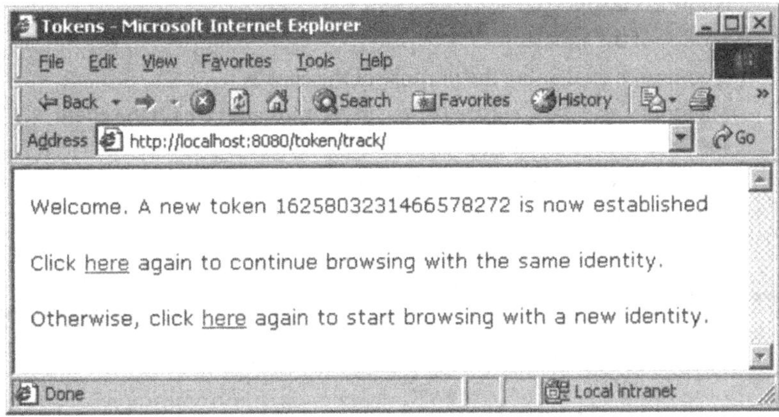

Figure 7-3. Greeting a new user

Although this technique can solve the problem of session tracking, it has the following two important limitations:

- Since the token is visible in the URL during a session, these sessions aren't very secure.
- Since links in static pages are hard-wired, they can't dynamically change for every user, so you can use this system only with servlets or other dynamic pages.

An alternative is to use cookies. As you'll see in the following section, cookies eliminate these limitations.

Session Tracking Using Cookies

Cookies provide a better alternative to explicit URL rewriting because cookies aren't sent as query strings but are exchanged within the bodies of HTTP requests and responses. A *cookie* is a string sent via the Hypertext Transfer Protocol (HTTP) request and HTTP response headers. Since there's no need to rewrite URLs, session handling via cookies doesn't depend on whether the content is static or dynamic.

All modern browsers can recognize and receive cookies from Web servers and then send them back along with requests. However, cookies have limitations. All browsers allow users to disable this functionality, which leads to browsers not recognizing cookies. This is because cookies have bad press—they have sometimes been used to gather information about consumers without their knowledge. Given this, it's worth simultaneously supporting an alternative technique such as URL rewriting. You'll see how you can do this with the Java Servlet API in the "Session Management Using the Servlet API" section.

A cookie has the parameters described in Table 7-1.

Table 7-1. Cookie Parameters

PARAMETER	DESCRIPTION
`Name`	Name of cookie.
`Value`	A value of the cookie.
`Comment`	A comment explaining the purpose of the cookie.
`Max-Age`	Maximum age of the cookie (a time in seconds after which the client shouldn't send the cookie back to the server).
`Domain`	Domain to which the cookie should be sent.
`Path`	The path to which the cookie should be sent.
`Secure`	Specifies if the cookie should be sent securely via secure HTTP (HTTPS).
`Version`	Version of the cookie protocol. Version 0 is meant for the original Netscape version of cookies. Version 1 is meant for cookies standardized via RFC 2109.

To send a cookie to a client, a server creates a cookie header and attaches it to the HTTP response. The client receives the request and extracts the cookie response header. This cookie data is usually stored in a file on the client's system.

When the client makes another request, two parameters help the client decide whether to send the cookie back to the server: `Domain` and `Path`. The path is given relative to the domain. For instance, in the URL `http://www.myserver.com/shop/top100`, `myserver.com` is the domain, and `/shop/top100` is the path. If the `Path` parameter isn't specified, the cookie applies to any path under the specified domain. Whenever the client makes a request to any URL matching the specified path within this domain, the client sends the cookie along with the request as a header. Say that the response from the server contains links to `http://www.myserver.com`, `http://sales.myserver.com`, and `http://support.myserver.com`, and the `Path` parameter hasn't been set. When the user clicks any of these links, the browser sends the cookie back to the server in the request header. Since all these links are under the same `myserver.com` domain, and any path in this domain is appropriate.

Working with Cookies in Servlets

The Java Servlet API includes a class `javax.servlet.http.Cookie` that abstracts the notion of a cookie. The `javax.servlet.http.HttpServletRequest` and `javax.servlet.http.HttpServletResponse` interfaces provide methods to add cookies to HTTP responses and to retrieve cookies from HTTP requests.

The `Cookie` class abstracts a cookie. A `Cookie` instance has the following constructor, which instantiates a cookie instance with the given name and value:

```
public Cookie(String name, String value)
```

This class has many methods that make working with cookies easier. It has getter and setter methods for all of the cookie parameters. For example:

```
public String getName()
public void setName(String name)
```

You can use these methods to access or change the name of a cookie. Similar methods exist to access or change other parameters (such as path, header, and so on) of a cookie.

To set cookies, the `javax.servlet.http.HttpServletResponse` interface has the following method:

```
public void addCookie(Cookie cookie)
```

You can call this method as many times as you want in order to set multiple cookies. To extract all cookies contained in the HTTP request, the `javax.servlet.HttpServletRequest` interface has this method:

```
public Cookie[] getCookies()
```

Now you can rewrite your TokenServlet servlet (now called CookieServlet) to track the user using cookies instead of URL rewriting. In this case, the servlet performs the following actions:

- Checks if there's a cookie contained in the incoming request.
- If there's none, it creates a cookie and sends it along with the response.
- If there's a cookie, it just displays the value of the cookie.

Listing 7-3 shows the source code for CookieServlet.

Listing 7-3. CookieServlet

```
package sessions;

import ava.io.*;
import java.util.Random;
import javax.servlet.http.*;
import javax.servlet.http.*;
import javax.servlet.ServletException;

public class CookieServlet extends HttpServlet {

  protected void doGet(HttpServletRequest request, HttpServletResponse response)
                                              throws ServletException, IOException {
    Cookie[] cookies = request.getCookies();
    Cookie token = null;
```

The servlet first retrieves all the cookies contained in the request object. If cookies are present, the servlet then checks each cookie to see if the name of the cookie is token. Listing 7-4 shows how to retrieve cookies.

Listing 7-4. Retrieving Cookies

```
if(cookies != null) {
  for(int i = 0; i < cookies.length; i++) {
    if(cookies[i].getName().equals("token")) {
      token = cookies[i];
      break;
    }
  }
}

response.setContentType("text/html");
PrintWriter writer = response.getWriter();
writer.println("<html><head><title>Tokens</title></head><body ");
writer.println("style=\"font-family:verdana;font-size:10pt\">");

String reset = request.getParameter("reset");
```

If the servlet doesn't find a cookie with the name token, the servlet creates a cookie called token and adds it to the response. The servlet creates a random number. The servlet then creates a cookie with the following parameters:

- **Name**: token
- **Value**: A random number (converted into a string)
- **Comment**: Token to identify user
- **Max-Age**: -1, indicating that the cookie should be discarded when the browser exits
- **Path**: /cookie/track, so the browser sends the cookie to only those requests under http://localhost:8080/cookie/track

Note that Listing 7-5 doesn't set Domain. As a matter of convention, it defaults to localhost. If you're deploying this application on a remote machine (server) and accessing it from another machine (client), you need to set the domain name to be that of the server.

Listing 7-5. Creating a Token

```
if(token == null || (reset != null && reset.equals("yes"))) {
  Random rand = new Random();
  long id = rand.nextLong();

  writer.println("<p>Welcome. A new token " +
                 id + " is now established</p>");

  token = new Cookie("token", Long.toString(id));
  token.setComment("Token to identify user");
  token.setMaxAge(-1);
  token.setPath("/cookie/track");
```

The servlet then adds the cookie to the Response object:

```
response.addCookie(token);
```

To facilitate re-creating the identity, the servlet also expects the request parameter reset. If this parameter is sent with a value of yes, the servlet re-creates the cookie as in Listing 7-5 so that the client gets a new token. Otherwise, the servlet doesn't set the cookie and just prints a message as shown in Listing 7-6.

Listing 7-6. Using an Existing Token

```
    else {
  writer.println("Welcome back. Your token is " + token.getValue() + ".</p>");
    }

    String requestURLSame = request.getRequestURL().toString();
    String requestURLNew = request.getRequestURL() + "?reset=yes";

    writer.println("<p>Click <a href=" + requestURLSame +
                   ">here</a> again to continue browsing with the " +
                   "same identity.</p>");
    writer.println("<p>Otherwise, click <a href=" + requestURLNew +
                   ">here</a> again to start browsing with a new identity.</p>");
    writer.println("</body></html>");
    writer.close();
  }
}
```

Now create a new Web application as you did for the URL rewriting example, and call it cookie. Compile the class shown previously, and place the class in the cookie/ WEB-INF/classes/sessions/ directory.

Create the simple deployment descriptor shown in Listing 7-7 for your Web application.

Listing 7-7. Deployment Descriptor

```
<?xml version="1.0"?>

<web-app xmlns="http://java.sun.com/xml/ns/j2ee"
xmlns:xsi="http://www.w3.org/2001/XMLSchema-instance"
xsi:schemaLocation="http://java.sun.com/xml/ns/j2ee web-app_2_4.xsd"
version="2.4">
  <servlet>
    <servlet-name>track</servlet-name>
    <servlet-class>CookieServlet</servlet-class>
  </servlet>

  <servlet-mapping>
    <servlet-name>track</servlet-name>
    <url-pattern>/track/*</url-pattern>
  </servlet-mapping>
</web-app>
```

Deploy the Web application, restart Tomcat, and navigate to http://localhost: 8080/cookie/track. You'll see a page just like the one in Figure 7-1, as shown in Figure 7-4.

Click the first link to get the page shown in Figure 7-5.

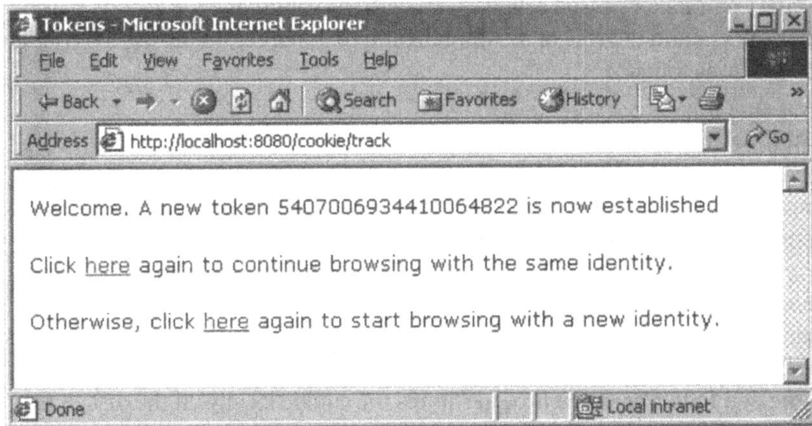

Figure 7-4. Creating a token

Figure 7-5. Recognizing a user

The token number is the same. The browser sent the cookie back to the server along with the request, and the server recognized it. Notice that the first link (in the second line) is the same as the one you entered in the address bar in the browser.

From the client perspective, this has the following two differences from URL rewriting:

- The token wasn't included in the query string.
- While displaying the page, the browser received a cookie from the server.

If you instead click the link on the third line, a fresh token will be created, and a new cookie will be set. For the server to re-create the token, you should note that there's an additional query parameter passed called `reset`, with the value yes.

To better understand the role of the domain and path names, in Listing 7-5 change the path to `/token`, as follows:

```
token.setPath("/token");
```

Recompile the servlet, and restart both Tomcat and the browser. This time, the browser doesn't send the cookie back when you click the links. This is because, while the cookie is set for path `/token`, the links point to `/cookie`. The servlet therefore can't track the user.

Try changing the maximum age to 86400 seconds (which equals one day). With this setting, even if you restart the browser and Tomcat, the servlet still recognizes the cookie for one day. In this case, the browser stores the cookie locally on the disk. A disadvantage of using cookies is that they're stored. What we mean by this is that you need to be careful (and aware) when a site may be storing something in a cookie that could be considered confidential. For example, sites could store a username/password pair so you don't have to type in your credentials every time. While this might be a convenience, the security holes far outweigh the ease of use.

Session Tracking Using Hidden Form Fields

The third alternative to session handling is via hidden form fields. Hypertext Markup Language (HTML) forms allow fields to be hidden, which means such fields aren't displayed when the form is rendered on the browser. While preparing a page with a form, the server can add one or more hidden fields within the form. When the client submits the form, the browser transfers the values in the hidden fields along with the other visible fields (if any) to the server. You can use this mechanism to track a user. `HiddenFieldServlet` illustrates this point (see Listing 7-8).

Listing 7-8. `HiddenFieldServlet`

```
package sessions;

import java.io.*;
import java.util.Random;
import javax.servlet.http.*;
import javax.servlet.ServletException;

public class HiddenFieldServlet extends HttpServlet {

  protected void doGet(HttpServletRequest request, HttpServletResponse response)
                                         throws ServletException, IOException {
```

First, you get the token from the request:

```
String token = request.getParameter("token");
```

Second, you prepare the response:

```
response.setContentType("text/html");
PrintWriter writer = response.getWriter();
writer.println("<html><head><title>Tokens</title></head><body ");
writer.println("style=\"font-family:verdana;font-size:10pt\">");
```

If the client didn't send any token, you create a new one:

```
if(token == null) {
  Random rand = new Random();
  token = Long.toString(rand.nextLong());
  writer.println("<p>Welcome. A new token " +
               token + " is now established</p>");
} else {
```

If the client sent a token, you acknowledge the client:

```
  writer.println("<p>Welcome back. Your token is " + token + ".</p>");
}
```

Then you prepare a URL for the client to send requests back:

```
String requestURL = request.getRequestURL().toString();
```

You finish by writing two forms. You first write a form with the token as a hidden field:

```
writer.println("<p>");
writer.println("<form method='GET' action='" + requestURL + "'>");
writer.println("<input type='hidden' name='token' value='" + token + "'/>");
writer.println("<input type='submit' value='Click Here'/>");
writer.println("</form>");
writer.println(" to continue browsing with the same identity.</p>");
```

Then you write another form without the hidden field:

```
    writer.println("<form method='GET' action='" + requestURL + "'>");
    writer.println("<input type='submit' value='Click Here'/>");
    writer.println("</form>");
    writer.println(" to start browsing with a new identity.</p>");
    writer.close();
  }
}
```

In this servlet, instead of using the usual <href> tags, you used buttons (within forms) so the user can respond to them. In the first form, the only parameter is a hidden field, and the second form has no parameters at all.

Again, to run the example, you need to create a new Web application as you did for the other examples; call this one hidden. Compile the previous class, and place the class file in the hidden/WEB-INF/classes/sessions/ directory.

Then create the simple deployment descriptor for the Web application (see Listing 7-9).

Listing 7-9. Deployment Descriptor

```
<?xml version="1.0"?>
<web-app xmlns="http://java.sun.com/xml/ns/j2ee"
xmlns:xsi="http://www.w3.org/2001/XMLSchema-instance"
xsi:schemaLocation="http://java.sun.com/xml/ns/j2ee web-app_2_4.xsd"
version="2.4">
  <servlet>
    <servlet-name>track</servlet-name>
    <servlet-class>sessions.HiddenFieldServlet</servlet-class>
  </servlet>

  <servlet-mapping>
    <servlet-name>track</servlet-name>
    <url-pattern>/track/*</url-pattern>
  </servlet-mapping>
</web-app>
```

Deploy the Web application, restart Tomcat, and go to http://localhost:8080/hidden/track. You should see the page shown in Figure 7-6.

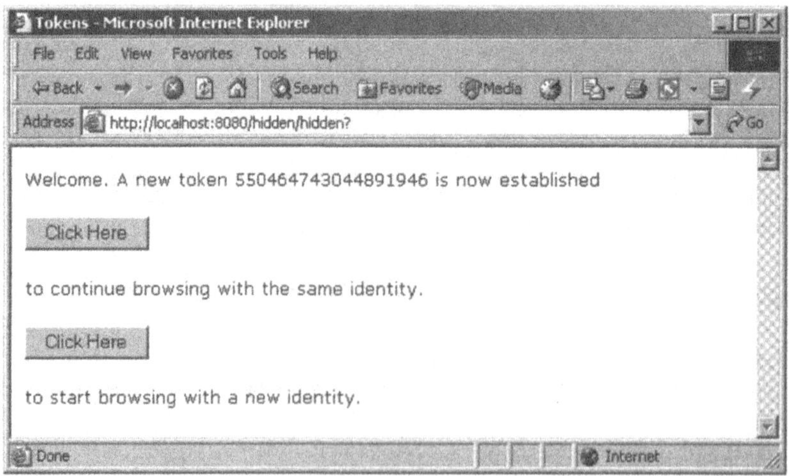

Figure 7-6. Creating a token

Instead of hyperlinks, the response contains two buttons. This is because the forms you created previously don't have any visible fields.

Click the first button to see a page similar to Figure 7-7.

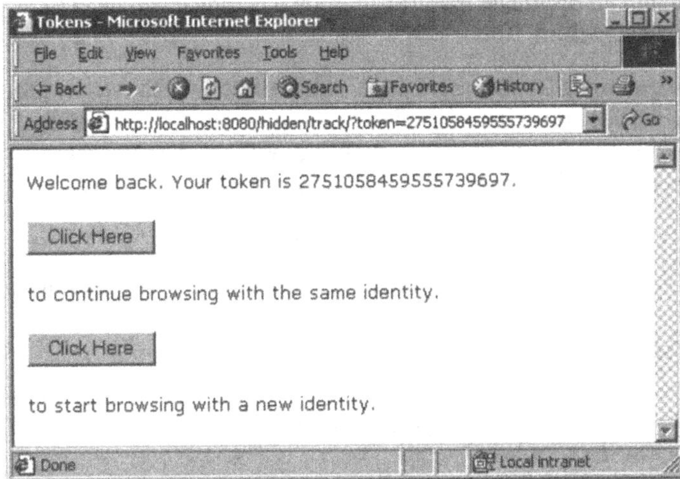

Figure 7-7. Recognizing the user

If you now click the second button, a new token is allocated.

As you can see from this example, a significant disadvantage to this technique of maintaining session is obviously that you need to create forms, which isn't particularly convenient when your content has hyperlinks and not forms.

Session Management Using the Servlet API

In the previous sections, we discussed three examples, each of which demonstrates how to track user sessions programmatically using URL rewriting, cookies, and hidden form fields. Each of these techniques required some unique string to be exchanged between the client and the server so the server could recognize the client. However, as you can infer from these examples, all three approaches have the following complications:

Reliability: Creating a unique ID programmatically isn't reliable, particularly in a multithreaded environment. For instance, what prevents two users from getting the same random number? This issue gets more complicated when you consider clustered environments where the ID is required to be unique across several Java virtual machines (JVMs); we'll discuss clustering later in the "Session Handling Within Clusters" section. You need a more robust and reliable approach for this.

Maintainability: Programmatically retrieving an ID (either from the request parameters or from cookies) is an additional task that each of your servlets must implement, which lowers the maintainability of the code and makes it more prone to errors.

Additional workload: This approach requires additional coding if you need to manage state with each session.

As far as servlet programming is concerned, these additional tasks make servlet programming more complex. The Java Servlet API, however, has provisions that eliminate the need to implement these tasks. In this section, you'll look at the session-handling interfaces of the Java Servlet API. The Servlet API provides the following facilities for managing sessions:

- Management of session life cycle, including session creation and termination
- Management of session state

The Java Servlet API includes interfaces and classes for session management in the `javax.servlet.http` package (see Table 7-2).

Table 7-2. Session Management Interfaces

INTERFACE	DESCRIPTION
`HttpSession`	Provides an abstraction of a session
`HttpSessionListener`	Handles events associated with session creation and termination (lifecycle events)
`HttpSessionBindingListener`	Handles events associated with binding and unbinding state for sessions
`HttpSessionActivationListener`	Handles events associated with session activation and passivation
`HttpSessionEvent`	Encapsulates lifecycle-specific session events
`HttpSessionBindingEvent`	Encapsulates session binding/unbinding events

We'll begin the discussion of these interfaces by talking about the `HttpSession` interface.

The HttpSession Interface

The `HttpSession` interface provides core functionality for session management. This interface abstracts a session. The container creates a session when a client first visits a server. Conceptually, an `HttpSession` object is an object that lives for the duration of a client session and is associated with the request objects.

J2EE Web containers use the following three mechanisms to establish sessions:

- **Cookies**: By default, most containers rely on cookies to establish sessions.
- **URL rewriting**: Web containers support URL rewriting to accommodate clients that don't accept or support cookies. However, in order for Web applications to work correctly with URL rewriting, you need to take an extra coding step by calling the `encodeURL()` method with each URL and using the return value in the content (instead of the original URL).
- **SSL-based sessions**: The Secure Socket Layer (SSL) protocol is used for HTTPS.

This interface also acts as a placeholder for storing data associated with the current session. Using this functionality, you can place client-specific objects in the session. This interface provides `java.util.Map`-like functionality to put and get objects. The `java.util.Map` interface can store objects, with each object linked to a name (which itself can be another object). You can put an object into the map with a name and retrieve the object using the same name. The `HttpSession` interface provides similar methods to manage state for each session. In this interface, each object (called an *attribute*) you add to the session should have a unique name (as a string). Servlets used during the course of a session may share these objects.

You'll now look at the methods provided by this interface. The first question is, how do you get an instance of this interface? The `HttpServletRequest` interface has the following methods to get instances of `HttpSession`:

```
public HttpSession getSession()
```

This method returns the session already associated with this request. However, if there's no session currently associated the request, supplying `true` to the following variant creates a new `Session` object and returns it:

```
public HttpSession getSession(boolean create)
```

If the argument is `false`, and there's no session currently associated with this request, this method returns `null`. If the argument is `true`, then a new session will be created if one doesn't already exist.

The following method returns a named attribute from the session:

```
public Object getAttribute(String name)
```

The `getAttributeNames()` method returns an `Enumeration` of names of all attributes placed into a session:

```
public java.util.Enumeration getAttributeNames()
```

The Web container creates a session when a client first accesses the container. The getCreationTime() method returns the time—in milliseconds since midnight January 1, 1970, Greenwich mean time (GMT)—at which the session was created. As you'll see, you can also re-create sessions programmatically:

```
public long getCreationTime()
```

The getId() method returns a unique identifier assigned to this session. This unique identifier is similar to the token you created in previous examples. Web containers use elaborate algorithms to create such identifiers so that the identifiers are unique even under concurrent requests:

```
public String getId()
```

The getLastAccessedTime() method returns the time the client last sent a request associated with this session. The time is expressed as milliseconds since midnight January 1, 1970, GMT:

```
public long getLastAccessedTime()
```

The following specifies the time, in seconds, between client requests before the servlet container will invalidate this session. A negative time indicates that the session should never time out:

```
public int getMaxInactiveInterval()
```

The getServletContext() method, unsurprisingly, returns the ServletContext associated with the application to which this session belongs:

```
public ServletContext getServletContext()
```

The invalidate() method invalidates this session and removes any attributes bound to it:

```
public void invalidate()
```

The isNew() method returns true if the client doesn't yet know about this session or if the client chooses not to join the session:

```
public boolean isNew()
```

The removeAttribute() method removes the named attribute from the session:

```
public void removeAttribute(String name)
```

The following method adds the named attribute to the session. If the named attribute already exists in the session, the method replaces the old attribute value with the new value:

```
public void setAttribute(String name, Object value)
```

This method sets the maximum allowed time (in seconds) between two consecutive client requests to participate in a session. After expiry of this interval, the container invalidates the session. If a client request arrives after this interval, the request results in a new session:

```
public void setMaxInactiveInterval (int interval)
```

The following logs the client out of the Web server and invalidates all sessions associated with this client. The scope of the logout is the same as the scope of the authentication. For example, if the servlet container implements single sign-on, the logout logs the client out of all Web applications on the servlet container and invalidates all sessions associated with the same client:

```
public void logout()
```

Session Tracking Performance Considerations

Each of the methods of session tracking impacts performance, depending on the amount of the data to be stored as session data and the number of concurrent users. Table 7-3 provides a basic guide.

Table 7-3. Comparing Session Tracking Techniques

SESSION MECHANISM	PERFORMANCE	DESCRIPTION
`HttpSession`	Good	There's no limit on the size of keeping session data.
Hidden fields	Moderate	There's no limit on the size of passing session data.
Cookies	Moderate	There's a limit for cookie size.
URL rewriting	Moderate	There's a limit for URL rewriting.
Persistent mechanism	Moderate to poor	There's no limit of keeping session data.

The persistent mechanism means that you store the session data in database or file storage. Persistent mechanisms give moderate to poor performance when compared to other approaches because of the overhead involved in database calls through Java Database Connectivity (JDBC) or file system accesses. Calls will be made to the database on every request in order to store that session data, and finally it needs to retrieve the whole session data from database, but it scales well when increasing session data and concurrent users.

URL rewriting gives moderate performance because the data has to pass between the client and server for every request, but there's a limitation on the amount of data that can be passed through URL rewriting. There's overhead involved on the network for passing data on every request. Cookies also give moderate performance because they need to pass the session data between client and server. It also has the size limit of 4 kilobytes for each cookie. Like URL rewriting and cookies, hidden fields need to pass the data between client and server. These three session mechanisms give moderate performance and are inversely proportional to the amount of session data.

The `HttpSession` mechanism provides better performance when compared to the other mechanisms because it stores the session data in memory and reduces overhead on network. Only the session ID will be passed between client and the server. But it doesn't scale well when the session data is huge and the concurrent number of users are more because of an increase in memory overhead and an increase in overhead for garbage collection.

Remember that choosing the session mechanism from one of the previous approaches depends on performance, scalability, and security. The best approach is to maintain a balance between performance, security, and scalability by choosing a mixed approach. Mixing the `HttpSession` mechanism with hidden fields gives both performance and scalability. By putting secure data in `HttpSession` and nonsecure data in hidden fields, you can achieve better security.

You'll now study the programming aspects of the session management API via a comprehensive example.

Implementing Session Management

The purpose of this example is to build a Web application that allows users to create notes and store them on the server. Each note has a title and associated text, both stored in a database. This example will allow the user to do the following:

- View the list of notes previously created (using the user's e-mail address to retrieve the list of notes).
- Create new notes.
- Edit existing notes.
- Change identity and create notes as a different user (identified by another e-mail address).

Figure 7-8 shows the flow of events and how you'll implement the previous functionality.

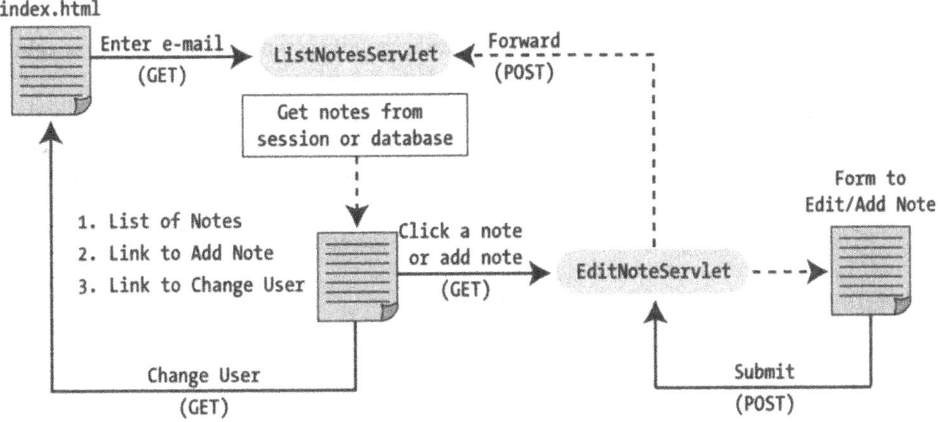

Figure 7-8. Implementing session management

In this figure, the normal arrows indicate the actions by the user, and the dotted arrows indicate the container responses. This application has the following three components:

index.html: This is a welcome page that collects the user's e-mail address.

ListNotesServlet: This servlet is responsible for obtaining the list of e-mails from the session. If the session is new, this servlet gets the list of e-mails from the database. This servlet then displays a page containing the list of notes (if any, with hyperlinks), a link to add a note, and another link to change the user. The arrows from this servlet show the possible user actions.

EditNoteServlet: This servlet performs two tasks. If the user clicks to edit a note, this servlet retrieves the note from the database and displays it in a form. If the user clicks to add a new note instead, this servlet displays an empty form. When the user submits this form, this servlet stores the note in the database, updates the list of notes in the session, and then forwards the request to the `ListNotesServlet`. The `ListNotesServlet` then displays the list of notes.

Therefore, this example relies on the session management API for the following tasks:

- Tracking a user entering notes
- Managing a list of notes
- Invalidating current sessions and creating new sessions

You'll start by creating the database schema.

Database Schema

You'll use the MySQL relational database management system (RDBMS) for managing the notes persistently. This RDBMS is available to download for free from `http://www.mysql.com`. To use this with your Web applications, you'll also need to download the JDBC driver `mm.mysql-2.0.8-bin.jar`. The database schema is simple—each note is associated with a `note_id` and an `email` address. The actual note data consists of a `note_title`, a `note`, and the `last_modified` time.

Use the following SQL to create the database schema:

```
CREATE DATABASE notepad;
USE notepad;

CREATE TABLE NOTES (
  note_id INT AUTO_INCREMENT PRIMARY KEY,
  email CHAR(50) NOT NULL,
  note_title CHAR(80) NOT NULL,
  note LONG VARCHAR,
  last_modified TIMESTAMP NOT NULL
);
```

This SQL creates a table called `NOTES` with the `note_id` as the primary key. You specify this column as an `AUTO_INCREMENT` key so that each insert will automatically increment the number. In the previous SQL script, you also create two indices on the `email` and `note_id` columns. These are the columns you use to query for the `NOTES` data.

You should note that this schema isn't exhaustive enough for use in a general production environment. At the end of this example, you'll see possible enhancements that could make this example more robust and usable.

Welcome Page

Listing 7-10 shows how to create the welcome page (`index.html`) for the notepad Web application.

Listing 7-10. The Notepad Application

```
<html>
  <head>
    <title>Notepad</title>
    <link rel="stylesheet" type="text/css" href="style/global.css" />
  </head>
  <body>
    <h3>NotePad</h3>
    <form action="/notepad/list" method="GET">
     <p>
```

```
        Enter your e-mail address:
        <input type="text" name="email" />
      </p>
      <p>
        <input type="submit" name="submit" value="Enter NotePad">
      </p>
    </form>
  </body>
</html>
```

This HTML displays a form for entering the user's e-mail address. When the user enters the e-mail address, the form sends a `GET` request to the `/notepad/list` servlet.

NotePadServlet

This servlet is abstract, and it doesn't directly handle HTTP requests. The purpose of this servlet is to provide the functionality to obtain database connections. You should note that in a production environment, you'd probably want to connect to your database through the Java Naming and Directory Interface (JNDI), but to keep things simple, for this example you'll connect to the database directly:

```
import java.sql.*;
import javax.servlet.http.HttpServlet;

public abstract class NotePadServlet extends HttpServlet {
```

The `getConnection()` method returns a database connection:

```
  protected Connection getConnection() throws NamingException, SQLException {
    Connection connection = null;
    try {
      Class.forName("org.gjt.mm.mysql.Driver").newInstance();
      connection = DriverManager.getConnection("jdbc:mysql://localhost/notepad");
    } catch(ClassNotFoundException cnfe) {
      throw new SQLException("Unable to load the driver: " + cnfe.getMessage());
    }
    return connection;
  }
}
```

ListNotesServlet

Listing 7-11 shows how to create the servlet to retrieve the notes and display them. This servlet extends from `NotePadServlet`.

Listing 7-11. `ListNotesServlet`

```
package sessions;

import java.util.*;
import java.io.*;
import java.sql.*;
import javax.naming.NamingException;
import javax.servlet.ServletException;
import javax.servlet.http.*;

public class ListNotesServlet extends NotePadServlet {
  protected void doGet(HttpServletRequest request, HttpServletResponse response)
                                          throws ServletException, IOException {
```

This servlet retrieves the parameter `email` from the incoming request and uses it to get a list of notes for that user. Note that the form in the welcome page contains an e-mail text field:

```
String email = request.getParameter("email");
```

The servlet then gets the current user session by calling the `getSession()` method on the `Request` object. When the user visits this notepad application for the first time, the container automatically creates a new session for the user. The `getSession()` method returns the same session to the servlet. When called for the first time, the session will be empty; it doesn't contain any attributes since you haven't yet added any:

```
HttpSession session = request.getSession();
```

This servlet then checks to see if there's an attribute called `email` in the session. As you'll see shortly, this Web application offers functionality to change the identity of the user. Say the user revisits the `index.html` page and enters a new e-mail address to see notes stored under a different e-mail address. In this case, the session would contain the old `email` attribute. The following code checks for this, and if the `email` is different from that retrieved from the request, it invalidates the current session and obtains a new session. This step also ensures that a user with a given e-mail address can't view the notes of another user with a different e-mail address. As discussed in the "Advanced Session Handling" section, you could also implement more robust security measures for this servlet:

```
String currentEmail = (String) session.getAttribute("email");
if(currentEmail != null) {
  if(!currentEmail.equals(email)) {
    session.invalidate();
    session = request.getSession();
  }
}
```

The servlet then puts the e-mail address in the session and checks if the list of notes is already available in the session. In this example, the list of notes is stored in a `java.util.Map` object. This object contains the `note_id` as the key and the `note_title` as the value. The actual note text is retrieved from the database only on demand. This step ensures that, for performance reasons, you store only the essential information in the `HttpSession` object. As you store more information in the session, the underlying JVM will have to allocate more and more memory, and as the number of concurrent users increases, it may limit the available memory for any processing. It's always a good practice to limit the number and size of attributes in the session. You should also remember to remove an attribute from the session if it's no longer required for this session:

```
session.setAttribute("email", email);
Map noteList = (Map) session.getAttribute("noteList");
Connection connection = null;
PreparedStatement statement = null;
if(noteList == null) {
```

When the user invokes this servlet for the first time, the `noteList` will be empty. The servlet then proceeds to retrieve the notes (only `note_id` and `note_title`) from the database and fill this map, as shown in Listing 7-12.

Listing 7-12. Retrieving Notes

```
try {
  String sql =
    "SELECT note_id, note_title FROM NOTES WHERE email = ?";
  connection = getConnection();
  statement = connection.prepareStatement(sql);
  statement.setString(1, email);
  ResultSet rs = statement.executeQuery();
  noteList = new HashMap();

  while(rs.next()) {
    noteList.put(new Integer(rs.getInt(1)), rs.getString(2));
  }
} catch(SQLException sqle) {
  throw new ServletException("SQL Exception", sqle);
} finally {
  try {
    if(statement != null) {
      statement.close();
    }
  } catch(SQLException ignore) {}
  try {
    if(connection != null) {
      connection.close();
    }
  } catch(SQLException ignore) {}
}
```

Listing 7-12 obtains a connection and executes a SQL SELECT statement using the email. It then initializes the noteList map and adds each note_title found into the noteList map using the note_id (converted to an Integer object) as the key. It then adds the noteList to the session under the name noteList as follows:

```
  session.setAttribute("noteList", noteList);
}
```

The rest of the doGet() method prepares a response. The response includes the list of note titles. Each note is associated with a hyperlink to edit the note. The response also includes a link to add a new note and another link to change the user. The former link takes the user to the EditNoteServlet, and the latter link takes the user back to the welcome page (see Listing 7-13).

Listing 7-13. Notes Link

```
  response.setContentType("text/html");
  PrintWriter writer = response.getWriter();
  writer.println("<html><head>");
  writer.println("<title>NotePad</title>");
  writer.println(
    "<link rel=\"stylesheet\" type=\"text/css\" href=\"style/global.css\" />");
  writer.println("</head><body>");
  writer.println("<h3>Notes</h3>");
  if(noteList.size() == 0) {
    writer.println("<p>You do not have any notes.</p>");
  } else {
    writer.println("<p>Click on the note to edit.</p><ul>");
    Iterator iterator = noteList.keySet().iterator();
    while(iterator.hasNext()) {
      Integer noteId = (Integer) iterator.next();
      String noteTitle = (String) noteList.get(noteId);
      writer.println("<li><a href='/notepad/edit?noteId=" +
      noteId.toString() + "'>" + noteTitle + "</a></li>");
    }
    writer.println("</ul>");
  }
  writer.println("<p><a href='/notepad/edit'>Add a New Note</a></p>");
  writer.println("<p><a href='/notepad/'>Change User</a></p>");
  writer.println("</body></html>");
  writer.close();
}
```

Finally, this servlet also implements a doPost() method. As you'll see in the next section, this method is required for the EditNoteServlet to forward to this servlet after saving a note in the database:

```
  protected void doPost(HttpServletRequest request, HttpServletResponse response)
    throws ServletException, IOException {
    doGet(request, response);
  }
}
```

EditNoteServlet

EditNoteServlet has two parts—a doGet() method to display a form with the note title and note text (empty for new notes) and a doPost() method to store/update the note in the database. The servlet also extends from the NotePadServlet. This servlet is rather long, as it implements two core features. First, given the note_id, it retrieves a note from the database and displays it in a form, and second, it stores the note into the database. The following shows the implementation more closely:

```
package sessions;

import java.util.Map;
import java.io.*;
import java.sql.*;
import javax.naming.NamingException;
import javax.servlet.*;
import javax.servlet.http.*;

public class EditNoteServlet extends NotePadServlet {
```

The doGet() method of this servlet is responsible for retrieving a note from the database. The same method is also used to display an empty form to enter a new note:

```
protected void doGet(HttpServletRequest request, HttpServletResponse response)
  throws ServletException, IOException {
```

This method first checks whether there's a noteId in the request. If you examine the ListNotesServlet, the link to add a new note doesn't include a noteId in the URL, but the links to existing notes include the noteId as a query parameter. This parameter helps the EditNoteServlet to determine if the request is for a new note or for an existing note:

```
String noteId = (String) request.getParameter("noteId");
String note = "";
String title = "";
boolean isEdit = false;
Connection connection = null;
PreparedStatement statement = null;

if(noteId != null) {
  try {
```

If there's no noteId in the request, the servlet generates an HTML form. Otherwise, this servlet retrieves the note from the database (see Listing 7-14).

Listing 7-14. Retrieve Note from Database

```
      String sql = "SELECT note_title, note FROM NOTES WHERE note_id = ?";
      connection = getConnection();
      statement = connection.prepareStatement(sql);
      statement.setInt(1, Integer.parseInt(noteId));
      ResultSet rs = statement.executeQuery();
      rs.next();
      title = rs.getString(1);
      note = rs.getString(2);
      isEdit = true;
    } catch(SQLException sqle) {
      throw new ServletException("SQL Exception", sqle);
    } finally {
      try {
        if(statement != null) {
          statement.close();
        }
      } catch(SQLException ignore) {}
      try {
        if(connection != null) {
          connection.close();
        }
      } catch(SQLException ignore) {}
    }
  }
```

Listing 7-14 retrieves the note title and the note text using the note_id. It then stores the results in the local variables title and note, respectively.

Listing 7-15 generates the form containing the note. In the case of a new note, the variables title and note will be empty.

Listing 7-15. Form Containing Note

```
  response.setContentType("text/html");
  PrintWriter writer = response.getWriter();
  writer.println("<html><head>");
  writer.println("<title>NotePad</title>");
  writer.println(
    "<link rel=\"stylesheet\" type=\"text/css\" href=\"style/global.css\" />");
  writer.println("</head><body>");
  writer.println("<h3>Notes</h3>");
  writer.println("<h1>Add/Edit a Note</h1>");
  if(isEdit) {
    writer.println("<form action='/notepad/edit?noteId=" + noteId +
                   "' method='POST'>");
  } else {
```

```
      writer.println("<form action='/notepad/edit' method='POST'>");
    }
    writer.println("<p>Title: <input type='text' name='title' size='40' value='" +
                   title + "'></p>");
    writer.println("<p><textarea name='note' cols='50' rows='15'>");
    writer.println(note);
    writer.println("</textarea></p>");
    writer.println("<p><input type='Submit' name='submit'
                   value='Save Note'></p>");
    writer.println("</form></body></html>");
    writer.close();
  }

  protected void doPost(HttpServletRequest request, HttpServletResponse response)
    throws ServletException, IOException {
```

The form makes a POST request for saving the note. When the user enters the note and clicks the Save button, they invoke the doPost() method of this servlet. The responsibility of the doPost() method is to store the note into the database. Before saving the note, this method retrieves all the necessary information from the Request and Session objects:

```
String noteId = (String) request.getParameter("noteId");
HttpSession session = request.getSession();
String email = (String) session.getAttribute("email");
Map noteList = (Map) session.getAttribute("noteList");
String title = request.getParameter("title");
String note = request.getParameter("note");
Connection connection = null;
PreparedStatement statement = null;
try {
```

This servlet uses the noteId parameter in the request to determine if this is a new note or an existing note. If the note is new, it inserts the note in the database (see Listing 7-16).

Listing 7-16. Insert Note

```
// new note
if(noteId == null) {
        String sql = "INSERT INTO NOTES (email, note_title, note, last_modified)"
                   + "VALUES(?, ?, ?, ?)";
        connection = getConnection();
        statement = connection.prepareStatement(sql);
        statement.setString(1, email);
        statement.setString(2, title);
        statement.setString(3, note);
        statement.setTimestamp(4, new Timestamp(System.currentTimeMillis()));
        statement.executeUpdate();
```

```
        // Retrieve the automatically inserted NOTE_ID
        // LAST_INSERT_ID() is a MySQL funtion
        sql = "SELECT LAST_INSERT_ID()";
        statement = connection.prepareStatement(sql);
        ResultSet rs = statement.executeQuery(sql);
        int id = 0;
        while(rs.next ()) {
          id = rs.getInt(1);
        }
        noteList.put(new Integer(id), title);
// existing note
      } else {
```

The note_id is retrieved from the database after executing the INSERT statement. The note_id column is a column automatically incremented by the database whenever a new note is inserted. You therefore must retrieve the inserted value from the database.

If the note already exists, the doPost() method simply updates it (see Listing 7-17).

Listing 7-17. Update Note

```
    String sql = "UPDATE NOTES SET note_title = ?, note = ?, " +
                 "last_modified = ? WHERE note_id = ?";
    connection = getConnection();
    statement = connection.prepareStatement(sql);
    statement.setString(1, title);
    statement.setString(2, note);
    statement.setTimestamp(3, new Timestamp(System.currentTimeMillis()));
    statement.setInt(4, Integer.parseInt(noteId));
    statement.executeUpdate();

    noteList.put(new Integer(noteId), title);
  }
} catch(SQLException sqle) {
  throw new ServletException("SQL Exception", sqle);
} finally {
  try {
    if(statement != null) {
      statement.close();
    }
  } catch(SQLException ignore) {}
  try {
    if(connection != null) {
      connection.close();
    }
  } catch(SQLException ignore) {}
try {
    if(rs != null) {
      rs.close();
    }
  } catch(SQLException ignore) {}

}
```

Whether you created or updated a note, this method puts the `note_id` and `note_title` in the `noteList` map so the `ListNotesServlet` can display the updated list of notes. After inserting/updating the note, the servlet forwards the request to the `ListNotesServlet` to display the updated list of notes:

```
    RequestDispatcher rd = request.getRequestDispatcher("/list?email=" + email);
    rd.forward(request, response);
  }
}
```

Since the call to the `forward()` method is performed via the `doPost()` method, the `ListNotesServlet` should implement the `doPost()` method. This is why you implemented the `doPost()` method in the `ListNotesServlet`.

This completes the coding required for this Web application. The next tasks are to write a deployment descriptor and configure Tomcat to deploy the servlets.

Deployment Descriptor

Listing 7-18 shows the deployment descriptor for your notepad application.

Listing 7-18. Deployment Descriptor

```
<?xml version="1.0"?>

<web-app xmlns="http://java.sun.com/xml/ns/j2ee"
xmlns:xsi="http://www.w3.org/2001/XMLSchema-instance"
xsi:schemaLocation=http://java.sun.com/xml/ns/j2ee web-app_2_4.xsd
version="2.4">

  <servlet>
    <servlet-name>listNotes</servlet-name>
    <servlet-class>ListNotesServlet</servlet-class>
  </servlet>

  <servlet>
    <servlet-name>editNote</servlet-name>
    <servlet-class>EditNoteServlet</servlet-class>
  </servlet>

  <servlet-mapping>
    <servlet-name>listNotes</servlet-name>
    <url-pattern>/list/*</url-pattern>
  </servlet-mapping>

  <servlet-mapping>
    <servlet-name>editNote</servlet-name>
    <url-pattern>/edit/*</url-pattern>
  </servlet-mapping>

</web-app>
```

Listening for Session Lifecycle Events

As the container creates sessions, and as you add, remove, or change attributes in sessions, the Web container instantiates event objects so that Web applications can be notified of these events. In this section, you'll look at how you can make applications receive notifications upon changes to `Session` objects.

Figure 7-9 shows the session life cycle with its associated event objects.

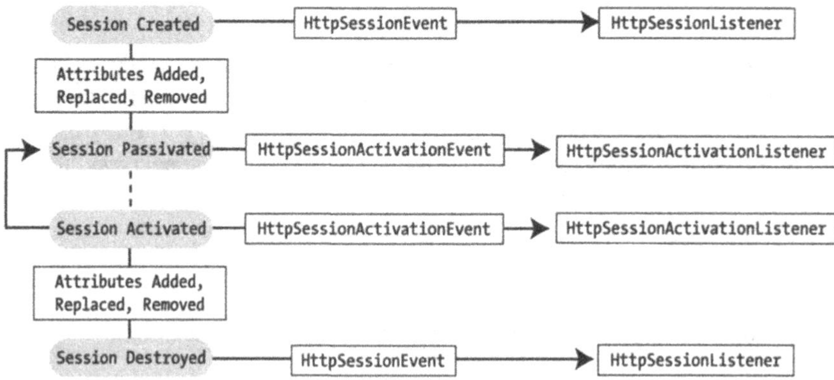

Figure 7-9. Session life cycle

This figure shows the life cycle of a session from creation to destruction. In between, servlets may add, remove, or replace attributes within the session. During its life cycle, a session may be passivated and activated zero or more times. In Figure 7-9, the rectangles on the right are the listeners that handle various events. In addition to the events shown previously, as attributes are added/replaced/removed, the container fires attribute-related events as shown in Figure 7-10.

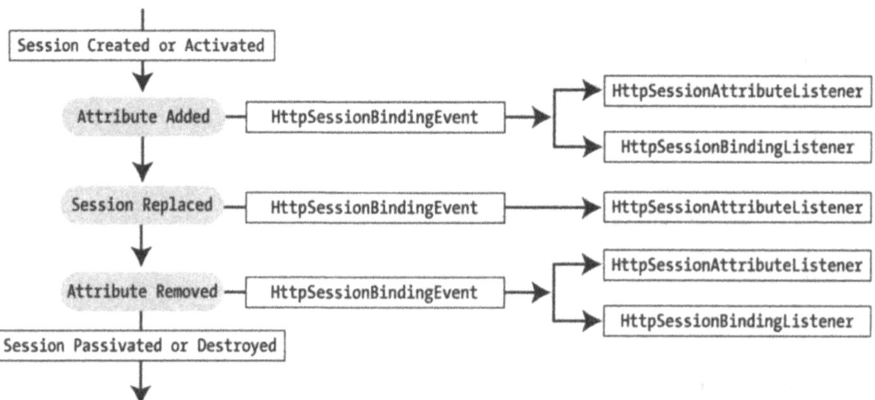

Figure 7-10. Associated events

The next section discusses these events and the associated listeners in more detail.

Listening for Session Creation and Termination

As discussed in the previous section, the container creates a session when the user accesses the server for the first time. The session is subsequently accessible to servlets in the application. But how long should the container keep the `Session` object alive? This question is important since no user is likely to use the application indefinitely. To conserve system resources, you need to instruct the container to terminate a session after some meaningful interval. You should consider the following while building and deploying a Web application:

Session lifetime: Based on the nature of the application, you should identify a suitable lifetime for a session. You can specify this interval in the deployment descriptor of the Web application. For instance, the following entry to the deployment descriptor of the notepad application sets the session lifetime for all users to 60 minutes. Add this element after `<servlet-mapping>` elements and before the `<resource-ref>` element. At the end of 60 minutes, the container automatically terminates the session. Here's the code:

```
<session-config>
  <session-timeout>60</session-timeout>
</session-config>
```

Session inactivity: In addition to the previous item, you can also instruct the container to terminate a session based on how long the session has been inactive. For instance, the user may leave the browser after using the notepad application for 30 minutes. You may want the container to wait for 15 more minutes before allowing the container to terminate the session. To do so, you should call the `setMaxInactiveInterval()` method on the `Session` object. To call this method, you should specify the interval in seconds.

Session logout: It's also possible to explicitly log out a session using the `logout()` method on the `Session` object. If the `logout()` method is called, all sessions associated with this client are invalidated.

The Java Servlet API includes an interface `javax.servlet.http.HttpSessionListener` that's notified when a session is created or destroyed.

The HttpSessionListener Interface

The `HttpSessionEvent` interface specifies methods to deal with session creation and session destruction:

```
public void sessionCreated(HttpSessionEvent event)
```

The container invokes the previous method when a session is created. The event is specified via the `javax.servlet.http.HttpSessionEvent` class. As you'll see next, this class encapsulates the `Session` object:

```
public void sessionDestroyed(HttpSessionEvent event)
```

The container invokes the `sessionDestroyed()` method right before the session is destroyed.

You'll now see the `HttpSessionEvent` class. The `HttpSessionEvent` class has only one method:

```
public HttpSession getSession()
```

This method returns the `Session` object associated with this event.

You can implement the `HttpSessionListener` interface, and deploy your implementation, via the Web application deployment descriptor:

```
<listener>
  <listener-class>YourListenerClassHere</listener-class>
</listener>
```

You should add this element before the `<servlet>` elements. When you specify a class implementing the `HttpSessionListener` interface, the container invokes the `sessionCreated()` method whenever a new session is created. The container similarly calls the `sessionDestroyed()` method whenever a session is destroyed.

What useful logic can you add to the implementation of these methods? Well, when the `sessionCreated()` method is called, your class gets access to the `Session` object via the `HttpSessionEvent` object passed. Since this session is newly created, it won't yet have any attributes. This precludes you from implementing any logic that relies on the state of a session. The same applies to the `sessionDestroyed()` event. This event is called after all the attributes have been removed from the session. Depending on your application, you may, however, implement any application logic that doesn't rely on any session data.

Note that you can specify more than one listener class by adding more `<listener>` elements to the deployment descriptor.

Listening for Session Activation and Passivation

Apart from creation and destruction, a container may generate objects when two other events occur—passivation and activation. In this section, you'll see what these events are and how they occur.

A container can trigger these events in two ways. In a realistic production environment, you may have one or more Web applications deployed on a container with several hundred (or more) users accessing the container. Of all the users, however, only a few may be actively sending requests while the other users are temporarily not accessing the system and there's still time left for terminating such sessions. In such cases, to conserve memory, the container may decide to copy all of the `Session` objects to a persistent storage area (such as a database or a file system) and remove the sessions from memory. This isn't the same as terminating the sessions. The sessions are valid, but they aren't there in memory. This process is *passivation*.

The container may load the session data when the user sends a request again (before the session timeout interval and before the session inactive interval) from the persistent area. This process is *activation*. The process of activation and passivation aren't deployment-time controlled—these events happen based on container implementation and the active load on the server. If you're familiar with the Enterprise JavaBean (EJB) life cycle, this should all sound a bit familiar.

The container uses session passivation and activation in another way. As we'll discuss in the "Session Handling Within Clusters" section, you can configure a set of Web containers as a cluster, with all of the container instances sharing the load between them. In this case, from time to time, the container may decide to shift the load of one session to another container instance. For this purpose, the container passivates the session on one container instance, sends the contents over the network to the other container instance, and activates the session there.

Both activation and passivation require that the attributes held in the session are serializable; otherwise, the container can't passivate the session. Since your application may add nonserializable attributes (such as objects related to network/file input/output) into a session, the Java Servlet API specifies an event listener that can be notified during activation and passivation. During these events, the event listener may close the network/file resources before passivation and may re-create the same resources during activation. The `javax.servlet.http.HttpSessionActivationListener` interface serves this purpose.

The HttpSessionActivationListener Interface

The `HttpSessionActivationListener` interface specifies methods to deal with session passivation and session activation.

The following container invokes the `sessionDidActivate()` method when a session is activated. You specify the event via the `HttpSessionEvent` class:

```
public void sessionDidActivate(HttpSessionEvent event)
```

The following container invokes the method shown previously before passivating a session:

```
public void sessionWillPassivate(HttpSessionEvent event)
```

You can implement this interface and deploy the implementation via the `<listener>` element in the deployment descriptor, as mentioned previously.

Listening for Attribute-Specific Events

The Java Servlet API includes another interface to deal with attributes. The `javax.servlet.http.HttpSessionAttributeListener` interface deals with the following events:

- A servlet adds an attribute to a session.
- A servlet removes an attribute from a session.
- A servlet replaces an attribute in a session with another attribute of the same name.

The HttpSessionAttributeListener Interface

This interface specifies several methods.

The following container calls the previous event when an attribute is added to the session. This method receives an `HttpSessionBindingEvent` object; we'll discuss this object in the next section:

```
public void attributeAdded(HttpSessionBindingEvent event)
```

The following container calls the `attributeRemoved()` method when an attribute is removed from the session:

```
public void attributeRemoved (HttpSessionBindingEvent event)
```

The following container calls the `attributeReplaced()` method when an attribute is replaced in the session:

```
public void attributeReplaced (HttpSessionBindingEvent event)
```

This happens when you call the `setAttribute()` method using the same attribute name.

All of these methods receive an instance of the `javax.servlet.http.HttpSessionBindingEvent` class. This class encapsulates the name of the attribute, the value of the attribute, and the associated `Session` object. You'll now take a closer look at the methods of this class.

The HttpSessionBindingEvent Class

This class contains the following getter methods:

```
public String getName()
public Object getValue()
```

These methods return the name and value of the attribute being added, replaced, or removed.

The following method returns the associated `Session` object:

```
public HttpSession getSession()
```

This class has two constructors. However, you should note that the container creates instances of these objects. As before, you can deploy this class via the `<listener>` element in the deployment descriptor.

The HttpSessionBindingListener Interface

You can handle attribute-related events in another way: via the `javax.servlet.http.HttpSessionBindingListener` interface. Unlike the other event-handling interfaces discussed previously, this interface may be implemented by the attributes themselves; an external listener isn't necessary. As an attribute is being added to a session, or removed from a session, this container invokes methods on this interface so that the attribute being added (known as *attribute binding*) or removed (known as *attribute unbinding*) to the session can handle this event.

The following container calls the `valueBound()` method when the attribute is added to the session:

```
public void valueBound (HttpSessionBindingEvent event)
```

Conversely, the following container calls the `valueUnbound()` method when the attribute is removed from the session:

```
public void  valueUnbound (HttpSessionBindingEvent event)
```

As discussed previously, any attribute may implement this interface to get notified by the container.

Advanced Session Handling

What if you were planning to deploy the previous notepad Web application for public use on an Internet Web site and expected thousands of users to concurrently use this application? You'd have to consider the following issues:

- How do you make sure the application/server doesn't fail to respond to such a heavy load?
- How do you make sure users don't lose their data if a server/operating system crash occurs?
- How do make sure your application code is suitable for deployment under such conditions?

Many aspects of application design can influence these issues, and a few aspects relate to session handling. In the following sections, you'll take a look at these.

Session Handling Within Clusters

Before discussing how to handle sessions for such scenarios, consider how you deploy such applications. Most Web servers are deployed in *clusters*. A cluster is a group of servers meant to share the incoming load of HTTP requests. In the most commonly used clustering configuration, a clustered Web container is configured behind a Web server such as Apache, SunOne Server, or Internet Information Services (IIS). Here the Web server acts as a proxy for the Web container cluster; all that the client sees is the Web server. Note that it's also common to find more than one Web server installed in a cluster. In the previous configuration, the Web server uses a plug-in to delegate incoming HTTP requests to a Web server within the cluster. A Web server *plug-in* is a piece of software installed on the Web server that sends requests to the Web container processes in the container. Note that it's also possible to configure clusters without using Web servers (although such configurations are rare).

You should note that Tomcat doesn't support clustering because it's meant to be only the reference implementation of the Java Servlet API. However, if you use Apache as the Web server and Tomcat as the servlet container, then you'll be fine.

Clustering introduces the following complexities that may affect your application:

- In a cluster, more than one container instance may handle the requests for a given session. This implies that the container should make the `Session` object available to all such instances; otherwise, the user may lose the session data, or the session data may be inconsistent. This process is called *session replication*.

- The container may swap a session from one container instance to another instance. This process requires the container to passivate and activate the session.

These issues involve copying `Session` objects from one machine to another machine, which implies further complexities.

Making Session Attributes Serializable

First, since you need to copy `Session` objects across machines, attributes stored in a session should be serializable. You can accomplish this in two ways. You can use simple Java classes such as `String` (which is already serializable), or, if you use your own custom objects, they must implement the `java.io.Serializable` interface. If any attribute isn't serializable, you should provide an implementation of the `HttpSessionActivationListener` interface so that the implementation may remove the nonserializable attributes from the session during passivation and re-create them during activation.

When to Replicate Sessions

Second, consider the question, what triggers session replication? Is there a chance that certain attributes don't get replicated? For example, consider the list of notes stored in the notepad Web application. To modify this list, you can retrieve it from the session and add or remove notes from it without the Web container being aware of such modifications. Since the container doesn't manage session attributes, it has no way to figure out that such changes have been made. In this case, you'll have to consider the following questions:

- Should the container replicate such an attribute immediately after it's set (via the `setAttribute()` method) or wait until the request is processed?
- What happens if your servlet modifies the attribute after adding it to the session?
- What happens if you retrieve an attribute, modify it, but don't set the attribute back in the session?

These situations arise because you can modify a session attribute via its reference. The Java Servlet specification isn't clear about these situations.

The answers to the previous questions depend on the specific container you're using. Most containers replicate the session attributes at the end of a request. However, to avoid replication of unchanged attributes, the container may expect you to call `setAttribute()` to set the attribute again. You should refer to the documentation of your Web container for more information about this issue.

Minimizing the Data Stored in Sessions

Since both replication and passivation involve network traffic and possibly storage, you should always make sure the number and the size of attributes in the session are as small as possible. Even in stand-alone deployments, session attributes consume memory, and the fewer attributes your applications maintain in sessions, the better. In effect, you should try to build your applications as stateless as possible. For instance, when you built your notepad application, although you could have put the note content in the session (along with the ID and the title), you didn't do so because it would've increased the size of the session. Since you have the `noteId` in the session (via the `noteList`), you can retrieve any note whenever required. This helps minimize the size of the session. Another way to avoid wasting resources is to remove attributes once they're no longer required to be in the session.

Failover Considerations

In addition to these considerations, you should understand the failover abilities that some containers support. Fail over allows another instance in the cluster to share the load of an instance in the event of a system failure. However, such a fail over is still susceptible to failures that happen while processing a request. When an instance crashes while processing a request, you may lose all the changes made to the session before the crash. In the case of mission-critical data, it's usually better to store the data immediately in a database instead of storing it in the session for long periods. Always remember—a session is a temporary area in the working memory, and it's not a data storage facility.

Working with Filters

Often certain tasks are common to multiple requests and/or sessions. To perform these tasks in such a way that they're components that can be used in any number of situations, you create a *filter*. Filters allow you to add functionality to your Web applications that previously would've required proprietary container enhancements or other nonportable extensions to your environment. Filters sit between the client and the underlying Web application, and they examine and modify the requests and responses that flow between them.

You can use filters to quickly prototype new concepts or to add new functionality to your applications, without having to alter the original application.

In the next couple of sections, you'll learn the following:

- You'll discover what a filter is and understand how they fit into the logical and physical design of your Web applications.
- You'll look at how you can configure and combine filters at deployment time.

Along the way, you'll design and code two practical filters to log access to your applications and to transform content for different types of clients.

What Is a Filter?

Like servlets, filters are Web application components that you can bundle into a Web application archive. However, unlike other Web application components, filters are "chained" to the container's processing pipeline. This means they have access to an incoming request before the servlet processor does, and they have access to the outgoing response before it's returned to the client. In Servlet 2.4, it's possible to put filters under the `RequestDispatcher`, as well, so that filters can process forwards and redirects. This access allows filters to examine and modify the contents of both requests and responses.

NOTE Filters *are Web components that add functionality to the request and response processing of a Web application.*

Because of their unique position in the request/response-processing pipeline, filters can be a useful addition to a developer's toolbox. You can use them for the following:

- Prototyping new functionality for a Web application
- Adding new functionality to legacy code

Filters are particularly useful in prototyping new concepts because their addition to the application occurs at deployment time. This means you can add and remove filters without having to rewrite the underlying application code.

Prototyping New Functionality

Imagine a Web site that wants to start charging for services it previously provided for free. To implement this, you'll need to add billing information to certain Web pages. In another attempt to increase revenue, you also want to add the site's best advertising banners to the pages that were most popular on the previous day.

This new functionality would be difficult to implement if the design of the original Web application hadn't anticipated this scenario. However, adding this type of new functionality is easy with filters. You could create the following two filters:

- The first filter would examine the incoming request to determine if the requested resource is one of the pages for which you want to charge. On completion of the standard page processing, the filter would append its own output (which details the billing information).
- The second filter would maintain a list of the most frequently used pages for the previous day (probably obtained at startup from a database). The filter would examine the incoming requests to determine if the request is for one of the popular pages; if it is, the filter would generate an advertisement banner and append it to the pages by modifying the output stream sent to the client.

By inserting these two filters into the Web application, you can quickly prototype your proposed implementation, and you can make any changes in the implementation by simply modifying the code in the two filters—you don't have to touch the underlying Web application.

Adding New Functionality

Imagine an application that's used by the accounting and sales departments of a company to obtain inventory information from a database. Both departments use the same servlets, JavaServer Pages (JSP) pages, and static Web pages to access the database information. However, because of the recent restructuring of the company, it's now necessary to hide certain information from the sales department but to continue to allow the accounting department unrestricted access. How can you do this without having to rewrite the logic contained in the servlets and JSP pages?

You could use a filter to apply a *patch* to the legacy code. The filter would determine from the incoming request if a user is a member of the sales department. After the underlying component has completed its processing, the filter can scan the output and remove any information that shouldn't be displayed. By inserting this single filter into the processing pipeline, you can avoid having to modify the original application.

Understanding Filters

You can look at a filter in two ways:

- **The logical view**: The conceptual view of where filters fit within the container architecture

- **The physical view**: How to actually implement, package, and deploy filters

To gain a full understanding of how filters operate, you need to understand both these views.

The Logical View of a Filter

A filter can examine and modify the request before it reaches the Web resource that the request applies to; it can also examine and modify the response after the Web resource has generated its output.

> **TIP** A Web resource *refers to a Web application or Web service component that's managed by the container—it could be a servlet, a JSP page, or even static content such as an HTML page.*

Figure 7-11 illustrates where filters fit into a container's processing pipeline. A filter intercepts the incoming request before the servlet has access to it and intercepts the outgoing request before it's returned to the client.

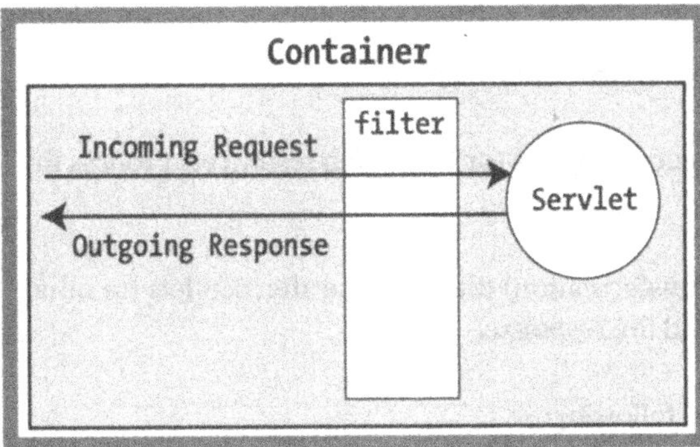

Figure 7-11. A container's processing pipeline

By coupling filters to specific Web resources, you can effectively combine the processing performed by the filters and the processing performed by the Web resource into a single unit.

Filters and Web Services

Consider a stock quote Web service for which the underlying Web resource is a servlet that provides real-time stock market quotes. This servlet accesses a cached database of recent quotes and generates quote data formatted in Extensible Markup Language (XML). Most Web service clients can access this data using Simple Object Access Protocol (SOAP). However, to accommodate clients on wireless cell phones with no SOAP capability, you also need to send the data formatted using Wireless Markup Language (WML). To further complicate the situation, the service must cater for a group of Web clients that have access only to the service via Web browsers. These clients need to have the data formatted with HTML.

One solution to this problem would be to create three versions of the servlet, one for each type of client. However, the logic of the servlet may be fairly complicated; replicating it will waste development time and won't be conducive to effective code reuse. It's better to isolate the non-client-specific logic in a servlet and put the client-sensitive logic in a filter.

Many clients send descriptive information in the `user-agent` attribute of the header, which you can use to determine if the client is capable of supporting various features. For clients that don't generate a `user-agent` header, you can use other properties of the request—for example, the subnet of the originating Internet Protocol (IP) address—to determine if the client is accessing your application via the Web or a wireless network.

Using one or more filters, you can easily process the XML generated by the servlet into SOAP, WML, or HTML as necessary. In addition, because filters can access the request before it reaches the servlet, you can identify the client type beforehand and then perform the necessary transformation after the servlet has finished its work. This will allow the SOAP clients, the phone clients, and the Web clients to access the stock quotes from a single URL.

Filter Actions

You've seen how you can use filters to do the following:

- Access request information before servlets (or other Web resources) process the request.
- Examine and modify (via a transformation) the response after servlets (or other Web resources) have processed the response.

You can also use filters to do the following:

- Generate a response and block access to the underlying Web resource—you could use this to create authorization filters.
- Dynamically redirect clients from an old resource to a new one.
- Expose additional functionality for the Web resource to use—for example, a filter could bundle a library that encapsulates data access methods, and a servlet could detect during run time if this filter is available and use the methods accordingly.

The Physical View of a Filter

The physical view of a filter is the view that a Web application deployer or assembler will see. It's the view that a filter developer works with when packaging the filter.

> **NOTE** *A filter is a Java class that you can add to a Web application just as you add a servlet.*

At deployment time, you have the option of associating a filter with a particular Web resource within the Web application.

The Life Cycle of a Filter

A filter follows a life cycle similar to that of a servlet. A filter has four stages: instantiate, initialize, filter, and destroy. These are analogous to the stages of a servlet: instantiate, initialize, service, and destroy. Refer to Chapter 6 to find more information about the life cycle of servlets.

The container will supply a reference to a configuration object (`FilterConfig`) that the filter instance can use to obtain additional initialization parameters. Since the filter is a Web resource, these initial parameters are set in the deployment descriptor. Like a servlet, a filter instance can throw an `UnavailableException` to indicate to the container that it's not ready to service any request.

The container then calls the `init()` method of the filter. Immediately after this call, the filter instance must be ready to handle simultaneous requests. Requests come into the filter via a `doFilter()` method, just like requests come into servlets via a `service()` method.

The container will call the filter's `destroy()` method once all outstanding `doFilter()` method calls have been returned. After the `destroy()` method call, the filter is considered inactive. You should implement all per-instance cleanup in the `destroy()` method, as the underlying Java object may be garbage collected shortly afterward.

Some containers may opt to pool instances of filters for performance reasons, which means that another `init()` method call may come shortly after the `destroy()` call on the *same* instance of a filter. If you're developing filters for containers that pool filter instances, you should be careful when designing your filters.

The Filter Classes and Interfaces

All filters must implement the `javax.servlet.Filter` interface, which defines three methods: `init()`, `doFilter()`, and `destroy()`.

The container calls the `init()` method to initialize the filter instance:

```
public void init(FilterConfig config) throws ServletException
```

The container passes this method a `FilterConfig` object, which contains configuration information (set using initialization parameters in the deployment descriptor).

This method is a good place to read any process and initialization parameters that may be associated with the filter because the container guarantees that this method will be called before `doFilter()`.

The `doFilter()` method contains the logic of your filter—just as the `service()` method contains the logic of your servlets:

```
public void doFilter(ServletRequest req, ServletResponse res,
                     FilterChain chain) throws IOException, ServletException
```

Remember that a single instance of a filter can be servicing many requests simultaneously. This means that any shared (nonlocal) variables must be accessed via synchronized blocks.

The `FilterChain` argument is vital for proper filter operations. The `doFilter()` logic is obliged to make a call to the `doFilter()` method of the `FilterChain` object, unless it wants to block further downstream processing (that is, prevent the request from reaching the underlying Web resource associated with the request). Typically, this call gives temporary control to the container before the nested call to the downstream processing is actually made.

The container will call the `destroy()` method before the container destroys the filter instance:

```
public void destroy()
```

In the doFilter() method implementation, any code that comes before the call to the doFilter() method of FilterChain is considered *preprocessing* filter logic. At this stage, the incoming request is available, but processing by the Web resource hasn't yet occurred.

The code after the call to the doFilter() method of FilterChain makes up the *postprocessing* filter logic. At this stage, the outgoing response contains the complete response from the Web resource.

> **NOTE** *The call to the* doFilter() *method of* FilterChain *will invoke the next filter (when chaining) or the underlying Web resource if there aren't any more filters.*

The actual processing by any downstream filters or underlying Web resources will occur *during* the call to the doFilter() method of FilterChain. From the point of view of the filter, all the nonfilter logic request processing is "folded" into the call to the doFilter() method of FilterChain. This allows you to do something that's typically difficult to perform in other request/response intercepting mechanisms. You can easily share variables between the preprocessing and the postprocessing logic.

Configuring Filters

A Web service deployer can control how the container loads and applies filters via the deployment descriptor. Just as you use <servlet> and <servlet-mapping> elements to configure servlets, you can use <filter> and <filter-mapping> elements to configure filters.

Defining Filters

A *filter definition* associates a filter name with a particular class. The association is specified using the <filter-name> and <filter-class> elements. For example, this filter instance is named Logger, and the class used is filters.LoggerFilter:

```
<filter>
  <filter-name>Logger</filter-name>
  <filter-class>filters.LoggerFilter</filter-class>
</filter>
```

You can also use a filter definition to specify initialization parameters. You specify parameters using the <init-param> element and pairs of <param-name> and <param-value> elements. For example:

```
<filter>
  <filter-name>XSLTFilter</filter-name>
  <filter-class>filters.SmartXSLFilter</filter-class>
  <init-param>
    <param-name>xsltfile</param-name>
    <param-value>/xsl/stockquotes.xsl</param-value>
   </init-param>
</filter>
```

Each occurrence of a filter definition in the `web.xml` file specifies a unique instance of a filter that will be loaded by the container. If *n* filter definitions refer to the same underlying Java class, the container will create *n* distinct instances of this class.

When the Web application starts, the container creates instances of filters according to the definitions within the deployment descriptor. Instances are created, and their `init()` methods are called according to the order they're defined within the deployment descriptor. Because a container will create a single instance of a filter per filter definition (per JVM managed by the container), it's imperative that the filter code is thread safe, as many requests may be processed simultaneously by the same instance.

Mapping Filters

A *filter mapping* specifies the Web resource to which a filter instance should be applied. You must specify filter mappings *after* the filter definitions. Mapping filters is similar to how you map servlets using the `<servlet-mapping>` element.

You specify filter mappings via the `<filter-mapping>` element. This element must have a `<filter-name>` element inside in order to specify the filter that's to be mapped. The filter that's referred to must have been named in an earlier filter definition.

In addition to the `<filter-name>` element, a filter mapping should also contain either a `<url-pattern>` element or a `<servlet-name>` element. Using the `<url-pattern>` element, you can specify wildcard symbols to define the range of Web resources to which the filter will apply. For example, the following `Logger` filter will be applied to every Web resource in the Web application:

```
<filter-mapping>
  <filter-name>Logger</filter-name>
  <url-pattern>/*</url-pattern>
</filter-mapping>
```

To apply the same filter to just the servlets in the application, you can use this mapping:

```
<filter-mapping>
  <filter-name>Logger</filter-name>
  <url-pattern>/servlet/*</url-pattern>
</filter-mapping>
```

To obtain even finer-grained control over the Web resource that's associated with a filter, you can use the <servlet-name> element to specify a specific servlet within the application. For example, the following filter mapping specifies that the XSLTFilter filter will be applied only to the XMLOutServlet servlet. No other request will trigger this filter:

```
<filter-mapping>
  <filter-name>XSLTFilter</filter-name>
  <servlet-name>XMLOutServlet</servlet-name>
</filter-mapping>
```

Chaining Filters

It's possible to specify that multiple filters should be applied to a specific resource. For example, the following set of filter mappings will apply both the XSLTFilter and AuditFilter filters to all the resources in an application:

```
<filter-mapping>
    <filter-name>XSLTFilter</filter-name>
    <url-pattern>/*</url-pattern>
</filter-mapping>
<filter-mapping>
    <filter-name>AuditFilter</filter-name>
    <url-pattern>/*</url-pattern>
</filter-mapping>
```

A Web application deployer can use such filter chaining as a "construction set," allowing it to build versatile services. For example, you could chain together an XML-to-HTML conversion filter, an encryption filter, and a compression filter to produce an encrypted, compressed stream of HTML output—all from a servlet that outputs only XML.

> **NOTE** *The container will construct filter chains based on the order of appearance of the filter mappings within the deployment descriptor.*

The order of filters within a chain is important for the proper operation of an application because filter chaining isn't transitive.

NOTE *Applying filter A and then applying filter B isn't necessarily equal to applying filter B and then applying filter A.*

Using Filters

We'll briefly describe some typical uses of filters. This should provide you with ideas for how you can use filters in your own applications. These examples demonstrate how filters provide a flexible, portable, modular method of adding functionality to your Web applications:

To implement the Adapter architectural pattern: You can use filters to implement the Adapter architectural pattern, which can be useful when the output from one system doesn't match the input requirement of another system (particularly when the systems aren't in your control). A filter can modify the request or response to adapt one system to another.

To measure traffic or enforce resource quotas: You can add logging and auditing filters to a set of resources within a Web application to measure traffic or enforce resource quotas.

To reduce bandwidth: You can use compression filters to reduce the bandwidth used on expensive network connections. For example, a metropolitan radio packet network used for sending digital information to radio-equipped personal digital assistants (PDAs) may be expensive. By using a compression filter on the server, along with a decompression library on the client, you can save costs.

To bridge a network of requests: You can use encryption and decryption filters to bridge a network of requests over the Internet. You could change encryption algorithms simply by changing the filter used. For example, you could add a gateway filter to support a hardware-based public key encryption filter. If the decryption logic is contained in a proxy, the client can access the server securely (even over an unsecured network such as the Internet), without having the decryption logic built in to it.

To add security: Authentication and authorization filters can add security features to basic Web services, which may have originally been written without authentication and authorization in mind. For example, you can quickly impose a fixed password to a set of Web resources by adding a filter that implements the Basic HTTP authentication protocol.

To present multiple views: Transformation filters are useful for presenting multiple views of the same content. For example, you could use a language translation filter that detects the country of origin of a client and then translates the content before sending it to the client.

A Logging Filter

The first filter you'll build is just about as simple as a filter can get—it's intended to get you acquainted with the design, coding, and deployment stages common to all filters. The filter will log access to the underlying Web resource. For example:

```
2003-02-14 11:26:40  Request Orginiated from IP 32.33.23.33
(remote.access.com), using browser (mozilla/4.0 (compatible; msie 6.0;
windows nt 5.0)) and accessed resource /filters/servlet/BasicServlet and used
40 ms
```

The general form of the log entry is as follows:

```
<date and time>  Request Originated from IP <xxx.xxx.xxx.xxx
(xxxx.xxx.xxx.xxx)>, using browser <browser's Agent ID>  and accessed
 resource <URL of resource> and used <duration> ms
```

Information will be extracted from the request, which will allow you to log the originating IP address, the date and time of request, the type of browser that makes the request, and the time spent by the underlying resource processing the request:

```
package filters;

import java.io.*;import javax.servlet.*;
import javax.servlet.http.*;

public final class LoggerFilter implements Filter {

  private FilterConfig filterConfig = null;
```

The doFilter() method is where the filter processing logic resides. A ServletRequest object is passed in with all the details of the incoming request. The ServletResponse object passed in is to what the output (if any) must be written. The filter is also obliged to call the doFilter() method of the FilterChain object passed in; this will pass the response and request (or their wrapper classes) downstream.

In this case, the doFilter() method performs preprocessing logic by storing the current time and extracting the remote address, the remote hostname, the user-agent header, and the uniform resource indicator (URI) of the request:

```
public void doFilter(ServletRequest request, ServletResponse response,
                     FilterChain chain)
    throws IOException, ServletException {
  long startTime = System.currentTimeMillis();
  String remoteAddress =  request.getRemoteAddr();
  String remoteHost = request.getRemoteHost();
  HttpServletRequest myReq = (HttpServletRequest) request;
  String reqURI = myReq.getRequestURI();
  String browserUsed = myReq.getHeader("User-Agent").toLowerCase();
```

After the preprocessing logic is complete, you must call the downstream filters (and/or resources). In this case, you simply pass the incoming `Request` and `Response` objects that were passed to you. Because your filter doesn't modify the `Request` or `Response` objects, there's no need to create wrappers for them:

```
chain.doFilter(request, response);
```

After the downstream `doFilter()` call, you're ready to perform the postprocessing logic. In this case, you simply write a log entry, reflecting the processed request. You couldn't have written this entry in the preprocessing logic because you needed to calculate the time the resource spent processing the request:

```
  filterConfig.getServletContext().log(
    "Request Originated from IP " + remoteAddress + "(" + remoteHost +
    "), using browser (" + browserUsed  + ") and accessed resource " +
    reqURI + " and used " + (System.currentTimeMillis() - startTime) +
    " ms"
  );
}
```

In the `destroy()` method, you release the `FilterConfig` reference:

```
public void destroy() {
  this.filterConfig = null;
}
```

In the `init()` method, the container passes in a `FilterConfig` object, which you store for later use:

```
  public void init(FilterConfig filterConfig) {
    this.filterConfig = filterConfig;
  }
}
```

Now, turn your attention to the Web resource to which you'll apply your filter. You'll create a simple servlet named `XMLOutServlet`, which will simply return the following XML when invoked:

```
<?xml version="1.0" ?>
<quote.set>
  <stock.quote><stock>IBM</stock><price>100.20</price></stock.quote>
  <stock.quote><stock>SUNW</stock><price>28.20</price></stock.quote>
</quote.set>
```

This XML contains data for two stock quotes. In a production application, of course, `XMLOutServlet` would obtain its data via a live data feed, a JDBC data source, or other Web services. However, as long as it outputs XML, the filtering logic will remain the same.

The code for the servlet is straightforward, as shown in Listing 7-19.

Listing 7-19. Servlet Code

```
package filters;

import java.io.*;
import javax.servlet.*;
import javax.servlet.http.*;

public class XMLOutServlet extends HttpServlet {

  public void doGet(HttpServletRequest request,
                   HttpServletResponse response)
      throws ServletException, IOException {
    PrintWriter out = response.getWriter();
    out.println("<?xml version=\"1.0\" ?>");
    out.println("<quote.set>");
    out.println("<stock.quote><stock>IBM</stock>" +
                "<price>100.20</price></stock.quote>");
    out.println("<stock.quote><stock>SUNW</stock>" +
                "<price>28.20</price></stock.quote>");
    out.println("</quote.set>");
  }
}
```

Deploying the Filter

The deployment descriptor, `web.xml`, must contain the filter definition and mapping information before you can use the filter:

```
<?xml version="1.0" encoding="ISO-8859-1"?>
<web-app xmlns="http://java.sun.com/xml/ns/j2ee"
    xmlns:xsi="http://www.w3.org/2001/XMLSchema-instance"
    xsi:schemaLocation="http://java.sun.com/xml/ns/j2ee web-app_2_4.xsd"
    version="2.4">
```

The name of the filter is set to `Logger`:

```
<filter>
  <filter-name>Logger</filter-name>
  <filter-class>filters.LoggerFilter</filter-class>
</filter>
```

The filter is mapped to all the resources served within this application context:

```
  <filter-mapping>
    <filter-name>Logger</filter-name>
    <url-pattern>/*</url-pattern>
  </filter-mapping>
  <servlet>
    <servlet-name>XMLOutServlet</servlet-name>
    <servlet-class>filters.XMLOutServlet</servlet-class>
  </servlet>
</web-app>
```

Compile all the classes. Then you need to create the Web archive (WAR) containing the required files. You should have the following file and directory structure:

```
WEB-INF/
        web.xml
        classes/filters/
                        XMLOutServlet
                        LoggerFilter
```

Create the WAR using the following command:

```
jar cvf filters.war WEB-INF/*
```

Deploy the Web application by moving `filters.war` to Tomcat's `webapps` folder, and restart the server.

Using the Filter

Before you access `XMLOutServlet`, check out the `logs` directory of Tomcat. You should find a log file with a name that follows the following scheme:

```
<hostname>_log_yyyy-mm-dd.txt
```

where `<hostname>` is the local host name and `yyyy-mm-dd` is the date of the `log`. This is the file to which your logging filter will write. Navigate to `http://localhost:8080/filters/servlet/XMLOutServlet`. The result you see will depend on whether your browser understands XML. Figure 7-12 shows the result in Internet Explorer 6.

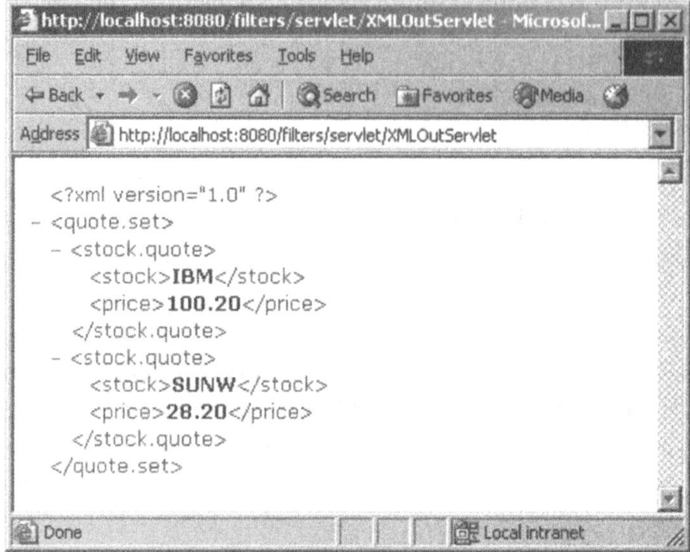

Figure 7-12. The result in Internet Explorer 6

Examine the end of the log file; you'll find that it contains the output from your logging filter. It will be similar to the output shown in Figure 7-13.

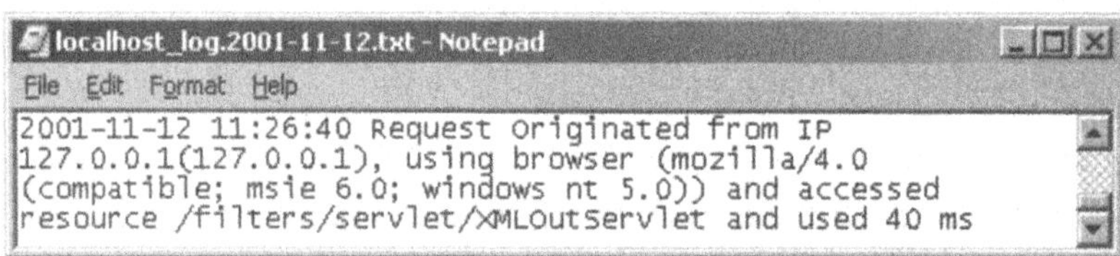

Figure 7-13. The output

A XSLT Transformation Filter

The second example filter will be more complex than the first, but you'll be applying this filter to the same `XMLOutServlet` servlet. This filter will first check the browser type of the client and then do the following:

- If the client's browser is Internet Explorer, the XML output is passed directly back to the browser.
- If the browser is any other type, you'll assume that it can't display XML properly. So, you'll use an XSL Transformations (XSLT) stylesheet to transform the XML into HTML and then pass the HTML back to the client.

Detecting the Browser Type

You'll use the `user-agent` header, which contains information about the browser version, the vendor, and the operating system of the client to detect the browser type. Internet Explorer 6 on Windows 2000 sends the following `user-agent` header:

```
mozilla/4.0 (compatible; msie 6.0; windows nt 5.0)
```

Unlike Internet Explorer, the `user-agent` headers of other browsers don't contain the `msie` string. You'll use this fact to detect if the browser is Internet Explorer. For example, the `user-agent` header for Netscape 6.1 on Windows 98 is as follows:

```
mozilla/5.0 (windows; u; win98; en-us; rv:0.9.2) gecko/20010726 netscape6/6.1
```

Converting XML to HTML

The XSLT stylesheet used to transform the content is named `stockquotes.xsl` and is stored in an `xsl` directory in the root directory of the Web application. It will transform the output from your `XMLOutServlet` servlet into an HTML page (see Listing 7-20).

Listing 7-20. XSLT Stylesheet

```
<?xml version="1.0"?>
<xsl:stylesheet xmlns:xsl=
    "http://www.w3.org/1999/XSL/Transform" version="1.0">
  <xsl:template match="/">
    <html>
      <head>
        <title>Apress Stock Quote Page</title>
      </head>
      <body>
        <h1>Apress Quote Service</h1>
        <table border="1">
          <tr>
            <td width="100">
              <b>Symbol</b>
            </td>
            <td width="100">
              <b>Price</b>
            </td>
          </tr>
          <xsl:for-each select="quote.set/stock.quote">
            <tr>
              <td><xsl:value-of select="stock"/></td>
              <td><xsl:value-of select="price"/></td>
            </tr>
          </xsl:for-each>
        </table>
      </body>
    </html>
  </xsl:template>
</xsl:stylesheet>
```

> **TIP** *You can learn more about how to use XML and XSLT in* XML Programming: Web Applications and Web Services with JSP and ASP *(Apress, 2002).*

Content Substitution Filters

In many filters, such as the earlier logging example, the `Request` and `Response` objects that you pass down are the same as those passed into the `doFilter()` method. Filters that replace content *don't* pass the same `Request` and `Response` objects downstream. Instead, they pass a wrapper `Request` object that can intercept calls by downstream components to provide access to a modified version of the request data.

In filters that modify or transform the response, you also pass a wrapper `Response` object that will capture the response from the next downstream component in a memory buffer. After the chained call returns, this buffer can be examined, and the transformed or replaced output is written to the actual response. This is what your XSLT transform filter will do.

Implementing the Filter

This XSLT filter requires an XSLT parser. The Java API for XML Processing (JAXP) library used by Tomcat will access the Xalan parser by default, so you should download the latest version of `xalan.jar` from `http://xml.apache.org/xalan-j/index.html` and place it in `%CATALINA_HOME%\common\lib\`.

Before you can implement your filter, you need to create a wrapper class for a buffer. You extend `HttpServletResponseWrapper`, which is a convenience class that contains the implementation of the `HttpServletResponse` interface:

```
package filters;

import java.io.*;
import javax.servlet.http.*;

public class OutputCapturer extends HttpServletResponseWrapper {
  private CharArrayWriter buffer;
```

The buffer allows you to easily convert between the output capture buffer and a string—allowing you to work with the captured output. This is the buffer that the filter will use to capture the output of the Web resource (or downstream filter). In this case, it will be the output of `XMLOutServlet`:

```
public OutputCapturer(HttpServletResponse resp) {
  super(resp);
  buffer = new CharArrayWriter();
}
```

Downstream filters and resources will actually write their output into the buffer via a call to getWriter(). This is how the output is effectively "captured:"

```
public PrintWriter getWriter() {
  return new PrintWriter(buffer);
}
```

The toString() method provides an easy way to access the buffer containing the captured output:

```
  public String toString() {
    return buffer.toString();
  }
}
```

The filter class is named SmartXSLFilter and has three instance variables:

- filterConfig stores the context and instance information passed in from the container.
- xsltFactory stores the JAXP XSLT transformation factory class used in this filter instance.
- xsltTemplates stores the preloaded XSLT transformation template used in this filter instance.

The filter's init() method will initialize these instance variables with the appropriate references and the destroy() method will release them:

```
package filters;

import java.io.*;
import javax.servlet.*;
import javax.servlet.http.*;
import javax.xml.transform.*;
import javax.xml.transform.stream.*;

public final class SmartXSLFilter implements Filter {
  private FilterConfig filterConfig = null;
  private TransformerFactory xsltFactory = null;
  private Templates xsltTemplates = null;
```

In the init() method you use JAXP to create an XSLT template for transformations. The XSLT template is based on an XSLT stylesheet source file, which is specified by an initialization parameter in the deployment descriptor. You can use the getInitParameter() method of the FilterConfig object to retrieve these initialization parameter values:

```
public void init(FilterConfig filterConfig) {
  this.filterConfig = filterConfig;
  this.xsltFactory = TransformerFactory.newInstance();
  String xsltfile = filterConfig.getInitParameter("xsltfile");
```

The template object allows the transformation to occur efficiently. By creating a template based on the XSLT source, you won't need to reread and reprocess the template for each incoming request:

```
    try {
      this.xsltTemplates = xsltFactory.newTemplates(new StreamSource(
        this.filterConfig.getServletContext().getRealPath(xsltfile)));
    } catch (Exception ex) {
      this.filterConfig.getServletContext()
        .log("SmartXSLFilter - can't create template - init failed - " +
             ex.toString());
    }
  }
}
```

The doFilter() method contains the core logic of the filter. The first section contains the preprocessing logic, in which you decode the user-agent header of the request and determine if the request is from an Internet Explorer browser:

```
public void doFilter(ServletRequest request,
                     ServletResponse response,
                     FilterChain chain)
                     throws IOException, ServletException {

  String browserUsed =
    ((HttpServletRequest) request).getHeader("User-Agent").toLowerCase();
  boolean isMSIE = (browserUsed.indexOf("msie") >= 0);
```

The exact way you call downstream filters will depend on whether you're dealing with Internet Explorer. If it's not Internet Explorer, you'll need to transform the output from XML to HTML. You do this by creating an instance of the OutputCapturer wrapper class and then handing it downstream:

```
if (!isMSIE) {
  PrintWriter realOutput = response.getWriter();
  OutputCapturer myCapture =
               new OutputCapturer((HttpServletResponse) response);
  chain.doFilter (request, myCapture);
```

After the chained call, myCapture now contains the output of XMLOutServlet. You'll now transform this XML into HTML using the XSLT template you obtained during initialization:

```
try {
  Source xfrmSrc =
          new StreamSource(new StringReader(myCapture.toString()));
  Transformer tpXfrmer = xsltTemplates.newTransformer();
  CharArrayWriter finalOut = new CharArrayWriter();
  StreamResult xfrmResult = new StreamResult(finalOut);
  tpXfrmer.transform(xfrmSrc, xfrmResult);
```

The transformed output is stored in `finalOut`, and you use this to write the actual response:

```
  response.setContentLength(finalOut.toString().length());
  realOutput.write(finalOut.toString());
  filterConfig.getServletContext().log(
                  "SmartXSLFilter activated - completed transform");
} catch (Exception ex) {
  filterConfig.getServletContext().log(
    "SmartXSLFilter - XSLT transformation failed - " + ex.toString());
}
```

If the request is from Internet Explorer, you simply pass the incoming request and response. The output from `XMLOutServlet` isn't touched at all, and you can use the browser to view the resulting XML data:

```
  } else {
    chain.doFilter(request, response);
  }
}
```

The `destroy()` method sets the instance variables to `null`, which will release the associated objects and enable a container to reuse this filter instance (if the functionality is implemented), avoiding the overhead of destroying and creating a new instance:

```
  public void destroy() {
    this.filterConfig = null;
    this.xsltFactory = null;
    this.xsltTemplates = null;
  }
}
```

Deploying the Filter

To configure the filter, you need to add the filter definition and mapping information to `web.xml`:

```
<?xml version="1.0" encoding="ISO-8859-1"?>
<web-app xmlns="http://java.sun.com/xml/ns/j2ee"
    xmlns:xsi="http://www.w3.org/2001/XMLSchema-instance"
```

```
    xsi:schemaLocation="http://java.sun.com/xml/ns/j2ee web-app_2_4.xsd"
    version="2.4">
   <filter>
    <filter-name>XSLTFilter</filter-name>
    <filter-class>
      filters.SmartXSLFilter
    </filter-class>
```

An initialization parameter named `xsltfile` is given a value of `/xsl/stockquotes.xsl` (which is the path to the XSLT stylesheet that the filter uses):

```
  <init-param>
    <param-name>xsltfile</param-name>
    <param-value>/xsl/stockquotes.xsl</param-value>
  </init-param>

</filter>
```

You create the filter mapping in this case via a `<servlet-name>` element, which will associate a specific servlet (`XMLOutServlet`) with the filter. The filter will be activated only when this servlet is accessed:

```
  <filter-mapping>
    <filter-name>XSLTFilter</filter-name>
    <servlet-name>XMLOutServlet</servlet-name>
  </filter-mapping>
  <servlet>
    <servlet-name>XMLOutServlet</servlet-name>
    <servlet-class>filters.XMLOutServlet</servlet-class>
  </servlet>
</web-app>
```

Compile all of the classes, making sure you include `jaxp.jar` and `xalan.jar` in your classpath. Then you need to create the WAR. You should have the following file and directory structure:

```
WEB-INF/
        web.xml
        classes/filters/
                        XMLOutServlet
                        SmartXSLFilter
                        OutputCapturer
xsl/
    stockquotes.xsl
```

Then, create the WAR with the following command:

```
jar cvf filters.war WEB-INF/* xsl/*
```

Deploy the Web application by copying `filters.war` to Tomcat's `webapps` folder and restarting the server.

Using the Filter

Use Internet Explorer to navigate to `http://localhost:8080/filters/XMLOutServlet` to access the servlet (and your filter). Your filter will have detected the browser and passed the XML output straight through, so you'll see the same output as you did during the logging example.

Now, try accessing the same URL using another type of browser. Your `SmartXSLFilter` will detect the non-IE browser and perform the XML-to-HTML conversion before sending back the response.

Chaining Filters

You can chain the `Logger` and `XSLTFilter` filters together by including both in `web.xml` (see Listing 7-21).

Listing 7-21. `web.xml`

```
<?xml version="1.0" encoding="ISO-8859-1"?>
<web-app xmlns="http://java.sun.com/xml/ns/j2ee"
    xmlns:xsi="http://www.w3.org/2001/XMLSchema-instance"
    xsi:schemaLocation="http://java.sun.com/xml/ns/j2ee web-app_2_4.xsd"
    version="2.4">
  <filter>
    <filter-name>Logger</filter-name>
    <filter-class>filters.LoggerFilter</filter-class>
  </filter>

  <filter>
    <filter-name>XSLTFilter</filter-name>
    <filter-class>filters.SmartXSLFilter</filter-class>
    <init-param>
      <param-name>xsltfile</param-name>
      <param-value>/xsl/stockquotes.xsl</param-value>
    </init-param>
  </filter>

  <filter-mapping>
     <filter-name>Logger</filter-name>
     <url-pattern>/*</url-pattern>
  </filter-mapping>

  <filter-mapping>
    <filter-name>XSLTFilter</filter-name>
    <servlet-name>XMLOutServlet</servlet-name>
  </filter-mapping>

  <servlet>
```

```
    <servlet-name>XMLOutServlet</servlet-name>
    <servlet-class>filters.XMLOutServlet</servlet-class>
  </servlet>
</web-app>
```

Restart Tomcat and try accessing `XMLOutServlet` using both Internet Explorer and Netscape once more. The `XSLTFilter` will work as before. Now check out the log file in the `logs` directory of Tomcat, and you'll see that the `Logger` filter logs every access to `XMLOutServlet`. The two filters have been chained together.

The log entry from the `Logger` filter always precedes the entry from the `XSLTFilter`, which indicates that the `Logger` filter is always upstream. All filters with `<filter-mapping>` elements that use `<url-pattern>` elements are chained (in the order they appear in the `web.xml` file) before the `<filter-mapping>` elements that use `<servlet-name>` elements (again in the order that they appear in the `web.xml` file).

Designing Filters

To round out the chapter, the following are a few guidelines you should keep in mind when you're developing filters:

- You should design filters to be easily configurable at deployment time. Often you can reuse a filter through the careful planning and use of initialization parameters.
- Filtering logic, unlike that of servlets, shouldn't depend on session state information that's maintained between requests because a single filter instance may be servicing many different requests at the same time.
- When mapping filters, always use the most restrictive mapping possible—use `<servlet-name>` instead of `<url-pattern>` if possible. You can significantly increase the overhead of filter operations if the filter is consistently applied to Web resources that don't need it.

Summary

You saw in this chapter how you can use filters to add functionality such as auditing, logging, authentication, transformation, compression, and encryption to your applications at deployment time. You can easily add and remove such functionality as business requirements change.

You can use filters without having to touch existing code. Filter definitions and filter mapping within the deployment descriptor indicate to the container how filters should be chained together and the Web resource to which the filters should apply. You can even configure multiple instances of the same underlying filter within the deployment descriptor together with different initialization parameters. The container manages the lifetime of a filter and will create and destroy instances of the filter as specified in the deployment descriptor.

To complete the chapter, you built two filters: a simple logging filter and a transformation filter. The transformation filter allowed the same underlying service logic to service a variety of different clients. Finally, you saw how these two filters could be chained together in order to combine their functionality.

CHAPTER 8

Handling Security in the Web Tier

THERE WAS A TIME when Web application security wasn't an issue to many developers. This is surely no longer the case. Security features are now one of the most important issues to consider when writing your applications. This is true not only for the security of your users but also for the security of the environment in which your application runs. The execution of third-party servlets is increasingly common. Consider an application service provider (ASP) that hosts many Web applications on virtual hosts supported by a single servlet container instance. You certainly don't want someone else's misbehaving servlet to bring down the entire server. The ability to restrict certain actions is vital to the well-being of a server and the Web applications running on it.

While the implementation details may vary from vendor to vendor, all servlet containers provide the following characteristics for your applications, as detailed in the Servlet 2.4 specification:

- **Authentication**: The means by which communicating entities prove to one another that they're acting on behalf of specific identities that are authorized for access.

- **Access control for resources**: The means by which interactions with resources are limited to collections of users or programs for the purpose of enforcing integrity, confidentiality, or availability constraints.

- **Data integrity**: The means used to prove that a third party hasn't modified information while in transit.

- **Confidentiality (data privacy)**: The means used to ensure that information is made available only to users who are authorized to access it.

In this chapter, you'll see how to address the various details of security using a combination of available technologies. You'll examine the following components of servlet security:

- How to use server-side policy files
- How to configure Tomcat to use Secure Socket Layer (SSL)
- How SSL relates to public key encryption, digital signatures, and transitive trust
- How to use Tomcat 5 realms, which provide a platform-independent way of performing authentication and role mapping
- How to implement container-managed security
- How to implement Basic, Form-based, Digest, and Client-Cert authentication
- How to implement Tomcat's single sign-on mechanism that eliminates multiple authentication requests

Understanding the Java 2 Security Model on the Server

The Java 2 security model provides a fine-grained, policy-based mechanism with which you can control programmatic access to system resources. You can set the level of protection by modifying a *policy file* for individual Java virtual machines (JVMs).

> **NOTE** *Once security is enabled, resources can't be accessed unless access is explicitly granted in a policy file.*

You can use policy files to do the following:

- Allow connections only to the host from which the code was originally loaded.
- Prevent access to the local file system.
- Prevent access to JVM and operating system properties.

A policy file contains *grant statements*, which grant permission for a specific type of access by a specific principal:

- A *security principal* is associated with a body of code.
- A *permission* encapsulates the action of accessing a protected system resource.

Table 8-1 describes some of the most frequently used permissions in typical policy files.

Table 8-1. Policy File Permissions

PERMISSION	DESCRIPTION
`java.lang.RuntimePermission`	Controls the runtime execution of vital system calls, such as `exitVM()`, `setSecurityManager()`, and `createClassLoader()`
`java.util.PropertyPermission`	Controls access (both read and write) to system properties
`java.io.FilePermission`	Controls access (read, write, delete, and execution) to files and directories
`java.net.SocketPermission`	Controls access (connect, listen, accept, and resolve) to network sockets
`java.security.AllPermission`	Enables access to *all* protected resources

You should keep a couple of concepts in mind when dealing with permission objects. First, a permission object represents, but doesn't grant access to, a system resource. Permission objects are constructed and assigned (*granted*) to code based on the policy in effect. When a permission object is assigned to some code, that code is granted the permission to access the system resource specified in the permission object in the specified manner. You can find a complete list of security permissions in the online documentation at `http://java.sun.com/security/` or `http://java.sun.com/j2se/1.4/docs/guide/security/permissions.html`.

Understanding Server-Side Policy Files

When you start Tomcat using the default `startup` script, it starts without security enabled, which is equivalent to a grant of `java.security.AllPermission`. Tomcat comes with a default policy file that's used when you start Tomcat with security enabled using the `-security` option. This policy file is named `catalina.policy` and is stored in the `%CATALINA_HOME%\conf` directory.

You'll now examine some interesting parts of this policy file, starting with the following system code permissions:

```
grant codeBase "file:${java.home}/lib/-" {
        permission java.security.AllPermission;
};
```

The Java compiler needs to be called from within Catalina (the servlet container used by Tomcat), and this policy will enable it to access everything (because you trust the Java compiler to consist of benevolent code). The same permission is granted to system extensions:

```
grant codeBase "file:${java.home}/jre/lib/ext/-" {
        permission java.security.AllPermission;
};
```

Although the Catalina server code isn't system library code, it's granted all permissions to facilitate its operation:

```
grant codeBase "file:${catalina.home}/bin/bootstrap.jar" {
        permission java.security.AllPermission;
};
```

The code in the `common` library will also be granted all permissions. These permissions apply to the Servlet API classes and those that are shared across all classloaders located in the `common` directory. This means you should pay careful attention about what you place into this directory:

```
grant codeBase "file:${catalina.home}/common/-" {
        permission java.security.AllPermission;
};
```

The policy file goes on to grant permissions to the container's core code, the JSP page compiler, the shared Web application libraries, and the shared Web application classes. It's probably worth your while to spend a couple of minutes looking over the contents of the `%CATALINA_HOME%\conf\catalina.policy` file to get familiar with it.

Using Server-Side Policy Files

You're now ready to try a malicious servlet to see how a server-side policy file can protect you from its mischief. Consider the following servlet:

```
import javax.servlet.*;
import javax.servlet.http.*;
```

```
public class ViciousServlet extends HttpServlet {

  public void doGet(HttpServletRequest request,
                  HttpServletResponse response)
      throws IOException, ServletException {
    System.exit(1);
  }
}
```

The `System.exit(1)` system call stops the execution of the JVM that's hosting the servlet container. This represents the type of mistake that an inexperienced developer could make when working in a shared servlet hosting environment.

Start Tomcat *without* security enabled, and access the servlet by navigating to `http://localhost:8080/policytest/vicious`. Tomcat will shut down; this is because with security not enabled, any servlet can shut down the JVM on which Tomcat is running.

Next, you'll start Tomcat *with* security enabled, which by default will grant the permissions specified in `catalina.policy`. This policy file doesn't grant `java.lang.RuntimePermission` for `exitVM()` to any Web application, which means that Web applications won't be able to successfully call the `exit()` method.

Use the following command to start Tomcat in security-enabled mode:

```
catalina start -security
```

Now, when you navigate to `http://localhost:8080/policytest/vicious`, you'll see something like Figure 8-1.

The servlet has committed an access violation, but in this case the server is spared a complete crash.

You'll now create another servlet that accesses a known uniform resource locator (URL) and passes its content to the client. This means it'll require permission to access a specific host and socket:

```
import java.net.*;
import java.io.*;
import javax.servlet.*;
import javax.servlet.http.*;

public class NetAccessServlet extends HttpServlet {

  public void doGet(HttpServletRequest request,
                  HttpServletResponse response)
      throws IOException, ServletException {
    PrintWriter out = response.getWriter();
    String tpString = null;
```

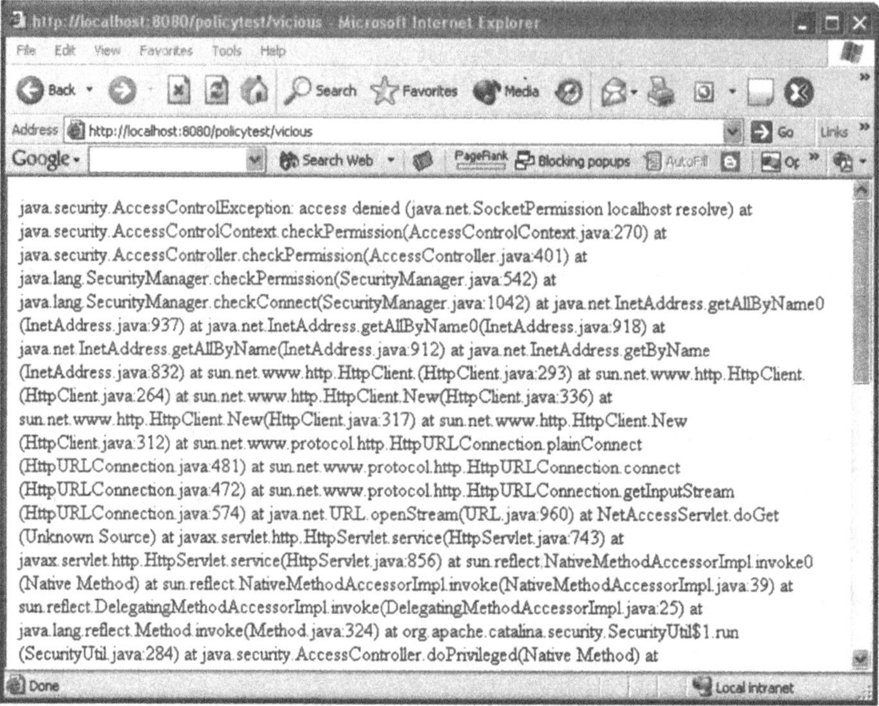

Figure 8-1. Tomcat with security enabled

The servlet creates a connection to `http://localhost:8080/` and then creates a `BufferedReader` from the contents of the URL connection. Once the connection is opened, it simply sends everything to the servlet's response:

```
    try {
      URL myConn = new URL("http://localhost:8080/");
      BufferedReader myReader =
        new BufferedReader((new InputStreamReader(myConn.openStream())));
      while ((tpString = myReader.readLine()) != null) {
        out.println(tpString);
      }
    } catch (Exception ex) {
      ex.printStackTrace(out);
    }
  }
}
```

Start Tomcat *without* security, and navigate to `http://localhost:8080/policytest/passthru`. You should be redirected to the Tomcat home page (although without the images because they're located at a different URL), as shown in Figure 8-2.

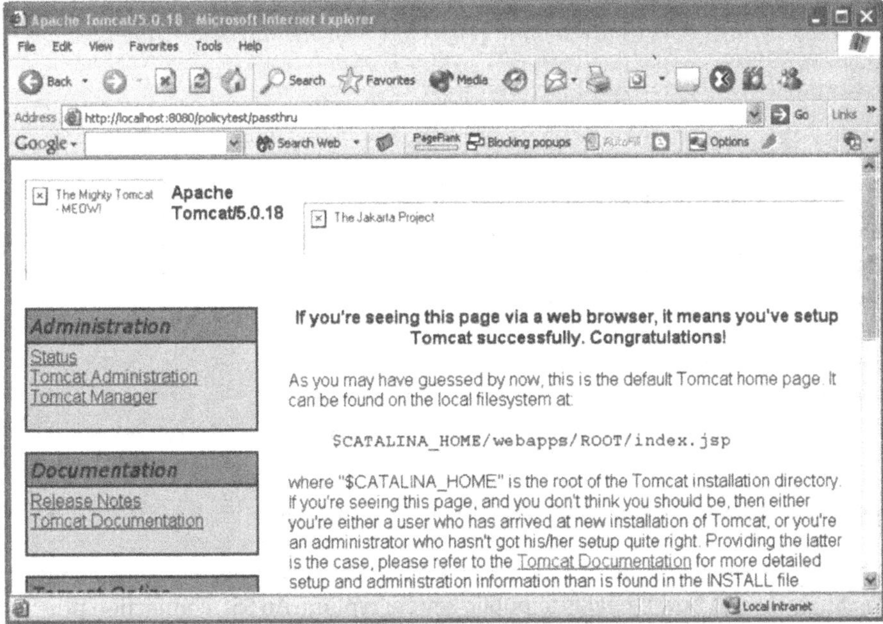

Figure 8-2. Tomcat home page without security

Shut down Tomcat, restart it *with* security, and navigate again to `http://localhost:8080/policytest/passthru`. Once more, you'll see an access exception, which means that, by default, servlets aren't allowed to directly access to any network resource. To enable the specific network access required by the `NetAccessServlet`, you must add the following entry to `catalina.policy`:

```
grant codeBase "file:${catalina.home}/webapps/policytest/WEB-
INF/classes/NetAccessServlet.class" {

  permission java.net.SocketPermission "localhost:8080", "connect";
};
```

This entry grants `NetAccessServlet` (but no other class) the privilege of connecting to `localhost` at port 8080. Make the addition to `catalina.policy`, restart Tomcat 5 with security, and navigate to `http://localhost:8080/policytest/passthru`. This time, you'll see Tomcat's home page.

Implementing Secure Socket Layer

Commercial Web sites extensively use Secure Socket Layer (SSL), which has emerged as the standard security mechanism on the Web. It provides a secure connection between the client and the server.

> **TIP** *SSL is an international standard, in the form of an Internet Engineering Task Force (IETF) Request for Comment (RFC) called Transport Layer Security (TLS) 1.0. You can find it at* `http://www.ietf.org/rfc/rfc2246.txt`.

You're probably familiar with the way SSL works on your browser—look for the "secure indicator" (typically a small padlock, depending on what browser you're using) when you visit a secure site. Once you've made a successful SSL connection, you can be sure that the following has happened:

- You've reached a legitimate Web site.
- The data sent between your browser and the server will be encrypted.

Understanding the SSL Operation Model

To understand how to configure SSL for servlet containers, you need to understand how SSL works and how it relates to public key encryption. An SSL connection provides the following three guarantees:

- The authenticity of the server
- The privacy of data transferred via encryption
- The integrity of the data when it's transferred (the data must not be modified during transfer between client and server)

The third guarantee provides protection against a "man-in-the-middle" security attack, in which the message is intercepted between the client and the server.SSL provides this authentication, privacy, and integrity using a combination of *public key encryption* and *shared secret encryption*.

The downside of using SSL is that it adds about 10 percent overhead to your network operations. Usually, you want to specify which pages in your application require SSL so that you can mitigate the performance hit.

Data Encryption Fundamentals

Encryption is the act of transforming a message (via some mathematical algorithm) into an unintelligible form. Typically, the encryption transformation is performed using a sequence of numeric values or a *key*, which is also used in the decryption process. Possession of the key enables the recipient to decode the message. This sort of encryption is frequently referred to as *shared secret encryption* because each party shares a common key.

SSL uses this simple form of encryption to encode the stream of data between the client and the server. Anyone who learns the shared key will be able to access the transmitted data, but both the client and the server need to know the key. Consequently, SSL depends on a considerably stronger form of encryption during its handshaking phase (prior to the creation of the shared secret session) in order to establish a secured session between a client and a server—which is called *public key encryption*.

Public Key Encryption

Unlike shared secret encryption, public key encryption uses two keys that differ in value. The keys are generated using a mathematical algorithm in which anything encrypted with one of the keys can be decrypted only with the other. Such keys are known as *asymmetric keys*. What makes public key encryption so strong is that having one of the keys in the key pair won't allow you to work out the other (at least not without trying different sequences for a long time.)

Having generated two keys with such a special property, you can then designate one of them as a *public key* and the other one as a *private key*. The private key is *never* shared with anyone else. Compromising the private key will leave your data unsecured. The public key, on the other hand, can be widely circulated; any client who wants to communicate with the server can use it.

During an encrypted communications session between the server and the client, the following happens:

1. The server can encrypt all the data going to the client using its private key.
2. The client can then use the public key to decrypt the data.

Going the other way, the following happens:

1. The client can use the server's public key to encrypt the data.
2. The server can use its private key to decrypt it.

Since the public key is the only key in the world that can decrypt data encrypted by the server's private key, the client can be assured that it's indeed talking to the server (because only the server possesses the private key).

This all sounds elegant and straightforward, but unfortunately there's a problem. Public key encryption requires tremendous processing power to encrypt and decrypt the data. For this reason, SSL uses the faster and simpler shared secret encryption for encrypting its data stream. Public key encryption is used only to exchange the key that's to be used for shared secret encryption.

Phases of SSL Communication

SSL utilizes public key encryption during its handshaking process (when a client wants to establish a secured session with a server). After that, SSL enters into a communication session in which shared secret encryption is used to encrypt the data.

The following occurs during the SSL handshaking phase:

1. The server is authenticated.
2. The client and server agree on a set of encryption algorithms to use.
3. Optionally, the client can also be authenticated (although this isn't done in the usual client to Web server connection).
4. The client and server negotiate a shared secret key, which encrypts the data during the second communications phase of the protocol.

NOTE *The key negotiated between the client and the server is valid only for a single session.*

In the next few sections, you'll take a closer look at how the first step of the handshaking phase—server authentication—happens in SSL.

Digital Signatures, Certificates, and Trust

Public key encryption requires the wide distribution of the public key. This is more difficult than it first appears. Imagine the hundreds of sites you may visit through an SSL connection. If you were to use public key encryption directly, you'd need to possess a site's public key before you can establish a session with that site. Storing and managing so many public keys would become a problem, particularly when a site changes its key pair.

One solution would be to have the server send its public key immediately upon connection, but this would mean you have a server handing a client its own public key, and the client would be using this public key to assert the server's identity, opening a large security loophole.

Although you may not trust a server handing out a public key that it claims as its own, you can collectively trust groups such as VeriSign (`http://www.verisign.com`) or Thawte (`http://www.thawte.com/`). These are Certification Authorities (CAs), and they provide a mechanism by which you can validate a server's public key as it's handed to you.

This mechanism uses transitive trust. First, you must assume that you've obtained the public key of the CA, obtained through some highly secured means (built right into modern browsers). Now you need to have faith in only the CA's public key because the CA will in turn vouch for the authenticity of a server's public key. This happens through a *digital certificate* (or *cert*).

A cert is an *unencrypted* message that contains a server's public key as well as other information such as domain name, Internet Protocol (IP), name of the issuing CA, and expiration date, together with a digital signature that's obtained from a CA. The CA will take the server's information and authenticate it via some external means (for example, human intervention) and will then vouch for the authenticity of that information by signing it with its own private key. This signing happens using a *digital signature*.

A digital signature is appended at the end of a message and ensures the integrity of the message during transmission. In this case, the message plus the signature forms the certificate. A digital signature is computed by putting the contents of the message through the one-way hash algorithm (MD5) that produces a *message digest*. MD5 is a frequently used algorithm; you find details at `http://www.ietf.org/rfc/rfc1321.txt`. The digest is then encrypted using the private key of the CA and appended to the message.

When it receives a certificate supplied by the server, a client can ascertain the validity of the information on the certificate by performing the same one-way hash on the content, decrypting the signature using the CA's well-known public key, and finally comparing the two hash values. In this way, the authenticity of the server is established through the transitive trust relationship between the client, the CA, and the server, as shown in Figure 8-3.

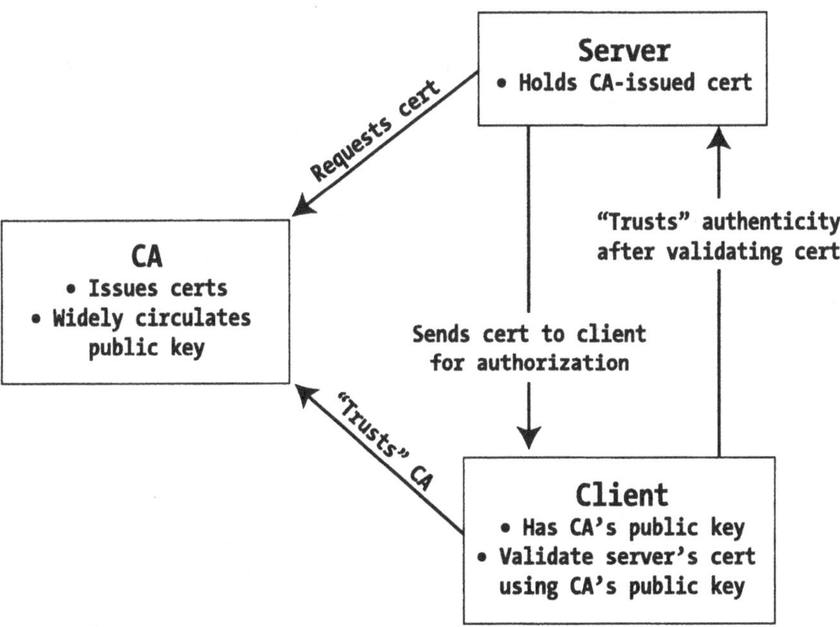

Figure 8-3. Authenticating a server

One of the most frequently used formats for certificates is based on the X.509 format, described at `http://www.ietf.org/rfc/rfc2459.txt`. Tomcat's SSL implementation supports using this standard format.

SSL Server Authentication

During SSL server authentication, a client checks the identity of the server to make sure it's contacting the genuine server. After the connection of a client via unencrypted sockets, the server sends a cert to the client. The client then performs a series of checks to authenticate the server, including the following:

- Verifying that the certificate hasn't expired
- Verifying that the CA issuing the certificate is to be trusted
- Verifying the domain name against the one on the certificate
- Validating the CA's digital signature on the certificate (by decrypting the signature with the CA's public key and comparing it against the message digest) to ensure that the certificate is issued by the CA and that the information hasn't been tampered with

After server authentication is performed, the client and server will check the set of cryptographic algorithms available to them and negotiate a *cipher suite* that represents the algorithms available to both of them. Finally, a key is generated (using one of the shared secret encryption algorithms from the cipher suite) and shared between the client and server for the communications phase of the protocol.

Possible SSL-Enabled Container Configurations

You can set up an SSL-enabled Web site based on Tomcat 5 (and most other servlet containers/application servers) in at least two ways: using a Web server front end and using a stand-alone configuration.

Using a Web Server Front End

When you use a Web server front end, you use a connector between the Web server and Tomcat. The establishment of the SSL connection, and encryption and decryption of the data stream, all occur between the client and the Web server. The connection between the Web server and Tomcat is via a physically secured network, and the data isn't encrypted when transferred, as shown in Figure 8-4.

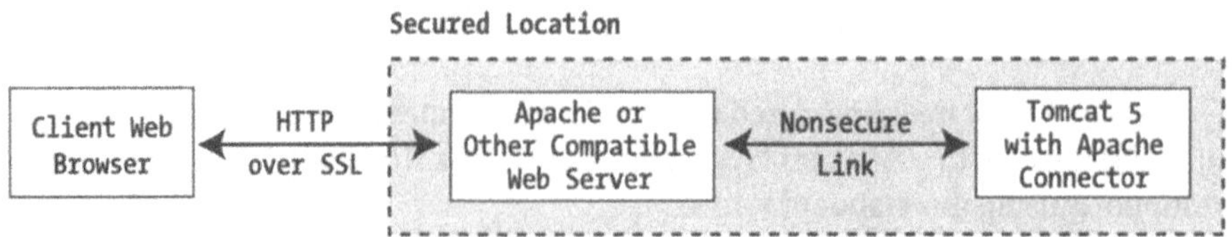

Figure 8-4. Using a connector

The exact configuration of the systems in this scenario is specific to the Web server. The documentation of all the leading Web servers such as Apache, JBoss, WebLogic, WebSphere, IIS, and SunOne Server[1] provide details of setting up an SSL server, so we won't cover them here.

Using the Stand-Alone Configuration of Apache Tomcat

You can also use a stand-alone configuration in which Tomcat is used as both the Web server (for serving static content) and the application server. In this case, you establish the SSL connection between a client's browser and Tomcat 4 directly, as shown in Figure 8-5.

Figure 8-5. Establishing the connection directly

Enabling SSL on Tomcat 5

Instead of reimplementing the complex SSL layer, Tomcat uses the Java Secure Socket Extension (JSSE) standard extension that's available from `http://java.sun.com/products/jsse/` (JSSE comes as an integral part of J2SE 1.4). JSSE provides a pure Java implementation of SSL, implemented as a set of custom socket factory classes that enable any non-SSL application to easily use them by simply specifying one of the factory classes when creating a socket.

Installing JSSE

JSSE consists of a set of JAR files: `jsse.jar`, `jcert.jar`, and `jnet.jar`. While Tomcat 5 can use an environment variable named `JSSE_HOME` for locating these extensions, the most reliable way is to install JSSE as a standard extension by copying these Java archive (JAR) files to the `%JAVA_HOME%\jre\lib\ext` directory or to make them available to Tomcat by copying them to `%CATALINA_HOME%\common\lib`.

Creating a Server-Side Keystore

JSSE obtains public key and cert information from a *keystore*. The keystore used by JSSE is in the proprietary format Java Key Store (JKS). Users can create a keystore, generate public key pairs, and create certificates using a tool that's part of the standard Java Development Kit (JDK): `keytool`, which has several options (see Table 8-2).

1. SunOne Server is formally known as iPlanet.

Table 8-2. keytool *Options*

OPTION	DESCRIPTION
-genkey	Generates a public and private key pair and creates a self-signed cert
-export	Exports a cert in binary or text format
-alias	Specifies a text alias that can be used to retrieve the keys after creation
-list	Lists the contents of the store
-keyalg	Specifies a key generation algorithm (RSA is usually used)
-keystore	Specifies the path to the keystore
-storepass	Specifies the password for the keystore
-validity	Lists the number of days for which the cert will be valid

Self-signed certificates represent a cert vouching for your authenticity whose signing CA is yourself. Although not useful in production environments, they're useful for testing because obtaining custom certs can be expensive.

To create a keystore that you can use on Tomcat, you can use the following command:

```
keytool -genkey -alias apress-keystore .\keystore -keyalg RSA -validity 365
```

When you execute this command, keytool will prompt for some additional information. Answer the questions according to Figure 8-6 (blank entries indicate that you don't need to enter any value and can simply press the Return key).

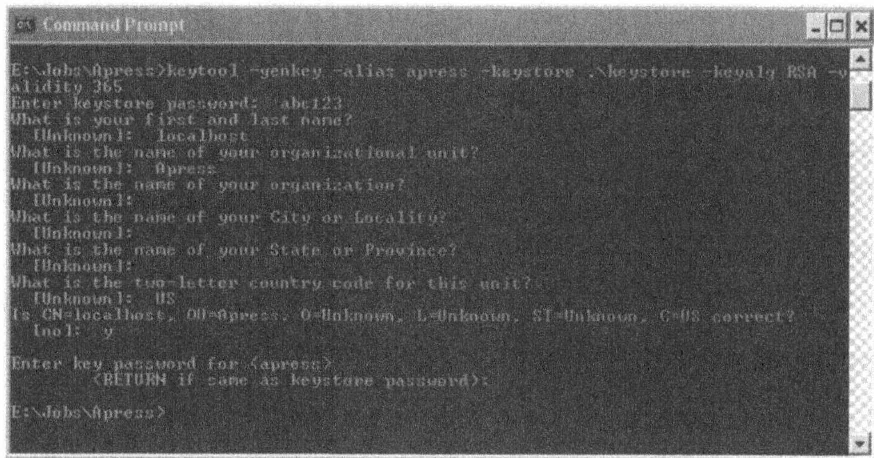

Figure 8-6. Creating a keystore

The fields for the cert are standard X.509 required fields. Because you're creating a cert for your server, it's important to use the server's name when prompted—in this case, `localhost`. You also need to be careful to set the same password for the keystore and for the cert entry (in this example, it's set to `abc123`). This is because Tomcat allows you to specify a single password for both.

You may see a significant delay during the generation of the public key pair and the creation of a self-signed cert, after which there will be a file named `keystore` in your working directory. You can see the contents of the keystore by running this command:

```
keytool -keystore .\keystore -list
```

You'll be prompted for the keystore password. The tool will then list the contents of the keystore (in this case, it contains only the self-signed cert you just created), as shown in Figure 8-7.

```
Command Prompt

E:\Jobs\Apress>keytool -keystore .\keystore -list
Enter keystore password:  abc123

Keystore type: jks
Keystore provider: SUN

Your keystore contains 1 entry

apress, Mar 15, 2004, keyEntry,
Certificate fingerprint (MD5): D0:06:6E:C2:29:90:37:50:CB:C4:78:6F:4C:ED:93:83

E:\Jobs\Apress>
```

Figure 8-7. The contents of the keystore

You need to move this keystore to a location where Tomcat can locate it. Create a `keystore` directory underneath `%CATALINA_HOME%`, and copy the keystore file to it.

Exporting a CA Certificate for a Client Browser

Next, you need to get your browser to recognize you as a CA. You do this by exporting your cert and then importing it into the browser you're using. The command to export a cert using `keytool` is as follows:

```
keytool -export -keystore .\keystore -alias apress -rfc -file apress.cer
```

The tool will prompt for your password and then generate a key file in RFC 1421, Base 64-encoded format (which is easily transportable). The key file is stored as `apress.key` in your working directory and will look something like this:

```
-----BEGIN CERTIFICATE-----
MIICQDCCAakCBDwLYykwDQYJKoZIhvcNAQEEBQAwZzELMAkGA1UEBhMCVUsxEDAOBgNVBAgTB1Vu
a25vd24xEDAOBgNVBAcTB1Vua25vd24xEzARBgNVBAoTCldyb3ggUHJlc3MxCzAJBgNVBAsTAklU
MRIwEAYDVQQDEwlsb2NhbGhvc3QwHhcNMDExMjAzMTEzNDAxWhcNMDIxMjAzMTEzNDAxWjBnMQsw
CQYDVQQGEwJVSzEQMA4GA1UECBMHVW5rbm93bjEQMA4GA1UEBxMHVW5rbm93bjETMBEGA1UEChMK
V3JveCBQcmVzczELMAkGA1UECxMCSVQxEjAQBgNVBAMTCWxvY2FsaG9zdDCBnzANBgkqhkiG9w0B
AQEFAAOBjQAwgYkCgYEA59pRG46XWhV7syzNeZqPvOONDSHYRO9zKOxWnxe3SNHUSNRhrVbRJ89y
E5jWmjXz4fZtE1W9DADN6NBgQVyYmbcu68hqeqmzsM4bGxYVMRNCkIFtkawgYBD9CKSgKdDGvean
nugTSiHBF6xRfkUy4wUbLoOECZ4utZQHFYcYCTMCAwEAATANBgkqhkiG9w0BAQQFAAOBgQAuQ66L
EXaCrNTI8jyw9TcOZsKS3+LWJNOnAnitURfSkejgzmOYkLYdwCagvU3eLPPe7BCOndqiYZQmuSod
o8C+wBaCyLYcg3BqBuOs/RLxUooNA5EpU5W2rhJotW9vkiEGPhRCjZGuM+jvAc3zIsVJCQFqrqKO
aaphYb5gre8t7g==
-----END CERTIFICATE-----
```


You'll import this as a CA to Internet Explorer (to import to other browsers, you should consult their documentation). Select Tools ➤ Internet Options. Click the Content tab, and you should see something similar to Figure 8-8.

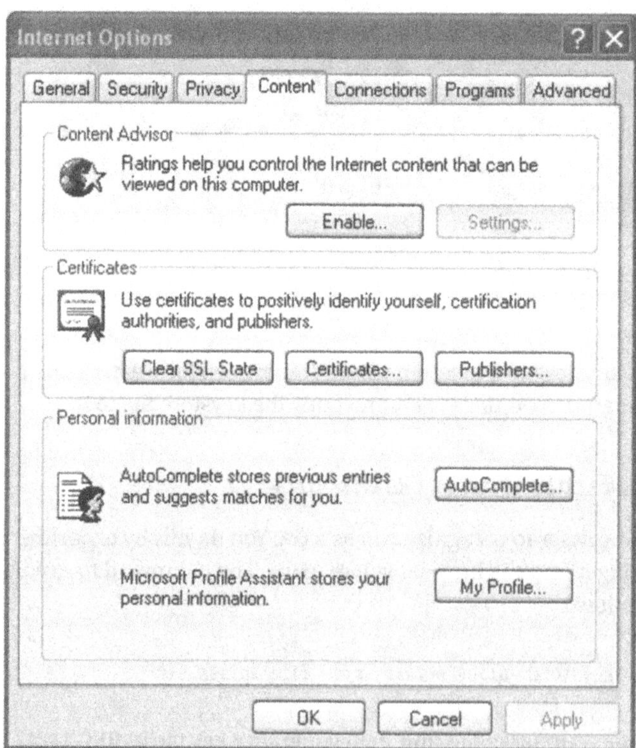

Figure 8-8. The Content tab

Click the Certificates button, and then click the Trusted Root Certification Authorities tab. You should see a list of already installed CAs, as shown in Figure 8-9.

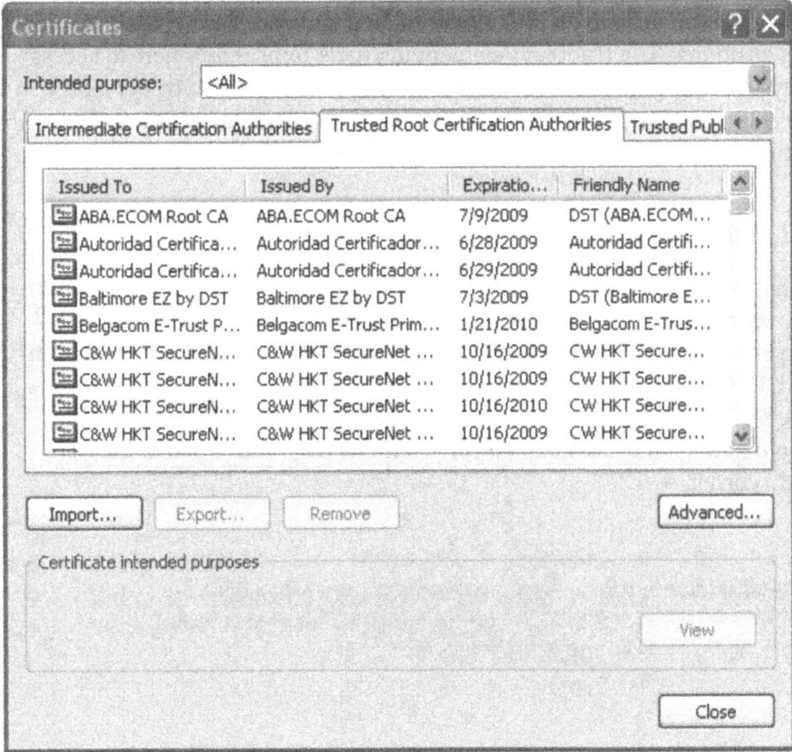

Figure 8-9. Already installed CAs

Click the Import button, and walk through the wizard, importing your `apress.cer` file. The wizard will recognize the certificate format and install it into the root certificate store.

Adding an SSL Connector to Tomcat 5

Finally, you can configure Tomcat to take advantage of the server-side SSL setup. You can do this by editing `server.xml` in Tomcat's `conf` directory:

```
<Connector className="org.apache.catalina.connector.http.HttpConnector"
           port="8443" minProcessors="5" maxProcessors="75"
           enableLookups="true" acceptCount="10" debug="0"
           scheme="https" secure="true">
<Factory className="org.apache.catalina.net.SSLServerSocketFactory"
           keystoreFile="keystore/keystore" keystorePass="abc123"
           clientAuth="false" protocol="TLS"/>
</Connector>
```

Within the `<Service name="Tomcat-Standalone">` element, you should find an entry already in place. All you need to do is to uncomment it and add the `keystoreFile` and `keystorePass` attributes. The `<Factory>` element instructs Tomcat on where to access the public key and certs required for the SSL session (as implemented by the JSSE socket factory classes). The protocol type is an encryption/decryption protocol to be used on this socket. The default value has no other options.

Trying SSL-Enabled Tomcat

Remember that the JSSE JAR files will need to be available to Tomcat for this to work. Using the browser you've added the CA cert to, navigate to `https://localhost:8443/`. The `8443` part is the port used by Tomcat, but you can reset it to `443`, which is the standard SSL port. However, doing so requires some special setup for Tomcat to use ports less than 443. You can refer to the current Tomcat documentation if you need to do this. You should now get the SSL-enabled Tomcat home page with a padlock icon in the lower-right corner.

> **NOTE** *Non-SSL access is still available via port 8080. The portion of an application that doesn't need a secure connection should avoid using SSL access because it's considerably more processor-intensive than non-SSL access.*

It's worth taking a moment to examine what's happening here. The browser authenticates the server by doing the following:

1. Receiving a certificate from Tomcat (`localhost`)
2. Validating the certificate against a trusted CA
3. Checking the host name used to access the resource (`localhost`)
4. Checking the expiration date of the certificate (a year from now)

All of these checks must be successful before a shared secret key is generated and used for communication. If you try to access `https://localhost:8443/index.html` using a browser that doesn't have your certificate installed, you'll see a warning.

Setting Up Servlet 2.4 Security

The Servlet 2.4 specification, consistent with J2EE philosophy, prescribes a model that separates the developers from the deployers of a Web application:

- It's the responsibility of the developers to anticipate how the application will be used after deployment and to make it flexible enough to adapt to different environments.

- A deployer is responsible for deploying the Web application to the actual environment within which it will run.

Developers will not know ahead of time the specific users who may be using the application, but there are many situations in which access to Web resources must be partitioned depending on the users involved. For example, if Jane and Jill are peers in the same department, they shouldn't be able to access each other's salary information. Accordingly, developers need to be able to build security into the Web applications without referring to the actual users who can use the application. The deployer understands the relationships in the deployment environment and so should decide who can access what.

You need to be able to map names to the final users and security principals. These mappable textual names are called *roles*. Figure 8-10 shows the mapping roles.

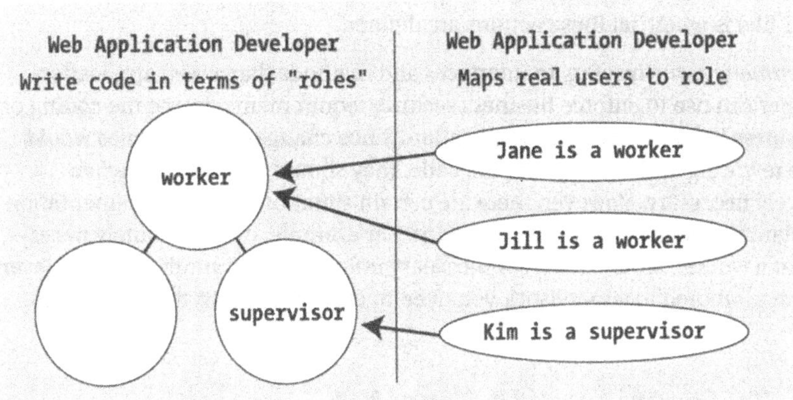

Figure 8-10. Mapping roles

NOTE Roles *serve as an indirect mapping to users and security principals in the deployed environment.*

Roles isolate developers from changes in the physical deployment. For example, a Web application developer need only write code that will prevent one worker from accessing another's salary record. The fact that Jane and Jill both map to the role of a worker isn't of concern to the developer. The decision to map Jane and Jill to worker is the responsibility of the deployer. Envision a real-life scenario in which Jane gets a promotion and therefore requires a supervisor role. In this case, Jane will be able to access Jill's salary information because the Web application developer has written the code to allow a supervisor role to access the information belonging to a worker.

Understanding Access Security and J2EE Business Logic

The fact that a supervisor can access worker's salary records is a *business rule*. The Servlet 2.4 specification provides mechanisms that make it possible (and easy) to code such business security logic without the need to implement a security infrastructure of your own. The combination of all the business security rules that are implemented in a Web application is referred to as the Web application's *security model*.

The Servlet 2.4 specification describes two ways that containers can help in implementing an application's security model. It's preferable to use declarative security as much as possible because it will be easier to maintain in your application. The indirect mapping offered by roles is essential in enabling both of the following:

Declarative security refers to security constraints that the deployer can configure at deployment time. This includes, but isn't limited to, mapping roles to users/principals, configuring authentication for certain resources, and restricting access to other resources. The deployment descriptor file of the Web application (the `web.xml` file) is where all these actions are defined.

Programmatic security refers to interfaces and methods that a Web application developer can use to enforce business security requirements during the coding of the business logic within a Web application. Since changes in these rules would require rewriting and recompiling the code, they should be used only when absolutely necessary. However, there are certain situations when implementation via declarative security may be insufficient. For example, if it's absolutely necessary that a worker shouldn't access the salary information of another worker (even if they're promoted to supervisor), you need to code this within the application.

Setting Up Security with Tomcat 5

The Servlet 2.4 specification is careful to avoid platform-specific features. This presents an interesting challenge for Tomcat, a product that's expected to run well across a variety of operating systems and platforms. While the Servlet 2.4 specification describes features in generic terms, the designers of Tomcat 5 must actually ensure that the features work on different platforms.

Figure 8-11 illustrates the Tomcat solution.

Users-to-roles mappings are maintained through *realms*. In programmatic terms, a realm is nothing more than a programming interface. By specifying this interface and not dictating the means by which this mapping is done, you can adapt Tomcat for new platforms. You can accommodate new means of authentication and roles mapping tracking by creating a new realms component, or you can provide access through standard data access interfaces such as Java Database Connectivity (JDBC).

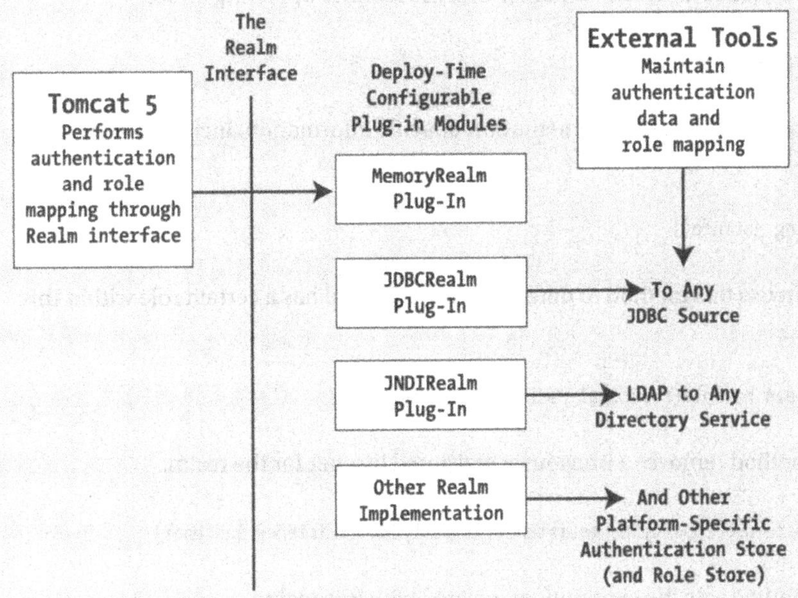

Figure 8-11. The Tomcat solution

> **NOTE** *By factoring out the means of authenticating a user, and retrieving the role mapping to a user, Tomcat is able to participate in server-managed security without being tied down to any specific operating system or platform implementation.*

Introducing Realms

Tomcat requires every implementation of a realm to support the `org.apache.catalina.Realm` programming interface. This interface defines the following methods:

```
public void addPropertyChangeListener()
```

This adds a listener to monitor property changes in the realm. These methods authenticate users and principals using simple credentials, passwords, RFC 2096, or chains of X.509 certs:

```
public Principal authenticate(String username, String credentials)
public Principal authenticate(String username, byte[] credentials)
public Principal authenticate(String username, String digest, String nonce,
                              String nc, String cnonce, String realm,
                              String md5a2,)
public Principal authenticate(java.security.cert.X509Certificate[] certs)
```

This method returns the container that the realm is operating under:

```
public Container getContainer()
```

This method returns implementation-specific information, including a version number:

```
public String getInfo()
```

You can use this method to determine if a principal has a certain role within this realm:

```
public boolean hasRole(Principal principal, String role)
```

This method removes a previously registered listener for the realm:

```
public void removePropertyChangeListener(PropertyChangeListener listener)
```

This method sets the container associated with this realm:

```
public void setContainer(Container container)
```

The operational model of realms is quite straightforward. On the first access by a user of any declaratively protected resource, the applicable realm's `authenticate()` method is called. Tomcat then caches the user's password and roles for the duration of the session. This means that any database changes won't be visible until the next time `authenticate()` is called.

While Tomcat provides a means to access realm information for authentication and role queries, it doesn't provide any way of creating and maintaining the information store.

Realm Implementations

By default, an in-memory realm based on an XML file will be used. This base realm is only loaded at Tomcat startup. The static nature of this in-memory realm means that it's really useful only for testing purposes.

Tomcat provides an implementation of a `JDBCRealm` for use in production systems. A `JDBCRealm` will access any JDBC source to obtain user-to-roles mapping information. You can store user authentication and role information in any information store that provides JDBC access.

Since much of the enterprise-based user and access information is accessible via directory services, Tomcat also provides an implementation of a `JNDIRealm` that can interface to any Lightweight Directory Access Protocol (LDAP)–accessible directory service.

Realms Association

In an application-hosting environment, you may want to have various levels of administrative users. You may grant some owners control over certain Web applications and others over a complete virtual server. A system-level user may want to have system-wide access to some resources across all virtual hosts and across all the Web applications running within the same engine instance. You can configure realms in Tomcat 5 to fulfill all these requirements.

You can define and associate a realm within the server configuration file (`server.xml`) with the following `<Context>`, `<Host>`, or `<Engine>` elements:

- When a realm is defined as a subelement of a `<Context>` element, it means that the group of users and roles managed by the realm is applicable only within the Web application that the `<Context>` element defines.

- When a realm is defined as a subelement of a `<Host>` element, it means that the group of users and roles managed by the realm is applicable across the Web applications running under the same virtual host.

- When a realm is defined as a subelement of a `<Engine>` element, it means that the group of users and roles managed by this realm is across all the applications running across all the virtual hosts running on the same Tomcat instance. You can use this to provide system administrator-level access to all the applications on a particular Tomcat instance.

Inner scope always overrides outer scope. So, if a `JDBCRealm` is defined in the `<Engine>` scope, but subsequently a `MemoryRealm` is defined in the `<Context>` scope, users' authentication will be done against the `MemoryRealm` (and not the global `JDBCRealm`) for the application associated with the specific `<Context>`.

Setting Up Container-Managed Security

Now that you have the authentication database and roles mapping, you need to put protection on some resources. The Servlet 2.4 specification defines two elements in the deployment descriptor to support this declarative security mechanism. They are `<security-constraint>` and `<login-config>`, described as follows:

- The `<security-constraint>` element specifies what Web resources need to be protected, the type of authentication required, and what roles should have access to the resource. This is declarative security in action, also known as *container-managed security*.

- There can be as many `<security-constraint>` entries in a `Web.xml` file as there are different sets of resources to protect. The `<login-config>` element specifies the style of authentication required by the application.

Under container-managed security, a J2EE application builder can specify security constraint and role mapping purely using graphical user interface (GUI) tools and have the container implement the actual access control. The GUI configuration process is the declarative means by which the application deployed can give instructions to the container on how to managed security. While GUI-based security administration tools exist for many commercial products, servlet containers aren't required to implement them in any standard manner. The Servlet 2.3 specification is the first revision to formalize this as a requirement for every compliant container.

Table 8-3 describes the subelements of a `<security-constraint>` element.

Table 8-3. `<security-constraint>` *Subelement*

SUBELEMENT NAME	DESCRIPTION
`<display-name>`	This is the name for the constraint, typically used by a GUI tool to refer back to this specific constraint.
`<web-resource-collection>`	This specifies a group of resources to protect within a Web application. You can use one or more `<url-pattern>` elements to specify the set(s) of resources. An `<http-method>` element can also specify the specific HTTP method to constrain (`GET`, `POST`, and so on).
`<auth-constraint>`	This contains `<role-name>` elements, each of which specifies the role that's allowed to access this constrained set of resources.
`<user-data-constraint>`	This specifies the transport guarantee (via a `<transport-guarantee>` element) that must be met when access to the resources is attempted. The transport guarantee can be `NONE`, `INTEGRAL`, or `CONFIDENTIAL`. If `INTEGRAL` or `CONFIDENTIAL` is applied, the access must usually be made through an SSL connection; otherwise the request is refused.

The `<login-config>` element specifies the authentication method to be used within an application when the container attempts to authenticate a user. Table 8-4 describes the subelements of `<login-config>`.

Table 8-4. `<login-config>` *Subelements*

SUBELEMENT	DESCRIPTION
`<auth-method>`	The value of this can be one of `BASIC`, `DIGEST`, `FORM`, or `CLIENT-CERT`.
`<realm-name>`	This isn't a Tomcat realm. It's simply a text string that's used when a Basic authentication dialog box is displayed.
`<form-login-config>`	If the `FORM` authentication method is specified, this provides more information on the Web page and the error page that will be used during the custom form authentication process.

Understanding Methods of Authentication

Since resources in a Web application are accessed via HTTP, authentication methods are restricted to those supported by HTTP. The authentication methods supported by Tomcat 5 (as defined in the Servlet 2.4 specification) include the following:

- Basic authentication
- Form-based authentication
- Digest authentication
- Client-Cert authentication

Basic Authentication

Basic authentication is the most popular form of HTTP authentication. You've probably experienced Basic authentication many times. When you reach a Web destination, the Web browser pops up a dialog box prompting you to enter username and password. The username is passed in clear text, and the password is transferred in easily decoded Base 64 encoding. This method of authentication is the least secure, but the most widely supported, of the four.

Form-Based Authentication

Form-based authentication uses a custom form supplied by the Web application deployer to perform the actual authentication. Once the user has completed the user and password information in the custom form, the information is sent back to the server for processing. If the authentication fails, an error page is displayed to the user. Because a standard `POST` is used to send password information back to the server, this is a weak form of authentication, but you can use the additional Basic authentication protection methods described in the previous section in conjunction with this type of authentication.

Digest Authentication

In Digest authentication, the password is transmitted in an encrypted digest form, using a one-way hash algorithm such as MD5. MD5 is one of more popular digest algorithms. If you want to learn more about it, visit `http://www.rfc-editor.org/rfc/rfc1321.txt`. At the server end, a prehashed digest is stored with the password and is compared to the one received. Since the actual password is never transmitted directly, this form of authentication is significantly more secure than Basic authentication. This form of authentication isn't in widespread use, but it's supported in the latest version of most Web browsers.

Client-Cert Authentication

Even though Basic and Form-based authentication aren't intrinsically strong methods of authentication, you can make them strong by deploying them over a secured transport such as SSL. You can use X.509 client-side certificates to perform client authentication. The server can authenticate a cert passed by the client by doing the following:

- Verifying that the certificate comes from a trusted CA
- Using the CA's public key to validate that the cert hasn't been tampered with
- Checking the cert's expiry date
- Checking the client information on the cert (to authenticate the client)

The latest versions of Internet Explorer and Netscape both support this feature.

Using Declarative Security

We've covered enough theory and background regarding the operation model of Tomcat 5's declarative container-managed security—it's time to put your knowledge to work with some examples. Keep in mind that although declarative security is preferred over programmatic security, it may force you to use application server-specific security mechanisms, which means it may not be as portable across application servers. You should evaluate if this is an issue for your project.

Using a MemoryRealm

The first example will use a `MemoryRealm`. You'll do the following:

- Protect the `NetAccessServlet` you worked with earlier in a new Web application called `apressrealms`.
- Set up a `MemoryRealm` to supply a username, password, and role to the Tomcat container.
- Set up the declarative security by adding a `<security-constraint>` and `<login-config>` entry to the deployment descriptor.
- Test declarative security by accessing the protected `NetAccessServlet`.

You'll define a `MemoryRealm`, based on the worker and supervisor scenario introduced earlier. The `MemoryRealm` implementation will take user authentication data and role information from an XML file (`apressUsers.xml`) when Tomcat starts. Tomcat requires the document element of this file to be `<tomcat-users>`:

```
<tomcat-users>
  <user name="jane" password="abc123" roles="worker" />
  <user name="jill" password="cde456" roles="worker"  />
  <user name="kim"  password="efg789" roles="worker,supervisor" />
</tomcat-users>
```

Next, you must configure a MemoryRealm to associate with your apressrealms Web application. You need to create a <Context> for your apressrealms application and associate a MemoryRealm with it. The following is what needs to be added to Tomcat's server.xml:

```
<Context path="/apressrealms" docBase="apressrealms" debug="0"
         reloadable = "true">
  <Realm className="org.apache.catalina.realm.MemoryRealm"
         pathname="webapps/apressrealms/WEB-INF/apressUsers.xml" />
</Context>
```

You use the pathname attribute of the realm element to point directly to the XML file that contains the user, password, and role information. The attributes supported by the realm element depend on the type of realm used.

You need to configure container-managed security in the web.xml deployment descriptor:

```
<?xml version="1.0" encoding="ISO-8859-1"?>

<web-app version="2.4" xmlns="http://java.sun.com/xml/ns/j2ee"
                       xmlns:xsi="http://www.w3.org/2001/XMLSchema-instance"
                       xsi:schemaLocation="http://java.sun.com/xml/ns/j2ee
                       http://java.sun.com/xml/ns/j2ee/web-app_2_4.xsd">
  <servlet>
    <servlet-name>passthru</servlet-name>
    <servlet-class>NetAccessServlet</servlet-class>
  </servlet>
```

Access is restricted to the role of supervisor only:

```
  <security-constraint>
    <web-resource-collection>
      <web-resource-name>Access Through Servlet Name</web-resource-name>
      <url-pattern>/servlet/passthru</url-pattern>
    </web-resource-collection>
    <auth-constraint>
      <role-name>supervisor</role-name>
    </auth-constraint>
  </security-constraint>
```

Using the `<login-config>` entry, you associate the Basic method of authentication with this Web application:

```
  <login-config>
    <auth-method>BASIC</auth-method>
    <realm-name>Apress Supervisors Only</realm-name>
  </login-config>

</web-app>
```

Start Tomcat 5, and navigate to `http://localhost:8080/apressrealms/servlet/passthru`. You'll then be prompted with a login dialog box.

The realm you've specified in the `<login-config>` shows up as a simple string label in this dialog box. This has nothing to do with the realm that you use in Tomcat; it's just an unfortunate coincidence in terminology.

Enter a username of **jane** and a password of **abc123**. When you do this, Tomcat will perform authentication by calling the `authenticate()` method of the associated realm (`org.apache.catalina.realm.MemoryRealm` in this case). It'll also call the `userInRole()` method of the realm to determine if the user belongs to a role that's needed to access this resource. The authentication succeeds, but Jane isn't allowed to access the protected resource because she doesn't map to the role of supervisor.

Now, try to access the servlet via an unprotected backdoor. Navigate to `http://localhost:8080/apressrealms/servlet/NetAccessServlet`. Jane can now access the protected servlet. The protection specified in deployment descriptor has a loophole since a servlet can be accessed directly with its class name. In the `<url-pattern>` specified in the `<security-constraint>` element, you should have been more thorough (by using `/*` or specifying `/servlet/*`).

Many browsers will cache the username and password once authentication succeeds, so you should restart the browser before attempting authentication with another username. Navigate to `http://localhost:8080/apressrealms/servlet/passthru`, and enter the username **kim** and password **efg789**. This time, you'll notice that authentication succeeds, and you'll be able to access `NetAccessServlet`.

Using Form-Based Authentication

It's possible to supply your own customized Web pages to authenticate the user, instead of using the default dialog box supplied by the browser. First you must modify the `<login-config>` element in the `web.xml` deployment descriptor. Instead of using the Basic authentication method, you now use the Form-based method. You specify `<form-login-page>` and `<form-error-page>` elements that will define your login and error pages. These paths are specified relative to the root of the Web application, as shown in Listing 8-1.

Listing 8-1. Form-Based Authentication

```
<login-config>
  <auth-method>FORM</auth-method>
  <realm-name>Apress Supervisors Only</realm-name>
  <form-login-config>
     <form-login-page>/formlogin/login.htm</form-login-page>
     <form-error-page>/formlogin/error.htm</form-error-page>
  </form-login-config>
  <auth-constraint>
    <role-name>supervisor</role-name>
  </auth-constraint>
</login-config>
```

You need to create additional Web pages to authenticate the user. Create `login.htm`, as shown in Listing 8-2.

Listing 8-2. Login Web Page

```
<html>
  <head>
    <title>Customized Page for Authentication</title>
    <style>
      body, table, td {background-color:#FFFFFF; color:#000000;
                       font-family:verdana; font-size:10pt;}
      input {font-family:verdana; font-size:10pt;}
    </style>
  </head>
  <body>
    <h3>Apress Login</h3>
    <form method="post" action="j_security_check">
      <table>
        <tr>
         <td>User Name:</td>
         <td><input type="text" name="j_username"></td>
        </tr>
        <tr>
          <td>Password:</td>
          <td><input type="password" name="j_password"></td>
        </tr>
      </table>
      <p><input type="submit" value="Authenticate"></p>
    </form>
  </body>
</html>
```

> **NOTE** *The action associated with the* `POST` *for the form must be* `j_security_check` *for the authentication to be handled properly. The username must be contained in a field called* `j_username` *and the password in* `j_password`.

The error page (`error.htm`) will indicate a login error, as shown in Listing 8-3.

Listing 8-3. Login Error

```
<html>
  <head>
    <title>Error Page for Authentication</title>
    <style>
      body {background-color:#FF3333; color:#FFFFFF;
            font-family:verdana; font-size:10pt;}
    </style>
  </head>
  <body>
    <h3>Apress Security</h3>
    <p><b>Sorry, your login request has been denied.</b></p>
  </body>
</html>
```

Start Tomcat 5, and navigate to `http://localhost:8080/apressrealms/servlet/passthru` to access the protected servlet. Instead of the rather mundane authentication dialog box, you should now see the custom form, as shown in Figure 8-12.

If you enter the username **jane** and the password **bbbccc**, your error page will be displayed, as shown in Figure 8-13.

Attempt to log in again. Enter the username **kim** and password **efg789** in `login.htm`. As expected, you're allowed to access the protected URL.

Finally, try again using **jane** and the correct password **abc123**—remember to restart your browser first, though, to flush the cashed credentials. When you try it this time, you'll (perhaps surprisingly) see an "access to the requested resource has been denied" error from Tomcat.

This is the correct behavior because the following is true:

- The authentication is successful, and the user `jane` is authenticated; therefore, there's a login error, so the error page isn't displayed.
- The user `jane` doesn't map to the `supervisor` role required to access the resource; therefore, she's denied access.

Figure 8-12. The custom form

Figure 8-13. The error page

Using Digested Passwords

Now, you'll modify the example to use digested passwords, which is supported by the MemoryRealm that you use. Shut down Tomcat, and make the following amendments to server.xml:

```
<Context path="/apressrealms" docBase="apressrealms" debug="0"
        reloadable="true">
  <Realm className="org.apache.catalina.realm.MemoryRealm"
        pathname="webapps/apressrealms/WEB-INF/apressUsersDigested.xml"
        digest="MD5" />
</Context>
```

The MemoryRealm implementation in Tomcat acts also as a stand-alone password-hashing utility. You can use the following command to obtain the hash string for abc123:

```
java -classpath %CATALINA_HOME%\server\lib\catalina.jar
 org.apache.catalina.realm.RealmBase -a MD5 abc123
```

apressUsersDigested.xml has replaced the clear-text password with the MD5-hashed equivalents:

```
<tomcat-users>
  <user name="jane" password="e99a18c428cb38d5f260853678922e03"
       roles="worker" />
  <user name="jill" password="b7e64172f775d1df1348da7e925be164"
       roles="worker"  />
  <user name="kim" password="236ef0ed108857aecd3d328485e402da"
       roles="worker,supervisor" />
</tomcat-users>
```

The other two passwords for users kim and jill are hashed in the same way. Start Tomcat, and navigate to http://localhost:8080/apressrealms/servlet/passthru. Entering the identities of **kim** and then **jane**, the behavior stays the same. Basic authentication is still used as specified by the <login-config> associated with the Web application. However, the apressUsers.xml file now contains the digested passwords, which are difficult to decode.

Using a JDBCRealm

A `JDBCRealm` accesses user login information and role mapping information through a JDBC source, instead of the simple XML file as in `MemoryRealm`. The utility of a `JDBCRealm` isn't restricted to only relational database management systems; it can access information from any storage facility that exposes a JDBC-compatible interface.

For a JDBC source to work with a `JDBCRealm`, the database storing the mapping information must have specific table layout, as shown in Figure 8-14.

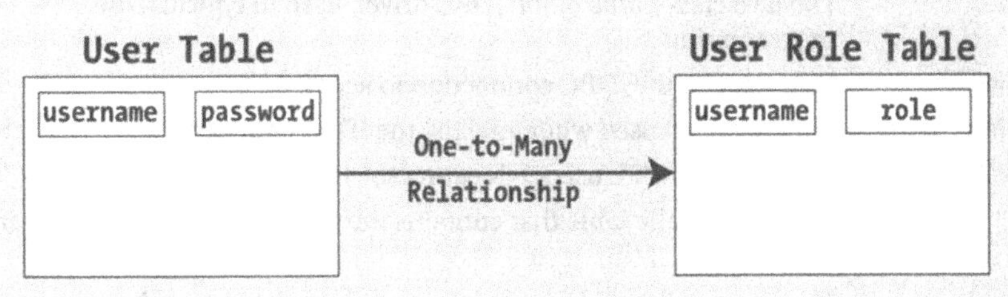

Figure 8-14. Table layout

The actual name of the table and columns in the JDBC source aren't specified by the `Realm` implementation but can be assigned at deployment time based on the attributes of the `<Realm>` element.

In the user table, the columns listed in Table 8-5 are mandatory.

Table 8-5. The User Table

REQUIRED COLUMN	DESCRIPTION
`username`	The name of the user for authentication
`password`	Contains the password associated with the user

The user role table consists of the mandatory columns listed in Table 8-6.

Table 8-6. The User Role Table

REQUIRED COLUMN	DESCRIPTION
`username`	The name of the user for authentication
`role`	One of the roles to which the user is mapped

In the user role table, there must be one row for each role with which a user is associated. The tables used can, in fact, contain other columns; however, the `JDBCRealm` implementation will use only the required columns noted previously.

As with the `MemoryRealm`, or any other realm implementation, the definition for the realm is associated with a `<Context>`, a `<Host>`, or a `<Engine>` and appears in the `server.xml` file. For `JDBCRealm`, the attributes of the `<Realm>` element listed in Table 8-7 are important.

Table 8-7. `<Realm>` *Attributes*

ATTRIBUTE NAME	DESCRIPTION
`classname`	Must be for `org.apache.catalina.realm.JDBCRealm`, Tomcat 4's `JDBCRealm` implementation
`driverName`	The Java class name of the JDBC driver, used in typical JDBC programming
`connectionName`	The name of the JDBC connection to access
`connectionPassword`	The password used when making the JDBC connection
`connectionURL`	The database URL used to locating the JDBC source
`userTable`	The name of the table that contains the two required fields of a user table
`userRoleTable`	The name of the table that contains the two required columns of a user role table
`userNameCol`	The name of the column, in both the `userTable` and the `userRoleTable`, which contains the username information (both columns must have the same name across the two tables)
`userCredCol`	The name of the column in the `userTable` that contains the password of the user
`roleNameCol`	The name of the column in the `userRoleTable` that contains a role associated with the user

You'll use `MySQL` and the `MM.MySQL` JDBC driver in the example, but you could easily adapt the example for any other database and JDBC driver. Use the SQL script shown in Listing 8-4 to create the database and tables and supply sample data.

Listing 8-4. SQL Script

```
CREATE DATABASE realmDB;
USE realmDB;

CREATE TABLE deptusers (
  apressusername VARCHAR(15) NOT NULL PRIMARY KEY,
  password      VARCHAR(15) NOT NULL
);

CREATE TABLE deptroles (
  apressusername VARCHAR(15) NOT NULL,
  apressrole     VARCHAR(15) NOT NULL,
  PRIMARY KEY (apressusername, apressrole)
);
```

```
INSERT INTO deptusers VALUES ('jane', 'abc123');
INSERT INTO deptusers VALUES ('jill', 'cde456');
INSERT INTO deptusers VALUES ('kim',  'efg789');
INSERT INTO deptroles VALUES ('jane', 'worker');
INSERT INTO deptroles VALUES ('jill', 'worker');
INSERT INTO deptroles VALUES ('kim',  'worker');
INSERT INTO deptusers VALUES ('kim',  'supervisor');
```

Now, you have everything to fill out the attributes of the `JDBCRealm`, as shown in Table 8-8.

Table 8-8. The `JDBCRealm` *Attributes to Use*

ATTRIBUTE	OUR VALUE
className	org.apache.catalina.realm.JDBCRealm
driverName	org.gjt.mm.mysql.Driver
connectionURL	jdbc:mysql://localhost/realmDB
userTable	deptusers
userRoleTable	deptroles
userNameCol	apressusername
userCredCol	password
roleNameCol	apressrole

You should replace the previously associated `MemoryRealm` for the `apressrealms` Web application with this new `JDBCRealm`. The following is the `<Realm>` element you must add to Tomcat's `server.xml` file:

```
<Context path="/apressrealms" docBase="apressrealms" debug="0"
        reloadable="true">
  <Realm className="org.apache.catalina.realm.JDBCRealm"
        driverName="org.gjt.mm.mysql.Driver"
        connectionURL="jdbc:mysql://localhost/realmDB"
        userTable="deptusers" userRoleTable="deptroles"
        userNameCol="apressusername" userCredCol="password"
        roleNameCol="apressrole" />
</Context>
```

Make sure you have the MySQL running, start Tomcat, and navigate to `http://localhost:8080/apressrealms/servlet/passthru`. The custom form-based login will be displayed, so enter **jill** for the user and **cde456** for the password. Access to the servlet will be denied.

Restart your browser to clear the credentials cached, and try entering **kim** and **efg789** for the user and password, respectively. Kim is allowed to access the protected servlet because she has a role of supervisor, which is authenticated this time through the newly configured `JDBCRealm`.

Imagine the scenario in which the user `jill` has been promoted to a supervisor. You simply need to use MySQL to add a single row to the deptroles table within the database:

```
INSERT INTO deptroles VALUES ('jill', 'supervisor');
```

Restart your browser, and try authenticating with **jill** and **cde456** as the user and password, respectively, once more. Immediately upon promotion, the user `jill` can now access the protected resource—without even having to restart Tomcat.

> **NOTE** *The ability to reflect dynamic change in the authentication data and role mapping is a prerequisite for any production environment—and Tomcat's* `JDBCRealm` *implementation satisfies this requirement.*

Using Multiple Authentication Requests

Now we'll illustrate a potential problem that users may encounter. You'll deploy two trivial Web applications, `apressapp1` and `apressapp2`, on the same virtual host (each will have its own context, of course). Each application contains a servlet and provides a link to the other Web application. The only difference between the servlets is their name. One is called `TrivialServlet1`, and the other is called `TrivialServlet2`. Listing 8-5 shows `TrivialServlet1`.

Listing 8-5. `TrivialServlet1`

```
import javax.servlet.*;
import javax.servlet.http.*;
import java.io.*;

public class TrivialServlet1 extends HttpServlet {

  public void doGet(HttpServletRequest request,
                  HttpServletResponse response)
      throws IOException, ServletException{
    PrintWriter out = response.getWriter();
    out.println("<html><head><style>");
    out.println("body {background-color:#FFFFFF;color:#000000;" +
              "font-family:verdana;font-size:10pt;}");
    out.println("</style></head>");
    out.println("<body>");
    out.println("Thank you for visiting Service <br><h1>#1</h1><p>");
    out.println("Please visit our " +
              "<ahref=\"http://localhost:8080/apressapp2/servlet/trivial\">"
              + other service</a>.");
    out.println("</body></html>");
  }
}
```

You have to associate the JDBCRealm with the <Host> entry instead of individual <Context> entries. Listing 8-6 shows the configuration for apressapp1 and apressapp2 that needs to be added to server.xml.

Listing 8-6. TrivialServlet1

```
<Realm className="org.apache.catalina.realm.JDBCRealm"
       driverName="org.gjt.mm.mysql.Driver"
       connectionURL="jdbc:mysql://localhost/realmDB"
       userTable="deptusers" userRoleTable="deptroles"
       userNameCol="apressusername" userCredCol="password"
       roleNameCol="apressrole" />

<Context path="/apressapp1" docBase="apressapp1" debug="0" reloadable = "true">
</Context>
<Context path="/apressapp2" docBase="apressapp2" debug="0" reloadable = "true">
</Context>
```

So, apressapp1 and apressapp2 have quite a few things in common: the same virtual host, the same authentication realm, and a similar servlet class. However, there's one key difference; the deployer of apressapp1 has opted to configure the Basic method of authentication, whereas the deployer of apressapp2 has chosen to configure the Form-based method of authentication. Listing 8-7 shows the web.xml deployment descriptor for apressapp1.

Listing 8-7. Deployment Descriptor for apressapp1

```
<?xml version="1.0" encoding="ISO-8859-1"?>

<web-app version="2.4" xmlns="http://java.sun.com/xml/ns/j2ee"
                       xmlns:xsi="http://www.w3.org/2001/XMLSchema-instance"
                       xsi:schemaLocation="http://java.sun.com/xml/ns/j2ee
http://java.sun.com/xml/ns/j2ee/web-app_2_4.xsd">

  <servlet>
    <servlet-name>trivial</servlet-name>
    <servlet-class>TrivialServlet1</servlet-class>
  </servlet>

  <security-constraint>
    <web-resource-collection>
      <web-resource-name>Protected Servlet</web-resource-name>
      <url-pattern>/servlet/trivial</url-pattern>
    </web-resource-collection>
    <auth-constraint>
       <role-name>supervisor</role-name>
       <role-name>worker</role-name>
    </auth-constraint>
  </security-constraint>
```

```
  <login-config>
    <auth-method>BASIC</auth-method>
    <realm-name>All Apress Users</realm-name>
  </login-config>
</web-app>
```

Listing 8-8 shows the `web.xml` deployment descriptor for `apressapp2`.

Listing 8-8. Deployment Descriptor for `apressapp2`

```
<?xml version="1.0" encoding="ISO-8859-1"?>

<web-app version="2.4" xmlns="http://java.sun.com/xml/ns/j2ee"
                       xmlns:xsi="http://www.w3.org/2001/XMLSchema-instance"
                       xsi:schemaLocation="http://java.sun.com/xml/ns/j2ee
http://java.sun.com/xml/ns/j2ee/web-app_2_4.xsd">

   <servlet>
    <servlet-name>trivial</servlet-name>
    <servlet-class>TrivialServlet2</servlet-class>
  </servlet>

  <security-constraint>
    <web-resource-collection>
      <web-resource-name>Protected Servlet</web-resource-name>
      <url-pattern>/servlet/trivial</url-pattern>
    </web-resource-collection>
    <auth-constraint>
       <role-name>Supervisor</role-name>
       <role-name>Worker</role-name>
    </auth-constraint>
  </security-constraint>

  <login-config>
    <auth-method>FORM</auth-method>
       <realm-name>All Apress Users</realm-name>
       <form-login-config>
        <form-login-page>/formlogin/login.htm</form-login-page>
        <form-error-page>/formlogin/error.htm</form-error-page>
      </form-login-config>
  </login-config>
</web-app>
```

Deploy the Web applications, and navigate to `http://localhost:8080/apressapp1/servlet/trivial`. You should be prompted to enter a username and password with a browser dialog box. Enter any one of **jane**, **jill**, or **kim**. You can see the output of the protected `TrivialServlet1` in Figure 8-15.

This servlet invites you to visit another service hosted on the same virtual host. You can try it by following the link.

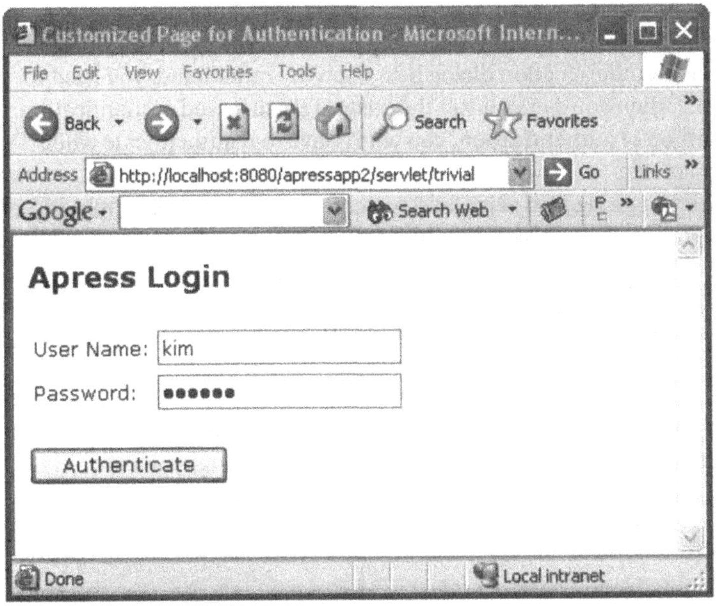

Figure 8-15. `TrivialServlet1` *output*

You're asked to authenticate yourself again, this time via the custom Form-based method of authentication; then you finally reach the requested service.

Imagine a virtual host with associated services such as travel, stock quotes, news, and so on. This requirement to authenticate each time a service is accessed even though the authentication is done against the same realm would be tedious. Fortunately, you can use an elegant solution to avoid this problem—*single sign-on.*

Using Single Sign-On

Single sign-on allows a single user authentication to work across all the Web applications within a single virtual host, as long as they're all authenticating against the same realm. This is a useful feature that avoids unnecessary calls to authentication.

> **NOTE** *The mechanism used to achieve single sign-on is Tomcat 5 specific, not part of the Servlet 2.4 specification requirements.*

You accomplish single sign-on using a *valve.* A valve is the system-level equivalent of a filter. A valve is inserted into the request-processing pipeline and given an opportunity to modify a request if necessary. The valve caches authentication information and role mappings across Web applications within the same virtual host, and it automatically uses the cached information for Web applications that require authentication.

This authentication and role information caching happens during the first authentication against a Web application. Therefore, if you access apressapp1 first, you'll encounter a Basic authentication dialog box. If, on the other hand, you tried to access apressapp2 first, then you'd encounter the custom Form-based authentication. Regardless of the method of authentication, you won't have to reauthenticate when you access the other service.

Install the Tomcat single sign-on valve, and see it in action. To do so, simply add the following <Valve> element to server.xml:

```
<Host name="localhost" debug="0" appBase="webapps" unpackWARs="true">
<Valve classname="org.apache.Catalina.authenticator.SingleSignOn"
       debug="0"/>
```

Restart Tomcat, and navigate to http://localhost:8080/apressapp1/servlet/trivial. Authenticate with one of the Apress user credentials through the Basic authentication box. You should now see the output of TrivialServlet1. Click the link to TrivialServlet2. You'll no longer be required to authenticate against this separate Web application.

> **NOTE** *The single sign-on valve uses HTTP cookies, so the client must have cookies enabled for it to work properly.*

Logging Out of an Application

When dealing with all the authentication methods in containers, both single sign-on and multiple sign-ons, you need to make sure that when a client logs out, their ability to access any resources is terminated. The following situations cause a logout:

- Invalidation or timeout of the last active session for this user
- An explicit call to HttpSession.invalidateAll method or HttpSession.logout method

For containers that aren't single sign-on, a session invalidation has no effect on login state or session state in other Web applications. For single sign-on containers, logout causes all other active sessions associated with the current user to be invalidated. When a session has been invalidated or a timeout of an individual session occurs, this will cause the termination of only that session. The user won't actually be logged out unless it's the last session for this user. This allows applications that may have multiple client sessions active to force the user to continually log back in if one of their sessions times out. If there's still at least one existing session for the user authenticated, the container may start a new session for one or more of the Web applications without reauthenticating the user.

Setting Up Programmatic Security

You should implement every aspect of the application security model via declarative security that you can because declarative security allows the deployer to change or alter a policy according to the deployment situation. In some cases, however, you must use programmatic security. To use programmatic security, you'll need to become familiar with three specific methods of the `HttpServletRequest` interface.

If the user has been authenticated, the following method returns the name of the user; otherwise, it returns `null`:

```
public java.lang.String getRemoteUser()
```

If the user has been authenticated, you can call the following method to determine if a specific role has been mapped to the user:

```
public boolean isUserInRole(java.lang.String role)
```

The following method returns a `java.security.Principal` object associated with the authenticated user. If no object is associated with the user, it returns `null`:

```
public java.security.Principal getUserPrincipal()
```

As an example, you'll create another servlet under the `apressapp1` application (see Listing 8-9).

Listing 8-9. Servlet Listing

```
import javax.servlet.*;
import javax.servlet.http.*;
import java.io.*;

public class SupersOnly extends HttpServlet {
  public void doGet(HttpServletRequest request,
                    HttpServletResponse response)
      throws IOException, ServletException {
    PrintWriter out = response.getWriter();
```

You call `getRemoteUser()` to obtain the authenticated username. You print the welcome message only if the user has been authenticated and indeed has a role of supervisor (see Listing 8-10).

Listing 8-10. Supervisor Role Check

```
    String user = request.getRemoteUser();
    out.println("<html><head><style>");
    out.println("body {background-color:#FFFFFF;color:#000000;" +
                "font-family:verdana;font-size:10pt;}");
    out.println("</style></head>");
    if (user != null) {
      if (request.isUserInRole("supervisor")) {
        out.println("<body><h3>Welcome, " + user +
                    ", you are a supervisor!</h3>");
      } else {
        out.println("<body><h3>Sorry, " + user +
                    ", but only supervisors can see the message.</h3>");
      }
      out.println("</body>");
    }
    out.println("</html>");
  }
}
```

Before trying this servlet, you need to make a servlet definition and a security constraint modification to the deployment descriptor of your application (see Listing 8-11).

Listing 8-11. Deployment Descriptor

```
<?xml version="1.0" encoding="ISO-8859-1"?>

<web-app version="2.4" xmlns="http://java.sun.com/xml/ns/j2ee"
                       xmlns:xsi="http://www.w3.org/2001/XMLSchema-instance"
                       xsi:schemaLocation="http://java.sun.com/xml/ns/j2ee
 http://java.sun.com/xml/ns/j2ee/web-app_2_4.xsd">

  <servlet>
    <servlet-name>trivial</servlet-name>
    <servlet-class>TrivialServlet1</servlet-class>
  </servlet>

  <servlet>
    <servlet-name>supercheck</servlet-name>
    <servlet-class>SupersOnly</servlet-class>
  </servlet>

  <security-constraint>
    <web-resource-collection>
      <web-resource-name>Protected Servlet</web-resource-name>
      <url-pattern>/servlet/*</url-pattern>
    </web-resource-collection>
    <auth-constraint>
       <role-name>supervisor</role-name>
    </auth-constraint>
  </security-constraint>
```

```
  <login-config>
    <auth-method>BASIC</auth-method>
    <realm-name>Apress Supervisors Only</realm-name>
  </login-config>
</web-app>
```

Restart Tomcat, and navigate to `http://localhost:8080/apressapp1/servlet/supercheck`. Log in by entering **kim** and **efg78**. You should see the welcome screen since Kim is a supervisor.

Restart your browser, and try again. This time, authenticate by entering **jane** and **abc123**. Since the user `jane` isn't a supervisor, you get the display indicating that only supervisors can view the message.

Summary

In this chapter, you saw how to use server-side policy files to protect against badly written or malevolent code. Such policy files are especially important when third-party code is hosted on a server.

The chapter covered SSL and the technologies that make it possible, including shared secret encryption and public key encryption. You saw how easy it is to configure SSL both on the server and the client side—you configured Tomcat to use SSL and created and imported a certificate into Internet Explorer.

You also explored both declarative and programmatic security. Tomcat 5 provides a highly customizable declarative security implementation, and it includes support for container-managed security. By using realms, Tomcat fulfills its authentication and security requirements without becoming platform dependent. Single sign-on with Tomcat demonstrated how you can make a system significantly more user-friendly by avoiding several tedious authentications when a service spans Web applications.

Although as much security as possible should be declarative in nature, you may sometimes need to define security programmatically. So, you took a quick look at programmatic security to see how you can use it to implement an application's security model.

CHAPTER 9

Building the Best Application You Can

IN PREVIOUS CHAPTERS, you saw that servlets are great at handling requests and responses, but they're not so good for generating content for end users. You also wouldn't use Java Server Pages (JSP) pages to process business logic—although they do handle content generation effectively. To make the most of servlets, or any other components within a Web application, you need to understand when and where you should use them—what tasks do they perform best?

In this chapter, you'll explore the design of Web applications, focusing particularly on when and where you should use servlets within the application.

The chapter begins by discussing the basics for good application design: maintainability, reusability, and extensibility. While this might not be groundbreaking news for most readers, developers frequently overlook many aspects of good application design. Usually, this happens in the name of getting a deliverable out the door. However, by skimping on these principles, you make your application worse off, you make your customers unhappy, and you basically create a bigger mess than if you spent the time to do it right in the first place. Every developer should have the words *maintainability*, *reusability*, and *extensibility* posted on their monitor. If you're working on coding something and it doesn't fit into those categories, stop what you're doing, revaluate, and find a better way to do it.

The chapter then moves on and covers the most commonly used Web application architecture, Model 2.

We'll also introduce design patterns, which you can use to recognize and solve common design problems. Then we'll demonstrate how you can apply these patterns to a Web application.

To put all these concepts into context, the chapter shows you how to create an example application, an online auction, to which you'll apply the designs and patterns.

You'll start by considering why good application design is important.

Why Is Good Application Design Important?

The design of applications is an important aspect of the project life cycle, but it's one that's often neglected. When you design an application, you should aim to enhance the following features:

- Maintainability
- Reusability
- Extensibility

You'll now take a closer look at each of these aspects of design.

Maintainability

Maintainability describes the amount of effort required to keep an application running correctly. Obviously, in a commercial sense, more maintenance means more time and more money spent. In reality, an application's maintainability is difficult to quantify, but you can use certain techniques to increase a system's maintainability.

So, what aspects of the application need to be maintained? First, you can maintain the source code itself. An undocumented, unstructured, and badly formatted body of source code will be harder to maintain than documented code with a clearly defined structure. If you make code easy to follow and understand, debugging and code modification usually become faster and easier. For example, trying to maintain a large method that performs a lot of processing will be much more complex than trying to maintain a collection of shorter methods that achieve the same result. When addressing maintainability, refactoring is an excellent way to continually simplify code structure. In addition to this, developers who have to maintain this in the future (be it bug fixing, cleaning up, or rebuilding) will have a hard job understanding code that isn't commented or indented/formatted well. Source code should be functional, but at the same time that doesn't mean it can't look nice, too!

The structure of the application also plays an important part. Designing a meaningful, logically partitioned application will greatly increase the maintainability of the application. In a typical application there might be several distinct parts; for example, the application may consist of the user interface, the classes that perform business processing, and the classes that represent business entities. Introducing structure and making a distinction between these types of classes will increase the maintainability because it'll be more apparent to developers how the application pieces fit together. Although creating neatly formatted source code is undoubtedly important, knowing how to quickly find the piece of functionality that needs to be fixed is just as important.

The naming of this structure is equally important. We can't count the number of projects we've been called upon as consultants and had to decipher poorly structured directories along with misnamed packages and classes. These types of issues may not seem like a big deal in smaller (30–50) class projects, but once you get passed that point for larger projects, it is.

Another requirement of maintainability is to have a set of acceptance tests for your product. Why? Because at any given point during development, you can run a suite of tests that will let you know, right then and there, what's working and what isn't. In a maintainable application, you should be able to pinpoint what your application status is continually. One approach to this type of acceptance testing is to use test-driven development (TDD). TDD is one of the principles behind the extreme programming (XP) methodology. It basically states that you should design your tests before you design or implement your program. You then incrementally add functionality to the program as it passes each test. Entire test frameworks (such as JUnit at `http://www.junit.org`) exist that provide a clean and easy way to create your tests and test suites. We won't go into the many details—and debates—about the different development methodologies (XP, Rational Unified Process [RUP], Scrum, and so on) you should (or should not) be using. However, each has sound principles, and you should spend some time deciding which approach best fits your development cycle and team. Following a methodology, or at least portions of a methodology, can greatly increase your chances of meeting your project's maintainability goals.

Reusability

One of the goals of object-oriented design and implementation is to strive for reusable components. Reusability is enhanced when a class has a low reliance on other objects, or *low coupling*, and provides a specialized set of tasks, or *high cohesion*.

Some degree of reusability is achievable without design, but thinking about the structure beforehand will help ensure that the classes you create are reusable across the application. Stepping back to look at the big picture will help in identifying those places in the system where you can reuse functionality later if you want to modify or enhance the application.

When doing TDD, you'll find that some of the components that are reusable will make themselves apparent while writing the test cases. This is usually an iterative cycle, but it's one that can result in a more module architecture.

Reusability also comes in the form of components used in design patterns. That's one of the reasons you'll spend a fair amount of time in this chapter identifying and using design patterns that meet your project's needs. It becomes possible to use various design patterns so they can all work together. This type of structure is one of the reasons that evaluating existing frameworks can also lead to reusability in your development. Keep in mind that even if you're taking advantage of such frameworks as Struts or Sun's Web Application Framework (WAF), you should still pay attention to not intrinsically tie your application to that framework. You'll likely gain a fair amount of reuse from the framework itself, but if you can use other components in your systems on other projects, keep that in mind.

Extensibility

Changes in the business require changes in software. The *extensibility* of your software determines how much it can be extended and enhanced after it has been put into production use.

Ideally, you'd like to add functionality to an application without altering the original code—much like you extend existing Java classes.

A good design will attempt to take extensibility into account. Of course, it's impossible to foresee every eventual circumstance, such as a drastic change in the business or other major changes in functional requirements. You can often enhance extensibility by logically partitioning the application into smaller parts, reducing the impact of changes on other parts of the system. By taking advantage of reusable components, it becomes possible to build extensibility into software architecture.

Symptoms of Poor Application Design

Although it's easy to say what a good design should look like, sometimes you can move forward by examining a current design and looking at its characteristics to determine how to improve it. Martin Fowler, an object-oriented patterns pioneer, has described this as "bad smells" in the code. Often it's the case that bad smells then turn into rotting code. You should become aware of a number of smells. If you pay attention to your olfactory sense, then you'll probably be able to avoid these smells. The following symptoms are other good candidates for that Post-it Note on the monitor so you can frequently remind yourself to take time and smell the roses:[1]

Rigidity: The software is difficult to change in any way. Simple changes cause cascading changes in other dependent components.

Fragility: When a change made in one functional area breaks another functional area that's seemingly unrelated. This causes unexpected problems. Usually developers try to stay away from these components because it creates a never-ending list of bug fixes.

Immobility: The difficulty in separating the systems components so they can be reused. Usually this involves a large amount of effort and risk to perform the separation of the parts from the original system.

Viscosity: When the design-preserving methods are harder to employ than the hacks to the system, the viscosity is high. It becomes easy to do the wrong thing, but hard to do the right thing.

Needless complexity: If there are elements in the system that aren't being used or infrastructure that adds no direct benefit. Typically, this happens when developers anticipate needed functionality and add a placeholder for it. Then the functionality never materializes, but there's still baggage being carried around.

Needless repetition: The design contains repeating structures that could be implemented as an abstraction. This is the cut-and-paste-when-editing syndrome in action.

Opacity: While the code might be written clearly, the purpose of the module is hard to understand.

---

1. These symptoms are adapted from *Agile Software Development: Principles, Patterns, and Practices* by Robert C. Martin (Prentice Hall, 2002).

If you notice any of these symptoms in applications you're working on, don't ignore them. Things will only get worse. Take a step back, and try to apply some of the design principles and patterns we're about to discuss.

Understanding J2EE Web Application Design

Servlets are just one component that you can use in building a Web application. You can also use JSP pages, JSP tag libraries, JavaBeans, and even business components such as Enterprise JavaBeans (EJBs) if you need or want to do so. Each of these components has its strengths and weaknesses, so each is suited to a different role. Identifying the roles needed within the application and finding the components most suitable for these roles are the first steps in understanding the design of your applications.

The most commonly used Web application architecture is Model 2. In the next few sections, we'll discuss Model 2 so you can understand where your different components will fit into the architecture. You may be familiar with Model 1 architecture. Model 1 was originally used to build Web applications and included much of the business logic within your presentation. This quickly led to some maintainability issues in larger applications. Hence, Model 2 emerged. Although Model 1 is the simpler of the two, it isn't commonly used much in application development. Model 1 promotes some practices that are no longer considered "good" from a large application perspective. These include combining presentation and business logic and having your JSP pages accessing data sources directly.

We won't talk about the details of Model 1 in this chapter other than when comparing it to Model 2.

Introducing Model 2 Architecture

The Model 2 architecture overcomes many of the problems of the Model 1 architecture. Model 2 is based upon the Model-View-Controller (MVC) architecture. In a Model 1 Web application, the pages are accessed directly; in a Model 2 architecture, all access is routed through a Controller component (typically implemented by a servlet). Figure 9-1 shows this architecture.

You can use the same Controller for the entire site or multiple Controllers that are each responsible for sections of the site. For both, the principle of the design is the same: Requests from clients are routed to a central Controller, which decides how the request should be serviced. Later in the "Using the Front Controller Pattern" section, you'll see how a Controller can delegate this task, but for now just assume that the Controller processes the request.

When it processes the request, the Controller may modify the underlying Model (often JavaBeans). Once the request has been serviced, the Controller delegates the task of sending back the response to a View component (often implemented by JSP pages). The View component generally contains a minimal amount of code and focuses on the task of presenting information to the end user. Both the Controller and the View components can access and modify Model components. However, it isn't advisable to modify the Model components from the View. Usually doing so means that you have some type of business logic in your View, and you should consider how to encapsulate the logic in a JavaBean.

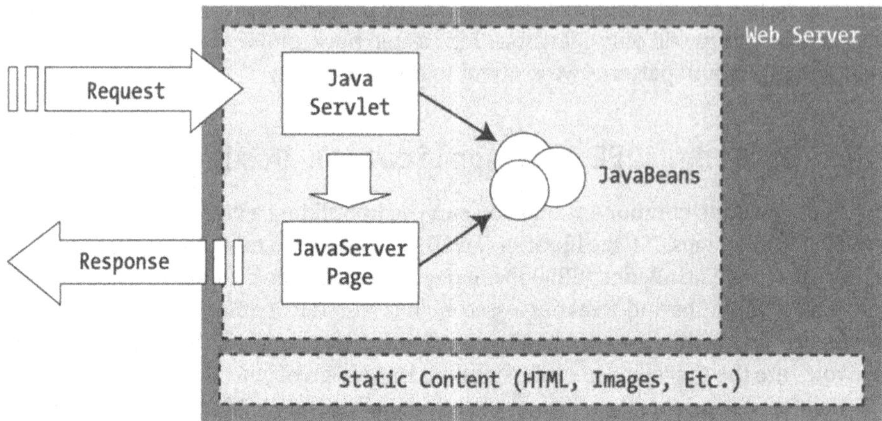

Figure 9-1. Model 2 architecture

Benefits of Model 2 Architecture

Using Model 2 architecture improves the design of your Web application in a number of ways.

Enhancing Maintainability

Because the Controller component in your architecture is responsible for determining which page in your Web application you should see next, as well as interpreting the user's actions, the structure of the Web application is defined in a single place. This increases the maintainability of the application, particularly if you go further, separating the structural definition from the Controller to make the structure externally configurable. Additionally, the processing and business logic associated with servicing requests is easy to find because it's not embedded and scattered throughout the pages of the system, which was common in Model 1–based applications.

Promoting Extensibility

The logic that processes each type of request in Model 2 is now much more centralized. This centralization, in conjunction with splitting the View components from the logic that services the request, means that the system is now much easier to extend. By introducing more componentization, you make extensions easier to write, and you make the chances of a ripple effect throughout the application much less likely.

For example, to extend the application by adding new pages, all you need to do is add new View components and make appropriate modifications to the Controller component—either directly or through external configuration files. Another advantage is that by separating the View components from the Model, you can accommodate different types of clients. It may that the client doesn't even have a View portion, such as in the case of a Web service.

Ensuring Security

Routing all requests through a single point of entry is a simple way to handle Web application security. In Model 2, you can use this technique because you can move all security processing to the Controller(s), reducing the burden on developers and the risk of accidental security breaches.

Using Other J2EE Components in Model 2 Architecture

For many applications, you use technologies other than JSP pages, servlets, and JavaBeans. You may want to introduce an EJB layer containing session and entity beans, where you place complex business processing or represent persistent business data, as shown in Figure 9-2.

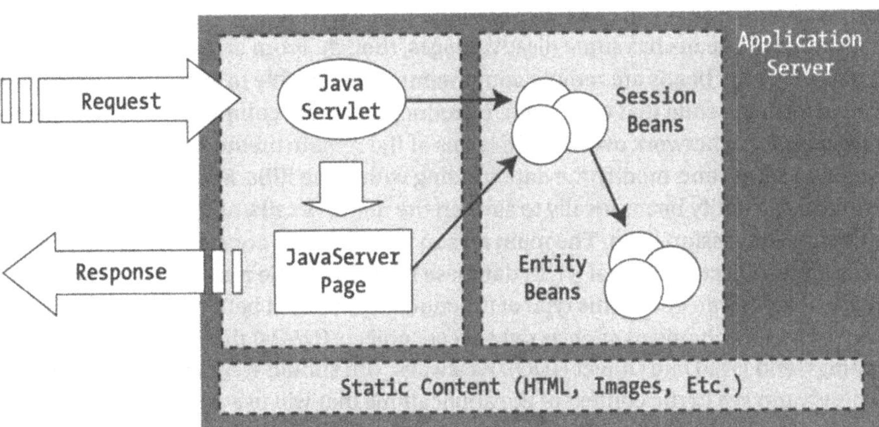

Figure 9-2. Using session and entity beans

While the basic architecture remains unchanged, introducing these additional components does, however, raise the following questions:

- How should the functionality of your application be split between the components?
- What effect does introducing these components have on performance and scalability?

You'll examine these issues more closely in the next two sections.

Using Entity Beans

Entity beans represent data that's stored in some type of persistent data store such as a relational database. In smaller applications, you'd probably have the Web components (your servlets and JSP pages) using Java Database Connectivity (JDBC) to communicate with the database instead (possibly with JavaBeans representing the data).

Introducing entity beans means that they become the Model on which your Web application operates. The components that handle the presentation of data on a Web page (in other words, the JSP pages and servlets in the Web container) will access and modify business data residing in the EJB tier.

From an architectural and design perspective, this separation of the components in your Web application is certainly beneficial. Splitting these makes for a more maintainable system since functionality has been logically partitioned across the application. When the entities in the business layer change, you instantly know which part of the application needs to change to reflect this. In addition, you may also end up with some components that you can reuse in future projects.

Using entity beans has some disadvantages, though. From an implementation perspective, entity beans are remote components that are able to execute on a separate machine from the code that calls them. Introducing remote components means introducing additional network overhead in terms of the remote method calls that are required to access and modify the data residing within the EJBs. Keep in mind that it's possible to call entity beans locally to save on the network calls, as is typically done from a stateless session bean. The main reason you'd want to consider using an entity bean is for its object/relational (O/R) database mapping, table relationships, and persistence. But you can get all this type of functionality handled better and faster by lighter-weight mechanisms such as data access objects (DAOs) that use JDBC, O/R mappings, and Java Data Object (JDO). As always, you should weigh the advantages and disadvantages in the context of the applications that will use entity beans before you decide to use them.

Using Session Beans

Traditionally, business logic has been embedded in client applications, whether they're desktop-based or Web-based applications. Session beans can instead encapsulate this logic in a robust and reusable manner. However, session beans, like entity beans, were intended to be remote components, so you may incur the same network overhead when using the functionality contained within session beans.

Typically, people don't use remote interfaces anymore, so this really isn't an issue. Rather than having a box that just runs the Web tier and another box that runs the EJB tier (vertical scaling), you put the entire Java 2 Enterprise Edition (J2EE) stack on each machine and run them in parallel (horizontal scaling). The reason for this is that remote calls can be tens if not hundreds of times slower than local calls. Calling a stateless session bean with a local interface doesn't have much more overhead than calling a plain old Java object (POJO). The reason you use stateless session beans is for declarative transaction demarcation/management. Think of each stateless session bean method as managing *taskflow*,[2] the set of steps necessary to carry out a use case or user story. The EJB manages a whole module or service in your architecture. One trend is that you just use a stateless session beans as a layering technology for managing transactions. So now each stateless session bean method just delegates off to a POJO to do the real work (this is known as an Application Service pattern).

With these issues in mind, you'll now look at roles and responsibilities in a Model 2 architecture.

Component Roles in Model 2 Architecture

Consider the role of the Controller in the Model 2 architecture. It should do the following:

- Act as a single point of entry for requests.
- Process the requests, accessing and modifying the underlying Model.
- Delegate the task of presenting information to a specific View component.

The Controller can process requests in a number of ways. It can process requests itself, which means that the Controller encapsulates business logic. However, this is probably not an effective solution, as the Controller would rapidly become bloated.

A more efficient system would be to delegate processing tasks to other components such as JavaBeans, session EJBs, or even standard Java classes. If you select this strategy, how do you determine where specific functionality is to be situated, including that associated with servicing the request, validating any data, and (of course) enforcing security? When you design your application, you need to answer these questions, deciding on the roles and responsibilities of components. This is often a tricky task, but fortunately many of the common problems encountered during the design process have been tackled before, and the solutions to these problems are well documented in the form of *design patterns*.

Documenting Design Principles

Industry-recognized standards and guidelines help those involved with a project to communicate in a consistent and effective way. For example, you can use the Unified Modeling Language (UML) to represent an application's design.

In the same way that coding conventions are important when writing source code, using a standard means of documenting designs is also important, especially when you undertake reviews and walkthroughs. Such documentation allows the developer to question the business and its methods by giving them a platform that nontechnical personnel can understand.

2. This was a term coined by Richard Monson-Haefel in *Enterprise JavaBeans*, Fourth Edition (O'Reilly, 2004).

Using Design Patterns

Design patterns capture reusable solutions to common design problems and provide a common language with which to describe them. The book *Design Patterns: Elements of Reusable Object-Oriented Software* (Addison-Wesley, 1995) describes 24 common design problems. Many other patterns in software development have been documented, including some directly related to J2EE development; see *Core J2EE Patterns: Best Practices and Design Strategies*, Second Edition (Prentice Hall, 2003). If you're planning on architecting or designing an application, it's imperative that you understand a variety of design patterns. Not only will it make your architectures more efficient, but you'll have a built-in vocabulary for describing the architecture to others.

J2EE Patterns

The J2EE patterns catalog documents a number of patterns that provide solutions to frequently encountered problems in the design and implementation of J2EE applications. This includes issues such as decreasing the number of fine-grained method calls across the network by using transfer data objects, encapsulating business logic and workflow into session beans through a session façade, and accessing large amounts of read-only data through DAOs. The catalog also contains patterns that are relevant when designing the presentation tier of J2EE applications.

> **TIP** *You can find detailed information on all of the patterns contained within the J2EE patterns catalog at* `http://java.sun.com/blueprints/patterns/index.html` *or at* `http://www.corej2eepatterns.com/index.htm`.

Why Use Patterns?

Without patterns, it's still possible to build fairly complex systems that achieve the desired goal. However, the problem with this approach is that more often than not, the way problems are tackled and subsequently solved within the application may not be consistent. This inconsistency decreases the application's maintainability.

Although using patterns does tend to increase the initial complexity of the implemented solution, patterns are important tools for helping you structure your applications in a proven and consistent manner. Each component has a predefined purpose and a predefined way in which to interact with the others involved in the system. This is good from a maintainability perspective because it's easier to become familiar with a system based upon familiar, common structures than one that isn't.

In addition to this, some of the patterns are optimized for high performance and scalability. Another important benefit of using patterns is that they also provide developers with a standard way of communicating design ideas.

Now you'll look at how you can use Model 2 architecture and a handful of J2EE patterns to design and build the Web portion of an online auction site.

Creating an Online Auction

In the following sections, you'll implement a small Web application in order to understand the concepts of good and bad design that we've been discussing. You'll create a Web site for an online auction, called Acme Auction. Before you can start designing your auction, you need to define its features. This is an important stage in the development process, and it's important to fully state the requirements of your application.

Stating the Requirements

The Acme Auction's requirements are as follows:

- Sellers can sell their items by registering them on the Web site with a description and asking price.
- Buyers can bid for the items through the Web site.
- The system will check the highest bid for each item since it was created and notify the seller about the highest bid on an hourly basis.
- Sellers can accept the bid through the Web site. The site then notifies the buyer about the bid acceptance. Once the buyer acknowledges the acceptance, the transaction is complete.
- The system will charge the seller a percentage of the highest bid.
- Once an item is for sale and a bid is made, the buyer and seller settle the transaction by exchanging a set of specific messages.
- Once the transaction is settled, the system removes the offer.
- Only registered users can use the system. Registered users can buy and sell items. Users need to provide contact, address, and credit card details during registration.

This is a fairly simple set of requirements, so building the application shouldn't be too difficult. However, before you start implementing the functionality, you need to understand the underlying domain on which the application will operate.

Understanding the Entities Within the Domain Model

An important aspect of object-oriented analysis and design is to identify the entities present in the application's domain. The domain model describes the entities that take part in the process. It isn't meant to define the object structure of the application. In the domain model for Acme Auction, you have the following three main domain objects:

- **Customer**: The customer can have one address and one credit card. A customer can offer one or more items and bid for one or more items.
- **Offer**: An offer can have one or more bids.
- **Bid**: A bid should be sent from one customer to zero or more customers that includes an offer for the relevant auction.

The next step is to model the entities and the relationships between them using UML. This allows you to represent the domain clearly and concisely so you can communicate it effectively to both developers and nondevelopers within the team.

> **TIP** *You can learn more about UML in* UML Distilled: A Brief Guide to the Standard Object Modeling Language, *Third Edition (Addison-Wesley, 2003), or* Instant UML *(Wrox Press, 1997).*

Building the Online Auction Using Model 2 Architecture

Patterns typically cooperate with one another. In other words, although each pattern addresses a certain aspect of recurring behavior, the patterns work together to help form a complete application solution. If you look at the total architecture of your online auction application, you can see the relationship between the various patterns (see Figure 9-3).

We won't go into detail about all of the patterns used throughout the complete architecture. Instead, we'll concentrate on some of the main patterns used in Web tier development. The Model 2 architecture accepts requests through a Controller component, where it can service the request itself or delegate this task to some other component. The task of rendering the response is then dispatched to the appropriate View component. Of course, you can implement this in various ways. The following sections present the following four design patterns:

- Front Controller
- Intercepting Filter
- View Helper
- Service to Worker, which is a combination of the previous three patterns

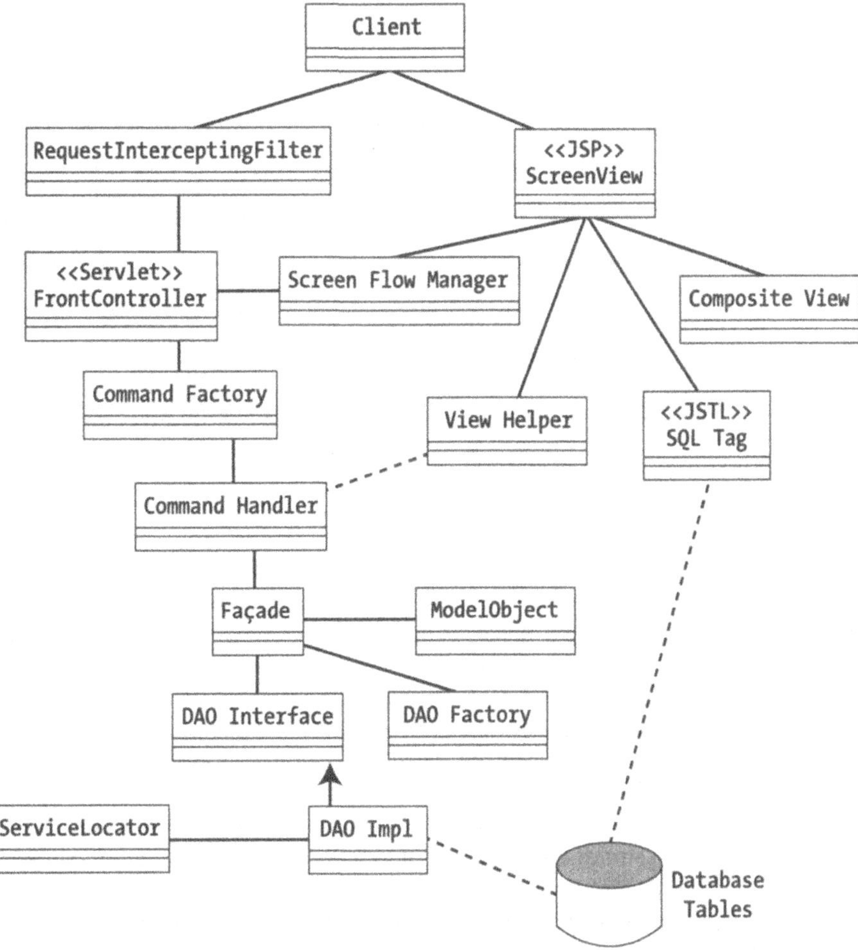

Figure 9-3. The patterns for the online auction application

Using the Front Controller Pattern

Your application, Acme Auction, has many views. JSP pages are often developed by two types of people: Web designers (who handle the look and feel of the site) and J2EE developers (who take care of the business logic). Placing too much Java code into the page usually makes it more difficult for Web designers to modify the look and feel as they battle with Java code that they may not understand. You've already learned in previous chapters about numerous ways to avoid this behavior.

Ideally, you'd like to place any logic in a single location to help you ensure that this type of functionality is consistent, maintainable, and extensible in the future. The Front Controller pattern can help you to achieve these goals. Figure 9-4 shows how it fits into the Model 2 architecture.

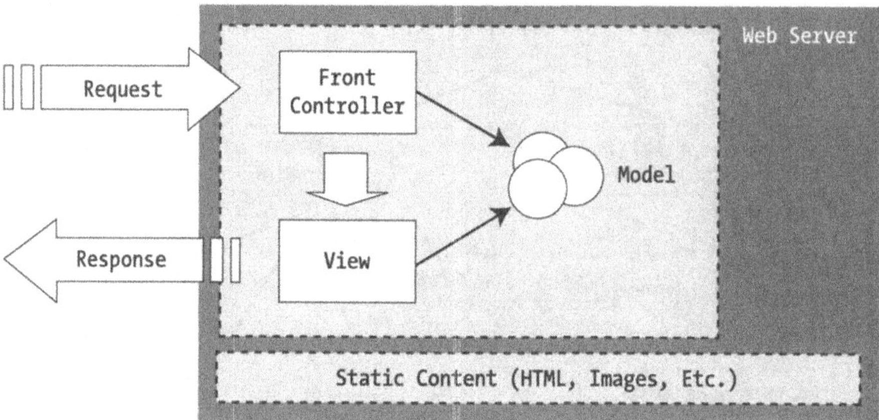

Figure 9-4. The Front Controller pattern

This is the same as the Model 2 architecture you saw in Figure 9-1 where a Controller component is the entry point for Web requests. The Controller performs some processing of the request and may make changes to the underlying Model. The task of rendering the response is then dispatched to a View component.

A Front Controller is also a good place in which to centralize services such as error handling and logging. The Front Controller may also have various servlet listeners implemented for handling certain session activities or requests. Centralizing system services and the flow between pages has many benefits because it moves business logic and other system-level service code out of JSP scriptlets and back into reusable components, therefore promoting reusability of functionality across different types of requests, as you'll see shortly as you progress through this section.

Various strategies exist by which a Front Controller can be implemented, with the typical strategy focusing on using a servlet. This role is better implemented using a servlet than a JSP for several reasons. As noted before, outputting content back to the client isn't an ideal use of a servlet because it involves writing lots of print statements—effectively tying together the content and the logic. JSP pages, on the other hand, are much better suited to delivering content because they're written as content containing small bits of logic wherever necessary. Because a Controller component doesn't actually deliver any content itself, implementing it as a JSP page results in a page containing no content—just the logic required to process the requests. For this reason, a servlet is the preferred strategy.

Of course, centralizing all of this functionality can lead to a large, bloated Controller component that has responsibilities for the entire Web application. You can solve this problem in a number of ways, one of which is to have several Front Controllers, each responsible for particular area of the site. Figure 9-5 shows an example of using several Front Controllers for the online auction.

For example, the auction site may have one Controller responsible for servicing all requests related to customers and another to service all portfolio requests. Another solution is to use the strategy discussed in the upcoming "The Command and Controller Strategy" section.

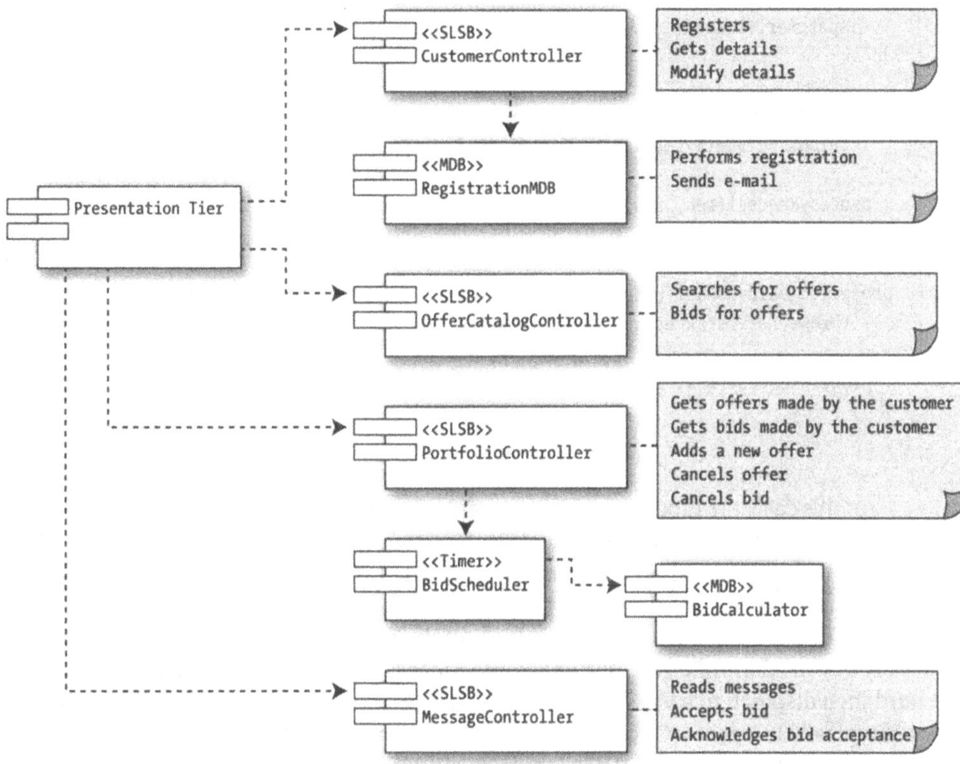

Figure 9-5. Front Controllers in the Acme Auction application

Implementing the Front Controller Pattern

For the moment, Listing 9-1 shows an example skeleton implementation of the Front Controller pattern.

Listing 9-1. Front Controller

```
package forum;

import java.io.IOException;

import javax.servlet.*;
import javax.servlet.http.*;

public class FrontController extends HttpServlet {

  protected void processRequest(HttpServletRequest req,
                                HttpServletResponse res)
                                throws ServletException, IOException {
    RequestDispatcher dispatcher =
```

```
      getServletContext().getRequestDispatcher("name of view component");
    dispatcher.forward(req, res);
  }

  protected void doGet(HttpServletRequest req, HttpServletResponse res)
      throws ServletException, IOException {

    processRequest(req, res);
  }

  protected void doPost(HttpServletRequest req, HttpServletResponse res)
      throws ServletException, IOException {

    processRequest(req, res);
  }
}
```

In this case, the Front Controller is simply an extension of `HttpServlet` with default implementations of the `doGet()` and `doPost()` methods that delegate processing of the request to another method called `processRequest()`. This ensures that no matter how the request is made, the Front Controller will service it.

We've left out the majority of the body of the `processRequest()` method, but essentially a Front Controller will perform some processing that's associated with a request and then dispatch to a View component to render the response. The View components are typically JSP pages. Once the Controller has completed performing its business logic, it can dispatch to a JSP page through the `RequestDispatcher`.

At this point, you may have a question. If the Controller is responsible for handling all requests, how does it know what the request is and therefore how to handle it?

The Command and Controller Strategy

In the Command and Controller strategy, the logic to handle each specific request is moved out into a separate component (see Figure 9-6).

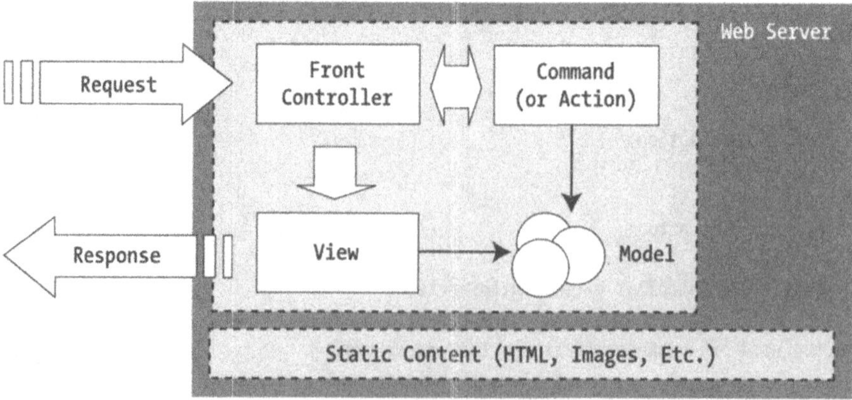

Figure 9-6. The Command and Controller strategy

Each of these extra components represents a specific command (or *action*), and the component encapsulates the logic to perform that action.

The Front Controller delegates the handling of requests to the appropriate command component, which may modify the state of the underlying Model. Once the command component has completed its work, the Controller again dispatches the task of rendering the response to the appropriate View component. But how does the Controller know which command component to use? We'll tackle this issue in a moment.

Action Classes

The first thing you need to do to implement the Command and Controller strategy is to define the interface between the Controller and action components. You can do this by creating an interface or an abstract class. For the purposes of this example, you'll define an abstract class that all actions in your Web application must extend (which means you have a single place in which to add common functionality for all actions in the future):

```
package forum;
import javax.servlet.http.*;

public abstract class Action {
```

Subclasses will implement their specific business and processing logic in the `process()` method. To ensure that the action classes have access to the same environment and information as servlets, the `process()` method takes a reference to the HTTP `Request` and `Response` objects in the same way that the `processRequest()` method in the `FrontController` class did. Once the processing has been completed, the action can return a string to identify the View component to which the Controller should dispatch to next:

```
  public abstract String process(HttpServletRequest request,
    HttpServletResponse response);
}
```

Defining the interface between the Controller and the action components helps to decouple them from each other, which means you can change the Controller or the actions without affecting the other.

The next stage is to put together the logic that will figure out what the request is and delegate the processing to the appropriate action component.

Communicating the Type of Request

You have a number of ways to communicate the type of request to the Controller servlet, and most focus on passing parameters to the servlet over HTTP. The problem with sending additional parameters to indicate the type of request is that the URLs need to be written carefully—after all, it's easy to misspell parameter names and get the query string syntax wrong.

Another mechanism is to use a string that represented the type of request you wanted to perform and pass this to the servlet as additional path information. You already know how you can define mappings between a servlet and a uniform resource indicator (URI) via the `web.xml` file. Listing 9-2 shows an example of this that defines a mapping between your `FrontController` servlet and the URI `/controller/*`.

Listing 9-2. Defining a Mapping

```
<?xml version="1.0" encoding="ISO-8859-1"?>

<web-app xmlns="http://java.sun.com/xml/ns/j2ee"
    xmlns:xsi="http://www.w3.org/2001/XMLSchema-instance"
    xsi:schemaLocation="http://java.sun.com/xml/ns/j2ee web-app_2_4.xsd"
    version="2.4">
  <servlet>
    <servlet-name>FrontController</servlet-name>
    <servlet-class>forum.FrontController</servlet-class>
  </servlet>

  <servlet-mapping>
    <servlet-name>FrontController</servlet-name>
    <url-pattern>/controller/*</url-pattern>
  </servlet-mapping>

</web-app>
```

Now you can make calls to the Controller by appending `controller/ViewTopic?id=0` to your URL. Here, `ViewTopic` is the additional path information (also known as *path info*) and represents the type of request you're making. You can use the query string as usual, with `id=0` providing the parameters for your specific request to view a topic. This is much cleaner than adding additional parameters to indicate the type of request. Instead, this information is now part of the URL that you use. With this side of the request figured out, how does the Controller know what do, and where does this logic reside?

What you need to do here is to map the string you obtain from the additional path info onto a specific action instance. Once again, you have many strategies for this, with the most flexible being externalizing this mapping, for example, through an XML file. Other examples here include hard-coding the mapping inside the Controller or perhaps using a properties file.

For simplicity, in this example you'll build a separate component in which this mapping will be encapsulated. In a production application, hard-coding such configuration information means that changes require the appropriate Java class to be modified, recompiled, and redeployed. In other words, it decreases the maintainability. However, hard-coding this information into a separate component will suffice for this simple example, and you'll call this class your `ActionHelper` (see Listing 9-3). The mapping information is stored in a `HashMap`.

Listing 9-3. ActionHelper

```
package forum;
import java.util.HashMap;

public class ActionHelper {

  private static HashMap actions = new HashMap();

  static {
    actions.put("ViewTopic", "forum.ViewTopicAction");
    actions.put("Login", "forum.LoginAction");
    actions.put("Logout", "forum.LogoutAction");
    actions.put("NewResponse", "forum.NewResponseAction");
    actions.put("ProcessNewResponse", "forum.ProcessNewResponseAction");
    actions.put("DeleteResponse", "forum.DeleteResponseAction");
  }
```

The `ActionHelper` class effectively maintains a mapping between request names (or types) and the fully qualified class names of the classes that can process the requests. Given the name of a request, the static `getAction()` method returns an instance of an `Action` class that can be used for processing (see Listing 9-4).

Listing 9-4. Action

```
  public static Action getAction(String name) {
    Action action = null;

    try {
      Class c = Class.forName((String)actions.get(name));
      action = (Action)c.newInstance();
    } catch (Exception e) {
      e.printStackTrace();
    }

    return action;
  }
}
```

The next step is to plug all of this into the `processRequest()` method of your `FrontController` because this will be the single entry point for all requests in your Web application (see Listing 9-5).

Listing 9-5. The `processRequest()` *Method*

```
package forum;
import java.io.IOException;

import javax.servlet.*;
import javax.servlet.http.*;
```

```
public class FrontController extends HttpServlet {

  protected void processRequest(HttpServletRequest req,
                                HttpServletResponse res)
                                throws ServletException, IOException {
```

Here you find which action should be used:

```
String actionName = req.getPathInfo().substring(1);
```

Now you use the helper class to locate the action:

```
Action action = ActionHelper.getAction(actionName);
```

The next step is to process the action so you can find out which View to show the user next:

```
String nextView = action.process(req, res);
```

Finally, you redirect to the appropriate View:

```
    RequestDispatcher dispatcher =
       getServletContext().getRequestDispatcher(nextView);
    dispatcher.forward(req, res);
  }

  protected void doGet(HttpServletRequest req, HttpServletResponse res)
      throws ServletException, IOException {

    processRequest(req, res);
  }

  protected void doPost(HttpServletRequest req, HttpServletResponse res)
      throws ServletException, IOException {

    processRequest(req, res);
  }
}
```

With the code to look up actions and process requests encapsulated elsewhere, your Controller servlet is fairly minimal. In fact, all the components you've implemented as part of the Command and Controller strategy have been fairly lightweight. This is good from both a maintainability and reusability perspective because small components are generally easier to maintain (and bug fix) and are also more likely to be reusable elsewhere. The framework you've built is also extensible because new request handlers (actions) can easily be built and added to the system.

The Jakarta Struts Framework

The implementation of the Front Controller pattern presented in this chapter is fairly simple and straightforward, but you can make many improvements. One such example is externalizing the mapping between action names and the `Action` classes that are going to service the request. Although such work isn't particularly complex, it's still time consuming nonetheless. For this reason, a number of third-party frameworks are available for developers to use as a starting point for their Web applications. Once such example is Struts from the Jakarta project (`http://jakarta.apache.org`).

Struts is an open-source framework providing an implementation of not only a Front Controller but a complete implementation (or *framework*) of the Model 2 architecture. The key components are similar to those presented here, including, for example, a Controller servlet (called `ActionServlet`), `Action` classes in which to place functionality for processing a request, and `ActionBean` classes in which to encapsulate data coming in from a request. In addition to this, Struts also contains a comprehensive collection of JSP tag libraries for the easy assembly of Hypertext Markup Language (HTML)–based forms and JSP pages in general. You can use these tag libraries in conjunction with the JSP Tag Library (JSTL).

One of the most important features of Struts is that pretty much everything about it is externally configured through the `struts-config.xml` file. This includes the mappings between action names and `Action` classes (called `ActionMappings`) and also the `ActionForwards` concept.

For the simple example presented in this chapter, the `Action` classes return a string representing the URI of the JSP page that should be displayed next. In Struts, however, the `Action` classes return a symbolic name (wrapped up in an `ActionForward` instance) representing which View component should be displayed next. As an example, consider a login form containing a username and password. On submission of the form, the login is either successful or not successful. In this case, the `Action` class could return symbolic names such as `success` or `failure`. These symbolic names are then configured in the `struts-config.xml` file, and it's here that the physical URI to the appropriate JSP is specified. This is a powerful feature and is yet another way in which you can take the flow and structure of the Web application out of the code to increase maintainability. After all, if the structure of the site changes, only the configuration file need to change.

> **TIP** *A full explanation of Struts is beyond the scope of this book, but you can find a more detailed study of this framework in* The Struts Framework: Practical Guide for Java Programmers *(Morgan Kaufmann, 2002).*

With the design and framework of a Model 2–based auction in place, you'll now see how you can implement the auction once again in Model 2 architecture.

Viewing the Responses

Previously, to view the responses to a topic, you made a direct request to the view-topic.jsp page, passing the id of the specific topic. At the top of this page was a JSP scriptlet that found this parameter and used it to look up the appropriate Topic instance for use further down the page when building the table of responses. One of the benefits of the Command and Controller strategy is that you can move this sort of code out of the JSP and back into a reusable component. With this in mind, you can implement the action to view a topic:

```
package forum;
import javax.servlet.http.*;

public class ViewTopicAction extends Action {

  public String process(HttpServletRequest request,
      HttpServletResponse response) {
```

In the process() method, you first get the id parameter and use it to look up the appropriate Topic instance:

```
String id = request.getParameter("id");
Topic topic = Topics.getTopic(Integer.parseInt(id));
```

Now that you have the topic, you place it in the request ready for use on the View:

```
    request.setAttribute("topic", topic);
    return "/view-topic.jsp";
  }
}
```

You've literally just moved the code into an Action subclass. Once the Topic instance has been located, you then need to make this available to the page so it can build the table of responses. To do this, you use the HTTP Request object as a temporary storage area for this object:

```
request.setAttribute("topic", topic);
```

Using the HTTP request (or even the session) is a useful and frequently used mechanism for passing information between the various components within Web applications. This works between two servlets, two JSP pages, or a mixture of both.

On completion of this action, the Controller will dispatch control to the view-topic.jsp page on which you can use the standard <jsp:useBean/> action to locate the object again. The remainder of the page remains unchanged:

```
<jsp:useBean id="topic" class="forum.Topic" scope="request"/>

<p>
<h2>Topic : <%= topic.getTitle() %></h2>
</p>
```

Following this, you just build the table of responses as before.

The final step in using this is to ensure that you change all direct links to the `view-topic` JSP page into links to the Controller, not forgetting to include the name of the action you want to perform:

```
/controller/ViewTopic?id=0
```

Although this particular action is fairly small, it illustrates the earlier point about enhanced maintainability and reusability. You can now use this action elsewhere in your application rather than coding a scriptlet on a JSP page. This means that should you want to modify this behavior, you'll know where to find it, and the modifications will be reflected elsewhere in your application automatically.

Processing the Login

In a similar way, you can encapsulate the logic associated with processing the user's login into an `Action` class, `LoginAction`, as shown in Listing 9-6.

Listing 9-6. `LoginAction`

```
package forum;

import javax.servlet.http.*;

public class LoginAction extends Action {

  public String process(HttpServletRequest request,
      HttpServletResponse response) {

    String id = request.getParameter("id");
    String password = request.getParameter("password");
    String view;
    if (Users.exists(id, password)) {
      request.getSession().setAttribute("user", Users.getUser(id));
      view = "/index.jsp";
    } else {
      view = "/login.jsp";
    }

    return view;
  }

}
```

As you can see, you've moved the code from the `process-login.jsp` page. This page didn't actually contain any presentation at all in the page-centric implementation, and this is another good reason for moving the code into a small reusable component. It's not only easier to find this code to maintain it in the future, but JSP pages are really suited to rendering responses rather than being containers for lots of Java code.

To ensure that your action gets called, you again need to change any references to the `process-login.jsp` page, including the `action` attribute of HTML form tags:

```
<form action="controller/Login" method="post">
```

Adding a New Response

You've already seen how the `view-topic.jsp` page has changed; the short scriptlet at the top of the page has been removed. The `new-response.jsp` page is effectively the same with an additional HTML form underneath the table of responses. For this reason, and rather than recoding the logic to look up the appropriate topic, you can extend the `ViewTopicAction` class, which helps to ensure that the functionality is consistent (see Listing 9-7).

Listing 9-7. `ViewTopicAction`

```
package forum;

import javax.servlet.http.*;

public class NewResponseAction extends ViewTopicAction {

  public String process(HttpServletRequest request,
      HttpServletResponse response) {

    super.process(request, response);

    return "/new-response.jsp";
  }
}
```

Although a simple example, this shows how you can reuse the action components across different types of requests. Here, you're using the same functionality but dispatching to a different View.

Processing a New Response

You can place the logic to add a new response from the HTML form within an `Action` class, as illustrated in Listing 9-8.

Listing 9-8. `Action`

```
package forum;

import javax.servlet.http.*;
```

```
public class ProcessNewResponseAction extends Action {

  public String process(HttpServletRequest request,
      HttpServletResponse response) {

    String text = request.getParameter("text");
    int id = Integer.parseInt(request.getParameter("id"));

    User user = (User)request.getSession().getAttribute("user");

    Topic topic = Topics.getTopic(id);
    topic.add(new Response(user, text));

    return "/controller/ViewTopic?id=" + id;
  }
}
```

Instead of dispatching to a JSP, you've asked that the request be forwarded onto the `ViewTopic` action. This is a useful way of chaining actions together and again shows the ability to reuse them across different types of requests.

Deleting an Existing Response

The final action you have in your Web application is the ability to delete an existing response. Once again, you can move the business logic associated with this into an `Action` component, as shown in Listing 9-9.

Listing 9-9. `DeleteResponseAction`

```
package forum;

import javax.servlet.http.*;

public class DeleteResponseAction extends Action {

  public String process(HttpServletRequest request,
      HttpServletResponse response) {

    int topicId = Integer.parseInt(request.getParameter("topic"));
    int responseId = Integer.parseInt(request.getParameter("response"));

    User user = (User)request.getSession().getAttribute("user");

    Topic topic = Topics.getTopic(topicId);
    Response res = topic.getResponse(responseId);
```

Only the original author of a response can delete it, and for this reason the `DeleteResponseAction` contains the appropriate logic to make this check. However, what it (or the other actions) doesn't check is whether the user is actually logged on. You'll deal with this issue in the "Using the Intercepting Filter Pattern" section:

```
    if (res.getUser().equals(user)) {
      // yes, so delete it
      topic.remove(res);
    }

    return "/controller/ViewTopic?id=" + topicId;
  }
}
```

Using the Intercepting Filter Pattern

Checking that the user is logged on is another common piece of functionality that's an ideal candidate to encapsulate into a reusable component. You could, of course, wrap this verification up into a small component and call it from the appropriate actions. However, what you really want is for unauthenticated requests to be redirected to the login page. You'll now learn how the Intercepting Filter pattern can help.

Exploring User Verification in Acme Auction

To place a bid on an auction, a user must be logged into the application. It's common to see application code that has code scattered throughout the Views checking for an attribute that indicates whether a user has an active session. It might look something similar to this:

```
<%
  if (session.getAttribute("user") == null) {
    // no, so redirect them to the login page
  }
%>
```

This code checks that the user is logged in before allowing them to see the page that they requested. If the user isn't logged in yet, you simply forward them to the login page.

The problem with this approach is that this code is scattered throughout the Views (pages) in an application. This means you may not be entirely sure which Views contain the code. Subsequently, some pages that should have this code may not, and if you need to update the verification code, you need to modify every page that contains it. Obviously, this isn't the most conducive way to ensure that the user has a valid session.

One way around this problem is to use Intercepting Filters. Intercepting Filters are a useful way of performing preprocessing on requests before they're handled by the components in your Web application. If you extend the architecture yet further, you can insert an Intercepting Filter to preprocess the requests, as shown in Figure 9-7.

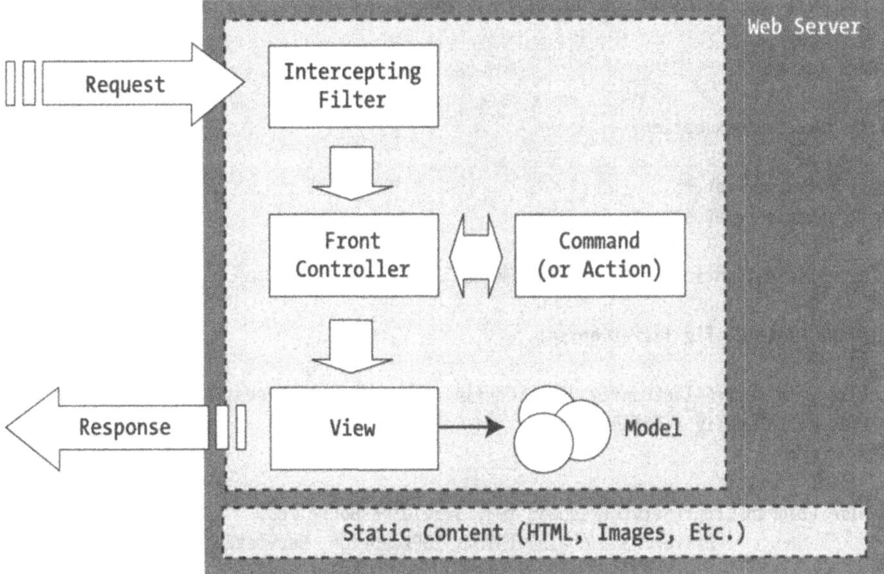

Figure 9-7. The Intercepting Filter pattern

The types of tasks you may want an Intercepting Filter to perform could be as follows:

- Checking the client type so that the appropriate type of site can be served up
- Checking whether the user has a valid session
- Checking that the user is logged in

In Acme Auction, you can use an Intercepting Filter to ensure that any requests to specific pages are authenticated. Having identified that an Intercepting Filter is a useful component to have in your Web application, how do you go about building one?

Implementing an Intercepting Filter

Chapter 7 introduced *filters*, a feature of the Servlet 2.4 specification. Using the same techniques described in that chapter, you can build a simple filter and define a handful of mappings, specifying those URLs on which you want them to operate.

Start with the filter class itself; call it `AuthenticationFilter` (see Listing 9-10).

Listing 9-10. `AuthenticationFilter`

```
package forum;

import java.io.IOException;

import javax.servlet.*;
import javax.servlet.http.*;

public class AuthenticationFilter implements Filter {

  private FilterConfig filterConfig;

  public void init(FilterConfig filterConfig) throws ServletException {
    this.filterConfig = filterConfig;
  }

  public void doFilter(ServletRequest req, ServletResponse res,
                 FilterChain chain) throws IOException, ServletException {

    HttpServletRequest request = (HttpServletRequest)req;
    HttpServletResponse response = (HttpServletResponse)res;
```

In the `doFilter()` method, you check to see if the current user logged in. If not, you redirect them to the login page, as shown in Listing 9-11.

Listing 9-11. Redirecting the User

```
    if (request.getSession().getAttribute("user") == null) {
      RequestDispatcher dispatcher =
        filterConfig.getServletContext().getRequestDispatcher("/login.jsp");
      dispatcher.forward(request, response);
    } else {
      chain.doFilter(request, response);
    }
  }

  public void destroy() {
  }
}
```

What's important here is that the functionality associated with this filter is almost identical to the scriptlet of code that probably appears in the numerous Views. All it does is check that the user is logged in and redirect them to the `login.jsp` page if this isn't the case. One of the goals of object orientation is to encapsulate reusable functionality, and that's exactly what you've done here. You've moved this logic out of the Views and back toward the front of the request-handling process.

With the filter built, you now need to plug it into your Web application. As you've seen before, you achieve this through the Web application deployment descriptor—the `web.xml` file (see Listing 9-12).

Listing 9-12. `web.xml`

```
<?xml version="1.0" encoding="ISO-8859-1"?>

<web-app xmlns="http://java.sun.com/xml/ns/j2ee"
    xmlns:xsi="http://www.w3.org/2001/XMLSchema-instance"
    xsi:schemaLocation="http://java.sun.com/xml/ns/j2ee web-app_2_4.xsd"
    version="2.4">

  <filter>
    <filter-name>AuthenticationFilter</filter-name>
    <filter-class>forum.AuthenticationFilter</filter-class>
  </filter>

  <filter-mapping>
    <filter-name>AuthenticationFilter</filter-name>
    <url-pattern>/controller/NewResponse</url-pattern>
  </filter-mapping>

  <filter-mapping>
    <filter-name>AuthenticationFilter</filter-name>
    <url-pattern>/controller/ProcessNewResponse</url-pattern>
  </filter-mapping>

  <filter-mapping>
    <filter-name>AuthenticationFilter</filter-name>
    <url-pattern>/controller/DeleteResponse</url-pattern>
  </filter-mapping>

  <servlet>
    <servlet-name>FrontController</servlet-name>
    <servlet-class>forum.FrontController</servlet-class>
  </servlet>

  <servlet-mapping>
    <servlet-name>FrontController</servlet-name>
    <url-pattern>/controller/*</url-pattern>
  </servlet-mapping>

</web-app>
```

You've already defined that all URLs starting with `/controller/` are directed to your `FrontController` servlet. Alongside this, you define a filter called `Authentication-Filter` and tell your Web application to use the `AuthenticationFilter` class from the `forum` package. Once you've set this up, you can specify the set of URLs that trigger the filter. In your application, you need to preprocess all requests coming in for the following actions:

- `NewResponse`
- `ProcessNewResponse`
- `DeleteResponse`

This is a powerful and flexible mechanism because you can easily reconfigure your filter should the security requirements of your application change.

The patterns just discussed cover much of your example application. A discussion about Web application design wouldn't be complete without a quick look at a few more patterns:

- View Helper
- Service to Worker

Using the View Helper Pattern

The View Helper pattern is a way of taking logic embedded in the View (for example, scriptlets inside a JSP) and wrapping it up as reusable functionality for use on other View components.

Advantages of the View Helper Pattern

In the same way that you've tried to move much of the functionality away from the View components and back toward the front of the request-handling cycle, some functionality still remains in the Views. A good example is the JSP scriptlets inside the `view-topic.jsp` page that determine whether a particular response has been deleted and should be hidden.

The purpose of the View component is to present information to the user. All the business processing associated with the request should have been performed by this stage, leaving the View component to perform any logic specifically related to presenting the information. While you can include business logic in a JSP page via scriptlets, we've already noted (numerous times at that!) that this isn't a wise approach because the code in the scriptlet isn't in a reusable form.

To solve this problem, you can move this type of functionality into helper components and subsequently reuse them across the Web application. On an implementation level, you can build these helpers as any of the following:

- JavaBeans for use in servlet/JSP Views
- Custom tags for use in JSP Views

Seeing an Example of the View Helper Pattern

In fact, you've already seen an example of the View Helper pattern in the `view-topic.jsp` page. The `ViewTopicAction` looks up the appropriate `Topic` instance and places it into the HTTP `Request` object, ready for the JSP to find it. To recap, here's the code for the `process()` method in the `ViewTopicAction`:

```
public String process(HttpServletRequest request,
                      HttpServletResponse response) {

  String id = request.getParameter("id");
  Topic topic = Topics.getTopic(Integer.parseInt(id));
  request.setAttribute("topic", topic);
  return "/view-topic.jsp";
}
```

To use the information that this action places into the HTTP request, you could have implemented this lookup in `view-topic.jsp` using a simple JSP scriptlet as follows:

```
<%
  Topic topic = (Topic)request.getAttribute("topic");
%>
```

Instead, however, you decided to use the `<jsp:useBean/>` action in `view-topic.jsp`:

```
<jsp:useBean id="topic" class="forum.Topic" scope="request"/>
```

This is just one such example, and it just happens that in this situation, the helper is already written for you. What's important is that you're removing as much logic from the View components in your Web application as possible and placing it inside reusable components.

Another example includes the JSP scriptlet that's used to iterate over a collection of `Response` objects in the `view-topic.jsp` page, as shown in Listing 9-13.

Listing 9-13. The `view-topic.jsp` *page*

```
<%
  Iterator it = topic.getResponses().iterator();
  Response res;

  while (it.hasNext()) {
    res = (Response)it.next();
    if (!res.isDeleted()) {
%>
      <tr>
        <td><%= res.getUser().getId() %></td>
        <td><%= res.getText() %><br><br></td>
        <td valign="top" align="center">
```

```
            [ <a href="controller/DeleteResponse?
              topic=<%= topic.getId() %>&response=<%= res.getId() %>">
              Delete</a> ]
          </td>
        </tr>
<%
    }
  }
%>
```

This example contains much more Java code, and therefore much more can go wrong. Ideally, you'd like to be able to reuse this type of functionality on other pages that build up the content by iterating over a collection of Java objects. In this situation, you could use a JSP custom tag as a View Helper, as follows:

```
<forum:iterate id="res"
               className="forum.Response"
               collection="<%= topic.getResponses() %>">
  <%
    if (!res.isDeleted()) {
  %>
      <tr>
        <td><%= res.getUser().getId() %></td>
        <td><%= res.getText() %><br><br></td>
        <td valign="top" align="center">
          [ <a href="controller/DeleteResponse?
            topic=<%= topic.getId() %>&response=<%= res.getId() %>">
            Delete</a> ]
        </td>
      </tr>
  <%
    }
  %>
</forum:iterate>
```

Here, the Java code responsible for performing the iteration has been moved inside a custom tag, moving it away from the page and resulting in a much cleaner JSP page containing much less Java code than before. In doing this, you've created a reusable View Helper that can be used on other pages in the Web application.

This pattern is applicable to the following types of functionality:

- Retrieval of data (for example, getting data from the Model to display)
- Logic related to presentation of data but not to formatting (for instance, determining whether a particular piece of data should be displayed)
- General presentation layer–related logic (such as iterating over a collection of data items)

Using the Service to Worker Pattern

The final pattern you'll consider is the Service to Worker pattern, which can be described as a "macro pattern." It's really just a combination of a Front Controller pattern, along with Views and View Helpers.

This pattern describes the architecture of your auction, where you've wrapped up a large amount of the processing and presentation logic into reusable components. In other words, you're delegating the task off to Worker components, as illustrated in Figure 9-8.

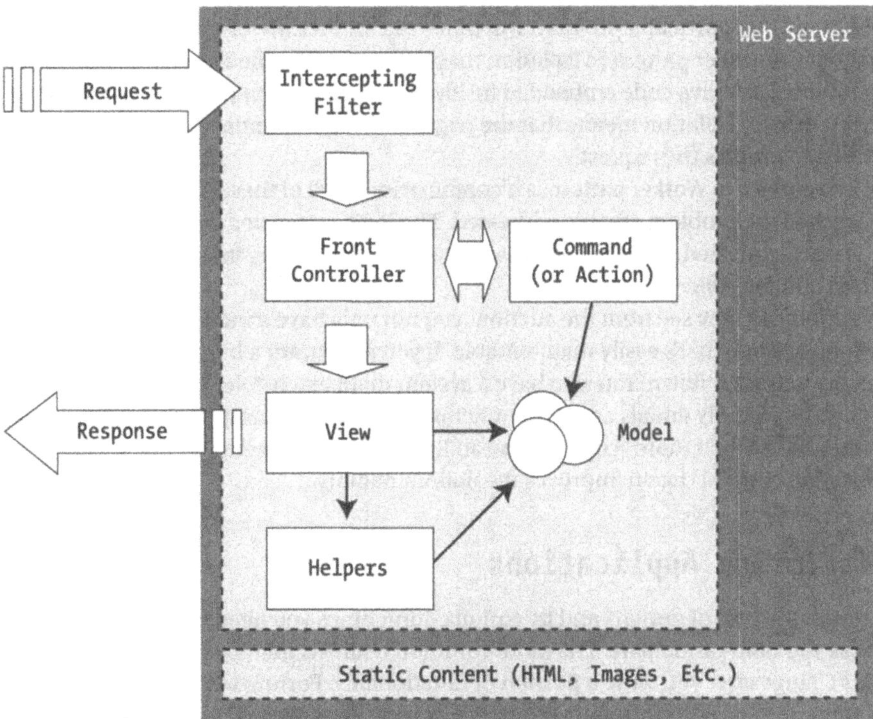

Figure 9-8. The Service to Worker pattern

As with your auction, the Controller delegates processing to the actions, which in turn perform processing associated with servicing the request. These actions may modify the underlying Model. The Controller then dispatches the request to the next View component, which will in turn use the underlying Model and helper components (such as JavaBeans and/or custom tags) to build and render the response.

Each of the patterns you've seen in this chapter focuses on one particular area of development:

- **The Front Controller pattern:** This pattern is a centralized place for logic associated with servicing requests; here Views are responsible only for the presentation of information to the user.

- **The Intercepting Filter pattern:** This pattern is a centralized place for intercepting requests, for example, to allow or disallow them.

- **The View Helper pattern:** This pattern wraps up reusable functionality used by the Views and moves unnecessary logic away from them.

Although each of these addresses a particular problem, using them in isolation means only that particular problem will be solved. In the case of your auction, using the Front Controller pattern in isolation may still mean that the View components contain unnecessary Java code embedded inside the JSP pages. On the other hand, using View Helpers in isolation means that the pages will contain unnecessary business logic required to process the request.

The Service to Worker pattern is a combination of all of these patterns and ensures that each of the problem areas is addressed. The logic associated with processing a request is centralized, and the logic associated with presenting information is also centralized and reusable.

As you can now see from the auction, you not only have a more structured system, but you have one that's easily maintainable. If you encounter a bug, it shouldn't take you long to track it down. You also have a system that's extensible. The addition of new functionality simply entails adding new actions into your request-handling framework. You now have much more scope for reusability of the components within in your application, and this again improves the maintainability.

Refactoring Applications

Even with the best of designs and intentions, sometimes you need to deal with circumstances you didn't anticipate. The more common reality is that the business requirements change after you write a portion of functionality. Fortunately, all is not lost. You can attempt to refactor the application. *Refactoring* basically means changing from one form to another, and although not strictly "design," it does promote some of the same thought processes. When you refactor a piece of software, it generally means you change the internal structure in some way without damaging the functionality it provides.

Refactoring is something everyone probably does already without realizing. Some of the reasons why you may want to refactor a particular piece of software include to tidy it up, to fix bugs, or to simply extend it. The downside to all this is that refactoring can be a time-consuming process. However, by having a complete test suite that can run at given time, developers can be confident that nothing is getting broken in the process. The ability to refactor and continually run tests is one of the most valuable details a developer can monitor. Refactoring also plays a role in keeping the nasty smells that we mentioned earlier in this chapter out of the code.

Summary

Application design is an important facet of software development and is often neglected because of the ever-decreasing timescales for Internet development and time to market. Including time in the development process to perform design will ultimately save time in the long term. While it's easy to put together a Web application representing the business needs of a company, a lack of good design will result in an application that's expensive to maintain and extend.

The most common architecture for building Web applications today is Model 2.

In this chapter, you looked at the typical implementation strategies, along with some of their characteristics, including the following:

- **Maintainability**: How easy it is to keep the application running smoothly
- **Extensibility**: The ease with which you can add new functionality to the system
- **Security**: Making sure the proper access is allowed at the proper time

The chapter then introduced some of the other J2EE components in the picture, and this led to a discussion about how to partition functionality within the Web application.

Following this, you looked more closely at application design. You considered how designs are documented, the concept of a design pattern, and the J2EE patterns catalog.

You then moved on to look at how you could build an online action application using a Model 2 architecture. By carefully using the appropriate design patterns, you were able to see how you could build an application while still maintaining the maintainability, extensibility, and reusability you desire.

You looked at a handful of Web tier–related J2EE patterns:

- Front Controller
- Intercepting Filter
- View Helper
- Service to Worker

Finally, you explored the purpose of these patterns and looked at how they're useful when you design your online auction application to maximize maintainability, extensibility, and reusability.

CHAPTER 10

Using Session Beans

ENTERPRISE JAVABEANS (EJBs) are one of the most important and widely used component types in Java 2 Enterprise Edition (J2EE) applications. EJBs free component developers from implementing system-level services such as security, transactions, and instance management within the component code. Instead, EJBs are managed components that run within the realms of an EJB container and rely on the container for the aforementioned system-level services. The requirements of the previous services are defined outside the component source using Extensible Markup Language (XML) deployment descriptors. This allows component developers to focus on implementing the business logic, and the deployer can configure the runtime behavior of the component in terms of utilizing services, such as security, at deployment time by editing the deployment descriptor.

The EJB 2.1 specification defines the following three types of EJBs:

- **Entity beans**: Entity beans provide an interface for persisting the state of the domain objects to a persistent store such as a relational database management system (RDBMS).

- **Message-driven beans**: Message-driven beans (MDBs) are components that can asynchronously listen for messages sent using a variety of messaging protocols.

- **Session beans**: Session beans act as an extension to the clients that connect to the EJB container. Session beans are mainly used for implementing the business logic and providing an interface to the business tier.

In this chapter, you'll look mainly at writing session beans. The coming chapters cover using entity beans, using MDBs, and configuring the runtime environment of EJBs by editing the deployment descriptors.

Introducing the Remote and Local Client Views

For clients, session beans are nonpersistent components that provide a piece of business logic, and entity beans provide any object-oriented view of a set of persistent business entities. MDBs are never accessed directly by the clients. Clients use the following two artifacts to access a session or an entity EJB:

The home object: The home object is the gateway for accessing a bean component. Home objects for a bean component are normally bound by the container in a Java Naming and Directory Interface (JNDI) namespace, which is looked at by the clients. Clients then use the home object to create or locate the component object (which is explained next). Methods that are invoked on the home object map to the lifecycle methods of the EJB.

The component object: The component object provides the interface to the business methods implemented by the EJB. Clients use the component object to invoke the business methods on the EJB component.

Whenever a client invokes a method on the home or component object, the container interposes the invocation to provide the services that are requested declaratively in the deployment descriptor such as transactions, security, and so on. The clients can be either local or remote. Remote clients use the Java Remote Method Invocation/Internet Inter-ORB Protocol (RMI/IIOP) invocation semantics for invoking methods on the home and component objects, and local clients use the Java pass-by-reference invocation semantics.

Remote clients are location transparent. The remote home object of a bean is required to implement an interface that extends `javax.ejb.EJBHome`, and the remote component object of a bean is required to implement an interface that extends `javax.ejb.EJBObject`. Both these interfaces in turn extend the `java.rmi.Remote` interface. The arguments and return values exchanged during remote invocations are passed by value.

Local clients can invoke only those EJBs collocated in the same Java virtual machine (JVM). The local home object of a bean is required to implement an interface that extends `javax.ejb.EJBLocalHome`, and the local component object of a bean is required to implement an interface that extends `javax.ejb.EJBLocalObject`. The arguments and return values exchanged during remote invocations are passed by reference.

NOTE *Great consideration should be given when deciding whether to use a local or remote view. In Web applications, where the servlet and EJB containers are collocated, having a local view highly improves performance because of the absence of the overhead involved in remote communication. However, in the future, if you decide to distribute the application to improve scalability, and your Web clients have been written to take advantage of the pass-by-reference semantics of local invocation, you'll need quite a lot of rework on the client side.*

NOTE *Similarly, collocating a distributed application will involve detailed analysis on whether the clients of beans mutate the value of the arguments and return objects directly. These changes wouldn't be visible in a distributed system because of the pass-by-reference semantics. However, as soon as you collocate it, you'll start noticing unexpected results.*

You need to consider the following points before you decide on a local or remote client view for your bean component:

Remote clients provide location transparency and decouple the clients from the bean components.

Remote invocations involve passing objects by value. Hence, any mutations made to the objects by the clients or the bean aren't visible to each other.

Arguments and return values used in remote invocations should be serializable and hence are potentially expensive because of the overheads involved in marshaling and unmarshaling the objects.

Remote calls can potentially fail for reasons outside the application logic because of problems in network communication. The clients need to be aware of this and should handle exceptions accordingly.

Remote objects aren't suitable for chatty fine-grained invocations.

Local invocations involve the pass-by-reference paradigm and can introduce tight coupling between the client and the bean component, where the clients started relying on modifications made to the objects passed by reference to the server. In such cases it will be difficult to migrate to a remote pass-by-value paradigm later.

The client and bean developers need to be highly careful that they don't inadvertently mutate the value of the objects that are passed as arguments and return values.

The points made in this section are common to both session and entity beans. The rest of the chapter focuses on session beans alone.

Introducing the Session Bean State

Session beans can be either stateful or stateless. Stateful session beans persist their state across multiple client invocations. Stateless session beans don't persist their state across multiple client invocations. Deciding whether to use stateful or stateless session beans is as important as deciding on using remote or local client views. Unless you have a telling reason for persisting state across multiple client invocations, we recommend using stateless session beans. Since stateless session beans don't have a client identity, containers often pool stateless session bean instances, which can highly enhance performance and scalability. Also, using stateful session beans can adversely impact performance in a clustered environment where the state will have to be replicated across the various nodes in the cluster.

Fortunately, deciding whether a bean is stateful or stateless is mainly a deployment-time option specified declaratively using the bean deployment descriptor. However, subtle differences exist in how you code a stateful session bean and a stateless session bean, which is explained later in the "Implementing the Session Bean Component Contract" section.

Using the Session Bean Client View

Session beans are an extension to the client that uses the bean instance. A session bean's logic is implemented using the bean class. However, the clients never access the bean class directly. Instead, they access the bean through its client view. The client view is defined using the bean's home and component objects. The home objects provide the lifecycle methods for the bean component, and the component object defines the business methods. Whenever the client invokes a method on the home or component object, the container interposes to provide the system-level services such as transactions and security as requested in the deployment descriptor before diverting the invocation to an instance of the bean class.

The home object of the session bean is made available for lookup in a JNDI namespace by the bean container. The home object should implement the home interface of the bean component described in its deployment descriptor. It's the responsibility of the bean provider to provide the home interface, and it's the responsibility of the container to provide the class that implements this interface. The home interface should extend `javax.ejb.EJBHome` or `javax.ejb.EJBLocalHome` depending on whether the client view is remote or local, respectively.

Once the client gets a reference to the home object, the client can use it to create an instance of the component object. The component object can then invoke business methods on the bean component. The component object should implement the component interface of the bean component described in its deployment descriptor. It's the responsibility of the bean provider to provide the component interface, and it's the responsibility of the container to provide the class that implements this interface. The component interface should extend `javax.ejb.EJBObject` or `javax.ejb.EJBLocalObject` depending on whether the client view is remote or local, respectively.

> **NOTE** *Different containers implement different strategies for providing the home and component objects. For example, WebLogic statically generates stubs and skeletons for the home and component interfaces either during deployment or during a separate step called* `ejbc` *prior to deployment. JBoss, on the other hand, doesn't statically generate these objects but relies on a more dynamic approach using dynamic proxies.*

Introducing the Home Object

A session bean's home interface can be either local or remote. The remote home interface extends the `EJBHome` interface, and the local home interface extends the `EJBLocalHome` interface. The client looks up the home object provided by the container using JNDI lookup.

Looking Up the Home Object

The following snippet shows how a remote client looks up the remote home object:

```
public CustomerHome getRemoteCustomerHome()
{
    java.util.Properties env = new java.util.Properties();
    env.put(javax.naming.Context.INITIAL_CONTEXT_FACTORY,
         "weblogic.jndi.WLInitialContextFactory");
    env.put(javax.naming.Context.PROVIDER_URL,
         "t3://al-aqsa:7001");

    javax.naming.Context ctx = new javax.naming.InitialContext(env);

    Object ref = ctx.lookup("java:comp/env/ejb/CustomerHome");
    return (CustomerHome)javax.rmi.PortableRemoteObject.narrow(
        ref, CustomerHome.class);
}
```

In the previous example, `CustomerHome` is the name by which the bean's remote home object is bound in the JNDI namespace. Since the client is remote, you need to somehow specify the JNDI properties to indicate the initial context factory, provider uniform resource locator (URL), security principal, credentials, and so on. In the previous example, these values are passed using a `Properties` object. You can also employ other techniques such as specifying these properties in a file called `jndi.properties` available in the classpath for the client.

The following code shows how to look up a local home object:

```
public CustomerHome getLocalCustomerHome()
{
    javax.naming.Context ctx = new javax.naming.InitialContext();
    return (CustomerHomeLocal)ctx.lookup(
         "java:comp/env/ejb/CustomerHome");
}
```

As you can see, the lookup is in-container lookup, and usually containers don't force you to provide the JNDI properties. Also, you can use a normal Java cast on the looked-up home object to cast it to your home interface.

Introducing the Remote Home Interface

The `EJBHome` interface provides the methods described in Table 10-1 that can be used by the clients.

Table 10-1. `EJBHome` *Methods*

METHOD	DESCRIPTION
`EJBMetaData getEJBMetaData()`	Obtains the `EJBMetaData` interface for the enterprise bean. The `EJBMetaData` interface allows a client to obtain the enterprise bean's metadata information. The metadata is intended for development tools used for building applications that use deployed enterprise beans and for clients using a scripting language to access the enterprise bean. The metadata includes the bean's home interface, component interface, whether a bean is a session bean, if it's a session bean or a stateless session bean, and so on.
`HomeHandle getHomeHandle()`	Obtains a handle for the remote home object. The `HomeHandle` interface is implemented by all home object handles. A handle is an abstraction of a network reference to a home object. A handle is intended to be used as a "robust" persistent reference to a home object.
`void remove(Handle handle)`	Removes an EJB object identified by its handle. The `Handle` interface is implemented by all EJB object handles. A handle is an abstraction of a network reference to a remote component object. A handle is intended to be used as a "robust" persistent reference to the remote component object.
`void remove(java.lang.Object primaryKey)`	This method is applicable only for home objects of entity bean components.

The home interface of a session bean defines methods that create the component object for the EJB component. The following snippet shows the remote home interface of the `Customer` EJB used in the auction application:

```
import javax.ejb.CreateException;
import javax.ejb.EJBHome;
import java.rmi.RemoteException;
```

```
public interface CustomerControllerHome extends EJBHome {

  public CustomerController create()
  throws CreateException, RemoteException;

}
```

The remote home interface extends `EJBHome` and defines one method for creating the component object. In the EJB vocabulary, these methods are called *create methods*. The home interface can have one or more create methods.

The method should return the remote component interface of the bean as defined in the deployment descriptor and should declare to throw both `RemoteException` and `CreateException`. The name of the method should start with the string `create`. For example, you can have a create method that's called `createSpecialCustomer`. If the bean is stateless, the create methods shouldn't have any arguments, whereas stateful session beans can take arguments in the create methods. All arguments should be valid Java RMI/IIOP types.

The following code shows how to create a component object:

```
CustomerHome home = getRemoteCustomerHome()
Customer customer = home.create();
```

To remove the component object, you can do the following:

```
CustomerHome home = getRemoteCustomerHome()
Customer customer = home.create();
home.remove(customer.getHandle());
```

Using the Remote Component Interface

The remote component interface should extend the `EJBObject` interface, which defines the methods described in Table 10-2.

Table 10-2. `EJBObject` *Methods*

METHOD	DESCRIPTION
`EJBHome getEJBHome()`	Obtains the enterprise bean's remote home interface.
`Handle getHandle()`	Obtains a handle for the EJB object.
`java.lang.Object getPrimaryKey()`	Obtains the primary key of the EJB object. This is relevant only for entity beans.
`boolean isIdentical(EJBObject obj)`	Tests if a given EJB object is identical to the invoked EJB object. This will always return `true` for stateless session beans with the same home objects, as they don't have any client identity.
`void remove()`	Removes the EJB object. You can use this as an alternative to the `remove(Handle)` method on the `EJBHome` interface.

The following snippet shows the remote component interface for the Customer EJB:

```
import javax.ejb.EJBObject;
import java.rmi.RemoteException;

public interface CustomerController extends EJBObject {

  public void createCustomer(CustomerData customer)
  throws CustomerException, RemoteException;

  public CustomerData getCustomer(String userId)
  throws CustomerException, RemoteException;

  public void updateCustomer(CustomerData customer)
  throws CustomerException, RemoteException;

}
```

All the methods should accept and return valid RMI/IIOP types and should declare to throw RemoteException.

Introducing the Local Home Interface

The EJBLocalHome interface provides the method described in Table 10-3 that can be used by the clients.

Table 10-3. EJBLocalHome *Method*

METHOD	DESCRIPTION
void remove(java.lang.Object primaryKey)	This method is applicable only for home objects of entity bean components.

The following snippet shows the local home interface of the Customer EJB used in the auction application:

```
import javax.ejb.CreateException;
import javax.ejb.EJBLocalHome;

public interface CustomerControllerLocalHome extends EJBLocalHome {

  public CustomerControllerLocal create() throws CreateException;

}
```

The remote home interface extends EJBLocalHome and defines one method for creating the component object. The method should return the local component interface of the bean as defined in the deployment descriptor and should declare to throw CreateException but shouldn't declare to throw RemoteException.

The following code shows how to create a component object:

```
CustomerHomeLocal home = getRemoteCustomerLocal()
CustomerLocal customer = home.create();
```

Using the Local Component Interface

The local component interface should extend the `EJBLocalObject` interface, which defines the methods described in Table 10-4.

Table 10-4. `EJBLocalObject` *Methods*

METHOD	DESCRIPTION
`EJBLocalHome getEJBHome()`	Obtains the enterprise bean's local home interface.
`java.lang.Object getPrimaryKey()`	Obtains the primary key of the EJB object. This is relevant only for entity beans.
`boolean isIdentical(EJBLocalObject obj)`	Tests if a given EJB object is identical to the invoked EJB object. This will always return `true` for stateless session beans with the same home objects, as they don't have any client identity.
`void remove()`	Removes the EJB object.

The following snippet shows the remote component interface for the `Customer` EJB:

```
import javax.ejb.EJBLocalObject;

public interface CustomerControllerLocal extends EJBLocalObject {

  public void createCustomer(CustomerData customer)
  throws CustomerException;

  public CustomerData getCustomer(String userId)
  throws CustomerException;

  public void updateCustomer(CustomerData customer)
  throws CustomerException;

}
```

The methods shouldn't declare to throw `RemoteException`.

Implementing the Session Bean Component Contract

So far you've seen how to write the client view of a session bean. Now you'll look at how the bean itself is implemented and how the bean behaves as a managed component within the realms of a container. The client view mainly defines the bean's home and component interfaces. The business methods defined in the bean's component interface are implemented in the bean class.

> **NOTE** *Note that it isn't recommended for bean classes to literally implement the component interface in Java semantics. However, each method defined in the component interface should be available as a nonabstract method in the bean class.*

Bean classes for session beans are required to implement the `javax.ejb.SessionBean` interface. This interface defines the various callback methods related to the bean's lifecycle events. The life cycle of a session bean instance is controlled by the various actions instigated by the client. The bean instance may choose to store conversational state across multiple client invocations in its instance variables, if the bean has been declared stateful in the deployment descriptor.

Listing 10-1 shows the code for the bean class used in the example for the customer controller session bean.

Listing 10-1. Session Bean Implementation

```
package com.apress.auction.customer.ejb;

import javax.ejb.*;

import com.apress.auction.entity.interfaces.*;
import com.sun.j2ee.blueprints.servicelocator.ejb.ServiceLocator;
import com.apress.auction.customer.client.*;

import java.rmi.server.UID;

public class CustomerControllerEJB implements SessionBean {

  private CustomerLocalHome customerHome;

  private SessionContext ctx;

  public void ejbCreate() {

    ServiceLocator sl = new ServiceLocator();
    customerHome = (CustomerLocalHome)
    sl.getLocalHome("java:comp/env/ejb/customer");

  }
```

```
public void ejbActivate() {}
public void ejbPassivate() {}
public void ejbRemove() {}
public void setSessionContext(SessionContext ctx) { this.ctx = ctx; }

public void createCustomer(CustomerData customerData)
  throws CustomerException {

  try {

    customerHome.create(
      customerData.getUserId(),
      customerData.getPassword(),
      customerData.getName(),
      customerData.getEmail());

  }catch(DuplicateKeyException ex) {
    // This will roll back the current transaction
    ctx.setRollbackOnly();
    throw new CustomerException("User id already exists");
  }catch(Exception ex) {
    /* Container translates EJBException to RemoteException
    to the client. Any runtime or remote exception thrown
    from the bean will roll back the current transaction. However,
    any checked exception other than RemoteException will commit
    the current transaction unless you call the setRollbackOnly
    method on the EJB context */
    throw new EJBException(ex);
  }

}

public CustomerData getCustomer(String userId) throws CustomerException {

  try {

    return customerHome.findByPrimaryKey(userId).getData();

  }catch(ObjectNotFoundException ex) {
    ctx.setRollbackOnly();
    throw new CustomerException("Customer not found");
  }catch(Exception ex) {
    throw new EJBException(ex);
  }

}

public void updateCustomer(CustomerData customerData)
  throws CustomerException {

  try {
```

```
        customerHome.findByPrimaryKey(
          customerData.getUserId()).setData(customerData);

      }catch(ObjectNotFoundException ex) {
        ctx.setRollbackOnly();
        throw new CustomerException("Customer not found");
      }catch(Exception ex) {
        throw new EJBException(ex);
      }

    }

}
```

In Listing 10-1, the methods can be classified as follows:

- Methods implemented by the `SessionBean` interface
- Business methods defined in the component interface of the bean
- `ejbCreate` methods corresponding to the create methods in the home interface of the bean

Create Methods

For every create method in the home interface, the bean class should have a method that takes the same number, type, and order of arguments. Also, the method name should be the string `ejb` prefixed to the name of the corresponding create method, returning `void`. For example, if the home interface has a method with the signature `CustomerController createSpecialCustomer(int id)`, the corresponding method in the bean class will be `void ejbCreateSpecialCustomer(int id)`.

When a client calls a create method on the session bean's home interface, the container calls `newInstance` on the bean class to create an instance of the bean class. To do this, the bean class should have a public no-argument constructor. Then the container calls the `setSessionContext` method on the bean instance, passing an instance of the `SessionContext` interface. You'll look at this interface in detail in the "Session Context" section. Then the container calls the `ejbCreate` method corresponding to the create method on the home interface that the client called.

If your bean is stateful, your create method can take arguments and use them to initialize instance variables, which can be used in later client invocations. This is because for stateful session beans, the bean instance created in response to the client invocation of the create method on the home interface is guaranteed to be the same instance that will serve further invocations by the client on the component object returned as a result of invoking the create method. However, for stateless session beans, the create methods shouldn't take any arguments because there's no state persisted between invocations. However, you can still use instance variables that are reused by various clients. This is because containers pool stateless session beans, and you can use the `ejbCreate` methods for performing expensive operations such as looking up entity bean home objects.

> **NOTE** *Containers guarantee that invocations to the bean instances are always serialized. This means the instance variables in a stateless session bean instance are always thread safe. However, this doesn't hold true for static variables.*

Figure 10-1 is from the EJB specification and shows how the bean instance is managed by the container for a stateful session bean in response to the various actions instigated by the client.

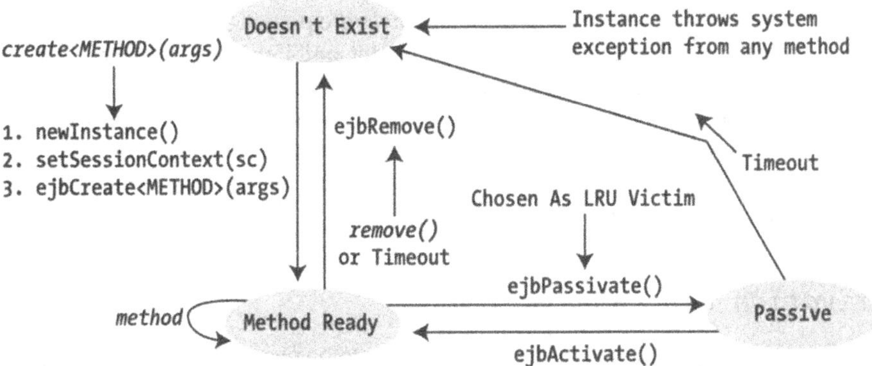

Figure 10-1. State chart for stateful session beans

When a client calls the create method on the home object, and if the bean instance doesn't exist, the container calls `newInstance` on the bean class, sets the session context, and calls the corresponding `ejbCreate` method. After that the bean instance can service only invocations made by through the component object that was returned as a result of the create method invocation. This means stateful session bean instances are tightly coupled to the client that created them and are hence highly nonscalable. Once the bean is in the method-ready state, it can service business method invocations from the client. A method can execute within the context of a transaction, depending on the transaction attribute defined for the method in the deployment descriptor. Chapter 13 covers transaction attributes in detail.

Figure 10-2 is from the EJB specification and shows how the bean instance is managed by the container for a stateless session bean in response to the various actions instigated by the client.

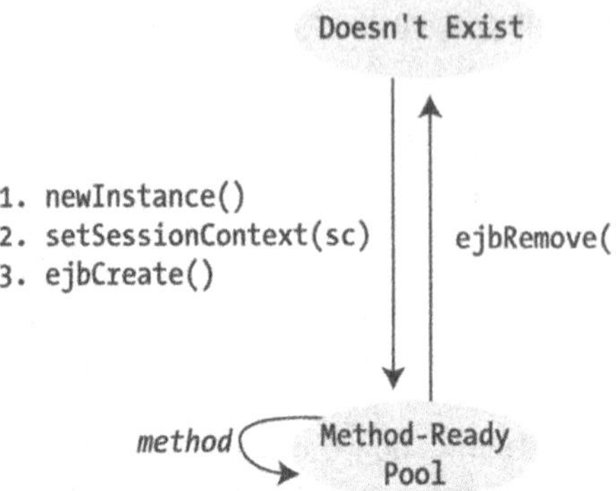

Figure 10-2. State chart for stateless session beans

As you can see, stateless session bean instances are pooled and reused. When a client invokes the create method on the home object, and if the bean instance isn't available, the container creates an instance, sets the session context, and calls the `ejbCreate` method. Then the instance is moved into the method-ready pool, where it's available for servicing any client. The fact that stateless session bean instances are pooled and don't carry any client state contributes heavily to the reason why they're the most scalable components in the J2EE world.

Activation and Passivation

The EJB specification allows session bean instances to be passivated when the container runs out of physical resources. The passivated instances are reactivated when a client request comes for the bean instance. During the process of activation and passivation, the following states are persisted:

- A serializable object
- A `null`
- A reference to another EJB's remote component object
- A reference to another EJB's remote home object
- A reference to an entity EJB's local component object
- A reference to an entity EJB's local home object

- A reference to `SessionContext`
- A reference to `UserTransaction`, which is a Java Transaction API (JTA) that can be used for bean-managed transaction demarcation
- A reference to the bean's JNDI environment naming context (ENC), which is covered in detail in Chapter 13

The `SessionBean` interface defines the following two callback methods that are used by the container for notifying the bean instances about activation and passivation:

- **ejbPassivate**: This method is called just before the bean instance is passivated. Bean developers can use this to close Java Database Connectivity (JDBC) connections, URL connections, and so on.
- **ejbActivate**: This method is called just after the bean instance is activated. You can use this for reinitializing physical connections.

NOTE *Note that stateless session beans are neither activated nor passivated.*

Session Context

The bean instances get a reference to the context that runs in the container through an object that's passed to it by the container. This object implements the interface `SessionContext`. This interface defines the following methods:

- **java.security.Principal getCallerPrincipal()**: This obtains the `java.security.Principal` method that identifies the caller. Chapter 13 covers security in further detail.
- **boolean isCallerInRole(java.lang.String roleName)**: This tests if the caller has a given security role.
- **EJBHome getEJBHome()**: This obtains the enterprise bean's remote home interface.
- **EJBLocalHome getEJBLocalHome()**: This obtains the enterprise bean's local home interface.
- **boolean getRollbackOnly()**: This tests if the transaction has been marked for rollback only. Chapter 13 covers transactions in further detail.

- **UserTransaction getUserTransaction()**: This obtains the transaction demarcation interface. You can use this only if the bean uses bean-managed transaction (BMT) demarcation.
- **void setRollbackOnly()**: This marks the current transaction for rollback.
- **EJBLocalObject getEJBLocalObject()**: This obtains a reference to the EJB local object that's currently associated with the instance.
- **EJBObject getEJBObject()**: This obtains a reference to the EJB object that's currently associated with the instance.

SessionSynchronization

The `javax.ejb.SessionSynchronization` interface can be optionally implemented by session bean classes that use container-managed transaction (CMT) demarcation to get notification about important transaction events. This isn't relevant for beans with BMT because they're in control of starting, committing, and rolling back the transactions. The instances can use these notifications, for example, to manage database data they may cache within transactions.

The container calls the `afterBegin` method before invoking the first business method on the bean instance in a transaction context. The `beforeCompletion` method is called just before the transaction commits. The `afterCompletion` is called after the current transaction has completed. A completion status of `true` indicates that the transaction has committed; a status of `false` indicates that a rollback has occurred.

The following list shows the signatures of the previous methods:

- **void afterBegin()**: The `afterBegin` method notifies a session bean instance that a new transaction has started and that the subsequent business methods on the instance will be invoked in the context of the transaction.
- **void afterCompletion(boolean committed)**: The `afterCompletion` method notifies a session bean instance that a transaction commit protocol has completed and tells the instance whether the transaction has been committed or rolled back.
- **void beforeCompletion()**: The `beforeCompletion` method notifies a session bean instance that a transaction is about to be committed.

Figure 10-3 shows the state chart of a stateful session bean with additional transaction notifications.

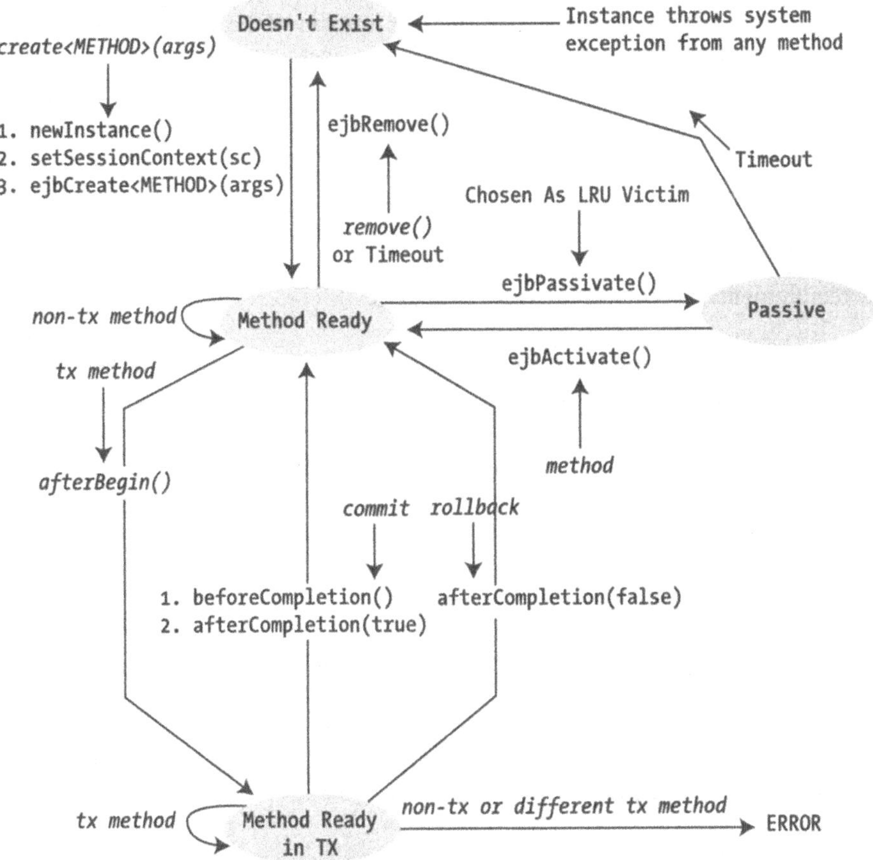

Figure 10-3. State chart for stateful session beans with transaction synchronization

Understanding the Session Bean Requirements

Now that we've covered most of the artifacts involved in writing session beans, the following sections summarize the requirements of writing session beans.

Session Bean Artifacts

The requirements for the session bean artifacts are as follows:

- The bean class that implements the `SessionBean` interface
- The remote home interface that extends `EJBHome` and the remote component interface that extends the `EJBObject` interface if the bean provides a remote client view

- The local home interface that extends `EJBLocalHome` and the local component interface that extends the `EJBLocalObject` interface if the bean provides a remote client view

- The bean deployment descriptors, both standard EJB deployment descriptor and application server–specific deployment descriptors

Session Bean Class

The requirements for the bean class are as follows:

- The class should implement the `SessionBean` interface or extend a class that implements that interface.

- The class must be public, nonfinal, and nonabstract.

- The class should have a public no-argument constructor.

- The class must not have a finalize method.

- The class isn't required and is recommended to not implement the component interface.

- The class must provide implementations for the business methods defined in the component interface.

- The class must provide implementations for the `ejbCreate` methods corresponding to the create methods defined in the home interface.

- Stateful session beans can optionally implement the `SessionSynchronization` method.

ejbCreate Methods

The requirements for the `ejbCreate` methods are as follows:

- The method names should be `ejbCreate`.

- The method should be public, nonstatic, and nonfinal.

- The method should return `void`.

- The method arguments should be legal RMI/IIOP types.
- Methods can declare to throw application-specific exceptions including `javax.ejb.CreateException`. However, these exceptions should be declared in the `throws` clause of the corresponding create methods in the home interface.

Business Methods

The requirements for the business methods are as follows:

- The method names shouldn't start with the prefix `ejb`.
- The method should be public, nonstatic, and nonfinal.
- The method arguments and return types should be legal RMI/IIOP types.
- Methods can declare to throw application-specific exceptions. However, these exceptions should be declared in the `throws` clause of the corresponding business methods in the component interface.

Remote Component Interface

The requirements for the remote component interface are as follows:

- The interface should directly or indirectly extend the `javax.ejb.EJBObject` interface.
- The method arguments and return types should be legal RMI/IIOP types.
- Methods should have `java.rmi.RemoteException` in their `throws` clause.
- Methods can declare to throw application-specific exceptions. Each method in the component interface should have a corresponding nonabstract method in the bean class with the same name, parameters, return types, and exception types (the `RemoteException` is optional in the methods in the bean class).
- These methods shouldn't expose a local component or home object as arguments or return types. This is quite obvious because remote types are used by remote clients, and the remote types shouldn't be exposing local types to remote clients.

Local Component Interface

The requirements for the local component interface are as follows:

- The interface should directly or indirectly extend the `javax.ejb.EJBLocalObject` interface.
- Methods can declare to throw application-specific exceptions. Each method in the component interface should have a corresponding nonabstract method in the bean class with the same name, parameters, return types, and exception types.
- The methods shouldn't declare to throw `java.rmi.RemoteException`.

Remote Home Interface

The requirements for the remote home interface are as follows:

- The interface should directly or indirectly extend the `javax.ejb.EJBHome` interface.
- The method arguments and return types should be legal RMI/IIOP types.
- Methods should have `java.rmi.RemoteException` in their `throws` clause.
- Methods should have `javax.ejb.CreateException` in the `throws` clause.
- Method names should start with the prefix `create`.
- Methods should declare to return the bean's remote component interface.
- Methods can declare to throw application-specific exceptions. Each method in the component interface should have a corresponding nonabstract method in the bean class with the same name and with the prefix `create` replaced with `ejbCreate`, parameters, return types, and exception types (the `RemoteException` and `CreateException` are optional in the methods in the bean class).

Local Home Interface

The requirements for the local home interface are as follows:

- The interface should directly or indirectly extend the `javax.ejb.EJBLocalHome` interface.
- Methods shouldn't have `java.rmi.RemoteException` in their `throws` clause.

- Methods should have `javax.ejb.CreateException` in the `throws` clause.
- Method names should start with the prefix `create`.
- Methods should declare to return the bean's local component interface.
- Methods can declare to throw application-specific exceptions. Each method in the component interface should have a corresponding nonabstract method in the bean class with the same name and with the prefix `create` replaced with `ejbCreate`, parameters, return types, and exception types (the `CreateException` is optional in the methods in the bean class).

Understanding the Session Bean Deployment Descriptor

Now you'll look at the relevant elements in the EJB deployment descriptor pertaining to session beans. Each session bean in the EJB Java archive (JAR) file should have an element called `session` under the `enterprise-beans` element in the deployment descriptor, as shown in Listing 10-2.

Listing 10-2. Deployment Descriptor

```
<?xml version="1.0" encoding="ISO-8859-1"?>

<ejb-jar
  version="2.1"
  xmlns="http://java.sun.com/xml/ns/j2ee"
  xmlns:xsi="http://www.w3.org/2001/XMLSchema-instance"
  xsi:schemaLocation="http://java.sun.com/xml/ns/j2ee
    http://java.sun.com/xml/ns/j2ee/ejb-jar_2_1.xsd">

  <display-name>CustomerJar</display-name>
  <enterprise-beans>
    <session>
      <display-name>CustomerController</display-name>
      <ejb-name>CustomerController</ejb-name>
      <home>com.apress.auction.customer.client.CustomerControllerHome</home>
      <remote>com.apress.auction.customer.client.CustomerController</remote>
      <ejb-class>
        com.apress.auction.customer.ejb.CustomerControllerEJB
      </ejb-class>
      <session-type>Stateless</session-type>
      <transaction-type>Container</transaction-type>
      <ejb-local-ref>
        <ejb-ref-name>ejb/customer</ejb-ref-name>
        <ejb-ref-type>Entity</ejb-ref-type>
        <local-home>
          com.apress.auction.entity.interfaces.CustomerLocalHome
        </local-home>
```

```
      <local>com.apress.auction.entity.interfaces.CustomerLocal</local>
      <ejb-link>Customer</ejb-link>
    </ejb-local-ref>
  </session>

 </enterprise-beans>

</ejb-jar>
```

The child elements of the `session` element are as follows:

- **display-name**: A display name that can be used by deployment tools.
- **ejb-name**: A unique name for the EJB in the deployment unit.
- **home**: The fully qualified name of the bean's remote home interface.
- **remote**: The fully qualified name of the bean's remote component interface.
- **local-home**: The fully qualified name of the bean's local home interface.
- **local**: The fully qualified name of the bean's local component interface.
- **ejb-class**: The fully qualified name of the bean class.
- **session-type**: The type of the session bean, whether it's stateful or stateless. The possible values are `Stateless` and `Stateful`.
- **transaction-type**: Used to define whether the bean uses container-managed transactions or bean-managed transactions. The possible values are `Container` and `Bean`.

> **NOTE** *Chapter 13 covers other relevant child elements of the session element in detail.*

Summary

This chapter covered how to write stateful and stateless session beans. You learned about the various artifacts involved in developing and deploying J2EE session beans. You also learned about session bean life cycles and component contracts.

CHAPTER 11

Introducing Entity Beans and Persistence

In this chapter you'll learn about the following:

- What entity beans are and how they've changed in Java 2 Enterprise Edition (J2EE) 1.4
- The interfaces and classes that make up an entity bean
- The Enterprise JavaBean (EJB) query language (QL)
- Container- and bean-managed persistence in detail
- The entity section of the EJB deployment descriptors
- Some implementation issues

What Are Entity Beans?

What are entity beans? The short answer is that they provide an object-oriented persistence mechanism with declarative security and transactions.

The longer answer is that entity EJBs represent the entity objects in an analysis model. They can correspond to real-world concepts, such as customers or products, or they can correspond to abstractions, such as manufacturing processes, company policies, or customer purchases.

This notion of representation is important to understand. After all, a session bean can access any data that an entity bean can. Although a session bean can access data, it can't provide an object-oriented representation of that data. How does an entity bean differ? Why can't you have a "customer" session bean or a "bid" session bean, like you can with entity beans?

The basic explanation is simple, even if the details are complicated. You've seen in the previous chapter that the state maintained by stateful session beans is private in the sense that only the client that's currently using the session bean can manipulate this state. Entity beans are different because their state is stored in the database; several clients can therefore access their state simultaneously. So the fundamental problem in representing an object with a session bean is in how that state is made available to clients of that bean. An entity bean is (logically, anyway) a single point of access for that data; any client that accesses the data will go through that entity bean. A session bean, on the other hand, is accessible only to a single client. If there are multiple clients, there will be multiple session beans.

Finally, session beans don't persist their state to a database. If the container crashes, the state of a session bean is nonrecoverable; however, the entity can get its state back from the database.

Understanding the Changes in J2EE 1.4

With regard to entity beans, the only specific change in J2EE is the new EJB 2.1 specification, which provides extra EJB QL extensions: `ORDER BY`, aggregation functions, and the `MOD` function.

Introducing the Bean

You'll now look at what makes up an entity bean.

Constructing an Entity Bean

Entity beans, like session beans, have up to four different interfaces: `Remote`, `RemoteHome`, `Local`, and `LocalHome`, as well as an abstract bean class (container-managed persistence) or a concrete bean class (bean-managed persistence) and a deployment descriptor, which is `ejb-jar.xml`. Additionally, it will usually be necessary to have an application server–specific deployment descriptor.

These interfaces, classes, and descriptor will be covered in detail throughout the chapter; however, let us now take a quick cursory glance at what we have in store.

The Remote Interface

Listing 11-1 shows the `Remote` interface.

Listing 11-1. The `Remote` *Interface*

```
package com.apress.auction.entity.interfaces;

import javax.ejb.EJBObject;
import java.rmi.RemoteException;
import java.util.Collection;

public interface Customer
        extends EJBObject {

    public String getUserId() throws RemoteException;

    public String getName() throws RemoteException;
```

```
    public void setName(String name) throws RemoteException;

    public String getPassword() throws RemoteException;

    public void setPassword(String password) throws RemoteException;

    public String getEmail() throws RemoteException;

    public void setEmail(String email) throws RemoteException;

    public Collection getBids() throws RemoteException;

    public void setBids(Collection bids) throws RemoteException;

    public CustomerData getData() throws RemoteException;

    public void setData(CustomerData data) throws RemoteException;

    public String getOffers() throws RemoteException;

    public void setOffers(Collection offers) throws RemoteException;
}
```

A remote interface for entity beans as with session beans extends `javax.ejb.EJBObject`. In Listing 11-1, you can see accessors for all the fields and mutators except the primary key; it wouldn't make any sense to change the primary key for a given entity, because it's the primary key that gives it its identity. You must always consider the primary key class or field as immutable when working with entity beans.

Because this is a remote object, you also declare all the methods as being capable of throwing a `java.rmi.RemoteException`, which is standard practice for any remote method calls.

You can divide the methods shown into the following three categories:

- Field accessors/mutators (for example, `getName()`/`setEmail()`, which returns/sets entity field values).

- Relationship accessors/mutators (for example, `getBids()` or `setOffers()`, which returns/sets other entities).

- Business methods (in this case, the `getData()` method that provides you with a Value Object representation of the entity that can then be passed to other layers of the application directly). However, this could be a method such as the following:

  ```
  public double getHighestBidValue() throws RemoteException;
  ```

The Remote Home Interface

Listing 11-2 shows the RemoteHome interface.

Listing 11-2. The RemoteHome *Interface*

```
package com.apress.auction.entity.interfaces;

import javax.ejb.CreateException;
import javax.ejb.FinderException;
import javax.ejb.EJBHome;
import java.rmi.RemoteException;

public interface CustomerRemoteHome
                         extends EJBHome
{
   public Customer create(String userId,
String password,
String name,
String email)
      throws RemoteException,
             CreateException;

   public Customer findByPrimaryKey(String pk)
      throws RemoteException, FinderException;

}
```

The remote home interface in Listing 11-2 extends EJBHome and has a create method as you'd find in session beans. The difference is that with entity beans, as you'll see, the create method will also create a record in the underlying data store as well as creating an instance of the bean class.

Another difference is that you now also have a finder method, which locates an instance of an entity within the data store.

The Local Interface

Listing 11-3 shows the Local interface.

Listing 11-3. The Local *Interface*

```
package com.apress.auction.entity.interfaces;

import java.util.Collection;

public interface CustomerLocal
   extends javax.ejb.EJBLocalObject
{
   public String getUserId();
```

```
    public String getName();
    public void setName(String name);

    public String getPassword();
    public void setPassword(String password);

    public String getEmail();
    public void setEmail(String email);

    public Collection getBids();
    public void setBids(Collection bids);

    public CustomerData getData();
    public void setData(CustomerData data) ;

    public Collection getOffers() ;
    public void setOffers(Collection offers) ;
}
```

The local interface is the same as the remote interface except that it doesn't declare `java.rmi.RemoteException` on each method.

The Local Home Interface

Listing 11-4 shows the `LocalHome` interface.

Listing 11-4. The `LocalHome` *interface.*

```
package com.apress.auction.entity.interfaces;

import javax.ejb.CreateException;
import javax.ejb.FinderException;
import javax.ejb.EJBLocalHome;

public interface CustomerLocalHome
        extends EJBLocalHome {

    public CustomerLocal create(String userId,
                               String password,
                               String name,
                               String email)
                               throws CreateException;

    public CustomerLocal findByPrimaryKey(String pk)
            throws FinderException;

}
```

Again, the local home interface is the same as the remote home interface except that you no longer throw `java.rmi.RemoteException` on each method.

The Abstract Bean Class

All entity bean classes must implement `javax.ejb.EntityBean`, as shown in Listing 11-5.

Listing 11-5. `javax.ejb.EntityBean`

```
package javax.ejb;

import java.rmi.RemoteException;

public interface EntityBean extends EnterpriseBean
{
    void ejbActivate() throws EJBException, RemoteException;

    void ejbLoad() throws EJBException, RemoteException;

    void ejbPassivate() throws EJBException, RemoteException;

    void ejbRemove() throws RemoveException,
                            EJBException,
                            RemoteException;

    void ejbStore() throws EJBException, RemoteException;

    void unsetEntityContext() throws EJBException, RemoteException;

    void setEntityContext(EntityContext entityContext) throws
                                   EJBException, RemoteException;
}
```

To continue the example of the customer bean, the container-managed version will look something like Listing 11-6.

Listing 11-6. The CMP Version

```
package com.apress.auction.entity.ejb;

import com.apress.auction.entity.interfaces.CustomerData;

import javax.ejb.EntityContext;
import javax.ejb.CreateException;
import java.util.Collection;

public abstract class CustomerBean implements javax.ejb.EntityBean {
```

```
public abstract String getUserId();
public abstract void setUserId(String userId);

public abstract String getPassword();
public abstract void setPassword(String password);

public abstract String getName();
public abstract void setName(String name);

public abstract String getEmail();
public abstract void setEmail(String name);

public abstract Collection getBids();
public abstract void setBids(Collection bids);

public abstract Collection getOffers();
public abstract void setOffers(Collection offers);

public String ejbCreate(String userId, String password,
         String name, String email) throws CreateException {
   setUserId(userId);
   setPassword(password);
   setName(name);
   setEmail(email);
   return null;
}

public void ejbPostCreate(String userId, String password,
         String name, String email) throws CreateException {
}


 public void ejbLoad() {}

 public void ejbStore() {}

 public void ejbActivate() {}

 public void ejbPassivate() {}

 public void setEntityContext(EntityContext ctx) {
     this.context= ctx;
 }

 public void unsetEntityContext() {
     this.context= null;
 }

 public void ejbRemove() {}

// Business Methods
```

```
    public CustomerData getData()
    {
        ........
    }

    public void setData(CustomerData dataHolder)
    {
        ........
    }

}
```

The first thing to note about the entity bean class is that you're dealing with an abstract class. With CMP, you don't in fact supply the concrete class; the container will do this for you as part of the EJB compilation. The accessors for both the fields and relationships are also abstract; the container again provides these methods. Next, you find the lifecycle callback methods for creating, loading, storing, removing, passivating, and activating that are similar to the callback methods found in session beans. Finally, you have the set and unset methods for the `EntityContext`.

For an example of a bean-managed bean, please refer to the "Introducing Bean-Managed Persistence (BMP)" section later in this chapter.

The Deployment Descriptor

Listing 11-7 shows the deployment descriptor.

Listing 11-7. The Deployment Descriptor

```
<entity>
 <description>Customer Bean for our auction application.</description>
 <ejb-name>Customer</ejb-name>
 <local-home>com.apress.auction.entity.interfaces.CustomerLocalHome</local-home>
 <local>com.apress.auction.entity.interfaces.CustomerLocal</local>
 <ejb-class>com.apress.auction.entity.ejb.CustomerBean</ejb-class>
 <persistence-type>Container</persistence-type>
 <prim-key-class>java.lang.String</prim-key-class>
 <reentrant>false</reentrant>
 <cmp-version>2.x</cmp-version>
 <abstract-schema-name>Customer</abstract-schema-name>
 <cmp-field>
    <description>Returns the userId</description>
    <field-name>userId</field-name>
 </cmp-field>
 <cmp-field>
    <description>Returns the password</description>
    <field-name>password</field-name>
 </cmp-field>
```

```
  <cmp-field>
    <description>Returns the name</description>
    <field-name>name</field-name>
  </cmp-field>
  <cmp-field>
    <description>Returns the email</description>
    <field-name>email</field-name>
  </cmp-field>
  <primkey-field>userId</primkey-field>
</entity>
```

That was a sneak preview at the type of code that's required to produce an entity bean. In the rest of this chapter, we'll go through all the code that makes up entity beans, both container-managed and bean-managed varieties.

Lifecycle Methods

Figure 11-1 summarizes information about container callbacks for entity beans. In the *pooled state*, an entity instance is initialized, but it isn't associated with a particular identity. In other words, it doesn't have a particular primary key, and it doesn't represent the state of any particular row in the database. In this state, it can be only used for finder methods (which apply to entity beans in the aggregate) or for home business methods.

In the *ready state*, the instance is associated with a particular identity and can be used for business methods. The EJB container can create an instance of an entity bean and move it to the pooled or ready state at its discretion, calling `ejbLoad()` and `ejb-Store` according to the rules described later in the "Caching" section. In practice, an EJB container will move an entity to the ready state only when a client wants to use it, and it'll leave that entity in the ready state, move it to the pooled state, or destroy the bean depending on the caching strategy in place.

Home Interface

When a client calls `create()` for an entity bean, state data is inserted into the corresponding data store (such as a relational database). This is transactional data that's accessible from multiple clients. In contrast, when a client calls `create()` for a stateful session bean, the EJB container creates a private, nontransactional store of data in the application server's temporary storage. This difference is important to understand.

> **NOTE** *When you call* `create()` *on a session bean's home interface, you're creating an instance of that session bean, but when you call* `create()` *on an entity bean's home interface, you're actually inserting a record into the data store.*

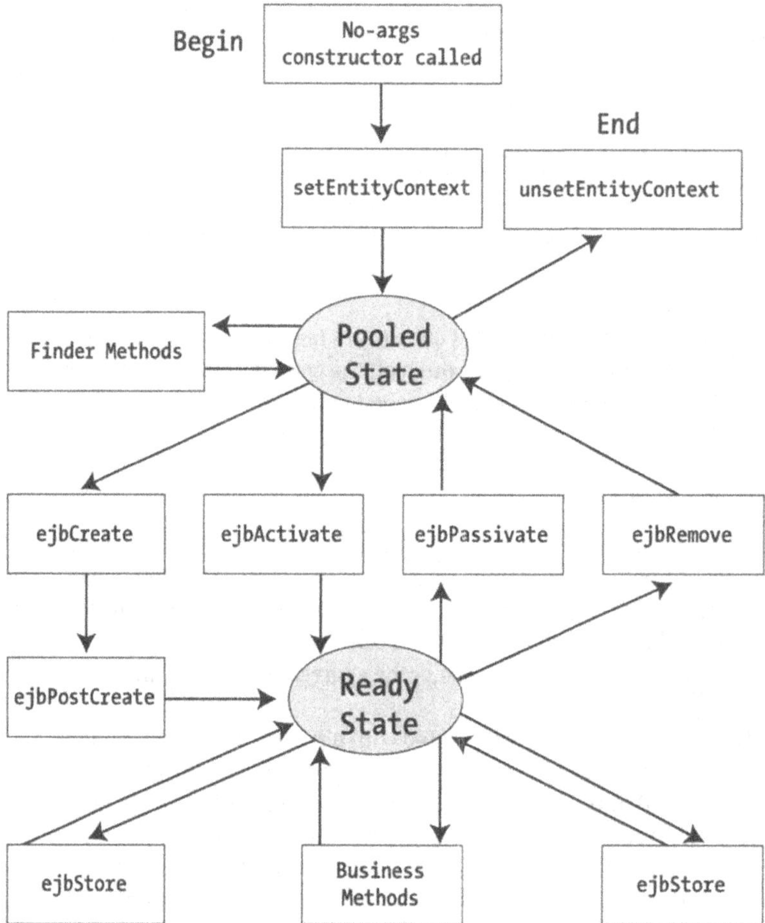

Figure 11-1. Entity bean life cycle

The `create()` method defined in the entity bean's home interface may be overloaded to provide several versions, and these `create()` methods may take different parameters, which correspond to the bean's state at the time of creation. The parameters must have enough information to at least initialize the primary key of the entity and any fields that are mapped to columns specified as `NOT NULL` in the database. All the `create()` methods must return the bean's remote interface, so when the client programmer calls `create()` on the home interface, they will have a reference to that bean on which business methods may be called.

All the `create()` methods must throw `java.rmi.RemoteException` because they can be remote methods. (This actually applies to all the methods on the remote interface.) They must also throw `javax.ejb.CreateException`, which indicates an application-level problem during the attempt at creation. (They can also throw user-defined exceptions.) Listing 11-8 shows an example of an application-level problem would be illegal parameters passed to `create()`.

Listing 11-8. Illegal Parameters

```
  public String ejbCreate(String userId,
                          String password,
                          String name,
                          String email)
                          throws javax.ejb.CreateException {
    setUserId(userId);
    setPassword(password);
    setName(name);
    setEmail(email);
    return null;
  }

public void ejbPostCreate( String userId, String password,
                          String name, String email )
                              throws javax.ejb.CreateException {
  }
```

The Abstract Bean Class

The two methods you write in the implementation class for each `create()` in the home interface must be named `ejbCreate()` and `ejbPostCreate()` and must have the same parameters in the same order as the home `create()` method. The methods must be declared `public` and must not be `final` or `static`. The return type of `ejbCreate()` is the primary key class of the entity bean, and the return type of `ejbPostCreate()` is `void`.

One point of confusion for many programmers is why an `ejbCreate()` and an `ejbPostCreate()` are both necessary. As a general rule, the bean programmer—for either BMP or CMP—will do all their work in `ejbCreate()`, leaving `ejbPostCreate()` empty. The fundamental reason that the `ejbPostCreate()` method exists is because the programmer is never allowed to pass `this` as a parameter to a remote method; they must always use the remote interface instead. The remote interface for the bean, however, isn't available until `ejbCreate()` returns. If they need the remote interface *during* the creation of the EJB component, they would have no way to proceed. Rather than leave this hole in the spec, an "after create" method was developed in which the remote interface would be available. This method is `ejbPostCreate()`.

The same situation exists with the primary key in CMP because the container creates the key. If the primary key is needed for some reason, that work also needs to be done in `ejbPostCreate()`. Why would you need to pass the EJB's remote reference or primary key to another EJB during its creation? A good reason is to set up relationships; for example, when you create the employee you want the boss to have a reference.

In a container-managed bean, the parameters passed in by the client will be used to initialize the entity bean's state. Although the return type of the `ejbCreate()` method is the same as the primary key, the bean developer should just return `null`. The container will ignore the returned value, regardless. The reason you should return `null` is that in the case of CMP the key will actually be created and initialized by the container based on the value of the fields you just initialized. You may wonder why `ejbCreate()` is returning a value at all. The reason is subtle; this way, you can create a BMP EJB class by extending a CMP EJB class. For this to work, the Java specification says that methods that need to be overridden in the child class must have the same return type; hence, you have this little trick.

In a bean-managed bean, the bean must insert its state into the underlying data store; for a relational database, this means the developer will write an `INSERT` statement in SQL. The bean developer should use the data to initialize the state variables of the bean, except in the unusual case that the BMP entity bean is storing its state directly in the database without using any instance variable intermediaries. Finally, the bean developer should construct an instance of its primary key and return it.

It is possible and sometimes appropriate to have an entity bean with no `create()` methods. An entity bean is just an object-oriented view on transactional shared data. In an environment with non-EJB applications, this data—and therefore, these entity beans—may exist without `create()` ever being called. If this data should be created *only* by these non-EJB applications, then the entity beans can be written without any `create()` methods. For instance, the customer records may be created exclusively by someone with a StarOffice spreadsheet linked to your database, with your EJB application being used to provide the online bidding facility for them in, say, an intranet environment. Because the EJB application is read-only, no `create()` methods would be required in this case.

The ejbLoad Method

The `ejbLoad()` callback method corresponds roughly to the read functionality of entity beans. A simple way to look at it is that the entity will load the data from the data store in correspondence to the container's `ejbLoad()` call. With CMP the EJB container will take care of transferring the entity's state from the data store to the entity's instance variables. In this case, the bean programmer will often leave the `ejbLoad()` method blank but may choose to do some postprocessing of the loaded data. With BMP, the bean programmer will write their data access code—probably Java Database Connectivity (JDBC) and Structured Query Language (SQL) code—in `ejbLoad()` to transfer the entity's state to instance variables.

This description is a good way to understand the process, but it's not the whole story. Technically, `ejbLoad()` doesn't tell the bean that it must actually load data; it just tells the bean that it must resynchronize its state with the underlying data store. This is a subtle but potentially important difference.

> **NOTE** *The bean's persistence implementation may choose to defer loading the state until that actual state is used.*

Consider this example: A customer entity bean may have a user ID, a customer name, password, and e-mail address, as well as a list of bids and offers. When `ejbLoad()` is called for an entity bean that represents a particular customer, the state of that order—

the ID, name, password, e-mail address, bids, and offers—must be synchronized with the database. In this example, the persistence logic may choose to update the ID, name, password, and e-mail address immediately from the database. Retrieving the list of bids and the lists of offers, though, is a potentially expensive operation, so a "dirty" flag is set instead. If the only method that is called on the customer bean is `getName()`, the bids and offers will never need to be loaded.

The ejbStore Method

The `ejbStore()` callback method corresponds roughly to the update functionality of entity beans. Of course, the actual modification of the entity bean's cached state will happen through calls to business methods, such as `setPassword()` or `setName()`. The container will call the `ejbStore()` method to notify the bean that it must synchronize its state with the database.

For a bean with container-managed persistence, this method will be called directly before the container writes the altered bean state to the database, and the programmer of a CMP bean may use this opportunity to preprocess the bean's data to ensure that it's in an appropriate state for persistent storage. Typically, however, this method will be left empty.

For a bean with bean-managed persistence, the programmer is responsible for providing in this method the logic that will transfer the bean's state to the underlying data store. For a relational database, this will typically mean that the bean programmer will write JDBC code and SQL `UPDATE` statements.

> **NOTE** *With* `ejbLoad()`, *the bean had the option to defer the actual loading of state until it was used.* `ejbStore()` *has no such option. Any modifications to the object's state must be written to the data store immediately. The equivalent optimization is something called* tuned updates. *In other words, only the modified state is written to the data store; if something hasn't changed, you can leave it alone.*

The remove Method

When a client calls `remove()` on an entity bean, data is deleted from the corresponding data store, which could be a row on an underlying database table. In contrast, when a client calls `remove()` for a stateful session bean, the EJB container discards the session bean instance in the application server's temporary storage. It's important to understand this difference. You should always call `remove()` when you're done using a stateful session bean; otherwise, the EJB container will waste resources managing this instance.

> **NOTE** *You should not call* `remove()` *on an entity bean unless you want to delete that record. The EJB container will manage the entity bean's instance in the container.*

For a CMP entity bean, the `ejbRemove()` method can usually be left empty, and the container will handle the deletion of the instance from the underlying data store. The programmer of an entity bean with container-managed persistence may use this method to implement any actions that must be done (such as updating related data or notifying other systems) before the entity object's representation is removed from the database. The following is the method for the customer bean with container-managed persistence.

```
public void ejbRemove()
```

For a BMP entity bean, the programmer is responsible for providing the logic that will remove the object from the underlying resource. For a relational database this will typically mean that the bean programmer will write JDBC code and SQL `DELETE` statements.

Activation and Passivation

Two of the callbacks for entity beans are `ejbActivate()` and `ejbPassivate()`. Session beans have these same callbacks, but they serve different purposes. Actually, for stateless session beans, they serve no purpose at all; they're there so that stateless and stateful session beans can implement the same interface. For stateful session beans, they indicate to the bean that it's about to be saved to or restored from secondary storage in order to help the EJB container manage its working set. Entity beans have no need to be saved to secondary storage; by definition, they already exist in persistent storage. If the container isn't using an entity bean, it doesn't need to worry about preserving its state before freeing its resources.

For entity beans, `ejbActivate()` provides a notification that the entity bean instance has been associated with an identity (a primary key) and its now ready for `ejbLoad()` to be called prior to business method invocation. A matching `ejbPassivate()` method will be called to notify the entity bean that it's being disassociated from a particular identity prior to reuse (with another identity or for finder methods), or perhaps prior to being dereferenced and made eligible for garbage collection.

The only case where the entity bean would care about the information provided by `ejbActivate()` and `ejbPassivate()` is if it were managing some resource that depended on a bean's identity. For example, you may need these callbacks to open and close database connections. Outside of this case, you can leave the implementation of these methods empty. An example of where the entity bean may need a resource associated with a particular identity is if it had a remote reference to a non-Java object whose state needed to be synchronized with the state of the entity bean, such as a business object in a proprietary application server belonging to a vendor of enterprise resource planning (ERP) systems.

If the resource needs to be associated with a particular identity, you must actually provide for initialization of that resource in both `ejbPostCreate()` and `ejbActivate()`, because the entity can become associated with an identity through either of these paths. Note that you need `ejbPostCreate()` rather than `ejbCreate()`, because `ejbPostCreate()` is where the identity becomes available. Similarly, you must use both `ejbPassivate()` and `ejbRemove()` for resource release.

It's also possible that the resource doesn't need to be associated with a particular identity, but just needs to be generally available to any identity. For instance, you may have a connection to a legacy ERP system that you can use to synchronize data for any object. You can use the `setEntityContext()` and `unsetEntityContext()` callback methods to allocate and deallocate the resource in this case.

So, for all the entities in this chapter, you'll be using the following:

```
public void ejbActivate() {}
public void ejbPassivate() {}
```

The Primary Key

Every entity bean has a primary key that represents a unique identity. This primary key must be represented by a primary key class, which the bean developer defines or specifies. In other words, this class contains the information necessary to find that entity in the persistent store. It's used internally by the EJB container and also by the client to find a particular instance of the entity. This class must abide by the following rules:

The primary key can be any legal value type in Remote Method Invocation/ Internet Inter-ORB Protocol (RMI-IIOP), which implies it must be serializable. Basically, you can use any Java object (as long as it's serializable) and also remote references. Types that don't make sense to be marshaled (such as Java interfaces) aren't legal RMI-IIOP types.

The EJB must also provide implementations of the `hashCode()` and `equals()` methods that respect the constraints explained in the documentation of `java.util.Hashtable`. For example, two identical objects must have a similar hash code, but two objects having the same hash code doesn't imply they're identical. For more details, please refer to the `Hashtable` (or `Collections`) application programming interface (API).

The primary key must have a unique value within the set of all beans of a particular type.

These are the only formal rules. Obviously, in practice the primary key class will have state fields that correspond to the values of the entity bean's primary key.

A few extra rules exist for a bean with container-managed persistence. The basic problem is that the container is responsible for managing the entity's creation, finding, loading, saving, and deletion. To do all these things, the container needs to be able to create a primary key, so the key class must have a no-arguments public constructor.

The container also needs to be able to map the bean's state to the state of the primary key class, and vice versa. So a few rules make this possible. The specification provides two methods for providing primary key classes for beans using CMP. One is a general case, good for primary keys with any number of fields; the other is a special case, for convenience in dealing with a primary key with one field.

The general case accomplishes the mapping using a naming convention; the public fields in the primary key class correspond to the equivalent public fields in the bean class.

Note that a primary key class must be immutable; once you've associated an entity bean with a primary key, you shouldn't reuse the same primary key object. This constraint is the same for Java containers in the `java.util.Collection` package; reusing the key you used to store an object in a `HashMap` will result in undefined behavior. When you do this, you're really changing the identity of the object, and the container has no way of knowing it.

Hence, abide by the following rule: Never provide setters in your primary key class. If you need a key with different values, create a new object.

Listing 11-9 shows an example of a primary key class for the customer bean. In this example, the customer bean will no longer be identified by an ID; instead, they will be identified by a combination of their e-mail address and name.

Listing 11-9. Primary Key Class

```
package com.apress.auction.entity.ejb;

public class CustomerKey implements java.io.Serializable {

   public String email;
   public String name;

   public CustomerKey() { };

   public CustomerKey(String email, String name) {
     this.email = email;
     this.name = name;
   }

   public String getEmail() {
      return email;
   }

   public String getName() {
      return name;
   }

   public boolean equals(Object other) {
      if (other instanceof CustomerKey) {
         return (email.equals(((CustomerKey)other).email)
                 && name.equals(((CustomerKey)other).name));
      }

      return false;
   }

   public int hashCode() {
      return email.hashCode();
   }
}
```

The fully qualified class of the primary key always has to be specified in the deployment descriptor for entity beans with bean-managed persistence. For example:

```
<prim-key-class> com.apress.auction.entity.ejb.CustomerKey</prim-key-class>
```

Or you can use the following:

```
<prim-key-class>java.lang.String</prim-key-class>
```

In the case of an entity bean with container-managed persistence that uses a simple type as its primary key, the bean developer specifies in the deployment descriptor the container-managed field of the entity bean that contains the primary key. The field's type must be the same as the primary key type. For example:

```
<primkey-field>bidId</primkey-field>
```

The EJB developer may want to use a synthetic key, such as an auto-incrementing key, as the primary key of their entity bean. Two possible strategies exist. The first is to generate the key using a session bean. This session bean may retrieve a block of keys from the database and distribute keys sequentially from this block to requesting entity beans. The second strategy is to depend on the database to automatically create the synthetic keys when the entity bean's state is inserted. If the entity bean uses container-managed persistence, the EJB container's object/relational-mapping tools must support this functionality for the target database.

The Finder Methods

Entity beans represent shared data. If this data is shared, there must be some mechanism for clients to get access to a particular entity bean. Notice that this problem doesn't come up for session beans; the client gets access to the bean when it's created, and no one else ever uses it. An entity bean, on the other hand, may be created by one client and used by any number of completely different clients (in this particular case, you'll have different instances of the EJB but they manipulate the same data in the database). Each of these clients must be able to find the bean for which they're looking.

As a solution for this problem, the EJB specification defines a mechanism called *finder methods*. One or more of these finder methods are declared in the entity bean's home interface, one for each way of locating that entity object or a collection of that type of entity object. These finder methods follow a certain naming convention: they all start with the prefix `find`.

Some examples are `findByNameOrDescription()`, `findLargestBidForCustomer()`, and `findBidsLargerThan()`. They can take any parameters that are necessary to specify the details of the search, as long as those parameters follow the normal rules of RMI/IIOP (the main rule, as mentioned before, is that they need to implement `java.io.Serializable`, be a primitive type, or be a remote interface).

Finder methods that will have at most one result will have a return type of the remote interface for that entity bean. For instance, the `findByNameOrDescription()` method defined on the `CustomerLocalHome` class has a return type of `Customer`. (The `findByPrimaryKey()` method in any entity bean is an example of this type of finder.) Finder methods that can have zero or more results will have a return type of either `java.util.Enumeration` or `java.util.Collection`. (The `findBidsLargerThan()` method is an example from the `BidLocalHome` interface.) If compatibility with JDK 1.1 is required, `Enumeration` must be chosen. Otherwise, it's probably better to a return a `Collection`, which provides a more flexible interface to the results.

In addition to the `java.rmi.RemoteException` thrown by all remote methods, every finder method must also declare that it throws the `javax.ejb.FinderException`. If a finder of that type that has zero or more results doesn't find any matching entities, the method will simply return an empty collection or an enumeration with zero elements.

Every entity bean must declare a certain "well-known" finder, named `findByPrimaryKey()`, that takes a single parameter of the same type as the entity's primary key class. This finder will either return the instance of the entity bean with that primary key or throw an `ObjectNotFoundException`. Additional finders beyond `findByPrimaryKey()` are optional. Some entities will have no other finders; others may have several.

Implementing Finder Methods

The implementation of the finding logic will be provided by the EJB container for beans with CMP, and the bean developer doesn't need to write supporting Java code of any sort. However, obviously not enough information exists in the finder's signature for the container to figure out the finder's intent and implement the logic. As you'll see in the section "Introducing Container-Managed Persistence (CMP)," EJB QL performs this task.

For entity beans with BMP, the EJB developer must provide a Java implementation of each finder's logic in the bean's implementation class. This method in the remote/local home interface is `findXXX()`, and the implementation of that finder method will be named `ejbFindXXX()` in the bean class. The return type for a finder method that has at most one result will be an instance of the primary key class for that entity, and the return type for a finder method implementation that has zero or more results will be either a concrete implementation of `Collection` or an `Enumeration`, depending on the return type of the corresponding finder method in the home interface. The items contained in the `Collection` or returned by the `Enumeration` will be instances of the primary key classes for the corresponding entities. Notice that the implementation of `findByPrimaryKey()` will take a primary key as a parameter, check to make sure the database record actually exists, and return that same primary key as the result if it does. Although the EJB container already has the primary key for this particular finder method, the EJB developer is asked to return it anyway so that its use is consistent with other finders that return at most one result.

You don't have any meaningful access to the state-related instance variables in the implementation of a finder method or any other identity-specific information. An entity bean that's used for a finder method won't be associated with a particular instance of state in the database. This is different from most other entity methods, such as the life-cycle methods and the business-logic methods. Although it must not be declared as static, you can think of it as having the same role as a static factory method in a non-EJB Java class.

The following example shows a typical finder; it's looking for an `Offer` whose name or description matches the text supplied (with wildcards). Listing 11-10 shows the entry to be placed in `ejb-jar.xml`.

Listing 11-10. `ejb-jar.xml` *Entry*

```
<query>
   <description></description>
   <query-method>
      <method-name>findByNameOrDescription</method-name>
      <method-params>
         <method-param>java.lang.String</method-param>
      </method-params>
   </query-method>
   <ejb-ql>SELECT DISTINCT OBJECT(o) FROM Offer AS o
       WHERE o.name like ?1 or o.description like ?1</ejb-ql>
</query>
```

The following is the addition to the local and/or remote home interface:

```
public String findByNameOrDescription(String searchText)
   throws javax.ejb.FinderException;
```

The Select Methods

Select methods in many ways are similar to finder methods; the essential differences are that they're local to the entity bean itself and that they can return results that aren't the EJB's `Local` or `Remote` interface. Basically, a select method allows you to perform fairly arbitrary `SELECT` statements on entity objects, returning any amount of any type of entities or any of their fields. With the addition in EJB 2.1 of aggregation functions such as `MIN()`, `MAX()`, and so on, the results of these functions are now also valid return values.

The following is an example of a query that can be used in a select method:

```
SELECT c.name FROM Customer AS c WHERE c.userId = ?1
```

This would translate into a method with the following signature on the abstract bean class:

```
public abstract String ejbSelectCustomerNameForId(String id)
        throws FinderException;
```

which would be defined within the deployment descriptor as the following:

```
<query>
    <query-method>
        <method-name>ejbSelectCustomerNameForId</method-name>
        <method-params>
            <method-param>java.lang.String</method-param>
        </method-params>
    </query-method>
    <ejb-ql>
        SELECT c.name FROM Customer AS c WHERE c.userId = ?1
    </ejb-ql>
</query>
```

Although the method is public on the abstract bean class, it won't be made available to the EJBs client and is only for the internal use of the bean class.

As with finder methods, you can also return a single `Remote` or `Local` interface; however, the default with select methods is to return the local interfaces. To override this behavior you'll need to either specify the `Remote` interface as the return type for single result queries or specify a `<result-type-mapping>` element within the `<query>` tags of your select method. The value of this element is, naturally, either `Remote` or `Local`.

If you want to return zero or more entities, then you may want to declare the method as returning either a `java.util.Set` or a `java.util.Collection`. A `Set` can contain only unique entries, and this also applies in the case of entities, therefore guaranteeing that you don't get duplicates returned by the method—a sort of implicit `SELECT DISTINCT`.

Introducing Container-Managed Persistence (CMP)

In your day-to-day usage of entity beans, it's likely you'll use CMP extensively. With CMP the container is responsible for most of the hard work you'd otherwise have to write yourself if you used BMP (for example, JDBC calls and SQL code). Services typically provided by the container include the following:

- Automatic conversion of `setXXX()` and `getXXX()` calls to SQL requests
- The selective loading of fields to avoid the unnecessary loading of data heavy fields for example images
- Conversion of object-based queries (EJB QL) to specific SQL requests

CMP Fields

A CMP entity bean is essentially defined by its CMP fields, which are Java fields that are mapped to tables in the database. The EJB 1.1 specification is vague in how these fields are supposed to be represented on the bean class. The EJB 2.1 specification implies that these CMP fields can be defined by abstract accessors instead of Java fields. For example, a CMP field called name would be declared as follows in an EJB 2.1 entity bean:

```
public abstract String getName();
public abstract void setName(String name);
```

> **NOTE** *In your database, you may not have a column named* name*; this is OK since it's only in the deployment descriptor that you specify how to map CMP fields.*

The most important point is that the container has total control of the access of fields. Since it will generate the code for each acccesor, it's able to make all kinds of decisions and optimizations on how to retrieve the data. The specification doesn't mandate any particular implementation, but the following are some benefits that EJB containers typically provide thanks to this design:

Lazy loading of beans: The container knows exactly when and what fields are being accessed; it doesn't have to load the entire state of the bean on `ejbLoad()`. It can decide to do nothing when the bean is initially fetched and decide to start loading the state on the first call of one of the getters. This can be especially important when your application starts and hundreds of beans are fetched in memory on startup.

Tuned updates: The container knows exactly what fields have been modified. Consequently, when the transaction commits, it's able to issue a "tuned update" to the database—a SQL request that will update only columns corresponding to fields modified during the transaction.

Container Manager Relationships (CMR)

A Java program typically manipulates graphs of objects, which are objects that contain objects that contain more objects. Obviously, when you use entity beans, you want the persistent store to reflect these complex relationships, but the task isn't very easy because relational databases store tables (rows and columns). Therefore, a certain amount of work is needed to map a graph of Java objects to tables.

EJB 1.1 doesn't specify anything in that area, so bean providers often resort to bean-managed persistence to store their Java objects. EJB 2.0 introduces the concept of container-managed relationships, which addresses this problem.

Briefly, all the bean providers have to do now is define the relationship between their beans in their deployment descriptors, and the EJB 2.0 container will generate all the Java code and SQL statements needed to persist and navigate the relations. Relationships can be either unidirectional (a customer having bids, but a bid not having a customer) or bidirectional (you can locate the customer from the bid as well as the bid from the customer), and they can be of the following three sorts:

- **One-to-one**: Customer and credit card
- **One-to-many**: Customer and their bids
- **Many-to-many**: Bids and offers

The container generates code that takes care of the following tasks:

- Maintaining referential integrity (if a person changes their address, the address bean should be destroyed as well)
- Handling addition and removal of beans from a many relationship and persisting the new state
- Enabling navigation through relationships by generating SQL statements that select the right fields

Implementation

One of the most common questions asked about entity beans is how to implement relationships between them. The good news is that relationships are an integral part of the EJB specification, which means the container will take care of all the low-level implementation details. The bad news is that you need to become familiar with a few more notions before you can fully exploit them.

The first thing you need to know is that beans can be connected with a CMR relationship only through their local interfaces. Therefore, you'll need to create a `Local` interface for each of these beans (a corollary to this rule is that beans connected by a relationship need to be in the same deployment unit—the same Java archive (JAR) or same enterprise archive (EAR) file. Creating a local interface to a bean is straightforward, and it involves the following steps:

1. Create a new interface that extends `javax.ejb.EJBLocalHome`. This class is similar to the remote home interface except that its methods aren't allowed to throw `RemoteException`.
2. Create a new interface that extends `javax.ejb.EJBLocalObjects`. This class is similar to the remote object interface except that its methods aren't allowed to throw `RemoteException`.

3. The local home interface can have the same methods as a remote home interface: create, finders, and so on. The only difference is that the objects it returns are `EJBLocalObjects`, not remote ones.

4. Add `<local-home>` and `<local>` elements to your `ejb-jar.xml` deployment descriptor, in place of `<home>` and `<remote>`. They must refer to the previous classes.

As well as these steps, you may have some additional deployment descriptors to modify depending on the application server you're using, such as giving a Java Naming and Directory Interface (JNDI) name to the local home interface, binding local references to EJBs, binding field names to database columns, and so on.

Now that you have local interfaces, your beans are allowed to participate in a relationship. Suppose you have two EJBs, `Customer` and `Bids`, and that a bid references a customer. You first need to figure out some characteristics of this relationship.

Cardinality

A relationship can be one-to-one, one-to-many, or many-to-many. In this case, the `Bid` to `Customer` relationship is many-to-one.

Direction

A relationship can be unidirectional or bidirectional. Then again, this is your decision. Obviously, when you have a `Bid`, you want to reach the `Customer`. Do you want the reverse to be true? In that case, the relationship will be bidirectional; otherwise, it'll be unidirectional. You'll opt for a bidirectional relationship.

CMR Fields

You need a field on the `Bid` EJB that will reference the customer. This field is called a CMR field. Call this field `customer`. Since the relationship is bidirectional, you also need a symmetric field on the `Customer` EJB (which you've called `bids`).

Now you have all the information you need to define the relationship in the `ejb-jar.xml` deployment descriptor. You should know one last detail before you see what it looks like: a relationship is defined by two roles, each role defining half of the relationship.

Listing 11-11 shows the CMR fields.

Listing 11-11. CMR Fields

```
<ejb-relation>
  <ejb-relation-name>CUSTOMER-BID</ejb-relation-name>

  <ejb-relationship-role>
    <ejb-relationship-role-name>BID-has-CUSTOMER</ejb-relationship-role-name>
```

```
        <multiplicity>Many</multiplicity>
        <cascade-delete/>
        <relationship-role-source>
          <ejb-name>Bid</ejb-name>
        </relationship-role-source>
        <cmr-field>
          <cmr-field-name>customer</cmr-field-name>
        </cmr-field>
      </ejb-relationship-role>

      <ejb-relationship-role>
        <ejb-relationship-role-name>CUSTOMER-has-BID</ejb-relationship-role-name>
         <multiplicity>One</multiplicity>
         <relationship-role-source>
            <ejb-name>Customer</ejb-name>
         </relationship-role-source>
         <cmr-field>
            <cmr-field-name>bids</cmr-field-name>
            <cmr-field-type>java.util.Collection</cmr-field-type>
         </cmr-field>
       </ejb-relationship-role>

    </ejb-relation>
```

Finally, you need to add the CMR methods to the abstract bean:

```
public abstract String getBids();
public abstract void setBids(String bids);
```

EJB Query Language (EJB QL)

EJB QL closely resembles a subset of SQL, and the designers of EJB QL have certainly made great efforts to keep it as close to possible to SQL. An example of this is the use of OBJECT(), which you'll see shortly. It's redundant as far as EJB QL is concerned but exists to maintain compatibility with the new SQL specification.

EJB QL is used in the ejbFindXXX() and the ejbSelectXXX() methods; therefore, the subset of SQL it emulates is that of the SELECT statement. In EJB 2.0 EJB QL supported SELECT, FROM, and WHERE. A very welcome addition in EJB 2.1/J2EE 1.4 is ORDER BY, which replaces the manual sorting of data retrieved by a finder or ejbSelect(). Since the ORDER BY request is made in EJB QL, the container is now free to optimize the ordering process that may be implemented by the database or other persistence mechanism directly. The From ClauseStarting at the beginning, the simplest EJB QL statement is the retrieval of all the customers from the customer database:

```
SELECT OBJECT(c) FROM Customer AS c
```

This would be equivalent to the SQL statement `SELECT * FROM CUSTOMER` if your `Customer` entity beans were to map directly to the `CUSTOMER` table. The resemblance to SQL is now quite obvious. However, you also can see immediately some differences; you don't refer directly to tables on the database. Instead, you refer to the abstract schema names of the entity beans. The abstract schema name is that which is defined in the `ejb-jar.xml` file. For example:

```
<abstract-schema-name>Customer</abstract-schema-name>
```

You have the slightly different `FROM` clause that uses the `AS` keyword; this is in fact optional but useful for clarity at this point. The `AS` clauses define *identification variables*. In the previous example, the identification variable is `c`. Unlike SQL, such variables are defined only in the `FROM` clause of EJB QL. Also, you have the additional keyword `OBJECT`; this keyword must precede stand-alone identification variables, but it can't precede a single-valued path expression. If an identification variable is part of a single-valued path expression, it's not stand-alone.

The previous example is perfectly acceptable for use as either a finder method (the `ejbFindByXXX()` methods) or a select method (the `ejbSelectXXX` methods) for a `Customer` entity bean. However, naturally, you couldn't apply this query to the `Bid` entity bean since you wouldn't expect to get `Bids` from a finder for `Customers`! This sensible restriction doesn't apply to select methods since they're for the private use of the EJB itself; they can return arbitrary EJB abstract schemas.

Avoiding Duplicates

By the simple addition of the `DISTINCT` keyword, you can now eliminate duplicates from being returned:

```
SELECT DISTINCT OBJECT (c) FROM Customer AS c
```

As you'd imagine, the `DISTINCT` keyword behaves the same as its SQL equivalent. The `DISTINCT` keyword, however, is relevant only if you've specified that your finder (`ejbFindByXXX()`) or your select method (`ejbSelectXXXX()`) returns `java.util.Collection`. Collections can have duplicate values, which you may want to eliminate with this keyword; however, if your methods return `java.util.Set`, then the `DISTINCT` keyword would be redundant, as sets may not have duplicate values anyway.

The Where Clause

It's unlikely that you're always going to want all the entities in a collection for your finder methods; in many cases, your finder methods may simply want to restrict records by a single field, for example, `ejbFindByUserId(String userId)`. The EJB QL for this would be as follows:

```
SELECT DISTINCT OBJECT (c) FROM Customer AS c WHERE c.userId = ?1
```

In the previous expression, you've used an input parameter ?1. Input parameters mirror the parameters passed to the finder or select method. So in the previous example, ?1 is equivalent to the userId parameter in the ejbFindByUserId(String userId) method. The expression c.userId specifies the userId attribute of the Customer entity bean and must be equal to the userId parameter.

Now we've also introduced the WHERE clause; again, as you'd expect, the WHERE clause is similar to its SQL equivalent. You're able to use a variety of expressions in your attempts to restrict the entities returned. You have access to the following basic operators:

- **Object navigation**: The . operator
- **Basic arithmetic**: +, -, *, and /
- **Comparison**: =, < >, >, <, >=, and <=
- **Logical**: AND, OR, and NOT

To make life a little easier, Sun has kindly provided a few more SQL style expressions: BETWEEN, IN, LIKE, IS NULL, NULL.

Now you requesting Offer entities that have an askPrice attribute between the first and second parameter supplied to a method:

```
SELECT  DISTINCT OBJECT (o) FROM Offer AS o WHERE o.askPrice BETWEEN ?1 AND ?2
```

A typical method signature would be ejbFindOffersInRange(Double min, Double max). You also have a converse example of this:

```
SELECT  DISTINCT OBJECT (o) FROM Offer AS o
     WHERE o.askPrice NOT BETWEEN ?1 AND ?2
```

This would return all the Offer entities that have an askPrice attribute that isn't between the first and second parameter supplied to the method and would therefore apply to a method such as ejbFindOffersNotInRange(Double min, Double max).

Should you want to make sure your customers haven't used any obvious passwords, you could, for example, find all the customers with obvious passwords and email them a warning that they may want to make their password more secure, like so:

```
SELECT DISTINCT OBJECT(c) FROM Customer AS c WHERE
       c.password IN
{'','password','PASSWORD','Password','mum','dad'}
```

Note the SQL style use of single quotes to delimit your string literals rather than the Java double quotes.

So your method would probably be something such as `ejbFindBadPasswords()`; of course, you may want to pass the list of bad passwords into the method and you'd specify the EJB QL as so:

```
SELECT DISTINCT OBJECT(c) FROM Customer AS c WHERE c.password IN {?1}
```

String Comparison

For direct string equivalence in EJB QL, you can use the = operator. But for pattern matching you have the more flexible `LIKE` operator. This operator provides two wildcard symbols `%`, which will match any number of characters, and `_`, which will match any one character. So the following are true:

- `'A' LIKE '_'`
- `'A' NOT LIKE 'A_'`
- `'A' LIKE 'A%'`
- `'Alf' LIKE 'A%'`
- `'Alf' LIKE 'A%f'`

If you need to use the `_` or `%` character without it having its wildcard meaning, then you need some way of specifying an escape character. For this you have the `ESCAPE` option in the `LIKE` expression, so the following will also hold true:

- `'A_' LIKE 'A\_' ESCAPE '\'`
- `'AB' NOT LIKE 'A\_' ESCAPE '\'`

Working with Relationships

In the world of entity beans, much like in our day-to-day lives, an entity can do little without its relationships. In fact, the true power of CMP becomes visible when you add these CMRs into your EJB QL.

If you'd like to find the address of a customer who you have a name for, then you could create a finder method for your `Address` entity called `ejbFindCustomersAddress(String customerName)`, like so:

```
SELECT c.address FROM Customer AS c WHERE c.name = ?1
```

Notice that you no longer require the `OBJECT()` around the return value as this is required for stand-alone identification variables; instead, you now have the path expression `c.address`. The path expression `c.address` specifies that you'd like the `Address` entity that the `Customer` has a CMR relationship with and that's accessed from the `Customer` entity via the CMR accessor `Address getAddress()`.

The equivalent Java would look something like this:

```
Customer customer= CustomerLocalHome.findByName(name);
Address customersAddress= customer.getAddress();
```

It's possible to have arbitrary length path expressions that allow you to access any related entity from any other related entity.

The relationships can also return collections in which case you may have an EJB QL expression to return the bids made by your `Customer`:

```
SELECT c.bids FROM Customer AS c WHERE c.name= ?1
```

This method could be a finder on the `Bids` entity called `ejbFindBidsForCustomer(String customerName)`. You may then want to identify the `Customers` with no bids outstanding, in which case you'd have the following:

```
SELECT OBJECT(c) FROM Customer AS c WHERE c.bids IS EMPTY
```

And, conversely, you may want to obtain all the `Customers` that have bids:

```
SELECT OBJECT(c) FROM Customer AS c WHERE c.bids IS NOT EMPTY
```

Finally, EJB QL also provides the ability to detect whether an entity is a member of a collection. So, if you want to find out which `Customers` a bid belongs to, you could potentially use a finder method `ejbFindCustomersForBid(Bid bid)`, like so:

```
SELECT OBJECT(c) FROM Customer AS c WHERE ?1 MEMBER OF c.bids
```

Although in reality you'd probably establish a bidirectional relationship between the bids and the customers. Of course, you also have the negative form so you can find those customers who haven't made the particular bid, like so:

```
SELECT OBJECT(c) FROM Customer AS c WHERE ?1 NOT MEMBER OF c.bids
```

Simple Functions

EJB QL provides you with a limited set of functions that you can use in your queries; the latest addition is `MOD`, which wasn't available in the EJB 2.0 specification. Table 11-1 describes the functions available, four string functions and three numeric functions.

Table 11-1. Simple Functions

FUNCTION	DESCRIPTION
`CONCAT(String a, String b)`	Concatenates two `String`s and produces a `String` as the result.
`SUBSTRING(String text, int start, int length)`	Returns the substring of text starting at character startup but not including the character at `start+length`. `NB` the first character in the `String` has an index of `1`.
`LOCATE(String substring, String string[, int offset])`	Attempts to locate the substring within a `String` with an optional offset (the EJB specification warns that this offset may not be compatible across containers and databases and therefore recommends avoiding its usage).
`LENGTH(String string)`	Returns the length of the `String` supplied.
`ABS(int/float/double number)`	Returns the absolute value of number as the same type as the argument.
`SQRT(double number)`	Returns the square root of the number supplied.
`MOD(int number, int divider)`	Returns the remainder from dividing number by divider.

The Aggregation Functions

In EJB 2.1 you now have a set of aggregation functions from SQL; they are `AVG`, `MIN`, `MAX`, `SUM`, and `COUNT`. Because these functions return a nonentity value, they can't be used in finder methods. However, you may want to have select methods that use them so you could find out the average bid a customer has made, like so:

```
SELECT AVG(bids) FROM Customer AS c, IN(c.bids) AS bids
```

You could find the minimum and maximum bids, like so:

```
SELECT MIN(bids) FROM Customer AS c, IN(c.bids) AS bids
SELECT MAX(bids) FROM Customer AS c, IN(c.bids) AS bids
```

You could find the total amount of all their bids, like so:

```
SELECT SUM(bids) FROM Customer AS c, IN(c.bids) AS bids
```

Or you could find how many bids they've made:

```
SELECT COUNT(bids) FROM Customer AS c, IN(c.bids) AS bids
```

> **NOTE** COUNT *accepts an identification variable (in this example,* c*), a single-valued CMR field (in other words, one that doesn't return a collection), or a CMP path expression, but all the other functions can take CMP only fields.*

The ORDER BY Clause

A painfully missing feature of EJB 2.0 was the lack of any ability to sort the returned EJBs, which resulted in superfluous sorting code being applied to the result of finders. Databases are fantastic at sorting data; after all, this is one of their main features, so obviously encouraging developers to do the sorting in the middle tier can lead to a grotesque waste of server resource. Fortunately, you now have this clause in CMP 2.1, and it will accept a list of persistent and orderable CMP fields; as long as the SELECT clause specifies an identification variable, a single-valued CMR expression, or a CMP expression.

So you can now get all the Customers sorted by their names, like so:

```
SELECT OBJECT(c) FROM Customer AS c ORDER BY c.name
```

Of course, you could sort by their credit card number, like so:

```
SELECT OBJECT(c) FROM Customer AS c ORDER BY c.creditCard.number
```

Note that if you're writing a select method that returns a CMP field, then it must be the same field specified in the ORDER BY. Therefore, the following is valid:

```
SELECT c.name FROM Customer AS c ORDER BY c.name
```

But this isn't valid:

```
SELECT c.name FROM Customer AS c ORDER BY c.creditCard.number
```

EJB QL in the Deployment Descriptor

To specify a finder query in the ejb-jar.xml file, you'll need to insert the following between the <entity> tags:

```
<query>
   <description></description>
   <query-method>
      <method-name>findByNameOrDescription</method-name>
      <method-params>
         <method-param>java.lang.String</method-param>
      </method-params>
   </query-method>
   <ejb-ql>SELECT DISTINCT OBJECT(o) FROM Offer AS o
      WHERE o.name like ?1 or o.description like ?1</ejb-ql>
</query>
```

These should be added for each query; remember, you don't need to write one for the primary key finder `ejbFindByPrimaryKey()`, which is defined by default. If the query contains characters that have special meanings in XML (for example, < or >), then you'll need to enclose the query in a CDATA section. CDATA sections alert the XML parser to not translate the contents but instead to accept them literally. For example:

```
<ejb-ql>
        <![CDATA[
        SELECT OBJECT(b) FROM Bids b WHERE b.bidPrice> ?1
       ]]>
 </ejb-ql>
```

What's Missing?

Sometimes it's just as valuable to look at what you can't do as to what you can do. In EJB QL there's a lot you can't do. But the following are omissions that may trip you up:

- **Date/time**: Date/time objects aren't valid in EJB QL comparisons; instead, you must use their `long` values.

- **Inheritance**: CMP 2.1 (and therefore EJB QL) doesn't support entity inheritance. The lack of inheritance support in EJBs is arguably one of their weakest characteristics. A noticeable failure, in fact, of many J2EE technologies is the loss of object-oriented features and the benefit those features bring.

- **Comparison of different entities**: An entity may be compared only with another entity of the same type.

Introducing Bean-Managed Persistence (BMP)

The purpose of bean-managed persistence is to allow the developer to define the persistence mechanism for some or all of their entity beans. In older versions of the EJB specification, entity beans could deal only with the simplest operations and therefore encouraged developers to work with BMP to provide their only persistence mechanisms. With the advent of CMP 2.1 it's much less likely that a developer would use BMP for database persistence. However, this doesn't render BMP redundant; you may want to persist your entity bean to a legacy system, in which case you'd use BMP to provide the persistence logic using a Java Connector Architecture (JCA) resource adapter.

Database Connection

In all the following examples, you'll use the method `getConnection()`, which deserves a short explanation. This method provides a database connection by referencing a data source from a JNDI context. The JNDI context used is the environment naming context (ENC). This context is available through the `<resource-ref>` entries in the `ejb-jar.xml`.

In the getConnection() method, you have a data source referenced by java:comp/env/jdbc/myDB, as in the following example:

```
<resource-ref>
    <description>Our data-source from the container.</description>
    <res-ref-name>jdbc/myDB</res-ref-name>
    <res-type>javax.sql.DataSource</res-type>
    <res-auth>Container</res-auth>
</resource-ref>
```

The mapping of the res-ref-name to an actual data source is vendor specific. Note that the res-ref-name is the JNDI name minus the java:comp/env part.

To get a connection, now all that is required is the following simple JNDI lookup:

```
private Connection getConnection() throws SQLException {
          try {
              Context context= new InitialContext();
              DataSource ds= (DataSource)context.lookup("java:comp/env/jdbc/myDB");
              return ds.getConnection();
          } catch (NamingException e) {
              throw new EJBException(e);
          }
      }
```

Lifecycle Methods

As mentioned earlier, the lifecycle methods for BMP are radically different from those for CMP. In each of the four CRUD methods (create, read, update, delete), you need to implement the actual data retrieval code yourself. In the case of the auction example, this would be directly executing queries against the database.

The Create Method

You'll start with ejbCreate(); here you're trying to construct a single bid with the id and price supplied. First, since ejbCreate() is similar to a constructor, you first set the member variables to the values supplied. Next, you simply open a connection using your utility method getConnection(). Then, using a prepared statement, you insert a row into the database containing your values. Don't forget to make sure that connection is closed! Once the row has been successfully added, you can now return the primary key for the class (instead of null as you do for CMP) to the container. Listing 11-12 shows the create method.

Listing 11-12. `ejbCreate()`

```
public String ejbCreate(String bidId, BigDecimal bidPrice) throws
                                                    CreateException {
    this.id = bidId;
    this.price = bidPrice;
    Connection con = null;
    PreparedStatement prepStmt = null;
    try {

        con = this.getConnection();
        String insertStatement =
                "insert into bids values (? , ?)";
        prepStmt = con.prepareStatement(insertStatement);

        prepStmt.setString(1, bidId);
        prepStmt.setBigDecimal(2, bidPrice);

        prepStmt.executeUpdate();
    } catch (SQLException e) {
        throw new EJBException(e);
    } finally {
        if (prepStmt != null) {
            try {
                prepStmt.close();
            } catch (SQLException e) { }
        }
        if (con != null) {
            try {
                con.close();
            } catch (SQLException e) { }
        }
    }
    return bidId;
}
```

It's really as straightforward as that.

The ejbLoad Method

The role of `ejbLoad()` in bean-managed persistence is to notify the bean that it must invalidate the current cached state and prepare for business method invocations. In practical terms, this usually means replacing the state by loading it from the database.

To find the entity bean's data in the database, you'll need the primary key. By the time that `ejbLoad()` is called, the primary key has been associated with the entity and is available from its context. This entity context is associated with the bean by a callback method, just as the session context is associated with a session bean. Listing 11-13 shows the `EntityContext` interface.

Listing 11-13. `EntityContext`

```
package javax.ejb;

public interface EntityContext extends EJBContext
{
    Object getPrimaryKey() throws IllegalStateException;

    EJBLocalObject getEJBLocalObject() throws IllegalStateException;

    EJBObject getEJBObject() throws IllegalStateException;
}
```

A bean that uses bean-managed persistence needs to use the entity context to retrieve its associated primary key in the implementation of `ejbLoad()`, using the `setEntityContext()/unsetEntityContext()` pair of callbacks when they're invoked by the container to save the entity context for use. For example:

```
public void setEntityContext(EntityContext ctx) {
    this.context = ctx;
}

public void unsetEntityContext() {
    this.context = null;
}
```

So now you have the primary key, you can retrieve the row associated with it, as shown in Listing 11-14.

Listing 11-14. Retrieving the Primary Key Row

```
public void ejbLoad() {
     Connection con = null;
     PreparedStatement prepStmt = null;
     try {
         String pk = (String) context.getPrimaryKey();
         con = this.getConnection();
         String selectStatement =
                 "select price " +
                 "from bids where bidId = ? ";
         prepStmt =
                 con.prepareStatement(selectStatement);
```

```
        prepStmt.setString(1, pk);

        ResultSet rs = prepStmt.executeQuery();

        if (rs.next()) {
            price = rs.getBigDecimal(1);
        } else {
            throw new NoSuchEntityException("Row for bidId " + pk +
                    " not found in database.");
        }
    } catch (SQLException e) {
        throw new EJBException(e);
    } finally {
        if (rs != null) {
            try {
                rs.close();
            } catch (SQLException e) { }
        }
        if (prepStmt != null) {
            try {
                prepStmt.close();
            } catch (SQLException e) { }
        }
        if (con != null) {
            try {
                con.close();
            } catch (SQLException e) { }
        }
    }
}
```

The ejbStore Method

The `ejbStore()` method doesn't add any further complexity to the bean-managed EJB. You don't require the use of the entity context to obtain the primary key because you already have the primary key as an instance variable (`id` in the example). So, Listing 11-15 shows the store method.

Listing 11-15. `ejbStore()`

```
public void ejbStore() {
  Connection con = null;
  PreparedStatement prepStmt = null;
  try {
      con = this.getConnection();
      String updateStatement =
              "update bids set bidPrice =  ? , " +
              "where bidId = ?";
      prepStmt = con.prepareStatement(updateStatement);
```

```
            prepStmt.setBigDecimal(1, price);
            prepStmt.setString(2, id);
            int rowCount = prepStmt.executeUpdate();

            if (rowCount == 0) {
                throw new EJBException("Storing row for bidId " +
                        id + " failed.");
            }
        } catch (SQLException e) {
            throw new EJBException(e);
        } finally {
            if (prepStmt != null) {
                try {
                    prepStmt.close();
                } catch (SQLException e) { }
            }
            if (con != null) {
                try {
                    con.close();
                } catch (SQLException e) { }
            }
        }
    }
```

The Remove Method

Finally, Listing 11-16 shows the ejbRemove() method.

Listing 11-16. ejbRemove()

```
public void ejbRemove() {
    Connection con = null;
    PreparedStatement prepStmt = null;
    try {

        con = this.getConnection();
        String deleteStatement =
                "delete from bids where bidId = ? ";
        prepStmt = con.prepareStatement(deleteStatement);
        prepStmt.setString(1, id);
        prepStmt.executeUpdate();

    } catch (SQLException e) {
        throw new EJBException(e);
    } finally {
        if (prepStmt != null) {
            try {
                prepStmt.close();
            } catch (SQLException e) { }
        }
```

```
        if (con != null) {
            try {
                con.close();
            } catch (SQLException e) { }
        }
    }
}
```

Exceptions

With bean-managed persistence, exception handling is quite important. Your bean should throw the following three types of exceptions:

- **Application exceptions**: These are the custom business logic exceptions of your system; these are unlikely to be thrown by the lifecycle, finders, or accessor methods, but may be thrown by other business methods or your bean.
- **Framework exceptions**: These are `CreateException`, `FinderException`, `RemoveException`, `DuplicateKeyException`, and `ObjectNotFoundException`. These are the EJB framework exceptions thrown by bean-managed entity beans.
- **Runtime exceptions**: If any serious error occurs in the entity bean directly or through a subsystem such as JDBC, then you'll need to catch the exception and rethrow it as an unchecked `EJBException`.

Finder Methods

Unlike container-managed persistence, with bean-managed persistence you must write an explicit `ejbFindByPrimaryKey()` method. Usually this method will simply establish that the record exists and will then return the primary key parameter if it does or throw an `ObjectNotFoundException` otherwise. Listing 11-17 shows the finder methods.

Listing 11-17. Finder Method

```
public String ejbFindByPrimaryKey(String bidId) throws FinderException {
    boolean found = false;
    Connection con = null;
    PreparedStatement prepStmt = null;
    ResultSet rs = null;
    try {
        con = this.getConnection();
        String selectStatement =
                "select bidId, " +
                "from bids where bidId = ? ";
        prepStmt = con.prepareStatement(selectStatement);
        prepStmt.setString(1, bidId);
```

```
            rs = prepStmt.executeQuery();
            found = rs.next();
        } catch (SQLException e) {
            throw new EJBException(e);
        } finally {
            if (rs != null) {
                try {
                    rs.close();
                } catch (SQLException e) { }
            }
            if (prepStmt != null) {
                try {
                    prepStmt.close();
                } catch (SQLException e) { }
            }
            if (con != null) {
                try {
                    con.close();
                } catch (SQLException e) { }
            }
        }

        if (found) {
            return bidId;
        } else {
            throw new ObjectNotFoundException("No bid with the id '" +
                    bidId + "' could be found.");
        }
    }
```

Listing 11-18 shows an example of a finder implementation that has zero or more results and returns a collection.

Listing 11-18. Finder Implementation

```
public Collection ejbFindBidsInRange(BigDecimal min, BigDecimal max)
                                              throws FinderException {
    Connection con = null;
    PreparedStatement prepStmt = null;
    ResultSet rs = null;
    ArrayList results = new ArrayList();
    try {
        con = this.getConnection();
        String selectStatement =
                "select bidId " +
                "from bids where bidId between ?1 and ?2 ";
        prepStmt =
                con.prepareStatement(selectStatement);

        prepStmt.setBigDecimal(1, min);
        prepStmt.setBigDecimal(2, max);
```

```
        rs = prepStmt.executeQuery();

        while (rs.next()) {
            String pk = rs.getString("bidId");
            results.add(pk);
        }
    } catch (SQLException e) {
        throw new EJBException(e);
    } finally {
        if (rs != null) {
            try {
                rs.close();
            } catch (SQLException e) { }
        }
        if (prepStmt != null) {
            try {
                prepStmt.close();
            } catch (SQLException e) { }
        }
        if (con != null) {
            try {
                con.close();
            } catch (SQLException e) { }
        }
    }
    return results;
}
```

Don't forget to add entries for these finders in your home interface:

```
Bid findByPrimaryKey(String bidId)
        throws RemoteException, FinderException;
Collection findBidsInRange(BigDecimal min, BigDecimal max)
        throws RemoteException, FinderException;
```

The Complete Bean

For your convenience Listing 11-19 shows the complete BMP entity bean.

Listing 11-19. BMP Entity Bean

```
package com.apress.auction.entity.ejb;


import javax.ejb.*;
import javax.naming.Context;
import javax.naming.InitialContext;
import javax.naming.NamingException;
import javax.sql.DataSource;
```

```
import java.math.BigDecimal;
import java.sql.Connection;
import java.sql.PreparedStatement;
import java.sql.ResultSet;
import java.sql.SQLException;
import java.util.ArrayList;
import java.util.Collection;

public class BidBMPBean {
    public String id;
    public BigDecimal price;
    private EntityContext context;

    public String ejbCreate(String bidId, BigDecimal bidPrice)
      throws CreateException {
        this.id = bidId;
        this.price = bidPrice;
        Connection con = null;
        PreparedStatement prepStmt = null;
        try {
            con = this.getConnection();
            String insertStatement =
                    "insert into bids values (? , ?)";
            prepStmt = con.prepareStatement(insertStatement);
            prepStmt.setString(1, bidId);
            prepStmt.setBigDecimal(2, bidPrice);
            prepStmt.executeUpdate();
        } catch (SQLException e) {
            throw new EJBException(e);
        } finally {
            if (prepStmt != null) {
                try {
                    prepStmt.close();
                } catch (SQLException e) { }
            }
            if (con != null) {
                try {
                    con.close();
                } catch (SQLException e) { }
            }
        }
        return bidId;
    }


    public void ejbPostCreate(String bidId, BigDecimal bidPrice)
      throws CreateException {
        // Make use of the primary key.....
    }

    public void ejbLoad() {
```

```
        Connection con = null;
        PreparedStatement prepStmt = null;
        try {
            String pk = (String) context.getPrimaryKey();
            con = this.getConnection();
            String selectStatement =
                    "select price " +
                    "from bids where bidId = ? ";
            prepStmt =
                    con.prepareStatement(selectStatement);
            prepStmt.setString(1, pk);
            ResultSet rs = prepStmt.executeQuery();
            if (rs.next()) {
                price = rs.getBigDecimal(1);
            } else {
                throw new NoSuchEntityException("Row for bidId " + pk +
                        " not found in database.");
            }
        } catch (SQLException e) {
            throw new EJBException(e);
        } finally {
            if (rs != null) {
                try {
                    rs.close();
                } catch (SQLException e) { }
            }
            if (prepStmt != null) {
                try {
                    prepStmt.close();
                } catch (SQLException e) { }
            }
            if (con != null) {
                try {
                    con.close();
                } catch (SQLException e) { }
            }
        }
    }

    public void ejbStore() {
        Connection con = null;
        PreparedStatement prepStmt = null;
        try {
            con = this.getConnection();
            String updateStatement =
                    "update bids set bidPrice =  ? , " +
                    "where bidId = ?";
            prepStmt = con.prepareStatement(updateStatement);
            prepStmt.setBigDecimal(1, price);
            prepStmt.setString(2, id);
            int rowCount = prepStmt.executeUpdate();
```

```
            if (rowCount == 0) {
                throw new EJBException("Storing row for bidId " +
                        id + " failed.");
            }
        } catch (SQLException e) {
            throw new EJBException(e);
        } finally {
            if (prepStmt != null) {
                try {
                    prepStmt.close();
                } catch (SQLException e) { }
            }
            if (con != null) {
                try {
                    con.close();
                } catch (SQLException e) { }
            }
        }
    }

    public void ejbRemove() {
        Connection con = null;
        PreparedStatement prepStmt = null;
        try {
            con = this.getConnection();
            String deleteStatement =
                    "delete from bids where bidId = ? ";
            prepStmt = con.prepareStatement(deleteStatement);
            prepStmt.setString(1, id);
            prepStmt.executeUpdate();
        } catch (SQLException e) {
            throw new EJBException(e);
        } finally {
            if (prepStmt != null) {
                try {
                    prepStmt.close();
                } catch (SQLException e) { }
            }
            if (con != null) {
                try {
                    con.close();
                } catch (SQLException e) { }
            }
        }
    }


    public String ejbFindByPrimaryKey(String bidId) throws FinderException {
        boolean found = false;
        Connection con = null;
        PreparedStatement prepStmt = null;
```

```
    ResultSet rs = null;
    try {
        con = this.getConnection();
        String selectStatement =
                "select bidId, " +
                "from bids where bidId = ? ";
        prepStmt = con.prepareStatement(selectStatement);
        prepStmt.setString(1, bidId);

        rs = prepStmt.executeQuery();
        found = rs.next();
    } catch (SQLException e) {
        throw new EJBException(e);
    } finally {
        if (rs != null) {
            try {
                rs.close();
            } catch (SQLException e) { }
        }
        if (prepStmt != null) {
            try {
                prepStmt.close();
            } catch (SQLException e) { }
        }
        if (con != null) {
            try {
                con.close();
            } catch (SQLException e) { }
        }
    }

    if (found) {
        return bidId;
    } else {
        throw new ObjectNotFoundException("No bid with the id '" +
                bidId + "' could be found.");
    }
}

public Collection ejbFindBidsInRange(BigDecimal min, BigDecimal max)
        throws FinderException {
    Connection con = null;
    PreparedStatement prepStmt = null;
    ResultSet rs = null;
        ArrayList results = new ArrayList();
    try {
        con = this.getConnection();
        String selectStatement =
                "select bidId " +
                "from bids where bidId between ?1 and ?2 ";
        prepStmt =
```

```
                con.prepareStatement(selectStatement);
        prepStmt.setBigDecimal(1, min);
        prepStmt.setBigDecimal(2, max);
        rs = prepStmt.executeQuery();

        ArrayList results = new ArrayList();
        while (rs.next()) {
            String pk = rs.getString("bidId");
            results.add(pk);
        }
    } catch (SQLException e) {
        throw new EJBException(e);
    } finally {
        if (rs != null) {
            try {
                rs.close();
            } catch (SQLException e) { }
        }
        if (prepStmt != null) {
            try {
                prepStmt.close();
            } catch (SQLException e) { }
        }
        if (con != null) {
            try {
                con.close();
            } catch (SQLException e) { }
        }
    }
    return results;
}

public String getBidId() {
    return id;
}

public void setBidId(String bidId) {
    this.id = bidId;
}

public BigDecimal getBidPrice() {
    return this.price;
}

public void setBidPrice(BigDecimal bidPrice) {
    this.price = bidPrice;
}


public void ejbActivate() {
}
```

```
    public void ejbPassivate() {
    }

    public void setEntityContext(EntityContext ctx) {
        this.context = ctx;
    }

    public void unsetEntityContext() {
        this.context = null;
    }

    private Connection getConnection() throws SQLException {
        try {
            Context context = new InitialContext();
            DataSource ds = (DataSource) context.lookup("java:comp/env/jdbc/myDB");
            return ds.getConnection();
        } catch (NamingException e) {
            throw new EJBException(e);
        }
    }

}
```

Deployment Descriptors

To be fully specified, an EJB must be accompanied by at least one deployment descriptor, called `ejb-jar.xml` (and stored in a directory `META-INF` in the JAR file). While the EJB 2.0 specification only mandates the existence of one deployment descriptor, it's not sufficient to actually provide enough information to the container to deploy the EJB.

The reason is that `ejb-jar.xml` is trying to remain as neutral as possible about what implementation means will be used to perform certain operations. For example, the following information isn't part of `ejb-jar.xml`:

- JNDI name of the remote home interface
- JNDI names of the destinations used by message-driven beans
- Names of the tables used by CMP entity beans
- Connection pools used by CMP entity beans
- What columns of the table map to what fields of CMP beans
- Other resources

This information must therefore be provided separately. Containers will typically expect you to enter this information in a container-specific deployment descriptor.

Persistence in the Deployment Descriptors

The type of persistence—bean managed or container managed—is specified in the XML deployment descriptor for the EJB. The `<persistence-type>` element of the `ejb-jar.xml` deployment descriptor will be either the following:

```
<persistence-type>Bean</persistence-type>
```

or the following:

```
<persistence-type>Container</persistence-type>
```

If the bean's persistence is container managed, the fields that are persisted must also be specified in the deployment descriptor. Each entry in the deployment descriptor has the name of the field in the class and may also have a description. The following is an example of two fields from the CMP version of the `Customer` entity bean:

```
<cmp-field>
    <description>The customers password .</description>
    <field-name>password</field-name>
 </cmp-field>
 <cmp-field>
    <field-name>name</field-name>
 </cmp-field>
```

All the container-managed fields listed in the deployment descriptor must be declared in the bean class under the form of accessors, as shown previously. Both get and set methods must be provided, and you must remember to capitalize the first letter of your field in the method name. Thus, the CMP field `name` becomes `getName()/setName()` in your bean class.

Listing 11-20 shows the entity section of the `ejb-jar.xml` deployment descriptor for the CMP version of the bean.

Listing 11-20. Entity Section

```
<entity>
 <description>Customer Bean for our auction application.</description>
 <ejb-name>Customer</ejb-name>
 <local-home>com.apress.auction.entity.interfaces.CustomerLocalHome</local-home>
 <local>com.apress.auction.entity.interfaces.CustomerLocal</local>
 <ejb-class>com.apress.auction.entity.ejb.CustomerBean</ejb-class>
 <persistence-type>Container</persistence-type>
 <prim-key-class>java.lang.String</prim-key-class>
 <reentrant>false</reentrant>
 <cmp-version>2.x</cmp-version>
 <abstract-schema-name>Customer</abstract-schema-name>
 <cmp-field>
    <description>Returns the userId</description>
    <field-name>userId</field-name>
```

```
 </cmp-field>
 <cmp-field>
    <description>Returns the password</description>
    <field-name>password</field-name>
 </cmp-field>
 <cmp-field>
    <description>Returns the name</description>
    <field-name>name</field-name>
 </cmp-field>
 <cmp-field>
    <description>Returns the email</description>
    <field-name>email</field-name>
 </cmp-field>
 <primkey-field>userId</primkey-field>
</entity>
```

Using Entity Beans

Entity beans are similar to session beans in how you use them; basically, you have a home interface that you find from a JNDI lookup. However, you then either obtain a reference to a bean (use the finder methods) or create a new bean instance (using the create method). This is the main difference between session beans and entity beans. With session beans, their identity is the Java class itself, whether a stateless class or a stateful class; entity beans, however, have a life outside of their Java class. In fact, you can consider the Java class a temporary representation of the underlying data for the convenience of your Java program.

Listing 11-21 demonstrates a simple controller-style session bean using the `Customer` entity bean.

Listing 11-21. Controller-Style Session Bean

```
package com.apress.auction.customer.ejb;

import javax.ejb.*;
import javax.naming.NamingException;
import javax.naming.InitialContext;

import com.apress.auction.entity.interfaces.*;
import com.apress.auction.customer.client.*;

public class CustomerControllerEJB implements SessionBean {

  private CustomerLocalHome customerHome;

  private SessionContext ctx;

  public void ejbCreate() throws CreateException{
      try {
          InitialContext ic = new InitialContext();
          customerHome = (CustomerLocalHome)ic.lookup(
```

```
                        "java:comp/env/ejb/customer");
        } catch (NamingException ne) {
            throw new EJBException(ne);
        }
    }

    public void ejbActivate() {}
    public void ejbPassivate() {}
    public void ejbRemove() {}
    public void setSessionContext(SessionContext ctx) { this.ctx = ctx; }

    public void createCustomer(CustomerData customerData) throws CustomerException {

      try {

        customerHome.create(customerData.getUserId(),
        customerData.getPassword(), customerData.getName(), customerData.getEmail());

      }catch(DuplicateKeyException ex) {
        ctx.setRollbackOnly();
        throw new CustomerException("User id already exists");
      }catch(Exception ex) {
        throw new EJBException(ex);
      }

    }

    public CustomerData getCustomer(String userId) throws CustomerException {

      try {

        return customerHome.findByPrimaryKey(userId).getData();

      }catch(ObjectNotFoundException ex) {
        ctx.setRollbackOnly();
        throw new CustomerException("Customer not found");
      }catch(Exception ex) {
        throw new EJBException(ex);
      }

    }

    public void updateCustomer(CustomerData customerData) throws CustomerException {

      try {
        customerHome.findByPrimaryKey(
                 customerData.getUserId()).setData(customerData);
      }catch(ObjectNotFoundException ex) {
        ctx.setRollbackOnly();
        throw new CustomerException("Customer not found");
      }catch(Exception ex) {
```

```
            throw new EJBException(ex);
        }

    }

}
```

This controller acts as a simple façade to our entity bean—protecting the client code from the underlying implementation and providing the face of a simple stateless service, which accepts a value object containing all of the state information for the entity bean.

It's good, however, to be judicious in the usage of such patterns. You may well recognize the procedural nature of the previous code. In the case of the controller bean, you can liken it to a *package* or collection of methods and the value objects as simple *structures*. This shows that the code is steering away from object-orientation. For the sake of dealing with the technical difficulties of remoting objects, you may often make this compromise.

Therefore, be sure to make any code beyond your session bean revert to more object-oriented behavior and consider if the benefits of increased efficiency even justify the degradation in code quality.

So, what was the efficiency reason for the previous code? Simply put, the previous example isn't chatty; it tends to keep the calls from a remote client to the server down to a minimum, and this reduces network bandwidth, latency, marshaling, and unmarshaling costs as well as active threads on the server. You have to be careful to avoid all these kinds of issues in real-world situations.

In fact, it's because of these real-world limitations that you now have local EJB interfaces, and furthermore, it's why you tend to see most entity beans only having local interfaces. It would be inefficient to make four requests (one finder and three accessor calls) between the client and the server to retrieve three fields when, if you use a pattern similar to the one previously, you can do it in a single request.

Footnotes

Before we conclude the chapter, we'll present a couple of remaining issues regarding the use of entity beans.

Caching

A *cache* is a secondary copy of data that's typically made for reasons of performance or convenience. The instance variables in your entity bean that represent the object's persistent state are actually a cache of the data whose permanent storage location is in your database. For instance, in your `Customer` entity bean, you may have three string variables for the customer's first name, middle name, and last name. These three variables may be secondary copies of the data from three columns in a relational database table named `customer`: `fname`, `mname`, and `lname`. Table 11-2 describes field caching to make this example clearer.

Table 11-2. Field Caching

DATA	PRIMARY COPY	CACHED COPY
Customer's first name	Database column `fname`	Entity bean field `fname`
Customer's middle name	Database column `mname`	Entity bean field `mname`
Customer's last name	Database column `lname`	Entity bean field `lname`

The cache consisting of your entity bean instance variables will suffer from the same potential problems that any cache does. It may get out of sync with the primary copy of the data. To continue with the simple customer example, the record in the database may have an `lname` of `Smith` after an update by a customer management system, but the corresponding entity bean field may still have the former name of `Jones`. With both bean-managed persistence and container-managed persistence, it's the combined responsibility of the EJB container and the underlying data store to manage the synchronization of an entity's cache. The topic of caching is closely related to the CRUD callbacks and the transfer of an entity object's state to and from the persistent data store. The EJB container will call `ejbLoad()` and `ejbStore()` at the times it's necessary to keep the local cache in sync with the primary copy of the data.

As a bean programmer, you don't need to concern yourself with exactly when the container will call `ejbLoad()` and `ejbStore()`. You must be prepared for either method call to happen at any time between business-logic methods. Still, it's nice to understand the common strategies that EJB containers will employ in various situations, so you can make informed decisions about application servers, deployment, and so on.

Say that a client wants to use a copy of your three-field customer bean. They want to call two methods on the bean: `setFirstName()` and `setMiddleName()`. These are two distinct cases you must consider, depending on whether these methods are called in the same transaction:

In the first case, these two methods are called in the same transaction: Before the first business-logic method is called, the container or the bean (depending on CMP vs. BMP) will load the state from the database corresponding with a call to `ejbLoad()`. Now the `setFirstName()` business method is called. At this point, the container has the option of calling `ejbStore()` and `ejbLoad()` again, before calling `setMiddleName()`. It may do this if it was part of an application server cluster, and it couldn't guarantee that the same entity bean instance would be used for both business methods. However, in the most common case, it'll simply go ahead and call `setMiddleName()` method right away. It can do this because both methods are part of the same transaction, and transactions are designed to ensure that modifications to a data store are isolated from other activities against that data. In other words, `ejbLoad()` and `ejbStore()` will be called for entity objects on transaction boundaries. (Note that this isn't mandated by the specification; it's simply a common implementation strategy.)

In the second case, these two methods are called in different transactions: Again, before the first business logic method is called, the container or the bean will load the state from the database corresponding with a call to `ejbLoad()`. Once `setFirstName()` has been called, the transaction completes and `ejbStore()` is called to update the data store. Now `setMiddleName()` is called. In the general case, the EJB container will simply repeat the process, calling `ejbLoad()` and `ejbStore()` around the invocation of `setMiddleName()`. The cache must be resynchronized with `ejbLoad()` because between the two transactions, some other process or application could have modified the data.

However, the following two special cases may allow the EJB container to avoid calling `ejbLoad()` on the entity instance at the start of the transactions subsequent to the first method call:

The first is that all access to the data goes through the EJB container and that entity bean. If this were the case, then the container knows that the cache in the entity bean and the data in the persistent data store are in sync. Every change to the data will happen in the cache before it's reflected in the data store, if all access is through the bean. However, if any non-EJB technology is used to modify the data (an ERP system), then this approach can't be used. This is because there's nothing to guarantee that the data won't change without the container and EJB knowing it.

The second case is when the particular application doesn't absolutely need the freshest data. Obviously this won't apply in the case of a banking system that must keep account information in sync. However, it will be the case for a surprising number of systems—an e-commerce system, perhaps. The cached data could be set to expire after a certain amount of time and would be refreshed after that period. If the prices for products were changed by some non-EJB demand-management software, this change wouldn't be reflected in the e-commerce application immediately. After the cached data expired, though (say, in five minutes), it would be. The benefit may be far fewer database accesses and much better application performance. The consequences—a five-minute delay in changed prices—would probably be negligible.

If your application server provides this optimization of data caching between transactions, you'd set this with an application server–specific configuration tool. Typically, the optimization is available if you indicate that the EJB container has "exclusive access to the database," or similar.

Although the EJB container can optimize away calls to `ejbLoad()` at the beginning of a transaction, it can never do this for `ejbStore()` at the completion of the transaction. The EJB specification absolutely requires that `ejbStore()` be called when a transaction in which the entity bean is participating completes. This is because one of the ACID guarantees that a transactional system makes is that a transaction is *durable*. If the modified data is held in a temporary cache in the entity bean, and the entity bean is subsequently destroyed before it gets the chance to finally write its data to permanent storage, the "durable" part of the transactional guarantee has been violated. This could happen because a subsequent call to the bean resulted in a nonapplication exception, or even because the application server crashed.

What about the case where no data has changed? In this case, since all field access goes through accessors that the EJB container generated, it knows that the entity bean is untouched and the `ejbStore()` operation will be an empty operation.

A bean that uses bean-managed persistence should implement a strategy to determine whether the data has been changed to see if any action needs to be taken. One possibility is to simply maintain a "modified" flag, which is checked in the `ejbStore()` method to see if any action needs to be taken. Another possibility is to keep "before" and "after" copies of the data and to compare them to build an `UPDATE` statement that affects only the data that has been changed.

Reentrancy

Unlike session beans, which are never reentrant, an entity bean can be specified as reentrant or not reentrant. A reentrant bean is one that allows a *loopback*—for example, a `Customer` bean calls a `Bid` bean that then calls the `Customer` bean; the initial call to the `Bid` "looped back" to the `Order`. Another use for reentrant beans is a recursive bean, which calls itself for whatever reason.

If the `Order` bean in this example were specified as reentrant, the call would be allowed. If the `Order` bean were specified as not being reentrant, the EJB container would disallow the call and throw a `java.rmi.RemoteException` (or `javax.ejb.EJBException` in the case of a local interface). Many programmers are used to a style of programming where child items (such as a line item) have a reference to their containing parent (such as an order). This is admittedly useful in a variety of situations and is allowed. Making entity beans reentrant, however, is discouraged (not forbidden) by the specification. This is because it can prevent the container from catching a particular class of error (for example, the container may no longer be able to tell a loopback from a concurrent access by another client).

If a bean is coded as reentrant, the EJB container can't prevent a multithreaded client operating within a single transaction from making multiple calls to the entity bean. Although entity beans are designed to be single-threaded, this could lead to a situation where two (or more) threads of control were operating on a single instance of an entity bean simultaneously. This is the type of system error that EJB technology was designed to free the business-logic programmer from worrying about, which is partly why the specification suggests that bean programmers avoid reentrant beans.

Whether a bean is reentrant is indicated in the XML deployment descriptor and looks like the following:

```
<re-entrant>True</re-entrant>
```

or the following:

```
<re-entrant>False</re-entrant>
```

Summary

In this chapter, you learned the difference between entity beans and session beans, the many classes and descriptors that come together to make a deployable EJB, and the basic structure of a general entity bean. You then looked closely at both container-managed and bean-managed persistence including the full life cycle of the beans and primary key classes. Having learned the basics of CMP, you then spent a little longer looking at container-managed relationships and the syntax of the EJB query language, including the new aggregation functions. Finally, you took a little time to understand deployment and development issues such as deployment descriptors, caching, and reentrancy.

CHAPTER 12

Introducing Messaging

MESSAGE-ORIENTED MIDDLEWARE (MOM) has been a vital element in integrating disparate and disconnected applications for a quite a long time. MOM systems allow participating applications to produce, consume, and exchange enterprise messages reliably. Messaging systems are based on applications delivering asynchronous events/notifications that are consumed by other applications.

You can use messaging in enterprise applications to achieve facilities such as integrating loosely coupled disparate applications across organizations, integrating disconnected operation between applications, enhancing scalability and throughput by using asynchronous operation, and so on.

For example, in the Acme Auction application from previous chapters, calculation of bids can take a lot of time. Thousands of bids may be calculated simultaneously. In such a scenario, rather than processing the bids synchronously, the component that accepts the bids can send asynchronous messages on the submitted bids to a messaging system. Another component can listen for these messages and evaluate the bids in an asynchronous mode and notify the interested parties about the results when the evaluations are done.

Traditionally, implementing MOM solutions involved using proprietary messaging software from various vendors and using proprietary code within the applications to integrate with those messaging products. This meant applications that used this software from vendors were tied to proprietary products. Java 2 Enterprise Edition (J2EE) 1.3 introduced a new application programming interface (API) into the arsenal of enterprise Java developer: Java Message Service (JMS). JMS provided a generic API that Java developers can use for producing, exchanging, and consuming asynchronous enterprise messages in a reliable and transactional environment. JMS provides a vendor-neutral way in which Java clients can implement messaging solutions using a standard API. However, JMS doesn't provide any interoperability standards between JMS providers. This means when a client application using WebLogic sends a JMS message to a server application running on JBoss, you'll need a custom piece in the middle that receives JMS messages from WebLogic and then resends them using JBoss's JMS service to the server application running JBoss.

NOTE *Messaging software providers that are compliant with the JMS specification and allow Java applications to access them using the JMS API are called* JMS providers. *Since J2EE 1.3, JMS 1.0.2 has been a mandatory API. This means every J2EE 1.3–compliant application server is required to provide a JMS provider. Popular JMS providers include IBM MQ Series, BEA WebLogic, Progress SonicMQ, JBoss JBossMQ from JBoss, and so on.*

Enterprise JavaBean (EJB) 2.0 introduced a new type of enterprise bean component called message-driven bean (MDB). MDBs are stateless components that can be asynchronously activated by messages that are delivered to the JMS provider. J2EE 1.4 and EJB 2.1 have enhanced the messaging capability of J2EE by leaps and bounds by allowing MDBs to provide support for messaging protocols other than JMS. This happens through the new version of Java Connector Architecture (JCA) 1.5 that allows closer integration of enterprise systems into J2EE application servers.

Previous versions of JCA supported only transactional and secure request/response mode integration with enterprise information systems (EISs) from the J2EE environment initiated from the J2EE side. However, JCA 1.5 enhances EIS integration by supporting asynchronous message reception as well. This allows EIS to deliver messages to J2EE components in asynchronous mode.

This chapter covers the messaging capabilities of the J2EE platform and concentrates on JMS and MDB. The first half concentrates on JMS, and the second half concentrates on consuming JMS and non-JMS messages using MDBs.

Regarding JMS, the chapter covers the following:

- JMS architecture
- Messaging models
- Administered objects
- Connections and sessions
- Message producers and consumers
- Messages types

Regarding MDBs, the chapter covers the following:

- MDB component contract
- Life cycle
- Messaging protocol support
- Deployment configuration

Introducing JMS Architecture

JMS allows Java clients and Java-based middleware systems to utilize the capabilities offered by enterprise messaging systems. JMS defines an API that Java clients can use to access the facilities provided by messaging systems. JMS applications are mainly composed of the messaging provider, JMS clients that exchange messages using the messaging provider, and a set of enterprise messages that they exchange. The JMS provider is responsible for implementing the interfaces that are defined by the JMS API. Figure 12-1 shows the JMS architecture.

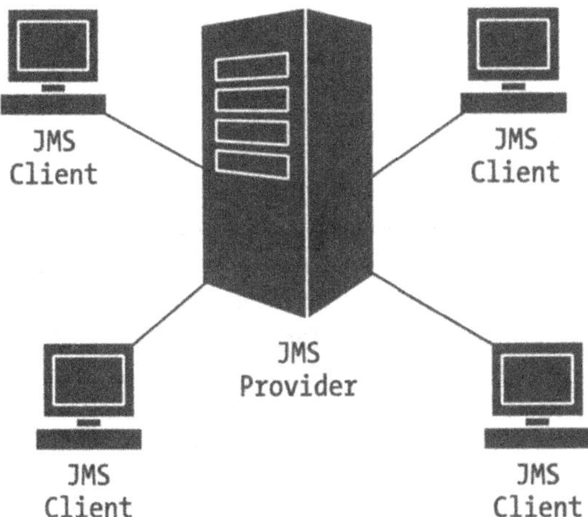

Figure 12-1. JMS architecture

JMS clients don't connect to each other to send messages. Instead, they all connect to a central messaging provider and send messages to what in JMS terms are called *destinations*. The JMS clients can register interest in specific destinations, and the provider is responsible for delivering messages to the JMS clients listening on those destinations to which messages are sent. This way JMS provides a loosely coupled architecture for integrating disparate and disconnected systems.

JMS relies highly on Java Naming and Directory Interface (JNDI) to provide portability across vendor implementations. The main constituents of a JMS application are as follows:

- JMS clients
- JMS provider
- JMS messages
- JMS administered objects

Two types of administered objects exist: connection factories and destinations. JMS provides interfaces for the connection factories and destinations. The clients use connection factories for creating physical connections to the messaging provider. Destinations identify where messages are sent to or received from. Messaging providers provide the implementations for the connection factory and destination interfaces. However, JMS clients shouldn't use the vendor implementation classes in their code. Instead, connection factory and destination instances are bound to a JNDI namespace using tools specific to the vendor, and the clients use standard JNDI calls to look up these objects.

> **NOTE** *The clients know the administered objects only through the standard JMS interfaces exposed by them.*

Once the clients look up the connection factories, they can use them for creating connections. Connections represent physical connections to the messaging server. You can use connections for creating one or more sessions. You can use sessions for creating messages, message producers, and message consumers. Message consumers and producers are created for specific destinations and are used for receiving and sending messages, respectively. Consumers can listen for messages asynchronously on destinations or can perform blocking reads. Figure 12-2 shows the JMS key interfaces.

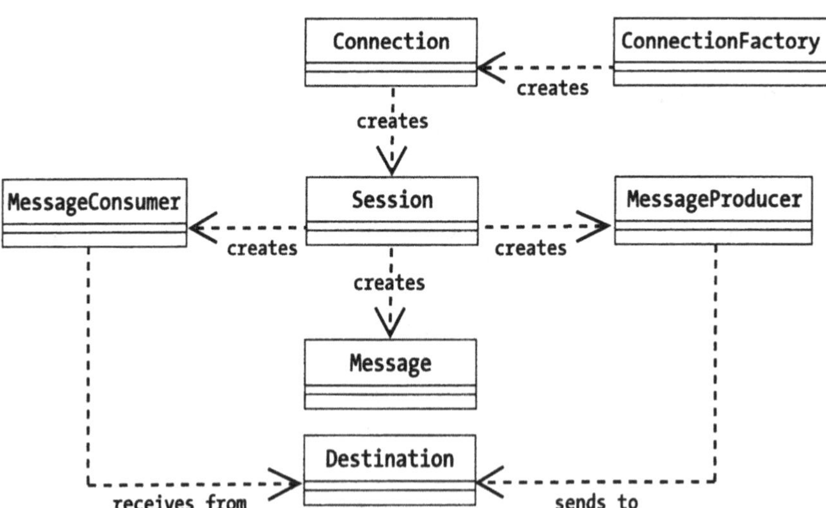

Figure 12-2. JMS key interfaces

Connection factories are represented by the interface `javax.jms.Connection`, connections by `javax.jms.Connection`, sessions by `javax.jms.Session`, destinations by `javax.jms.Destination`, message consumers by `javax.jms.MessageConsumer`, and message producers by `javax.jms.MessageProducer`. Connection factories, connections, and destinations support concurrent access.

Understanding Messaging Styles

JMS supports two modes of exchanging messages: Point-to-Point (P2P) and Publish-Subscribe (Pub-Sub). P2P messaging uses the concept of *queues*. Message producers send JMS messages to queues on which message receivers are listening synchronously or asynchronously. Clients address the messages to specific queues, and once another client reads the message from a queue, any other client can't access the same message. JMS provides specialized subinterfaces of the interfaces described in previous section for the various JMS artifacts related to P2P messaging. These are `QueueConnectionFactory`, `QueueConnection`, `Queue`, `QueueSession`, `QueueSender`, and `QueueReceiver` that extend `ConnectionFactory`, `Connection`, `Destination`, `Session`, `MessageProducer`, and `MessageConsumer`, respectively.

In Pub-Sub messaging, messages are addressed to topics. In Pub-Sub terms, this is called *publishing messages to the topic*. Multiple clients can subscribe to a topic and receive messages that are addressed to the topic. The main difference between P2P and Pub-Sub is that in P2P a message is received by only one consumer, and in Pub-Sub multiple consumers can receive a message. JMS provides specialized subinterfaces of the interfaces described in previous section for the various JMS artifacts related to Pub-Sub messaging. These are `TopicConnectionFactory`, `TopicConnection`, `Topic`, `TopicSession`, `TopicPublisher`, and `TopicSubscriber` that extend `ConnectionFactory`, `Connection`, `Destination`, `Session`, `MessageProducer`, and `MessageConsumer`, respectively.

NOTE *It's recommended to use the common interface rather than using message domain–specific interface wherever possible.*

Using Connection Factory

JMS clients use connection factories for creating physical connections to the JMS server. Connection factories are created, configured, and bound to a JNDI namespace using administration tools specific to the JMS server. The connection factories hide the vendor-specific details from the client. For example, with JBossMQ you can define different connection factories that identify the wire protocol that will be used by the clients for connecting to the JMS server and sending and receiving messages. Figure 12-3 shows the various connection factories provided in JMS.

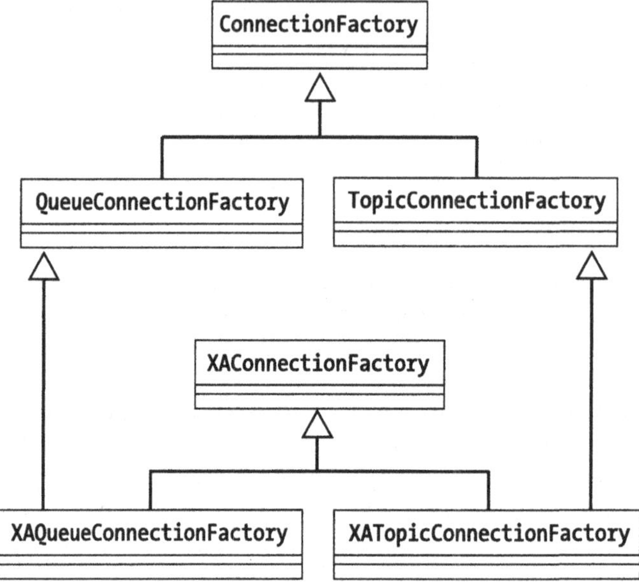

Figure 12-3. Connection factories

You use `QueueConnectionFactory`, `XAQueueConnectionFactory`, `TopicConnectionFactory`, and `XATopicConnection` factory for creating queue connections, queue connections that support distributed transactions, topic connections, and topic connections that support distributed transactions. Each of the previous interfaces provides two methods, `createXXXConnection()` and `createXXXConnection(String user, String passwd)`, for creating relevant connections. The methods throw a `JMSException` in case of an internal error and `JMSSecurityException` if authentication fails.

> **NOTE** *If you want to hide the message domain and transaction support details, you can use the base interface and configure a particular type of connection factory in the JNDI namespace using vendor-specific tools. The clients can perform the JNDI lookup to the* `ConnectionFactory` *reference, and the connections created using the factory will be relevant to the specific type of connection factory that was configured.*

For example, the following command creates a topic connection factory that can be looked up by the JNDI name `BidQueueConnectionFactory` using the J2EE Reference Implementation (RI). In a J2EE container environment you'd be using the JNDI Environment Naming Context (ENC) rather than the hard-coded JNDI name. Chapter 13 covers this in detail. Here's the code:

```
j2eeadmin -addJmsFactory BidQueueConnectionFactory queue
```

Listing 12-1 looks up the connection factory.

Listing 12-1. Looking Up the Connection Factory

```
package com.apress.projavaserver14.jms;

import javax.naming.*;
import javax.jms.*;

public class AdminObjects {

  public static void main(String args[]) throws Exception {

    InitialContext ctx = new InitialContext();
    ConnectionFactory cf = (ConnectionFactory)
      ctx.lookup("BidQueueConnectionFactory");
    Connection con = cf.createConnection();

    if(con instanceof TopicConnection)
      System.out.println("Got topic connection");

  }

}
```

In Listing 12-1, even though the looked-up JNDI object reference is cast to `ConnectionFactory`, the created connection using the factory is a topic connection because when you configured the connection factory, you specified it to be a topic connection factory.

> **NOTE** *Java Development Kit (JDK) 1.4 is a requirement for J2EE 1.4. When you run the previous client, please make sure to set the system property* `java.endorsed.dirs` *to* `%J2EE_HOME%\lib\endorsed` *and make sure you have the* `j2ee.jar` *file in the* `%J2EE_HOME\lib` *and* `jmsra.jar` *in* `%J2EE_HOME%\lib\system` *in the classpath.*

Understanding Destinations

JMS messages are sent to and received from destinations. You configure destinations in JNDI namespace using vendor-specific tools. JMS clients access the destinations using JNDI lookup and associate the message producers and consumers with the destinations. Figure 12-4 represents the interfaces that model destinations in JMS.

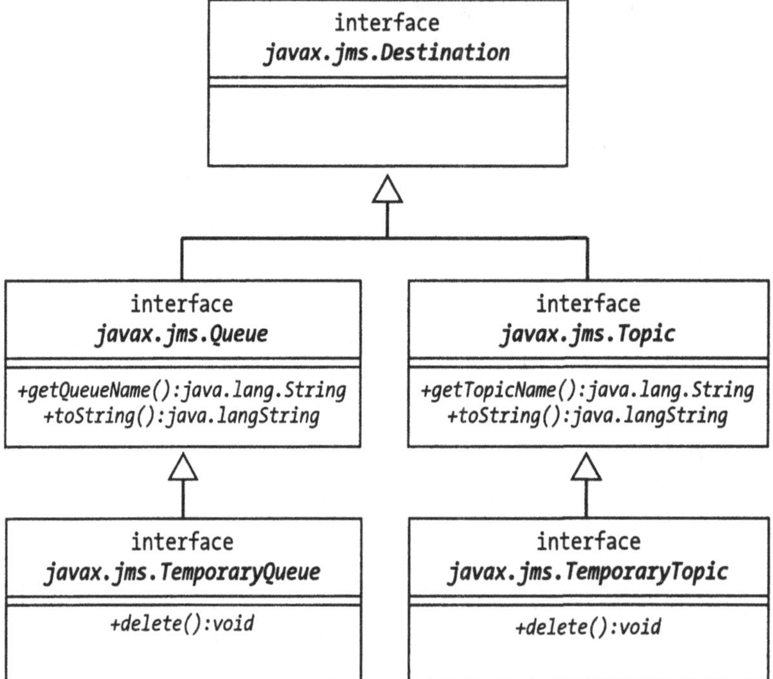

Figure 12-4. Destinations

The `Queue` interface represents destinations used in P2P. This interface defines the `getQueueName` and returns a nonportable vendor-specific name for the queue. A `TemporaryQueue` object is a unique `Queue` object created for the duration of a `Connection`. It's a system-defined queue that can be consumed only by the `Connection` that created it. The `Topic` interface represents the destination used in Pub-Sub. This interface defines the `getTopicName` and returns a nonportable vendor-specific name for the topic. A `TemporaryTopic` object is a unique `Topic` object created for the duration of a `Connection`. It's a system-defined `topic` that can be consumed only by the `Connection` that created it.

With JMS RI, destinations are added using the following command:

```
j2eeadmin -addJmsDestination <jndi-name> <queue|topic>
```

The following snippet adds a queue with the JNDI name `BidQueue`:

```
j2eeadmin - addJmsDestination BidQueue queue
```

You can look them up in the same way as looking up connection factories.

Using Connections

The `Connection` interface represents a physical connection to the JMS server. If you want your code to be message domain-neutral, you can use this base interface. However, if you want to use P2P or Pub-Sub–specific features, JMS also provides the following specific subinterfaces:

- **Connection**: This interface acts as the superinterface for the various types of connections.
- **QueueConnection**: This represents a connection in the P2P domain.
- **TopicConnection**: This interface represents a connection in the Pub-Sub domain.
- **XAConnection**: This interface represents connections that support distributed transactions.
- **XAQueueConnection**: This interface represents connections that support distributed transactions in the P2P domain.
- **XATopicConnection**: This interface represents connections that support distributed transactions in the Pub-Sub domain.

NOTE *In most of the cases, you'll be able to work with base interfaces. The only occasions you may need to know about the messaging domain you're working in is when you want to use domain-specific features. These scenarios include durable subscriptions in Pub-Sub and queue browsing P2P domains.*

Figure 12-5 shows the connections.

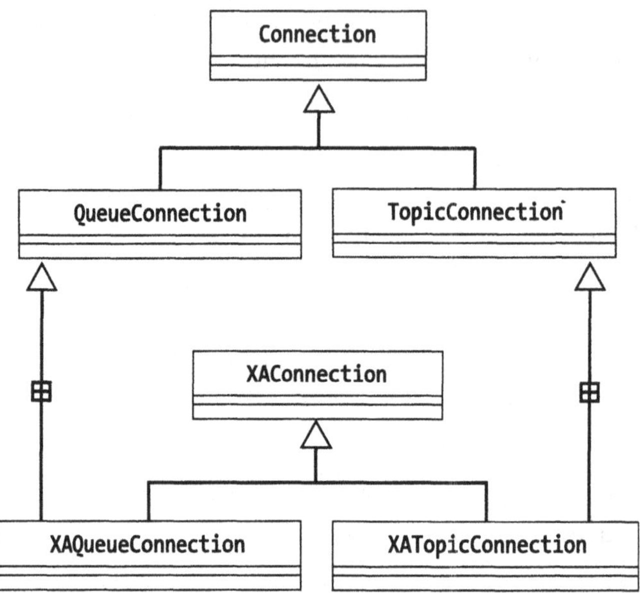

Figure 12-5. Connections

Connection State

When a connection is newly created, it can only send messages. Before you can receive messages using the connection, you need to start the connection by calling the `start` method. You can temporarily stop a connection by calling the `stop` method. Stopped connections can still send messages. You can permanently close the connection by calling the `close` method. Figure 12-6 shows the connection states.

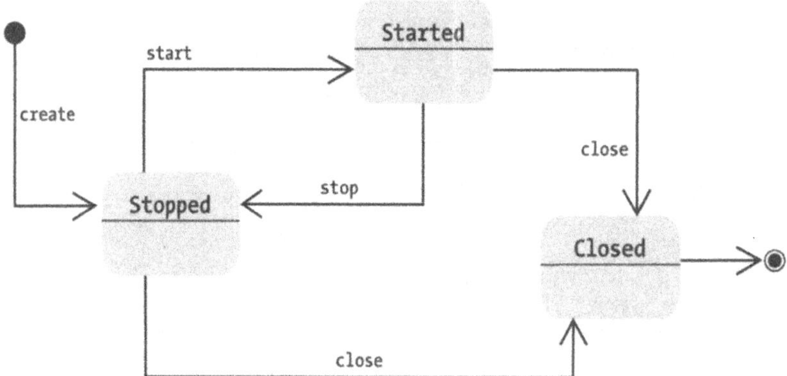

Figure 12-6. Connection states

> **NOTE** *Connections represent an open network connection to the JMS server. Hence, it's recommended to leave the connections open throughout the life of a JMS client. You can use a connection for creating multiple sessions. It's also recommended to start the connection only after the initialization of sessions, consumers, and producers associated with the connection. This is to avoid message delivery during the process of initialization.*

Connection Metadata

The `Connection` interface provides the method `getMetaData` to access the metadata associated with the connection. This method returns the interface `ConnectionMetaData`, which has the following methods:

- `int getJMSMajorVersion()`: Gets the JMS major version number.
- `int getJMSMinorVersion()`: Gets the JMS minor version number.
- `String getJMSProviderName()`: Gets the JMS provider name.
- `String getJMSVersion()`: Gets the JMS API version.
- `Enumeration getJMSXPropertyNames()`: Gets an enumeration of the JMSX property names. JMSX properties are message properties defined by JMS.
- `int getProviderMajorVersion()`: Gets the JMS provider major version number.
- `int getProviderMinorVersion()`: Gets the JMS provider minor version number.
- `String getProviderVersion()`: Gets the JMS provider version.

Listing 12-2 shows how to look up metadata.

Listing 12-2. Looking Up Metadata

```
package com.apress.projavaserver14.jms;

import javax.naming.*;
import javax.jms.*;

public class MetaData {

  public static void main(String args[]) throws Exception {

    InitialContext ctx = new InitialContext();
```

```
    ConnectionFactory cf = (ConnectionFactory)
      ctx.lookup("trainingCF");
    Connection con = cf.createConnection();

    ConnectionMetaData metaData = con.getMetaData();

    System.out.println("JMS Version:" +
      metaData.getJMSVersion());
    System.out.println("Provider Version:" +
      metaData.getProviderVersion());
    System.out.println("Provider:" +
      metaData.getJMSProviderName());

  }

}
```

The class in Listing 12-2 produces the following output with J2EE 1.4 RI:

```
JMS Version:1.1
Provider Version:1.1
Provider:Sun Microsystems
```

Exception Listeners

Most of the JMS operations declare to throw `JMSException` or one of its subclasses. However, if you want more extensive error handling, you can register an exception listener to the connection by calling the `setExceptionListener(ExceptionListener listener)` method. You need to implement the `ExceptionListener` interface that defines the method `onException(JMSException ex)` for hooking custom error handling. The `JMSException` class allows you to retrieve a vendor-specific error code.

Client Identifiers

Connections also allow you to set and get client identifiers using the methods `getClientID()` and `setClientID()`, respectively. Client identifiers are useful for durable subscriptions. Durable subscriptions allow clients to receive unexpired messages that were sent when they were inactive. You can set client identifiers for individual connection factories when you configure them or programmatically set them immediately after the connection is created. You should set the client identifier programmatically immediately after the creation of the connection before any other operation is performed on the connection. Attempts to set a client identifier for a connection that already possess an administratively configured client identifier will throw a `javax.jms.llegalStateException`.

Using Sessions

Connections also act as factories for sessions. The session uses the underlying connection for sending and receiving messages. You can have one or more sessions associated with a connection. Sessions are single-threaded objects used for the following purposes:

- Creating message consumers and producers
- Creating messages
- Providing transaction support for messages
- Asynchronously consuming messages for the message consumers associated with it
- Creating temporary destinations, and so on

The interface `Session` represents a session. This has specialized subinterfaces specific to the message domain and support for distributed transactions. These interfaces are as follows:

- **QueueSession**: These are used in P2P domain.
- **TopicSession**: These are used in Pub-Sub domain.
- **XASession**: These are used for distributed transaction support.
- **XAQueueSession**: These are used in P2P domain with support for distributed transactions.
- **XATopicSession**: These are used in Pub-Sub domain with support for distributed transactions.

Figure 12-7 shows the sessions.

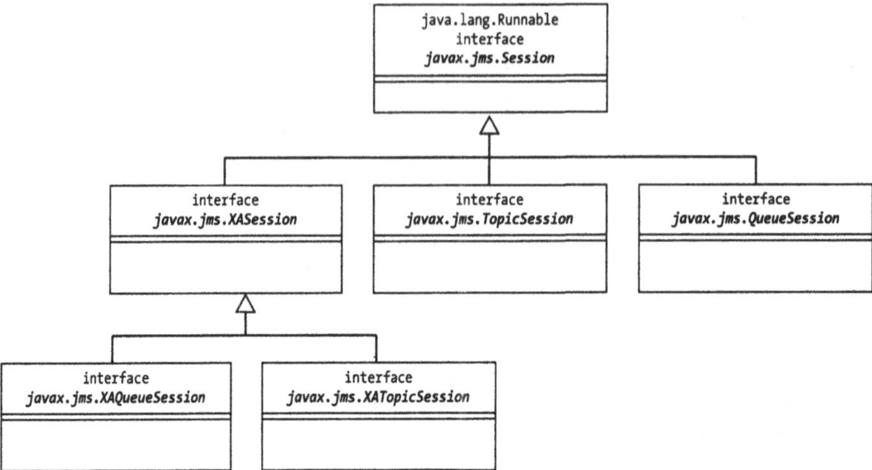

Figure 12-7. Sessions

Creating Sessions

Sessions are created using connection objects. You can create sessions using the following method defined on the `Connection` interface in a messaging model–neutral way:

```
public Session createSession(boolean transacted,
  int acknowledgmentMode);
```

The following snippet shows how to create a session:

```
Session sess = con.createSession(false,
  Session.AUTO_ACKNOWLEDGE);
```

Transaction Support

You can specify transaction support for sessions during the time of session creation. Transacted sessions group a set of produced and consumed messages into a single transaction. The session acknowledges all the messages consumed within a transaction and sends all the messages received within a transaction when the transaction is committed. However, if the transaction is rolled back, all the produced messages are destroyed, and the consumed messages are recovered. The transaction is committed by calling the `commit` method and rolled back using the `rollback` method. You can call the `getTransacted` method to check whether the session is transacted.

> **NOTE** *If you're relying on Java Transaction API (JTA) for transaction demarcation, you shouldn't be calling the* `commit` *and* `rollback` *methods to commit and roll back transactions. Instead, you should be using user transaction. In container-managed transaction demarcation scenarios, you should be relying on the container for committing and rolling back transactions. When a transacted session commits, all the messages consumed in that transaction are acknowledged.*

Acknowledgment Mode

If a session isn't transacted, you can specify three modes for acknowledging the messages it consumes. Clients can receive messages in synchronous mode by specifying a blocking read or register message listeners for asynchronous message delivery. You can specify these modes during the session creation using the enumerated constants specified in the `Session` interface:

- **DUPS_OK_ACKNOWLEDGE**: With this option, the session lazily acknowledges message receipt. This can cause duplicate message delivery.
- **AUTO_ACKNOWLEDGE**: With this option, the session automatically acknowledges the message when either the blocking read returns or the asynchronous message reception method on the message listener returns successfully.
- **CLIENT_ACKNOWLEDGE**: The client explicitly acknowledges the receipt by calling the `acknowledge` method on the message.

> **NOTE** *With the* `CLIENT_ACKNOWLEDGE` *mode it's possible that the client may accumulate huge amounts of unacknowledged messages. You can call the recover method on the session to restart from the last unacknowledged message.* `DUPS_OK_ACKNOWLEDGE` *can reduce overheads on the session object. The clients should be prepared to process duplicate delivery of messages. In* `AUTO_ACKNOWLEDGE` *mode, if a failure occurs after the client has processed the message and before the session has acknowledged the receipt, the provider will redeliver the message. However, the redelivered message will be marked so using a message header.*

You can call the `getAcknowledgeMode` method to determine the acknowledgment mode used by the session.

Concurrency Issues

Sessions are single-threaded in JMS. This means a session can receive a message or send one at the same time. If you want concurrent production and consumption of messages, you can use multiple sessions of the same connection. As mentioned earlier, connections are multithreaded. The message consumers associated with the same session can't perform a blocking read concurrently on multiple threads. However, you can have any number of message consumers with asynchronous message listeners for a given session. The session serializes the message delivery to the asynchronous message listeners.

Creating Consumers and Producers

You can use the following methods to create message consumers that will consume messages within the session in a messaging model–neutral way. The actual type of the message consumer that's created will depend on the type of messaging model you're using. In the P2P domain it will be `QueueReceiver`, and in Pub-Sub it will be a `TopicSubscriber`.

The following creates a `MessageConsumer` for the specified destination:

```
MessageConsumer createConsumer(Destination destination)
```

The following creates a `MessageConsumer` for the specified destination, using a message selector:

```
MessageConsumer createConsumer(Destination destination,
  String messageSelector)
```

Message selectors filter messages based on message headers and properties. Message selectors, message headers, and properties are covered in detail in the section on messages.

The following creates `MessageConsumer` for the specified destination, using a message selector:

```
MessageConsumer createConsumer(Destination destination,
  String messageSelector, boolean noLocal)
```

The `boolean` argument `noLocal` specifies whether the consumer can receive messages produced by the producers in the same session as the consumer.

You can use the following method for creating a messaging model–neutral message producer:

```
MessageProducer createProducer(Destination destination);
```

Pub-Sub–Specific Consumers

Since Pub-Sub messaging provides durable subscriptions, the `Session` interface provides a couple of methods specific to Pub-Sub messaging for creating durable topic subscribers.

> **NOTE** *If you don't need durable subscriptions, it's recommended you use one of the* `createConsumer` *methods for Pub-Sub to make your code messaging model neutral.*

The following creates a durable subscriber to the specified topic:

```
TopicSubscriber createDurableSubscriber(Topic topic,
  String name)
```

The name argument specifies a unique name for the durable subscription. Clients performing a durable subscription should use the same client identifier and specify the same subscription identifier across the subscriptions.

The following creates a durable subscriber to the specified topic, using a message selector and specifying whether messages published by its own connection should be delivered to it:

```
TopicSubscriber createDurableSubscriber(Topic topic,
  String name, String messageSelector, boolean noLocal)
```

In this section, you'll write a small example to illustrate the durable subscription capabilities of JMS. A message consumer will connect to the JMS server and create a durable subscription and disconnect. The message producer will then publish a message to a topic to which the consumer created the durable subscription. The consumer will then connect again and read the message that was published when it was inactive.

Before you run the programs, create a topic with the JNDI name `premier-LeagueScore` and a topic connection factory with the JNDI name `tcf`.

Listing 12-3 shows the code for the producer.

Listing 12-3. The Producer

```
package com.apress.projavaserver14.jms;

import javax.naming.*;
import javax.jms.*;

public class LiveScoreProducer {

  public static void main(String args[]) throws Exception {
```

```
    // Create the initial context
    InitialContext ctx = new InitialContext();
    // Look up the connection factory
    ConnectionFactory cf =
      (ConnectionFactory)ctx.lookup("tcf");
    // Look up the destination
    Destination dest =
      (Destination)ctx.lookup("premierLeagueScore");

    // Create the connection and session.
    Connection con = cf.createConnection();
    Session sess = con.createSession(false,
      Session.AUTO_ACKNOWLEDGE);

    // Create a message producer and message.
    MessageProducer prod = sess.createProducer(dest);
    Message msg = sess.createTextMessage(
      "Chelsea 5 - Man United 0");

    // Send the message and close the connection.
    prod.send(msg);

    con.close();

    System.out.println("Connection closed");

  }

}
```

NOTE *Listing 12-3 uses messaging model–neutral code for producing the messages. Until J2EE 1.3, it was difficult to write messaging model–neutral code because of the way various JMS interfaces were structured. However, with J2EE 1.4 onward, unless you're using queue browsing or durable subscriptions, you don't need to use messaging model–specific interfaces.*

Listing 12-4 shows the code for the message consumer.

Listing 12-4. The Consumer

```
package com.apress.projavaserver14.jms;

import javax.naming.*;
import javax.jms.*;

public class LiveScoreConsumer {
```

```
  public static void main(String args[]) throws Exception {

    // Create initial context
    InitialContext ctx = new InitialContext();
    // Look up the connection factory and destination.
    ConnectionFactory cf =
      (ConnectionFactory)ctx.lookup("tcf");
    Destination dest =
      (Destination)ctx.lookup("premierLeagueScore");

    // Create the connection
    Connection con = cf.createConnection();
    // Set the client id for durable subscriptions.
    con.setClientID("Meeraj");

    // Create the session.
    Session sess = con.createSession(false,
      Session.AUTO_ACKNOWLEDGE);

    // Create the topic subscriber to use durable
    // subscriptions.
    TopicSubscriber sub = sess.createDurableSubscriber(
      (Topic)dest, "liveScore");
```

Start the connection to receive messages (see Listing 12-5).

Listing 12-5. Starting the Connection

```
    con.start();

    // Do a blocking read for five seconds
    TextMessage msg = (TextMessage)sub.receive(5*1000);
    if(msg != null)
      System.out.println(msg.getText());
    con.start();

    // Close the connection.
    con.close();

    System.out.println("Connection closed");

  }
}
```

If you run the consumer first, then the producer, and then the consumer, the consumer will receive the message that was produces when it was inactive. This wouldn't have happened if the subscription weren't durable.

Queue Browser

Queue browsers are used in the P2P domain for looking at the messages in the queue without actually removing them. The Session interface defines methods for creating queue browsers for specified queues.

The following method creates a queue browser for the specified queue:

```
public QueueBrowser createBrowser(Queue queue)
```

The following method creates a queue browser for the specified queue and specified message selector:

```
public QueueBrowser createBrowser(Queue queue,
  String selector)
```

The QueueBrowser interface defines a method called getEnumeration to get an enumeration of the messages it can access.

> **NOTE** *This can be useful for writing admin clients that can monitor the queues without actually removing the messages.*

Temporary Destinations

Temporary destinations are created only for the duration of the session. You can have temporary queues and topics. Temporary queues and topics can be consumed only by the sessions and message consumers owned by the connection within which it was created.

> **NOTE** *Temporary destinations are useful in using JMS in a request/response mode. The sender can send the message and set a temporary destination as one of the JMS standard message header and perform a blocking read on it. The recipient can send the reply to this temporary destination.*

The Session interface provides the following methods for creating temporary destinations:

```
Public TemporaryQueue createTemporaryQueue();
Public TemporaryTopic createTemporaryTopic();
```

Both TemporaryQueue and TemporaryTopic provide the delete method to remove them.

Message Listener

Messages are normally consumed using message consumers created using sessions. These consumers can either perform a synchronous read or register a message listener for receiving asynchronous messages. Sessions allow you to register a message listener for all the message consumers associated with the session. You do this by calling the `setMessageListener(MessageListener listener)` method. The `MessageListener` interface defines a single `onMessage(Message msg)` method that will be invoked on an asynchronous message delivery.

> **NOTE** *When you have a message listener registered with the session, no other form of message reception is allowed for this session using its message consumers. However, the message producers can still send messages.*

Creating Message Domain-Specific Sessions

If you want to create sessions specific to the messaging domain, you can use the specific connections for creating them.

QueueSession

The `QueueSession` interface represents sessions in the P2P domain, and you can create it using the `QueueConnection` interface. You can use `QueueSession` for creating `QueueSender` and `QueueReceiver` that represent message producer and message sender, respectively, in the P2P domain. You can use queue senders for sending messages to queues, and you can use queue receivers for receiving messages from queues.

TopicSession

The `TopicSession` interface represents sessions in the Pub-Sub domain, and you can create it using the `TopicConnection` interface. You can use `TopicSession` for creating `TopicPublisher` and `TopicSubscriber` instances that represent message producer and message sender, respectively, in the Pub-Sub domain. You can use topic publishers for publishing messages to topics, and you can use topic subscribers for creating durable and nondurable subscriptions to topics.

XA Sessions

If you want to create sessions that support distributed transactions, you can use `XAConnection`, `XAQueueConnection`, and `XATopicSession` to create `XASession`, `XAQueueSession`, and `XATopicSession`, respectively.

Using Message Producers and Consumers

You use message producers and consumers for producing and consuming messages, respectively. Message producers are represented by the interface MessageProducer, and message consumers are represented by the interface MessageConsumer. In most scenarios, you'll be able to use these messaging domain-neutral interfaces for consuming and producing messages. You create message producers and consumers using the methods defined in the Session interface.

JMS also provides message producer and consumer interfaces specific to the messaging domains. QueueSender and QueueReceiver represent the producer and consumer in the P2P domain, and TopicPublisher and TopicSubscriber represent the same in the Pub-Sub domain. Figure 12-8 shows message consumers and producers.

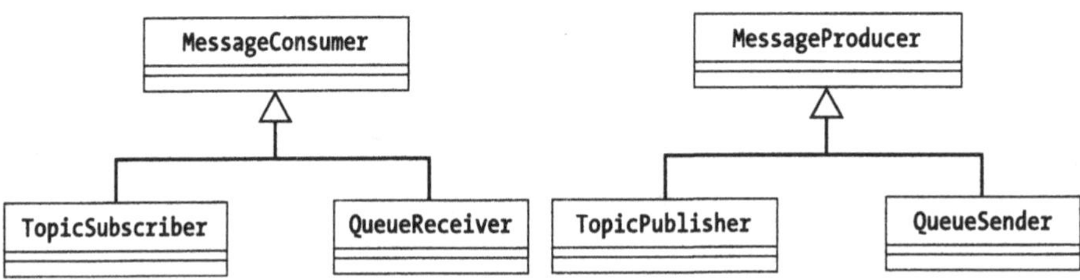

Figure 12-8. Message consumers and producers

Message ID

A message identifier that's set after the producer sends the message uniquely identifies messages in JMS. However, creating unique message IDs can create an overhead on the message providers' side. Message producers can provide a hint to the message providers that the messages sent by them don't need a message ID. You do this by calling the setDisableMessageID(boolean flag) on the message producer. You can check whether message ID generation is disabled by calling the method getDisableMessageID().

Message Time Stamp

Messages normally contain a time stamp indicating when the sender handed over the message to the provider. However, creating time stamps can create an overhead on the message providers' side. Message producers can provide a hint to the message providers that the messages sent by them don't need a time stamp. You do this by calling the setDisableMessageTimestamp(boolean flag) on the message producer. You can check whether time stamp generation is disabled by calling the method getDisableMessageTimestamp().

Message Priority

Messages that are sent by producers can have priorities ranging from values 0 to 10. You can set this either for individual messages that are sent or for all the messages sent by a producer. You can set the global priority for a producer by calling the `setPriority(int priority)` method on the producer. You can get the current priority by calling the `getPriority()` method. The constant `Message.DEFAULT_PRIORTY` defines the default priority.

NOTE *Priorities 0–5 are considered as normal and 6–10 are considered higher priority.*

Delivery Mode

You can specify the delivery mode for each message that's sent or globally to all the messages that are sent by a producer. The two delivery modes are defined by the constants `DeliveryMode.PERSISTENT` and `DeliveryMode.NON_PERSISTENT`. Clients can mark the message as persistent to make sure the message isn't lost in transit. You can set the delivery mode globally by calling the `setDeliveryMode(int mode)` method and get the current delivery mode by calling the `getDeliveryMode()` method.

NOTE *The default delivery mode is persistent. The delivery mode doesn't guarantee the retention of the message at the provider's end in a persistent store until it's acknowledged. It guarantees persistence only in transport.*

Time to Live

You can set a time to live in milliseconds for the messages that define the time for which the message provider will retain the message after the producer sends it. You can set this for individual messages or globally for all messages sent by a producer. You can set it globally by calling the `setTimeToLive(long time)` method on the message producer and call the `getTimeToLive()` to get the current message expiry time.

NOTE *A value of 0 means the message never expires. The constant* `Message.DEFAULT_TIME_TO_LIVE` *defines the default value.*

Sending Messages

You can send messages using the MessageProducer interface or the messaging domain–specific interfaces QueueSender and TopicPublisher.

MessageProducer

The MessageProducer interface defines the following methods for sending messages.

The following sends a message to the specified destination:

```
void send(Destination destination, Message message)
```

The following sends a message to the specified destination, specifying delivery mode, priority, and time to live:

```
void send(Destination destination, Message message,
  int deliveryMode, int priority, long timeToLive)
```

The following sends a message to the destination associated with message producer using the default delivery mode, priority, and time to live:

```
void send(Message message)
```

The following sends a message to the destination associated with message producer, specifying delivery mode, priority, and time to live:

```
void send(Message message, int deliveryMode, int priority,
  long timeToLive)
```

QueueSender

The QueueSender interface defines the following methods for sending messages.

The following sends a message to the queue associated with the queue sender:

```
void send(Message message)
```

The following sends a message to the queue associated with the queue sender, specifying delivery mode, priority, and time to live:

```
void send(Message message, int deliveryMode, int priority,
  long timeToLive)
```

The following sends a message to the specified queue:

```
void send(Queue queue, Message message)
```

The following sends a message to the specified queue, specifying delivery mode, priority, and time to live:

```
void send(Queue queue, Message message, int deliveryMode,
  int priority, long timeToLive)
```

TopicPublisher

The `TopicPublisher` interface defines the following methods for sending messages.

The following publishes a message to the topic associated with the publisher:

```
void publish(Message message)
```

The following publishes a message to the topic associated with the publisher, specifying delivery mode, priority, and time to live:

```
void publish(Message message, int deliveryMode, int priority,
  long timeToLive)
```

The following publishes a message to the specified topic:

```
void publish(Topic topic, Message message)
```

The following publishes a message to the specified topic, specifying delivery mode, priority, and time to live:

```
void publish(Topic topic, Message message, int deliveryMode,
  int priority, long timeToLive)
```

> **NOTE** *Delivery mode, priority, and expiry specified during the sending of a message will override the same set globally for the message producer.*

Receiving Messages

Message consumers can receive messages synchronously be performing blocking reads. The `MessageConsumer` interface defines the following methods for synchronous reads.

The following receives the next message produced for this message consumer:

```
Message receive()
```

The following receives the next message that arrives within the specified timeout interval in milliseconds:

```
Message receive(long timeout)
```

The following receives the next message if one is immediately available:

```
Message receiveNoWait()
```

Understanding Messages

The main component in JMS applications is the messages that are exchanged between the JMS clients. The `javax.jms.Message` interface represents messages. JMS messages can hold different content models such as objects, text, byte stream, maps, and so on. The provider implements the message interfaces defined by JMS. You create messages using the session object. The `Session` interface defines a set of factory methods for creating various types of messages.

Message Structure

The main design goals of JMS message model as defined by the specification are as follows:

- A single unified interface for messaging
- An interface for creating messages that match the format used by existing non-JMS applications
- An interface that supports heterogeneous applications that span across operating systems and machine architectures
- An interface that supports the creation of messages that can hold Java objects in their content

Specialized subinterfaces of the `Message` interface represent specific types of messages in JMS. Figure 12-9 shows the structure of a JMS message.

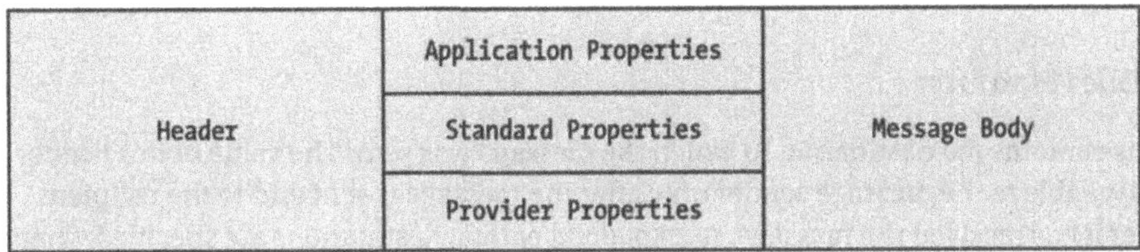

Figure 12-9. Message structure

Regardless of the specific message type, JMS messages are composed of the message header, the message properties, and the message body.

The header contains a set of standard fields defined by the JMS specification. Providers provide access to all the standard headers in their implementation classes. You use the header fields for proper routing and processing of messages. Message headers include message ID, delivery mode, time stamp, priority, and so on.

You use properties to add additional header fields to messages. Properties are classified into the following types:

- **Standard properties**: These are same as the header fields except that they're optional. Standard properties have `JMSX` as the property name prefix.
- **Application properties**: These are custom properties that JMS clients can set.
- **Provider properties**: These are additional properties supported by the provider. These are useful in integrating JMS clients with the providers' non-JMS clients.

JMS supports messages that can carry different content models. The following interface extends the `Message` interface to support various content models:

- **BytesMessage**: You use this for exchanging a stream of uninterpreted bytes.
- **TextMessage**: You use this for exchanging plain-text messages.
- **ObjectMessage**: You use this for exchanging serialized Java objects.
- **StreamMessage**: You use this for exchanging stream of Java primitives, strings, and objects of Java wrapper types.
- **MapMessage**: You use this for exchanging messages containing a map of name/value pairs.

Message Header

The clients can set message headers using the message implementation class or by the provider. The following sections explain the message headers supported by JMS.

JMSDestination

This contains the destination to which the message was sent. The value of this header is available to the message sender only after the message is sent and to the recipient after it has received the message. As explained earlier, destinations are specified when the producer is created from the session or when the producer sends the message. The send method sets this.

JMSDeliveryMode

This indicates the delivery modes. The possible delivery modes are `PERSISTENT` or `NON_PERSISTENT`. The send method sets this.

JMSPriority

This indicates the priority with which the message was sent. This is set by the send/publish method of the message producer. The send method sets this.

JMSExpiration

This indicates the sum time to live set for the message and the current time in Greenwich mean time (GMT). However, if the time to live is set as `0` for the message, then the expiration is also `0`, indicating the message will not expire. The send method sets this.

JMSMessageID

This indicates a unique message ID for the message. As explained earlier, the client can provide a hint to the provider to disable message ID generation. The send method sets this.

JMSCorrelationID

JMS clients operating in a request/response paradigm can use this. The client that replies to a message can set the `JMSCorrelationID` header to the message ID of the message for which it's replying. The original sender can use this value for correlating messages. The client sets this.

JMSReplyTo

JMS clients operating in a request/response paradigm can use this. Message senders can set this to a destination on which they will expect the reply message. JMS clients can use temporary destinations for this purpose. The client sets this.

JMSTimestamp

This indicates the time at which the JMS client handed the message over to the provider. As explained earlier, the client can provide a hint to the provider to disable message time stamp generation. This is set by the send method.

JMSRedelivered

The provider will set this header if the message was redelivered because of a failure in acknowledgment. The provider sets this.

JMSType

Providers that maintain a repository of application-specific messages can set this header to provide a hint to the JMS client on how to decode the message. The client sets this.

Message Header Methods

The `Message` interface provides the following methods for getting/setting message headers.

The following gets/sets the correlation ID for the message:

```
String getJMSCorrelationID()
void setJMSCorrelationID(String correlationID)
```

The following gets/sets the `DeliveryMode` value specified for this message:

```
int getJMSDeliveryMode()
void setJMSDeliveryMode(int deliveryMode)
```

The following gets/sets the `Destination` object for this message:

```
Destination getJMSDestination()
void setJMSDestination(Destination dest)
```

The following gets/sets the message's expiration value:

```
long getJMSExpiration()
void setJMSExpiration(long expiration)
```

The following gets/sets the message ID:

```
String getJMSMessageID()
void setJMSMessageID(String messageID)
```

The following gets/sets the message priority level:

```
int getJMSPriority()
void setJMSPriority(int priority)
```

The following gets/sets an indication of whether this message is being redelivered:

```
boolean getJMSRedelivered()
void setJMSRedelivered(boolean redelivered)
```

The following gets/sets the `Destination` object to which a reply to this message should be sent:

```
Destination getJMSReplyTo()
void setJMSReplyTo(Destination replyTo)
```

The following gets/sets the message time stamp:

```
long getJMSTimestamp()
void setJMSTimestamp(long timestamp)
```

The following gets/sets the message type identifier supplied by the client when the message was sent:

```
String getJMSType()
void setJMSType(String type)
```

Using JMS in Request/Response Paradigm

In the following sections, you'll develop two JMS applications. The first one sends a message to the second one specifying the reply to header and then performs a blocking read on the queue on which the reply is expected. The second one reads the message and sends a reply to the destination identified by the reply to header. The clients will use a correlation ID header to link replies to requests.

Requester

Listing 12-6 shows the client that sends the requests.

Listing 12-6. Requester

```
package com.apress.projavaserver14.jms;

import javax.naming.*;
import javax.jms.*;

public class Requester {

  public static void main(String args[]) throws Exception {
    // Look up the connection factory and destination.
    InitialContext ctx = new InitialContext();
    ConnectionFactory cf =
      (ConnectionFactory)ctx.lookup("qcf");
    Destination dest = (Destination)ctx.lookup("queue");
    // Create the connection and session
    Connection con = cf.createConnection();
    Session sess = con.createSession(false,
      Session.AUTO_ACKNOWLEDGE);
    // Start the connection.
    con.start();
    // Create a message producer for the destination.
    MessageProducer prod = sess.createProducer(dest);
    // Create a message.
    Message req = sess.createTextMessage();
    // Create a temporary queue.
    TemporaryQueue replyTo = sess.createTemporaryQueue();
    // Set the reply to header to the temporary queue.
    req.setJMSReplyTo(replyTo);
    // Send the message.
    prod.send(req);
    // Create a consumer for the temporary queue
    MessageConsumer cs = sess.createConsumer(replyTo);
    // Perform a blocking read.
    Message res = cs.receive();
    // Compare the correlation ID of the response to
    // the message ID of the request
    if(req.getJMSMessageID().equals(
      res.getJMSCorrelationID())) {
      System.out.println("Response received");
      System.out.println("Request ID: " +
        req.getJMSMessageID());
      System.out.println("Response Correlation ID: " +
      res.getJMSCorrelationID());
      System.out.println("Response ID: " +
        res.getJMSMessageID());
    }
```

Listing 12-7 removes the temporary queue.

Listing 12-7. Removing the Temporary Queue

```
    replyTo.delete();

    con.close();

  }

}
```

Responder

Listing 12-8 shows the client that sends the response.

Listing 12-8. The Responder

```
package com.apress.projavaserver14.jms;

import javax.naming.*;
import javax.jms.*;

public class Responder {

  public static void main(String args[]) throws Exception {
    // Look up the connection and destination.
    InitialContext ctx = new InitialContext();
    ConnectionFactory cf =
      (ConnectionFactory)ctx.lookup("qcf");
    Destination dest = (Destination)ctx.lookup("queue");
    // Create the connection and the session.
    Connection con = cf.createConnection();
    Session sess = con.createSession(false,
      Session.AUTO_ACKNOWLEDGE);

    con.start();
    // Create a consumer for the destination.
    MessageConsumer cs = sess.createConsumer(dest);
    // Perform a blocking read.
    Message msg = cs.receive();
    // Get the reply to and message ID headers.
    Destination replyTo = msg.getJMSReplyTo();
    String messageID = msg.getJMSMessageID();

    System.out.println("Request ID:" + messageID);
    // Create the response message and set the
    // correlation ID to the message ID of the request.
    Message reply = sess.createTextMessage();
```

```
    reply.setJMSCorrelationID(messageID);
    // Create a message producer and send the response.
    MessageProducer prod = sess.createProducer(replyTo);
    prod.send(reply);

    System.out.println("Response ID:" +
      reply.getJMSMessageID());

  }

}
```

The following text shows a sample output from the responder:

```
Request ID:ID:_meeraj_1044316656199_4.2.1.1
Response ID:ID:_meeraj_1044316637242_3.2.1.1
```

The following text shows the sample output from the requester:

```
Response received
Request ID: ID:_meeraj_1044316656199_4.2.1.1
Response Correlation ID: ID:_meeraj_1044316656199_4.2.1.1
Response ID: ID:_meeraj_1044316637242_3.2.1.1
```

You can see from this output that the response correlation ID matches the request ID.

QueueRequestor and TopicRequestor

JMS provides the helper classes `QueueRequestor` and `TopicRequestor` for implementing the request/response paradigm in the P2P and Pub-Sub domains, respectively. The `QueueRequestor` takes a nontransacted `QueueSession` and a `Queue` in the constructor and provides the method `Message request(Message req)` for sending service requests. The `TopicRequestor` takes a nontransacted `TopicSession` and a `Topic` in the constructor and provides the method `Message request(Message req)` for sending service requests.

Using a queue requester can simplify the requester code, as shown in Listing 12-9.

Listing 12-9. Queue Requester

```
package com.apress.projavaserver14.jms;

import javax.naming.*;
import javax.jms.*;

public class RequestResponse {

  public static void main(String args[]) throws Exception {
    // Create the initial context
    InitialContext ctx = new InitialContext();
```

```
    // Look up the connection factory
    QueueConnectionFactory cf =
      (QueueConnectionFactory)ctx.lookup("qcf");
    // Look up the destination
    Queue dest = (Queue)ctx.lookup("queue");
    // Create the connection
    QueueConnection con = cf.createQueueConnection();
    // Create a nontransacted session
    QueueSession sess = con.createQueueSession(false,
    Session.AUTO_ACKNOWLEDGE);
    // Start the connetcion
    con.start();
    // Create a queue requestor, send the message
    // and wait for response
    QueueRequestor requester = new QueueRequestor(sess, dest);
    Message req = sess.createTextMessage();
    Message res = requester.request(req);

    System.out.println("Response received");
    System.out.println("Request ID: " +
      req.getJMSMessageID());
    System.out.println("Response Correlation ID: " +
    res.getJMSCorrelationID());
    System.out.println("Response ID: " +
      res.getJMSMessageID());

    con.close();

  }

}
```

Message Body

JMS messages are categorized based on the type of content that the messages can have in their body. Accordingly, the JMS specification defines five types of messages that will cover most of the enterprise messaging requirements. The `Message` interface acts as an upper interface for these interfaces and defines the common methods. The common methods are categorized into the following:

- Methods for handling message headers
- Methods for handling message properties

In addition to the previous methods, two extra methods exist. One is for acknowledging messages when the acknowledgment mode is set to CLIENT_ACKNOWLEDGE:

```
public void acknowledge();
```

You use the second method for clearing the body content:

```
public void clearBody();
```

Bytes Messages

Bytes messages carry a stream of uninterpreted bytes in their body. It's the responsibility of the recipient to interpret the byte stream. You can use byte messages in conjunction with the JMSType header to define a custom repository of messages. The recipient can choose an appropriate decoding algorithm to interpret the byte stream based on the JMSType header.

The Session interface defines the following method creating bytes messages:

```
public BytesMessage createBytesMessage();
```

The BytesMessage interface defines a set of methods for reading and writing primitive types and strings to the byte stream.

Text Messages

Text messages contain plain text as the message body. They're useful for exchanging XML documents between applications. The Session interface defines the following methods for creating text messages:

```
public TextMessage createTextMessage()
public TextMessage createTextMessage(String text)
```

The TextMessage interface defines methods for getting and setting the message text.

Object Messages

You use object messages for exchanging serializable Java objects. The Session interface defines the following methods for creating object messages:

```
public ObjectMessage createObjectMessage()
public ObjectMessage createObjectMessage(Serializable object)
```

The ObjectMessage interface defines methods for getting and setting the message text.

Stream Messages

You use stream messages for exchanging sequential stream of Java primitives. The `Session` interface defines the following method-creating stream messages:

```
public StreamMessage createStreamMessage();
```

The `StreamMessage` interface defines methods similar to those defined in `BytesMessage`.

Map Messages

You use map messages for exchanging a map of Java primitives as name/value pairs. The `Session` interface defines the following method-creating map messages:

```
public MapMessage createMapMessage();
```

The `MapMessage` interface defines methods for getting and setting the named primitives in the map.

Message Properties

You use properties for adding additional header fields to the messages. Property names are strings, and property values should be one of the Java primitives or `String`. You should set properties before the message is sent, and a JMS client can't change the properties of received messages. Properties are predominantly used for enabling message selection and message header customization. Consumers to filter the messages they receive use message selectors.

> **NOTE** *You can also set properties as objects of Java primitive wrapper types.*

Calling the `clearProperties` method on the message object can clear the properties set for the message. The `Message` interface also defines get and set methods for getting and setting properties of various types.

Standard Properties

JMS defines a set of standard properties with property names prefixed by JMSX. You can retrieve these property names from the connection metadata. Table 12-1 shows the properties defined by the JMS 1.1 specification.

Table 12-1. JMS Properties

NAME	TYPE	SET BY	DESCRIPTION
`JMSXUserID`	`String`	Provider on send	The identity of the user sending the message
`JMSXAppID`	`String`	Provider on send	The identity of the application sending the message
`JMSXDeliveryCount`	`int`	Provider on receive	The number of message delivery attempts
`JMSXGroupID`	`String`	Client	The identity of the message group of which this message is a part
`JMSXGroupSeq`	`int`	Client	The sequence number of this message within the group
`JMSXProducerTXID`	`String`	Provider on send	The transaction identifier of the transaction within which this message was produced
`JMSXConsumerTXID`	`String`	Provider on receive	The transaction identifier of the transaction within which this message was consumed
`JMSXRcvTimestamp`	`long`	Provider on receive	The time JMS delivered the message to the consumer

Provider Properties

Usually you use provider properties for integrating JMS clients with the provider's non-JMS clients. Property names starting with `JMS_vendor_name` are reserved for the provider where `vendor_name` is specific to the provider.

Application Properties

JMS clients can set application properties for implementing application logic such as message header customization, message selection, and so on.

Message Selectors

Message selectors are specified as strings during the creation of message consumers. These are SQL predicate-like strings used for filtering messages. They conform to the standard ANSI SQL-92 syntax for predicates. They're evaluated using message headers and properties. For example, you set the message selector `course = 'Java Primer'` when creating the consumer. Then the consumer will receive only those messages that have the property called `course` with the value set to `Java Primer`.

Message Selector Examples

In this section, you'll look at a few message selector examples.

The following selects all messages with the examId property set to 1 and the grade property value greater than 10:

```
examId = 1 and grade > 10
```

The following selects all the messages with the courseName property beginning with the String Java:

```
courseName like 'Java%'
```

JMS message selectors support all the ANSI SQL-92-compliant combinations for predicates. Please refer to an ANSI SQL reference for an exhaustive list. The Session interface provides the functionality to specify a message selector when creating a consumer in the following methods:

```
createConsumer(Destination dest, String messageSelector)
```

Understanding Message-Driven Beans

So far you've seen the JMS artifacts for sending and receiving messages in the P2P and Pub-Sub domains. However, for message reception, you need to programmatically create the message consumer and associate it with a destination. JMS doesn't provide a component type that can be activated by asynchronous messages sent to destinations. This is a key requirement in J2EE server-side applications where clients can send messages and components can receive the messages and process them.

> **NOTE** *JMS does provide support for message consumptions in application server environments using connection consumers and server sessions. However, the JMS specification defines these features as optional. This means you can't expect every JMS provider to support these features.*

However, EJB 2.0 introduced MDBs that would listen on configured JMS destinations and that can be asynchronously activated by JMS messages arriving in those destinations. EJB 2.1 has furthered this support for messaging by supporting non-JMS messages. EJB 2.1 MDBs are tightly related to the JCA 1.5 specification. MDBs can be activated by non-JMS messages such as Simple Mail Transfer Protocol (SMTP) messages, JAXM messages, and so on.

MDB Overview

MDBs are stateless components that function in a secure, transactional, scalable environment that can be activated by messages arriving on destinations or endpoints serviced by the MDB components. Unlike session and entity beans, MDBs don't have any client identity. In other words, the client doesn't have any direct interaction with an MDB. The clients just sends messages to destinations or endpoints supported by the MDB's messaging protocol without being aware that those messages will be processed by an MDB.

MDBs offer a solution for building high-performance scalable applications. In scenarios where clients don't expect a synchronous response, the requests can be sent to a destination or endpoint supported by the MDB's messaging protocol, and the control can be immediately returned to the client. The message can be later processed by an MDB monitoring the destination or endpoint. Figure 12-10 shows the MDB.

> **NOTE** *Even though this can provide a perceived performance gain to the client, it doesn't reduce the load on the server. This is because processing the message within the MDB can take the same processing power as processing it using a synchronous component.*

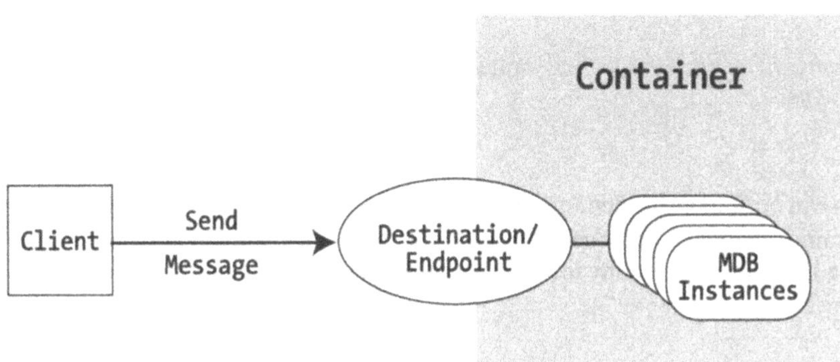

Figure 12-10. MDB

MDB Component Contract

All MDBs are required to implement the interface `javax.ejb.MessageDrivenBean`. In addition to this, they should implement the message listener interface specific to the messaging protocol they support. For example, an MDB listening for JMS messages should also implement the interface `javax.jms.MessageListener`. MDBs use the services provided by the container, such as transactions, security, concurrency, and so on. The container will also manage the bean life cycle and notify the bean instances when messages arrive in the destinations monitored by them.

The `MessageDrivenBean` instance defines two methods.

You can use the following message-driven context for getting the timer services, marking the transaction for rollback, and so on:

```
public void setMessageDrivenContext(MessageDrivenContext ctx)
```

The following method is called just before the bean instance is removed:

```
public void ejbRemove()
```

NOTE *The bean instance can use this for releasing resources such as removing database connections.*

The message listener interface implemented by the bean identifies the messaging protocol supported by the bean. JMS MDBs should use the `javax.jms.MessageListener` interface, and JAXM MDBs should use one of the JAM interfaces `javax.xml.messaging.OneWayListener` or `javax.xml.messaging.ReqRespListener`.

MDBs are required to provide a no-argument public `ejbCreate` method. The container creates a message bean instance by calling the `newInstance` method on the class and then sets its message-driven context. Then it calls the `ejbCreate` method.

NOTE *You can use this method for initializing resources such as opening database connections.*

MDBs can optionally implement the `TimedObject` interface if it wants to be the target of container-managed timer service.

Listing 12-10 shows the code for the MDB used in the auction application for calculating the bids.

Listing 12-10. Calculating the Bids

```
package com.apress.auction.message.ejb;

import javax.ejb.*;
import javax.jms.*;
import java.util.Iterator;
import java.math.BigDecimal;

import com.apress.auction.entity.interfaces.*;
import
  com.sun.j2ee.blueprints.servicelocator.ejb.ServiceLocator;
```

Since the MDB expects JMS messages, it implements the `MessageListener` interface (see Listing 12-11).

Listing 12-11. Bid Calculator MBean

```
public class BidCalculatorEJB implements MessageDrivenBean, MessageListener {

  private OfferLocalHome offerHome;

  public void ejbCreate() {

    ServiceLocator sl = new ServiceLocator();
    offerHome = (OfferLocalHome)
    sl.getLocalHome("java:comp/env/ejb/offer");

  }
  // These methods are implemented from the
  // MessageDrivenBean interface.
  public void ejbRemove() {}

  public void setMessageDrivenContext(MessageDrivenContext mdc) { }
  // This method is implemented from the
  // MessageListener interface.
  public void onMessage(Message inMessage) {

    try {
       // MDB expects an ObjectMessage.
      ObjectMessage msg = (ObjectMessage)inMessage;
      // Get the offer id.
      String offerId = (String)msg.getObject();
// Find the offer details.
      OfferLocal offer = offerHome.findByPrimaryKey(offerId);
      String offerName = offer.getName();
      String offerDescription = offer.getDescription();
      BigDecimal offerAskPrice = offer.getAskPrice();
// Get the offering customer details.
      CustomerLocal offerCustomer = offer.getCustomer();
      String offerCustomerName = offerCustomer.getName();
      String offerCustomerEmail = offerCustomer.getEmail();
// Get the highest bid.
      BidLocal highestBid = null;
      BigDecimal maxBid = new BigDecimal(0.0);

      Iterator bids = offer.getBids().iterator();
      while(bids.hasNext()) {
        BidLocal bid = (BidLocal)bids.next();
        if(bid.getBidPrice().compareTo(maxBid) > 0) {
          maxBid = new
            BigDecimal(bid.getBidPrice().doubleValue());
          highestBid = bid;
        }
      }

      if(highestBid == null) return;
```

```
// Get the highest bidding customer.
      CustomerLocal bidCustomer = highestBid.getCustomer();
      String bidCustomerName = bidCustomer.getName();
      String bidCustomerEmail = bidCustomer.getEmail();
// Print the details.
      //Send an email to the offer customer
      System.out.println("offerName:" + offerName);
      System.out.println("offerDescription:" +
        offerDescription);
      System.out.println("offerAskPrice:" + offerAskPrice);
      System.out.println("offerCustomerName:" +
        offerCustomerName);
      System.out.println("offerCustomerEmail:" +
        offerCustomerEmail);
      System.out.println("maxBid:" + maxBid);
      System.out.println("bidCustomerName:" +
        bidCustomerName);
      System.out.println("bidCustomerEmail:" +
        bidCustomerEmail);

    }catch(FinderException ex) {
      throw new EJBException(ex);
    }catch(JMSException ex) {
      throw new EJBException(ex);
    }

}
```

Message-Driven Context

The MessageDrivenContext interface extends EJBContext and doesn't define any additional methods to the ones provided by the superinterface. However, not all operations defined in the superinterface can be invoked from the MDB. Table 12-2 shows the methods that are allowed and not allowed.

Table 12-2. Methods

ALLOWED	NOT ALLOWED
setRollbackOnly	
getRollbackOnly	
getUserTransaction	
getTimerService	getCallerPrincipal
isCallerInRole	

NOTE *Security-related methods aren't allowed because MDBs don't have a client identity and are invoked by the container.*

Deployment Descriptor

MDBs are defined in the `ejb-jar.xml` file using the `message-driven` bean element. Prior to EJB 2.1, this element used to have a subelement specific to JMS. However, since EJB 2.1 supports non-JMS messages, the subelements of this element are more generic. Figure 12-11 depicts some of the more important subelements of the message-driven element, relevant to configuring the MDB.

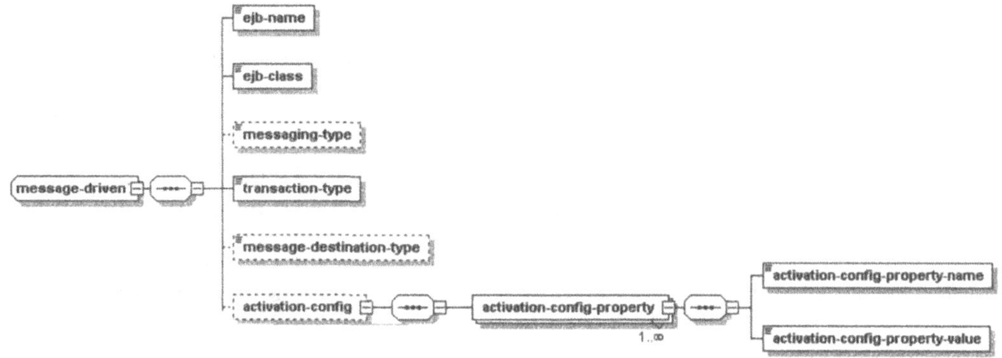

Figure 12-11. MDB deployment descriptor structure

> **NOTE** *Please note that Figure 12-11 doesn't depict the entire content model for the message-driven element. Some of the optional elements that have been omitted are specific to configuring the* `java:comp/env` *environment for the MDB. This is covered in detail in Chapter 17.*

The following are the elements used in the deployment descriptor for defining an MDB:

- The `ejb-name` element defines the name of the EJB.
- The `ejb-class` element specifies the fully qualified name of the MDB class.
- The `transaction-type` element specifies whether you use bean-managed or container-managed transactions.
- The `messaging-type` element specifies the fully qualified name of the message listener interface that the MDB uses. The default value is `javax.jms.MessageListener`.

- The `message-destination-type` element specifies the fully qualified name of the class/interface that represents the destination or endpoint monitored by the MDB, such as `java.jms.Queue`.
- The `activation-config` element provides any additional information required for the bean, such as acknowledgment mode, message selectors, and so on, that are passed to the underlying JCA resource adapter. The activation configuration properties you use are specific to the messaging protocol you use, and the vendors can add their own activation properties for a given protocol as well.

Table 12-3 shows the activation configuration properties available for JMS.

Table 12-3. Activation Configuration Properties

PROPERTY	VALUES	DESCRIPTION
`acknowledgeMode` `dups-ok-acknowledge`	`auto-acknowledge`	Defines the acknowledgment mode for the message. The MDB shouldn't call the method on the received message for acknowledgment. A message is acknowledged on transaction commit.
`messageSelector`		Message selector for the MDB.
`destinationType` `javax.jms.Topic`	`javax.jms.Queue`	The type of destination that's monitored. This is a bit redundant for JMD MDBs since the same information is present in the message destination-type element. However, for non-JMS MDBs, this activation configuration property may not be available and hence will have to rely on the message destination-type element to specify the message destination type.
`subscriptionDurability` `NonDurable`	`Durable`	Indicates the durability of topic subscription.

NOTE *How you specify the JNDI name of the destination monitored by the MDB is specific to the application server you use. However, EJB 2.1 introduces a powerful way of linking messages between message producers to destinations or MDBs. The "Introducing Message Linking" section explains this in detail.*

Listing 12-12 shows the deployment descriptor for the MDB used in the auction application.

Listing 12-12. Deployment Descriptor

```
<?xml version="1.0" encoding="UTF-8"?>
<ejb-jar xmlns="http://java.sun.com/xml/ns/j2ee"
         xmlns:xsi="http://www.w3.org/2001/XMLSchema-instance"
         xsi:schemaLocation="http://java.sun.com/xml/ns/j2ee
         http://java.sun.com/xml/ns/j2ee/ejb-jar_2_1.xsd"
         version="2.1">
  <display-name>BidCalculatorJAR</display-name>
  <enterprise-beans>
    <message-driven>
      <display-name>BidCalculator</display-name>
      <ejb-name>BidCalculator</ejb-name>
      <ejb-class>
        com.apress.auction.message.ejb.BidCalculatorEJB
      </ejb-class>
      <messaging-type>
        javax.jms.MessageListener
      </messaging-type>
      <transaction-type>Container</transaction-type>
      <message-destination-type>
        javax.jms.Queue
      </message-destination-type>
      <message-destination-link>
        LogicalQueue
      </message-destination-link>
      <activation-config>
        <activation-config-property>
          <activation-config-property-name>
            destinationType
          </activation-config-property-name>
          <activation-config-property-value>
            javax.jms.Queue
          </activation-config-property-value>
        </activation-config-property>
        <activation-config-property>
          <activation-config-property-name>
            destination
          </activation-config-property-name>
          <activation-config-property-value>
            BidQueue
          </activation-config-property-value>
        </activation-config-property>
      </activation-config>
      <ejb-local-ref>
        <ejb-ref-name>ejb/offer</ejb-ref-name>
        <ejb-ref-type>Entity</ejb-ref-type>
        <local-home>
          com.apress.auction.entity.interfaces.OfferLocalHome
        </local-home>
        <local>
```

```
            com.apress.auction.entity.interfaces.OfferLocal
          </local>
          <ejb-link>Offer</ejb-link>
        </ejb-local-ref>
      </message-driven>
    </enterprise-beans>

    <assembly-descriptor>
      <container-transaction>
        <method>
          <ejb-name>BidCalculator</ejb-name>
          <method-name>*</method-name>
          <method-params/>
        </method>
        <trans-attribute>Required</trans-attribute>
      </container-transaction>
      <message-destination>
        <message-destination-name>
          LogicalQueue
        </message-destination-name>
      </message-destination>
    </assembly-descriptor>
  </ejb-jar>
```

In Listing 12-12, the activation configuration property destination is specific to J2EE 1.4 RI and specifies the JNDI name of the destination watched by the MDB.

Introducing Message Linking

Message linking is one of the hidden gems in EJB 2.1. Message linking allows you to route messages sent by a J2EE component to an MDB in the same application. This is useful for implementing workflow in J2EE applications.

Any J2EE component wanting to produce or consume JMS messages can make the destinations they use available in their environment namespace, `java:comp/env`, using the `message-destination-ref` element whose structure is shown in Figure 12-12. This element is available for Web applications, session beans, entity beans, MDBs, and application clients.

In the structure shown in Figure 12-12, the `message-destination-ref-name` defines the coded name used by the component for looking up the reference. The `message-destination-type` element defines the fully qualified class name of the destination type, such as `javax.jms.Queue`, for example. The possible values for the `message-destination-usage` element are `Produces`, `Consumes`, and `ProducesConsumes`, which indicates the component produces messages for the destination, consumes messages from the destination, and both produces and consumes messages, respectively. The `message-destination-link` element is the key element for linking the messages sent to the destination by a component to an MDB. The `message-driven` element for MDBs has an immediate child element called `message-destination-link` that should have the same value of the message-destination-link element of the component that produces messages.

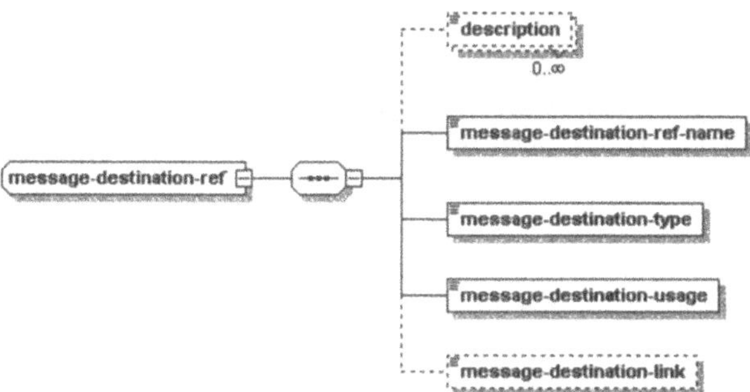

Figure 12-12. Message linking deployment descriptor structure

The message-destination-link value is a logical name for the destination that should match the message-destination-name element under the message-destination element under the assembly-descriptor element for the module. The linking of this logical name to a real destination in the operational environment is performed in an application server–specific manner during deployment. Figure 12-13 shows the message destination deployment descriptor structure.

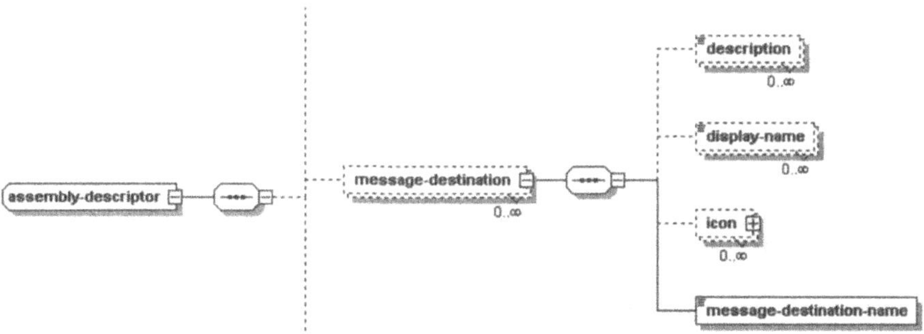

Figure 12-13. Message destination deployment descriptor structure

Listing 12-13 shows the excerpts from the deployment descriptors of the offer session bean that sends the JMS message when the offer times out and the MDB that calculates the highest bid for the offer. The session bean produces messages that are linked to a MDB.

Listing 12-13 shows the deployment descriptor for the session bean.

Listing 12-13. Session Bean Deployment Descriptor

```
<?xml version="1.0" encoding="US-ASCII"?>
<ejb-jar xmlns="http://java.sun.com/xml/ns/j2ee"
        xmlns:xsi="http://www.w3.org/2001/XMLSchema-instance"
        xsi:schemaLocation="http://java.sun.com/xml/ns/j2ee
        http://java.sun.com/xml/ns/j2ee/ejb-jar_2_1.xsd"
        version="2.1">
  ........................
  <enterprise-beans>
    <session>
      <display-name>OfferController</display-name>
      <ejb-name>OfferController</ejb-name>
      ...................
      <message-destination-ref>
        <message-destination-ref-name>
          jms/bidQueue
        </message-destination-ref-name>
        <message-destination-type>
          javax.jms.Queue
        </message-destination-type>
        <message-destination-usage>
          Produces
        </message-destination-usage>
        <message-destination-link>
          LogicalQueue
        </message-destination-link>
      </message-destination-ref>
    </session>
  </enterprise-beans>
  <assembly-descriptor>
    ..........................
    <message-destination>
      <message-destination-name>
        LogicalQueue
      </message-destination-name>
    </message-destination>
  </assembly-descriptor>
</ejb-jar>
```

The session bean can look up the topic by the name `java:comp/env/jms/bidQueue`. It uses the message link to define a logical name `LogicalQueue` that's defined in the assembly descriptor. Listing 12-14 shows the deployment descriptor for the MDB.

Listing 12-14. Deployment Descriptor

```
<?xml version="1.0" encoding="UTF-8"?>
<ejb-jar xmlns="http://java.sun.com/xml/ns/j2ee"
         xmlns:xsi="http://www.w3.org/2001/XMLSchema-instance"
         xsi:schemaLocation="http://java.sun.com/xml/ns/j2ee
         http://java.sun.com/xml/ns/j2ee/ejb-jar_2_1.xsd"
         version="2.1">
  ........................
  <enterprise-beans>
    <message-driven>
      <display-name>BidCalculator</display-name>
      <ejb-name>BidCalculator</ejb-name>
      <ejb-class>
        com.apress.auction.message.ejb.BidCalculatorEJB
      </ejb-class>
      .....................
      <message-destination-link>
        LogicalQueue
      </message-destination-link>
      <activation-config>
        ......................
      </activation-config>
    </message-driven>
  </enterprise-beans>
  <assembly-descriptor>
    .......................
    <message-destination>
      <message-destination-name>
        LogicalQueue
      </message-destination-name>
    </message-destination>
  </assembly-descriptor>
</ejb-jar>
```

The message destination link for the MDB matches the message destination link defined in the message destination reference for the session bean. The messages sent by the session bean to the destination identified by the message destination reference will be hence routed to the MDB. The actual mapping of `LogicalTopic` to a real destination will happen in an application server–specific manner.

MDBs and Transactions

MDBs can use either bean-managed transactions or container-managed transactions. They shouldn't be using the JMS API for acknowledging messages. The messages are automatically acknowledged when the transaction is committed. In the case of an error, the beans should mark the current transaction for rollback so that the message is redelivered. MDBs with bean-managed transactions can access the user transaction through their message-driven context. The only transaction attributes that are relevant to MDBs with container-managed transaction are `Required` and `NotSupported`. This is because the container always invokes MDBs, and there won't be an existing transaction associated with the caller.

MDBs and Security

Since the containers always invoke MDBs, there's no security identity associated with the caller. Hence, if you specify an explicit security identity in the deployment descriptor, you can't use the caller identity, and you should specify a run as identity. Because of the same reasons, you can't call `getCallerPrincipal` and `isCallerInRole` methods on the message-driven context.

Summary

This chapter provided a comprehensive coverage of the messaging capabilities of J2EE. It started with JMS and covered the messaging domains supported by JMS. Then you looked at the various JMS artifacts for implementing enterprise-messaging solutions in Java. The chapter covered transaction support in JMS and the various message types supported by JMS. You looked at durable subscriptions and then moved on to MDBs. The chapter also covered how MDBs support JMS and non-JMS messages. Finally, the chapter concluding by covering message linking in J2EE.

CHAPTER 13
Using EJB Container Services

One of the main reasons Enterprise JavaBeans (EJBs) have evolved into the most popular component model for distributed computing over the past few years is because of the way EJBs externalize system-level services such as transactions, scheduling, instance pooling, caching, and so on, from application logic. EJBs allow application developers to concentrate on writing the application logic and rely on the container services to make their application components transactional, persistent, secure, performing, and scalable. In this chapter, you'll learn about the services that the components can expect from the containers. The topics covered in this chapter include the following:

- Security services
- Transaction services
- Scheduling services

You'll also learn about value-added services provided by containers such as the following:

- Instance pooling
- Instance caching

Introducing Security

Security is one of the key aspects of enterprise application development. Security addresses a variety of enterprise application aspects, including the following:

- Authentication
- Authorization
- Data integrity
- Data confidentiality

- Nonrepudiation
- Auditing

Authentication is the process by which the claims of an entity's identity are verified when it participates in communication with another entity. The authenticated entity is called a *subject* and may comprise one or more principals. To perform the authentication, the entity that has to be authenticated presents private information, called *credentials*, to the authenticating entity. The credentials can be simple passwords, digital certificates, security cards, and so on. For example, a student trying to access the training application may need to present her username and password before accessing the enrolled courses. In the Java 2 Enterprise Edition (J2EE) stack, the Web application layer provides extensive support for various authentication mechanisms. The EJB specification doesn't specify anything about authentication. In most cases, the EJBs are accessed from the Web tier, and the Web tier takes care of authentication. This is acceptable in a colocated architecture. However, in scenarios where the Web tier and EJB tier are distributed across different application server instances, you may need to establish trust between the servers that are involved. If you have thick clients directly accessing the EJB layer, you can either perform authentication when you create the Java Naming and Directory Interface (JNDI) initial context by passing the principal identity and credentials or use Java Authentication and Authorization Service (JAAS) to perform the login and associate the retuned JAAS subject with the EJB invocations. The second method is preferred and recommended by most of the application server vendors.

NOTE *You can use JAAS in the Web tier for colocated architectures as well. In this case, you use* `Subject.doAs()` *to call the EJB, and you don't pass in the security credentials using JNDI. However, the web containers are required to propogate the credentials transparently.*

Once the entity is authenticated, the next process is *authorization*. Authorization checks the access rights of the authenticated subject. The authorization process ensures that the authenticated subject has the appropriate authority to access the requested resource. Both J2EE Web and EJB tiers provide extensive support for role-based authorization. In the Web tier, roles restrict access to uniform resource indicator (URI) patterns, whereas in the EJB tier they restrict access to the methods defined against the client view of the EJB.

When two parties are involved in exchanging data electronically, it's of the utmost importance that the data isn't modified in anyway while in transit. The most common way by which the *integrity* of the data is compromised by what, in security terms, is called a *man-in-the-middle attack*. In this case, someone intercepts the data sent by the sender, alters it, and resends it to the receiver. The receiver would have no idea that the original data was tampered with. Data integrity is normally ensured using message digests and digital signatures. Even though the EJB specification doesn't specify anything about ensuring the integrity of data during invocation, most of the leading application servers, such as WebLogic, JBoss, and so on, support EJB and JNDI invocation over a secure protocol such as Secure Socket Layers (SSL).

Data *confidentiality* is another security aspect that's as important as data integrity. Where data integrity makes it extremely difficult for the interceptor to tamper with the data, data confidentiality makes sure that the interceptor can't even read the data. This is important in exchanging confidential details such as credit card numbers, Social Security numbers, financial transactions, and so on. Again, EJB specification doesn't specify anything about ensuring the confidentiality of data during invocation. Data confidentiality is normally ensured using symmetric or asymmetric cryptography and is offered by industry-standard secure protocols such as SSL.

Security solutions that provide *nonrepudiation* services prove the occurrence of a transaction. Nonrepudiation leaves digital trails identifying the originator and recipient of a transaction and the information that was exchanged. This makes originating entities accountable for the transactions. Nonrepudiation is normally achieved through digital signatures, signature chains, and certificate authorities.

It's impossible to write a system that's perfectly secure. It's always striking a balance between the cost involved in implementing the security mechanism and the effort involved in security intrusion. However, one important point is when the system security is compromised, there should be clear *audit trail* on how, when, who, and what was compromised. Even though the EJB specification doesn't say anything about auditing, most of the mainstream application vendors provide various auditing services to log important security events related to authentication and authorization.

EJB security mainly focuses on the following aspects:

- Allowing component developers to concentrate on writing application logic and allowing the container to provide security services
- Allowing security to be configured at deployment time in a declarative manner
- Allowing portability of security policies of enterprise applications across server vendors

Security in EJBs is mainly associated with authorization and is based on declarative roles. *Roles* are logical groupings of permissions. For example, in the auction application, you can define a role called `customer` that can view the list of offers, details of a selected offer, and so on, and an `admin` role for adding, removing and updating customers. These roles are declared declaratively in the deployment descriptor so that the bean providers don't need to hard-code security policies in their business methods. The bean provider or application assembler will specify the roles in the deployment descriptor. The bean deployer can define method permissions and map the roles to principals in the operational environment at deployment time. The EJB specification doesn't say anything about mapping the logical roles to physical principals in the operational environment. The operational environment that defines the physical users and roles is called a *security realm*. Often you do this in an application server–specific manner. For example, in WebLogic, you define the mapping of roles to WebLogic users and/or groups in the WebLogic-specific EJB deployment descriptor `weblogic-ejb-jar.xml`.

Defining Security Roles

The security roles used for method permissions on the client views of EJBs are defined in the standard EJB deployment descriptor `ejb-jar.xml` for the EJB module. The security roles are defined within the `assembly-descriptor` element, as shown in Figure 13-1.

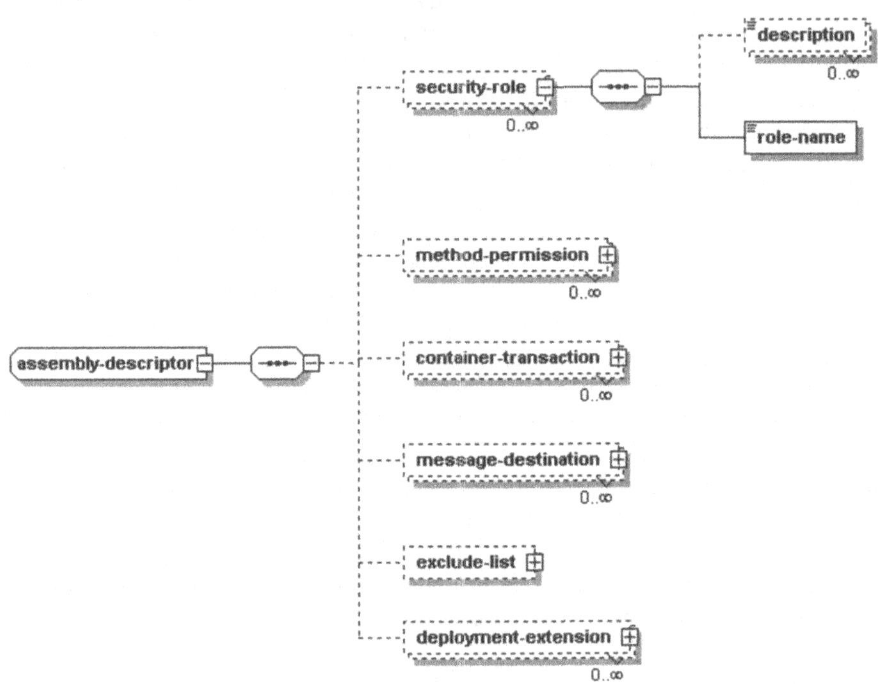

Figure 13-1. Defining security roles

The assembly descriptor can contain zero or more `security-role` elements, as shown in Listing 13-1. The `security-role` element should contain a `role-name` element providing a unique role name in the module and an optional `description` element for a meaningful description for the role.

Listing 13-1. Defining the Security Role

```
<assembly-descriptor>

  <security-role>
    <description>
      The role includes all the registered customers
    </description>
    <role-name>CUSTOMER<role-name>
  </security-role>
```

```
  <security-role>
    <description>
      The role includes all the valid administrators
    </description>
    <role-name>ADMIN<role-name>
  </security-role>

  ...
</assembly-descriptor>
```

Listing 13-1 defines two roles: CUSTOMER and ADMIN.

> **NOTE** *When you define role names, make sure you give meaningful names for your roles in the context of your application. Also make sure that your roles don't conflict with some of the system roles within the operational environment. For example, WebLogic uses some system roles such as* admin, deployer, operator, monitor, *and so on. However, conflicting role names won't cause a big problem in WebLogic. Because WebLogic scopes roles local to the deployment unit or resource, it's good practice to give roles names that makes sense in the context of the application. I tend to prefix my application roles with some application-specific string. For example, in Listing 13-1, you could name your role* AU CUSTOMER *and* AU ADMIN, *where* AU *stands for* auction.

Defining Method Permissions

Method permissions associate roles with methods that the authenticated users with those roles are allowed to access. Suppose you have two EJBs in your deployment unit, one implementing use cases related to listing available offers, viewing offer details, and so on, and the second one for editing, creating, updating, and deleting customer details. You can define method permissions so that only authenticated users with the customer role can access the methods defined for the first EJB and only users with the admin role can access the methods defined on the second EJB. This means the container will verify that the principal associated with an invocation possess the defined role before the invocation is permitted.

Method permissions are also defined within the assembly-descriptor element for the deployment descriptor, as shown in Figure 13-2.

The assembly-descriptor element can contain zero or more method-permission elements. Each method-permission element links one or more logical roles to one or more methods. The methods defined here can be from the home, component, and/or Web service endpoint interface. The method permissions ensure that only an invoker with the specified role can invoke that method. If you don't specify the role names using the role-name element and instead choose to use the unchecked element, the container won't check for authorization before the method is invoked.

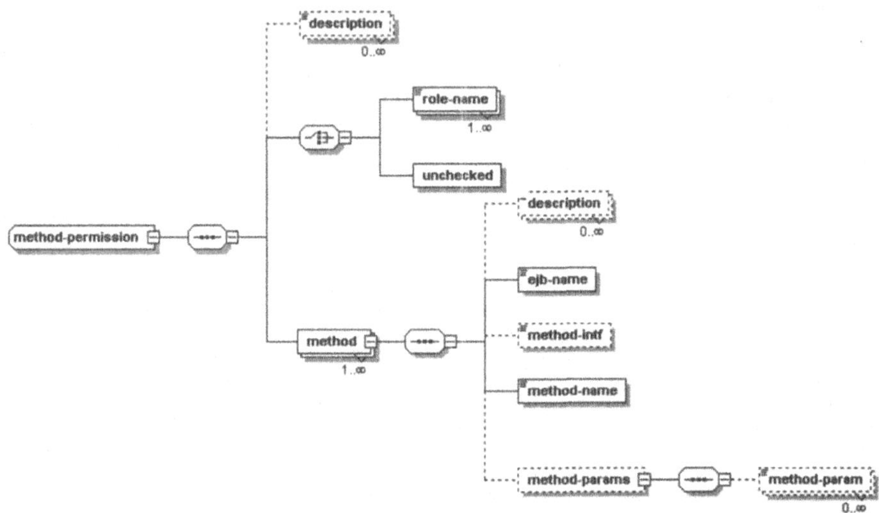

Figure 13-2. Method permissions

> **NOTE** *Typically the application assembler or bean provider defines the logical roles in the context of the application in the deployment descriptor. The bean provider, application assembler, or deployer can define the method permissions for the roles. However, the deployer in a mechanism specific to the operational environment in which the bean is deployed performs the mapping of those logical roles into principals.*

Listing 13-2 specifies that users with `CUSTOMER` or `admin` role can invoke all the methods on the `OfferController`, and only users with the `ADMIN` role can invoke methods on the `CustomerController`.

Listing 13-2. Defining the Security Role

```
<assembly-descriptor>

  <security-role>
    <description>
      The role includes all the registered customers
    </description>
    <role-name>CUSTOMER<role-name>
  </security-role>

  <security-role>
    <description>
      The role includes all the valid administrators
    </description>
    <role-name>ADMIN<role-name>
  </security-role>
```

```
  <method-permission>
    <role-name>CUSTOMER></role-name>
    <role-name>ADMIN></role-name>
    <method>
      <ejb-name>CustomerController</ejb-name>
      <method-name>*</method-name>
    </method>
  </method-permission>

  <method-permission>
    <role-name>ADMIN></role-name>
    <method>
      <ejb-name>CustomerController</ejb-name>
      <method-name>*</method-name>
    </method>
  </method-permission>

  ...
</assembly-descriptor>
```

NOTE *EJB 2.0 introduced the notion of* local references. *Local references are accessible only from the same JVM as the caller. This means the external interface for the local reference will be accessed indirectly through the some remote references. Typically in a distributed environment, remote Session Façades will be implementing the course-grained use cases and using helper classes and/or local entity references to realize the use case. In such scenarios, it's often efficient to define the method permissions on the remote Session Façade layer and leave the methods on the local references unchecked to improve performance. Another architectural pattern that's becoming increasingly popular is collocated architecture. Here the entire J2EE stack is on the physical node and uses local references even for Session Façade. Then, deploy the application on several machines in parallel to gain the scalability you want.*

Specifying Methods

You can specify the methods for which the permissions are defined in a variety of ways. In Listing 13-2, the permissions were defined for all the methods exposed by the relevant EJBs using the wildcard character * for the `method-name` element. This will define permission for all the methods exposed by the home, component, and Web service interfaces.

However, if you want to define the permission for a specific method, you can do so as follows:

```
<method>
  <ejb-name>OfferController</ejb-name>
  <method-name>searchOffers</method-name>
</method>
```

The previous snippet defines permissions for all the methods by the name `searchOffers` in the EJB's home, component, and Web service interfaces. However, if you want to refer to a specific instance of a method, rather than setting permissions for all the overloaded versions, you can use the following `method-params` element:

```
<method>
  <ejb-name>OfferController</ejb-name>
  <method-name>searchOffers</method-name>
  <method-params>
    <method-param>java.lang.String</method-param>
  </method-params>
</method>
```

The `method-params` element lists all the method parameters using an ordered list of `method-param` elements. In the previous snippet, all `serachOffers` methods that take a single argument of type `java.lang.String` are included. However, if you have the same method signature defined across the client view interfaces, all of them are included. If you want to use a specific client view interface, you can use the `method-intf` element to specify the interface you want. The allowed values for this element are as follows:

- **Home**: Specifies methods defined in the remote home interface
- **LocalHome**: Specifies methods defined in the local home interface
- **Remote**: Specifies methods defined in the remote component interface
- **Local**: Specifies methods defined in the local component interface
- **ServiceEndpoint**: Specifies methods defined in the Web service interface

In the following snippet, the `searchOffers` methods that take a single argument of type `java.lang.String` defined in the bean's remote component interface are included:

```
<method>
  <ejb-name>OfferController</ejb-name>
  <method-name>searchOffers</method-name>
  <method-params>
    <method-param>java.lang.String</method-param>
  </method-params>
  <method-inf>Remote</method-intf>
</method>
```

Programmatic Security

One of the main objectives of EJB security is to externalize security services from application code, using declarative security. However, when it comes to implementing instance-based security, this technique fails miserably. For example, when an authenticated customer requests the list of items she has made available for auction, nothing in the EJB specification allows you to return only those items offered by the customer.

> **NOTE** *Application servers such as JBoss allow you to have security logic externalized from the bean code by using security interceptors. JBoss uses an interceptor-based container architecture where you can declaratively configure the interceptors through which the invocations travel before they hit the target bean instance. If your application server doesn't supply this type of functionality, then you need to provide instance-based security yourself.*

> **NOTE** *Another upcoming technology that can aid immensely in implementing instance-based security is Aspect-Oriented Programming (AOP).*

To enable programmatic security to implement instance-based checks, the EJB API provides two methods in the `javax.ejb.EJBContext` interface. `SessionContext`, `EntityContext`, and `MessageDrivenContext` interfaces extend this interface.

This method returns the primary principal associated with identity of the caller:

```
public java.security.Principal getCallerPrincipal();
```

You can obtain the distinguished name of the caller by invoking the `getName` method on the returned principal. The runtime type of the principal instance that's returned is specific to the application server.

> **NOTE** *The principal doesn't need to correspond to the original username used by the user to log on to the system. However, in most scenarios,* `getCallerPrincipal().getName()` *will give you the username used by the user to log in to the system.*

Listing 13-3 shows how `OfferControllerBean` can use this to implement instance-based security.

Listing 13-3. `OfferControllerBean`

```
public class OfferControllerBean implements SessionBean {

  private SessionContext ctx;

  .....................

  public OfferData[] listOffers() {

    try {
      // Look up the entity EJBs local home.
      ServiceLocator sl = new ServiceLocator();
      OfferLocalHome offerHome =
          (OfferLocalHome)sl.getLocalHome("java:comp/env/ejb/offer");
      // Get the user's principal.
      Principal userPrincipal = ctx.getCallerPrincipal();
     // Get the principal's distinguished name.
      String customerId = userPrincipal.getName();
      // Select the courses by student id.
      Collection col = customerHome.findByPrimaryKey(userId).getOffers();
      OfferData offerData[] = new OfferData[col.size()];

      Iterator it = col.iterator();
      for(int i = 0;i < offerData.length && it.hasNext();i++)
        offerData[i] = ((OfferLocal)it.next()).getData();

      return offerData;

    }catch(ObjectNotFoundException ex) {
      throw new OfferException("Customer not found");
    }catch(FinderException ex) {
      throw new EJBException(ex);
    }

  }

}
```

NOTE *The principal returned is the invoker's called identity and not the run-as identity if there's one specified. Run-as identity is covered in detail in the next section.*

The following method—which is defined in the interface `EJBContext` that's the superinterface for the interfaces `SessionContext`, `EntityContext`, and `MessageDriven-Context`—is used to check whether the caller has the specified role:

```
public boolean isCallerInRole(String roleName);
```

However, if you have coded roles in the bean, these roles should be mapped to the security roles defined by the `security-role` element using the `security-role-ref` element. The `security-role` elements are defined at deployment unit level (EJB JAR file), and the `security-role-ref` elements are defined at bean level in the deployment descriptor (`ejb-jar.xml`), as shown in Figure 13-3.

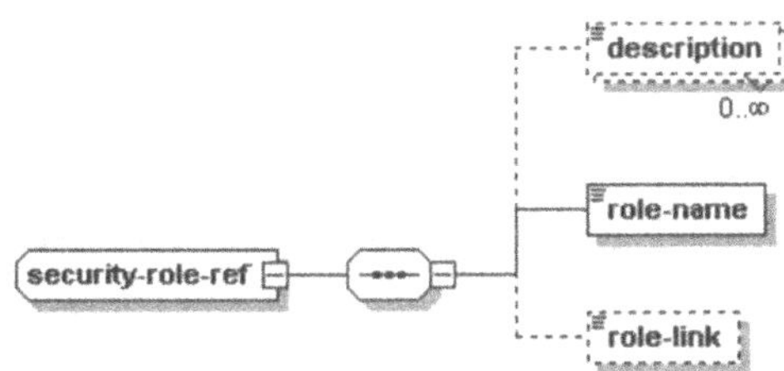

Figure 13-3. Security role reference

The entity and session elements in the deployment descriptor can have zero or more `security-role-ref` elements. The `role-name` element should have the coded role name used in the bean. This is the value that's passed to the `isCallerInRole` method. The `role-link` element should have the same value as the `role-name` element in the security-role defining the role to which the coded role is mapped.

> **NOTE** *You should use the* `security-role-ref` *element even if the coded name and the role defined in the deployment descriptor using the* `security-role/role-name` *element are the same. The deployer performs the mapping of the coded roles to roles specified in the deployment descriptor.*

Listing 13-4 shows how the logical role defined in the deployment descriptor is mapped to the coded role.

Listing 13-4. Security Role Reference

```
<session>
  <ejb-name>CustomerController</ejb-name>
  .............
  <security-role-ref>
    <role-name>ADMIN</role-name>
    <role-link>AU ADMIN</role-link>
  </security-role-ref>
  .............
</session>

<assembly-descriptor>
  <security-role>
    <role-name>AU ADMIN</role-name>
  </security-role>
</assembly-descriptor>
```

Now in the code you can use `sessionContext.isCallerInRole("ADMIN")` to check whether the authenticated principal has the role `AU ADMIN`.

> **NOTE** *You can invoke the methods* `getCallerPrincipal` *and* `isCallerInRole` *only from those methods that have a client security context associated with them. For session beans, these methods include* `ejbCreate`, `ejbRemove`, `ejbActivate`, `ejbPassivate`, *all the business methods defined in the component interface, and, if it implements the* `SessionSynchronization` *interface, the* `afterBegin`, `beforeCompletion`, *and* `afterCompletion` *methods. For entity beans, these methods include* `ejbCreate`, `ejbPostCreate`, `ejbRemove`, `ejbHome`, `ejbLoad`, `ejbStore`, *and any business methods defined in the component interface.*

Run-As Identity

In normal scenarios, you invoke bean methods within the security context of the caller's identity. However, sometimes you may want to execute a method under the security context of a different security identity. For example, in the auction application you have a session bean responsible for customer registration, which is unrestricted. In the method for registering the customer, the bean would call another EJB to get a list of all the registered customers to make sure the details are unique. The method on the second EJB has a permission set so that only those principals with the `ADMIN` role can invoke that method. This means if you invoke the registration method in the security context of the caller's identity, the second invocation would fail.

To avoid this, you can specify a run-as identity at bean level in the deployment descriptor for the first bean using the `security-identity` element, as shown in Figure 13-4.

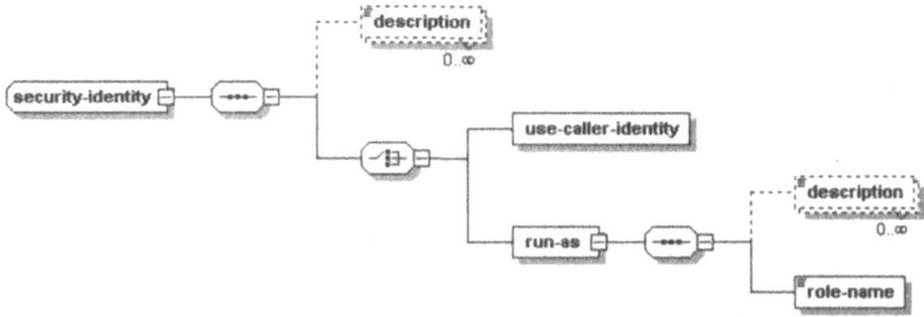

Figure 13-4. Run-as identity

If you want to use a run-as identity, you should specify the `run-as` element as the child for the `security-identity` element, as shown in Listing 13-5. The `role-name` should match one of the logical roles defined using the `security-role` element.

Listing 13-5. Run-As Identity

```
<enterprise-beans>
  .............
  <session>
    <ejb-name>CustomerController</ejb-name>
    .............
    <security-identity>
      <run-as>
        <role-name>AU ADMIN</role-name>
      </run-as>
    </security-identity>
  .............
  </session>
     .............
</enterprise-beans>
```

The mapping of the role used for run-as identity to a principal in the operational environment happens in an operational environment–specific manner.

> **NOTE** *The enterprise bean uses the run-as identity specified when it makes a call. This means it doesn't affect the method permissions set on the enterprise bean for which the run-as identity was set. If you have an MDB or an enterprise bean that uses the container-managed timer service calling another secure EJB in the* `onMessage` *or* `ejbTimeout` *method, respectively, you should specify the run-as identity in the deployment descriptor. This identity will be used when the method is invoked by the MDB's* `onMessage` *method or the scheduled EJB's* `ejbTimeout` *method.*

Mapping Roles to Principals

Mapping the roles to principals in the operational environment happens in a manner specific to the operational environment.

For example, in JBoss this is performed using the JBoss-specific EJB deployment descriptor jboss.xml, as shown in Listing 13-6. This deployment descriptor has an element called security-domain that will have the JNDI name of a login module used to perform authentication and authorization. This element registers a security realm with JBoss. The login modules are based on JAAS, and JBoss comes with a variety of login modules that can read security information from files, databases, directory services, and so on.

Listing 13-6. JBoss Security Mapping

```
<jboss>
  .............
  <security-domain>java:/auctionDomain</security-domain>
  <enterprise-beans>
    <session>
      <ejb-name>CustomerController</ejb-name>
      .............
    </session>
    .............
  </enterprise-beans>
  .............
</jboss>
```

Listing 13-6 defines a security domain for all the beans at deployment unit level. You can override this at bean level using JBoss container configurations. Refer to *JBoss 3.2 Deployment and Administration* (Apress, 2003) for more details.

WebLogic uses the weblogic-ejb-jar.xml file to map the roles to a list of principal names using the security-role-assignment element, as shown in Listing 13-7. In WebLogic principal names can be either user names or group names. Groups allow you to assign roles to a group of users.

Listing 13-7. WebLogic Security Mapping

```
<weblogic-ejb-jar>

  <weblogic-enterprise-bean>
    <ejb-name>CustomerController</ejb-name>
    .............
    <security-role-assignment>
      <role-name>AU ADMIN</role-name>
      <principal-name>Administrators</principal-name>
      <principal-name>Fred Flintstone</principal-name>
    </security-role-assignment>
    .............

  </weblogic-enterprise-bean>

</weblogic-ejb-jar>
```

In Listing 13-7 the `AU ADMIN` role is assigned to the `Administrators` group and the user `Fred Flintstone`.

Introducing Scheduling

Scheduling is one of the important tasks used in enterprise applications, especially in workflow-type applications. Prior to EJB 2.1, J2EE developers relied on proprietary services provided by the container such as WebLogic scheduling survives, JBoss scheduling MBeans, and so on, to schedule tasks. However, one of the coolest features introduced by EJB 2.1 is scheduling, or the container-managed timer service. This allows J2EE developers to implement timer-based event notifications in their applications in a standard, portable manner.

The EJB 2.1 container-managed timer service allows you to make an EJB instance the target of a timer.

> **NOTE** *The container-managed timer service allows you to make an entity bean, stateless session bean, or an MDB the target of timed callbacks. In the case of entity beans, the timed callback is sent to an instance with the same identity that scheduled the timer. For stateless session and message-driven instances, the timed callback is invoked on any instance in the ready-pooled state.*

The main classes and interfaces involved in container-managed timer service are as follows:

- **javax.ejb.TimedObject**: An enterprise bean instance that needs to be notified by the timer service should implement this interface.
- **javax.ejb.TimerService**: This interface provides the EJB instances access to the container-managed timer service. This can then be used for scheduling new timers and getting a collection of all instances of the timers associated with the bean instance.
- **javax.ejb.Timer**: An instance of this interface is passed to the timed callback method of the EJB instance. You can use this for cancelling the timer, getting the next timeout, getting any information that was passed when the timer was created, and so on.
- **javax.ejb.TimerHandle**: This allows you to serialize a timer to a persistent store.
- **javax.ejb.EJBContext**: Bean instances accessed the container-managed timer service through this interface.

Figure 13-5 shows the main classes and interfaces involved in the EJB 2.1 container-managed timer service.

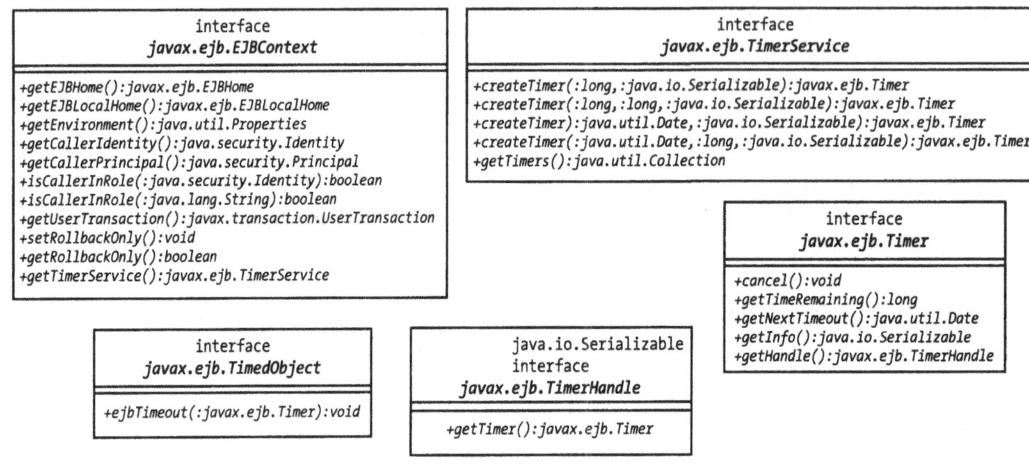

Figure 13-5. Timer services classes and interfaces

TimerService

This interface provides access to the container-managed timer service. Enterprise bean instances requiring a new timer create one by accessing the timer services using the `getTimerService` method provided by `javax.ejb.EJBContext`. This interface provides methods for creating both recurring and nonrecurring timers. For stateless session beans, the timer service can be accessed from the session context in the `ejbCreate` and `ejbRemove` methods, the business methods defined in the component and Web service endpoint interfaces, and the `ejbTimeout` method. The `ejbTimeout` method is called on a bean instance when the current timer times out. For MDBs, this can be done in the `ejbCreate` and `ejbRemove` methods, the message listener method, and the `ejbTimeout` method. For container-managed persistent entity beans, these methods include `ejbCreate`, `ejbPostCreate`, `ejbHome`, `ejbRemove`, `ejbActivate`, `ejbPassivate`, `ejbLoad`, `ejbStore`, `ejbTimeout`, and the business methods defined in the component interface.

You use the following methods for creating the timers. Specifically, the following creates an interval timer whose first expiration occurs at a given point in time and whose subsequent expirations occur after a specified interval:

```
Timer createTimer(Date initialExpiration, long intervalDuration,
  Serializable info)
```

Use the following to create a single-action timer that expires at a given point in time:

```
Timer createTimer(Date expiration, Serializable info)
```

Use the following to create an interval timer whose first expiration occurs after a specified duration and whose subsequent expirations occur after a specified interval:

```
Timer createTimer(long initialDuration, long intervalDuration, Serializable info)
```

Use the following to create a single-action timer that expires after a specified duration:

```
Timer createTimer(long duration, Serializable info)
```

Use the following to get all the active timers associated with this bean:

```
Collection getTimers()
```

The serializable object that's passed to all the methods for creating the timer can be used for passing contextual information that's passed back to the bean when the timer times out. The following snippet shows how to create a recurring timer that will expire every 30 seconds and expires for the first time 30 seconds after creation:

```
TimerService service = context.getTimerService();
Timer timer = service.createTimer(30*1000, 30*1000, null);
```

The duration is specified in milliseconds. Here the variable context can be a reference to a session, entity, or message-driven context.

In the auction application, timers keep track of offer expiry and send a Java Message Server (JMS) message. The JMS message is picked up by an MDB that calculates the highest bid and notifies the relevant parties. When the customer creates an offer, the timer starts. To send the message back to the customers, the stateless session bean that provides the callback for the timer can send a JMS message to a topic, which is monitored by an MDB, as shown in Figure 13-6.

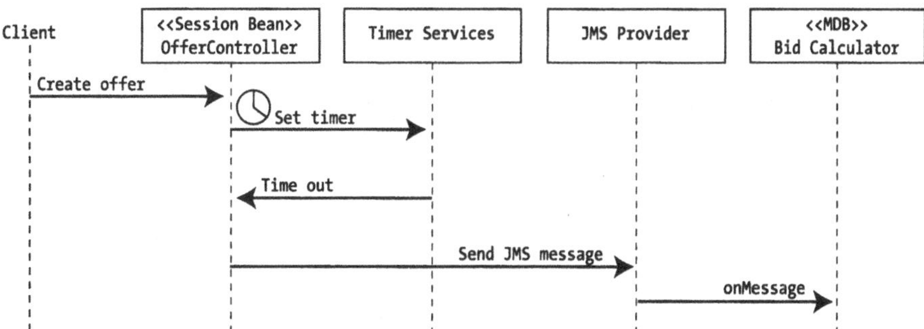

Figure 13-6. Timer sequence diagram

Listing 13-8 shows how to create a timer from the business method for creating the offer that will expire only once to achieve this purpose. The duration of the offer is configured as an EJB environment entry.

Listing 13-8. Create Offer Method

```
public void createOffer(OfferData offerData, String userId)
  throws OfferException {

    try {

      OfferLocal offer = offerHome.create(new UID().toString(),
      offerData.getName(), offerData.getDescription(),
      offerData.getAskPrice(), customerHome.findByPrimaryKey(userId));

      ctx.getTimerService().createTimer(delay,
        interval, offer.getOfferId());

    }catch(ObjectNotFoundException ex) {
      throw new OfferException("Customer not found");
    }catch(FinderException ex) {
      throw new EJBException(ex);
    }catch(CreateException ex) {
      throw new EJBException(ex);
    }

  }
```

In Listing 13-8, the offer ID is passed back to the timed callback of the bean instance when the timer expires.

TimedObject

All EJB instances that create a timer service should implement the `TimedObject` interface that defines the timed callback method that's invoked by the container on timer expiry. This interface a has the following single method:

```
public void ejbTimeout(Timer timer);
```

The argument that's passed to this method is an instance of `javax.ejb.Timer` interface that provides the following methods. Specifically, this causes the timer and all its associated expiration notifications to be cancelled:

```
void cancel()
```

The following gets a serializable handle to the timer:

```
TimerHandle getHandle()
```

The following gets the information associated with the timer at the time of creation:

```
Serializable getInfo()
```

The following gets the point in time at which the next timer expiration is scheduled to occur:

```
Date getNextTimeout()
```

The following gets the number of milliseconds that will elapse before the next scheduled timer expiration:

```
long getTimeRemaining()
```

Listing 13-9 shows the `ejbTimeout` method from the stateless session beans to send a JMS message to the MDB.

Listing 13-9. EJB Timer Implementation

```
public void ejbTimeout(Timer timer) {

  try {
    // Get the student ID that was stored when the timer was created.
    String offerId = (String)timer.getInfo();
    // Call the private method to send the JMS message.
    offerHome.findByPrimaryKey(offerId);
    System.out.println("Processing offer:" + offerId);

    sendMessage(offerId);

  }catch(ObjectNotFoundException ex) {
    System.out.println("Cancelling offer:" + offerId);
    timer.cancel();
  }catch(FinderException ex) {
    throw new EJBException(ex);
  }
  // Private method sends the JMS message.
  private void sendMessage(String offerId) {

    QueueConnection con = null;

    try {

      con = qcf.createQueueConnection();
      QueueSession sess = con.createQueueSession(false,
        Session.AUTO_ACKNOWLEDGE);
```

```
      QueueSender sender = sess.createSender(bidQueue);

      Message msg = sess.createObjectMessage(offerId);
      sender.send(msg);

    }catch(JMSException ex) {
      throw new EJBException(ex);
    }finally {
      try {
        if(con != null) con.close();
      }catch(JMSException ex) {
        throw new EJBException(ex);
      }
    }

}
```

NOTE *Two main shortcomings of the timer service are that there's no automatic way to create a timer service and there's no fine-grained control on how the timer intervals are set. Creating a timer service for a stateless session or entity EJB involves the client explicitly invoking a method on the client view and a timer service being created in the corresponding callback on the bean class. For MDBs this involves a message being sent to a destination monitored by the MDB. Currently the onus is on the bean providers to create a long value or date object that represents the initial delay and recurring intervals for the timer. However, if you compared this to the rich functionality provided by Microsoft Windows Scheduled Tasks or Unix Cron jobs, this falls short in functionality.*

Introducing Transactions

Support for transactions, especially distributed transactions, is one of the key container services mandated by J2EE.

Transactions are required to be atomic, consistent, isolated, and durable (ACID). Transactions allow business operations to execute in an atomic, consistent, isolated, and durable manner.

They're *atomic* in the sense that the tasks performed within that unit of work either commit fully or are rolled back fully. If any of the tasks in the operation fail, transactions make sure that the effect of all the tasks executed before the failed task are rolled back.

Consistency ensures that the integrity of data isn't violated after a business operation. For example, in a banking operation involving the transfer of funds, transactions ensure that the source account is always debited and the receiving account is credited by the same amount.

Isolation ensures that every business operation executes in a system, as if it were the only single operation executing at that time. This means when an operation is modifying the underlying data, it can be ensured that no other process is affecting the same data.

Durability of transactions makes sure that the changes made during the business operations are committed to a persistent storage.

Traditionally, database systems have provided the ACID characteristics of transactions by providing various locking and concurrency mechanisms. The advent of middleware systems advanced enterprise application development by moving some of the traditional database services such as caching into the application tier and thereby improving performance and throughput. They also avoid unnecessary disk access, eager loading data, and delaying writes only when it's absolutely necessary. However, this also brought in an added layer of complexity for managing transactions and concurrencies. The following sections show how EJBs support transactions.

EJB Transactions

The EJB specification mandates that the underlying containers manage transactions, allowing the bean providers to concentrate on the application logic. However, it also gives the choice to the developers to whether programmatically demarcate the transactions or delegate it to the container to demarcate the transactions. In either case, the container handles the actual task of managing the transactions.

The EJB specification also requires containers to support distributed transactions. Distributed transactions use a two-phase commit (2PC) protocol to span transactions across multiple resource managers. For example, you can write a record to a relational database and send a message to a JMS provider and be assured that both the tasks will execute in the same transaction. In other words, if the database write fails, the message isn't sent to the JMS provider, and if the message delivery fails, the database write is rolled back.

The EJB specification also requires transactions to be propagated across multiple EJB servers. For example, when a customer registers on the auction Web site, she provides the payment details. The client calls an EJB residing in the auction EJB container that will write a record to the auction database and calls another EJB in the account processing EJB server to debit the customer's account. EJB transactions make sure that both the tasks execute as a single atomic unit of work, without any additional programming overhead on the bean providers.

NOTE *The EJB specification requires containers provide support for the Java Transaction API (JTA). JTA defines an API for interfacing the underlying transaction manager with the other entities involved in distributed transactions such as resource managers, application programs, components, and containers.*

NOTE *Currently the EJB specification requires containers to support only flat transaction and not nested transactions. Nested transactions allow you to have multiple active transactions that are nested. In J2EE when a transaction starts within the context of another transaction, the enclosing transaction is suspended. This means rolling back or committing the nested transaction doesn't have any impact on the enclosing transaction.*

Container-Managed Transaction Demarcation

With container-managed transaction demarcation, the transactional behavior of an EJB method is defined in the deployment descriptor. Transactions attributes are defined in the deployment descriptors in a similar way to method permissions. You need to specify in the deployment descriptor for the bean whether the bean or the container should demarcate the transactions. You do this using the `transaction-type` element that's the subelement of `session-bean` or `message-driven-bean` elements. The possible values are `Container` or `Bean`. For container-managed transaction demarcation, you should set this to `Container`.

> **NOTE** *You can have only container-managed transactions for entity beans.*

You define the transaction attribute for a method or a set of methods using the `container-transaction` element within the `assembly-descriptor` element, as shown in Figure 13-7. You can have zero or more `container-transaction` elements within the `assembly-descriptor` element.

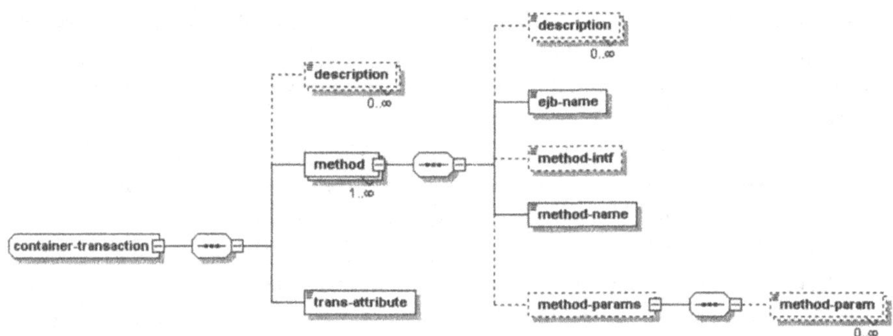

Figure 13-7. Container transactions

The method or set of methods for which the transaction attribute is identified is the same as explained earlier for method permissions. You can apply the transaction attributes for the following methods:

- All the methods exposed by a session bean's component interface apart from the ones defined by `javax.ejb.EJBObject` or `javax.ejb.EJBLocalObject`
- The `ejbTimeout` method for session, entity, and message-driven beans

- The methods exposed by a stateless session bean's Web service endpoint methods
- The message listener methods for the MDBs
- Methods defined by the component interface for entity beans excluding `getEJBHome`, `getEJBLocalHome`, `getHandle`, `getPrimaryKey`, and `isIdentical`
- All the methods defined in an entity bean's home interface excluding `getHomeHandle` and `getEJBMetadata`

The value for the `trans-attribute` attribute should be one of the values shown in Table 13-1.

Table 13-1. Values for the `trans-attribute` *Attribute*

VALUE	BEHAVIOR
`NotSupported`	The method with this transaction attribute is invoked in an unspecified transaction context. If there's a transaction context associated with the invoker, the container should suspend that transaction context before invoking the method.
`Required`	The container must invoke methods with this transaction attribute in the context of a transaction. If there's no transaction context associated with the thread, the container should start a new transaction.
`Supports`	Methods with this transaction attribute behave in the same way as that for `Required` if there's already a transaction context associated with thread and as `NotSupported` if there's no transaction context associated with the thread.
`RequiresNew`	With this transaction attribute, container starts a new transaction regardless of whether there's already a transaction context associated with the thread. If there is one, the container suspends that and starts a new transaction and, after completing the method, invokes the suspended transaction.
`Manadatory`	Methods with this transaction attribute should always be executed in the context of a transaction. If there's no transaction context that's already associated with the transaction, for remote references the container throws `javax.transaction.TransactionRequiredException` and throws `javax.transaction.TransactionRequiredLocalException` for local references.
`Never`	Methods with this transaction attribute can never be executed in a transaction context. If there's a transaction attribute associated with the thread, the container should throw `java.rmi.RemoteException` for remote clients and `javax.ejb.EJBException` for local clients.

Not all transaction attributes are applicable for all method types. Table 13-2 explains the exceptions.

Table 13-2. Supported Transaction Attributes

METHOD TYPE	VALID ATTRIBUTE
Web service endpoint methods	Required, RequiresNew, Supports, Never, NotSupported
MDBs	Required, NotSupported
CMP 2.0 entity beans	Required, RequiresNew, Manadatory

> **NOTE** *Containers may support* NotSupported, Supports, *or* Never *for entity beans requiring nontransactional access to data stores. A typical scenario is if you have a Session Façade with a set of methods, some performing only data reads and others performing reads and writes. You may not want the read methods to execute in a transaction context to improve concurrency and may want the read-write methods to execute with a transaction context to improve isolation. One solution would be to set the read methods on the Session Façade with the transaction attribute as* NotSupported, *the read-write methods with the transaction attribute as* Required, *and leave the transaction attribute for the entity bean methods as* Supports. *However, entity beans with* NotSupported, Supports, *or* Never *transaction attributes may not be portable.*

Listing 13-10 shows setting the transaction attribute for the updateOffer method on the remote interface for the SessionBean to Required.

Listing 13-10. Container Transaction

```
<container-transaction>
  <method>
    <ejb-name>OfferController</ejb-name>
    <method-intf>Remote</method-intf>
    <method-params>
      <method-param>com.apress.auction.dto.OfferDTO</method-param>
    </method-params>
  </method>
  </trans-attribute>Required</trans-attribute>
</container-transaction>
```

Rolling Back Transactions

When you use container-managed transaction, the container commits the transaction when the invocation successfully leaves the boundary at which the transaction was started. For example, if method A on bean X has the transaction attribute set to RequiresNew, the container starts the transaction before the thread enters the method and commits it after the thread leaves that method.

However, if an exception is thrown, the container may decide to roll back the transaction depending on the type of the exception. If the exception is an instance of `RuntimeException` or `RemoteException`, the container will automatically roll back the transaction. However, for other types of exceptions, the container won't roll back the transaction.

If you want to explicitly mark the transaction for rollback, you can use the following methods defined in the `EJBContext` interface. Specifically, this method marks the transaction context in which the current thread is executing for rollback:

```
public void setRollbackOnly(boolean flag);
```

This following checks whether the current transaction is marked for rollback:

```
public boolean getRollbackOnly();
```

> **NOTE** *You can't use the previous two methods if you're using bean-managed transaction demarcation. The container will throw* `IllegalStateException` *if* `setRollbackOnly` *is called from a method executing with the* `Supports`, `Never`, *or* `NotSupported` *transaction context.*

Listing 13-11 shows how to mark the transaction for rollback.

Listing 13-11. Update Offer Method

```
public void updateOffer(OfferDTO dto) throws OfferException {

  if(dto.getName() == null || !!.equals(dto.getName().trim()) {
    ctx.setRollbackOnly(true);
    throw new OfferException(OfferException.INVALID_OFFER_NAME);
  }

   ...........................

}
```

> **NOTE** *When you're using container-managed transaction demarcation, you can't use a resource manager–specific API for manipulating the transaction such as calling* `setAutocommit`, `commit`, *and* `rollback` *methods on* `java.sql.Connection`.

Bean-Managed Transaction Demarcation

Session beans and MDBs requiring demarcating the transactions themselves can do so by setting the `transaction-type` to `Bean` in the deployment descriptor. They can use the JTA interface `javax.sql.UserTransaction` interface for starting, committing, and rolling back transactions. The container should make an instance of user transaction available through the `EJBContext.getUserTransaction` method in the bean's environment under the JNDI name `java:comp/UserTransaction`. J2EE containers are required to make the user transaction instance available for lookup in the JNDI namespace by this well-known name.

> **NOTE** *The container will throw* `IllegalStateException` *if the user transaction is accessed from beans that use container-managed transaction demarcation.*

The interface defines the following methods. Specifically, the following creates a new transaction and associates it with the current thread:

```
void begin()
```

The following completes the transaction associated with the current thread:

```
void commit()
```

The following obtains the status of the transaction associated with the current thread:

```
int getStatus()
```

The statuses are enumerated in the `javax.transaction.Status` interface (see Table 13-3).

Table 13-3. Transaction Statuses

TRANSACTION STATUS	DESCRIPTION
STATUS_ACTIVE	A transaction is associated with the target object, and it's in the active state.
STATUS_COMMITTED	A transaction is associated with the target object, and it has been committed.
STATUS_COMMITTING	A transaction is associated with the target object, and it's in the process of committing.
STATUS_MARKED_ROLLBACK	A transaction is associated with the target object, and it has been marked for rollback, perhaps as a result of a setRollbackOnly operation.

continued

Table 13-3. Transaction Statuses (continued)

TRANSACTION STATUS	DESCRIPTION
STATUS_NO_TRANSACTION	No transaction is currently associated with the target object.
STATUS_PREPARED	A transaction is associated with the target object, and it has been prepared.
STATUS_PREPARING	A transaction is associated with the target object, and it's in the process of preparing.
STATUS_ROLLEDBACK	A transaction is associated with the target object, and the outcome has been determined to be a rollback.
STATUS_ROLLING_BACK	A transaction is associated with the target object, and it's in the process of rolling back.
STATUS_UNKNOWN	A transaction is associated with the target object, but its current status can't be determined.

The following rolls back the transaction associated with the current thread:

```
void rollback()
```

The following modifies the transaction associated with the current thread so that the only possible outcome of the transaction is to roll back the transaction:

```
void setRollbackOnly()
```

The following modifies the timeout value that's associated with transactions started by subsequent invocations of the begin method:

```
void setTransactionTimeout(int seconds)
```

All transactional resource manager access between the `begin` and `commit/rollback` calls are enlisted as a single transaction. Listing 13-12 shows how to demarcate transactions within the beans.

Listing 13-12. Programmatic Transaction Demarcation

```
Context ctx = new InitialContext();

//Look up the user transaction
UserTransaction utr = (UserTransaction)ctx.lookup("java:comp/env/UserTransaction");

//Start the transaction
Utr.begin();

DataSource oracleDS = (DataSource)ctx.lookup("java:comp/env/jdbc/OracleDS");
Connection oracleCon = oracleDS.getConnection();
//Perform some data access with the Oracle data store
DataSource sybaseDS = (DataSource)ctx.lookup("java:comp/env/jdbc/SybaseDS");
```

```
Connection sybaseCon = sybaseDS.getConnection();
//Perform some data access with the sybase data store

QueueConnectionFactory qcf =
(QueueConnectionFactory) ctx.lookup("java:comp/env/jms/qcf");
//Send some messages

//Commit the transaction
ctx.commit();
```

In Listing 13-12, data access to the Oracle and Sybase databases and message delivery to the JMS destination are performed in a single transaction.

> **NOTE** *You can't start a transaction without committing or rolling back a transaction that has already been started. When you're demarcating transactions using user transaction, you can't use resource manager–specific API for starting, committing, and rolling back transactions. Stateless session and MDBs are required to commit or roll back the transaction before the method that started the transaction returns. However, with stateful session beans, the transaction may span multiple client invocations. This means you can start the transaction in one method and commit it in another. EJBs with bean-managed transactions can't call the* `getRollbackOnly` *and* `setRollbackOnly` *methods on* `EJBContext`.

Client-Managed Transaction Demarcation

You can also get the client applications to demarcate transactions. The J2EE specification requires containers to expose the user transaction to remote clients by the JNDI name `java:/UserTransaction`, and the clients can use this for demarcating transactions. If an EJB is invoked within a client-demarcated transaction, the transaction context is propagated to the container.

Concurrency and Isolation Levels

Transactions allow business operations to be isolated from each other. In normal cases transactions ensures consistency by serializing access to data. The level of isolation can impact the performance and concurrency of applications. Databases have traditionally used isolation levels to specify the level of isolations required for transactions. The various isolation levels are as follows:

Read Uncommitted: With this isolation level, a transaction can read the data modified by another transaction that hasn't been committed. Hence, if the second transaction chose to rollback, the data read by the first transaction will be incorrect. This causes dirty reads and can perform well. However, the data accessed between multiple transactions may be inconsistent.

Read Committed: In this case, transactions can read only data that has been committed. This means dirty reads will never occur. However, if the transaction read the data and reread it after awhile, and in the meanwhile another transaction came and modified and committed the data, the data between the first and second reads won't match. This condition is called a *nonrepeatable read*. Also, if the first transaction is in process, another transaction could come and add new records that become visible to the first transaction when it rereads the data. This condition is called a *phantom read*.

Repeatable Read: With this isolation, a transaction can't modify the data that's read by another transaction. In database terms this is similar to pessimistic locking by using a `SELECT FOR UPDATE`. This can avoid nonrepeatable reads; however, phantom reads can still occur.

Serializable: With this isolation level, a transaction that has read the data prevents any other transactions from reading or writing the same data until it commits or rolls back. Even though this provides the highest level of isolation, the concurrency is poor.

You set the isolation level in a resource-specific manner. Hence, the EJB specification doesn't provide any method for setting the transaction isolation level. If you're using bean-demarcated transaction, you can use a resource manager–specific API for setting the isolation level. For example, the `java.sql.Connection` interface provides the method `setIsolationLevel` and the enumerated constants `TRANSACTION_UNCOMMITTED`, `TRANSACTION_READ_COMMITTED`, `TRANSACTION_REPEATABLE_READ`, and `TRANSACTION_SERIALIZABLE` for setting database-level isolation levels.

NOTE *Application servers such as BEA WebLogic and JBoss allow you to specify the isolation level at bean method level in the proprietary deployment descriptors.*

Concurrency and Locking

The EJB specification allows container providers the flexibility to implement the best possible concurrency and locking strategies. Since how the life cycle of entity beans is managed between transactions influences the concurrency options for entity beans, it's important that you have a good understanding of the commit options that are available for entity beans. The EJB 2.0 specification provides compliant containers with the flexibility to associate the object identity of entity beans to bean instances. The specification provides the following options to the containers:

Option A: The container caches entity bean instances in a ready state between transactions. The container ensures that the instance has exclusive access to the state of the entity in the persistent storage. Hence, the container doesn't need to synchronize the state of the bean at the beginning of each transaction.

Option B: This is similar to Option A in the sense that the ready instances are cached between transactions. However, the container doesn't assume that the instance has exclusive access to the state in the persistent storage. This means the state of the bean is synchronized at the start of each transaction.

Option C: With this option, the container doesn't cache the instance at all. The instance is returned to the pool at the end of each transaction.

The JBoss EJB container allows you to have a fourth commit option specified in the JBoss-specific deployment descriptor called Option D, which is similar to Option A but also allows you a refresh rate to specify how often the entity bean state should be refreshed. By default, JBoss uses Option A, with a single instance for an entity identity, and serializes access to the instance in transactions. However, this can cause frequent deadlocks if you have unordered access to entity beans across use cases. JBoss also allows you to have an instance per transaction policy, where each transaction will have its instance of the entity and the access isn't serialized.

> **NOTE** *It's recommended to maintain a lock tree document where lock hierarchies are defined to enforce developers to access entity beans in a particular lock order to avoid deadlocks. However, developers should adhere to the lock hierarchies, and the document should be updated when new use cases are added.*

BEA WebLogic provides the following variety of concurrency options:

Exclusive: In this case, WebLogic assumes it has exclusive access to the data and can be configured to cache instances between transactions. WebLogic ensures that the data integrity isn't violated across transactions. However, this won't work in a clustered environment where multiple server instances can access the data or some other application can access the backend data.

Database: This is the default strategy where the locking mechanisms are delegated to the underlying databases. To use this, you need to have a good understanding of how the underlying relationship database management system (RDBMS) locks data during transactions.

Optimistic: With this scheme, WebLogic doesn't hold any lock on the data and makes sure the state of the entity bean that's being updated hasn't changed by other transactions since it was first access in the current transaction. If it has, the current transaction is rolled back.

Optimistic Locking

Optimistic locking is a strategy often used in enterprise applications to improve performance and throughput. With optimistic locking the data that's accessed during a transaction isn't locked. However, before it's updated, it's checked that the state of the data isn't changed by another transaction since it was accessed for the first time in the transaction.

In most cases, optimistic locking involves having an extra column in the database whose value is read during the transaction. Any transaction that updates the data changes the value of this column for the row that's updated. However, before updating, it checks that the value of the column is the same as it read before in order to make sure the data wasn't changed by another transaction between the current transaction read and updated the data.

You can implement optimistic locking in the application using a container-specific service or using a database trigger. All three options have pros and cons. With the first option the onus is on the bean provider to write the code to implement the optimistic locking strategy. If you're using CMP 2.0, for example, you can have a root interface that's extended by all the component interfaces and a root bean class extended by all the bean classes. You can define a business method called `checkLock`, as shown in Listing 13-13.

The root local interface exposes the business method and CMP accessor to the optimistic lock column.

Listing 13-13. Version Numer Fields

```
public interface Local extends EJBLocalObject {

  public int getVersion();

  public void checkLock(int oldVersion);

}
```

The root entity bean class provides the abstract accessor and mutator for the optimistic lock column and the implementation for the business method that checks the lock, as shown in Listing 13-14.

Listing 13-14. Optimistic Locking Logic

```
public class AbstractEntity implements EntityBean {

  .........
  public abstract int getVersion();
  public abstract void setVersion(int version);

  public void checkLock(int oldVersion) {
    if(oldVersion !!= getVersion()) throw new OptimisticLockException();
  }

  .........

}
```

Any Session Façade or helper that updates the entity will call the checkLock method before updating the entity. The flip side of this is there's no way you can enforce the developers to call this method before updating the entity. One way to provide limited discipline is make sure that entities are always updated through a thin layer of helper class that will check the lock validation, as shown in Listing 13-15.

Listing 3-15. Using Entity Helpers

```
public class OfferEntityHelper {

  .........
 public void updateOffer(OfferDTO dto) {

    try {

      Context ctx = new InitialContext();
      OfferLocalHome home =
      (OfferLocalHome)ctx.lookup("java:comp/env/ejb/OfferLocalHome");

      Offer offer =
       home.findByKeyAndVersion(dto.getId(), dto.getVersion());

      course.setName(dto.getName());
      course.setDescription(dto.getDescription());
      course.setVersion(++dto.getVersion());

  }catch(ObjectNotFoundException ex) {
    throw new OptimisticLockException();
  }
 }

}
```

Here the helper tries to find the entity by specifying the key and the optimistic lock column, and if the entity isn't found, it was either removed or updated since it last read the entity. If the entity is found, it updates the entity and increments the value of the optimistic lock column.

However, this technique relies heavily on exactly when the container issues the update. This may also perform a buried update if the entity was changed by another transaction after the current transaction called the finder. The advantage of implementing optimistic locking is then that it isn't dependent on the application server or database vendor.

If you choose to use an application server–specific method such as the one explained for WebLogic, your logic will become nonportable across application servers. This will also involve changing all the proprietary deployment descriptor for entity beans to add optimistic locking support.

We like to use database triggers to check the lock and increment it because optimistic locking is a database issue and should be performed closest to the database. Of course, this isn't portable across database vendors; however, it's less likely you'd decide to change the database vendor in big enterprise applications. Even if you decide to change the database vendor, porting the triggers would be less tedious than porting the custom deployment descriptors.

> **NOTE** *If the only thing you want is to allow concurrent reads and disallow concurrent writes or reads on uncommitted writes, you can classify your use case realization methods on the Session Façade and set the transaction isolation level for read methods to* `READ COMMITTED` *and read-write methods to* `SERIALIZABLE` *and rely on the database's locking strategies for those isolation levels, rather than using optimistic locking. However, optimistic locking is the only way to go if you want to check data modifications across round trips to clients.*

Summary

This chapter covered EJB container services in detail. The chapter started with security services and looked at declarative security. Then you saw how it fell short on instance-based security and learned about programmatic security. Next you looked at the new feature introduced in EJB 2.1, timer service. The chapter covered the timer API in detail and looked at using the timer service in conjunction with JMS for sending timed notifications to remote clients. Then the chapter moved on to one of the key aspects of the EJB technology, transactions. The chapter covered container-managed and bean-managed transactions in detail. Finally, the chapter covered various concurrency and locking strategies in detail.

CHAPTER 14

Processing XML Documents

IN THE PAST two years Extensible Markup Language (XML) has evolved as the de facto standard for document markup with human readable tags. Since its advent, XML has found its way into a variety of applications, including the following:

- Configuration information
- Publishing
- Electronic Data Interchange (EDI)
- Voicemail systems
- Vector graphics
- Remote Method Invocation (RMI)
- Object serialization

You can use XML to customize tags that are relevant to the domain on which you work. As a result of this extensibility, XML has been adopted by horizontal and vertical industries for representing data that's relevant to their domain. What makes XML an integral element of enterprise computing is that XML documents are simple text documents with a platform-neutral way of representing the data. For example, an XML document that produces by an application running on Microsoft Windows can easily be consumed by an application running on Sun Solaris.

Using XML and Java Together

The cross-platform way of representing data using XML complements the cross-platform programming model of the Java platform quite well. Since XML became a World Wide Web Consortium (W3C) recommendation in1998, it has gained wide acceptance in the Java community. Over the last few years, a variety of vendors have offered Java-based application programming interfaces (APIs) for processing XML documents. The two prevalent APIs within J2EE that exist for processing XML documents are as follows:

- Document Object Model (DOM)
- Simple API for XML (SAX)

> **NOTE** *DOM and SAX are low-level APIs and are seldom used in real-world projects for marshaling/unmarsaling XML and Java. Castor from* `http://www.exolab.org` *has been widely used in the industry for this purpose. Another upcoming standard that isn't part of the Java 2 Enterprise Edition (J2EE) that's used for XML binding is Java API for XML Binding (JAXB).*

Parsers have been available in Java since the introduction of the aforementioned APIs that support SAX and DOM. In addition to the proprietary parsers available for processing XML, numerous Java specification request (JSRs) have come through the Java Community Process (JCP) that support XML and various XML-related technologies.

XML is used quite extensively in J2EE with the various component types using XML for describing deployment attributes and supporting Simple Object Access Protocol (SOAP), Web Services Description Language (WSDL), and Web services in J2EE 1.4. However, one of the XML APIs that has evolved through JCP and acts as the cornerstone for most of the other APIs is Java API for XML Processing (JAXP). JAXP provides a vendor-neutral API for the following:

- Processing XML using DOM
- Processing XML using SAX
- Transforming XML using XSL Transformations (XSLT)

JAXP has been around as an independent API for a while, and it became part of the J2EE 1.3 suite of APIs. The current version of JAXP is now part of the Java 2 Standard Edition (J2SE) 1.4.

JAXP 1.2 supports the following specifications:

- XML 1.0 (second edition)
- XML Namespaces 1.0
- Simple API for XML 1.0
- DOM Level 2
- XSLT 1.0
- XML Schema

> **NOTE** *J2SE 1.4 comes with Apache Crimson, which is an XML parser that supports both SAX/DOM and Xalan, which is an XML transformer. Crimson provides the JAXP support for XML parsing using SAX and DOM, and Xalan provides the support for XML transformations compliant with JAXP. In this chapter, we'll be using the aforementioned default parser and transformer that comes with the Java Development Kit (JDK). However, JAXP caters to pluggable parsers and transformers.*

Using the Document Object Model

DOM is a W3C recommendation that provides an API for treating an XML document as a tree of objects. It loads an entire XML document into memory and allows you to manipulate the structure of XML document by adding, removing, and amending the elements and/or attributes. The following illustrates the various levels of the DOM that has evolved over the past few years:

- **DOM Level 1**: This became a W3C recommendation in mid-1998. It defined the basic interfaces that represent the various components of an XML document such as the document itself, elements, attributes, processing instructions (PIs), and CDATA sections.
- **DOM Level 2**: This became a recommendation in late 2000 and, most important, added support for XML namespaces. Level 2 also modularized DOM into the following:
  - **Core**: This builds on Level 1, defining the interfaces for manipulating the structure of XML documents.
  - **Views**: This covers presentation of XML documents in different types of views.

- **Events**: This allows events and event listeners to be associated with XML nodes.
- **Style**: This deals mainly with stylesheets.

- **Traversal and Range**: This deals with traversal of XML documents and the definition of ranges between arbitrary points in an XML document.
- **DOM Level 3**: This is currently a working draft and builds on Level 2. Main additions include the loading and storing of Extended Markup Language (XML) documents from and to external sources.

> **NOTE** *JAXP 1.2 supports only DOM Level 2 Core. The Java bindings for the interfaces defined for the DOM Level 2 Core are made available by reference in the JDK in the package* `org.w3c.dom`.

DOM Level 2 Core Architecture

Figure 14-1 depicts the Java bindings for the main interfaces defined in the DOM Level 2 Core module.

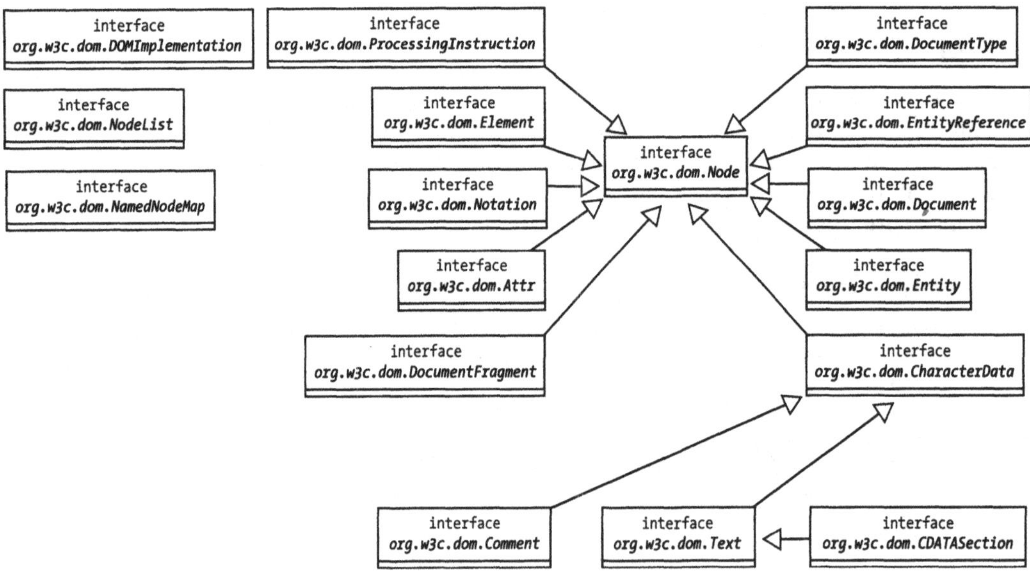

Figure 14-1. Java bindings for the main interfaces defined in the DOM Level 2 Core module

Table 14-1 describes the main interfaces that form the DOM Level 2 Core module.

Table 14-1. DOM Interfaces

INTERFACE	DESCRIPTION
Attr	The Attr interface represents an attribute in an Element object.
CDataSection	CDATA sections escape blocks of text containing characters that would otherwise be regarded as markup.
CharacterData	The CharacterData interface extends Node with a set of attributes and methods for accessing character data in the DOM.
Comment	This interface inherits from CharacterData and represents the content of a comment (in other words, all the characters between the starting <!-- and ending -->).
Document	The Document interface represents the entire Hypertext Markup Language (HTML) or XML document.
DocumentFragment	DocumentFragment is a "lightweight" or "minimal" Document object.
DocumentType	Each Document has a doctype attribute whose value is either null or a DocumentType object.
DOMImplementation	The DOMImplementation interface provides a number of methods for performing operations that are independent of any particular instance of the DOM.
Element	The Element interface represents an element in an HTML or XML document.
Entity	This interface represents an entity, either parsed or unparsed, in an XML document.
EntityReference	EntityReference objects may be inserted into the structure model when an entity reference is in the source document or when the user wants to insert an entity reference.
NamedNodeMap	Objects implementing the NamedNodeMap interface represent collections of nodes that can be accessed by name.
Node	The Node interface is the primary data type for the entire DOM.
NodeList	The NodeList interface provides the abstraction of an ordered collection of nodes, without defining or constraining how this collection is implemented.
Notation	This interface represents a notation declared in the document type definition (DTD).
ProcessingInstruction	The ProcessingInstruction interface represents a PI, which is used in XML as a way to keep processor-specific information in the text of the document.
Text	The Text interface inherits from CharacterData and represents the textual content (termed *character data* in XML) of an Element or Attr.

Every interface that represents a node in the DOM tree extends the Node interface.

Node

The Node interface defines a set of enumerated constants representing the specific type of the node. This is a short integer and corresponds to the value returned by calling the getNodeType method on the Node interface. Table 14-2 describes these constants.

Table 14-2. DOM Node Types

CONSTANT	NODE TYPE INTERFACE
ELEMENT_NODE	Element
ATTRIBUTE_NODE	Attr
TEXT_NODE	Text
CDATA_SECTION_NODE	CDATASection
ENTITY_REFERENCE_NODE	EntityReference
ENTITY_NODE	Entity
PROCESSING_INSTRUCTION_NODE	ProcessingInstruction
COMMENT_NODE	Comment
DOCUMENT_NODE	Document
DOCUMENT_TYPE_NODE	DocumentType
DOCUMENT_FRAGMENT_NODE	DocumentFragment
NOTATION_NODE	Notation

The methods defined in the Node interface can be mainly categorized into the following:

- Navigation methods
- Information methods
- Manipulation methods

Navigation Methods

The methods defined in the Node interface navigate from one node to another (see Table 14-3).

Table 14-3. Node Navigation Methods

METHOD	DESCRIPTION
Node getParentNode	Gets the parent of this node
Node getFirstChild	Gets the first child node of this node
Node getLastChild	Gets the last child node of this node
Node getNextSibling	Gets the next sibling node of this node
Node getPreviousSibling	Gets the previous sibling of this node
NodeList getChildNodes	Gets a NodeList representing all the child nodes of this node

The NodeList interface iterates through a list of nodes and provides the method getLength to get the number of nodes in the list and item(int index) to get a node in the list at the specified index.

Information Methods

Table 14-4 describes the methods provided to get information on a given node.

Table 14-4. Node Information Methods

METHOD	DESCRIPTION
`NamedNodeMap getAttributes`	Returns a `NamedNodeMap` representing the attributed available for `Element`-type nodes and `null` for the all other node types

`String getLocalName`	Returns the local name of the node. The actual value that's returned depends on the type of the node:
	`Element`: The tag name
	`Attr`: The attribute name
	`Text`: `#text`
	`CDataSection`: `#cdata-section`
	`EntityReference`: The name of the referenced entity
	`ProcessingInstruction`: The target of the PI
	`Comment`: `#comment`
	`Document`: `#document`
	`DocumentType`: Document type name
	`DocumentFragment`: `#document-fragment`
	`Notation`: The name of the notation

`String getNamespaceURI`	The namespace uniform resource indicator (URI) for this node
`String getNodeName`	Same as `getLocalName`
`String getNodeType`	Returns the type of the node as enumerated in the `Node` interface

`String getNodeValue`	Gets the value of the node. The returned value depends on the type of the node:
	Node Type: Value
	`Element`: `null`
	`Attribute`: Value of the attribute
	`Text`: Contents of the text node
	`CDATASection`: Contents of the CDATA section
	`EntityReference`: `null`
	`Entity`: `null`
	`Notation`: `null`
	`Document`: `null`
	`DocumentType`: `null`
	`DocumentFragment`: `null`
	`Comment`: Contents of the comment
	`ProcessingInstruction`: Contents of the PI excluding the target

`Document getOwnnerDocument`	Gets the document to which this node belongs
`String getPrefix`	Gets the namespace prefix for this node
`boolean hasAttributes`	Returns whether this attribute has children
`boolean hasChildren`	Returns whether this node has children

Manipulation Methods

Manipulation methods are mainly used for setting node values and amending the content model of nodes (see Table 14-5).

Table 14-5. Node Manipulation Methods

METHOD	DESCRIPTION
`Node appendChild(Node child)`	Adds the specified node to the end of the list of children to this node
`Node insertBefore(Node new, Node old)`	Inserts the node specified as the first argument before the node as specified as the second argument in the list of child nodes for this node
`Node removeChild(Node child)`	Removes the specified child from this node
`Node replaceChild(Child new, Child old)`	Replaces the node specified as the second argument with the node as specified as the first argument in the list of child nodes for this node
`void setValue(String value)`	Sets the value for this node

Document

The `Document` interface represents the entire document. It also acts as a factory for creating the various types of nodes. The nodes created by a given instance of `Document` can belong only to that document. However, the interface also supports methods for importing documents owned by other documents into the content model of a given document.

Table 14-6 describes the factory methods provided by this node for creating the various types of XML nodes.

Table 14-6. Document Methods

METHOD: `Attr createAttribute(String name)`
DESCRIPTION: Creates an `Attr` of the given name

METHOD: `Attr createAttributeNS(String namespaceURI, String qualifiedName)`
DESCRIPTION: Creates an attribute of the given qualified name and namespace URI

METHOD: `CDATASection createCDATASection(String data)`
DESCRIPTION: Creates a `CDATASection` node whose value is the specified string

METHOD: `Comment createComment(String data)`
DESCRIPTION: Creates a `Comment` node given the specified string

METHOD: `DocumentFragment createDocumentFragment()`
DESCRIPTION: Creates an empty `DocumentFragment` object

METHOD: `Element createElement(String tagName)`
DESCRIPTION: Creates an element of the type specified

METHOD: `Element createElementNS(String namespaceURI, String qualifiedName)`
DESCRIPTION: Creates an element of the given qualified name and namespace URI

METHOD: `EntityReference createEntityReference(String name)`
DESCRIPTION: Creates an `EntityReference` object

METHOD: `ProcessingInstruction createProcessingInstruction(String target, String data)`
DESCRIPTION: Creates a `ProcessingInstruction` node given the specified name and data strings

METHOD: `Text createTextNode(String data)`
DESCRIPTION: Creates a `Text` node given the specified string

`Element`

The `Element` interface represents an XML element, and most of the methods defined in this interface are related to manipulating the attributes for the element (see Table 14-7).

Table 14-7. Element Methods

METHOD: `String getAttribute(String name)`
DESCRIPTION: Retrieves an attribute value by name.

METHOD: `Attr getAttributeNode(String name)`
DESCRIPTION: Retrieves an attribute node by name.

METHOD: `Attr getAttributeNodeNS(String namespaceURI, String localName)`
DESCRIPTION: Retrieves an `Attr` node by local name and namespace URI.

METHOD: `String getAttributeNS(String namespaceURI, String localName)`
DESCRIPTION: Retrieves an attribute value by local name and namespace URI.

METHOD: `NodeList getElementsByTagName(String name)`
DESCRIPTION: Returns a `NodeList` of all descendant `Elements` with a given tag name, in the order in which they're encountered in a preorder traversal of this `Element` tree.

METHOD: `NodeList getElementsByTagNameNS(String namespaceURI, String localName)`
DESCRIPTION: Returns a `NodeList` of all the descendant `Elements` with a given local name and namespace URI in the order in which they're encountered in a preorder traversal of this `Element` tree.

METHOD: `String getTagName()`
DESCRIPTION: The name of the element.

METHOD: `boolean hasAttribute(String name)`
DESCRIPTION: Returns `true` when an attribute with a given name is specified on this element or has a default value. It returns `false` otherwise.

METHOD: `boolean hasAttributeNS(String namespaceURI, String localName)`
DESCRIPTION: Returns `true` when an attribute with a given local name and namespace URI is specified on this element or has a default value. It returns `false` otherwise.

METHOD: `void removeAttribute(String name)`
DESCRIPTION: Removes an attribute by name.

METHOD: `Attr removeAttributeNode(Attr oldAttr)`
DESCRIPTION: Removes the specified attribute node.

METHOD: `void removeAttributeNS(String namespaceURI, String localName)`
DESCRIPTION: Removes an attribute by local name and namespace URI.

METHOD: `void setAttribute(String name, String value)`
DESCRIPTION: Adds a new attribute.

METHOD: `Attr setAttributeNode(Attr newAttr)`
DESCRIPTION: Adds a new attribute node.

METHOD: `Attr setAttributeNodeNS(Attr newAttr)`
DESCRIPTION: Adds a new attribute.

METHOD: `void setAttributeNS(String namespaceURI, String qualifiedName, String value)`
DESCRIPTION: Adds a new attribute.

Offer Data As XML

Now that you're comfortable with the DOM API, you'll look at a small example that uses the DOM API to build an XML structure that represents the offers offered by the auction application (see Listing 14-1). The example will use the various interfaces and methods explained in the previous sections.

Listing 14-1. OfferReader

```
package com.apress.projavaserver14.chapter17.dom;
// Import the DOM interfaces.
import org.w3c.dom.Document;
import org.w3c.dom.Element;
import org.w3c.dom.Attr;
import org.w3c.dom.Node;
import org.w3c.dom.NodeList;
import org.w3c.dom.NamedNodeMap;
// Import the Crimson class that implements the Document interface.
import org.apache.crimson.tree.XmlDocument;

public class OfferReader {

     // Variable that holds the list of offers.
    static String offers[][] = {
        {"1", "MP3 Player", "256 Mb MP3 Player"},
        {"2", "iPod", "15 Gb Mini iPod"}
    };

    public static void main(String args[]) throws Exception {

        // Call the private method to build the offer list as an XML.
        Document offers = buildDOM();

        /* Print the contents of the XML document. This uses a vendor-specific
            method  of the Crimson implementation since DOM Level 2 doesn't
            specify any API for
        loading and storing XML from external sources. */
        ((XmlDocument)offers).write(System.out);

        /* Get the root element of the document and pass it a method that
            prints the contents of the document. */
        Element root = offers.getDocumentElement();
        printContents(root);

    }

    private static Document buildDOM() {
```

```
// Create an instance of the Crimson class that implements the Document
        // interface.
        Document dom = new XmlDocument();

        // Create the root element.
        Element root = dom.createElement("offers");
        // Append the root element to the document.
        dom.appendChild(root);

        // Iterate through the list of offers.
        for(int i = 0;i < offers.length;i++) {
            // Create an XML element that represents the offer.
            Element offer = dom.createElement("offer");
            // Set the course attributes as the element attributes.
            offer.setAttribute("id", offers[i][0]);
            offer.setAttribute("name", offers[i][1]);
            offer.setAttribute("description", offers[i][2]);
            // Append the course element to the root element.
            root.appendChild(offer);
        }
        // Return the XML document.
        return dom;

    }

    private static void printContents(Element root) {
        // Get the list of children for the root node.
        NodeList offerList = root.getChildNodes();

        for(int i = 0;i < offerList.getLength();i++) {

            System.out.print("Offer[" + i + "]: ");
            // Get the current offer in the list.
            Node course = offerList.item(i);
            // Get the attributes for the current course.
            NamedNodeMap offerAttributes = offer.getAttributes();
            // Print the attributes.
            for(int j = 0;j < offerAttributes.getLength();j++) {
                Node offerAttribute = offerAttributes.item(j);
                System.out.print(offerAttribute.getNodeName() + "=" +
                offerAttribute.getNodeValue() + " ");
            }
            System.out.println();

        }

    }

}
```

If you're using JDK 1.4, you don't need any external JAR file for compiling and running Listing 14-1. Otherwise, you need to download the Crimson JAR file from `http://xml.apache.org`. Running Listing 14-1 will produce the following output:

```
<?xml version="1.0" encoding="UTF-8"?>
<offers>
  <offer id="1" name="MP3 Player" description="256 Mb MP3 Player" />
  <offer id="2" name="iPod" description="15 Gb Mini iPod" />
</offers>
Offer[0]: id=1 name=MP3 Player description=256 Mb MP3 Player
Offer[1]: id=2 name=iPod description=15 Gb Mini iPod
```

Knowing When to Use the DOM

The following sections provide you with an overview of scenarios when you'd want to use the DOM and when you wouldn't.

> **NOTE** *Some of the ideas in the following sections have been adopted from J2EE tutorial addendum for version 1.4 from Sun.*

The DOM is a W3C standard, and JAXP 1.2 supports DOM and many other W3C standards such as XML Schema and namespaces. Hence, if you want to have a standards-based approach in your application, it's best to use DOM. However, for more object-oriented third-party APIs, JDOM and DOM4J will be a better fit. Compared to some of the other APIs, DOM doesn't fully utilize the object-oriented features of Java; DOM has always been designed to be language neutral, and it had to cater for non-object-oriented languages such as C and Perl.

Documents vs. Data

The document model for DOM differs from JDOM in the following ways:

- The kind of nodes in the hierarchy
- Support for mixed content

It's the difference in what constitutes a "node" in the data hierarchy that primarily accounts for the differences in programming with these two models. However, it's the capacity for mixed-content that, more than anything else, accounts for the difference in how the standards define a "node."

Mixed Content Model

Text and elements can be freely intermixed in a DOM hierarchy, which is called *mixed content*. Mixed content occurs frequently in documents and articles.

For example, to represent this structure:

```
<p>Click <a href="#12">here</a>to see details</p>
```

the hierarchy of DOM nodes would look something like this, where each line represents one node:

```
ELEMENT: p
  +  TEXT: Click
  +  ELEMENT: a
    + TEXT: here
  + TEXT: see details
```

Kinds of Nodes

The DOM API is kept simple to support mixed content. In the previous example, `getNodeName` for the element `p` returns the literal `p`, and `getNodeValue` returns `null`. However, for its first child, `getNodeName` returns the literal `#text`, and `getNodeValue` returns `Click`. As shown in earlier sections, the return values for `getNodeName` and `getNodeValue` depend on the type of the node.

Instead, obtaining the content you care about when processing a DOM means inspecting the list of subelements the node contains, ignoring those you aren't interested in and processing the ones you do care about. With DOM, you're free to create the semantics you need. However, you are also required to do the processing necessary to implement those semantics. Standards such as JDOM and DOM4J, on the other hand, make it a lot easier to do simple things because each node in the hierarchy is an object.

Although JDOM and DOM4J make allowances for elements with mixed content, they aren't primarily designed for such situations. Instead, they're targeted for applications where the XML structure contains data. As described in traditional data processing, the elements in a data structure typically contain either text or other elements, but not both. For example, here's some XML that represents a simple address book:

```
<offers>
  <offer>
    <id>1</id>
    <name>MP3 Player</name>
    <name>256 Mb MP3 Player</name>
  </offer>
    ...
</offers>
```

With JDOM and DOM4J, once you get to the nodes you're interested in, you can get the text content by a simple method call. However, with DOM you need to inspect the child elements and build the logic for interpreting the element content.

> **NOTE** *DOM is more suitable if your application predominantly uses XML to represent documents. However, if your applications are more data oriented, it's better to use a more object-oriented API such as JDOM or DOM4J.*

Using Simple API for XML (SAX)

DOM is a powerful API for loading an XML document into memory and inspecting and manipulating its contents. However, this isn't very efficient for processing large documents or in cases where you're not interested in the contents of the whole document or where you just want to verify the validity of the document. This is where SAX comes into picture.

Members of the `xml-dev` mailing list defined the SAX 1.0 API in mid-1998. The current release of SAX 2.0 provides advanced features, including support for namespaces, which is significantly different from version 1.0. This book concentrates on the 2.0 API.

SAX provides an event-driven approach for parsing XML documents. SAX parsers parse XML documents sequentially and emit events indicating the start and end of document, elements, text content, and so on. Applications that are interested in processing these events can register implementations of callback interfaces provided by the SAX API with the parser.

SAX Architecture

In SAX, you can configure the parser with a variety of callback handlers, as shown in Figure 14-2.

When the parser scans an external stream that contains XML markup, it'll report the various events involved to those callback handlers. These events include the following:

- Beginning of the document
- End of the document
- Namespace mapping
- Errors in well-formedness
- Validation errors
- Text data
- Start of an element
- End of an element

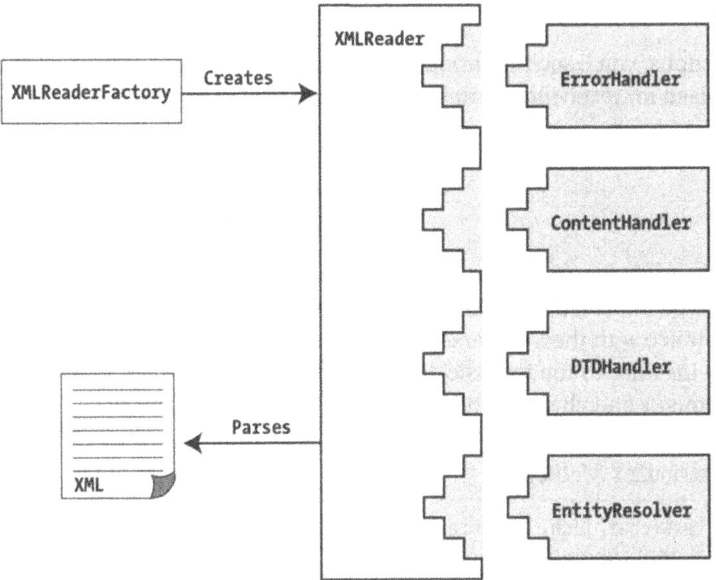

Figure 14-2. SAX architecture

The SAX API provides interfaces that define the contract for these callback handlers. When you write XML applications that use SAX, you can write implementations for these interfaces and register them with a SAX parser. Figure 14-3 depicts the important classes and interfaces in the SAX API.

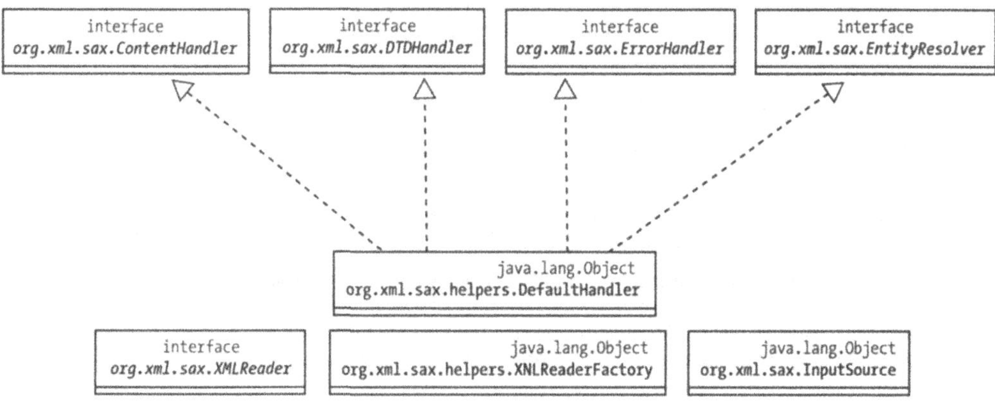

Figure 14-3. Important classes and interfaces in the SAX API

SAX Event Handlers

In the following sections, you'll see the various event handlers available in the SAX 2.0 API, which can be used for receiving relevant events associated with parsing XML documents.

ContentHandler

`ContentHandler` is the main interface that most SAX applications implement. If the application needs to be informed of basic parsing events, it implements this interface and registers an instance with the SAX parser using the `setContentHandler` method. The parser uses the instance to report basic document-related events such as the start and end of elements and character data. Table 14-8 describes its methods.

Table 14-8. `ContentHandler` *Methods*

METHOD: `void characters(char[] ch, int start, int length)`
DESCRIPTION: Receives notification of character data

METHOD: `void endElement(String namespaceURI, String localName, String qName)`
DESCRIPTION: Receives notification of the end of an element

METHOD: `void endPrefixMapping(String prefix)`
DESCRIPTION: Ends the scope of a prefix-URI mapping

METHOD: `void ignorableWhitespace(char[] ch, int start, int length)`
DESCRIPTION: Receives notification of ignorable whitespace in element content

METHOD: `void processingInstruction(String target, String data)`
DESCRIPTION: Receives notification of a processing instruction

METHOD: `void setDocumentLocator(Locator locator)`
DESCRIPTION: Receives an object for locating the origin of SAX document events

METHOD: `void skippedEntity(String name)`
DESCRIPTION: Receives notification of a skipped entity

METHOD: `void startDocument()`
DESCRIPTION: Receives notification of the beginning of a document

METHOD: `void startElement(String namespaceURI, String localName, String qName, Attributes atts)`
DESCRIPTION: Receives notification of the beginning of an element

METHOD: `void startPrefixMapping(String prefix, String uri)`
DESCRIPTION: Begins the scope of a prefix-URI namespace mapping

METHOD: `void endDocument()`
DESCRIPTION: Receives notification of the end of a document

DTDHandler

If a SAX application needs information about notations and unparsed entities, then the application implements the `DTDHandler` interface and registers an instance with the SAX parser using the parser's `setDTDHandler` method. The parser uses the instance to report notation and unparsed entity declarations to the application. Table 14-9 describes the `DTDHandler` methods.

Table 14-9. `DTDHandler` *Methods*

METHOD: `void notationDecl(String name, String publicId, String systemId)`
DESCRIPTION: Receives notification of a notation declaration event

METHOD: `void unparsedEntityDecl(String name, String publicId, String systemId, String notationName)`
DESCRIPTION: Receives notification of an unparsed entity declaration event

EntityResolver

If a SAX application needs to implement customized handling for external entities, it must implement the `EntityResolver` interface and register an instance with the SAX driver using the `setEntityResolver` method. Table 14-10 describes the `EntityResolver` method.

Table 14-10. `EntityResolver` *Method*

METHOD: `InputSource resolveEntity(String publicId, String systemId)`
DESCRIPTION: Allows the application to resolve external entities

ErrorHandler

If a SAX application needs to implement customized error handling, it must implement the `ErrorHandler` interface and then register an instance with the XML reader using the `setErrorHandler` method. The parser will then report all errors and warnings through this interface. Table 14-11 describes the `ErrorHandler` methods.

Table 14-11. `ErrorHandler` *Methods*

METHOD: `void error(SAXParseException exception)`
DESCRIPTION: Receives notification of a recoverable error

METHOD: `void fatalError(SAXParseException exception)`
DESCRIPTION: Receives notification of a nonrecoverable error

METHOD: `void warning(SAXParseException exception)`
DESCRIPTION: Receives notification of a warning

InputSource

The InputSource class allows a SAX application to encapsulate information about an input source in a single object, which may include a public identifier, a system identifier, a byte stream (possibly with a specified encoding), and/or a character stream. The application will deliver this input source to the parser in one of two places: as the argument to the parse method of XmlReader or as the return value of the resolveEntity method of EntityResolver. The SAX parser will use the InputSource object to determine how to read XML input. If a character stream is available, the parser will read that stream directly; if not, the parser will use a byte stream, if available. If neither a character stream nor a byte stream is available, the parser will attempt to open a URI connection to the resource identified by the system identifier.

Table 14-12 describes the constructors provided for this class.

Table 14-12. InputSource *Constructors*

CONSTRUCTOR	DESCRIPTION
InputSource()	Zero-argument default constructor
InputSource(InputStream byteStream)	Creates a new input source with a byte stream
InputSource(Reader characterStream)	Creates a new input source with a character stream
InputSource(String systemId)	Creates a new input source with a system identifier

DefaultHandler

The DefaultHandler class is an adapter class provided by SAX that implements all the callback interfaces. Hence, instead of implementing the callback interfaces directly, you'd extend this class and override the methods as required. The following example shows a callback handler that's interested in only the start and end of the document:

```
import org.xml.sax.helpers.DefaultHandler;

public class MyDocumentHAndler extends DefaultHandler {

  public void startDocument() { ... }

  public void endDocument() { ...... }

}
```

XMLReader

XMLReader is the interface that an XML parser's SAX2 driver must implement. This interface allows an application to set and query features and properties in the parser, to register event handlers for document processing, and to initiate a document parse. The interface defines the methods shown in Table 14-13.

Table 14-13. XMLReader *Methods*

METHOD	DESCRIPTION
ContentHandler getContentHandler()	Returns the current content handler
DTDHandler getDTDHandler()	Returns the current DTD handler
EntityResolver getEntityResolver()	Returns the current entity resolver
ErrorHandler getErrorHandler()	Returns the current error handler
boolean getFeature(String name)	Looks up the value of a feature
Object getProperty(String name)	Looks up the value of a property
void parse(InputSource input)	Parses an XML document
void parse(String systemId)	Parses an XML document from a system identifier (URI)
void setContentHandler(ContentHandler handler)	Allows an application to register a content event handler
void setDTDHandler(DTDHandler handler)	Allows an application to register a DTD event handler
void setEntityResolver(EntityResolver resolver)	Allows an application to register an entity resolver
void setErrorHandler(ErrorHandler handler)	Allows an application to register an error event handler
void setFeature(String name, boolean value)	Sets the state of a feature
void setProperty(String name, Object value)	Sets the value of a property

Factory-Based Approach to Parsing

If you want to parse an XML document using SAX, you need to use a class that implements the SAX XMLReader interface. The following snippet shows how to use a vendor-specific SAX parser:

```
org.xml.sax.XMLReader reader = new org.apache.crimson.parser.XMLReaderImpl();
```

However, one issue with the previous code is you'll be hard-coding the parser implementation in your code. This will make the code vendor dependent. To circumvent this problem, SAX provides a factory class called org.xml.sax.helpers.XMLReaderFactory. This class provides the methods shown in Table 14-14.

Table 14-14. XMLReader *Factory Methods*

METHOD	DESCRIPTION
XMLReader createXMLReader()	This method returns an XMLReader implementation specified by the system property org.xml.sax.driver.
XMLReader createXMLReader(String cls)	This method returns an XMLReader implementation specified by the method argument.

The following snippet shows how to use the factory-based approach:

```
XmlReader reader = XmlReaderFactory.createXMLReader(
  "org.apache.crimson.parser.XMLReaderImpl");
```

If you want to use the empty argument factory method, you can use the following option when you invoke the JVM:

```
-D=org.xml.sax.driver=org.apache.crimson.parser.XMLReaderImpl
```

Parsing Offer Data Using SAX

Now you'll write a simple application that will parse an XML document containing the offer data and generate a DOM representing the XML from the events fired to the callback handlers. The SAX `XMLReader` interface doesn't have any methods to return the DOM representing the parsed XML. Hence, if you need to create a DOM from the parsed document, you need to implement the logic using callback handlers.

OfferHandler.java

First, Listing 14-2 shows the `DefaultHandler` subclass that will handle the contents and parsing error–related callbacks.

Listing 14-2. `DefaultHandler`

```
package com.apress.projavaserver14.chapter17.sax;
// Import the SAX classes and interfaces.
import org.xml.sax.helpers.DefaultHandler;
import org.xml.sax.SAXParseException;
import org.xml.sax.SAXException;
import org.xml.sax.Attributes;
// Import the DOM interfaces.
import org.w3c.dom.Document;
import org.w3c.dom.Element;

import java.util.Stack;
// Import the Crimson Document implementation.
import org.apache.crimson.tree.XmlDocument;

public class OfferHandler extends DefaultHandler {
    // The stack is used to keep track of the elements when they re parsed.
    private Stack elements;
    // This is the Document that will hold the DOM.
    private Document offerDOM;
    // A method to return the course DOM.
    public Document getOfferDOM() { return offerDOM; }
    /* The next three methods handle parsing errors. The exceptions are
      just bubbled back and hence will be thrown out of the XMLReader's
     parse method. */
```

```
    public void error(SAXParseException ex) throws SAXException {
        throw ex;
    }

    public void fatalError(SAXParseException ex) throws SAXException {
        throw ex;
    }

    public void warning(SAXParseException ex) throws SAXException {
        throw ex;
    }
    /* This method is called when character data is parsed. The parsed data is
    appended as a text node to the element that was last parsed. */
    public void characters(char[] ch, int start, int length) {
        Element current = (Element)elements.peek();
        current.appendChild(offerDOM.createTextNode(new String(ch,
        start, length)));
    }
    /* When the parser finishes parsing the document, get the last
        element availablein the stack and append it as the root element for
        the DOM. */
    public void endDocument() {
        offerDOM.appendChild((Element)elements.pop());
    }
    // When the parser finished parsing an element pop it out of the stack.
    public void endElement(String nsURI, String localName, String qName) {
        if(elements.size() != 1) elements.pop();
    }
    // When the parser starts parsing the document create the DOM and the stack.
    public void startDocument() {
        elements = new Stack();
        offerDOM = new XmlDocument();
    }
    /* When the parser starts parsing an element, create the element, set the
    attributes, append it to the element on the top of the stack, and push the new
    element to the top of the stack. */
    public void startElement(String nsURI, String localName, String qName,
    Attributes atts) {

        Element child = offerDOM.createElement(qName);

        for(int i = 0;i < atts.getLength();i++)
            child.setAttribute(atts.getQName(i), atts.getValue(i));

        if(elements.isEmpty())
            elements.push(child);
        else {
            ((Element)elements.peek()).appendChild(child);
            elements.push(child);
        }

    }

}
```

OfferReader.java

Second, Listing 14-3 shows the class that does the parsing.

Listing 14-3. `OfferReader`

```
package com.apress.projavaserver14.chapter17.sax;
// Import the SAX classes and interfaces.
import org.xml.sax.XMLReader;
import org.xml.sax.InputSource;
import org.xml.sax.helpers.XMLReaderFactory;
// Import the Crimson Document implementation.
import org.apache.crimson.tree.XmlDocument;

public class OfferReader {

    public static void main(String args[]) throws Exception {
        // Create an instance of the Crimson SAX2 parser.
        XMLReader reader = XMLReaderFactory.createXMLReader(
        "org.apache.crimson.parser.XMLReaderImpl");
        // Create an instance of the handler class.
        OfferHandler handler = new OfferHandler();
        // Set the error and content handlers for the parser.
        reader.setContentHandler(handler);
        reader.setErrorHandler(handler);
        // Create an input source that reads the XML document from the classpath.
        InputSource in = new InputSource(OfferReader.class.getClassLoader()
        .getResourceAsStream("offers.xml"));
        // Parse the document.
        reader.parse(in);
        // Retrieve the DOM from the handler and print the contents.
        ((XmlDocument)handler.getOfferDOM()).write(System.out);
    }

}
```

Properties and Features

Even though the SAX helper API provides a vendor-neutral way of creating parsers, the vendors may need to provide specific features and properties in their parser implementations. You can do this in a vendor-neutral way by specifying them using the `setFeature()` and `setProperty()` methods available in the `XMLReader` interface. Both these methods will throw `SAXNotRecognizedException` if the specified feature/property isn't recognized and `SAXNotSupportedException` if it's recognized but not supported. You set the features using the Boolean values `true` or `false`, and you set properties as Java objects.

Features usually turn on the following:

- Validation
- Namespace support
- External general and parameter entity support

Properties usually specify schema location. The following snippet shows how to turn on validation for the SAX parser:

```
reader.setFeature("http://xml.org/sax/features/validation", true);
```

Knowing When to Use SAX

SAX is a fast and memory efficient way of processing XML data. However, SAX doesn't construct an in-memory data structure that represents the XML data being parsed. Hence, it's up to the developers to interpret the SAX events to construct an in-memory structure. SAX is efficient for checking the validity of an XML document or you're interested in only parts of the document. However, if you have complex requirements that need in-memory modification of XML structure, DOM is more suitable.

Using Java API for XML Processing (JAXP)

JAXP provides a high-level API for writing vendor-neutral applications that process XML. JAXP provides an extra layer of adapter around the vendor-specific parser and transformer implementation. The pluggability layer is available for the following:

- SAX-based XML processing
- DOM-based XML processing
- XML transformations

DOM Pluggability

JAXP provides DOM pluggability through the following:

- `javax.xml.parsers.DocumentBuilderFactory`
- `javax.xml.parsers.DocumentBuilder`

The `DocumentBuilder` instance allows you to parse an XML document and obtain an instance `org.w3c.dom.Document` interface representing the XML data that's parsed. The class that implements the previous interface hides the parser vendor's DOM implementation. This class also provides factory methods for creating empty instances of `org.w3c.dom.Document`.

DocumentBuilderFactory

`DocumentBuilderFactory` acts a factory for creating `DocumentBuilder` instances. Table 14-15 describes the methods provided by this class.

Table 14-15. `DocumentBuilderFactory` *Methods*

METHOD: `abstract Object getAttribute(String name)`
DESCRIPTION: Allows the user to retrieve specific attributes on the underlying implementation

METHOD: `boolean isCoalescing()`
DESCRIPTION: Indicates whether the factory is configured to produce parsers, which converts `CDATA` nodes to `Text` nodes and appends it to the adjacent (if any) `Text` node

METHOD: `boolean isExpandEntityReferences()`
DESCRIPTION: Indicates whether the factory is configured to produce parsers, which expand entity reference nodes

METHOD: `boolean isIgnoringComments()`
DESCRIPTION: Indicates whether the factory is configured to produce parsers, which ignores comments

METHOD: `boolean isIgnoringElementContentWhitespace()`
DESCRIPTION: Indicates whether the factory is configured to produce parsers, which ignore ignorable whitespace in element content

METHOD: `boolean isNamespaceAware()`
DESCRIPTION: Indicates whether the factory is configured to produce parsers, which are namespace aware

METHOD: `boolean isValidating()`
DESCRIPTION: Indicates whether the factory is configured to produce parsers, which validate the XML content during parsing

METHOD: `abstract DocumentBuilder newDocumentBuilder()`
DESCRIPTION: Creates a new instance of `DocumentBuilder` using the currently configured parameters

METHOD: `static DocumentBuilderFactory newInstance()`
DESCRIPTION: Obtains a new instance of `DocumentBuilderFactory`

METHOD: `abstract  void setAttribute(String name, Object value)`
DESCRIPTION: Allows the user to set specific attributes on the underlying implementation

METHOD: `void setCoalescing(boolean coalescing)`
DESCRIPTION: Specifies that the parser produced by this code will convert `CDATA` nodes to `Text` nodes and append it to the adjacent (if any) text node

(continued)

Table 14-15. `DocumentBuilderFactory` *Methods (continued)*

METHOD: `void setExpandEntityReferences(boolean expandEntityRef)`
DESCRIPTION: Specifies that the parser produced by this code will expand entity reference nodes

METHOD: `void setIgnoringComments(boolean ignoreComments)`
DESCRIPTION: Specifies that the parser produced by this code will ignore comments

METHOD: `void setIgnoringElementContentWhitespace(boolean whitespace)`
DESCRIPTION: Specifies that the parsers created by this factory must eliminate whitespace in element content (sometimes known loosely as *ignorable whitespace*) when parsing XML documents.

METHOD: `void setNamespaceAware(boolean awareness)`
DESCRIPTION: Specifies that the parser produced by this code will provide support for XML namespaces

METHOD: `void setValidating(boolean validating)`
DESCRIPTION: Specifies that the parser produced by this code will validate documents as they're parsed

The `newInstance` method uses one of the following methods to get a vendor-specific instance of `DocumentBuilderFactory`:

- Use the `javax.xml.parsers.DocumentBuilderFactory` system property.
- Use the properties file `lib/jaxp.properties` in the `lib` directory of the Java runtime environment (JRE), which is a standard Java properties file with the key being the system property mentioned previously.
- Use the JAR Services API, if available, to look for the class name in the file `META-INF/services/javax.xml.parsers.DocumentBuilderFactory` in the JAR files that are available at run time.
- Use the platform's default instance. Sun's JDK uses Crimson by default.

If an instance can't be instantiated at run time, a `FactoryConfigurationError` is thrown.

DocumentBuilder

Once you get an instance of `DocumentBuilderFactory`, you can set various properties on the instance to configure the behavior of the DOM parser that will be created by the factory. Then you can call the `newDocumentBuilder` method to get an instance of the DOM parser, `DocumentBuilder`. If the factory can't provide a parser with the requested behavior (for example, you ask the factory to give you a namespace-aware parser and the implementation doesn't support namespaces), a `ParserConfigurationException` is thrown.

This `DocumentBuilder` interface defines the methods shown in Table 14-16.

Table 14-16. `DocumentBuilder` *Methods*

METHOD: `abstract DOMImplementation getDOMImplementation()`
DESCRIPTION: Obtains an instance of a `DOMImplementation` object

METHOD: `abstract boolean isNamespaceAware()`
DESCRIPTION: Indicates whether this parser is configured to understand namespaces

METHOD: `abstract boolean isValidating()`
DESCRIPTION: Indicates whether this parser is configured to validate XML documents

METHOD: `abstract Document newDocument()`
DESCRIPTION: Obtains a new instance of a DOM `Document` object with which to build a DOM tree

METHOD: `Document parse(File f)`
DESCRIPTION: Parses the content of the given file as an XML document and returns a new DOM `Document` object

METHOD: `abstract Document parse(InputSource is)`
DESCRIPTION: Parses the content of the given input source as an XML document and returns a new DOM `Document` object

METHOD: `Document parse(InputStream is)`
DESCRIPTION: Parses the content of the given `InputStream` as an XML document and returns a new DOM `Document` object

METHOD: `Document parse(InputStream is, String systemId)`
DESCRIPTION: Parses the content of the given `InputStream` as an XML document and returns a new DOM `Document` object

METHOD: `Document parse(String uri)`
DESCRIPTION: Parses the content of the given URI as an XML document and returns a new DOM `Document` object

METHOD: `abstract void setEntityResolver(EntityResolver er)`
DESCRIPTION: Specifies the `EntityResolver` to be used to resolve entities present in the XML document to be parsed

METHOD: `abstract void setErrorHandler(ErrorHandler eh)`
DESCRIPTION: Specifies the `ErrorHandler` to be used to report errors present in the XML document to be parsed

Offer Data As XML Using JAXP

The first example in this chapter used the Crimson-specific implementation for creating a document instance. You can rewrite that code using JAXP with the following:

```
DocumentBuilderFactory dbf = DocumentBuilderFactory.newInstance();
DocumentBuilder builder = dbf.newDocumentBuilder();

Document offerDOM = builder.newDocument();
```

SAX Pluggability

JAXP provides DOM pluggability through the following:

- `javax.xml.parsers.SAXParserFactory`
- `javax.xml.parsers.SAXParser`

The `SAXParser` instance allows you parse XML documents. The class that implements the `SAXParser` interface hides the parser vendor's SAX `XMLReader` implementation.

SAXParserFactory

The `SAXParserFactory` acts a factory for creating `SAXParser` instances. Table 14-17 describes the methods provided by this class.

Table 14-17. `SAXParserFactory` *Methods*

METHOD: `abstract boolean getFeature(String name)`
DESCRIPTION: Returns the particular property requested in the underlying implementation of `org.xml.sax.XMLReader`

METHOD: `boolean isNamespaceAware()`
DESCRIPTION: Indicates whether the factory is configured to produce parsers, which are namespace aware

METHOD: `boolean isValidating()`
DESCRIPTION: Indicates whether the factory is configured to produce parsers, which validate the XML content during parse

METHOD: `static SAXParserFactory newInstance()`
DESCRIPTION: Obtains a new instance of `SAXParserFactory`

METHOD: `abstract  SAXParser newSAXParser()`
DESCRIPTION: Creates a new instance of `SAXParser` using the currently configured factory parameters

METHOD: `abstract  void setFeature(String name, boolean value)`
DESCRIPTION: Sets the particular feature in the underlying implementation of `org.xml.sax.XMLReader`

METHOD: `void setNamespaceAware(boolean awareness)`
DESCRIPTION: Specifies that the parser produced by this code will provide support for XML namespaces

METHOD: `void setValidating(boolean validating)`
DESCRIPTION: Specifies that the parser produced by this code will validate documents as they're parsed

The newInstance method uses one of the following methods to get a vendor-specific instance of SAXParserFactory:

- Use the javax.xml.parsers.SAXParserFactory system property.
- Use the properties file lib/jaxp.properties in the lib directory of the JRE, which is a standard Java properties file with the key being the system property mentioned previously.
- Use the JAR Services API, if available, to look for the class name in the file META-INF/services/javax.xml.parsers.SAXParserFactory in the JAR files that are available at run time.
- Use the platform's default instance. Sun's JDK uses Crimson by default.

If an instance can't be instantiated at run time, FactoryConfigurationError is thrown.

SAXParser

Once you get an instance of SAXParserFactory, you can set various properties on the instance to configure the behavior of the DOM parser that will be created by the factory. Then you can call the newSAXParser method to get an instance of the SAX parser, SAXParser. If the factory can't provide a parser with the requested behavior (for example, you ask the factory to give you a namespace-aware parser and the implementation doesn't support namespaces), ParserConfigurationException is thrown.

This SAXParser interface defines the methods described in Table 14-18 to support SAX 2.

Table 14-18. SAXParser *Methods*

METHOD: Object getProperty(String name)
DESCRIPTION: Returns the particular property requested for the underlying implementation of XMLReader

METHOD: XMLReader getXMLReader()
DESCRIPTION: Returns the XMLReader that's encapsulated by the implementation of this class

METHOD: boolean isNamespaceAware()
DESCRIPTION: Indicates whether this parser is configured to understand namespaces

METHOD: boolean isValidating()
DESCRIPTION: Indicates whether this parser is configured to validate XML documents

METHOD: void parse(File f, DefaultHandler dh)
DESCRIPTION: Parses the content of the file specified as XML using the specified DefaultHandler

METHOD: void parse(InputSource is, DefaultHandler dh)
DESCRIPTION: Parses the content of the given InputSource instance as XML using the specified DefaultHandler

(continued)

Table 14-18. SAXParser *Methods (continued)*

METHOD: void parse(InputStream is, DefaultHandler dh)
DESCRIPTION: Parses the content of the given InputStream instance as XML using the specified DefaultHandler

METHOD: void parse(InputStream is, DefaultHandler dh, String systemId)
DESCRIPTION: Parses the content of the given InputStream instance as XML using the specified DefaultHandler

METHOD: void parse(String uri, DefaultHandler dh)
DESCRIPTION: Parses the content described by the given URI as XML using the specified DefaultHandler

METHOD: void setProperty(String name, Object value)
DESCRIPTION: Sets the particular property in the underlying implementation of XMLReader

Parsing Offer Data Using JAXP

The first example in this chapter used the SAX XMLReaderFactory for creating the parser. You can rewrite that code using JAXP with the following:

```
SAXParserFactrory spf = SAXParserFactrory.newInstance();
SAXParser parser = dbf.new SAXParser();

InputSource in = new InputSource(OfferReader.class.getClassLoader()
getResourceAsStream("offers.xml"));

parser.parse(in, new OfferHandler());
```

Schema-Based Validation

JAXP specifies a set of properties and features that should be supported by implementing vendors to support XML schema–based validation for both SAX- and DOM-based parsing. To enable schema validation, you need to do the following:

1. **Turn on validation**: You can do this by calling setValidating(true) on DocumentBuilderFactory for DOM parsing and SAXParserFactory for SAX parsing.

2. **Set the schema language**: Calling setProperty on SAXParser for SAX and setAttribute on the DocumentBuilderFactory for DOM can do this. The property to set the schema language is http://java.sun.com/xml/jaxp/properties/schemaLanguage. The value for this property should match the schema language that's used (for example, http://www.w3c.org/2001/MChema).

3. **Set the schema source**: Calling setProperty on SAXParser for SAX and setAttribute on the DocumentBuilderFactory for DOM can do this. The property to set the schema language is http://java.sun.com/xml/jaxp/properties/schemaSource. The value for this property is the URL of the schema file that's used (for example, http://www.apress.com/trainingApp/courses.xsd).

The following snippet shows the code for turning schema validation on for SAX parsing:

```
SAXParserFactory spf = SAXParserFactory.newInstance();
spf.setValidating(true);
spf.setNamespaceAware(true);

SAXParser sp = spf.newSAXParser();
sp.setProperty(
  "http://java.sun.com/xml/jaxp/properties/schemaLanguage",
  "http://www.w3c.org/2001/XMLSchema");
sp.setProperty(
  "http://java.sun.com/xml/jaxp/properties/schemaSource",
  "http://www.apress.com/Auction/offers.xsd");

sp.parse(
  "http://www.apress.com/Auctionoffers.xml",
  new DefaultHandler());
```

The following snippet shows the code for turning schema validation on for DOM parsing,

```
DocumentBuilderFactory dbf = DocumentBuilderFactory.newInstance();

dbf.setValidating(true);
dbf.setNamespaceAware(true);
dbf.setAttribute(
  "http://java.sun.com/xml/jaxp/properties/schemaLanguage",
  "http://www.w3c.org/2001/XMLSchema");
dbf. setAttribute (
  "http://java.sun.com/xml/jaxp/properties/schemaSource",
  "http://www.apress.com/trainingApp/offers.xsd");

DocumentBuilder db = dbf.newDocumentBuilder();

sp.parse("http://www.apress.com/Auction/offers.xml");
```

Schema Source

If the target namespace of the schema identified by the `schemaSource` (`http://java.sun.com/xml/jaxp/properties/schemaSource`) property matches the target namespace specified in the instance document using the `schemaLocation` attribute, the parser is required to ignore the schema specified in the instance document using the `schemaLocation` attribute and use the schema specified by the `schemaSource` property. However, if they don't match, the parser may choose to use the schema specified by the `schemaLocation` attribute. The `schemaSource` property can be one of the following:

- A string representing the URI of the schema
- An `InputStream` with the contents of the schema
- A SAX `InputSource`
- A `File` pointing to the schema
- An array of objects with any of the previously mentioned items. You can use this only when the schema language has the ability to assemble a schema at run time. In such cases no two schemas that are specified should have the same target namespace.

If the instance document doesn't have a target namespace, the parser should behave in the same way as if the instance document used a `noNamespaceSchemaLocation` attribute.

Transformer Pluggability

JAXP also provides transformer pluggability by allowing an abstraction layer over vendors' transformer implementations. This allows you not to hard-code vendor-specific classes in your application. Transformer pluggability in JAXP works in the same way as DOM and SAX pluggability. The interface to the vendor-specific implementations is through a factory class called `javax.xml.transformer.TransformerFactory`. This class provides a `newInstance` method to get an instance of the transformer factory. JAXP picks a transformer factory in one of the following ways:

- Using the `javax.xml.transformer.TransformerFactory` system property
- Using the properties file `lib/jaxp.properties` in the `lib` directory of the JRE, which is a standard Java properties file with the key being the system property mentioned previously
- Using the JAR Services API, if available, to look for the class name in the file `META-INF/services/javax.xml.transformer.TransformerFactory` in the JAR files available at run time
- Using the platform's default instance. Sun's JDK uses Xalan by default.

If an instance can't be instantiated at run time, `TransformerFactoryConfigurationError` is thrown. Figure 14-4 shows the main classes and interfaces in the JAXP transformer pluggability layer.

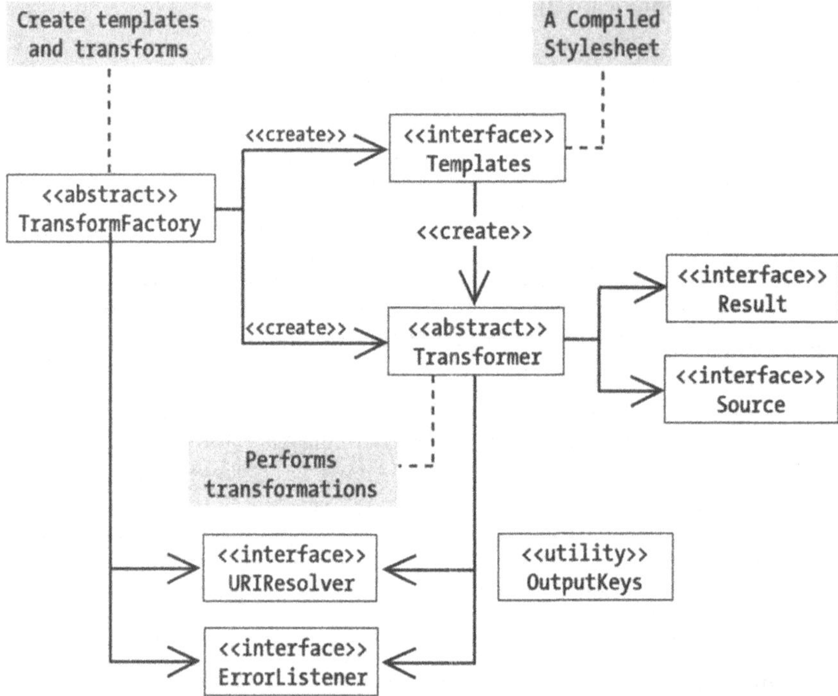

Figure 14-4. Classes and interfaces in the JAXP transformer pluggability layer

The following explains this layer:

- `TransformerFactory` acts as an abstraction layer over the vendor-specific `Transformer` implementations. You can use this class for creating `Transformer` and `Templates` instances.
- The `Transformer` interface defines methods for performing the actual transformation.
- The `Templates` interface represents a compiled stylesheet and can be used for creating `Transformer` instances.
- The `Result` interface abstracts the entity to which the transformed result is written. JAXP provides implementations based on writing the result to a DOM node, a SAX content handler, and a stream.
- The `Source` interface abstracts the entity from which the stylesheet and XML to be transformed can be read. JAXP provides implementations on based reading the result from a DOM node, a SAX XML reader, and a stream.

- The `OutputKeys` class enumerates a set of property names that can be passed to the transformer or templates object to control the properties of the output.
- The `ErrorListener` interface is used for implementing custom error handling.
- The `URIResolver` is an interface that can be used to resolve URIs specified in the stylesheet for `xsl:import` and `xsl:include`.

Now you'll look at some of the more important interfaces and classes in further detail.

TransformerFactory

Table 14-19 lists some of the important methods defined in this class.

Table 14-19. `TransformerFactory` *Methods*

METHOD: `abstract ErrorListener getErrorListener()`
`abstract void setErrorListener(ErrorListener listener)`
DESCRIPTION: These methods get and set error event listeners for `TransformerFactory`, which is used for the processing of transformation instructions, not for the transformation itself.

METHOD: `abstract URIResolver getURIResolver()`
`abstract void setURIResolver(URIResolver resolver)`
DESCRIPTION: These methods get and set the object that's used by default during the transformation to resolve URIs used in `document()`, `xsl:import`, or `xsl:include`.

METHOD: `static TransformerFactory newInstance()`
DESCRIPTION: Obtains a new instance of `TransformerFactory`.

METHOD: `abstract Templates newTemplates(Source source)`
DESCRIPTION: Processes the `Source` into a `Templates` object, which is a compiled representation of the source.

METHOD: `abstract Transformer newTransformer()`
DESCRIPTION: Creates a new `Transformer` object that performs a copy of the source to the result.

METHOD: `abstract Transformer newTransformer(Source source)`
DESCRIPTION: Processes the `Source` into a `Transformer` object.

METHOD: `boolean getFeature(String name)`
DESCRIPTION: This verifies whether the underlying transformer implementation supports a particular source or result implementation such as DOM, SAX, and Stream.

The following snippet shows how you'd normally use the `TransformerFactory`:

```
TransformerFactory tf = TransformerFactory.newInstance();
Transformer t = tf.newTransformer(<<Source Implementation>>);
```

The `Source` implementation passed to the `newTransformer` method identifies the Extensible Stylesheet Language (XSL) source as a DOM node, a SAX XML reader, or an input stream.

Transformer

An instance of this abstract class can transform a source tree into a result tree. You can obtain an instance of this class with the `TransformerFactory.newTransformer` method. You can then use this instance to process XML from a variety of sources and write the transformation output to a variety of sinks. Table 14-20 lists some of the important methods defined by `Transformer`.

Table 14-20. `Transformer` *Methods*

METHOD: `abstract void clearParameters()`
DESCRIPTION: Clears all the parameters.

METHOD: `abstract Object getParameter(String name)`
DESCRIPTION: Gets an XSLT parameter.

METHOD: `abstract void setParameter(String name, Object value)`
DESCRIPTION: These methods are used for clearing, getting, and setting parameters passed to the stylesheet.

METHOD: `abstract ErrorListener getErrorListener()`
DESCRIPTION: Gets the error listener.

METHOD: `abstract void setErrorListener(ErrorListener listener)`
DESCRIPTION: Gets and sets the error listener as in `TransformerFactory`.

METHOD: `abstract URIResolver getURIResolver()`
DESCRIPTION: Gets the URI resolver.

METHOD: `abstract void setURIResolver(URIResolver resolver)`
DESCRIPTION: Gets and sets the URI resolver as in `TransformerFactory`.

METHOD: `abstract Properties getOutputProperties()`
DESCRIPTION: Gets the output properties.

METHOD: `abstract String getOutputProperty(String name)`
DESCRIPTION: Gets a named output property.

METHOD: `abstract void setOutputProperties(Properties oformat)`
DESCRIPTION: Sets the output properties for formatting.

METHOD: `abstract void setOutputProperty(String name, String value)`
DESCRIPTION: Gets and sets output properties that configure how the output is produced. The keys for the properties are defined in `OutputPropertyKeys`.

METHOD: `abstract void transform(Source xmlSource, Result outputTarget)`
DESCRIPTION: Processes the source tree to the output result.

The following snippet shows how to use `Transformer`:

```
TransformerFactory tf = TransformerFactory.newInstance();
Transformer t = tf.newTransformer(<<Source Implementation>>);

t.transform(<<Source Implementation>>, <<Result Implementation>>);
```

The `Source` implementation passed to the `transform` method identifies the XML source that needs to be transformed as a DOM node, a SAX XML reader, or an input stream and written to the `Result` implementation as a DOM node, a SAX content handler, or an output stream.

Templates

An object that implements this interface is the runtime representation of processed transformation instructions. You can create a `Templates` instance using `TransformerFactory`, and then you can use it to create a `Transformer` instance, as follows:

```
TransformerFactory tf = TransformerFactory.newInstance();
Templates tmp = tf.newTemplates(<<Source Implementation>>);

Transformer t = tmp.newTransformer();

t.transform(domSource, streamResult);
```

The `Source` implementation passed to the `newTemplates` method identifies the XSL source as a DOM node, a SAX XML reader, or an input stream. The `Source` implementation passed to the `transform` method identifies the XML source that needs to be transformed as a DOM node, a SAX XML reader, or an input stream and written to the `Result` implementation as a DOM node, a SAX content handler, or an output stream.

JAXP Transformer Input/Output

JAXP allows the following sources for the XML that's transformed and XSL that's used for the transformation:

- A DOM node
- A SAX XML reader or input source
- A file, input stream, or reader

The following implementations are provided for the sinks, to which the result tree of transformation is written:

- A DOM node
- A SAX content handler
- A file, output stream, or writer

Figure 14-5 shows the JAXP transformer input/output classes.

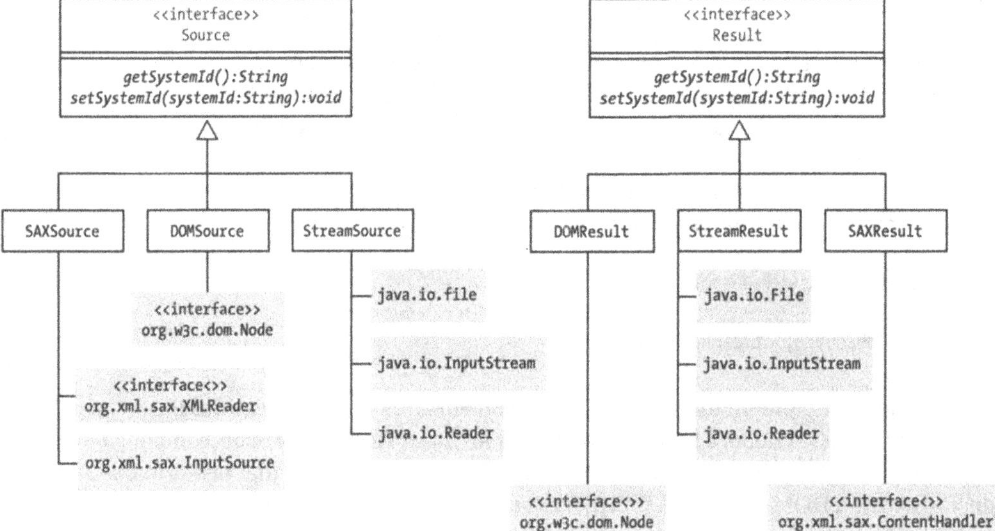

Figure 14-5. JAXP transformer input/output classes

The SAXSource class can be instantiated by passing an XMLReader or InputSource, DOMSource by a DOM Node, and StreamSource by a File, InputStream, or Reader. The SAXResult can be instantiated by passing a ContentHandler, a DOMResult by a DOM Node, and a StreamResult by a File, OutputStream, or Writer.

All the aforementioned Source and Result implementations have a static variable called FEATURE that can check whether the underlying transformer implementation supports a particular mode of input or output. You do this by calling the getFeature method on TransformerFactory by passing the relevant feature. The following snippet checks whether DOM-based input is supported:

```
if(tf.getFeature(DOMSource.FEATURE) {
  //perform DOM source-based processing
}
```

The fastest way to perform transformation is to present a DOM that represents the data to be transformed to the transformer. However, this isn't always feasible with memory-intensive, large documents. Stream input/output is quite efficient when the data that's transformed is streamed in as in a servlet or written out to a stream. SAX-based input is quite powerful if you want to transform non-XML data. Here you can write an `XMLReader` implementation that will read non-XML data and fire SAX events to the listening JAXP-compliant transformer.

Transform Offer Data

In this section, you'll write an example that will transform the offer XML you've seen in earlier sections to HTML. Listing 14-4 shows the stylesheet that's used.

Listing 14-4. Stylesheet

```
<?xml version="1.0" encoding="ISO-8859-1"?>

<xsl:stylesheet
  version="1.0"
  xmlns:xsl="http://www.w3.org/1999/XSL/Transform">

  <xsl:output method="html" indent="yes"/>

  <xsl:template match="offers">
    <html>
      <head><title>Offers</title></head>
      <body>
        <table>
          <tr>
            <th>Id</th>
            <th>Name</th>
            <th>Description</th>
          </tr>
          <xsl:apply-templates select="offer"/>
        </table>
      </body>
    </html>
  </xsl:template>

  <xsl:template match="offer">
    <tr>
      <td><xsl:value-of select="@id"/></td>
      <td><xsl:value-of select="@name"/></td>
      <td><xsl:value-of select="@description"/></td>
    </tr>
  </xsl:template>

</xsl:stylesheet>
```

The stylesheet in Listing 14-4 will format the offers data into a HTML table. The example accepts the XSL as a DOM node, accepts the XML as an input stream, and writes the result tree to a SAX content handler. Listing 14-5 shows `OfferTransformer`.

Listing 14-5. `OfferTransformer`

```
package com.apress.projavaserver14.chapter17.jaxp.transform;

import javax.xml.parsers.DocumentBuilder;
import javax.xml.parsers.DocumentBuilderFactory;

import javax.xml.transform.Transformer;
import javax.xml.transform.TransformerFactory;
import javax.xml.transform.TransformerConfigurationException;

import javax.xml.transform.dom.DOMSource;
import javax.xml.transform.stream.StreamSource;
import javax.xml.transform.sax.SAXResult;

import org.xml.sax.helpers.DefaultHandler;
import org.xml.sax.Attributes;
import org.w3c.dom.Document;

public class OfferTransformer {
    // The constants point to the URL of the XML and XSL files.
    private static final String XML_SYSTEM_ID = "file:///c:/offers.xml";
    private static final String XSL_SYSTEM_ID = "file:///c:/offers.xsl";

    public static void main(String args[]) throws Exception {
        // Create a document builder using the standard JAXP calls.
        DocumentBuilderFactory dbf = DocumentBuilderFactory.newInstance();
        dbf.setNamespaceAware(true);
        DocumentBuilder db = dbf.newDocumentBuilder();
        // Parse the XSL file into a DOM.
        Document xsl = db.parse(XSL_SYSTEM_ID);
        // Create a new transformer factory.
        TransformerFactory tf = TransformerFactory.newInstance();
        // Check whether DOM input is supported.
        if(!tf.getFeature(DOMSource.FEATURE))
            throw new TransformerConfigurationException(
            "DOM Source not supported");
        // Create a DOM source representing the XSL.
        DOMSource xslSource = new DOMSource(xsl, XSL_SYSTEM_ID);
        Transformer t = tf.newTransformer(xslSource);
        // Check whether stream input is supported.
        if(!tf.getFeature(StreamSource.FEATURE))
            throw new TransformerConfigurationException(
            "Stream Source not supported");
        // Create a stream source representing the XML that is to be transformed.
        StreamSource xmlSource = new StreamSource(XML_SYSTEM_ID);
```

```
        // Check whether SAX output is supported.
        if(!tf.getFeature(SAXResult.FEATURE))
            throw new TransformerConfigurationException(
            "SAX Result not supported");
        /* Create a SAX output with a content handler writing the transformed
            data to the system output. */
        SAXResult result = new SAXResult(new DefaultHandler() {

            public void startElement(String namespaceURI, String localName,
            String qName, Attributes atts) {

                System.out.print("<" + localName);
                if(atts.getLength() > 0) {
                    System.out.print(" ");
                    for(int i = 0;i < atts.getLength();i++) {
                        System.out.print(atts.getLocalName(i) + "=\"" +
                        atts.getValue(i) + "\"");
                    }
                }
                System.out.println(">");

            }

            public void endElement(String namespaceURI, String localName,
            String qName) {
                System.out.println("</" + localName + ">");
            }

            public void characters(char[] ch, int start, int length) {
                System.out.println(new String(ch, start, length));
            }

        });
        // Perform the transformation.
        t.transform(xmlSource, result);

    }

}
```

Listing 14-6 shows the generated HTML.

Listing 14-6. The Generated HTML

```
<html>
  <head><title>Courses</title></head>
  <body>
    <table>
      <tr><th>Id</th><th>Name</th><th>Description</th></tr>
      <tr>
```

```
        <td>1</td>
        <td>Java Primer</td>
        <td>Java Beginner Level</td>
      </tr>
      <tr>
        <td>2</td>
        <td>C++ Primer</td>
        <td>C++ Beginner Level</td>
      </tr>
    </table>
  </body>
</html>
```

Summary

This chapter covered how to process XML within J2EE in detail. It started by covering the two most prevalent APIs for processing XML, SAX and DOM. Then you learned how to use JAXP for writing vendor-neutral XML parsing code. You looked at both SAX and DOM pluggability. Then you moved onto writing vendor-neutral XML transformations using JAXP. You learned how JAXP can transform XML from a variety of sources into a variety of sinks.

CHAPTER 15

Introducing Enterprise Java Web Services

Web services are a technology that has gained enormous popularity in the industry over the past two years. Web services introduce a new paradigm in the field of distribute computing where the emphasis is on the protocol that's used rather than how the technology is implemented. The main advantage Web services have over other technologies that support distributed computing is that Web services are based on open standards such as Extensible Markup Language (XML), Simple Object Access Protocol (SOAP), Web Services Description Language (WSDL), Hypertext Transfer Protocol (HTTP), and so on, and hence are widely accepted in the industry. More than any other distributed computing technologies in the past, Web services promote interoperability between heterogeneous and incompatible systems.

Like most of its competitors, Sun Microsystems has extended a huge amount of support for Web service technologies including XML, SOAP, WSDL, and so on, in the Java 2 Standard Edition (J2SE) and Java 2 Enterprise Edition (J2EE), as well as other independent application programming interfaces (APIs).

This chapter covers the various J2EE 1.4 features that enable Java developers to add Web service capabilities to their applications. The chapter starts with an introduction to Web services, including the associated specifications and standards. Then you'll look at the support for these standards in the J2EE 1.4 suite of specifications. The chapter covers various J2EE Web services standards including Java API for XML-based RPC (JAX-RPC), Java API for XML Registries (JAX-R), SOAP with Attachment API for Java (SAAJ), and so on. It also covers how to expose Web services using the servlet and Enterprise JavaBean (EJB) endpoints. Next, the chapter covers the various models available for writing Web service clients; and finally, the chapter concludes by describing the J2EE support for interoperability standards.

An Overview of the Example

Throughout this chapter we'll present two of the use cases from the auction application in the examples to illustrate how to use Web services in J2EE. The use cases allow users to search the list of offers by keywords and also get the description of an offer for the specified offer ID.

The following snippet shows the methods that are exposed as Web services:

```
public OfferData[] searchOffer(String keyword);
public String getOfferDescription(int offerId);
```

You'll look at how to expose the previous use cases as Web services using both servlet and EJB endpoints. With the servlet endpoint, the implementation class will access the local entity EJBs to extract the required data. With the EJB endpoint, the implementation class is a stateless session EJB, and the bean class uses local entity EJBs to access the underlying database.

Listing 15-1 shows the definition of `OfferData`, which is a data transfer object.

Listing 15-1. `OfferData`

```
package com.apress.auction.entity.interfaces;

public class OfferData extends Object implements java.io.Serializable
{
   private int offerId;
   private String name;
   private String description;

   public int getOfferId() { return this.offerId; }
   public void setOfferId(int offerId) { this.offerId = offerId; }

   public String getName() { return this.name; }
   public void setName(String name) { this.name = name; }

   public String getDescription() { return this.description; }
   public void setDescription(String description) {
    this.description = description;
  }

}
```

An Overview of Web Services

Web services provide the integration of disparate, heterogeneous, and loosely coupled applications, using a service-oriented architecture. The services offered by the applications are accessible through industry-standard protocols such as HTTP, SOAP, XML, WSDL, and Universal Description Discovery and Integration (UDDI), and so on. In simplistic terms, *Web services* are distributed applications that use SOAP and WSDL to exchange data in XML format.

Web service–based distributed systems mainly contain the following entities:

- Applications that expose their services using Web services
- Registries that are used by the Web services provider to publish these services
- Web service clients that look up the services from the registries and send service requests to the Web service providers

Figure 15-1 illustrates the Web service architecture.

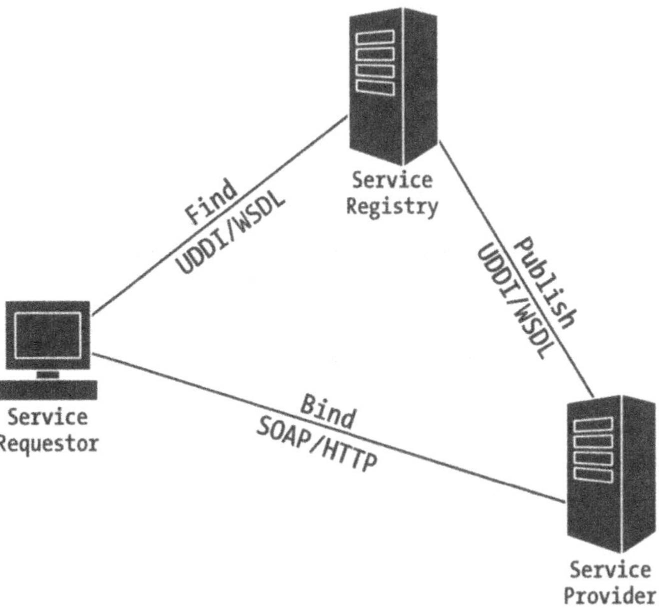

Figure 15-1. Web service architecture

In Figure 15-1 the service provider implements the service and registers the service description with a service registry. The service requester finds the details about the service from the registry and invokes the service using standard protocols.

WSDL is a standard XML application that's used to describe the service. WSDL defines abstract interface definitions for the service as well as concrete implementation and protocol binding details.

UDDI is a standard protocol for publishing and finding Web services from a registry of providers and services.

SOAP is an XML-based protocol that can be used to represent requests and responses in a Remote Procedure Call (RPC)–based interaction. For Web service invocation, you need to bind the abstract service definition to a data representation and transport protocol. Currently, SOAP over HTTP is the most predominant protocol binding. However, that doesn't mean it's the only available protocol binding.

The next two sections cover two of the more important technologies that constitute Web services: SOAP and WSDL.

Web Services Description Language

WSDL is a World Wide Web Consortium (W3C) standard for describing Web services. WSDL describes the following properties for the Web services:

- The types used in the Web service
- The message structures sent and received by the Web service
- The operations supported by the Web service
- The protocol bindings for the Web service in terms of how the data is represented and how it's transported
- Concrete service definitions for accessing the Web service

NOTE *You should have a good understanding of WSDL in order to understand the mapping from the Web service described by WSDL to how it's implemented using the various enterprise Java APIs such as JAX-RPC.*

Figure 15-2 depicts the structure of a WSDL document.

Before going into the details of the individual elements of the WSDL document, we'll present a sample WSDL document. The Web service for which the WSDL is defined provides the following functionality to search the offers in the auction application:

```
public OfferData[] searchOffer(String text)
public String getDescription(int offerId)
```

The Web service exposes two methods. One takes a search string and returns an array of objects representing offers. The second one takes the offer ID as an `int` and returns the offer description as a string. Listing 15-2 shows the WSDL for the Web service that is exposing the previous functionality.

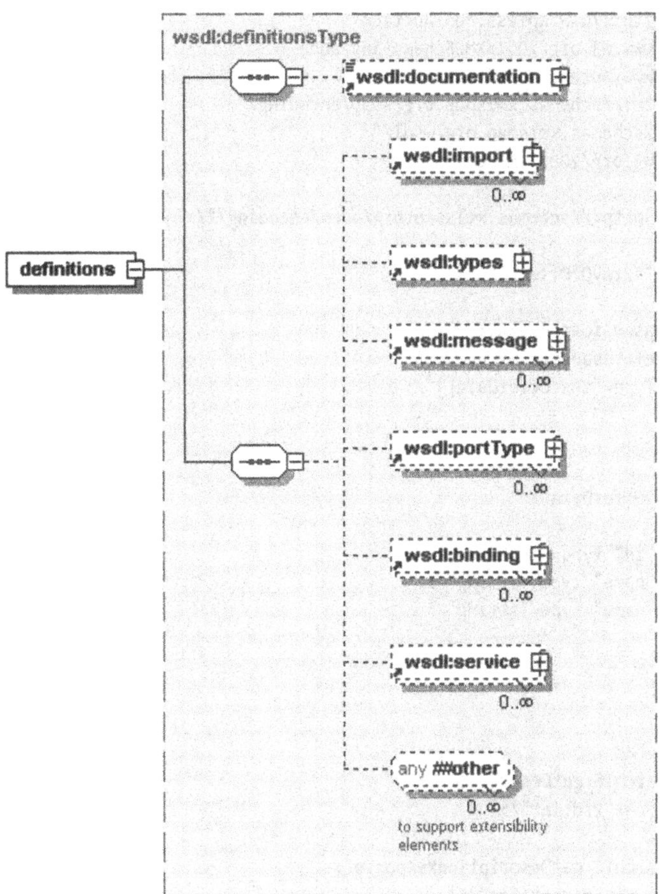

Figure 15-2. WSDL structure

Listing 15-2. The Web Service

```
<?xml version="1.0" encoding="UTF-8"?>

<definitions
  name="OfferSearchSEP"
  targetNamespace="http://www.apress.com/Auction"
  xmlns:tns="http://www.apress.com/Auction"
  xmlns="http://schemas.xmlsoap.org/wsdl/"
  xmlns:soap="http://schemas.xmlsoap.org/wsdl/soap/"
  xmlns:xsd="http://www.w3.org/2001/XMLSchema">

  <types>
    <schema
      targetNamespace="http://www.apress.com/Auction"
      xmlns:xsi="http://www.w3.org/2001/XMLSchema-instance"
      xmlns:tns="http://www.apress.com/Auction"
      xmlns:soap-enc="http://schemas.xmlsoap.org/soap/encoding/"
      xmlns:wsdl="http://schemas.xmlsoap.org/wsdl/"
      xmlns="http://www.w3.org/2001/XMLSchema">

      <import namespace="http://schemas.xmlsoap.org/soap/encoding/"/>

      <complexType name="ArrayOfOfferData">
        <complexContent>
          <restriction base="soap-enc:Array">
            <attribute ref="soap-enc:arrayType"
              wsdl:arrayType="tns:OfferData[]"/>
          </restriction>
        </complexContent>
      </complexType>
      <complexType name="OfferData">
        <sequence>
          <element name="id" type="int"/>
          <element name="name" type="string"/>
          <element name="name" type="string"/>
        </sequence>
      </complexType>
    </schema>
  </types>

  <message name="OfferSearchIF_getDescription">
    <part name="int_1" type="xsd:int"/>
  </message>
  <message name="OfferSearchIF_getDescriptionResponse">
    <part name="result" type="xsd:string"/>
  </message>
  <message name="OfferSearchIF_searchOffers">
    <part name="String_1" type="xsd:string"/>
  </message>
  <message name="OfferSearchIF_searchOffersResponse">
    <part name="result" type="tns:ArrayOfOfferData"/>
  </message>
```

```
  <portType name="OfferSearchIF">
    <operation name="getDescription" parameterOrder="int_1">
      <input message="tns:OfferSearchIF_getDescription"/>
      <output message="tns:OfferSearchIF_getDescriptionResponse"/>
    </operation>
    <operation name="searchOffers" parameterOrder="String_1">
      <input message="tns:OfferSearchIF_searchOffers"/>
      <output message="tns:OfferSearchIF_searchOffersResponse"/>
    </operation>
  </portType>

  <binding name="OfferSearchIFBinding" type="tns:OfferSearchIF">
    <operation name="getDescription">
      <input>
        <soap:body
          encodingStyle="http://schemas.xmlsoap.org/soap/encoding/"
          use="encoded"
          namespace="http://www.apress.com/Auction"/>
      </input>
      <output>
        <soap:body
          encodingStyle="http://schemas.xmlsoap.org/soap/encoding/"
          use="encoded"
          namespace="http://www.apress.com/Auction"/>
      </output>
      <soap:operation soapAction=""/>
    </operation>
    <operation name="searchOffers">
      <input>
        <soap:body
          encodingStyle="http://schemas.xmlsoap.org/soap/encoding/"
          use="encoded"
          namespace="http://www.apress.com/Auction"/>
      </input>
      <output>
        <soap:body
          encodingStyle="http://schemas.xmlsoap.org/soap/encoding/"
          use="encoded"
          namespace="http://www.apress.com/Auction"/>
      </output>
      <soap:operation soapAction=""/>
    </operation>
    <soap:binding
      transport="http://schemas.xmlsoap.org/soap/http" style="rpc"/>
  </binding>

  <service name="OfferSearchSEP">
    <port name="OfferSearchIFPort" binding="tns:OfferSearchIFBinding">
      <soap:address
        location="http://localhost:8000/Auction/offerSearch"/>
    </port>
  </service>

</definitions>
```

The document element of the WSDL document is `definitions`, and it declares the following namespaces:

- **http://www.apress.com/Auction**: This namespace qualifies the new message formats, types, operations, and so on, relevant to the Web services defined in the WSDL document.
- **http://schemas.xmlsoap.org/wsdl/**: This is used as the default namespace and qualifies the markup specific to WSDL such as `service`, `binding`, `portType`, `message`, and so on.
- **http://schemas.xmlsoap.org/wsdl/soap/**: This namespace qualifies markup specific to SOAP binding.
- **http://www.w3.org/2001/XMLSchema**: This namespace qualifies markup specific to the XML Schema language used to define the types of messages that are exchanged in the Web services.

In addition to the namespace declarations listed, the document element also has a `name` attribute that defines the name for the Web service definitions. The WSDL document uses the following six elements to describe the Web services.

types

The `types` element provides the data type definitions for the messages that are exchanged in the Web services. For maximum interoperability and platform neutrality XML Schema is the preferred as the canonical type system. However, the `types` element supports any content model to support extensible type systems (see Figure 15-3).

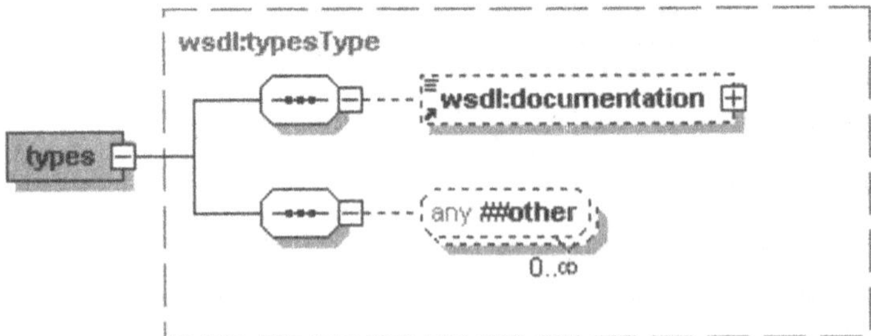

Figure 15-3. Type structure

In the previous example, you use XML Schema Definition (XSD) to define the complex types for OfferData and array of OfferData types. Listing 15-3 shows the XSD.

Listing 15-3. The XSD

```
<types>
  <schema
    targetNamespace="http://www.apress.com/Auction"
    xmlns:xsi="http://www.w3.org/2001/XMLSchema-instance"
    xmlns:tns="http://www.apress.com/Auction"
    xmlns:soap-enc="http://schemas.xmlsoap.org/soap/encoding/"
    xmlns:wsdl="http://schemas.xmlsoap.org/wsdl/"
    xmlns="http://www.w3.org/2001/XMLSchema">

    <import namespace="http://schemas.xmlsoap.org/soap/encoding/"/>

    <complexType name="ArrayOfOfferData">
      <complexContent>
        <restriction base="soap-enc:Array">
          <attribute
            ref="soap-enc:arrayType"
            wsdl:arrayType="tns:OfferData[]"/>
        </restriction>
      </complexContent>
    </complexType>

    <complexType name="OfferData">
      <sequence>
        <element name="description" type="string"/>
        <element name="id" type="int"/>
        <element name="name" type="string"/>
      </sequence>
    </complexType>
  </schema>
</types>
```

message

The message element defines the messages that are received and sent by the Web services. The message element has a name attribute whose value uniquely identifies a message among all the messages defined in the WSDL document. Messages contain one or more logical parts (see Figure 15-4).

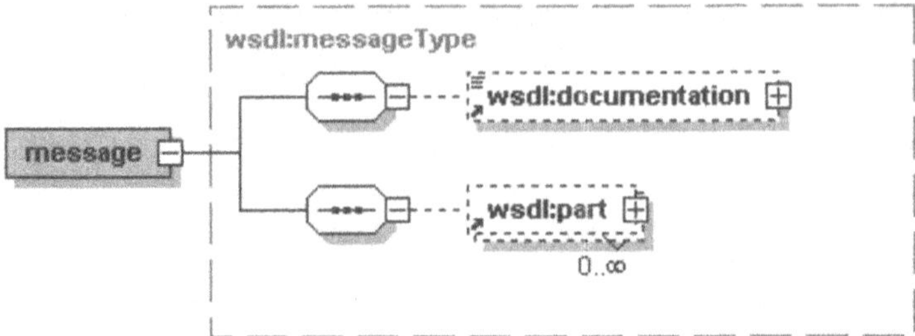

Figure 15-4. Message structure

Each part in the message is associated with a type either from the intrinsic type system (XSD) or a new type defined within the types element. Each part has name and type attributes. Listing 15-4 shows the message parts.

Listing 15-4. Message Parts

```
<message name="OfferSearchIF_getDescription">
  <part name="int_1" type="xsd:int"/>
</message>
<message name="OfferSearchIF_getDescriptionResponse">
  <part name="result" type="xsd:string"/>
</message>
<message name="OfferSearchIF_searchOffers">
  <part name="String_1" type="xsd:string"/>
</message>
<message name="OfferSearchIF_searchOffersResponse">
  <part name="result" type="tns:ArrayOfOfferData"/>
</message>
```

Listing 15-4 defines the following four messages:

- Arguments passed to the getDescription method, xsd:int
- The return type from the getDescription method, xsd:string
- Arguments passed to the searchOffers method, xsd:string
- The return type from the searchOffers method, a custom complex type representing the offer data transfer object

portType

This element defines the abstract set of operations and messages that are supported by the Web services. The name attribute of this element uniquely identifies the port type among all the port types defined in the WSDL document. This element contains one or more `operation` elements representing an operation that is supported by the Web service. The operation elements contain a combination of `input`, `output`, and `fault` elements depending on the type of the operation, as explained next. All three aforementioned elements have `name` and `type` attributes where the `type` should correspond to one of the messages defined using the `message` element. The following four types of operations are supported:

- **One-way**: Here the Web service endpoint receives a message from the client. In this case the operation consists of a single input message.
- **Request-response**: Here the client sends a message and receives a response. The operation consists of one input, one output, and zero or more fault messages.
- **Solicitor-response**: Here the endpoint sends a message to the client, and the client sends the response. In this case the operation consists of an output message followed by an input message and zero or more fault messages.
- **Notification**: Here the endpoint sends a notification message to the client, and the operation consists of a single output message.

Figure 15-5 shows the structure of the `portType` element.

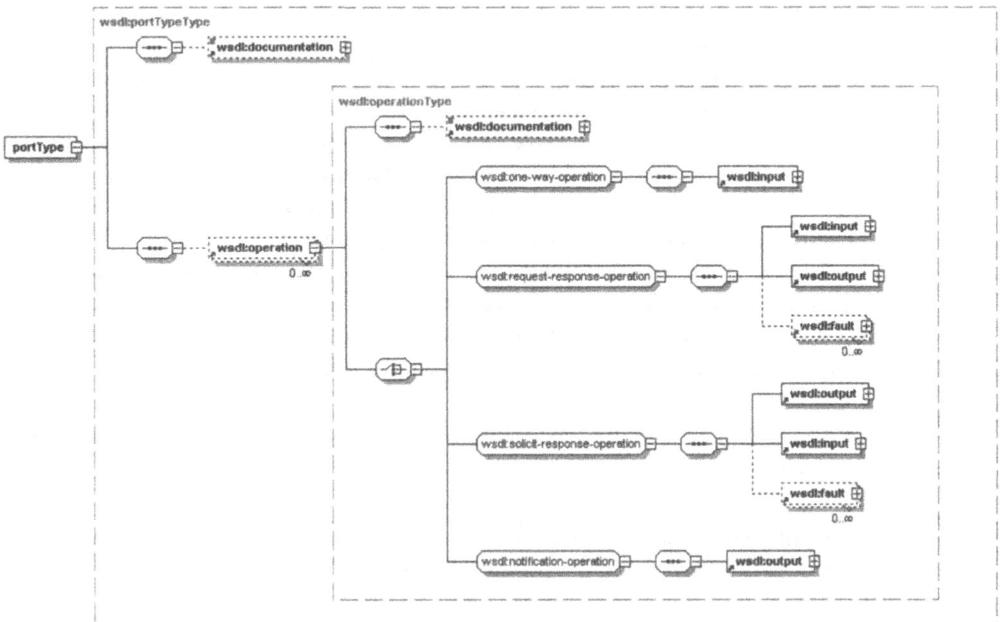

Figure 15-5. Port type structure

Listing 15-5 defines the abstract operation for the searchOffers and getdescription methods exposed by the Web service.

Listing 15-5. searchOffers *and* getdescription *Methods*

```
<portType name="OfferSearchIF">
  <operation name="getDescription" parameterOrder="int_1">
    <input message="tns:OfferSearchIF_getDescription"/>
    <output message="tns:OfferSearchIF_getDescriptionResponse"/>
  </operation>
  <operation name="searchOffers" parameterOrder="String_1">
    <input message="tns:OfferSearchIF_searchOffers"/>
    <output message="tns:OfferSearchIF_searchOffersResponse"/>
  </operation>
</portType>
```

The parameterOrder attribute may optionally specify the order in which the constituent parts of a message are passed during the operation.

binding

The types, message, and portType elements define the abstract operations supported by the Web services, and the binding, port, and service elements define the concrete implementation details for these operations. The implementation details include protocol bindings for data representation and transport, a concrete endpoint address for the Web service, and so on.

This binding element specifies the concrete transport and data representation protocols used for operations defined by the portType. This element uses an extension mechanism for supporting pluggable data representation and transport bindings. One of the predominantly used combinations is SOAP over HTTP, where SOAP is the data representation protocol and HTTP is the transport protocol.

Figure 15-6 shows the structure of the binding element.

The binding element contains zero or more operation elements corresponding to the abstract operations defined using the port type. There are mainly five extension points with the XSD type any content model to support pluggable protocol bindings.

The elements used for protocol bindings are as follows:

- An immediate child for the binding element to specify the protocol binding that is used.
- An immediate child for each operation element to specify how the operation will be modeled under the protocol binding.
- A child element each for input, output, and fault to represent how the input, output, and fault will be modeled, respectively, under the protocol binding.

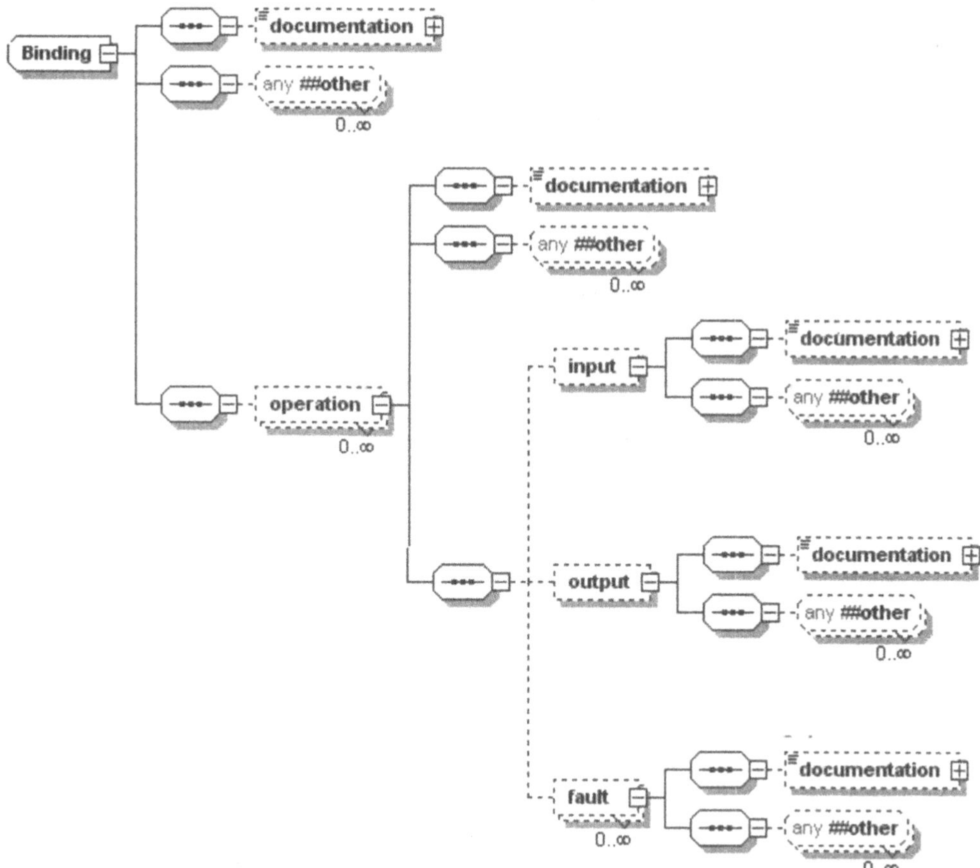

Figure 15-6. Binding structure

The `binding` element has a `name` element that uniquely identifies the binding and a `type` element that identifies the port type for which the binding is specified. You can have any number of bindings for a port type. The `name` attribute of each `operation` in the binding should match the same for the corresponding abstract operation defined in the port type.

Listing 15-6 shows the SOAP-HTTP binding for the Web service.

Listing 15-6. SOAP-HTTP Binding

```
<binding name="OfferSearchIFBinding" type="tns:OfferSearchIF">
  <operation name="getDescription">
    <input>
      <soap:body
        encodingStyle="http://schemas.xmlsoap.org/soap/encoding/"
        use="encoded"
```

```
            namespace="http://www.apress.com/Auction"/>
      </input>
      <output>
        <soap:body
          encodingStyle="http://schemas.xmlsoap.org/soap/encoding/"
          use="encoded"
          namespace="http://www.apress.com/Auction"/>
      </output>
      <soap:operation soapAction=""/>
    </operation>
    <operation name="searchOffers">
      <input>
        <soap:body
          encodingStyle="http://schemas.xmlsoap.org/soap/encoding/"
          use="encoded"
          namespace="http://www.apress.com/Auction"/>
      </input>
      <output>
        <soap:body
          encodingStyle="http://schemas.xmlsoap.org/soap/encoding/"
          use="encoded"
          namespace="http://www.apress.com/Auction"/>
      </output>
      <soap:operation soapAction=""/>
    </operation>
    <soap:binding
      transport="http://schemas.xmlsoap.org/soap/http" style="rpc"/>
</binding>
```

Listing 15-6 defines the protocol binding as RPC-style SOAP over HTTP and specifies that the input and output messages will be represented as SOAP body parts and the target namespace for the body parts will be `http://www.apress.com/Auction`.

service and port

The `port` defines a physical endpoint for a binding. A `port` has a `name` attribute to uniquely identify the port and a `binding` attribute to specify the binding for which the port is defined. The `port` element also supports pluggable extensions with any content model. The `service` element acts as an aggregation of ports (see Figure 15-7).

Listing 15-7 defines the port for the Web service.

Listing 15-7. The Port

```
<service name="OfferSearchSEP">
  <port name="OfferSearchIFPort" binding="tns:OfferSearchIFBinding">
    <soap:address
      location="http://localhost:8000/Auction/offerSearch"/>
  </port>
</service>
```

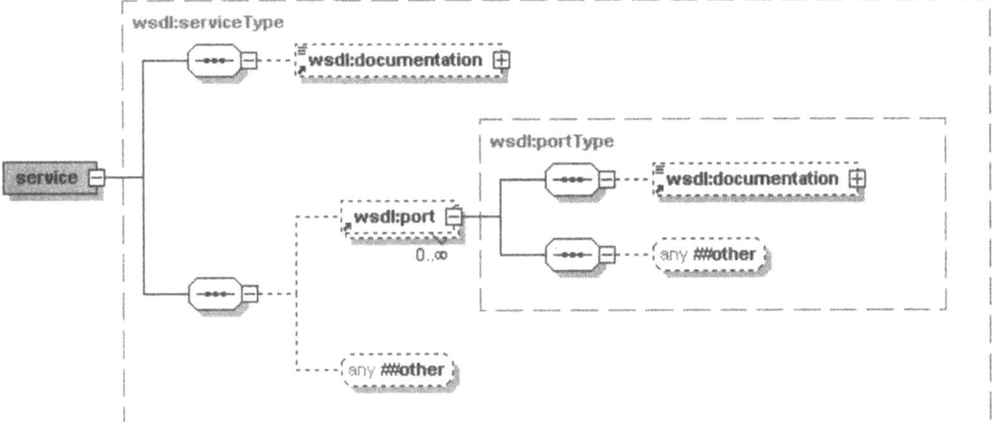

Figure 15-7. Service structure

Simple Object Access Protocol

In the previous section you saw how to describe a Web service using WSDL. You also saw that you can use various protocol bindings for representing and transporting the Web service. SOAP is the most widely used data representation protocol that's used in Web services. The SOAP 1.1 specification says this:

> *SOAP provides a simple and lightweight mechanism for exchanging structured and typed information between peers in a decentralized, distributed environment using XML.*

SOAP consists of mainly the following three parts:

- The SOAP envelope construct defines an overall framework for expressing what is in a message, who should deal with it, and whether it's optional or mandatory.
- The SOAP encoding rules define a serialization mechanism that can be used to exchange instances of application-defined data types.
- The SOAP RPC representation defines a convention that can be used to represent remote procedure calls and responses.

SOAP Message Structure

SOAP is an XML-based protocol for representing data. AN XML document that's authored according to the SOAP constructs is normally called a SOAP *envelope*. Figure 15-8 shows the structure of the SOAP envelope.

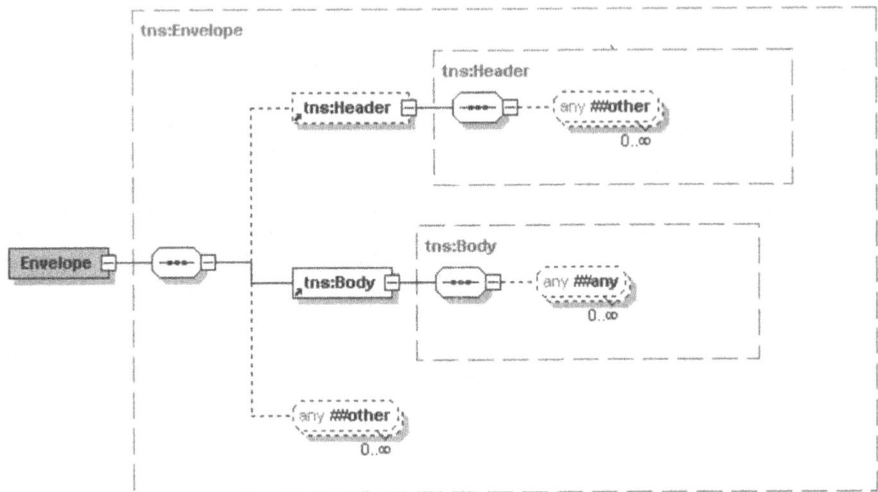

Figure 15-8. Envelope structure

A SOAP message is an XML document that consists of a mandatory SOAP envelope, an optional SOAP header, and a mandatory SOAP body. The namespace identifier for the markup specific to SOAP envelopes is `http://schemas.xmlsoap.org/soap/envelope/`.

A SOAP message contains the following:

The `Envelope` is the top element of the XML document. The `Envelope` element may contain namespace declarations as well as additional attributes that are namespace qualified. The `Envelope` element may contain additional subelements to `Header` and `Body` that are namespace qualified and must follow the `Body` element.

The `Header` is a generic mechanism for adding features to a SOAP message in a decentralized manner without prior agreement between the communicating parties. SOAP defines a few attributes that can indicate who should deal with a feature and whether it's optional or mandatory. The `Header` element may be present in a SOAP message. If present, the element must be the first immediate child element of a SOAP `Envelope` element. The element may contain a set of namespace-qualified header entries, each being an immediate child element of the SOAP `Header` element.

The `Body` is a container for mandatory information intended for the ultimate recipient of the message. SOAP defines one element for the body, which is the `Fault` element used for reporting errors. The `Body` element must be present in a SOAP message and must be an immediate child element of a SOAP `Envelope` element. It must directly follow the SOAP `Header` element if present. Otherwise, it must be the first immediate child element of the SOAP `Envelope` element. The element may contain a set of body entries that may be namespace qualified, each being an immediate child element of the `Body` element.

Listing 15-8 shows an example SOAP envelope that represents the request for the search offer Web service.

Listing 15-8. Search Offers

```
<soap-env:Envelope
  xmlns:soap-env="http://schemas.xmlsoap.org/soap/envelope/"
  xmlns:env="http://schemas.xmlsoap.org/soap/envelope/"
  xmlns:xsd="http://www.w3.org/2001/XMLSchema"
  xmlns:xsi="http://www.w3.org/2001/XMLSchema-instance"
  xmlns:enc="http://schemas.xmlsoap.org/soap/encoding/"
  xmlns:ns0="http://www.apress.com/Auction"
  env:encodingStyle="http://schemas.xmlsoap.org/soap/encoding/">
  <soap-env:Body>
    <ns0:searchOffer>
      <String_1 xsi:type="xsd:string">MP3</String_1>
    </ns0:searchOffer>
  </soap-env:Body>
</soap-env:Envelope>
```

In Listing 15-8 the envelope contains no headers, and the body contains the request for the search offer Web service. In the section "SOAP RPC," you'll look at how RPC calls and responses are represented as SOAP body elements.

Encoding Style

The encodingStyle attribute defines the encoding rules used to serialize application-specific data to the SOAP message. In Listing 15-8 the encoding style that's used is SOAP encoding represented by the uniform resource locator (URL) http://schemas.xmlsoap.org/soap.encoding. SOAP encoding is covered shortly.

SOAP Header

You can use SOAP headers for a variety of purposes including authentication, transactions, payment for the service, and so on. Immediate children of the Header element are called *header entries.* Header entries may use the mustUnderstand and actor attributes. Zero or more intermediaries may process a SOAP message before it reaches its ultimate recipient. The actor attribute gives a hint on which intermediary is required to process the entry, and the mustUnderstand attribute indicates whether intended intermediary should understand the header entry or whether it can ignore the entry. If the actor attribute isn't present, the header entry is intended to the ultimate recipient.

The following snippet shows an example of a header entry:

```
<SOAP-ENV:Header>
  <apress:Authentication xmlns:apress="http://www.apress.com"
    SOAP-ENV:mustUnderstand="1">
    <user>Fred</user>
    <password>******</password>
  </apress:Authentication>
</SOAP-ENV:Header>
```

The previous header entry is addressed to the ultimate recipient, and the recipient is required to understand it.

SOAP Fault

The `Fault` element carries error and/or status information within a SOAP message. If present, this should appear as a body entry and appear only once within a `Body` element.

This element can contain the following subelements:

- The `faultcode` element is intended for use by software to provide an algorithmic mechanism for identifying the fault.
- The `faultstring` element is intended to provide a human-readable explanation of the fault and isn't intended for algorithmic processing.
- The `faultactor` element is intended to provide information about who caused the fault to happen within the message path.
- The `detail` element is intended for carrying application-specific error information related to the `Body` element.

SOAP Encoding

SOAP encoding provides a simple type system that generalizes the common features of the popular type systems. In SOAP encoding a type is either a scalar type or a compound type composed of one or more parts, each with a scalar type. Arrays are also treated as compound types. In SOAP encoding all values are represented as element content.

These are the encoding rules as defined by the SOAP 1.1 specification:

> All values are represented as element content. A multireference value must be represented as the content of an independent element.
>
> For each element containing a value, the type of the value must be represented by at least one of the following conditions: the containing element instance contains an `xsi:type` attribute, the containing element instance is itself contained within an element containing a (possibly defaulted) `SOAP-ENC:arrayType` attribute, or the name of the element bears a definite relation to the type, which is then determinable from a schema. For example:

```
<description xsi:type="xsd:string">
  256 Mb MP3 Player
</description>
```

> A simple value is represented as character data, that is, without any subelements. Every simple value must have a type that is either listed in the XML Schema specification, part 2, or whose source type is listed therein (see also section 5.2 of the specification).

A *compound value* is encoded as a sequence of elements, each accessor represented by an embedded element whose name corresponds to the name of the accessor. Accessors whose names are local to their containing types have unqualified element names; all others have qualified names. For example:

```
<ns0:OfferData
  xsi:type="ns0:OfferData"
  xmlns:ns0="http://www.apress.com/Auction">
  <description xsi:type="xsd:string">256 Mb MP3 Player</description>
  <id xsi:type="xsd:int">2</id>
  <name xsi:type="xsd:string">MP3 Player</name>
</ns0:OfferData>
```

A multireference simple or compound value is encoded as an independent element containing a local, unqualified attribute named `id` of type `ID` per the XML specification. Each accessor to this value is an empty element having a local, unqualified attribute named `href` of type `uri-reference` per the XML Schema specification, with an `href` attribute value of a uniform resource identifier (URI) fragment identifier referencing the corresponding independent element. For example:

```
<ns0:ArrayOfOfferData
  id="ID1"
  xsi:type="enc:Array"
  enc:arrayType="ns0:OfferData[2]"
  xmlns:ns0="http://www.apress.com/Auction"
  xmlns:enc="http://schemas.xmlsoap.org/soap/encoding/">
  <item href="#ID2"/>
  <item href="#ID3"/>
</ns0:ArrayOfOfferData>
<ns0:OfferData id="ID2" xsi:type="ns0:OfferData">
  <description xsi:type="xsd:string">256 Mb MP3 Player</description>
  <id xsi:type="xsd:int">1</id>
  <name xsi:type="xsd:string">MP3 Player</name>
</ns0:OfferData>
<ns0:OfferData id="ID3" xsi:type="ns0:OfferData">
  <description xsi:type="xsd:string">128 Mb MP3 Player</description>
  <id xsi:type="xsd:int">2</id>
  <name xsi:type="xsd:string">MP3 Player</name>
</ns0:OfferData>
```

Strings and byte arrays are represented as multireference simple types, but special rules allow them to be represented efficiently for common cases. An accessor to a string or byte-array value may have an attribute named `id` and the type `ID` per the XML specification. If so, all other accessors to the same value are encoded as empty elements having a local, unqualified attribute named `href` and the type `uri-reference` per the XML Schema specification, with a `href` attribute value of a URI fragment identifier referencing the single element containing the value.

It's permissible to encode several references to a value as though these were references to several distinct values, but only when from context it's known that the meaning of the XML instance is unaltered.

Arrays are compound values. SOAP arrays are defined as having a type of `SOAP-ENC:Array` or a type derived from there. SOAP arrays have one or more dimensions (rank) whose members are distinguished by ordinal position. An array value is represented as a series of elements reflecting the array, with members appearing in ascending ordinal sequence. For multidimensional arrays the dimension on the right side varies most rapidly. Each member element is named as an independent element. SOAP arrays can be single-reference or multireference values and consequently may be represented as the content of either an embedded or independent element. SOAP arrays *must* contain a `SOAP-ENC:arrayType` attribute whose value specifies the type of the contained elements as well as the dimension(s) of the array. For example:

```
<ns0:ArrayOfOfferData
  id="ID1"
  xsi:type="enc:Array"
  enc:arrayType="ns0:OfferData[2]"
  xmlns:ns0="http://www.apress.com/Auction"
  xmlns:enc="http://schemas.xmlsoap.org/soap/encoding/">
```

SOAP RPC

SOAP is used in Web services as one of the data representation protocol bindings for the Web service requests and responses. In this section you'll see how to use SOAP body entries for representing RPC requests and responses.

In the case of using HTTP as the transport protocol binding, an RPC call maps naturally to an HTTP request, and an RPC response maps to an HTTP response. However, HTTP isn't the only protocol binding that can be used with SOAP RPC.

To make a method call, you need the following:

- The URI of the target object
- A method name
- An optional method signature
- The parameters to the method
- Optional header data

SOAP relies on the protocol binding to provide a mechanism for carrying the URI. For example, for HTTP the request URI indicates the resource against which the invocation is being made.

RPC method calls and responses are both carried in the SOAP `Body` element. The body entry that represents the method should have the following properties:

- A method invocation is modeled as a struct.
- The method invocation is viewed as a single struct containing an accessor for each `[in]` or `[in/out]` parameter.
- The struct is both named and typed identically to the method name.
- Each `[in]` or `[in/out]` parameter is viewed as an accessor, with a name corresponding to the name of the parameter and type corresponding to the type of the parameter. These appear in the same order as in the method signature.

Listing 15-9 shows the SOAP representation for the search offer Web service request.

Listing 15-9. SOAP Representation for Request

```
<soap-env:Envelope
  xmlns:soap-env="http://schemas.xmlsoap.org/soap/envelope/"
  xmlns:env="http://schemas.xmlsoap.org/soap/envelope/"
  xmlns:xsd="http://www.w3.org/2001/XMLSchema"
  xmlns:xsi="http://www.w3.org/2001/XMLSchema-instance"
  xmlns:enc="http://schemas.xmlsoap.org/soap/encoding/"
  xmlns:ns0="http://www.apress.com/Auction"
  env:encodingStyle="http://schemas.xmlsoap.org/soap/encoding/">
  <soap-env:Body>
    <ns0:searchOffer>
      <String_1 xsi:type="xsd:string"></String_1>
    </ns0:searchOffer>
  </soap-env:Body>
</soap-env:Envelope>
```

In Listing 15-9 the Web service request is modeled as the body entry `searchOffer` belonging to the namespace `http://www.apress.com/Auction`. The only parameter that's expected is of type `xsd:string` by the name `String_1`.

The body entry that represents the method response should have the following properties:

- A method response is also modeled as a struct.
- The method response is viewed as a single struct containing an accessor for the return value and each `[out]` or `[in/out]` parameter.
- The first accessor is the return value followed by the parameters in the same order as in the method signature.

- Each parameter accessor has a name corresponding to the name of the parameter and type corresponding to the type of the parameter.
- The name of the return value accessor isn't significant.
- Likewise, the name of the struct isn't significant. However, a convention is to name it after the method name with the string "Response" appended.
- A method fault is encoded using the SOAP Fault element.

Listing 15-10 shows the SOAP representation for the search offer Web service response.

Listing 15-10. SOAP Representation for Response

```
<env:Envelope
  xmlns:env="http://schemas.xmlsoap.org/soap/envelope/"
  xmlns:xsd="http://www.w3.org/2001/XMLSchema"
  xmlns:xsi="http://www.w3.org/2001/XMLSchema-instance"
  xmlns:enc="http://schemas.xmlsoap.org/soap/encoding/"
  xmlns:ns0="http://www.apress.com/Auction"
  env:encodingStyle="http://schemas.xmlsoap.org/soap/encoding/">
  <env:Body>
    <ns0:searchOfferResponse>
      <result href="#ID1"/>
    </ns0:searchOfferResponse>
    <ns0:ArrayOfOfferData
      id="ID1"
      xsi:type="enc:Array"
      enc:arrayType="ns0:OfferData[2]">
      <item href="#ID2"/>
      <item href="#ID3"/>
    </ns0:ArrayOfOfferData>
    <ns0:OfferData id="ID2" xsi:type="ns0:OfferData">
      <description xsi:type="xsd:string">Java Offer</description>
      <id xsi:type="xsd:int">1</id>
      <name xsi:type="xsd:string">Java Primer</name>
    </ns0:OfferData>
    <ns0:OfferData id="ID3" xsi:type="ns0:OfferData">
      <description xsi:type="xsd:string">C++ Offer</description>
      <id xsi:type="xsd:int">2</id>
      <name xsi:type="xsd:string">C++ Primer</name>
    </ns0:OfferData>
  </env:Body>
</env:Envelope>
```

In Listing 15-10 the Web service response is represented by the body entry searchOfferResponse, and the return value is represented by the element result, which has an attribute called href. This actually acts as an XML IDREF and refers to the element with an attribute of XML `ID` type and the same value. In this example, it refers to the element `ns0:ArrayOfOfferData`, which encodes an array of `OfferData` types (again by reference) .

Web Services in J2EE

Now with information on underlying technologies that constitute Web services, you're ready to look at the Web service support offered in J2EE 1.4. With J2EE 1.4, most of the specifications that constituted the Java Web service stack have become part of the J2EE suite. These specifications include the following:

Java API for XML RPC (JAX-RPC): JAX-RPC is the formal specification for JSR-101 and describes a client- and server-side model for implementing XML-based RPC in a protocol-agnostic manner. Server-side applications based on JAX-RPC can describe and export a Web service as an RPC-based service.

SOAP with Attachment API for Java (SAAJ): SAAJ specifies an API for processing raw SOAP messages. Historically, SAAJ used to be part of Java API for XML Messaging (JAXM). However, SAAJ has been separated from JAXM and is now included as a part of the J2EE 1.4 specification.

Java API for XML Registries (JAX-R): JAX-R is the formal specification for JSR-093 that enables Java software programmers to use a single, easy-to-use abstraction API to access a variety of XML registries. A unified JAXR information model describes content and metadata within XML registries. An XML registry is an infrastructure that enables the building, deployment, and discovery of Web services. JAXR provides an API for a set of distributed registry services that enables business-to-business integration between business enterprises, using the protocols being defined by ebXML.org, Oasis, and ISO 11179. JAXR is analogous to Java Naming and Directory Interface (JNDI) but designed specifically for Internet sharing of XML-related business information. Currently there are numerous open standards for distributed registries. Examples include OASIS, eCo Framework, and ebXML. In addition there also exists industry consortium efforts such as UDDI, which may eventually be donated to a standard body. JAXR will provide a uniform and standard API for accessing information from these registries within the Java platform.

Web Services for J2EE: The Web Services for J2EE API is the formal specification for JSR-109, and it describes an architectural model of Web services for J2EE. The specification focuses on leveraging the J2EE component model to provide a client and server programming model that's portable and interoperable across application servers. This specification relies heavily on the JAX-RPC specification and extends it to define a Web service architectural model within the J2EE realm.

In addition to these technologies, J2EE 1.3 has supported JAXP for parsing and transforming XML documents, which is now part of the J2SE 1.4. All of these APIs form a powerful toolset for a Web service developer in building Web services from scratch as well as leveraging the power of existing J2EE components and exposing them as Web services.

Figure 15-9 depicts the role of Web services in J2EE 1.4.

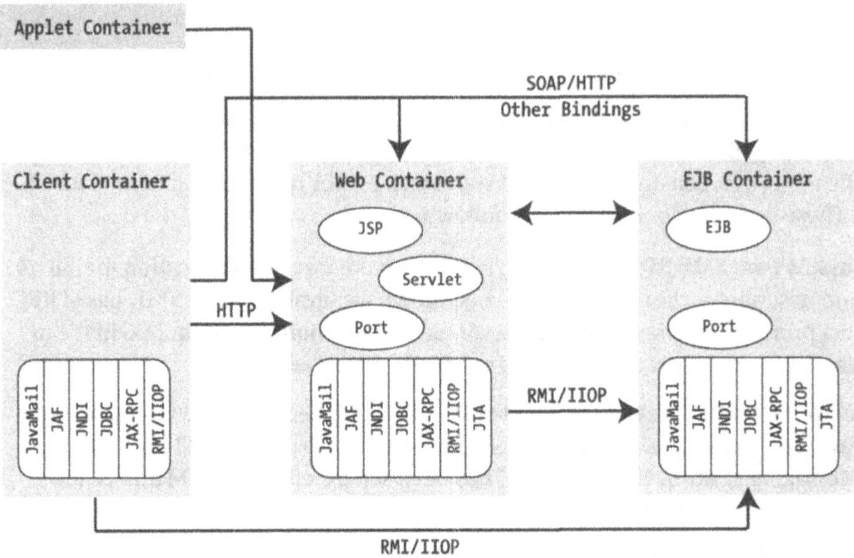

Figure 15-9. Web services support in J2EE

JAX-RPC introduces a programming model that allows the mapping of a WSDL document to Java. The JAX-RPC interface `javax.xml.rpc.Service` models the WSDL service element that acts as a factory for the ports it aggregates. The JAX-RPC client-side run time allows various methods for the clients to access the service. The port components are deployable in J2EE Web and EJB containers whereas they're accessible from Web, EJB, and application containers.

The protocol bindings supported by the port is transparent to the client. The clients access the port through the service endpoint interface exposed by the port. The operations on the service endpoint interface reflect the abstract operations defined by the port type in the WSDL document (see Figure 15-10).

J2EE supports the following two types of service endpoints:

- **Servlet endpoint**: In this case the service endpoint interface is represented by a Java interface that extends `java.rmi.Remote`, and the Web service itself is implemented by a Java class.

- **EJB endpoint**: In this case the service endpoint interface is represented by a Java interface that extends `java.rmi.Remote`, and the Web service itself is implemented by a stateless session class.

We'll cover both servlet and EJB endpoints in detail later in the chapter.

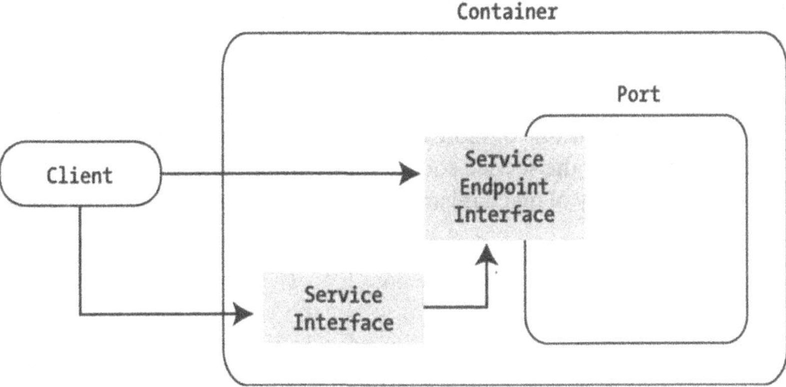

Figure 15-10. JAX-RPC model

JAX-RPC Architectural Model

JAX-RPC specifies an API and server-side and client-side programming model for performing XML-based RPC. Even though the only protocol binding that's supported is SOAP, the API itself is designed in a protocol-agnostic manner. Figure 15-11 depicts the architectural model for JAX-RPC using a stub-based client.

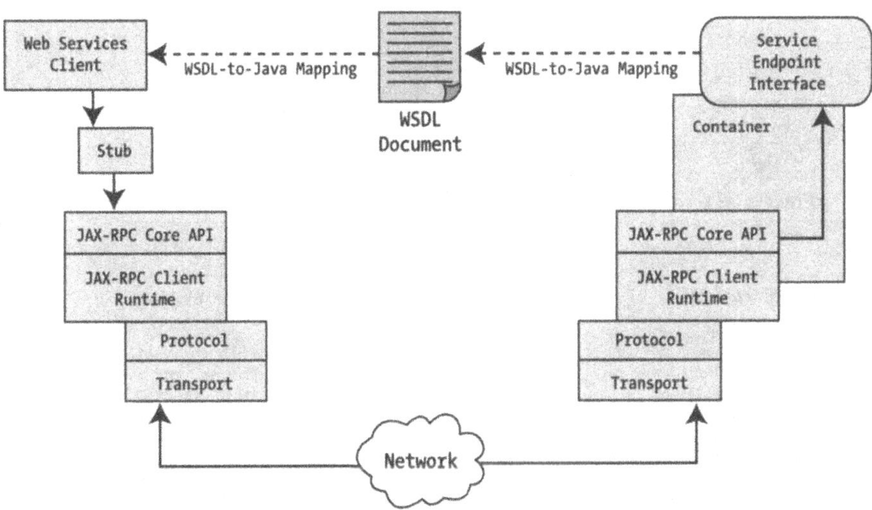

Figure 15-11. JAX-RPC architectural model

The services endpoint interface defines the operations that are supported by the Web service. The J2EE 1.4 containers would generally provide tools that can be used to generate the service endpoint interface from a WSDL document or vice versa. The endpoint interface is realized either as a servlet or EJB endpoint. Once the service endpoint is deployed in the target container—this can be a Web archive (WAR) file for the servlet endpoint or an EJB Java archive (JAR) file for an EJB endpoint—the container exports the WSDL document that describes Web service so that the clients can access it. The container will also define one or more concrete protocol bindings for the abstract operations defined by the service endpoint interface.

JAX-RPC provides a variety of mechanisms for the clients to access the port component:

- Static-generated stub-based invocation
- Dynamic proxy-based invocation
- Dynamic invocation interface

We'll explain these in detail later.

Invocation Process

Figure 15-12 shows the steps involved in an RPC-based invocation. The figure assumes the protocol binding that's used is SOAP over HTTP.

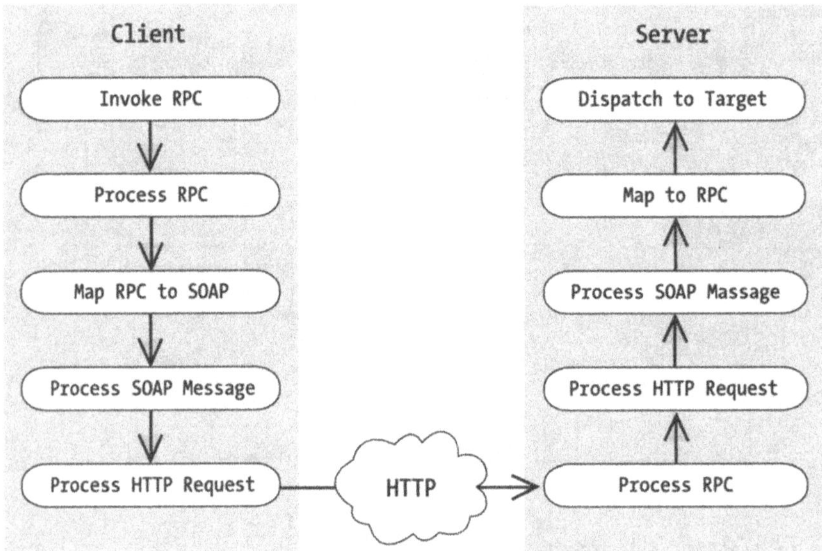

Figure 15-12. JAX-RPC invocation

On the client side, the following happens:

- The remote method call is first mapped to a SOAP message based on the serialization/deserialization rules between Java and XML data types.
- The SOAP messaging processing step involves representing the RPC as a SOAP message (the method name, parameters, and so on) based on the encoding scheme.
- Next the SOAP message is sent to the server as an HTTP request.

On the server side, the following happens:

- The HTTP request is processed to extract the SOAP message.
- The SOAP message is processed to identify the target object, method, and method parameters.
- The invocation is dispatched to the target object.
- The result/exceptions are again encoded as a SOAP message and sent back to the client with the HTTP response.

Java to WSDL Mapping

The following sections show how JAX-RPC maps the various Java artifacts such as data types, endpoint interface, and so on, to WSDL.

Type Mapping

The following sections show how Java types are mapped to XML types, and vice versa.

Simple Types

JAX-RPC supports all the Java primitive types and the corresponding wrapper classes. Table 15-1 shows the Java types to XML types mapping.

Table 15-1. Java Types to XML Types Mapping

JAVA TYPE	XML TYPE
boolean	xsd:boolean
byte	xsd:byte
short	xsd:short
int	xsd:int
long	xsd:long
float	xsd:float
double	xsd:double

For example, the id field in the OfferData class maps to the XML type xsd:int, as follows:

```
<id xsi:type="xsd:int">123</id>
```

If an XML type that corresponds to a Java primitive is defined with the nillable attribute set to true, it's then mapped to the corresponding Java wrapper class.

Standard Java Classes

Table 15-2 shows the mappings for some of the standard Java classes.

Table 15-2. Standard Java Class Mappings

JAVA CLASS	XML TYPE
java.lang.String	xsd:string
java.math.BigInteger	xsd:integer
java.math.BigDecimal	xsd:decimal
java.util.Calendar	xsd:dateTime
java.uril.Date	xsd:dateTime

For example, the name field in the OfferData class maps to the XML type xsd:string, as follows:

```
<name xsi:type="xsd:string">Java Primer</id>
```

Java Arrays

Java arrays are mapped to one of the following XML types:

- An array derived from soapenc:ArrayType using the wsdl:ArrayType attribute. The following snippet shows how an int array is encoded using this scheme:

  ```
  <!--Schema Fragment -->
  <complexType name="intArray">
    <complexContent>
      <restriction base="soapenc:Array">
        <attribute ref="soapenc:ArrayType" wsdl:ArrayType="xsd:int[]"/>
      </restriction>
    </complexContent>
  </complexType>
  ```

- An array with soapenc:ArrayType specified in the instance document. The following snippet shows how an int array is encoded using this scheme:

```
<!--Schema Fragment -->
<element name="numbers" type="soapenc:Array"/>
<!"Instance document -->
<numbers soapenc:ArrayType="xsd:int[2]">
  <member>1</member>
  <member>2</member>
</numbers>
```

Value Types

JAX-RPC defines a value type as an entity that can be moved between the service and the client. A value type should have the following properties:

- It should have a public default constructor.
- It shouldn't implement the java.rmi.Remote interface.
- It may implement any other interface or extends another Java class.
- The types of public fields must be one of the types supported by JAX-RPC.
- Bean properties should have accessors and mutators conformant with JavaBeans specification, and their types should be the ones supported by JAX-RPC.

Value types are mapped to XML complexType with xsd:all-based unordered grouping. The following snippet shows how the OfferData is mapped to an XML type:

```
<complexType name="OfferData">
  <sequence>
    <element name="description" type="string"/>
    <element name="id" type="int"/>
    <element name="name" type="string"/>
  </sequence>
</complexType>
```

In this example, the following is true:

- The name attribute of the complex type is mapped to the name of the Java class.
- Every public nonfinal nontransient field is mapped to an element within the complex type. The name and type of the attribute are mapped to the name of the field and mapped XML type of the field's Java type.

- Every JavaBean-style read-write property is mapped to an element within the complex type. The name and type of the property are mapped to the name of the property and mapped XML type of the property's Java type.
- Inheritance is mapped using complex type derivation.
- None of the methods are mapped.
- There's no support for indexed properties.

Support for Collections

JAX-RPC 1.0 supports the implementations shown in Table 15-3 for the `java.util.Collection` interface.

Table 15-3. JAX-RPC Collection Implementations

COLLECTION	IMPLEMENTATION
List	ArrayList, LinkedList
Stack	Vector
Map	HashMap, Hashtable
Properties	TreeMap
Set	HashSet, TreeSet

> **NOTE** *In addition to the default type mappings explained previously, JAX-RPX also allows you to have extensible type mapping implementations.*

Service Endpoint Mapping

The service endpoint interface in JAX-RPC maps to a port type in WSDL. As mentioned earlier, the endpoint interface should extend `java.rmi.remote` for both servlet- or EJB-based endpoints. Listing 15-11 shows how a servlet-based service endpoint interface maps to a port type in WSDL.

Listing 15-11. Service Endpoint Mapping

```
package com.apress.projavaserver14.ws;

import java.rmi.Remote;
import java.rmi.RemoteException;

public interface OfferSearchIF extends Remote {
```

```
  public OfferData[] searchOffer(String text)
  throws RemoteException;

  public String getDescription(int OfferId)
  throws RemoteException;

}
```

The corresponding WSDL port type will look like Listing 15-12.

Listing 15-12. WSDL Port Type

```
<portType name="OfferSearchIF">
  <operation name="getDescription" parameterOrder="int_1">
    <input message="tns:OfferSearchIF_getDescription"/>
    <output message="tns:OfferSearchIF_getDescriptionResponse"/>
  </operation>
  <operation name="searchOffers" parameterOrder="String_1">
    <input message="tns:OfferSearchIF_searchOffers"/>
    <output message="tns:OfferSearchIF_searchOffersResponse"/>
  </operation>
</portType>
```

The name of the port type maps to the name of the interface. The methods defined in the service point interface maps to the abstract operations aggregated by the port type. The name of each operation within the port type should map to the corresponding method name in the service point interface. JAX-RPC supports only request/response and one-way operations.

The methods in the service point interface are required to declare `RemoteException` in their `throws` clause. Any other Web service–specific exception should be mapped to WSDL fault messages.

WSDL supports the notion of out and in-out message parts. To support this, JAX-RPC provides holder classes. The holder classes provided by JAX-RPC are as follows:

- `javax.xml.rpc.holders.BigDecimalHolder`
- `javax.xml.rpc.holders.BigIntegerHolder`
- `javax.xml.rpc.holders.BooleanWrapperHolder`
- `javax.xml.rpc.holders.ByteArrayHolder`
- `javax.xml.rpc.holders.ByteHolder`
- `javax.xml.rpc.holders.ByteWrapperHolder`
- `javax.xml.rpc.holders.CalendarHolder`
- `javax.xml.rpc.holders.DoubleHolder`

- `javax.xml.rpc.holders.DoubleWrapperHolder`
- `javax.xml.rpc.holders.FloatHolder`
- `javax.xml.rpc.holders.FloatWrapperHolder`
- `javax.xml.rpc.holders.IntHolder`
- `javax.xml.rpc.holders.IntegerWrapperHolder`
- `javax.xml.rpc.holders.LongHolder`
- `javax.xml.rpc.holders.LongWrapperHolder`
- `javax.xml.rpc.holders.ObjectHolder`
- `javax.xml.rpc.holders.ShortHolder`
- `javax.xml.rpc.holders.ShortWrapperHolder`
- `javax.xml.rpc.holders.StringHolder`

The previous holder classes will be used for message parts that are defined as `out` or `in-out` in the WSDL. The Java-to-WSDL mapping tool provided by the provider is required to generate holder classes for any other custom value type used as an out or in-out message part. These holders are required to implement the `javax.xml.rpc.holders.Holder` interface.

Service Interface

The WSDL `port` element defines a concrete protocol binding and an endpoint address for an abstract port type. In JAX-RPC, a port is represented by a port component that can be accessed through one of the following ways:

- A static stub generated by the WSDL-to-Java mapping tool
- Using dynamic proxies
- A `javax.xml.rpc.Call` object for Dynamic Invocation Interface (DII)

The WSDL `service` element aggregates all the ports (service endpoints). HAX-RPC maps this element to a service class. This class acts as a factory for the port components. This class is required to implement the interface `javax.xml.rpc.Service` directly or indirectly. This interface supports the methods shown in Table 15-4 for accessing the ports aggregated by the service.

Table 15-4. Service Interface Methods

Method	Description
`java.rmi.Remote getPort(Qname portName, Class serviceEndpointInterface) throws ServiceException;`	This method returns a dynamic proxy or a generated stub class for the specified port. The retuned object can be cast to the service endpoint interface.
`java.rmi.Remote getPort(Class serviceEndpointInterface) throws ServiceException;`	This method returns a dynamic proxy or a generated stub class for the specified port. The retuned object can be cast to the service endpoint interface.
`Call createCall() throws ServiceException;`	Creates a call object not associated with specific operation or target service endpoint. This call object needs to be configured using the setter methods on the `Call` interface.
`Call createCall(Qname portName) throws ServiceException;`	Creates a call object for the specified port.
`Call createCall(Qname portName, Qname operationName) throws ServiceException;`	Creates the call object for the specified port and operation.
`Call[] getCalls(Qname portName) throws ServiceException;`	Gets call objects for all the operations supported by the specified port.
`Java.net.URL getWSDLDocumentLocation();`	Gets the location of the WSDL document for this service.
`Qname getServiceName();`	Gets the name of this service.
`java.util.Iterator getPorts() throws ServiceException;`	Returns an `Iterator` for the list of `QName` of service endpoints grouped by this service.

`QName` is a class that identifies an element or an attribute by its local part and namespace URI. Clients using DII use the methods that are related to the `javax.xml.rpc.Call` interface. These methods are explained in detail in the section on the "Dynamic Invocation Interface" section. This interface is implemented in a vendor-specific manner.

The WSDL-to-Java mapping tool provided by the vendor will generate a service implementation class based on the WSDL `service` element. This class will act as the factory for generated static stubs. The service implementation class should implement either `javax.naming.Referenceable` or `java.io.Serializable` so that instances can be registered in a JNDI namespace. In addition to the methods defined by the implemented interfaces, this class is required to provide strongly typed methods for accessing the service endpoint. The signature of this method is as follows:

```
<Service Endpoint Interface> get<Name of WSDL Port>() throws ServiceException;
```

In the search offer Web service scenario, this method is as follows:

```
OfferSearchIF getOfferSearchIFPort() throws ServiceException;
```

Here the name of the method is the string `get` followed by the name of the WSDL port that defines the concrete protocol binding and endpoint address for the abstract port type. The following snippet shows how the service implementation class is created and the service endpoint is accessed:

```
OfferSearchIF OfferSearch = new OfferSearchService_Impl().getOfferSearchIFPort();
OfferData result[] = OfferSearch.searchOffer("");
```

In the previous snippet `OfferSearchService_Impl` is a vendor-specific service implementation generated by the WSDL-to-Java mapping tool. The next section covers Web service client programming models in detail.

Servlet Endpoints

In this section you'll learn how to build, package, deploy, and invoke Web services with servlet endpoints in detail. Web services with servlet endpoints are deployed as standard J2EE WAR components. The WAR component you deploy is required to include the following files:

- The compiled service endpoint interface
- The compiled service implementation bean class that implements the methods defined in the services endpoint interface
- The WSDL document
- The Web service deployment descriptor
- The type mapping deployment descriptor
- The Web application deployment descriptor

The following sections explain the aforementioned entities in detail.

Service Endpoint Interface

We've already covered the requirements for the servlet-based service endpoint interface in earlier sections. In this section, we'll just round up the following requirements:

- Servlet service endpoint interfaces are required to extend the interface `java.rmi.Remote`.

- The methods declared on the interface should declare to throw `java.rmi.RemoteException`.
- The methods may declare to throw any other application-specific exceptions.
- The arguments to the methods and the return types should be valid JAX-RPC supported types.

Most of the Java-to-WSDL compilation tools that come with the containers support generation of WSDL from service endpoint interface and vice versa. This chapter's examples use `wscompile`, which comes with the J2EE 1.4 RI beta.

Listing 15-13 shows the service endpoint interface for the search offer Web service.

Listing 15-13. Service Endpoint Interface

```
package com.apress.projavaserver14.ws;

import java.rmi.Remote;
import java.rmi.RemoteException;

public interface OfferSearchIF extends Remote {

  public OfferData[] searchOffer(String text)
  throws RemoteException;

  public String getDescription(int OfferId)
  throws RemoteException;

}
```

You've already seen the definition for the class `OfferData`.

Service Implementation Bean

The service implementation bean is the class that implements the methods provided by the service endpoint interface. For servlet endpoints, it's a plain Java class.

> **NOTE** *The JAX-RPC specification mandates that the service implementation bean for servlet endpoints should implement the service endpoint interface. However, the Web Services for J2EE (JSR-109) specification has removed this requirement to make it consistent with EJB endpoints. But the service implementation bean is required to implement all the methods defined in the service endpoint interface.*

The service implementation bean should have a default public constructor, should be public, and should be nonabstract. It shouldn't implement the `finalize` method and shouldn't store any state in instance variables across invocation. The service implementation bean for a servlet endpoint can optionally implement the following interfaces:

- **javax.Servlet.SingleThreadModel**: You should implement this interface if you want the service to operate in a single-threaded mode.
- **javax.xml.rpc.server.ServiceLifecycle**: You should implement this interface if the bean requires to be notified on changes in its state such as after initialization, before it's destroyed, and so on.

Listing 15-14 shows the service implementation bean for the Web service with a servlet endpoint.

Listing 15-14. Service Implementation Bean

```
package com.apress.projavaserver14.ws;

import javax.naming.InitialContext;
import javax.rmi.PortableRemoteObject;
import com.apress.auction.entity.interfaces.*;
import com.sun.j2ee.blueprints.servicelocator.ejb.ServiceLocator;
import com.apress.auction.offer.client.*;

public class OfferSearchImpl implements OfferSearchIF {

  private OfferLocalHome offerHome;

  // The constructor looks the entity EJB local home
  public void OfferSearchImpl() {
    ServiceLocator sl = new ServiceLocator();
    offerHome = (OfferLocalHome) sl.getLocalHome("java:comp/env/ejb/offer");
  }

  // The method calls the entity EJB to get the data
  public  OfferData[] searchOffers(String text)  throws RemoteException {
    try {
      Collection col = offerHome.findByNameOrDescription("%" + searchText + "%");
      OfferData offerData[] = new OfferData[col.size()];
      Iterator it = col.iterator();
      for(int i = 0;i < offerData.length && it.hasNext();i++)
        offerData[i] = ((OfferLocal)it.next()).getData();
      return offerData;
    }catch(FinderException ex) {
      throw new RemoteException(ex.getMessage());
    }
  }
```

```
// The method calls the entity bean to get the data.
  public String getDescription(int OfferId) throws RemoteException {
    try {
      return offerHome.findByPrimaryKey(new Integer(offerId)).getDescription();
    }catch(Exception ex) {
      throw new RemoteException(ex.getMessage());
    }
  }

}
```

Generate WSDL

Once you've done the service endpoint interface and the service implementation class, you need to generate the WSDL for the Web service. Alternatively, you can author the WSDL first and then generate the service endpoint interface from the WSDL. Most of the vendors will provide tools for performing Java-to-WSDL and WSDL-to-Java compilation. The J2EE 1.4 RI comes with the tool `wscompile` that can be used for a variety of purposes, including the following:

- Generating WSDL from the service endpoint interface
- Generating the service endpoint interface from WSDL
- Generating static client stubs, serializers, and so on, that can be used to access the Web service from WSDL, for example

Please refer to the J2EE 1.4 tools documentation for more information about `wscompile`. To generate the WSDL for the example Web service, you need to issue the following command:

```
wscompile.bat -define -d <output dir> -nd <output dir> -classpath
<classpath> <config file>
```

In the previous command, the classpath should contain the definitions for the service endpoint interface, the service implementation bean, and the value type classes. The WSDL is written to the directory specified by `<output dir>`. The config file is specific to the J2EE 1.4 RI implementation, and for generating the WSDL it should contain the information shown in Listing 15-15.

Listing 15-15. Config File

```
<?xml version="1.0" encoding="UTF-8"?>
<configuration
  xmlns="http://java.sun.com/xml/ns/jax-rpc/ri/config">
  <service
      name="OfferSearchSEP"
```

```
        targetNamespace="http://www.apress.com/Auction"
        typeNamespace="http://www.apress.com/Auction"
        packageName="com.apress.projavaserver14.ws">
        <interface name="com.apress.projavaserver14.ws.OfferSearchIF"/>
    </service>
</configuration>
```

This will generate the WSDL called `OfferSearchSEP.wsdl` with the namespace for the messages, port types, and so on, in the WSDL as `http://www.apress.com/Auction`, and the target namespace for the new types is defined in the WSDK as `http://www.apress.com/Auction`. The local name of the service element in the WSDL will be `OfferSearchSEP` (SEP is the acronym we've used for servlet endpoint).

Web Services Deployment Descriptor

Servlet endpoint Web services are packaged as standard WAR files, and EJB endpoints are packaged as EJB JAR files. Both EJB and servlet endpoint–based Web services are required to include the Web service deployment descriptor, `webservices.xml`, in the `META-INF` or `WEB-INF` directories, respectively. Figure 15-13 shows the high-level structure of this file.

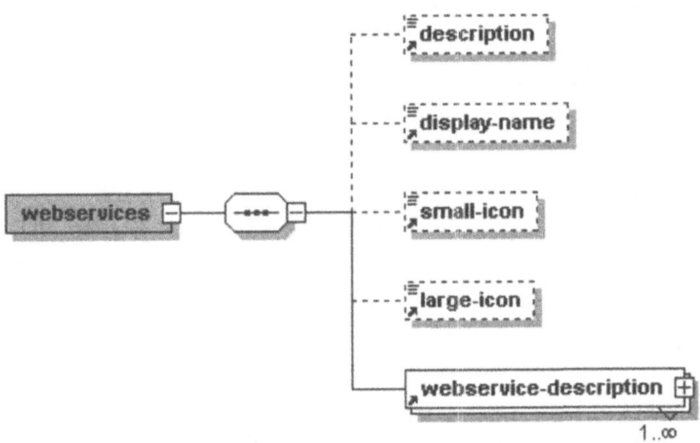

Figure 15-13. Web service deployment descriptor

Each `webservice-description` element describes a Web service packaged in the WAR or EJB module. Figure 15-14 shows the mandatory children for this element.

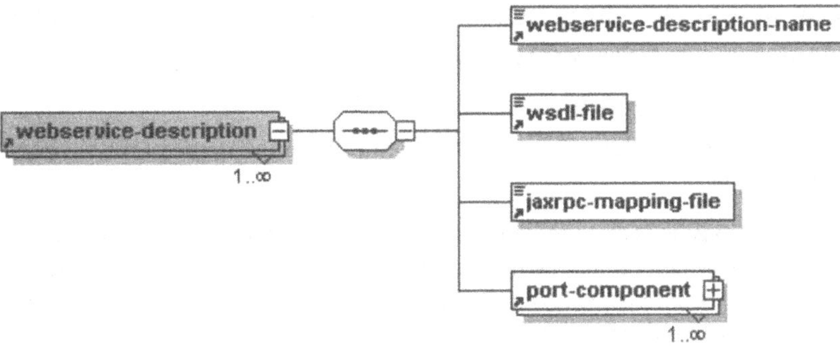

Figure 15-14. Web service description

This example has the following parts:

webservice-description-name: This name identifies a collection port components associated with a WSDL file and JAX-RPC mapping.

wsdl-file: This specifies the name and location of the WSDL file within the packaged module.

jaxrpc-mapping-file: This specifies the name and location of the file that describes the mapping between the Java interfaces used by the application and the WSDL artifacts within the packaged module.

port-component: This element associates a WSDL port with the JAX-RPC endpoint interface and implementation. Figure 15-15 shows the mandatory children for the `port-component` element.

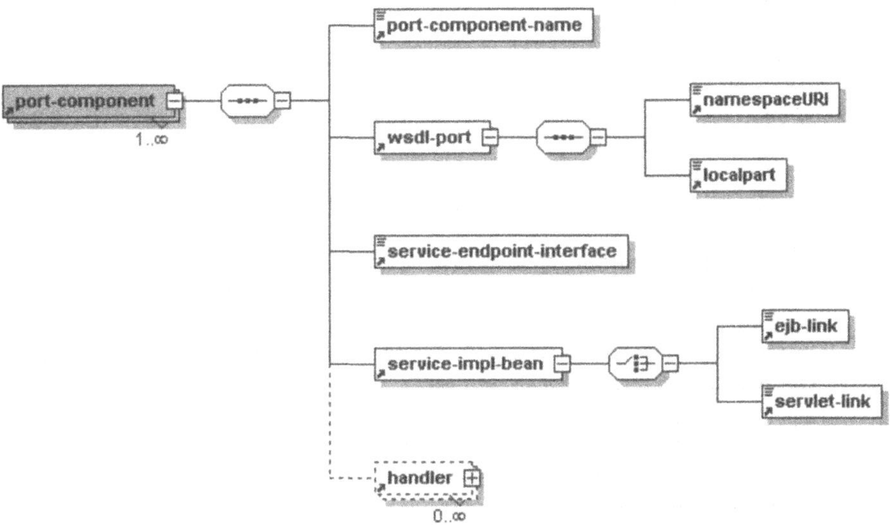

Figure 15-15. Port component structure

port-component-name: This is a unique name associated with the port component.

wsdl-port: This element specifies the namespace URI and local name of the WSDL port for which this port component is defined.

service-endpoint-interface: This defines the fully qualified name of the service endpoint interface.

service-impl-bean: This element defines the service implementation bean. For EJB endpoints the `ejb-link` should be used to specify the name of the EJB as defined in `ejb-jar.xml` for which the port component is defined. For servlet endpoints, the `servlet-link` should be used to specify the name of the servlet that will accept the calls for this port component as defined in the `web.xml` file. During packaging, the servlet class for this servlet should be the fully qualified name of the service implementation bean. However, during deployment the container will generate a servlet that will accept the requests on behalf of the service implementation bean. How the container does this is left to the container vendor.

handler: Handlers are components similar to servlet filters that can preprocess and postprocess requests and responses both on the client and server side. Handlers are declared using this element and are covered in detail in the "Using Message Handlers" section.

Listing 15-16 shows the Web service deployment descriptor for the servlet endpoint–based Web service.

Listing 15-16. Deployment Descriptor

```
<!DOCTYPE webservices PUBLIC "-//IBM Corporation, Inc.//DTD J2EE Web services
  1.0//EN" "http://www.ibm.com/standards/xml/webservices/
  j2ee/j2ee_web_services_1_0.dtd">
<webservices>
  <webservice-description>
    <webservice-description-name>
      OfferSearchSEP
    </webservice-description-name>
    <wsdl-file>OfferSearchSEP.wsdl</wsdl-file>
    <jaxrpc-mapping-file>WEB-INF/mapping.xml</jaxrpc-mapping-file>
    <port-component>
      <description>port component description</description>
      <port-component-name>OfferSearchIFPort</port-component-name>
      <wsdl-port>
        <namespaceURI>http://www.apress.com/Auction</namespaceURI>
        <localpart>OfferSearchIFPort</localpart>
      </wsdl-port>
      <service-endpoint-interface>
        com.apress.projavaserver14.ws.OfferSearchIF
      </service-endpoint-interface>
      <service-impl-bean>
        <servlet-link>OfferSearchSEPServlet</servlet-link>
      </service-impl-bean>
```

```
    </port-component>
  </webservice-description>
</webservices>
```

Listing 15-16 defines the following properties:

- The name of the service is defined as `OfferSearchSEP`.
- The location of the WSDL is defined as the root of the WAR file and is called `OfferSearchSEP.wsdl`.
- The location of the JAX-RPC file is defined as the `WEB-INF` directory and is called `mapping.xml`.
- The name of the port component is defined as `OfferSearchIFPort`.
- The port component is mapped to corresponding port in the WSDL using the namespace URI and local part.
- The service endpoint interface is defined as `com.apress.projavaserver14.ws.OfferSearchIF`.
- The service implementation bean is defined using the `servlet-link` as `OfferSearchSEPServlet`. You'll later see how this servlet is defined in the `web.xml` file.

Type Mapping Deployment Descriptor

The JAX-RPC mapping file describes the mapping between the Java interfaces used by the application and the WSDL artifacts within the packaged module. This file has no standard name, and its name and location are defined in the Web service deployment descriptor. A one-to-one correspondence exists between the WSDL files and the mapping files in a module. The deployment tool generally uses the information in this file for generating the stubs and ties.

In most of the cases, you need to specify only the mapping between the namespace used in WSDL for the locally declared elements and the Java package. You don't need to specify anything else in this file if the following conditions are met:

- The WSDL has exactly one `service` element.
- The `service` element has exactly one `port`.
- The port binding is SOAP 1.1, the invocation style is RPC, and the encoding style is SOAP encoding.

- Operations have exactly one `input` message with zero or more parts, zero or one `output` message with zero or one part, and zero or more `fault` messages.
- Faults must not map to subclasses of `RuntimeException`.
- Part types in messages are types identified by JAX-RPC.

If any of these conditions aren't met, you can use the JAX-RPC mapping file to define the required mapping. Listing 15-17 shows the mapping descriptor used for this Web service.

Listing 15-17. Mapping Descriptor

```
<?xml version="1.0" encoding="UTF-8"?>
<!DOCTYPE java-wsdl-mapping PUBLIC
  "-//IBM Corporation, Inc.//DTD J2EE JAX-RPC mapping 1.0//EN"
  "http://www.ibm.com/standards/xml/webservices/j2ee/j2ee_jaxrpc_mapping_1_0.dtd">
<java-wsdl-mapping>
    <package-mapping>
        <package-type>com.apress.projavaserver14.ws</package-type>
        <namespaceURI>http://www.apress.com/Auction</namespaceURI>
    </package-mapping>
</java-wsdl-mapping>
```

Web Deployment Descriptor

As explained earlier, servlet endpoints are packaged as WAR components and obviously need a Web deployment descriptor. This deployment descriptor defines the servlet corresponding to the servlet-link defined in the Web service deployment descriptor. You may also specify a URI mapping for this servlet, which will be the URI used to access the port. Please note that the URI mapping should be an exact match. Please note that you may also define other things such as security constraints if you want to restrict access to the Web service.

Listing 15-18 shows the Web deployment descriptor used for the `Offer` search Web service.

Listing 15-18. `Offer` *Deployment Descriptor*

```
<?xml version="1.0" encoding="UTF-8"?>

<!DOCTYPE web-app
    PUBLIC "-//Sun Microsystems, Inc.//DTD Web Application 2.3//EN"
    "http://java.sun.com/j2ee/dtds/web-app_2_3.dtd">

<web-app>
  <display-name>Auction</display-name>
  <servlet>
```

```
    <servlet-name>OfferSearchSEPServlet</servlet-name>
    <servlet-class>
      com.apress.projavaserver14.ws.OfferSearchImpl
    </servlet-class>
    <load-on-startup>0</load-on-startup>
  </servlet>
  <servlet-mapping>
    <servlet-name>OfferSearchSEPServlet</servlet-name>
    <url-pattern>/OfferSearch</url-pattern>
  </servlet-mapping>
  <session-config>
    <session-timeout>60</session-timeout>
  </session-config>

  <!-- Reference for offer entity -->
  <ejb-local-ref>
    <ejb-ref-name>ejb/offer</ejb-ref-name>
    <ejb-ref-type>Entity</ejb-ref-type>
    <home>com.apress.auction.entity.interfaces.OfferLocalHome</home>
    <remote>com.apress.auction.entity.interfaces.Offer</remote>
    <ejb-link>Offer</ejb-link>
  </ejb-local-ref>
</web-app>
```

Please note that the servlet class matches the service implementation bean class, and the servlet is mapped to the URI `offerSearch`. Hence, if the context path for the Web application is `Auction`, for example, the endpoint address to access the service will be `http://host:port/Auction/OfferSearch`.

Packaging and Deploying

Servlet endpoints are packages as WAR components. In this case, you need to deploy an EAR file that contains the servlet endpoint WAR file and the EJB JAR file containing the entity beans.

Service Lifecycle

Servlet endpoints that want to be notified about lifecycle events can get the service implementation class to implement the `javax.xml.rpc.server.ServiceLifecycle` interface. This interface supports two methods, described in Table 15-5.

Table 15-5. `javax.xml.rpc.server.ServiceLifecycle` *Methods*

`init(Object context)`	This method is called after the endpoint is initialized.
`destroy()`	This is called before the endpoint is destroyed.

In the `init` method, an endpoint context is passed. This should be cast to a context specific to the JAX-RPC runtime environment. For a Web container–based environment the context can be cast to `javax.xml.rpc.server.ServletEndpointContext`. This interface defines the methods described in Table 15-6.

Table 15-6. `javax.xml.rpc.server.ServletEndpointContext` *Methods*

`HttpSession getSession()`	Returns the session associated with the invocation.
`ServletContext getServletContext()`	Gets a reference to the underlying servlet context.
`MessageContext getMessageContext()`	Gets the message context for the invocation. For SOAP-based invocation, this can be cast to `SOAPMessageContext` to get a reference to the SOAP message itself. Message contexts can also get and set properties that can be shared between the handlers in the chain leading to the target and the target itself.
`Principal getUserPrincipal()`	Gets the currently authenticated user principal.

Web Service Clients

J2EE 1.4 requires vendors to support a variety of J2SE and J2EE clients for Web services. Clients always access the Web services through the service endpoint interface. The services endpoints themselves are accessed through the `javax.xml.rpc.Service` interface. The clients can use this interface directly or may choose to use a subinterface that provides strongly typed methods for accessing specific service endpoint interfaces.

You can get hold of an instance of the `javax.xml.rpc.Service` interface in the following three ways:

Using the `javax.xml.rpc.ServiceFactory` class. This class provides methods to create objects that implement the `javax.xml.rpc.Service` interface. These objects may implement a subinterface of the `javax.xml.rpc.Service` interface to provide strongly typed access.

Directly instantiate a vendor-specific implementation of the `javax.xml.rpc.Service` interface or its subinterface.

J2EE clients such as EJBs, Web applications, and application clients can include a Web service client deployment descriptor that contains references to the services they want to use. The containers will then make these references available for JNDI lookup in the `java:comp/env` namespace.

The `javax.xml.rpc.ServiceFactory` class provides the methods described in Table 15-7.

Table 15-7. `javax.xml.rpc.ServiceFactory` *Methods*

`Service createService(QName serviceName)` Creates the services specified by the qualified name.
`Service createService(URL wsdlLocation, QName serviceName)` Creates the services for the specified WSDL location and qualified service name.
`static ServiceFactory newInstance()` Factory method to get an instance of the service factory.

You'll see all the previous methods in detail. Once the clients get the service object, they can access the Web service in the following three possible ways:

- Using strongly typed statically generated stubs
- Using dynamic proxy-based service endpoint implementation
- Using JAX-RPC DII

Static Stubs

Static stubs are normally generated from the WSDL document for the Web service. Vendors provide tools for generating static stubs from WSDL locations. The static stubs access as a proxy to the Web service endpoint. The runtime type of the static stub is assignable to both the service endpoint interface as well as to the JAX-RPC interface, which is `javax.xml.rpc.Stub`. Normally, clients using static stubs will use a strongly typed subinterface of the `Service` interface to get a reference to the stub.

With J2EE 1.4 RI, you can generate static stubs from the WSDL document using `wscompile` tool. The following command will generate the static stubs, custom serializers, and the strongly typed `Service` subinterface and implementation:

```
wscompile.bat -gen:client -d <output dir> <configuration file>
```

This command writes the generated classes to the specified output directory. Listing 15-19 shows the contents of the configuration file.

Listing 15-19. Configuration File

```
<?xml version="1.0" encoding="UTF-8"?>
<configuration
    xmlns="http://java.sun.com/xml/ns/jax-rpc/ri/config">
  <wsdl location="dd/OfferSearchSEP.wsdl"
       packageName="com.apress.projavaserver14.ws"/>
</configuration>
```

The tool uses Listing 15-19 to generate the client artifacts from the WSDL file `OfferSearchSEP.wsdl`. Listing 15-20 shows the code for using static stubs.

Listing 15-20. Using Static Stubs

```
package com.apress.projavaserver14.ws;

import javax.xml.rpc.Stub;

public class StaticClient {

    private String endpointAddress;

    public static void main(String[] args) {
    /* The service endpoint address is passed as a command-line argument (for
        example, http://localhost:8000/Auction/OfferSearch). */
        System.out.println("Endpoint address = " + args[0]);
        try {
            // This calls a private method to get the static stub.
            Stub stub = createProxy();
            // Set the endpoint address for the web service.
            stub._setProperty(javax.xml.rpc.Stub.ENDPOINT_ADDRESS_PROPERTY,
                args[0]);
            // Cast the stub to endpoint interface.
            OfferSearchIF OfferSearch = (OfferSearchIF)stub;
            System.out.println(OfferSearch.searchOffers("").length);
        } catch (Exception ex) {
            ex.printStackTrace();
        }
    }

    private static Stub createProxy() {
     /* OfferSearchSEP_Impl is a class generated by wscompile that implements the
     Interface OfferSearchSEP again generated by wscompile. This interface
     extends the JAX-RPC Service interface and provides strongly typed interface to
     access the service endpoint. */
        return (Stub)(new OfferSearchSEP_Impl().getOfferSearchIFPort());
    }
}
```

NOTE *Note that the code shown in Listing 15-20 is vendor specific and hence not portable.*

Stub

This section shows the `javax.xml.rpc.Stub` interface in closer detail. The interface provides the methods described in Table 15-8.

Table 15-8. `javax.xml.rpc.Stub` *Methods*

`_setProperty(String name, Object value)`	Sets a stub property
`Iterator _getPropertyNames()`	Gets all the property names
`Object _getProperty(String name)`	Gets the named property value

Table 15-9 describes the standard stub properties.

Table 15-9. Standard Stub Properties

`ENDPOINT_ADDRESS_PROPERTY`	Endpoint address for the Web service
`USER_NAME_PROPERTY`	Username for authentication
`PASSWORD_PROPERTY`	Password for authentication
`SESSION_MAINTAIN_PROPERTY`	A Boolean property to indicate whether the client wants to maintain a session with the service

Dynamic Proxies

Dynamic proxies were introduced in JDK 1.3 and can generate runtime classes that implement a specified set of interfaces. The invocation logic is handled by an implementation of the `InvocationHandler` interface. JAX-RPC runtime is required to support dynamic proxy-based access to the service endpoint to the clients. Here a dynamic proxy class will implement the service endpoint interface and mediate access to the Web service.

Listing 15-21 shows the code using dynamic proxies.

Listing 15-21. Using Dynamic Proxies

```
package com.apress.projavaserver14.ws;

import java.net.URL;
import javax.xml.rpc.Service;
import javax.xml.rpc.JAXRPCException;
import javax.xml.namespace.QName;
import javax.xml.rpc.ServiceFactory;

public class DynamicProxyClient{

  public static void main(String[] args) throws Exception {

    /* Create the URL to get the WSDL by appending the string ?WSDL to the
    endpoint address. */
    String UrlString = args[0] + "?WSDL";
    // This is the namespace URI for the service and port elements in the WSDL.
    String nameSpaceUri = "http://www.apress.com/Auction";
    // This is the local name of the service element.
    String serviceName = "OfferSearchSEP";
```

```
    // This is the local name of the port element.
    String portName = "OfferSearchIFPort";

    URL helloWsdlUrl = new URL(UrlString);
    // Get an instance of the service factory.
    ServiceFactory serviceFactory = ServiceFactory.newInstance();
    // Pass the WSDL URL and qualified name of the service to get the service.
    Service helloService = serviceFactory.createService(helloWsdlUrl,
    new QName(nameSpaceUri, serviceName));
    /* Call the getPort method on the service to get the port. This returns
      the dynamic  proxy and can be cast to the service endpoint interface. */
    OfferSearchIF myProxy = (OfferSearchIF ) helloService.getPort(
    new QName(nameSpaceUri, portName), OfferSearchIF.class);
    // Invoke the web service.
    System.out.println(myProxy.getDescription(1));


  }

}
```

> **NOTE** *To make dynamic proxy-based invocation, the clients should have some knowledge of the WSDL.*

Dynamic Invocation Interface

DII clients use the `Call` interface to access the port and invoke the Web service. To use DII, the clients should have good knowledge of the WSDL. Before going into the details of DII you'll quickly look at an example using DII (see Listing 15-22).

Listing 15-22. Using DII

```
package com.apress.projavaserver14.ws;

import javax.xml.rpc.Call;
import javax.xml.rpc.Service;
import javax.xml.rpc.JAXRPCException;
import javax.xml.namespace.QName;
import javax.xml.rpc.ServiceFactory;
import javax.xml.rpc.ParameterMode;

import com.apress.projavaserver14.ws.*;

public class DIIClient {
   // Name of the service in the WSDL document.
   private static String qnameService = "OfferSearchSEP";
```

```
    // Name of the port in the WSDL document.
    private static String qnamePort = "OfferSearchIFPort";
    // Namespace URI for the service and port defined in the WSDL document.
    private static String BODY_NAMESPACE_VALUE =
    "http://www.apress.com/Auction";
    // Property to set the encoding style namespace URI.
    private static String ENCODING_STYLE_PROPERTY =
    "javax.xml.rpc.encodingstyle.namespace.uri";
    // Namespace URI for markup from XML Schema.
    private static String NS_XSD =
    "http://www.w3.org/2001/XMLSchema";
    // Namespace URI for SOAP encoding.
    private static String URI_ENCODING =
    "http://schemas.xmlsoap.org/soap/encoding/";

    public static void main(String[] args) throws Exception {
      // The endpoint address is passed in as a commandline argument.
      System.out.println("Endpoint address = " + args[0]);
      // Get a reference to the service.
      ServiceFactory factory = ServiceFactory.newInstance();
      Service service = factory.createService(new QName(qnameService));
      // Get the port from the service.
      QName port = new QName(qnamePort);
      // Create a call object for the port.
      Call call = service.createCall(port);
      // Set the target endpoint address.
      call.setTargetEndpointAddress(args[0]);
      // Set the SOAP action and the encoding style that is used.
      call.setProperty(Call.SOAPACTION_USE_PROPERTY, new Boolean(true));
      call.setProperty(Call.SOAPACTION_URI_PROPERTY, "");
      call.setProperty(ENCODING_STYLE_PROPERTY, URI_ENCODING);
      // Set the return type for the call.
      QName QNAME_TYPE_STRING = new QName(NS_XSD, "string");
      call.setReturnType(QNAME_TYPE_STRING);
      // Set the operation name and register the IN parameter type.
      QName QNAME_TYPE_INT = new QName(NS_XSD, "int");
      call.setOperationName(
        new QName(BODY_NAMESPACE_VALUE, "getDescription"));
      call.addParameter("int_1", QNAME_TYPE_INT, ParameterMode.IN);
      System.out.println(call.invoke({ new Integer(1) }));

    }

}
```

The main interface used for DII is `javax.xml.rpc.Call`. This interface defines the methods shown in Table 15-10.

Table 15-10. `javax.xml.rpc.Call` *Methods*

`void addParameter(String paramName, QName xmlType, Class javaType, ParameterMode parameterMode)`
Adds a parameter for the call by specifying the parameter name, XML type, Java type, and the parameter mode (`IN`, `IN-OUT`, or `OUT`)

`void addParameter(String paramName, QName xmlType, ParameterMode parameterMode)`
Adds a parameter for the call by specifying the parameter name, XML type, and the parameter mode (`IN`, `IN-OUT`, or `OUT`)

`QName getOperationName()`
Gets the name of the operation to be invoked using this `Call` instance

`List getOutputValues()`
Returns a `List` values for the output parameters of the last invoked operation

`QName getParameterTypeByName(String paramName)`
Gets the XML type of a parameter by name

`QName getPortTypeName()`
Gets the qualified name of the port type

`Object getProperty(String name)`
Gets the value of a named property

`Iterator getPropertyNames()`
Gets the names of configurable properties supported by this `Call` object

`QName getReturnType()`
Gets the return type for a specific operation

`String getTargetEndpointAddress()`
Gets the address of a target service endpoint

`Object invoke(Object[] inputParams)`
Invokes a specific operation using a synchronous request/response interaction mode

`Object invoke(QName operationName, Object[] inputParams)`
Invokes a specific operation using a synchronous request/response interaction mode

`void invokeOneWay(Object[] inputParams)`
Invokes a remote method using the one-way interaction mode

`boolean isParameterAndReturnSpecRequired(QName operationName)`
Indicates whether `addParameter` and `setReturnType` methods are to be invoked to specify the parameter and return type specification for a specific operation

`void removeAllParameters()`
Removes all specified parameters from this `Call` instance

`void removeProperty(String name)`
Removes a named property

`void setOperationName(QName operationName)`
Sets the name of the operation to be invoked using this `Call` instance

`void setPortTypeName(QName portType)`
Sets the qualified name of the port type

`void setProperty(String name, Object value)`
Sets the value for a named property

`void setReturnType(QName xmlType)`
Sets the return type for a specific operation

`void setReturnType(QName xmlType, Class javaType)`
Sets the return type for a specific operation

`void setTargetEndpointAddress(String address)`
Sets the address of the target service endpoint

The `Call` interface supports the properties described in Table 15-11.

Table 15-11. `Call` *Interface Properties*

ENCODINGSTYLE_URI_PROPERTY	Property for encoding `Style: Encoding` style specified as a namespace URI.
OPERATION_STYLE_PROPERTY	Property for operation style.
PASSWORD_PROPERTY	Property for password for authentication.
SESSION_MAINTAIN_PROPERTY	A Boolean property is used by a service client to indicate whether it wants to participate in a session with a service endpoint.
SOAPACTION_URI_PROPERTY	Property for `SOAPAction`.
SOAPACTION_USE_PROPERTY	Property for `SOAPAction`.
USERNAME_PROPERTY	Property for username for authentication.

J2EE Clients

Web service components that are referenced by J2EE components running in Web, EJB, or application client containers can use a logical name to access the Web service using JNDI lookup. This service reference is defined in the Web service client deployment descriptor `webservicesclient.xml` that's present in the same directory as the module deployment descriptor (`WEB-INF` for WAR and `META-INF` for EJB and application clients). These references should be bound in the `java:comp/env` namespace of the component by the container during deployment.

Web Services Client Deployment Descriptor

Figure 15-16 shows the high-level structure of the deployment descriptor.

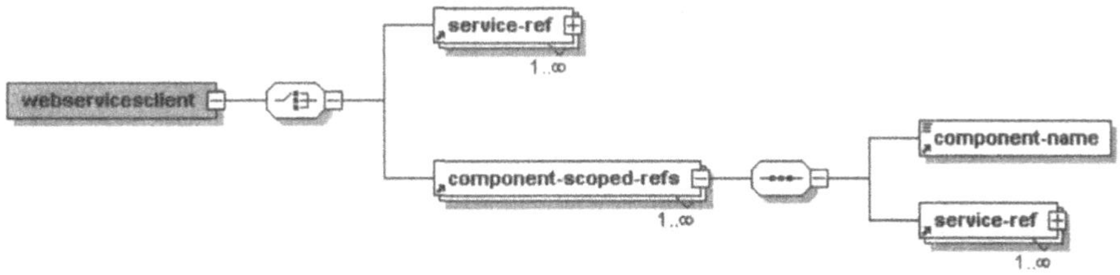

Figure 15-16. Web service client deployment descriptor

For components running in Web and application client containers, the service references should be defined as immediate children to the document element. However, for EJB components this should be defined in the `component-scope-refs` element with the `component-name` element referring to the EJB name in whose `java:comp/env` namespace the reference is made available.

Figure 15-17 shows the main subelements of the `service-ref` element.

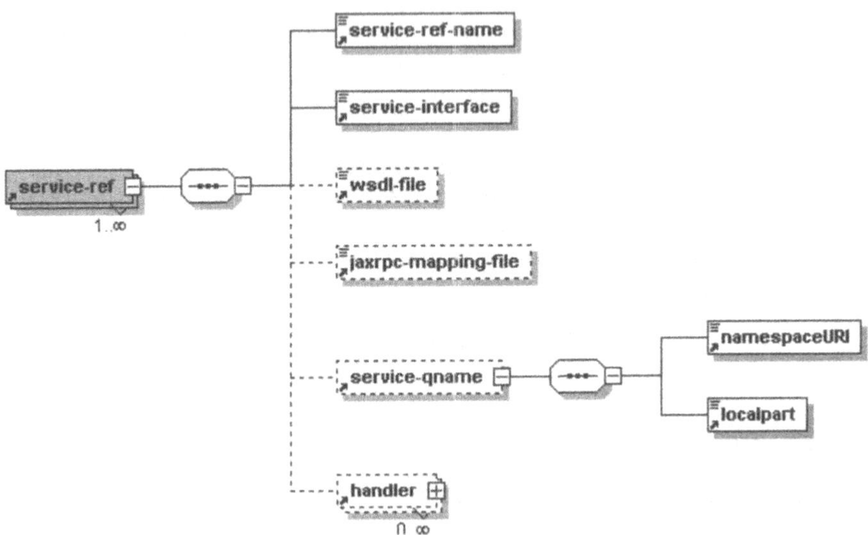

Figure 15-17. Service reference

This example has the following parts:

- **service-ref-name**: This defines the logical name by which the service reference is looked up.
- **service-interface**: This defines the fully qualified class name of the JAX-RPC service that's returned from the lookup. This can be either the JAX-RPC interface `javax.xml.rpc.Service` or a strongly typed subinterface.
- **wsdl-file**: This defines the relative location of the WSDL file that defines the service in the module.
- **jaxrpc-mapping-file**: This defines the JAX-RPC mapping file to use.
- **service-qname**: This defines the namespace URI and local name of the services defined in the WSDL document.
- **handler**: This defines the handlers in the same way as for Web services.

Listing 15-23 shows the Web service client deployment descriptor for the search `Offers` Web service.

Listing 15-23. `Offers` *Deployment Descriptor*

```
<?xml version="1.0" encoding="UTF-8"?>
<!DOCTYPE webservicesclient PUBLIC "-//IBM Corporation, Inc.//
  DTD J2EE Web services client 1.0//EN"
"http://www.ibm.com/standards/xml/webservices/j2ee/
  j2ee_web_services_client_1_0.dtd">
<webservicesclient>
  <service-ref>
    <service-ref-name>service/OfferSearch</service-ref-name>
    <service-interface>
      com.apress.projavaserver14.ws.OfferSearchService
    </service-interface>
    <wsdl-file>OfferSearchSEP.wsdl</wsdl-file>
    <jaxrpc-mapping-file>mapping.xml</jaxrpc-mapping-file>
  </service-ref>
</webservicesclient>
```

The class `com.apress.projavaserver14.ws.OfferSearchService` is a strongly typed subinterface of the `javax.xml.rpc.Service` interface. The clients can use the Web service as follows:

```
OfferSearchService service = (OfferSearchService)new InitialContext().lookup(
  "java:comp/env/service/OfferSearch");
OfferSearchIF endpoint = service.getOfferSearchIFPort();
endpoint.getDescription(1) ;
```

Working with SOAP Messages

So far you've been using the higher-level API provided by JAX-RPC that encapsulated the complex underlying protocols such as SOAP and WSDL to access the Web services. J2EE 1.4 provides another API SAAJ to work directly with the SOAP messages for a higher level of flexibility. The API in the `javax.xml.soap` package allows you to do the following:

- Create a point-to-point connection to a specified endpoint.
- Create a SOAP message.
- Create an XML fragment.
- Add content to the header of a SOAP message.
- Add content to the body of a SOAP message.
- Create attachment parts and add content to them.

- Access/add/modify parts of a SOAP message.
- Create/add/modify SOAP fault information.
- Extract content from a SOAP message.
- Send a SOAP request-response message.

NOTE *This package isn't specific to JAX-RPC, but is shared with other J2EE APIs such as JAX-R as well as non-J2EE APIs such as JAXM. In fact, SAAJ was originally part of JAXM.*

In this section you'll write a client that will use raw SOAP messages to access the search `Offers` Web service. Before you do that you'll look quickly at the interfaces and classes provided by SAAJ (see Figure 15-18).

Table 15-12 describes the SAAJ classes and interfaces.

Table 15-12. SAAJ Classes and Interfaces

`SOAPConnection`	A point-to-point connection that a client can use for sending messages directly to a remote party (represented by a URL, for instance).
`SOAPFactory`	`SOAPFactory` is a factory for creating various objects that exist in the SOAP XML tree.
`SOAPConnectionFactory`	A factory class for creating SOAP connections.
`MessageFactory`	A factory for creating SOAP messages.
`SOAPMessage`	An interface that represents the SOAP message.
`Node`	Common ancestor for all the other interface that represents various SOAP elements such as body, header, body entry, header entry, and so on.
`SOAPElement`	An object representing the contents in a `SOAPBody` object, the contents in a `SOAPHeader` object, the content that can follow the `SOAPBody` object in a `SOAPEnvelope` object, or what can follow the detail element in a `SOAPFault` object.
`SOAPBody`	An object that represents the contents of the SOAP body element in a SOAP message.
`SOAPBodyElement`	A `SOAPBodyElement` object represents the contents in a `SOAPBody` object.
`SOAPHeader`	A representation of the SOAP header element.
`SOAPHeaderElement`	An object representing the contents in the SOAP header part of the SOAP envelope.
`SOAPFault`	An element in the `SOAPBody` object that contains error and/or status information.
`SOAPFaultElement`	A representation of the contents in a `SOAPFault` object.

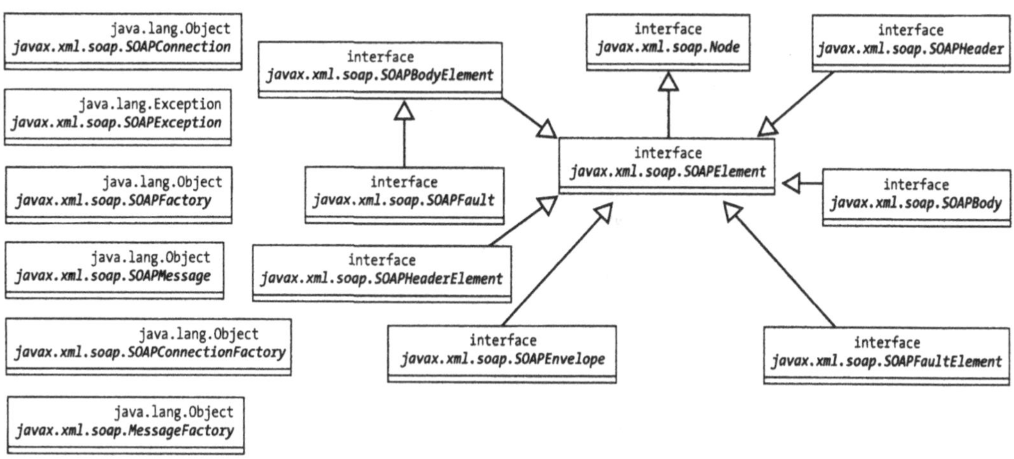

Figure 15-18. SAAJ classes and interfaces

Now you'll see the client for accessing the Web service by processing raw SOAP messages (see Listing 15-24).

Listing 15-24. Processing Raw SOAP Messages

```
package com.apress.projavaserver14.ws;

import javax.xml.soap.*;
import java.net.URL;

public class SOAPClient {

  public static void main(String[] args) throws Exception {
    // The endpoint address is passed in as a commandline argument.
    System.out.println("Endpoint address = " + args[0]);
    // Call the method to send the request.
    SOAPMessage reply = sendMessage(args[0]);
    // Process the response SOAP message.
    processResponse(reply);


  }

  private static SOAPMessage sendMessage(String endpoint) throws Exception {
    /* Create a SOAP connection factory and a SOAP connection. SOAP connection
    is used to send P2P messages.*/
    SOAPConnectionFactory scf = SOAPConnectionFactory.newInstance();
    SOAPConnection connection = scf.createConnection();
    /* Create a message factory that will be used to create the various SOAP
    artifacts. */
```

```
        MessageFactory msgFactory = MessageFactory.newInstance();
        // Create the SOAP message.
        SOAPMessage msg = msgFactory.createMessage();
        // Use the SOAP message to get the SOAP envelope.
        SOAPEnvelope envelope = msg.getSOAPPart().getEnvelope();
        // Add the required namespace declarations in the document element.
        envelope.addNamespaceDeclaration("env",
        SOAPConstants.URI_NS_SOAP_ENVELOPE);
        envelope.addNamespaceDeclaration("xsd",
        "http://www.w3.org/2001/XMLSchema");
        envelope.addNamespaceDeclaration("xsi",
        "http://www.w3.org/2001/XMLSchema-instance");
        envelope.addNamespaceDeclaration("enc",
        SOAPConstants.URI_NS_SOAP_ENCODING);
        envelope.addNamespaceDeclaration("ns0",
        "http://www.apress.com/Auction");
        // Create a qualified name for the encoding style attribute.
        Name encodingAttribute = envelope.createName("env:encodingStyle");
        // Set the encoding style attribute in the document element.
        envelope.addAttribute(encodingAttribute,
        SOAPConstants.URI_NS_SOAP_ENCODING);
        // Get the SOAP body.
        SOAPBody body = envelope.getBody();
        /* Create a qualified name for the body entry that will represent
           the method call getDescription on the Web service. */
        Name methodElement = envelope.createName("ns0:getDescription");
        // Add the body entry that represents the method.
        SOAPBodyElement getDescription = body.addBodyElement(methodElement);
        /* Create a qualified name for the element that will represent the method
        argument for the call getDescription on the Web service. */
        Name paramElement = envelope.createName("int_1");
        /* Add the argument element with the body content set to the value 1,
          which is the argument value. */
        SOAPElement methodParam = getDescription.addChildElement(paramElement);
        methodParam.addTextNode("1");
        // Set the type attribute for the method argument.
        Name typeAttribute = envelope.createName("xsi:type");
        methodParam.addAttribute(typeAttribute, "xsd:int");
        // Save the message changes.
        msg.saveChanges();
        // Print the input SOAP message to the standard output.
        System.out.println("*****************Request************");
        msg.writeTo(System.out);
        // Send the message to the endpoint and receive the reply.
        return connection.call(msg, new URL(endpoint));

    }

    private static void processResponse(SOAPMessage reply) throws Exception {
        // Print the response SOAP message to the standard out.
        System.out.println("*****************Response************");
```

```
    reply.writeTo(System.out);
    // Get the SOAP envelope and body.
    SOAPEnvelope envelope = reply.getSOAPPart().getEnvelope();
    SOAPBody body = envelope.getBody();
    // Get the body entry that represent the method response.
    SOAPElement response = (SOAPElement)body.getChildElements().next();
    // Get the result from the Web service call and print the value.
    SOAPElement result = (SOAPElement)response.getChildElements().next();

    System.out.println();
    System.out.println("Offer Description:" + result.getValue());

  }

}
```

Listing 15-25 shows the output of running the code in Listing 15-24. The SOAP messages have been indented to improve readability.

Listing 15-25. Output

```
Endpoint address = http://localhost:8000/Auction/OfferSearch
*****************Request***********
<soap-env:Envelope
  xmlns:soap-env="http://schemas.xmlsoap.org/soap/envelope/"
  xmlns:env="http://schemas.xmlsoap.org/soap/envelope/"
  xmlns:xsd="http://www.w3.org/2001/XMLSchema"
  xmlns:xsi="http://www.w3.org/2001/XMLSchema-instance"
  xmlns:enc="http://schemas.xmlsoap.org/soap/encoding/"
  xmlns:ns0="http://www.apress.com/Auction"
  env:encodingStyle="http://schemas.xmlsoap.org/soap/encoding/">
  <soap-env:Header></soap-env:Header>
  <soap-env:Body>
    <ns0:getDescription>
      <int_1 xsi:type="xsd:int">1</int_1>
    </ns0:getDescription>
  </soap-env:Body>
</soap-env:Envelope>
*****************Response***********
<?xml version="1.0" encoding="UTF-8"?>
<env:Envelope
  xmlns:env="http://schemas.xmlsoap.org/soap/envelope/"
  xmlns:xsd="http://www.w3.org/2001/XMLSchema"
  xmlns:xsi="http://www.w3.org/2001/XMLSchema-instance"
  xmlns:enc="http://schemas.xmlsoap.org/soap/encoding/"
  xmlns:ns0="http://www.apress.com/Auction"
  env:encodingStyle="http://schemas.xmlsoap.org/soap/encoding/">
  <env:Body>
    <ns0:getDescriptionResponse>
      <result xsi:type="xsd:string">
```

```
            256 Mb MP3 Player
          </result>
        </ns0:getDescriptionResponse>
    </env:Body>
</env:Envelope>

Description: 256 Mb MP3 Player
```

Please note that to write a client that uses raw SOAP messages to invoke the Web service, you need to have good knowledge about the WSDL as well as how the requests and responses are encoded using SOAP.

EJB Endpoints

So far in this chapter you've been using servlet endpoints in your Web service to access the stateless session EJB. However, with J2EE 1.4 you can directly expose stateless session EJBs as Web services using EJB endpoints. Building, packaging, and deploying EJB endpoints are similar to servlet endpoints with the following major differences:

- EJB endpoints are packaged as standard EJB JAR files.
- The service implementation bean is a class that implements `javax.ejb.SessionBean` that provides implementations for methods defined in the service endpoint interface.
- In the Web service deployment descriptor you use `ejb-link` instead of `servlet-link` in the `service-implementation-bean` element to specify the EJB name as defined in the EJB deployment descriptor.

EJB Deployment Descriptor

EJB 2.1 introduces some new elements to the standard deployment descriptor to support Web service endpoints. Listing 15-26 shows the deployment descriptor for the session bean to expose it as an EJB endpoint.

Listing 15-26. Session Bean Deployment Descriptor

```
<?xml version="1.0" encoding="UTF-8"?>
<ejb-jar version="2.1" xmlns="http://java.sun.com/xml/ns/j2ee"
xmlns:xsi="http://www.w3.org/2001/XMLSchema-instance"
xsi:schemaLocation="http://java.sun.com/xml/ns
  /j2ee http://java.sun.com/xml/ns/j2ee/ejb-jar_2_1.xsd">
  <display-name>Ejb1</display-name>
  <enterprise-beans>
    <session>
      <display-name>OfferSearchEEPEJB</display-name>
      <ejb-name>OfferSearchEEPEJB</ejb-name>
```

```
        <service-endpoint>
          com.apress.projavaserver14.ws.OfferSearchIF
        </service-endpoint>
      <ejb-class>com.apress.projavaserver14.ws.OfferSearchBean</ejb-class>
      <session-type>Stateless</session-type>
      <transaction-type>Container</transaction-type>
    </session>
  </enterprise-beans>
</ejb-jar>
```

Here the client view is the service endpoint interface, and hence the `service-endpoint` interface is used instead of specifying the home and component interfaces. The EJB name should link to the `ejb-link` element in the Web service deployment descriptor.

Web Services Deployment Descriptor

The Web service deployment descriptor is similar to that for the servlet endpoint with a minor difference (see Listing 15-27).

Listing 15-27. Web Service Deployment Descriptor

```
<!DOCTYPE webservices PUBLIC "-//IBM Corporation, Inc.//DTD J2EE Web services
1.0//EN" "http://www.ibm.com/standards/xml/webservices/j2ee/
  j2ee_web_services_1_0.dtd">
<webservices>
  <webservice-description>
    <webservice-description-name>
      OfferSearchEEP
    </webservice-description-name>
    <wsdl-file>OfferSearchEEP.wsdl</wsdl-file>
    <jaxrpc-mapping-file>META-INF/mapping.xml</jaxrpc-mapping-file>
    <port-component>
      <description>port component description</description>
      <port-component-name>OfferSearchIFPort</port-component-name>
      <wsdl-port>
        <namespaceURI>http://www.apress.com/Auction</namespaceURI>
        <localpart>OfferSearchIFPort</localpart>
      </wsdl-port>
      <service-endpoint-interface>
        com.apress.projavaserver14.ws.OfferSearchIF
      </service-endpoint-interface>
      <service-impl-bean>
        <ejb-link>OfferSearchEEPEJB</ejb-link>
      </service-impl-bean>
    </port-component>
  </webservice-description>
</webservices>
```

This example has the following changes:

- The name of the service has now been changed.
- The name of the WSDL file has now been changed.
- Now the service implementation bean is linked using the `ejb-link` element.
- The mapping deployment descriptor is now stored in the `META-INF` directory of the module. However, the contents of the mapping deployment descriptor are the same as for servlet endpoint.

> **NOTE** *To deploy a stateless session bean, because you don't need the home and component interfaces, you need only the bean class and the service endpoint interface.*

Packaging and Deploying

The endpoint address of the EJB is specified in a vendor-specific manner in `sun-ri-j2ee.xml`, as shown in Listing 15-28.

Listing 15-28. `sun-ri-j2ee.xml`

```
<?xml version="1.0" encoding="UTF-8"?>

<!DOCTYPE j2ee-ri-specific-information PUBLIC '-//Sun Microsystems Inc.//DTD J2EE
Reference Implementation 1.3//EN'
  'http://localhost:8000/sun-j2ee-ri_1_3.dtd'>

<j2ee-ri-specific-information>
  <server-name></server-name>
  <rolemapping />
  <enterprise-beans>
    <module-name>OfferSearchEEP.jar</module-name>
    <unique-id>0</unique-id>
    <ejb>
      <ejb-name>OfferSearchEEPEJB</ejb-name>
      <webservice-endpoint>
        <port-component-name>OfferSearchIFPort</port-component-name>
        <endpoint-address-uri>OfferSearch</endpoint-address-uri>
      </webservice-endpoint>
    </ejb>
  </enterprise-beans>
</j2ee-ri-specific-information>
```

You can access the service using any of the clients explained earlier by specifying the endpoint address as `http://server:port/OfferSearch`.

Using Message Handlers

Message handlers are similar to servlet filters in that they can be used to preprocess and postprocess requests and responses. The only difference is that with Web services, you can configure handlers at both the client and server side (see Figure 15-19).

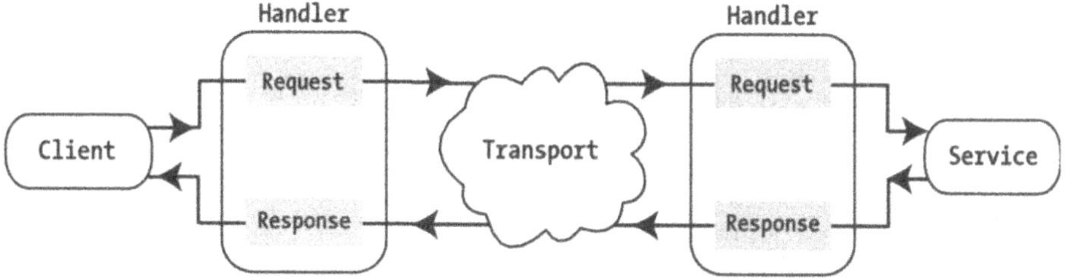

Figure 15-19. Message handlers

> **NOTE** *Handlers are JAX-RPC specific and aren't part of standard WSDL.*

JAX-RPC supports handlers only for requests and responses with SOAP binding. However, there's no restriction on the transport binding. On the client side, handler execution occurs after the stub/proxy has marshaled the request into the SOAP message, before the container and transport services for requests, after container and transport services, and before demarshaling of the SOAP message for responses. For the server side, handlers are run after container services, before demarshaling of the SOAP message for requests, after marshaling of the SOAP message, and before container and transport services for responses.

Handlers can access the messages through the message contexts that are passed to them. They can add/remove header entries but aren't allowed to alter the SOAP body structure. They can change the values for element text content as long as they don't change the type.

Usage Scenarios

Handlers can be used in the following variety of scenarios:

- Pre-agreed SOAP header processing between client and service.
- Caching.
- Logging.
- Handlers have a limited amount of support for XML encryption and XML digital signatures.

Implementation

Handlers are packaged with the service or service client component. Handlers are executed in an ordered chain as specified in the Web services or Web service client deployment descriptor. Figure 15-20 shows the content model for how a handler is configured.

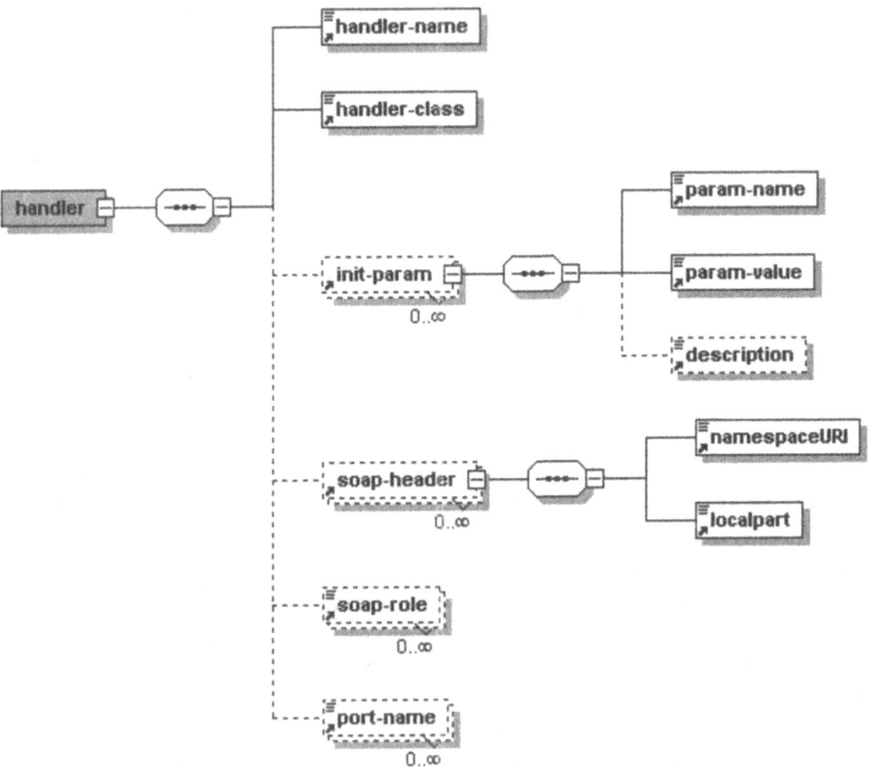

Figure 15-20. Handler structure

The example has the following parts:

- **handler-name**: This specifies a unique name for the handler.
- **handler-class**: This specifies the fully qualified name of the handler class.
- **init-param**: This passes initialization parameters for the handler.
- **soap-header**: This specifies the SOAP header entries that are processed by the handler.
- **soap-role**: This specifies the SOAP actor role played by the handler.

In the Web service deployment descriptor, handlers are specified for the port component, and in Web service client deployment descriptors, they're defined for service references. The following snippet shows a simple handler definition:

```
<handler>
  <handler-name>LoggingHandler</handler-name>
  <handler-class>com.apress.projavaserver14.ws.LoggingHandler</handler-class>
</handler>
```

Figure 15-21 depicts the classes and interfaces involved in implementing handlers. Table 15-13 describes the handler classes and interfaces.

Table 15-13. Handler Classes and Interfaces.

`Handler`	All the handlers should directly or indirectly implement this interface. The container calls the `init` method, passing the `HandlerInfo` for the handler after the handler is initialized. The `HandlerInfo` can access the declarative information defined in the deployment descriptor such as init parameters, SOAP headers that are processed by the handler, and so on. The `destroy` method is called just before the handler instance is destroyed. The `getHeaders` method should return all the SOAP header entries processed by the handler. The handler can get this information from the `HandlerInfo`. The three important methods are `handleRequest`, `handleResponse`, and `handleFault` that are called during request, response, and fault processing. All the three methods are passed a `MessageContext` that can be cast to `SOAPMessageContext`. For handling requests, if the method returns `true`, the container dispatches the request to the next handler in the chain; if it returns `false`, the request is blocked, and the `handleResponse` method is called on the same instance with the same SOAP message context.
`GenericHandler`	This is an adapter class that provides default implementation for all the `Handler` interface methods except the `getHeaders` method.
`HandlerChain`	This represents a chain of handlers.
`MessageContext`	This represents the context in which messages are passed. This can be used to share information between the handlers in a chain.
`SOAPMessageContext`	This is specialized message context for SOAP messages.
`HandlerInfo`	This contains the declarative information defined for the handler in the deployment descriptor.

Listing 15-29 shows a simple logging handler that can be used for debugging. The handler simply writes the request and response SOAP messages to the standard output.

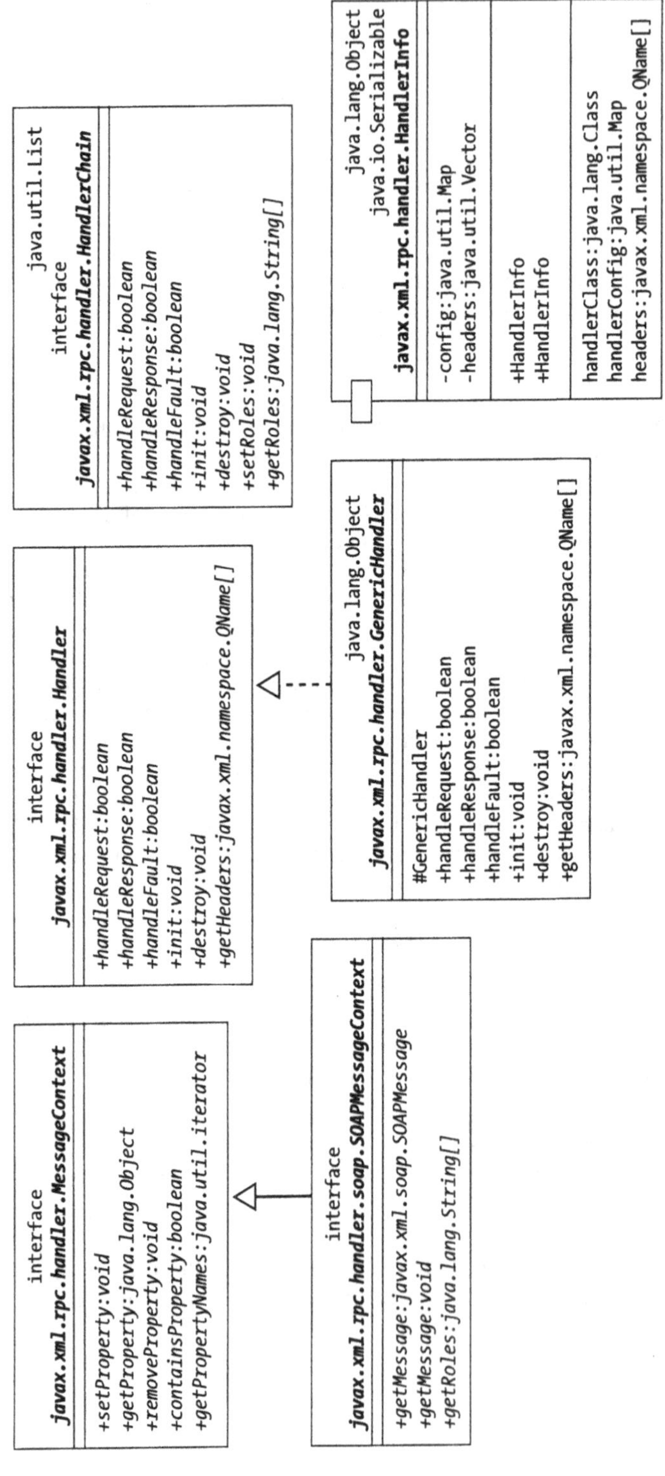

Figure 15-21. Handler classes and interfaces

Listing 15-29. Simple Logging Handler

```
package com.apress.projavaserver14.ws;

import javax.xml.rpc.handler.*;
import javax.xml.rpc.handler.soap.*;
import javax.xml.soap.SOAPMessage;
import javax.xml.namespace.QName;

public class LoggingHandler extends GenericHandler {

  private HandlerInfo handlerInfo;
  // Store a reference to the handler info.
  public void init(HandlerInfo handlerInfo) {
    this.handlerInfo = handlerInfo;
  }

  public void destroy() {
    handlerInfo = null;
  }

  public QName[] getHeaders() {
    return handlerInfo.getHeaders();
  }
  // Log the request messages.
  public boolean handleRequest(MessageContext ctx) {
    try {
      ((SOAPMessageContext)ctx).getMessage().writeTo(System.out);
    }catch(Exception ex) {
      ex.printStackTrace();
    }
    return true;
  }
  // Log the response messages.
  public boolean handleResponse(MessageContext ctx) {
    try {
      ((SOAPMessageContext)ctx).getMessage().writeTo(System.out);
    }catch(Exception ex) {
      ex.printStackTrace();
    }
    return true;
  }

}
```

Deployment Process

The following provides insight into the deployment of Servlet and EJB endpoints:

- The endpoints can be deployed as a service-enabled module or as part of an EAR file.
- Servlet endpoints are deployed as WAR and EJB endpoints or are deployed as EJB JAR files.
- For every concrete port defined in the WSDL, there should be a port component in the Web service deployment descriptor.
- For EJB endpoints the transaction attributes shouldn't be mandatory for methods.
- For EJB endpoints the bean class should implement all the methods defined in the service endpoint interface.
- For servlet endpoint the service implementation class should implement the methods defined in the service endpoint interface.
- Bindings defined in the WSDL should be supported by the container runtime.
- For servlet endpoints, the container generates a servlet that will accept the HTTP requests and replace the servlet class defined in the Web deployment descriptor from the service implementation bean class name to the generated servlet class name. The port address for servlet endpoint will be a combination of the context root of the Web application and the URI for the servlet mapping.
- The WSDL is updated to reflect the correct port endpoint address.

Web Service Interoperability

Web Services Interoperability Organization (WS-I) is an organization that has been formed recently to support interoperability between Web service platforms implemented using different technologies. The organization focuses on conformance tests and best-practice guidelines for vendors and developers for writing interoperable Web services.

The WS-I Web site (`http://www.ws-i.org`) has published the following as the following deliverables as part of the activities of the organization:

- **Profiles**: Sets of Web service specifications that work together to support specific types of solutions. For more information, read the short white paper.
- **Sample implementations**: With the context of a profile, the teams will work to define a set of Web services that are implemented by multiple team members to identify where interoperability issues exist.

- **Implementation guidelines**: Recommendations for uses of specifications in ways that have been proven to be most interoperable. These guidelines also provide the set of test cases that the sniffer and analyzer tools detect for compliance verification.

- **Sniffer**: Tools to monitor and log interactions with a Web service. This tool generates a file that can later be processed by the analyzer.

- **Analyzer**: Tools that processes sniffer logs and verify that the Web service implementation is free from errors.

Profiles

WS-I profiles specify a set of Web service specifications at specific versions and how they work together. This means Web service platforms that support the same profile level are interoperable. Similarly a Web service that's compliant with a given profile level can be deployed on a platform that supports that profile level.

The basic profile supports the following Web service specification:

- XML Schema 1.0
- SOAP 1.1
- WSDL 1.1
- UDDI 2.0
- XML 1.0
- HTTP 1.1

J2EE 1.4–compliant application servers are required to support the WS-I basic profile.

Summary

This chapter covered the support for Web services in J2EE 1.4. The chapter started with an overview of the underlying Web service technology and explained WSDL and SOAP in detail. Then it moved onto the various APIs available in J2EE 1.4 that support the various Web service technologies. The chapter covered JAX-RPC in detail and showed how the various WSDL artifacts mapped to JAX-RPC and Java. You then implemented one of the use cases from the auction application as a Web service using a JAX-RPC servlet endpoint. The chapter covered servlet endpoints in detail and showed the service implementation life cycle. Next the chapter covered the different ways J2EE and J2SE clients can access Web services. The chapter then introduced SAAJ and presented an example on how to use SAAJ to access Web services. Then it covered EJB endpoints in detail and rounded out the chapter by covering message handlers and deployment process.

CHAPTER 16

Managing Applications, Components, and Resources

Over the past three years Java 2 Enterprise Edition (J2EE) has evolved into the most predominant platform for building enterprise-class server-side applications. During this time, the need for a standards-based approach for administering, monitoring, and configuring J2EE applications, components, and resources has become more demanding. For example, you'll find it extremely useful in a production environment to monitor how well a stateless session bean pool or a Java Message Server (JMS) connection factory is performing in real time. The same holds true for the bespoke J2EE components and applications you've built and deployed. It's also extremely important that error conditions are properly monitored and corrective actions are adopted in production environments.

Java Management Extensions (JMX) is a specification that evolved through the Java Community Process (JCP)—JSR-03—and has started playing a key role in bringing out an open standard for the management of J2EE applications and application infrastructures. The JMX specification says the following:

> *JMX defines an architecture, the design patterns, the APIs and the services for application and network management and monitoring in the Java language. The JMX specification provides Java developers across all industries with the means to instrument Java code, create smart Java agents, implement distributed management middleware and managers, and smoothly integrate these solutions into existing management and monitoring systems.*

Some of the popular J2EE application and Web servers/containers use JMX for the core management functions of the server and associated components. These servers include the following:

- JBoss
- BEA WebLogic
- Sybase EAServer
- Tomcat

JMX is a generic specification and application programming interface (API) that vendors can implement to provide a standards-based management solution. It's designed in such a way that it can be used for bridging existing and future management protocols.

Another specification that has evolved more recently through JCP is the J2EE Management API (JSR-77). The J2EE Management API builds on JMX to provide a J2EE management model that identifies the information model of the managed objects, their attributes, the operations, and the events within a J2EE server. These managed objects include the J2EE server, domain, Java virtual machine (JVM), J2EE applications, application components, J2EE resources such as Java Database Connectivity (JDBC) connection pools, and so on. The specification defines a standard set of attributes that need to be supported by these managed objects and also allows vendor-specific managed objects and attributes. Furthermore, it provides a remote API to query these managed objects and register to events in an interoperable manner.

NOTE *J2EE 1.4 includes both JMX and the J2EE Management API. However, the main reason JMX is included is the dependency of the J2EE Management API on JMX. Complete support for the JMX specification isn't mandated from the J2EE vendors according to the J2EE 1.4 specification. However, most of the leading J2EE servers completely support JMX. The J2EE Management API is mandatory in J2EE 1.4 and also acts as an optional add-on with J2EE 1.3.*

In this chapter, you'll look at JMX and the J2EE Management API in detail. You'll see how to use JMX to monitor the auction application components and the J2EE Management API to monitor the performance of the various components used in the application.

NOTE *We'll use the JMX reference implementation available from* `http://java.sun.com/products/JavaManagement` *for the JMX examples and the J2EE 1.4 reference implementation for the Java Management API.*

Using Java Management Extensions

JMX is a specification and API for monitoring and managing resources from the Java language. These resources are managed using management applications. The resources can be software components and hardware devices. Management applications manage and monitor the attributes of these resources. For example, you can use a JMX-based management application to manage the Internet Protocol (IP) address, port number, forwarded ports, and so on, for a router.

The JMX architecture offers the following benefits:

- Enables application management without heavy investment
- Provides a scalable management architecture
- Integrates existing management solutions
- Leverages existing Java technologies
- Can leverage future management concepts
- Defines only the interfaces required for management

JMS provides an efficient management solution by providing the following three fundamental issues related to management:

- How to make resources manageable
- How to make manageable resources available for management
- How management applications access the manageable resources

JMX addresses these issues with an architecture composed of the following three levels:

Instrumentation level: This level defines the artifacts for making resources manageable. The resources are made manageable using managed beans or MBeans. MBeans provide an interface to the resources that are actually managed.

Agent level: This level is responsible for providing a run time for aggregating all the MBean components representing the resources that are managed. The management applications access the MBean components through the agent level. The agent level also provides agent-level MBeans for services such as monitors, timers, dynamic loading, relationship management, and so on.

Distributed services level: This level is responsible for connecting the agent level to the management applications. JSR-03 addresses only the instrumentation and agent levels. Other JSRs address connectivity to the agent level. JSR-160 is about standardizing the distributed services level for JMX.

You'll look at the JMX architecture in detail in the next section.

JMX Architecture

Figure 16-1 illustrates the high-level architecture for JMX.

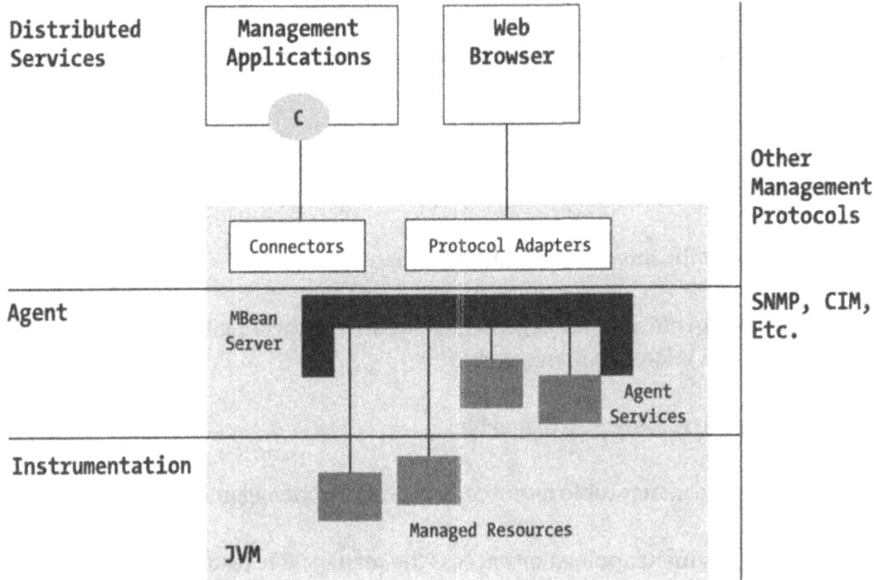

Figure 16-1. JMX architecture

The instrumentation level provides the interface to the resources that are managed. The resources can be applications, application components and resources, hardware devices, users, and so on. The resources are either required to be written in Java or provide a Java-based wrapper. The instrumentation for the resource is provided through one or more MBeans. The MBeans are required to provide the following information to the agent level:

- The attributes that represent the state of the resource
- Constructors that can be used by management applications and JMX agents to create the MBean instances
- The operations that can be performed on the resources through the MBeans
- The arguments that are passed to the constructors and operations
- Notifications that are emitted by the MBeans

JMX defines the following four ways of implementing the MBeans to communicate this information:

Standard: Standard MBeans communicate the previous information to agents and management applications using statically bound Java interfaces and classes.

Dynamic: Dynamic MBeans communicate the previous information to agents and management applications using metadata classes provided by the JMX specification.

Model: Model MBeans are generic MBeans that can be used by anyone to instrument any resource rapidly. They're dynamic MBeans with some additional functionality. JMX providers are required to provide a model MBean implementation.

Open: Open MBeans use a set of metadata that can describe complex types that are used in implementation. This means that the agents don't need to know about the specific complex types that are used by the instrumentation and interpret them at run time.

Instrumentation level is covered in detail in the "Instrumentation Level" section.

The agent level mainly consists of the MBean server and the agent-level services. The MBean server acts as a registry for all the MBeans that are registered with it. It also brokers the communication between the MBeans and management applications. Management applications seldom access the MBeans directly; instead the MBeans are always accessed through the MBean server. The agent level is also required to provide a set of agent-level services for loading MBeans dynamically and monitoring MBean attributes, timers, and relations between MBeans. These agent-level services are themselves implemented as MBeans (and are covered in the "Agent-Level Services" section).

Distributed services level provides the interfaces for implementing the JMX managers. This level defines management interfaces and components that can operate on agents. These components provide a transparent mechanism for the management applications to interact with the agents through a connector. They can also provide protocol adapters that can be used to expose the management view to external systems. An example is an HTTP adapter to display the agent view as HTML.

MBean Server

The MBean server is the core of the JMX agent level. It acts as the registry for the MBeans registered with it. The management applications access the MBeans through the MBean server. The MBean server is represented by the interface `javax.management.MbeanServer`. This interface defines methods for the following:

- Creating MBeans
- Registering MBeans
- Deserializing MBeans from a byte stream

- Adding and removing notification listeners for MBeans
- Manipulating by MBeans by getting/setting attributes and invoking operations
- Querying MBeans

The MBeans are registered with the MBean server against object names. The JMX object name uniquely identifies an MBean within an MBean server.

ObjectName

Every MBean that's registered with an MBean server is uniquely identified by an object name represented by the class `javax.management.ObjectName`. Object names follow this format:

```
domain-name:key1-value1[,key2=value2,...,keyX=valueX]
```

The portion of the object name before the colon is called the *domain name*, and the colon is followed by at least one key-value pair. The combination of domain name and key-value pairs should be unique within an MBean server. You specify the object name for the MBean when you register it with an MBean server. This is an example of an object name:

```
AuctionApplication:type=Offer,name=MP3 Player
```

The object name shown has the domain name `AuctionApplication` and two keys, `type` and `name`, with properties set to `Offer` and `MP3 Player`, respectively. You can consider the domain name a namespace mechanism for scoping MBeans. JMX implementations should provide a default domain name. The `MbeanServer` interface provides a method called `getDefaultDomain()` to get the default domain name for the implementation. The name `JMSImplementation` is reserved and shouldn't be used as a domain name.

The `ObjectName` class provides the constructors described in Table 16-1.

Table 16-1. `ObjectName` *Constructors*

CONSTRUCTORS	DESCRIPTION
`ObjectName(String name)`	Allows an object name to be created from the given string.
`ObjectName(String domain, Hashtable table)`	Allows an object name with several key properties to be created.
`ObjectName(String domain, String key, String value)`	Allows an object name to be created using only one key property.

The following snippet shows how to construct the object name shown in the previous example:

```
Hashtable prop = new Hashtable();
prop.put("type", "Offer");
prop.put("name", "MP3 Player");

ObjectName mp3PlayerMBeanName =
  new ObjectName("AuctionApplication", properties);
```

The class also provides methods to get the domain name, named property value, property list, and so on, for a given `ObjectName` instance.

MbeanServerFactory

The class `javax.management.MbeanServerFactory` provides a set of static methods for creating, finding, and releasing MBean server instances.

The following methods create instances of the MBean server, the first one with the implementation-specific default domain name and the second one with the specified default domain name, and they keep a reference to the MBean server so that it isn't garbage collected:

```
static MbeanServer createMBeanServer();
static MbeanServer createMBeanServer(String domainName);
```

The following methods create instances of the MBean server, the first one with the implementation-specific default domain name and the second one with the specified default domain name, without keeping a reference to the MBean server:

```
static MbeanServer newMBeanServer();
static MbeanServer newMBeanServer(String domainName);
```

The following method releases reference to an `MbeanServer` instance created by one of the `createMBeanServer` methods:

```
static void releaseMBeanServer(MbeanServer server)
```

The following method returns a list of registered `MBeanServer` objects. A registered `MBeanServer` object is one that was created by one of the `createMBeanServer` methods and not subsequently released with `releaseMBeanServer`:

```
static ArrayList findMBeanServer(String agentId)
```

The `agentId` is the agent identifier of the `MBeanServer` to retrieve. If this parameter is `null`, all registered `MBeanServers` in this Java virtual machine (JVM) are returned.

Otherwise, only MbeanServer instances whose ID is equal to agentId are returned. The agent ID is specific to the implementation; however, JMX specifies an MBean called MBeanServerDelegateMBean that provides the metadata about the implementation.

The following snippet shows how to create a new MBean server:

```
MBeanServer server =
  MbeanServerFactory.createMBeanServer("AuctionApplication");
```

Next you'll take a closer look at some of the important methods defined in the MBeanServer interface.

Instantiating, Registering, and Unregistering MBeans

The MbeanServer interface provides a set of methods for instantiating, registering, and unregistering MBeans. The methods you'll see are the methods for instantiating MBeans. These methods are as follows:

```
Object instantiate(String className)
Object instantiate(String className, Object[] params,
  String[] signature)
Object instantiate(String className, ObjectName loaderName)
Object instantiate(String className, ObjectName loaderName,
  Object[] params, String[] signature)
```

All the four methods listed previously create an MBean instance whose class is specified by className. The second and fourth overloaded versions create the MBean that invokes the constructor that's identified by the signature parameter, passing the parameters specified by the params argument. The third and fourth overloaded versions allow you to specify a classloader to use to load the MBean class. However, this classloader should also be registered as an MBean with the MBean server. The following snippet shows how to instantiate an MBean representing an offer in the auction application:

```
String offerMBeanClass =
  "com.apressprojavaserver14.chapter19.standard.Offer";
MBeanServer  server =
  MbeanServerFactory.createServer("OfferApplication");
Object offer = server.instantiate(offerMBeanClass);
```

The previous snippet expects a public no-argument constructor for the MBean class. The following snippet shows how to specify an explicit constructor:

```
String offerMBeanClass =
  "com.apress.projavaserver14.chapter19.standard.Offer";
MBeanServer  server =
  MbeanServerFactory.createServer("OfferApplication");

Object[] params = new Object[] {new Integer(1),
  "MP3 Player", "256 Mb MP3 Player"};
```

```
String[] signature = {Integer.TYPE.getName(),
  "java.lang.String", "java.lang.String"};
Object course = server.instantiate(offerMBeanClass,
  params, signature);
```

The previous code uses the constructor `Offer(int, String, String)`.

Once you've instantiated the MBean, you need to register it with the MBean server. To do this, the MBeanServer interface provides the following methods:

```
ObjectInstance registerMBean(Object object,
  ObjectName ObjectName)
```

This method registers the MBean instance under the specified object name. The return type of this method is the `ObjectInstance` class, which encapsulates the object name and the class name of the registered MBean. One important exception this method declares to throw is the `NotCompliantException` if the passed object instance doesn't comply with the JMX specification. In the "Instrumentation Level" section, you'll see in detail the requirements for an object instance to be a fully compliant MBean. The following snippet shows the code for registering an MBean:

```
String offerMBeanClass =
  "com.apress.projavaserver14.chapter19.standard.Offer";
MBeanServer  server =
  MbeanServerFactory.createServer("OfferApplication");

Object[] params = new Object[] {new Integer(1), "MP3 Player",
  "256 Mb MP3 Player"};
String[] signature = {Integer.TYPE.getName(),
  "java.lang.String", "java.lang.String"};
Object offerMBean = server.instantiate(offerMBeanClass,
  params, signature);

Hashtable prop = new Hashtable();
prop.put("type", "Offer");
prop.put("name", "MP3 Player");

ObjectName mp3PlayerMBeanName =
  new ObjectName("OfferApplication", properties);

server.registerMBean(offerMBean, mp3PlayerMBeanName);
```

Once the MBean is registered, it can be manipulated by the management applications through its MBean server. The `MBeanServer` interface also defines a set of methods that combine the instantiation and registration functionality, as shown below:

```
Object createMBean(String className, ObjectName objectName)
Object createMBean(String className, ObjectName objectName,
  Object[] params, String[] signature)
Object createMBean(String className, ObjectName objectName,
```

```
  ObjectName loaderName)
Object createMBean(String className, ObjectName objectName,
  ObjectName loaderName, Object[] params, String[] signature)
```

All the four methods listed previously are similar to the corresponding instantiate methods except that these methods also perform registration in addition to instantiation. The following snippet shows how to use these methods:

```
server.createMBean(offerMBeanClass, mp3PlayerMBeanName,
  params, signature);
```

To unregister a registered MBean, you can call `unregisterMBean(ObjectName ObjectName)`, passing the object name of the MBean to be unregistered.

Querying MBeans

The MBean server allows you to search and get information about the MBeans that are hosted by it, through a set of methods defined in the `MBeanServer` interface. The following are two methods used to query MBeans:

```
public Set queryMBeans(ObjectName, QueryExp exp)
public Set queryNames(ObjectName, QueryExp exp)
```

The first method gets MBeans controlled by the MBean server. This method allows any of the following to be obtained:

- All MBeans
- A set of MBeans specified by pattern matching on the `ObjectName` and/or a `Query` expression
- A specific MBean

When the object name is `null` or no domain and key properties are specified, all objects are to be selected (and filtered if a query is specified). It returns the set of `ObjectInstance` instances for the selected MBeans. The behavior of the second method is similar to that of the first; the only difference being is that it returns a set of `ObjectName` instances.

The `QueryExp` interface is an interface that models a set of predicates and is constructed using the `Query` class. The following snippet selects all the course MBeans in the `OfferApplication` domain, with a `name` attribute set to a value starting with the string `MP3`:

```
ObjectName ob = new
  ObjectName("OfferApplication:type=Offer,*");
QueryExp exp = Query.initialSubstring(Query.att("name"),
  Query.value("MP3")
Set res = mbeanServer.queryNames(ob, exp);
```

Here the Query class creates a predicate that filters all the name MBean attributes with values starting with MP3. The initialSubstring method creates an expression that filters objects selected by the object name filter, with attribute values starting with the value specified. For example, the object name OfferApplication:type=Offer,* will select all the MBeans with object names matching the pattern. The query expression will then filter from that set, selecting only those MBeans whose name attribute starts with the string MP3.

The Query class provides a plethora of methods for creating various query expressions and combining them using logical and and or operators. The following snippet creates a query expression where the name equals MP3 Player and the asking price is less than or equal to 100:

```
QueryExp exp1 = Query.eq(Query.att("name",
  Query.value("MP3 Player"));
QueryExp exp2 = Query.gt(Query.att("askPrice",
  Query.value(100));
QueryExp exp3 = Query.and(exp1, exp2);
```

The method eq generates an equals expression, the method gt generates a greater-than expression, and the function and generates a logical and operator.

Manipulating MBeans

The only way management applications can set and get attributes and invoke operations on the MBean components are through the MBean server that hosts the components. To perform these tasks, the MBeanServer interface defines a set of methods. Management applications access the MBeans through the hosting MBean server by specifying the relevant object names. The MBean server is responsible for finding the required MBean, invoking the relevant operation, and returning the results:

```
public Object getAttribute(ObjectName name, String attribute)
  throws
  MBeanException,
  AttributeNotFoundException,
  InstanceNotFoundException,
  ReflectionException,
  RuntimeOperationsException
```

The method returns the value of the attribute specified in the argument attribute on the MBean with the specified object name. The attribute should follow the standard JavaBeans property pattern. The method throws the following exceptions:

- **MBeanException**: This wraps any exception thrown by the MBean's attribute accessor method.
- **AttributeNotFoundException**: This is thrown if the specified attribute isn't defined on the MBean identified the object name.
- **InstanceNotFoundException**: This is thrown if the MBean specified the object name isn't registered with the MBean server.

- **ReflectionException**: This wraps any reflection exception caused in trying to invoke the attribute accessor.
- **RuntimeOperationsException**: This wraps an `IllegalARgumentException` if any of the arguments passed to this method is `null`.

The following snippet gets the name attribute of the offer MBean:

```
String offerName = (String)
  mbeanServer.getAttribute(mp3PlayerMBeanName, "name");
```

```
public void setAttribute(ObjectName name, Attribute attribute)
  throws MBeanException, AttributeNotFoundException,
  InstanceNotFoundException, ReflectionException,
  RuntimeOperationsException, InvalidAttributeValueException
```

The method sets the value of the attribute specified by the argument `attribute` on the MBean with the specified object name. The attribute should follow the standard JavaBeans property pattern. The class `javax.management.Attribute` encapsulates the name and value of an attribute. The method throws all the exceptions declared by the `getAttribute` method and in addition throws the `InvalidAttributeValueException` if the specified value doesn't match the type of the MBean attribute.

The following snippet sets the name attribute of the offer MBean:

```
mbeanServer.setAttribute(mp3PlayerMBeanName,
  new Attribute("name", "MP3 Player");
```

Instead of getting and setting attributes individually, you can perform bulk access and mutation of the MBean attributes using these methods:

```
AttributeList getAttributes(ObjectName name,
  String[] attributes)
```

The string array specifies the attribute names you want to get. The `AttributeList` class acts as an aggregation of `Attribute` instances. This class extends `ArrayList` to add strongly typed operations to manipulate the collection by adding and removing `Attribute` objects. The following snippet gets the name and description attributes for the offer MBean:

```
Iterator it = mbeanServer.getAttributes(mp3PlayerMBeanName,
  new String[] {"name", "description"};
while(it.hasNext()) {
  Attribute att = (Attribute)it.next();
  System.out.println(att.getName() + "::" att.getValue();
}
```

The class `Attribute` provides the methods `getName` and `getValue` to get the name and value of the attribute, respectively. You can set multiple attributes by calling the following methods:

```
public void setAttribute(ObjectNAme name,
  AttributeList attributes);
```

Now you'll look at the method to invoke MBean operations. You can use these methods to invoke operations on MBeans.

The following method invokes the operation specified the name and signature passing the arguments specified by the argument `params` to the MBean identified by the object name. This method throws `InstanceNotFoundException`, `MBeanException`, and `ReflectionException`:

```
public Object invoke(ObjectName name,
  String operationName, Object params[], String signature[])
```

The following snippet shows how the `bid` method on the offer MBean is invoked passing a double parameter specifying the bid value:

```
Double bidPrice = new Double(10);

Object params[] = new Object[] {bidPrice};
String signature[] = new String[] {Double.TYPE.getName()};
...........
...........
mbeanServer.invoke(mp3PlayerMBeanName, "bid",
  params, signature);
```

Notification

JMX allows MBeans to emit notifications that can be received by notification receivers. In this section, you'll briefly look at the methods provided by the `MBeanServer` interface for registering and removing notification listeners. We'll cover JMX notification in detail.

The following method adds the `NotificationListener` to the MBean identified by the object name:

```
void addNotificationListener(ObjectName name,
  NotificationListener listener, NotificationFilter filter,
  Object handback)
```

The MBean itself is required to implement the `NotificationBroadcaster` interface. The `NotificationFilter` interface specifies the types of notifications the listener is interested in, and `handback` is an opaque object that's passed back to the listener by the broadcaster as part of the notification. The listener can use this object to associate a context with the notification.

```
void addNotificationListener(ObjectName name, ObjectName
  listener, NotificationFilter filter, Object handback)
```

In this case, both the listener and broadcaster are MBeans registered with the MBean server. In this case, the MBean identified by the `listener` argument should implement the `NotificationListener` interface.

```
void removeNotificationListener(ObjectName name, NotificationListener listener)
void removeNotificationListener(ObjectName name,
NotificationListener listener,
NotificationFilter filter,
  Object handback)
void removeNotificationListener(ObjectName name, ObjectName
  listener)
void removeNotificationListener(ObjectName name, ObjectName
  listener, NotificationFilter filter, Object handback)
```

The previous methods remove the specified listener from the broadcaster.

Miscellaneous Methods

Table 16-2 describes some of the other methods defined in the `MBeanServer` interface.

Table 16-2. Other `MBeanServer` *Methods*

METHODS	DESCRIPTION
`String getDefaultDomain()`	Returns the default domain used for naming the MBean.
`String[] getDomains()`	Returns the list of domains in which any MBean is currently registered.
`Integer getMBeanCount()`	Returns the number of MBeans registered in the MBean server.
`ObjectInstance getObjectInstance(ObjectName name)`	Gets the `ObjectInstance` for a given MBean registered with the MBean server.
`boolean isRegistered(ObjectName name)`	Checks whether an MBean, identified by its object name, is already registered with the MBean server.
`MBeanInfo getMBeanInfo(ObjectName name)`	This method discovers the attributes and operations that an MBean exposes for management.

Auction Application: JMX Incarnation

In this chapter, you'll develop an application that will manage and monitor all the courses in the training application. In this section, you'll start the example by writing the framework for starting the MBean server and setting up a Hypertext Transfer Protocol (HTTP) adapter that can be used to manage and monitor the MBeans registered in the server through a browser window (see Listing 16-1).

For the example we'll be using the JMX Reference Implementation (RI) from Sun for writing the application. You can download this from `http://java.sun.com/products/JavaManagement`. The RI provides an HTTP adapter that itself is an MBean that can be registered with the MBean server.

NOTE *To run all the examples in this chapter you need to have the* `jmxri.jar` *and* `jmxtools.jar` *files in the* `lib` *directory of the exploded RI software bundle in the classpath.*

Listing 16-1. The Framework

```
package com.apress.projavaserver14.chapter19.server;
// Import the JMX classes and interfaces.
import javax.management.MBeanServer;
import javax.management.MBeanServerFactory;
import javax.management.MalformedObjectNameException;
import javax.management.Attribute;
import javax.management.ObjectName;
// Import the Sun JMX RI HTTP adapter.
import com.sun.jdmk.comm.HtmlAdaptorServer;

public class TrainingServer {

  public static void main(String[] args) throws Exception {
    // Create an MBean server instance.
    MBeanServer server =
      MBeanServerFactory.createMBeanServer();
    // Create an HTML adapter server instance.
    // This is implemented as a dynamic MBean.
    final HtmlAdaptorServer adaptorMBean =
      new HtmlAdaptorServer();
    // Create the object name under which the HTML
    // adapter MBean will be registered.
    ObjectName adaptorMBeanName =
      new ObjectName("Adaptor:name=html,port=8000");
    // Register the HTML adapter MBean.
    server.registerMBean(adaptorMBean, adaptorMBeanName);
    // Change the port number of the adapter
    // from the default value to 8000.
    server.setAttribute(adaptorMBeanName,
    new Attribute("Port", new Integer(8000)));
    // Start the adapter server.
    adaptorMBean.start();

    System.out.println("Auction server started");


  }

}
```

Now if you point the browser to the address `http://localhost:8000`, you'll get the page shown in Figure 16-2.

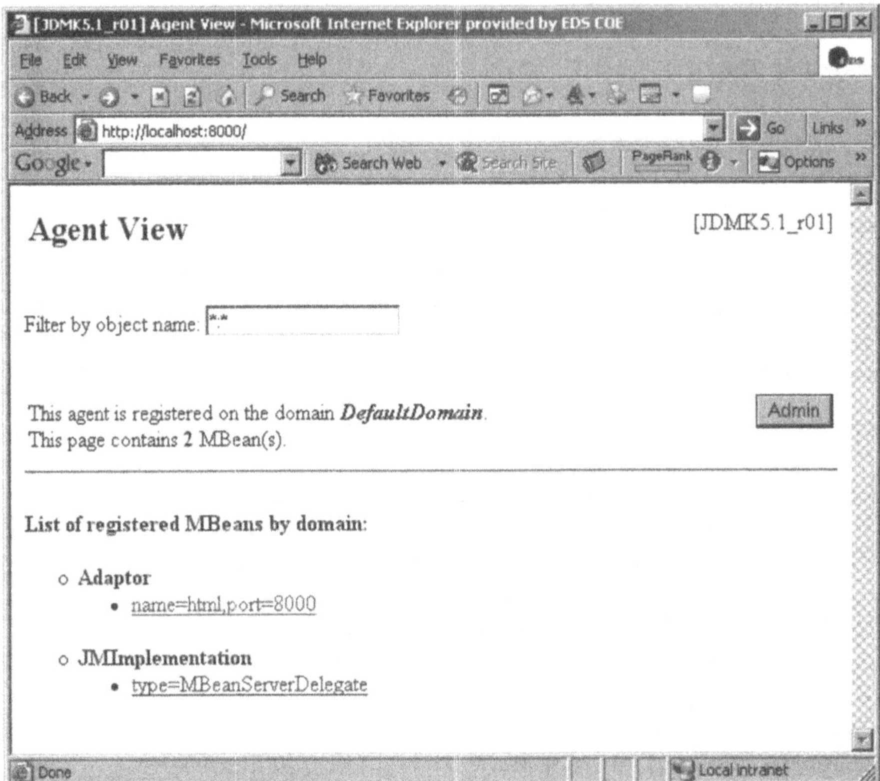

Figure 16-2. Agent view

The page allows you to filter the registered MBeans and by default displays all the MBeans. It also displays the default domain name as `DefaultDomain` and lists the two MBeans that are currently registered by displaying their object names as hyperlinks. The MBeans are grouped by their domain names. You can click them to go to the page to get/set the MBean attributes and invoke the operations. The first MBean is the HTML adapter you registered. If you click it, the page shown in Figure 16-3 will display.

Here you can read/write the HTML adapter MBean attributes and invoke the operations. You can stop the HTML adapter server by invoking the `stop` operation from the MBean view for the adapter MBean.

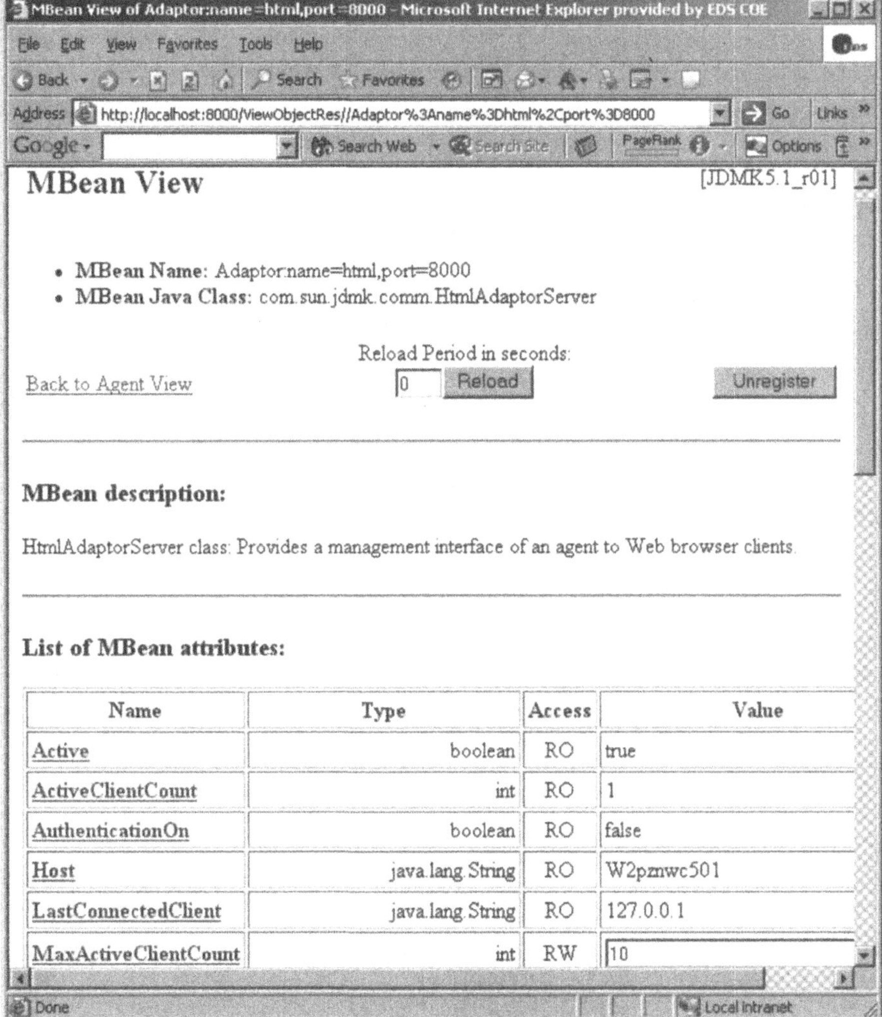

Figure 16-3. MBean view

The second MBean is registered with the name `JMImplementation:type=MBeanServerDelegate` whose management interface is `javax.management.MBeanServerDelegateMBean`. If you click the MBean, you'll get the page shown in Figure 16-4.

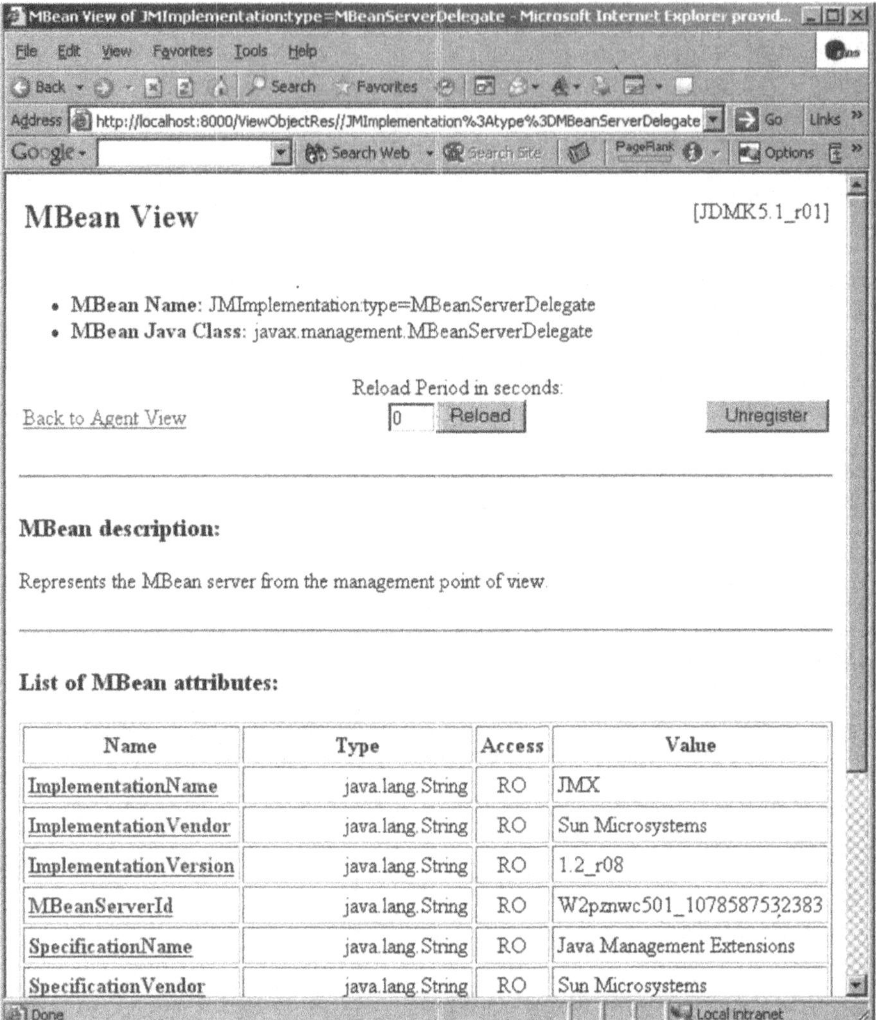

Figure 16-4. MBean attributes

This page displays agent properties such as server ID, implementation name, vendor name, specification name, and so on. The HTML adapter also allows you to create and remove MBeans by clicking the Admin button in the home page, as shown in Figure 16-5.

You need to specify the object name by specifying the domain name and one or more key-value pairs, the fully qualified name of the MBean class, and the optional object name of the classloader.

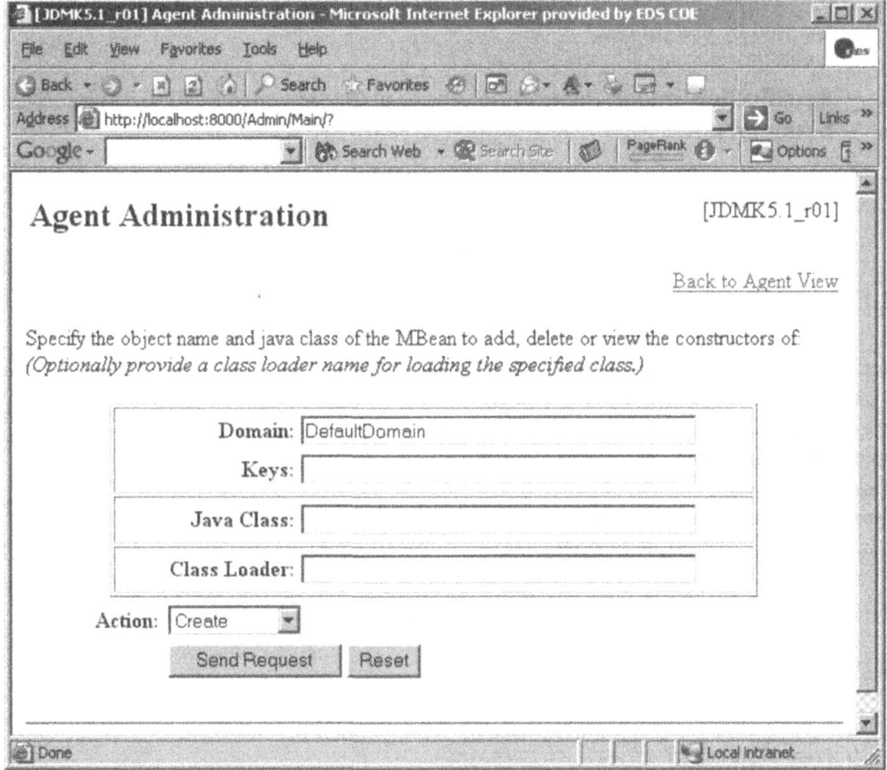

Figure 16-5. Agent administration

Agent Details

Before concluding the discussion of the MBean server, you'll write a small example to read the agent details using `MBeanServerDelegateMBean` (see Listing 16-2). This MBean should be registered with the object name `JMImplementation:type=MbeanServer-Delegate` by all vendors and should expose the following read-only properties:

- **ImplementationName**: Returns the JMX implementation name (the name of this product)
- **ImplementationVendor**: Returns the JMX implementation vendor (the vendor of this product)
- **ImplementationVersion**: Returns the JMX implementation version (the version of this product)
- **MBeanServerId**: Returns the MBean server agent identity

- **SpecificationName**: Returns the full name of the JMX specification implemented by this product
- **SpecificationVendor**: Returns the vendor of the JMX specification implemented by this product
- **SpecificationVersion**: Returns the version of the JMX specification implemented by this product

Listing 16-2. AgentDetails

```
package com.apress.projavaserver14.chapter19.server;
// Import the JMX classes and interfaces.
import javax.management.MBeanServer;
import javax.management.MBeanServerFactory;
import javax.management.Attribute;
import javax.management.AttributeList;
import javax.management.ObjectName;

import java.util.Iterator;

public class AgentDetails {

  public static void main(String[] args) throws Exception {
    // Create the MBean server.
    MBeanServer server =
      MBeanServerFactory.createMBeanServer();
    // Create the object name for the delegate MBean.
    ObjectName delegateMBeanName = new
      ObjectName("JMImplementation:type=MBeanServerDelegate");
    // Get the attributes specified the delegate
    // MBean's management interface.
    AttributeList attribs =
      server.getAttributes(delegateMBeanName,
        new String[] {
          "ImplementationName",
          "ImplementationVendor",
          "ImplementationVersion",
         "MBeanServerId",
          "SpecificationName",
          "SpecificationVendor",
          "SpecificationVersion"
      });
    // Iterate through the attributes and
    // print the name and value.
    Iterator it = attribs.iterator();
    while(it.hasNext()) {
        Attribute att = (Attribute)it.next();
        System.out.println(att.getName() + ":" +
```

```
            att.getValue());
        }

    }

}
```

Running the class in Listing 16-2 will produce the following output:

```
ImplementationName:JMX
ImplementationVendor:Sun Microsystems
ImplementationVersion:1.2_r08
MBeanServerId:meeraj_1041798298466
SpecificationName:Java Management Extensions
SpecificationVendor:Sun Microsystems
SpecificationVersion:1.2 Maintenance Release
```

Instrumentation Level

So far, you've been looking at the agent level in detail. In the following sections, you'll look at another important level in the JMX architecture, instrumentation level. Instrumentation level is responsible for making the management interface of the managed resource to the agent level. The management interface exposes the attributes that can be read and written on the managed resource as well as the operations that can be invoked. For example, to expose an offer as a managed resource, you may want to expose the attribute's ID, name, description, and asking price for the offer and an operation to send a bid for the offer.

JMX specification provides four different ways of instrumenting the management interface.

Standard MBeans

A standard MBean explicitly defines a management interface in order to be manageable. The management interface is defined as a Java interface that provides accessors and mutators to the attributes and defines operations to the resource that's managed. The managed resource is required to implement the management interface using the `implements` keyword. The management interface and the instrumenting class are required to comply with a set of design patterns that provide the following information to the hosting agent:

- The public constructors available for the instrumenting class
- The read-only and read-write attributes that are available
- The operations that are exposed by the instrumenting class
- The notifications that are broadcast

Naming and Implementing the MBean Interface

The management interface should be defined as a public Java interface, and its name should be the name of the instrumenting class followed by the string `MBean`. For example, if the instrumenting class is called `Offer`, the management interface should be called `OfferMBean`. Hence, the management interface for the offer would look like this:

```
public interface OfferMBean {
  ........
}
```

The instrumenting class should implement the management interface using the Java implements keyword as follows:

```
public class Offer implements OfferMBean {
  ........
}
```

> **NOTE** *Only those methods and attributes exposed by the management interface are accessible through the agent level.*

Public Constructors

The instrumenting class is required to have at least one public constructor; however, the constructor doesn't need to be a no-argument constructor. The class can have any number of public constructors. For example:

```
public class Offer implements OfferMBean {

  public Offer(int id, String name, String description) {
  ........
  }

}
```

Attribute Accessors and Mutators

The accessors and mutators for attributes should follow the JavaBeans naming pattern. You can have read-only attributes with only accessors defined and read-write attributes with accessors and mutators. For example:

```
public interface OfferMBean {

  public int getId();
```

```
  public String getName();
  public void setName(String newName);
  ........

}
```

Defining and Instrumenting the Offer MBean

Now that you know how to write a standard MBean, you'll learn how to define and instrument a course as an MBean. Listing 16-3 shows the management interface for the course MBean.

Listing 16-3. `OfferMBean`

```
package com.apress.projavaserver14.chapter19.mbean.standard;

public interface OfferMBean {

    public int getId();

    public String getName();
    public void setName(String newName);

    public String getDescription();
    public void setDescription(String newDescription);

    public double getAskPrice();

    public void bid(double bidPrice);

}
```

The management defines the read-only attributes `id` and `askPrice`, representing the ID of the offer and the asking price, respectively; read-write attributes `name` and `description`, representing the name and description for the offer, respectively; and an operation `bid` that accepts a double specifying the bid price. Listing 16-4 shows the standard MBean instrumentation class.

Listing 16-4. `Offer`

```
package com.apress.projavaserver14.chapter19.mbean.standard;

public class Offer implements OfferMBean {

  private int id;

  private String name;
```

```
  private String description;

  private double askPrice;

  public Offer(int newId, String newName,
    String newDescription) {

    id = newId;
    name = newName;
    description = newDescription;

  }

  public int getId() { return id; }

  public String getName() { return name; }
  public void setName(String newName) { name = newName; }

  public String getDescription() { return description; }
  public void setDescription(String newDescription) {
      description = newDescription;
  }

  public double getAskPrice() { return askPrice; }

  public void bid(double bidPrice) {
      System.out.println("Bid received:" + bidPrice);
  }

}
```

The instrumentation class implements the management interface. Now you'll look at how to register an instance of this MBean with the MBean server. For this you need to add the following code to the `TrainingServer` class after creating the MBean server:

```
Offer offerMBean = new Offer(1, "MP3 Player",
  "256 Mb MP3 Player");
ObjectName mp3PlayerMBeanName = new ObjectName(
  "AuctionApplication:type=Course,name=MP3
    Player,mBeanType=standard");

server.registerMBean(offerMBean, mp3PlayerMBeanName);
```

The previous code creates an instance of the `Offer` class and registers it with the MBean server by the object name `AuctionApplication:type=Offer,Name=MP3 Player,mBeanType=standard`.

NOTE *Please note that you can have any key-value pair you like as long as the object name is valid and unique. For example, you can call the previous MBean by the object name* `BuffaloClub:firstName=Fred,secondName=Flintstone`.

Now if you access the HTML adapter server, the offer MBean will be listed as shown in Figure 16-6.

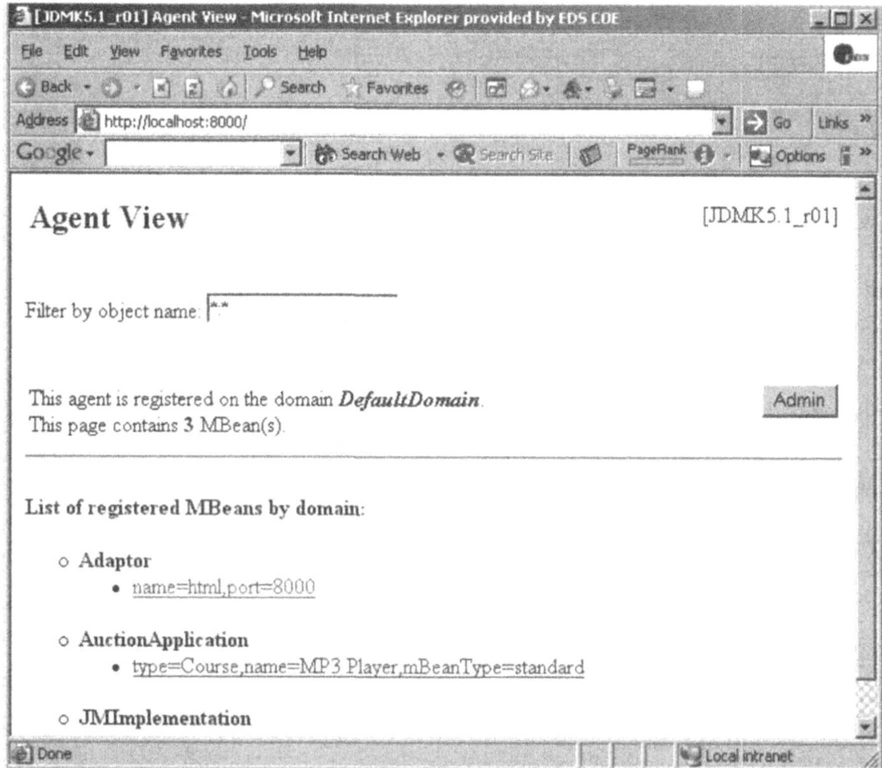

Figure 16-6. Agent view

If you click the hyperlink for the MBean, you'll be able to access the page for accessing the MBean attributes and operations, as shown in Figure 16-7.

If you enter a value for the `bid` method and click the button, you'll get the screen shown in Figure 16-8, and the message will be displayed in the command prompt running the MBean server.

MBean View of AuctionApplication:type=Course,name=MP3 Player,mBeanType=standard - Microsoft In...
http://localhost:8000/ViewObjectRes//AuctionApplication%3Atype%3DCourse%2Cname%3DMP3
List of MBean attributes:
Name
Type
Access
Value
AskPrice
double
RO
0.0
Description
java.lang.String
RW
256 Mb MP3 Player
Id
int
RO
1
Name
java.lang.String
RW
MP3 Player
Apply
List of MBean operations:
Description of bid
void bid (double)p1
Done
Local intranet

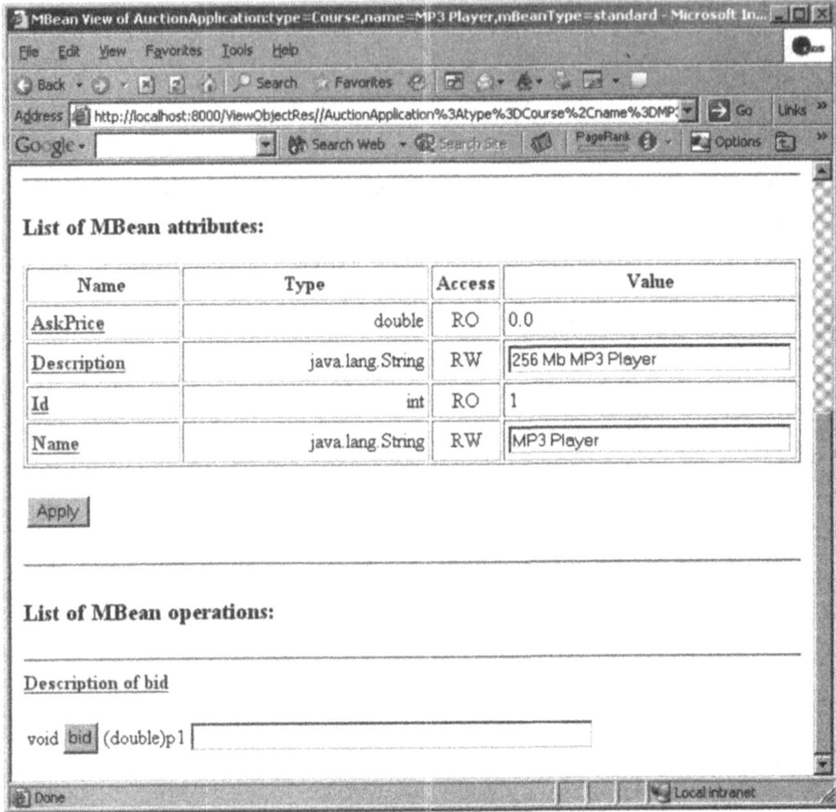

Figure 16-7. MBean attributes and operations

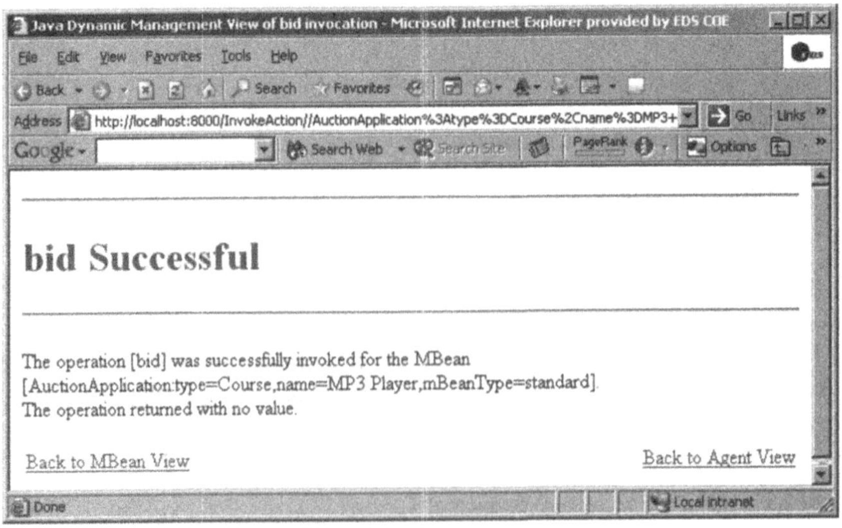

Java Dynamic Management View of bid invocation - Microsoft Internet Explorer provided by EDS COE
http://localhost:8000/InvokeAction//AuctionApplication%3Atype%3DCourse%2Cname%3DMP3+
bid Successful
The operation [bid] was successfully invoked for the MBean
[AuctionApplication:type=Course,name=MP3 Player,mBeanType=standard].
The operation returned with no value.
Back to MBean View
Back to Agent View
Done
Local intranet

Figure 16-8. Result of invoking the method

Standard MBeans and Inheritance

In the following sections, you'll briefly look at how management interfaces can be inherited, which is subtly different from Java inheritance.

Case #1

Suppose you have a management interface XMBean with an instrumenting class X, as shown in Figure 16-9. Listing 16-5 shows the code.

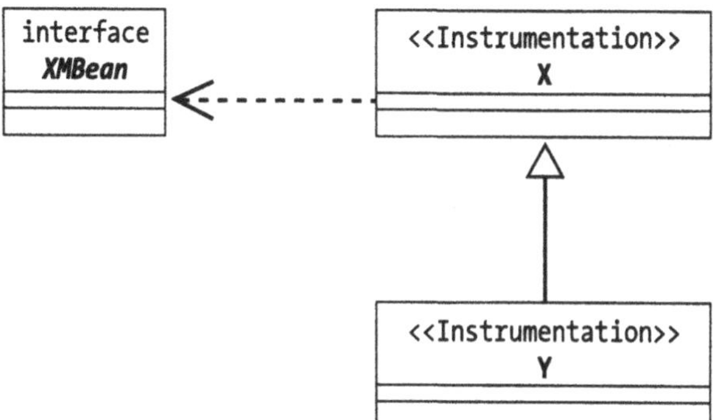

Figure 16-9. MBean inheritance 1

Listing 16-5. MBean Inheritance 1

```
public interface XMBean {
  ........
}

public class X implements XMBean {
  ........
}
```

Now if you have a class Y that extends X as follows:

```
public class Y extends X {
  ........
}
```

then the management interface for Y as interpreted by the MBean server is XMBean.

Case 2

Suppose you have a management interface YMBean that's implemented by the instrumentation class Y, and Y extends the class X as shown in Figure 16-10. Listing 16-6 shows the code.

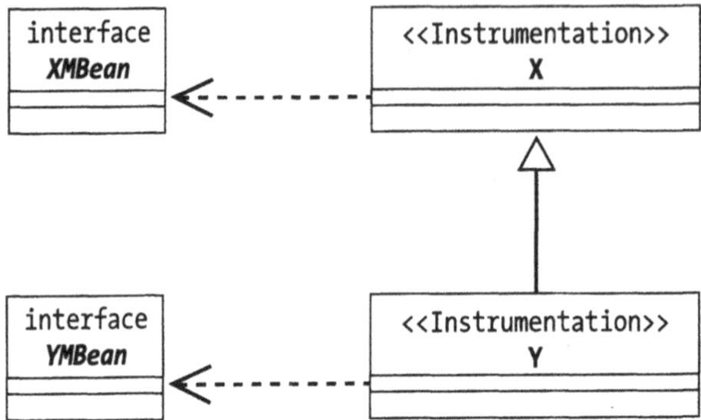

Figure 16-10. MBean inheritance 2

Listing 16-6. MBean Inheritance 2

```
public interface YMBean {
  ........
}

public class Y extends X {
  ........
}
```

Here, even though Y extends X, and X implements the interface XMBean, the management interface for Y includes only those attributes and operations defined in YMBean and none in XMBean.

Case 3

Suppose YMBean extends XMBean. Now the management interface of Y includes all the attributes and operations defined by the interfaces XMBean and YMBean, as shown in Figure 16-11. Listing 16-7 shows the code.

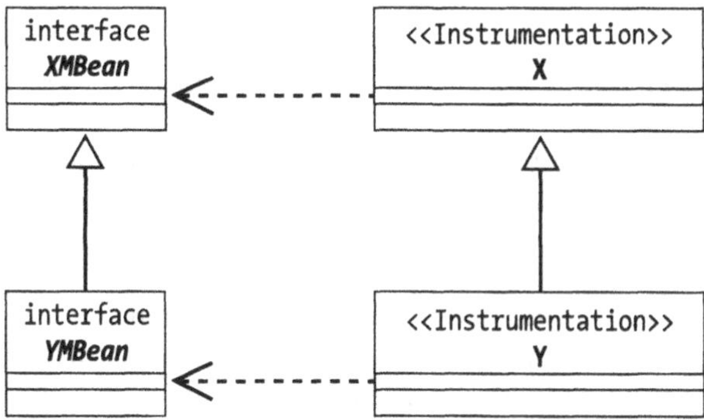

Figure 16-11. MBean inheritance 3

Listing 16-7. MBean Inheritance 3

```
public interface YMBean extends XMBean {
  ........
}
```

Case 4

Now if Y doesn't extend X and implement YMBean, which in turn extends XMBean, the management interface of Y includes all the attributes and operations defined by the interfaces XMBean and YMBean, as shown in Figure 16-12. The only difference from the "Case 3" section is that with Case 3 Y doesn't need to explicitly implement the methods defined in XMBean as X implements them.

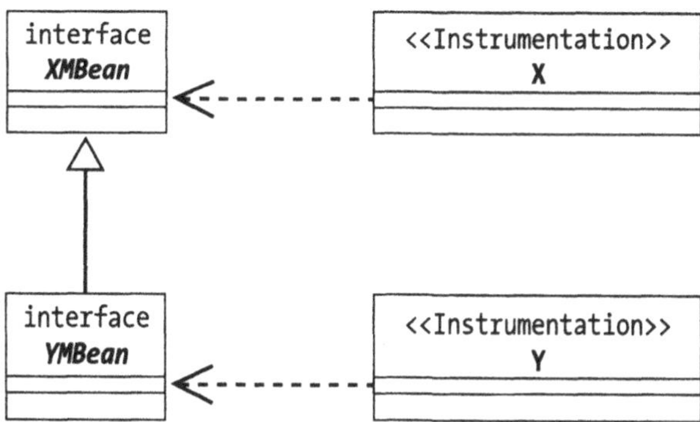

Figure 16-12. MBean inheritance 4

Dynamic MBeans

Standard MBeans are useful where the structure of the managed resources is known beforehand and is pretty straightforward. However, if the data structures are expected to evolve, dynamic MBeans provide the flexibility to instrument them. Unlike standard MBeans that define their management interface statically, dynamic MBeans provide information about the attributes, constructors, operations, and notifications using metadata classes.

Dynamic MBean instrumentation classes are required to implement the `javax.management.DynamicMBean` interface. Dynamic MBeans aren't supposed to follow the design patterns discussed for standard MBeans. This interface defines the following methods.

Specifically, the following methods are similar to the methods with the same name defined in the `MBeanServer` interface. The instrumentation class should provide implementations for these methods so that the agent can dynamically get/set attributes and invoke operations:

```
public Object getAttribute(String attribute)
public AttributeList getAttributes(String[] attributes)
public void setAttribute(Attribute attribute)
public void setAttributes(AttributeList attributes)
public Object invoke(String name, Object params[],

  String signature[])
```

This is the class that provides the metadata information about the MBean's management interface to the agent:

```
public MBeanInfo getMBeanInfo()
```

This class provides the following information about the instrumentation class:

- Constructors
- Operations
- Parameters that are passed to constructors and operations
- Attributes
- Notifications

The MBeanInfo class comprises five other classes to provide this information, as shown in Figure 16-13.

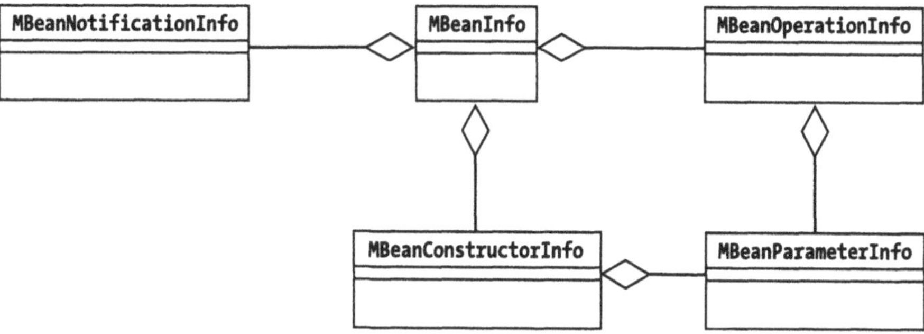

Figure 16-13. Dynamic MBean classes and interfaces

MBeanParameterInfo

This class represents an argument that's passed to an MBean constructor or operation. The class provides the following constructor:

```
public MBeanParameterInfo(String name, String type,
  String description)
```

For reference types that aren't arrays, the type should match the fully qualified class name. For example, you'd construct the name parameter for the course as follows:

```
MBeanParameterInfo nameParam = new MBeanParameterInfo("name",
  "java.lang.String", "The name of the item");
```

For primitive types, you should use the getName() function on the static variable TYPE of java.lang.Class defined on the corresponding wrapper type. The following snippet shows how to represent a Java int:

```
MBeanParameterInfo askPriceParam = new
  MBeanParameterInfo("askPrice", Double.TYPE.getName(),
    "Ask price for the item");
```

For single-dimensional arrays of reference types, the format is [L<<class name>>;. For multi-dimensional arrays the number of left square brackets should match that of the dimension of the array. For example, a two-dimensional string array is represented as [[Ljava.lang.String;.

Table 16-3 shows the types for single-dimensional primitive arrays.

Table 16-3. Primitive Array Types

PRIMITIVE	ARRAY TYPE
boolean[]	[Z
byte[]	[B
char[]	[C
short[]	[S
int[]	[I
long[]	[J
float[]	[F
double[]	[D

MBeanConstructorInfo

This class represents a constructor that's available for the MBean. The class provides the following two constructors:

```
MBeanConstructorInfo(String description,
  Constructor constructor)
```

In this case, the class is instantiated by passing the constructor object, which can be retrieved, from the instrumentation class using reflection. The class provides the following two constructors:

```
MBeanConstructorInfo(String name, String description,
  MBeanParameterInfo[] signature)
```

In this case, the constructor is created by specifying the name, description, and an array for objects representing the ordered list constructor parameters. The good thing about this constructor is that you can specify descriptions for individual parameters that can be visible from the management application. Listing 16-8 shows how to construct the constructor for the offer MBean.

Listing 16-8. Creating `MBeanConstructorInfo`

```
MBeanConstructorInfo con = new MBeanConstructorInfo(
  "Offer",
  "Creates a new Offer",
  new MBeanParameterInfo[] {
    new MBeanParameterInfo(
      "newId",
      Integer.TYPE.getName(),
      "Offer ID"
    ),
```

```
    new MBeanParameterInfo(
      "newName",
      "java.lang.String",
      "Offer Name"
    ),
    new MBeanParameterInfo(
      "newDescription",
      "java.lang.String",
      "Offer Description")
  }
);
```

MBeanOperationInfo

This class represents a single operation that's exposed by the MBean. The class provides the following constructors:

```
MBeanOperationInfo(String description, Method method)
```

This is similar to the corresponding constructor for `MBeanConstructorInfo`. The `java.lang.reflect.Method` for the MBean operation instantiates an instance of the class:

```
MBeanOperationInfo(String name, String description,
  MBeanParameterInfo[] signature, String type, int impact)
```

Here the method signature is specified by the name and an ordered list of `MBeanParameterInfo` objects representing the method parameters. The `type` parameter specifies the type of the operation's return value. The impact argument is specified using one of the following four enumerated variables present in the `MBeanParameterInfo` class:

- **INFO**: This means the state of the MBean remains unchanged after invoking the operation.
- **ACTION**: The state of the MBean will be changed in some way.
- **ACTION_INFO**: The operation will return some information about the MBean as well as change the state.
- **UNKNOWN**: The impact is unknown.

Listing 16-9 shows how an `MBeanParameterInfo` instance is created for the bid method.

Listing 16-9. Creating `MBeanParameterInfo`

```
MBeanParameterInfo bidInfo = new MBeanParameterInfo(
  "bid",
  new MBeanParameterInfo[] {
    new MBeanParameterInfo(
      "askPrice",
      Integer.TYPE.getName(),
      "Ask Price"
    )
  },
  Void.TYPE.getName(),
  MBeanParameterInfo.INFO
);
```

MBeanAttributeInfo

This represents a single attribute for the MBean. The class provides the following constructors:

```
MBeanAttributeInfo(String name, String description,
  Method getter, Method setter)
```

The constructor initializes the name, description, and accessor/mutator methods for the attributes:

```
MBeanAttributeInfo(String name, String type,
  String description, boolean isReadable,
    boolean isWritable, boolean isIs)
```

This constructor allows you to specify the name, type, description, and whether the attribute is readable, writable, and whether the accessor name starts with string is if the type is a Boolean. This method assumes the accessor and mutator follows the standard Java beans design pattern.

The following snippet shows how to construct the description attribute for the course MBean:

```
MBeanAttributeInfo descriptionInfo =
  new MBeanAttributeInfo("description", "Offer description",
    true, true, false);
```

MBeanNotificationInfo

This class represents the notifications broadcasted by the MBean. We'll cover MBean notifications in the "Notification" section.

MBeanInfo

Now that you've seen all the classes that comprise MBeanInfo, you'll look at how to construct the MBeanInfo instance itself. The class provides a single constructor that has the following signature to pass information about the constructors, attributes, operations, and notifications:

```
MBeanInfo(String className, String description,
  MBeanAttributeInfo[] attributes, MBeanConstructorInfo[]
    constructors, MBeanOperationInfo[] operations,
      MBeanNotificationInfo[] notifications)
```

The constructor also expects the fully qualified class name of the instrumenting class and a description.

Offer Dynamic MBean

Now that you've looked at instrumenting dynamic MBeans, you'll rewrite the course MBean as a dynamic MBean. You'll first write a utility class that will create the required metadata information for the dynamic course MBean,

The OfferMBeanHelper.java class provides metadata information regarding the attributes, constructors, operations, and notifications for the MBean, as shown in Listing 16-10.

Listing 16-10. OfferMBeanHelper.java

```
package com.apress.projavaserver14.chapter19.mbean.dynamic;

import javax.management.MBeanAttributeInfo;
import javax.management.MBeanConstructorInfo;
import javax.management.MBeanParameterInfo;
import javax.management.MBeanInfo;
import javax.management.MBeanNotificationInfo;
import javax.management.MBeanOperationInfo;

public class OfferMBeanHelper {
/* This method constructs the metadata information for the MBean attributes.
You have two read-only attributes, id and noOfStudents, and two read-write
attributes, name and description. Please note that unlike standard MBeans,
now you can specify description for each attribute that can be accessed from
the management applications. Similarly you can specify descriptions for methods,
constructors, parameters, and notifications as well as for the MBean itself. */
  private static MBeanAttributeInfo[] getAttributeInfo() {

    return new MBeanAttributeInfo[] {
      new MBeanAttributeInfo("id", Integer.TYPE.getName(),
        "Offer Id", true, false, false),
      new MBeanAttributeInfo("name", "java.lang.String",
```

```
        "Offer Name", true, true, false),
      new MBeanAttributeInfo("description",
        "java.lang.String",
        "Offer Description", true, true, false),
      new MBeanAttributeInfo("noOfStudents",
        Double.TYPE.getName(),
        "Ask Price", true, false, false)
    };

  }
/* This methods provides information about the only constructor that
takes id, name and description as arguments. */
  private static MBeanConstructorInfo[] getConstructorInfo() {

    return new MBeanConstructorInfo[] {
      new MBeanConstructorInfo("Offer", "Creates an offer",
        new MBeanParameterInfo[] {
          new MBeanParameterInfo("newId",
          Integer.TYPE.getName(),
          "Offer Id"),
          new MBeanParameterInfo("newName",
            "java.lamg.String",
            "Offer Name"),
          new MBeanParameterInfo("newDescription",
            "java.lamg.String",
            "Offer Description")
        }
      )
    };

  }
/* This method creates the metadata for the sendAssignmentReminder
operation that accepts an int and returns void. */
  private static MBeanOperationInfo[] getOperationInfo() {

    return new MBeanOperationInfo[] {
      new MBeanOperationInfo("bid",
        "Bids for the offer",
        new MBeanParameterInfo[] {
          new MBeanParameterInfo("bidPrice",
          Double.TYPE.getName(),
          "Bid price")
        },
        Void.TYPE.getName(),
        MBeanOperationInfo.INFO
      )
    };

  }
/* This method creates the notifications broadcasted by the dynamic
MBean. Currently our MBean doesn't broadcast any notifications. */
```

```
  private static MBeanNotificationInfo[]
    getNotificationInfo() {
    return new MBeanNotificationInfo[0];
  }
/* The method aggregates all the metadata information into an
MBeanInfo instance. */
  public static MBeanInfo getMBeanInfo() {

    return new MBeanInfo(
      "com.apress.projavaserver14.chapter19.mbean.
        dynamic.Offer",
      "Dynamic offer MBean",
      getAttributeInfo(),
      getConstructorInfo(),
      getOperationInfo(),
      getNotificationInfo()
    ) ;

  }

}
```

Now you'll look at the dynamic offer MBean class. This class implements the DynamicMBean interface, as shown in Listing 16-11.

Listing 16-11. `Offer.java`

```
package com.apress.projavaserver14.chapter19.mbean.dynamic;

import javax.management.DynamicMBean;

import javax.management.AttributeNotFoundException;
import javax.management.MBeanException;
import javax.management.ReflectionException;
import javax.management.InvalidAttributeValueException;
import javax.management.RuntimeOperationsException;

import javax.management.AttributeList;
import javax.management.MBeanInfo;
import javax.management.Attribute;

import java.util.Iterator;

public class Offer implements DynamicMBean {
/*These are the MBean attributes. You don't need to have them as separate
instance variables. You can choose any data structure to store the state of
the MBean as long as you can get and set the state for each attribute from the
corresponding DynamicMBean callback methods.*/
  private int id;
  private String name;
```

```
  private String description;
  private double askPrice;
/*The constructor initializes the MBean with id, name and description.
With dynamic MBeans operations, attributes and constructors are defined as
metadata. Hence it is entirely up to the developers how they choose to
implement the attributes and operations as long the instrumenting class can
take an appropriate action when the agent tries to get\set attributes or
invoke operations through the callback methods defined on the DynamicMBean
interface. This means the class doesn't need to have attributes and operations
corresponding to those specified by the metadata according to Java language
semantics. However the class should have the constructor defined by the
metadata.*/
  public Course(int newId, String newName,
    String newDescription) {

    id = newId;
    name = newName;
    description = newDescription;

  }
/* The agent to get the MBean metadata calls this method defined
in the DynamicMBean interface. */
  public MBeanInfo getMBeanInfo() {
    return CourseMBeanHelper.getMBeanInfo();
  }
/* The agent to get an MBean attribute calls this method defined
in the DynamicMBean interface. */
  public Object getAttribute(String attribute) throws MBeanException,
  AttributeNotFoundException, ReflectionException {
/* If the attribute is null throw an IllegalARgumentException wrapped in a
RuntimeOperationException. This is a standard JMX practice. */
    if (attribute == null)
      throw new RuntimeOperationsException(
      new IllegalArgumentException("Attribute name " +
        "cannot be null"));
// Return the value of the requested attribute.
    if (attribute.equals("id"))
      return new Integer(id);
    else if (attribute.equals("name"))
      return name;
    else if (attribute.equals("description"))
      return description;
    else if (attribute.equals("askPrice"))
      return new Double(askPrice);
/* If the request attribute is not found, throw an exception. */
    throw new AttributeNotFoundException("Cannot find " +
      attribute);

  }
/* The agent to get an MBean attribute calls this method defined in
the DynamicMBean interface. */
```

```
  public void setAttribute(Attribute attribute) throws MBeanException,
  AttributeNotFoundException, InvalidAttributeValueException,
  ReflectionException {

    if(attribute == null) {
      throw new RuntimeOperationsException(
      new IllegalArgumentException(
        "Attribute cannot be null"));
    }
// Get the attribute name and value.
    String name = attribute.getName();
    Object value = attribute.getValue();

    if (name == null) {
      throw new RuntimeOperationsException(
      new IllegalArgumentException(
        "Attribute name cannot be null"));
    }

    try {
// The only two mutable attributes are name and description.
      if (name.equals("name"))
        name = (String)value;
      else if (name.equals("description"))
        description = (String)value;
      else
        throw new AttributeNotFoundException(
          "Attribute not found " + name);
    }catch(ClassCastException ex) {
// If the passed value is not a string, throw an exception.
      throw new InvalidAttributeValueException(
        "Invalid value for " + name);
    }

  }
// This method returns a collection of attributes.
  public AttributeList getAttributes(String[] attributeNames) {

    if (attributeNames == null)
      throw new RuntimeOperationsException(
        new IllegalArgumentException(
          "attributeNames[] cannot be null"));

    AttributeList resultList = new AttributeList();

    if (attributeNames.length == 0)
      return resultList;

    for(int i=0 ;i<attributeNames.length ;i++){
      try {
        Object value =
```

```
          getAttribute((String)attributeNames[i]);
        resultList.add(new
          Attribute(attributeNames[i],value));
      } catch (Exception e) {
        e.printStackTrace();
      }
    }

    return resultList;

  }
// This method sets a collection of attributes.
  public AttributeList setAttributes(
  AttributeList attributes) {

    if (attributes == null)
      throw new RuntimeOperationsException(
      new IllegalArgumentException(
        "attributeNames[] cannot be null"));

    AttributeList resultList = new AttributeList();

    if (attributes.isEmpty()) return resultList;

    for (Iterator i = attributes.iterator(); i.hasNext();) {

      Attribute attr = (Attribute) i.next();
      try {
        setAttribute(attr);
        String name = attr.getName();
        Object value = getAttribute(name);
        resultList.add(new Attribute(name,value));
      } catch(Exception e) {
        e.printStackTrace();
      }

    }

    return resultList;

  }
/* The agent calls this method when the management application
tries to invoke an MBean operation. */
  public Object invoke(String operationName, Object params[],
    String signature[]) throws MBeanException,
      ReflectionException {

    If (operationName == null) {
      throw new RuntimeOperationsException(
      new IllegalArgumentException(
        "Operation name cannot be null"));
    }
```

```
/* If the operation name is sendAssignmentReminder, print the value
of the only argument. */
    if (operationName.equals("bid")){
      System.out.println("Bid price:" + params[0]);
      return null;
    } else
// Throw an exception if the operation is not recognized.
      throw new ReflectionException(
        new NoSuchMethodException(operationName));

  }

}
```

If you register the previous MBean with an MBean server with the JMX RI, you'll get the MBean view with HTML adapter that's shown in Figure 16-14.

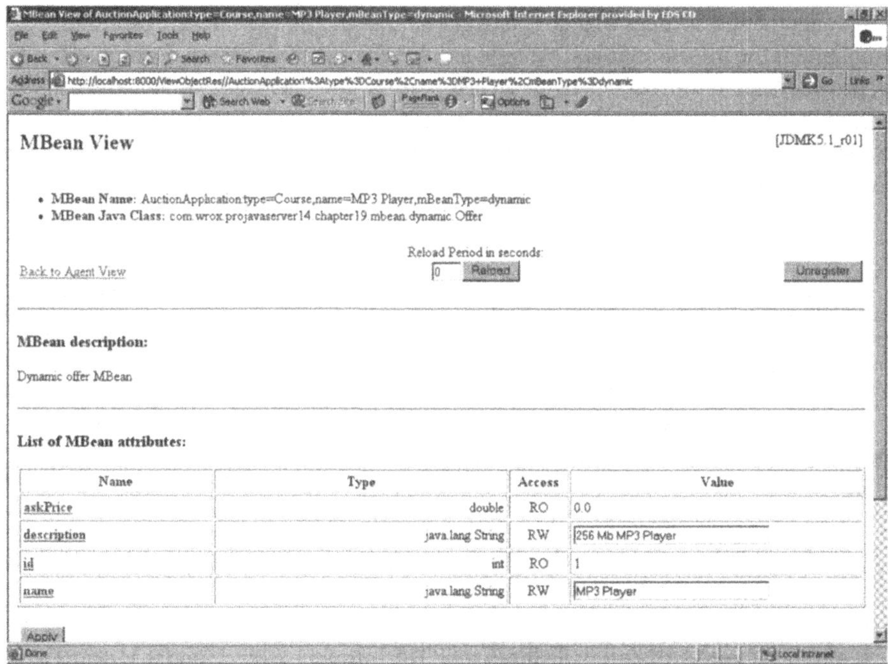

Figure 16-14. Agent view

You can click the hyperlinks for attributes, operations, and parameters to get the description. For example, if you click the Description hyperlink, you'll get the pop-up window shown in Figure 16-15.

Figure 16-15. MBean view

Model MBeans

Model MBeans provide the most powerful way of instrumenting manageable resources. Model MBeans are dynamic MBeans in the sense that they provide metadata classes to expose the various manageable aspects of the resources, such as attributes, operations, constructors, and notifications. However, they also provide additional features to configure the runtime behavior of the MBeans in a declarative manner.

Management resources that are instrumented as model MBeans are required to implement the interface `javax.management.modelmbean.ModelMBean`. Compliant JMX providers are required to provide a class named `javax.management.modelmbean.RequiredModelMBean` that implements the `ModelMBean` interface. Instrumentation providers can use this class as an easy-to-use template for instrumenting managed resources as model MBeans.

> **NOTE** *An exhaustive coverage of model MBeans is beyond the scope of this chapter and the book. This section provides an overview of model MBeans.*

The classes that instrument managed resources as model MBeans are required to implement the `ModelMBean` interface. This interface in turn extends the following interfaces:

- **DynamicMBean**: This interface defines methods for exposing the management interface using a set of metadata classes.
- **ModelMBeanNotificationBroadcaster**: The interface allows model MBeans to send automatic notifications on attribute changes.
- **PersistentMBean**: This interface defines methods for persisting the state of the model MBean.

Like dynamic MBeans, model MBeans also provide information about the management interface of the resource using a set of metadata classes. The only difference is that dynamic MBeans expose the management information using the `MBeanInfo` class; model MBeans use the `ModelMBeanInfo` interface. The JMX specification provides a class `ModelMBeanInfoSupport` that implements this interface. The interface uses the following classes to describe the management information of the resource:

- **ModelMBeanConstructorInfo**: This class provides information about the constructors provided by the model MBean and extends the dynamic MBean counterpart `MBeanConstructorInfo`.
- **ModelMBeanAttribuiteInfo**: This class provides information about the attributes provided by the model MBean and extends the dynamic MBean counterpart `MBeanAttributeInfo`.
- **ModelMBeanOperationInfo**: This class provides information about the operations provided by the model MBean and extends the dynamic MBean counterpart `MBeanOperationInfo`.
- **ModelMBeanNotificationInfo**: This class provides information about the notifications provided by the model MBean and extends the dynamic MBean counterpart `MBeanNotificationInfo`.
- **MBeanParameterInfo**: Similar to dynamic MBeans, this class describes the parameters that are passed to the MBean constructors and operations.

Figure 16-16 shows the model MBean metadata classes.

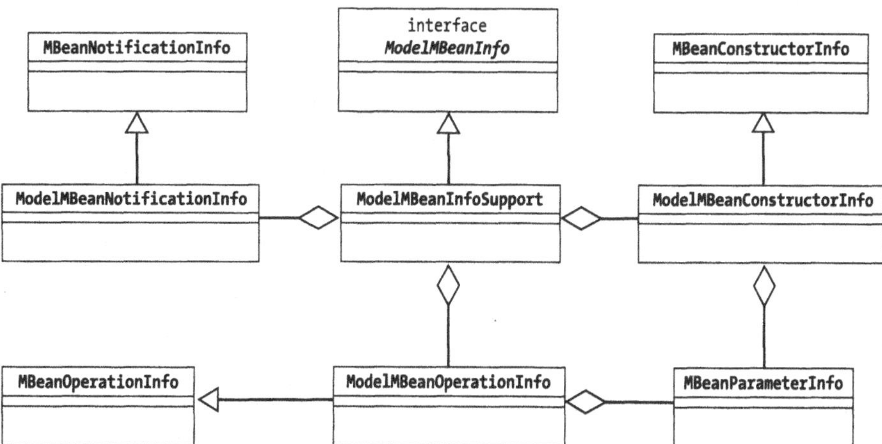

Figure 16-16. Model MBean classes and interfaces

From what you've seen so far, model MBeans aren't dramatically different from normal dynamic MBeans apart from the facts that they provide state persistence and automatic attribute change notification. Then what makes them such a special breed of instrumentation mechanism? You'll look at that next.

Descriptors

Each of the model MBean–specific metadata classes uses a descriptor that can configure the runtime behavior of the instrumenting class. A *descriptor* is basically a set of key-value pairs. You can associate descriptors with `ModelMBeanInfo`, `ModelMBeanNotificationInfo`, `ModelMBeanOperationInfo`, `ModelMBeanAttributeInfo`, and `ModelMBeanConstructorInfo` classes.

The key-value pairs stored in the descriptor can control a variety of runtime behavior, such as the following:

- Mapping attribute getter/setter to a different method on the managed resource. The `ModelMBean` interface defines the `setManagedResource(Object resource, String type)` method to register a managed resource with the instrumenting class; using the descriptor, you can map the getter/setter of an attribute that's exposed using the metadata classes to an actual method on the managed resource.
- Setting state persistence policies
- Setting caching policies for MBean attributes and operation results
- Setting logging policies, and so on

The descriptor is represented by the interface `javax.management.Descriptor`, which defines the methods in Table 16-4.

Table 16-4. Descriptor Methods

METHOD	DESCRIPTION
`Object clone()`	Returns a new descriptor, which is a duplicate of this descriptor.
`String[] getFieldNames()`	Returns all the fields names in the descriptor.
`String[] getFields()`	Returns all of the fields contained in this descriptor as a string array
`Object getFieldValue(String fieldName)`	Returns the value for a specific field name
`Object[] getFieldValues(String[] fieldNames)`	Returns all the field values in the descriptor as an array of objects
`boolean isValid()`	Returns `true` if all of the fields have legal values given their names
`void removeField(String fieldName)`	Removes a field from the descriptor
`void setField(String fieldName, Object fieldValue)`	Sets the value for a specific field name
`void setFields(String[] fieldNames, Object[] fieldValues)`	Sets all fields in the list to the new value with the same index in the `fieldValues` array

The JMX specification provides the DescriptorSupport class that implements interface. The model MBean metadata classes provide constructors that take a Descriptor instance as one of the arguments. This instance can configure the runtime behavior of the operation, attribute, constructor, notification, or the MBean itself to which the descriptor is associated. Further, these classes implement the DescriptorAccess interface that provides the following methods for accessing the descriptor associated with the metadata:

```
public Descriptor getDescriptor()
public void setDescriptor(Descriptor descriptor)
```

For example, suppose you have a legacy resource that doesn't comply with the requirements for a standard MBean. If you want to expose this resource for management, you can wrap the resource in a model MBean implementation and use descriptors to map the management interface exposed by the metadata to the corresponding methods on the managed resource.

Suppose you have a legacy class as follows:

```
public class LegacyOffer {
  ........
  public String readDescription() {
    ........
  }
  public String writeDescription(String val) {
    ........
  }
  ........
}
```

The methods readDescription and writeDescription are accessor and mutator for the offer description. To instrument the previous class as a model MBean, first you need to expose the management interface using model MBean metadata classes. The following snippet shows how you create the metadata for the description attribute:

```
ModelMBeanAttributeInfo descriptionATtribute =
new ModelMBeanAttributeInfo("description", "java.lang.String",
  "Offer Description", true, true, false);

Descriptor descriptor = descriptionATtribute.getDescriptor();
descriptor.setFeature("getMethod", "readDescription");
descriptor.setFeature("setMethod", "writeDescription");
```

The constructor for ModelMBeanAttributeInfo is similar to that of MBeanAttributeInfo. After the instance is created, its descriptor is accessed, and the read and write methods on the managed resource are set by the descriptors getMethod and setMethod. The JMX specification provides a standard set of field names for descriptors. However, vendors are allowed to extend this. Table 16-5 lists the standard fields defined by the specification. Descriptor field names aren't case sensitive.

Table 16-5. Descriptors

FEATURE	APPLICABLE TO	DESCRIPTION
`Name`	MBean, attribute, operation, notification	The case-sensitive name of the MBean, attribute, operation, or notification.
`DescriptorType`	MBean, attribute, operation, notification	The type of the descriptor. MBean, attribute, operation, or notification.
`DisplayName`	MBean, attribute, operation	Display name of the MBean, attribute, or operation.
`PersistPolicy`	MBean, attribute	The persistence policy for all the attributes in the MBean that can be overridden by individual attributes. Possible vales are `Never`, `OnTimer`, `OnUpdate`, `NotMoreOftenThan`, and `Always`.
`PersistePeriod`	MBean, attribute	Time period between persistence if the policy is set as `OnTimer` or `NotMoreOftenThan`.
`PersistLocation`	MBean	A value to assist the persistence mechanism. The RI uses this to specify the directory to which the attributes are persisted.
`PersistName`	MBean	A value to assist the persistence mechanism. The RI uses this to specify the filename to which the attributes are persisted.
`Log`	MBean, notification	A Boolean value to indicate whether all the notifications for this MBean should be logged. This can be overridden for individual notifications.
`LogFile`	MBean, notification	The file to which notifications are logged.
`CurrencyTimeLimit`	MBean, attribute, operation	The value in seconds from the attribute value or operation result is current and not stale. During this period the MBean is required to return the cached value rather than getting it from the original attribute or invoking the operation.
`Export`	MBean	A serializable object that will make the MBean locatable.
`Visibility`	MBean, attribute, operation	A value between 1–4 indicating how often the MBean, attribute, or the operation is accessed.
`PresentationString`	MBean, attribute, operation, notification	An XML-encoded string on how to present the MBean, attribute, operation, or notification to the user.

(continued)

Table 16-5. Descriptors (continued)

FEATURE	APPLICABLE TO	DESCRIPTION
`Value`	Attribute, operation	The value that was returned from the attribute or operation the last time it was accessed.
`Default`	Attribute	The default value for the attribute.
`GetMethod`	Attribute	The get method for the attribute.
`SetMethod`	Attribute	The set method for the attribute.
`LastUpdatedTimestamp`	Attribute, operation	Time stamp when the value was last updated.
`TargetObject`	Operation	The target object on which the operation should be invoked.
`TargetType`	Operation	The type of the target object.
`Severity`	Notification	The severity of the notification.
`MessageId`	Notification	The message ID of the notification.

Required Model MBean

Another added advantage of model MBeans is that all compliant providers are required to provide the class `javax.management.modelmbean.RequiredModelMBean`, which implements the `ModelMBean` interface. This means developers can easily instrument the managed resources by using `RequiredModelMBean` as a template. This class provides a constructor that accepts `ModelMBeanInfo` instances that describe the management interface as arguments. The following snippet shows an example:

```
ModelMBeanInfo info = getModelMBeanInfo();
RequiredModelMBean rmb = new RequiredModelMBean(info);

rmb.setManagedResource(new LegacyOffer(), "ObjectReference");

//Register the MBean
```

The other possible value for object types when you set the managed resource are `EJBHandle`, `RMIReference`, `IOR`, and `Handle`. This means the managed resource doesn't always need to be a local object reference.

Open MBeans

Open MBeans allows managed resources to be instrumented in such a way that they're accessible to a variety of management applications. Open MBeans use a small set of predefined types for their attributes and arguments passed to the constructors and operations. Thus, management applications can interpret the MBeans' management interface quite easily without prior knowledge of the complex types that are used by the MBean. This means the management applications don't need to have access to the custom types used by the agent and instrumentation levels.

Open MBeans are required to implement the DynamicMBean interface. The getMBeanInfo method defined in the DynamicMBean method is required to return an instance of the interface javax.management.openmbean.OpenMBean for open MBean classes. JMX provides an implementation of this interface OpenMBeanSupport. The classes that implement this interface hence should extend MBeanInfo class. Figure 16-17 shows the interfaces and classes that describe the metadata for open MBeans and their relation to the normal dynamic MBean metadata classes.

The OpenMBeanInfo interface provides metadata for the beans and provides information on the constructors, attributes, operations, and notifications for the MBean. The classes that implement this interface are required to extend the MBeanInfo class and are returned from the getMBeanInfo method defined in the DynamicMBean interface and implemented in the open MBean instrumenting class. JMX provides an implementation for this class called OpenMBeanInfoSupport.

The OpenMBeanParameterInfo interface provides metadata for the arguments that are passed to open MBean constructors and operations. The classes that implement this interface are required to extend the MBeanParameterInfo. JMX provides an implementation for this class called OpenMBeanParameterInfoSupport.

The OpenMBeanAttributeInfo interface provides metadata for the open MBean attributes. The classes that implement this interface are required to extend the MBeanAttributeInfo. JMX provides an implementation for this class called OpenMBeanAttributeInfoSupport.

The OpenMBeanOperationInfo interface provides metadata for the open MBean operations. The classes that implement this interface are required to extend the MBeanOperationInfo. JMX provides an implementation for this class called OpenMBeanOperationInfoSupport.

The OpenMBeanConstructorInfo interface provides metadata for the open MBean constructors. The classes that implement this interface are required to extend the MBeanConstructorInfo. JMX provides an implementation for this class called OpenMBeanConstructorInfoSupport.

So far you've seen the JMX classes and interfaces that provide the metadata information for the open MBeans' management interfaces. Now you'll see how open MBeans are made "open." You achieve the openness through using a rich set of metadata and using only a predefined set of types for attributes and operations/constructors arguments.

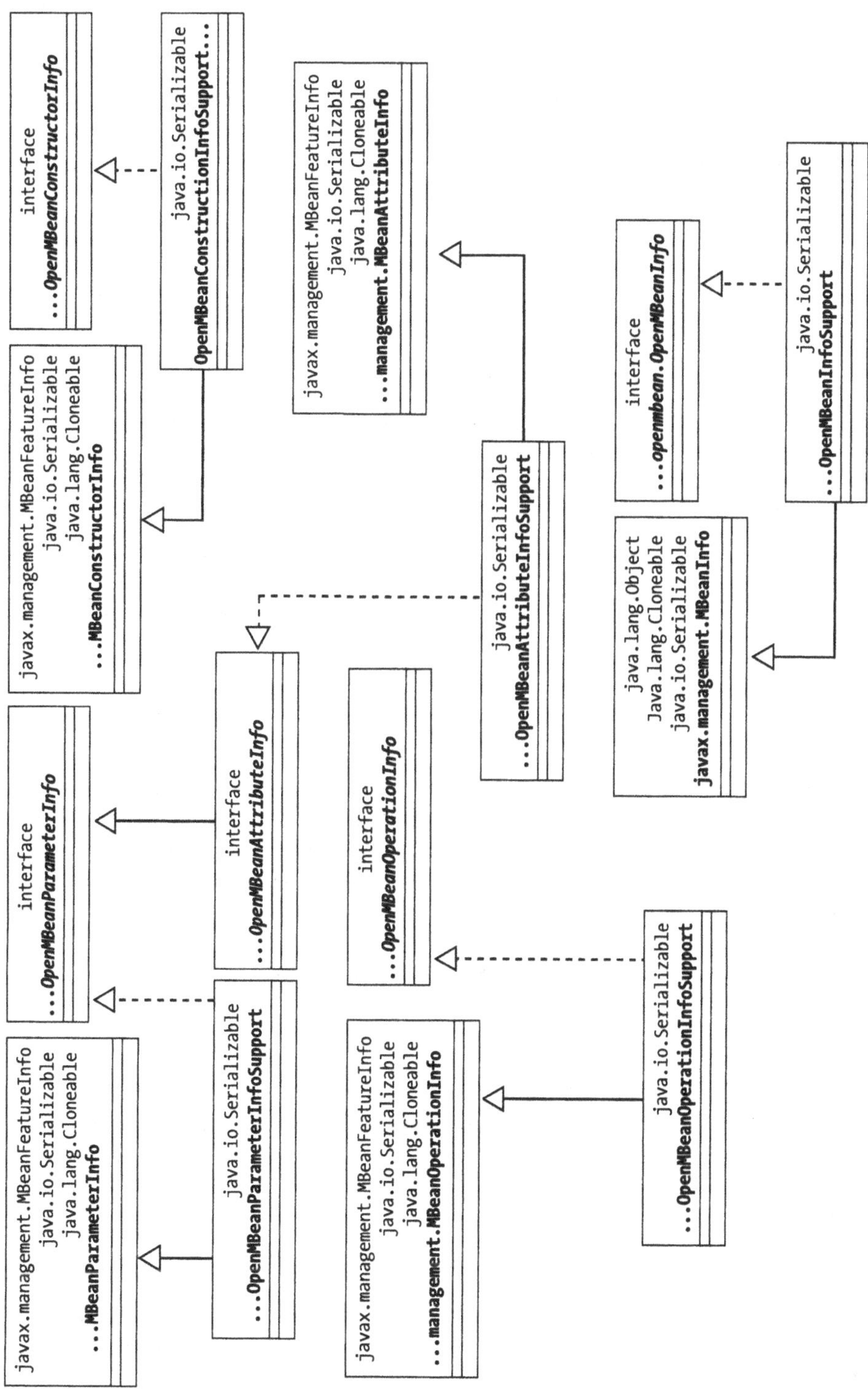

Figure 16-17. Open MBean classes and interfaces

Open MBean Types

To allow maximum interoperability between the agents and management applications, open MBeans are required to use only the types shown in Figure 16-18 for attributes and method parameters.

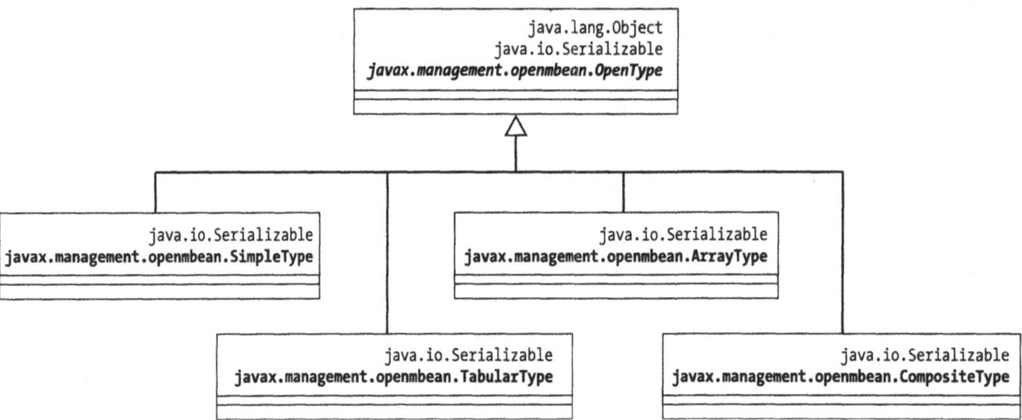

Figure 16-18. Open MBean types

The types used by open MBeans should be defined as a `SimpleType`, `CompositeType`, `ArrayType` or `TabularType`. All these classes extend the abstract class `OpenType`. Both `OpenMBeanAttributeInfoSupport` and `OpenMBeanParameterInfoSupport` classes provide constructors that accept the open type of the attribute or parameter as one of the arguments. Two of the overloaded constructors are shown below:

```
OpenMBeanAttributeInfoSupport(String name, String description,
  OpenType openType, boolean isReadable,
    boolean isWritable, boolean isIs)
```

Constructs an `OpenMBeanAttributeInfoSupport` instance, which describes the attribute of an open MBean with the specified name, open type and description, and the specified read/write access properties.

```
OpenMBeanParameterInfoSupport(String name,
  String description, OpenType openType)
```

Constructs an `OpenMBeanParameterInfoSupport` instance, which describes the parameter used in one or more operations or constructors of a class of open MBeans, with the specified name, open type and description.

SimpleType

This class is used to represent the following types,

- `java.math.BigDecimal`
- `java.math.BigInteger`
- `java.lang.Byte`
- `java.lang.Char`
- `java.lang.Integer`
- `java.lang.Short`
- `java.lang.Float`
- `java.lang.Double`
- `java.lang.String`
- `java.lang.Void`
- `java.util.Date`
- `javax.management.ObjectName`

CompositeType

This class represents composite data. Composite data is represented as key-value pairs, where the key is a string representing the name of a member and the value is an object representing its value. The value itself can be one of the open MBean types. The class provides the following constructor:

```
CompositeType(String typeName, String description,
  String[] itemNames, String[] itemDescriptions,
    OpenType[] itemTypes)
```

This constructs a `CompositeType` instance, checking for the validity of the given parameters. For example, if you want to construct a type called `course` that has the three members ID, name, and description of types `int`, string, and string, respectively, you'd use the following code:

```
CompositeType offerType = new CompositeType(
  "Offer",
  "Describes an offer",
  new String[] {"id", "name", "description"},
  new String[] { "Offer Id", "Offer Name",
    "Offer Description"},
 new OpenType[] {SimpleType.INTEGER, SimpleType.STRING, SimpleType.STRING});
```

In the previous example, all the member items in the type are of simple types. However, you can also have nested composite types.

ArrayType

This class represents an i-dimension array of an open type. Instances of this class are initialized by specifying the dimension and open type of the array members, as follows:

```
ArrayType arrayOfStrings =
  new ArrayType(2, SimpleType.STRING);
```

The previous snippet creates a type for a two-dimensional string array.

TabularType

This class represents tabular data structures. The type allows you to specify a key by which the rows in the tabular data structure are indexed and specifies the type of each row in the table. The class provides the following constructor:

```
TabularType(String typeName, String description,
  CompositeType rowType, String[] indexNames)
```

The following code creates a type used to represent a table of course types indexed by course ID:

```
TabularType offerTableType = new TabularType("offerTable",
  "A table of offers", offerType, new String[] {id});
```

The values of the index array should be valid item names present in the composite type.

Type Instances

JMX provides the following interfaces and classes to represent instances of composite and tabular types, as shown in Figure 16-19.

The `TabularData` interface defines methods for classes that represent data of type `TabularType`. JMX provides the implementation class `TabularDataSupport` that has a `Map` as the underlying data structure.

The `CompositeDataSupport` class provides the following constructors.

Specifically, the following constructs a `CompositeDataSupport` instance with the specified composite type, whose item names and corresponding values are given by the mappings in the map items:

```
CompositeDataSupport(CompositeType compositeType, Map items)
```

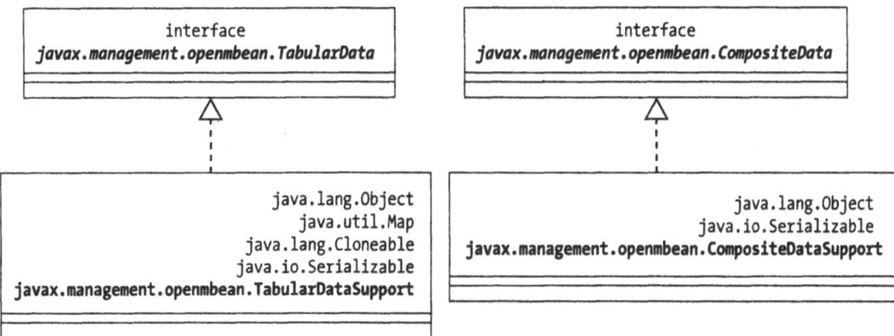

Figure 16-19. Type instances

The following constructs a CompositeDataSupport instance with the specified composite type, whose item values are specified by itemValues[], in the same order as in itemNames[]:

```
CompositeDataSupport(CompositeType compositeType,
  String[] itemNames, Object[] itemValues)
```

The following snippet creates an instance of composite type offerType:

```
CompositeData offerData = new CompositeDataSupport(
  courseType,
  new String[] {"id", "name", "description"},
  new Object[] {new Integer(10), "MP3 Player",

    "256 Mb MP3 Player"};
```

The TabularDataSupport class provides the following constructors.

Specifically, the following creates an empty TabularDataSupport instance whose open type is tabularType and whose underlying HashMap has a default initial capacity (101) and default load factor (0.75):

```
TabularDataSupport(TabularType tabularType)
```

The following creates an empty TabularDataSupport instance whose open type is tabularType and whose underlying HashMap has the specified initial capacity and load factor:

```
TabularDataSupport(TabularType tabularType,
  int initialCapacity, float loadFactor)
```

Open MBean Student Report

Now that you've seen all the classes and interface used to represent open MBean metadata and open MBean types, you'll write an example that will use open MBeans to provide a report of all offers available in the auction application. The report will show all the offers that are available.

The report will have one or more offers, each student will see the details of the customers who have offered the item, and an item may be jointly offered by multiple customers. The open MBean will expose the offer report as a read-only attribute. Listing 16-12 shows the instrumentation code.

Listing 16-12. `OfferReport.java`

```
package com.apress.projavaserver14.chapter19.mbean.open;

import javax.management.DynamicMBean;

import javax.management.AttributeNotFoundException;
import javax.management.MBeanException;
import javax.management.ReflectionException;
import javax.management.InvalidAttributeValueException;
import javax.management.RuntimeOperationsException;

import javax.management.AttributeList;
import javax.management.MBeanInfo;
import javax.management.MBeanNotificationInfo;
import javax.management.Attribute;

import javax.management.openmbean.ArrayType;
import javax.management.openmbean.CompositeData;
import javax.management.openmbean.CompositeDataSupport;
import javax.management.openmbean.CompositeType;
import javax.management.openmbean.OpenDataException;
import javax.management.openmbean.OpenMBeanAttributeInfo;
import javax.management.openmbean.OpenMBeanAttributeInfoSupport;
import javax.management.openmbean.OpenMBeanConstructorInfo;
import javax.management.openmbean.OpenMBeanInfo;
import javax.management.openmbean.OpenMBeanInfoSupport;
import javax.management.openmbean.OpenMBeanOperationInfo;
import javax.management.openmbean.OpenType;
import javax.management.openmbean.SimpleType;
import javax.management.openmbean.TabularData;
import javax.management.openmbean.TabularDataSupport;
import javax.management.openmbean.TabularType;

import java.util.Iterator;
/* Open MBeans are required to implement the DynamicMBean interface. */
public class OfferReport implements DynamicMBean {
/* This is the composite type for the customer who has offered the item. */
  private static CompositeType customerType;
```

```
/* This is the composite type for offer. */
  private static CompositeType offerType;
// This is the tabular type for report.
  private static TabularType offerReportType;
/* This is the metadata for the MBean. The runtime type of this
class should implement the OpenMBeanInfo interface. This means
that class will be extending the MBeanInfo class and implementing
the OpenMBeanInfo interface. One such class provided by JMX is
OpenMBeanInfoSupport. */
  private static MBeanInfo offerReportInfo;
// This is the tabular data for the report.
  private static TabularData reportData;

  static {
/* The static initializer builds the types, metadata
and the original report data. */
    try {
      buildTypes();
      buildMetadata();
      buildData();
    } catch(OpenDataException ex) {
      ex.printStackTrace();
      throw new RuntimeException(ex.getMessage());
    }

  }
/* The only attribute that is supported is report and
returns the tabular data for the report. */
  public Object getAttribute(String attribute)
    throws AttributeNotFoundException,
      MBeanException, ReflectionException {

    if (attribute == null)
      throw new RuntimeOperationsException(
      new IllegalArgumentException(
        "Attribute name cannot be null"));

    if (attribute.equals("report")) return reportData;

    throw new AttributeNotFoundException(
      "Cannot find " + attribute);

  }

  public AttributeList getAttributes(
    String[] attributeNames) {

    if (attributeNames == null)
      throw new RuntimeOperationsException(
      new IllegalArgumentException(
        "attributeNames[] cannot be null"));
```

```
        AttributeList resultList = new AttributeList();

        if (attributeNames.length == 0) return resultList;

        for (int i=0 ;i<attributeNames.length ;i++){
          try {
            Object value =
              getAttribute((String)attributeNames[i]);
            resultList.add(
              new Attribute(attributeNames[i],value));
          } catch (Exception e) {
            e.printStackTrace();
          }
        }

        return resultList;

      }
    // Returns the MBean metadata.
      public MBeanInfo getMBeanInfo() {
        return offerReportInfo;
      }
    // The MBean doesn't support any operation.
      public Object invoke(String operationName, Object[] obj,
        String[] str2)
      throws MBeanException, ReflectionException {
        throw new ReflectionException(new
          NoSuchMethodException(operationName));
      }
    // The MBean doesn't have any writable attributes.
      public void setAttribute(Attribute attribute)
        throws MBeanException, AttributeNotFoundException,
          InvalidAttributeValueException, ReflectionException {
        throw new AttributeNotFoundException(
          "No settable attributes");
      }

      public AttributeList setAttributes(
        AttributeList attributeList) {
        return new AttributeList();
      }
    // The private method builds the required types.
      private static void buildTypes() throws OpenDataException {
    /* The assignment type is composed of two simple types for the name and score. */
        customerType = new CompositeType(
          "customerType",
          "Customer",
          new String[] {"name", "email"},
          new String[] {"Name", "E-Mail"} ,
          new OpenType[] {SimpleType.STRING, SimpleType.String});
    // This defines an array of customer types.
```

```
    ArrayType customersType = new ArrayType(1, customerType);
/* The offer type is composed of the simple and composite types. */
    offerType = new CompositeType(
      "offerType",
      "Offer",
      new String[] {
        "name", "description", "askPrice", "customers"
    },
    new String[] {
      "Name", "Description", "Ask Price", "Customers"
    },
    new OpenType[] {
      SimpleType.STRING,
      SimpleType.STRING,
      SimpleType.DOUBLE,
      customersType
    });
/* Offer report type is a tabular type for storing offer types
indexed by offer names. */
    offerReportType = new TabularType(
      "offerReportType ",
      "Offer Report",
      offerType,
      new String[] {"name"}
    );

  }
// This method builds the metadata.
  private static void buildMetadata() {
/* The only metadata that is required is for the read-only report
attribute. Please note that the runtime type is OpenMBeanInfoSupport
and all the metadata classes except the one for notification are
specific to open MBeans. Also the metadata class for the attribute
accepts the open type for the attribute. */
    offerReportInfo = new OpenMBeanInfoSupport(
     "com.apress.projavaserver14.
       chapter19.mbean.open.OfferReport",
     "Offer report metadata",
     new OpenMBeanAttributeInfo[] {
       new OpenMBeanAttributeInfoSupport(
       "report",
       "Offer report",
       offerReportType,
       true,
       false,
       false)},
     new OpenMBeanConstructorInfo[] {},
     new OpenMBeanOperationInfo[] {},
     new MBeanNotificationInfo[] {}) ;

  }
```

```
// The utility method builds the data.
  private static void buildData() throws OpenDataException {
// This is the composite data for a customer.
    CompositeData customer1 =
      new CompositeDataSupport(
        offerType,
        new String[] {"name", "email"},
        new Object[] {
          "Fred Flintstone", "fred@waterbuffalos.com"}});
// This is the composite data for another customer.
    CompositeData customer2 =
      new CompositeDataSupport(
        offerType,
        new String[] {"name", "email"},
        new Object[] {"Barney Rubble",
          "barney@waterbuffalos.com"}});
/* Composite data for the offer is created by specifying the
offer name, description, ask price and an array of composite
data for customers. */
    CompositeData offer1 =
      new CompositeDataSupport(
        offerType,
        new String[] {
          "name", "description", "askPrice", "customers"
        },
        new Object[] {
          "MP3 Player", "256 Mb MP3 Player", new Double(100),
          new CompositeData[]{customer1, customer2}}
    );
/* The tabular data for offers is created and the individual
composite data for each offer is added. */
    reportData = new TabularDataSupport(offerReportType);
    reportData.put(offer1);

  }

}
```

Now that you've instrumented the report, you'll write a small class that will act as the agent and the management application (see Listing 16-13). The agent bit will start the MBean server and register the MBean, and the management side will read the report and print it as XML. The reason you're writing the management side is that currently the HTML adapter for RI doesn't support open types.

Listing 16-13. `OfferReportRenderer.java`

```
package com.apress.projavaserver14.chapter19.mbean.open;

import javax.management.MBeanServer;
import javax.management.MBeanServerFactory;
import javax.management.ObjectName;
```

```
import javax.management.openmbean.TabularData;
import javax.management.openmbean.CompositeData;
import javax.management.openmbean.TabularType;
import javax.management.openmbean.CompositeType;
import javax.management.openmbean.OpenType;
import javax.management.openmbean.SimpleType;

import java.util.Set;
import java.util.Iterator;

public class OfferReportRenderer {

  public static void main(String args[]) throws Exception {
// Create the MBean server.
    MBeanServer server =
      MBeanServerFactory.createMBeanServer();
// Register the report MBean.
    ObjectName reportName =
      new ObjectName("AuctionApplication:type=report");
    server.registerMBean(new OfferReport(), reportName);
/* Read the report attribute, which is returned as a tabular data structure. */
    TabularData report =
      (TabularData)server.getAttribute(reportName, "report");
/* Get the tabular type and type description. The getTabularType()
method on TabularData returns the type of the individual rows in
the table. */
    TabularType reportType = report.getTabularType();
    String reportDescription = reportType.getDescription();
/* Iterate through the rows and print each composite data representing
the row. The values() method on TabularData will give a reference to the
underlying collection of composite data that make up the table. */
    Iterator rows = report.values().iterator();

    System.out.print("<" + reportDescription + ">");
    while(rows.hasNext()) {
      printComposite((CompositeData)rows.next());
    }
    System.out.print("</" + reportDescription + ">");

  }
/* This is a utility method that prints the information in a
composite data structure. */
  private static void printComposite(CompositeData comp) {
// Get the type of the composite data.
    CompositeType type = comp.getCompositeType();
// Get the description of the type.
    String description = type.getDescription();
    System.out.print("<" + description + ">");
// Get the items in the composite structure.
    Iterator itemNames = type.keySet().iterator();
    while(itemNames.hasNext()) {
```

```
// Get the name, type and description of the item.
      String itemName = (String)itemNames.next();
      OpenType itemType = type.getType(itemName);
      String itemDescription = type.getDescription(itemName);
/* If an array, recursively print each element in an array. The code
assumes arrays are always of composite type. This code will throw a
ClassCastException if the array is of simple types. */
      if(itemType.isArray()) {
        System.out.print("<" + itemDescription + ">");
        CompositeData[] values =
          (CompositeData[]) comp.get(itemName);
        for (int i = 0;i < values.length;i++)
          printComposite(values[i]);
        System.out.print("</" + itemDescription + ">");
// If simple type, print the simple type.
      } else if (itemType instanceof SimpleType) {
        System.out.print("<" + itemDescription + ">");
        System.out.print(comp.get(itemName));
        System.out.print("</" + itemDescription + ">");
// If composite type, recursively print its contents.
      }else {
        printComposite((CompositeData)comp.get(itemName));
      }
    }
    System.out.print("</" + description + ">");

  }

}
```

Listing 16-14 shows the output of running this program. The output is intended to improve readability.

Listing 16-14. Offer Report in XML

```
<Offer Report>
  <Offer>
    <Ask Price>100.0</Ask Price>
    <Customers>
      <Customer>
        <E-Mail>fred@waterbuffalos.com</E-Mail>
        <Name>Fred Flintstone</Name>
      </Customer>
      <Customer>
        <E-Mail>barney@waterbuffalos.com</E-Mail>
        <Name>Barney Rubble</Name>
      </Customer>
    </Customers>
    <Description>256 Mb MP3 Player</Description>
    <Name>MP3 Player</Name>
  </Offer>
</Offer Report>
```

This example demonstrated how open MBeans can achieve very low dependencies between the agent/instrumentation level and management applications.

Notification Infrastructure

JMX allows MBeans to send notifications to the agent, other objects, and management applications on important events and state changes (see Figure 16-20).

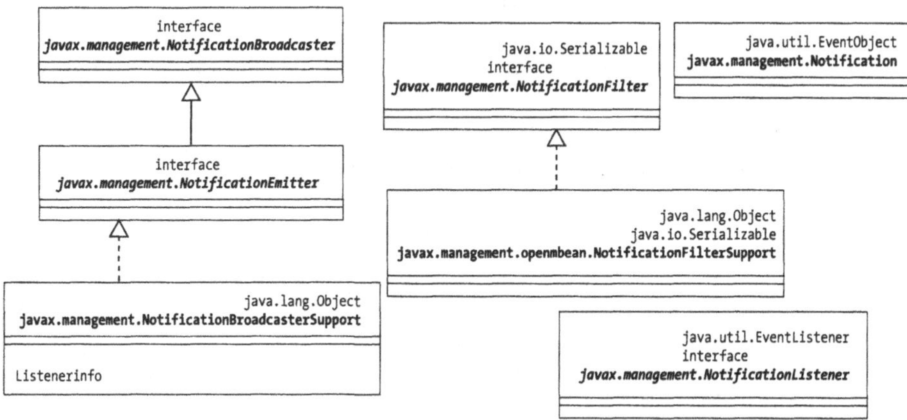

Figure 16-20. Notification classes and interfaces

These are the main classes and interfaces used by JMX for implementing the notification model:

- **Notification**: This class represents a generic notification. You can either use this class directly or subclass it.
- **NotificationListener**: This is an interface that should be implemented by objects interested in listening to notifications emitted by MBeans.
- **NotificationFilter**: Notification listeners can use implementations of this interface to filter the notifications that are sent to them.
- **NotificationBroadcaster**: All the MBeans capable of broadcasting notifications should implement this interface. This interface defines methods for registering listeners with the broadcaster.

MBeans can be both notification listeners and broadcasters. You've already seen that it defines methods for registering listeners to broadcasters in the "MBean Server" section.

Notification

The class `javax.management.Notification` represents notifications. Notifications have a notification type associated with them, which is assigned by the broadcaster and assign a meaning to the notification. The type is actually a string recommended to be represented as a series of dot-separated strings.

An example of the type is `training.course.assignment.sendReminder`. All notification types are prefixed with the string `JMX` and are reserved. You can use types for categorizing and scoping the various notifications you use in your applications. The `Notification` class also provides the following attributes:

- **Sequence number**: A unique number identifying the notification in the context of the broadcaster
- **Time stamp**: Indicates when the notification was broadcasted
- **Message**: A string message that's sent to the listener
- **User data**: Any other information that the broadcaster wanted to send to the user

The class also lets you pass a reference to the source of the notification. The constructors provided by this class are as follows:

```
Notification(String type, Object source, long sequenceNumber)
Notification(String type, Object source,
  long sequenceNumber, long timeStamp)
Notification(String type, Object source,
  long sequenceNumber, long timeStamp, String message)
Notification(String type, Object source,
  long sequenceNumber, String message)
```

The following snippet shows how to create a notification object:

```
Notification bidReceivedNotification = new Notification(
  "auction.bid",
  this,
  seqNo++,
  System.currentTimeMiilis(),
  "Send bid notification");

Double bidPrice = new Double(10);
bidReceivedNotification.setUserData(bidPrice);
```

NotificationBroadcaster

All the MBeans that broadcast notification should implement this interface. The interface defines methods that will allow the MBean server to register listeners with it. This interface defines the following methods.

Specifically, the following method adds a listener to the broadcaster:

```
void addNotificationListener(NotificationListener listener,
  NotificationFilter filter, Object handback)
```

The filter filters notifications, and `handback` is an opaque object that's returned to the listener. The listeners can use this object to keep track of the context in which the listener was registered. You can register the same listener with different filters with the same broadcaster passing different `handback` objects. The listener can later use the `handback` objects when it receives the notifications to identify in what context was the interest in the notification registered.

The following returns an array indicating, for each notification this MBean may send, the name of the Java class of the notification and the notification type. The `MBeanNotification` class is instantiated by passing a string array of notification types it emits, the fully qualified Java class name of the notification, and a meaningful description:

```
MBeanNotificationInfo[] getNotificationInfo()
```

The following removes a listener from this MBean:

```
void removeNotificationListener(
  NotificationListener listener)
```

This will remove the listener from broadcaster. However, if a listener has registered with a broadcaster more than once with different filters and handbacks, this method will remove all the instances of registration for the listener. However, if you want more control on how the listeners are removed, you need to implement the `NotificationEmitter` interface that extends the `NotificationBroadcaster` interface and defines the following additional method:

```
removeNotificationListener(NotificationListener listener,
  NotificationFilter filter, Object handback)
```

This method removes the listener for the filter and handback.

JMX provides the adapter class `NotificationBroadcasterSupport` that implements the `NotificationEmitter` interface. MBeans that send notification can extend this class. In addition to the methods defined in the implemented interface, this class provides the following utility methods that can be used by extending MBeans:

```
public void sendNotification(Notification notification)
```

This will send the notification to all the relevant listeners based on the filters passing the relevant handbacks.

NotificationListener

Objects that are interested in receiving notifications from broadcasting MBeans should implement this interface. This interface defines a single method that's invoked when a notification occurs. The method passes the notification object and the `handback` that was passed to the broadcaster during registration:

```
void handleNotification(Notification notification,
  Object handback)
```

NotificationFilter

Instances of classes that implement this interface are passed to the broadcaster during registration to filter notifications. The interface defines the following method:

```
boolean isNotificationEnabled(Notification notification)
```

The broadcaster invokes this method to decide whether a particular notification should be sent to a listener. JMX provides the `NotificationFilterSupport` class that implements this interface by filtering notifications based on notification types. The class provides the methods shown in Table 16-6.

Table 16-6. `NotificationFilterSupport` *Methods*

METHOD	DESCRIPTION
`void disableAllTypes()`	Disables all notification types
`void disableType(String prefix)`	Removes the given prefix from the prefix list
`void enableType(String prefix)`	Enables all the notifications, the type of which starts with the specified prefix to be sent to the listener
`Vector getEnabledTypes()`	Gets all the enabled notification types for this filter
`boolean isNotificationEnabled(Notification notification)`	Invoked before sending the specified notification to the listener

Bid Reminder Using Notification

In the example on standard MBeans, we saw the MBean operation for placing a bid on the offer. In the example in this section, we will extend it to implement the sending of a notification to the customer who has offered the item when a bid is received. When the operation is invoked, the MBean will send a notification that will be captured by a listener and processed.

Offer MBean

You can use the same instrumentation class you used for the standard MBean example with the changes shown in bold, as shown in Listing 16-15.

Listing 16-15. Offer

```
.............................
// Now the class extends the NotificationBroadcasterSupport.
public class Offer extends
  NotificationBroadcasterSupport implements CourseMBean {

  ........................
/* This variable is used to keep track of notification sequence numbers. */
  private int seq;

  ........................

  public double getAskPrice() { return askPrice; }
// The MBean operation now sends the notification.
  public void bid(double bidPrice) {
/* The notification is created by specifying the type, time stamp,
and sequence number. */
    Notification notification = new Notification(
    "auction.bid",
    this, System.currentTimeMillis(), seq++, "Bid received");
    notification.setUserData(new Double(bidPrice));
// The user data is set to the number of days remaining.
    this.sendNotification(notification);

  }

}
```

BidSender

Listing 16-16 shows the class that listens for the notification.

Listing 16-16. BidSender

```
package com.apress.projavaserver14.chapter19.notification;

import javax.management.NotificationListener;
import javax.management.Notification;
// The class implements NotificationListener.
public class BidSender implements NotificationListener {
/* This method is invoked whenever a notification matching the
filter is broadcasted. */
  public void handleNotification(
    Notification notification, Object obj) {

    System.out.println("Received notification");
    Double bidPrice = (Integer)notification.getUserData();

  }

}
```

Registering the Listener

Listing 16-17 shows how to register the listener with the broadcaster.

Listing 16-17. Registering the Listener with the Broadcaster

```
MBeanServer server = MBeanServerFactory.createMBeanServer();
// Create the MBean.
Offer offerMBean =
  new Offer(1, "MP3 Player", "256 Mb MP3 Player");
// Create the object name.
ObjectName mp3PlayerMBeanName = new ObjectName(
  "AuctionApplication:type=Offer,name=MP3
    Player,mBeanType=notification");
// Register the MBean with the agent.
server.registerMBean(courseMBean, mp3PlayerMBeanName);
// Create a filter that filters by notification type.
NotificationFilterSupport filter =
  new NotificationFilterSupport();
filter.enableType("auction.bid");
// Add the listener to the broadcaster.
server.addNotificationListener(mp3PlayerMBeanName,
  new BidSender(), filter, null);
```

Agent-Level Services

Agent-level services are MBeans that providers offer to provide utility services. The JMX specification requires the following set of agent-level services:

- **Dynamic loading**: This allows the service to load MBeans from a set of uniform resource locators (URLs). The URLs will point to text files that will contain MBean definitions. The MBeans definitions are specified using an XML language. Each MBean definition is called an m-let (which means *management applet*).

- **Monitors**: JMX also requires agent-level MBeans that can monitor the attribute of other MBeans at specified intervals when either the attribute value or the change in attribute value between two measurements exceeds a specified value.

  JMX requires the following three types of monitors:

  - **Counter monitor**: This monitors an increasing attribute value of type `int`, `long`, `short` and sends a notification when the value exceeds a certain threshold.

  - **Gauge monitor**: This monitors attribute value changes between two measurements.

  - **String monitor**: This monitors patterns for string attributes.

  - **Timers**: You can use these agent-level MBeans for sending notifications at predefined time periods.

  - **Relations**: You can use this for maintaining relations between MBeans registered in a server.

NOTE *An exhaustive coverage of agent-level services is beyond the scope of this book and chapter.*

Introducing the J2EE Management Specification

So far you've seen a generic model for exposing and instrumenting resources so they can be made available for management on a standard platform and can be managed by managed applications. J2EE 1.4 adds another important tool to the arsenal of J2EE developers, deployers, and administrators: the J2EE Management specification. J2EE Management specification has evolved through JCP, and Sun released it for public review in late 2001, with JSR-77. Unlike JMX, which provides an API for exposing managed resources to management applications that discover and interpret the interfaces exposed by the management resources at run time, the J2EE Management specification defines a concrete set of information models that describes the management interface for the various J2EE resources running in a J2EE server. These resources include the J2EE server, JVM, deployed components, resource factories, and so on. The J2EE Management specification also mandates the requirement of a remote session Enterprise JavaBean (EJB), called a management EJB (MEJB), that can be used by remote management clients for accessing the management information for the various J2EE components running in a server. It also defines specifications for other management protocols such as Simple Network Management Protocol (SNMP) and Common Interface Model (CIM).

Information Model

The J2EE Management specification defines the management interfaces for the resources in terms of objects. However, these aren't Java classes; rather, an object represents a collection information exposed by a particular resources. Figure 16-21 illustrates the managed objects defined by the J2EE Management specification.

The information model for all the managed objects defined by JSR-77 extend that of `J2EEManagedObject`. Each managed object is uniquely identified by an object name that's similar to the JMX object name. Additionally, managed objects can provide metadata-related information about their state, providing performance statistics and events.

The various managed objects within a J2EE server form a hierarchical graph of objects with parent-child relationships. For example, a `J2EEServer` may have zero or more stand-alone `J2EEModule` and/or `J2EEApplication` objects. The `J2EEModule` objects could be an `EJBModule`, `WebModule`, `AppClientModule`, or `ResourceAdaptorModule` object. The `J2EEApplication` object may in turn comprise zero or more `J2EEModule` objects. An `EJBModule` may contain one or more EJB objects, which can be `StatelessSessionBean`, `StatefulSessionBean`, `MessageDrivenBean`, or `EntityBeanObjects`. Here an `EJB` object is said to be the child of an `EJBModule` object, which could be a child of a `J2EEApplication`, an object for EAR, or a `J2EEServer` object for stand-alone EJBs. Similarly, a `J2EEApplication` object is the child of the `J2EEServer` object. Figure 16-22 shows these relations.

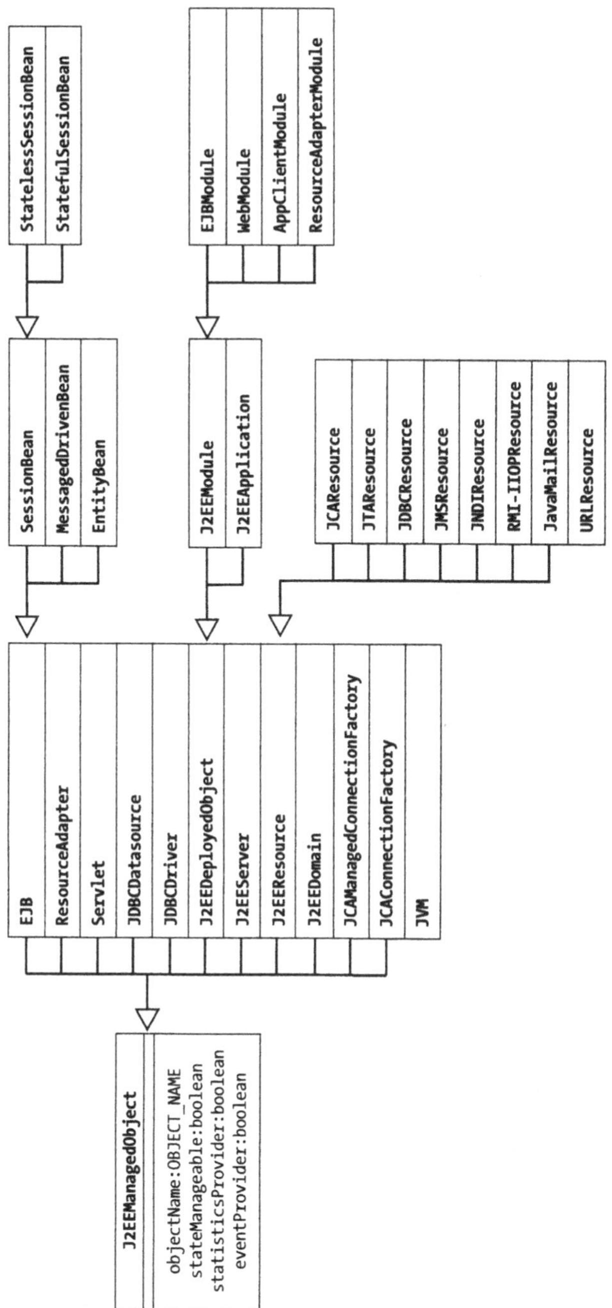

Figure 16-21. Management model

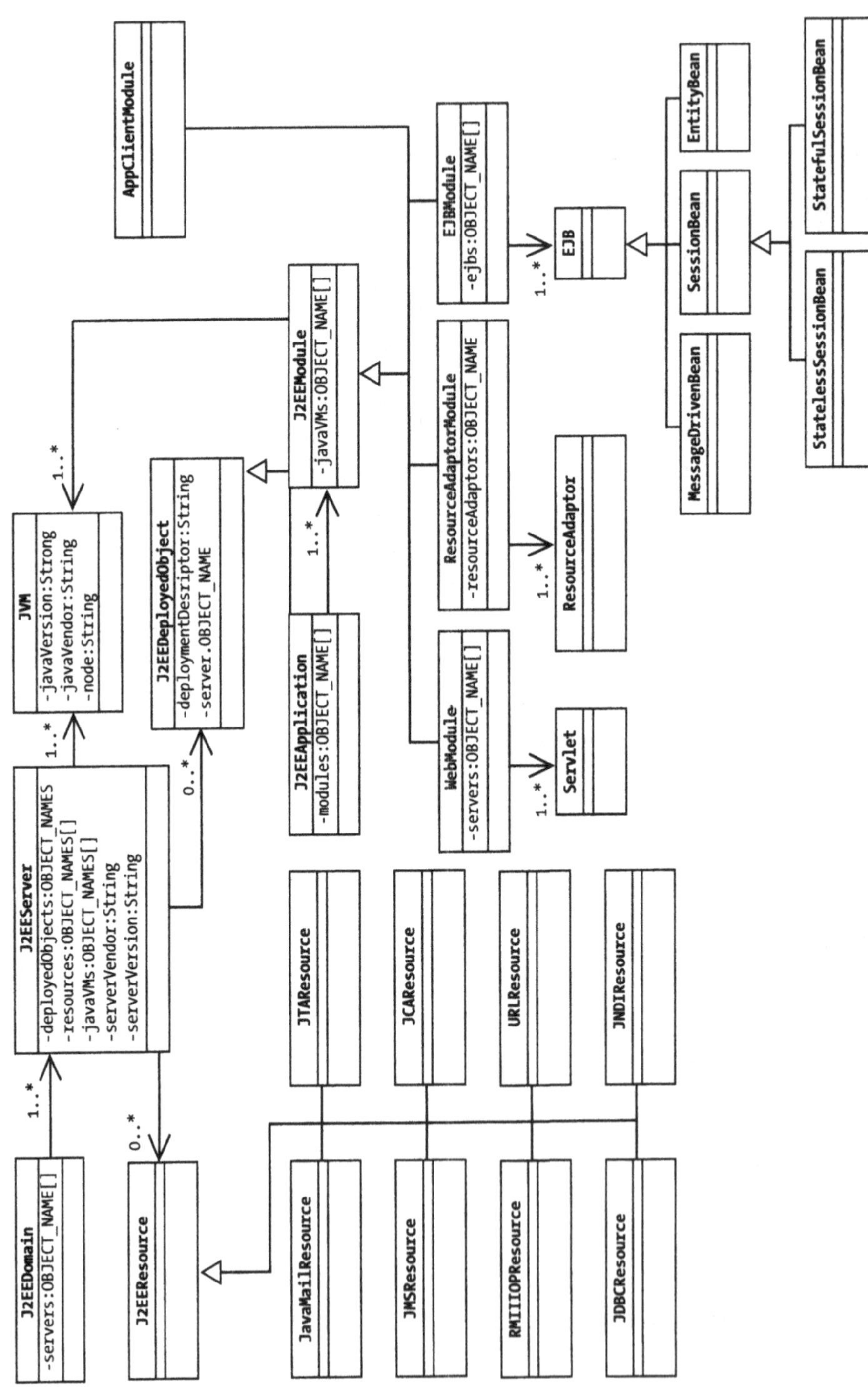

Figure 16-22. Management information model

Object Name

The object name uniquely identifies a managed object in the J2EE server and is similar to JMX object names. An object name comprises a domain name and a set of key-vale pairs. A colon separates the domain name and the key-value pairs. A comma separates each key-value pair. The following three key-value pairs are mandatory:

j2eeType: This key identifies the type of the managed object. The valid values are as follows:

- `J2EEDomain`
- `J2EEServer`
- `J2EEApplication`
- `AppClientModule`
- `EJBModule`
- `WebModule`
- `ResourceAdaptorModule`
- `EntityBean`
- `StatefulSessionBean`
- `StatelessSessionBean`
- `MessageDrivenBean`
- `Servlet`
- `ResourceAdaptor`
- `JavaMailResource`
- `JCAResource`
- `JCAConnectionFactory`
- `JCAManagedConnectionFactory`
- `JDBCDataSource`
- `JDBCDriver`

- `JMSResource`
- `JNDIResource`
- `JTAResource`
- `RMI_IIOPResource`
- `URLResource`
- `JVM`

name: This specifies the name of the J2EE managed object. The naming scheme is entirely up to the vendor.

J2EEServer: The third attribute is mandatory for all objects other than `J2EEDomain`. This attribute will provide a path from the manage object to its ancestor `J2EEServer` object. This in fact a series of key-value pairs instead of a single key-value pair. For example, if the object name of the J2EEServer is `TrainingApplication:j2eeType=J2EEServer,name=TrainingServer`, then an application hosted by the server will have the object name `TrainingApplication:j2eeType=J2EEApplication,name=CourseManager,J2EEServer=TrainingServer`. And an EJB module within the application will have the object name `TrainingApplication:j2eeType=J2EEApplication,name=AssignmentEJB,J2EEApplication=CourseManager,J2EEServer=TrainingServer`. This means the object name comprises the domain name and key-value pairs for the `name`, `j2eeType`, and a set of key-value pairs each for an ancestor of the current object until its `J2EEServer` ancestor, with the key representing the value of the ancestor's `j2eeType` key and the value representing the value of the ancestor's `name` key.

Management EJB

So far, you've seen the information model defined by the J2EE Management specification. But how do managed applications use this model? The specification supports a host of standard management protocols. However, for a Java application needing to access a J2EE server and query its J2EE managed objects, the specification provides the remote and home interface for a session EJB. As mentioned, this EJB is called a management EJB (MEJB). The EJB should be implemented and deployed by the compliant server providers, and the home objects should preferably be bound to the JNDI name `ejb/mgmt/MEJB`.

The home interface is `javax.management.j2ee.ManagementHome`, which provides a single `create` method to create the remote object. The component interface for the remote object is `javax.management.j2ee.Management`. This interface depends heavily on the JMX classes and interfaces, and the methods defined by this interface are similar to those in the `MBeanServer` interface (see Table 16-7).

Table 16-7. Management EJB Methods

METHOD: `Object getAttribute(ObjectName name, String attribute)`
DESCRIPTION: Gets the value of a specific attribute of a named managed object.

METHOD: `AttributeList getAttributes(ObjectName name, String[] attributes)`
DESCRIPTION: Enables the values of several attributes of a named managed object.

METHOD: `String getDefaultDomain()`
DESCRIPTION: Returns the default domain name of this MEJB.

METHOD: `ListenerRegistration getListenerRegistry()`
DESCRIPTION: This method gives a handle to the listener registration so that remote management applications can listen to the notifications emitted by the J2EE managed objects.

METHOD: `Integer getMBeanCount()`
DESCRIPTION: Returns the number of managed objects registered in the MEJB.

METHOD: `MBeanInfo getMBeanInfo(ObjectName name)`
DESCRIPTION: This method discovers the attributes and operations that a managed object exposes for management.

METHOD: `Object invoke(ObjectName name, String operationName, Object[] params, String[] signature)`
DESCRIPTION: Invokes an operation on a managed object.

METHOD: `boolean isRegistered(ObjectName name)`
DESCRIPTION: Checks whether a managed object, identified by its object name, is already registered with the MEJB.

METHOD: `Set queryNames(ObjectName name, QueryExp query)`
DESCRIPTION: Gets the names of managed objects controlled by the MEJB. The return value is a collection of object names.

METHOD: `void setAttribute(ObjectName name, Attribute attribute)`
DESCRIPTION: Sets the value of a specific attribute of a named managed object.

METHOD: `AttributeList setAttributes(ObjectName name, AttributeList attributes)`
DESCRIPTION: Sets the values of several attributes of a named managed object.

Getting the Vendor Details

In this section, you'll write a small example that will connect to the J2EE server and get the vendor information (see Listing 16-18).

Listing 16-18. `DomainDetails.java`

```
package com.apress.projavaserver14.chapter19.jsr77;
// Import the MEJB home and component interfaces.
import javax.management.j2ee.ManagementHome;
import javax.management.j2ee.Management;

import javax.naming.InitialContext;
import javax.rmi.PortableRemoteObject;

import java.util.Iterator;
// Import the JMX ObjectName class.
import javax.management.ObjectName;
```

```
public class DomainDetails {

  public static void main(String args[]) throws Exception {
// Create the initial context and lookup the MEJB.
    InitialContext ctx = new InitialContext();
    Object obj = ctx.lookup("ejb/mgmt/MEJB");
    ManagementHome home = (ManagementHome)
      PortableRemoteObject.narrow(obj, ManagementHome.class);
    Management mejb = home.create();
/* Query the MEJB for the object name pattern *:j2eeType=J2EEServer,*.
This will return all the J2EE managed objects with the j2eeType attribute
set to J2EEServer. */
    ObjectName pattern = new
      ObjectName("*:j2eeType=J2EEServer,*");
    Iterator j2eeServers = mejb.queryNames(pattern,
      null).iterator();

    if (j2eeServers.hasNext()) {
// Get the object name of the server.
      ObjectName serverName = (ObjectName)j2eeServers.next();
// Print the serverVendor and serverName attributes.
      System.out.println("Vendor:" +
        mejb.getAttribute(serverName, "serverVendor"));
      System.out.println("Version:" +
        mejb.getAttribute(serverName, ="serverVersion"));

    }

    ctx.close();

  }

}
```

With J2EE 1.4 RI, this will produce the following output:

```
Vendor:Sun Microsystems, Inc.
Version:1.4-beta-b35
```

Statistics, Events, and State

J2EE managed objects can also specify whether they can provide performance statistics, events, and state information through the Boolean attributes `statisticProvider`, `eventProvider`, and `stateManageable`, respectively.

Statistics

A J2EE object that provides performance statistics is required to implement the information model defined by `StatisticsProvider`. Any managed object that implements this information model should provide an attribute called `stats` whose type is defined by one of the subtypes of `Stats`. Figure 16-23 shows the `Stats` subtype for the various managed objects.

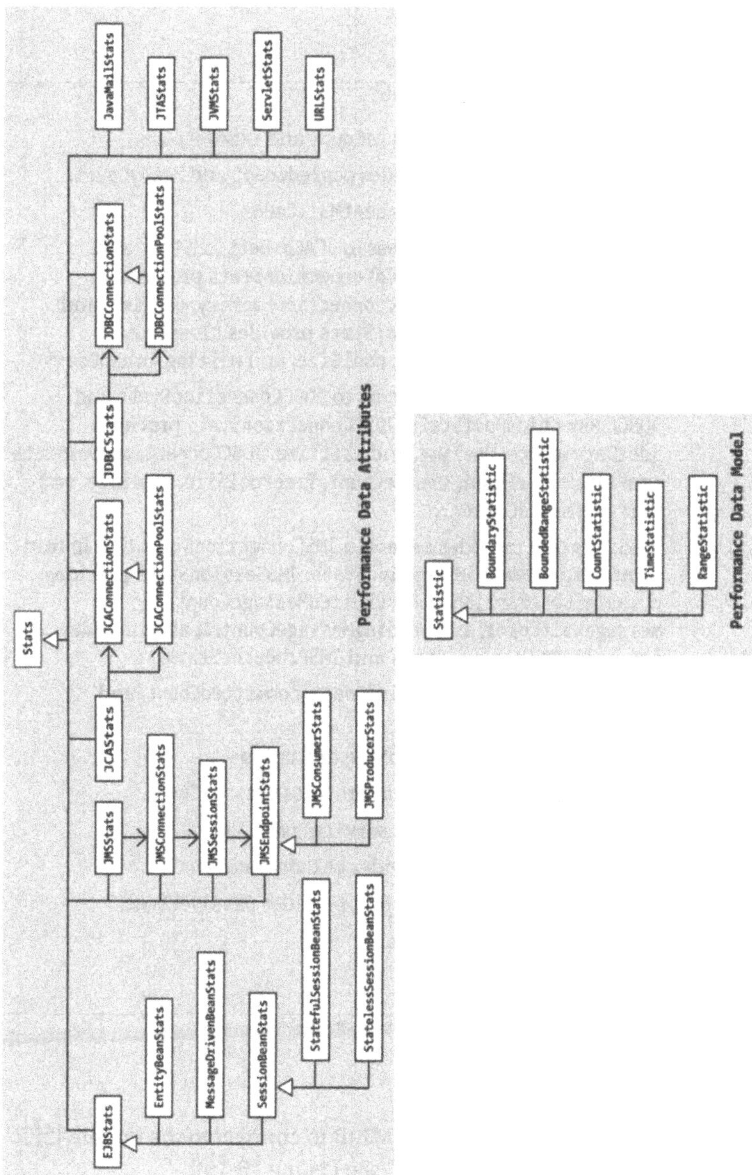

Figure 16-23. Statistics

The Stats model and its submodel specify the attributes exposed by the various J2EE managed objects to expose the various performance data. The Stats model and submodels define the type of the performance data exposed through these attributes. For example, an EJB that provides statistics will provide two attributes, createCount and removeCount, through the EJBStats model. The CountStatistic model defines the type of both these attributes.

Table 16-8 relates the performance attribute model shown in Figure 16-23 to the J2EE managed object model.

Table 16-8. Management Model Resources

METHOD	DESCRIPTION
EJB	EJBStats that provides createCount and removeCount.
EntityBean	EntityBeanStats that provides pooledCount and readyCount.
JavaMail	JavaMailStats that provide sentMailCount.
JCAResource	JCAStats that provides access to JCAConnectionStats and JCAConnectionPoolStats. JCAConnectionStats provides connectionFactory, managedConnectionFactory, useTime, and waitTime. JCAConnectionPoolStats provides closeCount, createCount, freePoolSize, poolSize, and waitingThreadCount.
JDBCResource	JDBCStats that provides access to JDBCConnectionStats and JDBCConnectionPoolStats. JDBCConnectionStats provides jdbcDataSource, useTime, and waitTime. JDBCConnectionPoolStats provides closeCount, createCount, freePoolSize, poolSize, and waitingThreadCount.
JMSResource	JMSStats that provides access to JMSConnectionStats that in turn provides access to JMSSessionStats. JMSSessionStats provides durableSubscriptionCount, expiredMessageCount, messageWaitCount, and pendingMessageCount. It also provides access to JMSConsumerStats and JMSProducerStats.
JTAResource	JTAStats that provides activeCount, committedCount, and rolledBackCount
JVMResource	JVMStats that provides heapSize and uptime.
MessageDrivenBean	MessageDrivenBeanStats that provides messageCount.
Servlet	ServletStats that provides serviceTime.
SessionBean	SessionBeanStats that provides methodReadyCount.
StatefulSessionBean	StatefulSessionBeanStats that provides passiveCount.
StatelessSessionBean	StatelessSessionBeanStats.
URLResource	URLStats.

JVM Monitor

Now you'll write a small program that will use the MEJB to connect to the remote J2EE server and monitor the JVM uptime and heap size (see Listing 16-19).

Listing 16-19. `JVMMonitor.java`

```
package com.apress.projavaserver14.chapter19.jsr77;

import javax.management.j2ee.ManagementHome;
import javax.management.j2ee.Management;
/* These are the two statistics provided by J2EE managed objects of type JVM. */
import javax.management.j2ee.statistics.BoundedRangeStatistic;
import javax.management.j2ee.statistics.CountStatistic;

import javax.naming.InitialContext;
import javax.rmi.PortableRemoteObject;

import java.util.Iterator;

import javax.management.ObjectName;
import javax.management.Query;

public class JVMMonitor {

  public static void main(String args[]) throws Exception {
// Look up and create the MEJB.
    InitialContext ctx = new InitialContext();
    Object obj = ctx.lookup("ejb/mgmt/MEJB");
    ManagementHome home = (ManagementHome)
      PortableRemoteObject.narrow(obj, ManagementHome.class);
    Management mejb = home.create();
// Query all the J2EE managed objects of type JVM.
    //ObjectName pattern = new ObjectName("*:j2eeType=JVM,*");
    ObjectName pattern = new ObjectName("*:*");
    Iterator j2eeServers = mejb.queryNames(pattern,
      Query.eq(Query.attr("j2eeType"),
      Query.value("JVM"))).iterator();

    While (j2eeServers.hasNext()) {

      ObjectName serverName = (ObjectName)j2eeServers.next();
// Check whether the JVM provides statistics.
      Boolean statisticsProvider =
      (Boolean)mejb.getAttribute(serverName,
        "statisticsProvider");

      if (!statisticsProvider.booleanValue()) continue;

/* If the JVM provides statistics get the heap size and up time.
Heap size is provided as a boundary statistic and up time is provided
as a count statistic. */
      BoundedRangeStatistic heapSize =
        (BoundedRangeStatistic)
          mejb.getAttribute(serverName, "heapSize");
      CountStatistic upTime = (CountStatistic)
```

```
        mejb.getAttribute(serverName, "upTime");
// Print the up time, minimum and maximum heap size.
       System.out.println("Up Time:" + upTime.getCount());
       System.out.println("Min Heap:" +
         heapSize.getLowerBound());
       System.out.println("Max Heap:" +
         heapSize.getUpperBound());

    }

    ctx.close();

  }

}
```

NOTE *The J2EE 1.4 beta RI doesn't provide statistics for J2EE managed objects of type JVM.*

Events

J2EE managed objects that are capable of broadcasting events will send JMX-style notifications to remote management clients. If you're using MEJB, you can use the `getListenerRegistry` method to get a reference to the `ListenerRegistration` object. You can use this for registering interest in notifications by specifying the listener, notification filter, and handback object.

State

J2EE managed objects that are state manageable can send important notifications related to state changes to registered management applications.

Summary

In this chapter, you looked at JMX and the J2EE Management specification in detail. The chapter started with JMX and covered the JMX instrumentation and agent levels in detail. You learned how to use JMX to make the resources manageable through an open and standard API. You instrumented courses in the training application as standard and dynamic MBeans. Then you implemented the report as an open MBean. The chapter then covered the JMX notification model and concluded by covering the agent services.

After covering JMX, the chapter moved onto the J2EE Management specification to show how you can use it for managing and monitoring J2EE servers. You looked at the J2EE managed object information model and then looked at monitoring and managing statistics, events, and the state of the managed objects.

CHAPTER 17

Packaging and Deploying Your Applications

JAVA 2 ENTERPRISE EDITION (J2EE) is a platform for building enterprise-class Java applications that are comprised of a variety of technologies and component types. A typical enterprise application that's built using J2EE contains the following:

- Entity beans that model the application's domain
- Session beans that model the application's business processes
- Message-driven beans (MDBs) that model an application's asynchronous messaging requirements
- Servlets, JavaServer Pages (JSPs), and tag libraries that provide browser-based access to the application
- Application clients that provide a rich user interface
- Web services that provide platform- and technology-agnostic access to the services
- Resource adapters for accessing external enterprise information systems

These components in turn use a variety of resources and system-level services provided by the container run time to offer the necessary services. The resources include the following:

- Connection factories to Java Database Connectivity (JDBC) databases
- Java Message Service (JMS) connection factories
- Mail sessions
- Uniform resource locator (URL) connection factories
- Other Java Connector Architecture (JCA) connection factories
- JMS destinations

The system-level services include the following:

- Transaction demarcation and management
- Security
- Resource pooling
- Resource caching

One of the main reasons behind the overwhelming popularity of J2EE as a platform for building enterprise applications is that the J2EE components externalize application behavior from application logic using deployment descriptors. Accordingly, J2EE introduced the notion of *roles* that have well-defined responsibilities at various stages of application development. These roles include component providers, application assemblers, deployers, and so on. The component providers provide hints to application assemblers about how a particular component can fit into the bigger picture of the whole application, using the component deployment descriptors. The application assemblers and component providers provide hints to the deployers about how the components and applications need to be configured in the operational environment to use the various services and resources provided by the operational environment.

This chapter covers the various aspects of deployment and packaging. Specifically, it covers the following topics:

- J2EE application roles
- The J2EE packaging model
- How to configure a component's environment
- How to resolve dependencies

Understanding J2EE Platform Roles

J2EE defines a set of roles for people in regard to the activities involved in developing, assembling, deploying, running, and administering J2EE applications. These roles don't need to be mapped to different individuals. However, in big enterprises you'll often find individuals with the specific responsibilities of developing the components, assembling the components into applications, deploying the applications, and administering the applications. The J2EE specification defines the platform roles covered in the following sections.

Product Provider

J2EE product providers provide the operational environment in which the J2EE applications and components can run. The product provider implements the J2EE specifications and application programming interfaces (APIs). In addition to the runtime environment for running the applications and components, the product providers may provide tools for configuring, deploying, and administering applications and components.

> **NOTE** *Prior to J2EE 1.4, these tools used proprietary APIs and protocols. However, J2EE 1.4 makes a big step forward by including standard specifications and APIs as part of the platform, which enable deployment and administration of applications and components. The specifications include Java Management Extensions (JMX), the J2EE Management API, and the J2EE Deployment API.*

Application Component Provider

Application component providers have the responsibility of developing application components. These components include servlets, JSPs, tag libraries, Web services, Enterprise JavaBeans (EJBs), resource adapters, and so on. Typically, application component developers hand over the components to application assemblers to assemble the components provided by various application components into bigger applications. The application component developers may use a variety of integrated development environments (IDEs) and tools for accomplishing this task. They also provide hints to the application assemblers about how the component can be integrated into the application using the component's deployment descriptor.

Application Assembler

Application assemblers accept components from different providers and integrate them into a functional application. They use the information present in the deployment descriptors to configure the components within the applications. The components are assembled into a J2EE application as an enterprise archive (EAR) file. Application assemblers may use tools provided by the container provider to perform this task. The application assemblers provide instructions to the deployer on how the application's external dependencies can be resolved in the operational environment using the application and component deployment descriptors.

Deployer

Deployers accept assembled applications from application assemblers and deploy them in the operational environment. They follow the instructions provided by application assemblers and component providers to resolve the application's external dependencies. These dependencies include making resource factories and resource environment references available to the components in the application. Deployers use platform-specific deployment descriptors and tools to perform these tasks. The deployment also generates any additional classes that are required for the components. These generated classes include generated classes for JSPs, Web services static stubs, EJB stubs and ties, and so on.

System Administrator

System administrators are responsible for monitoring and managing the components and applications and the runtime environments within which the components and applications run. J2EE product providers provide tools based on standard APIs and protocols for performing these tasks.

Tool Providers

Tool providers are responsible for providing a variety of tools that can be used in various points in a J2EE application's life cycle. These tools can be used for the following:

- Developing components
- Configuring components
- Assembling applications
- Configuring applications
- Deploying applications
- Monitoring and managing applications

System Component Providers

System component providers are responsible for providing system-level components that can integrate the J2EE applications with external systems. Examples for system components are JCA resource adapters for connecting to external enterprise information systems (see Figure 17-1).

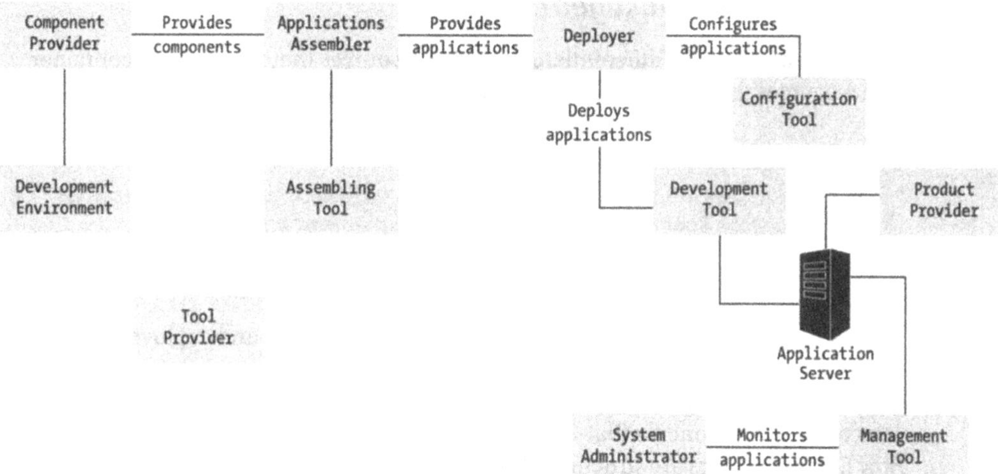

Figure 17-1. J2EE roles

> **NOTE** *In Figure 17-1, the J2EE product and tool providers can be the same or different. A typical application you may use is Borland JBuilder to develop the components. The application assemblers may use the same tool for assembling the applications. The deployer can then use Sitraka Deployment Director to configure and deploy the application on a WebLogic server provided by BEA Systems. Then the system administrator can use a tool from another vendor that uses JMX and JSR-77 (the J2EE Management API) to monitor and manage the application.*

Understanding the J2EE Packaging Model

A J2EE application is composed of the following:

- One or more J2EE components
- A J2EE application deployment descriptor

When one or more heterogeneous J2EE components need to use one another, a J2EE application must be created. You must take into account many considerations when building a J2EE application, including the following:

- The types of J2EE components that can be packaged into a J2EE application
- The roles that people play when creating J2EE packages
- The current limitations of J2EE packaging
- The classloading approaches that different vendors use to meet the needs of J2EE component interactions

What Can Be Packaged?

The J2EE specification differentiates between resources that run within a container and resources that can be packaged into a J2EE EAR file.

> **NOTE** *An EAR file is used to package one or more J2EE modules into a single module so that they can have aligned classloading and deployment into a server.*

J2EE clarifies the difference between runtime containers and deployment modules. *Runtime* containers are request-level interceptors that provide infrastructure services around the components of the system. A *deployment* module is a packaging structure for components that will ultimately execute in a runtime container. Recall how J2EE containers are structured (see Figure 17-2).

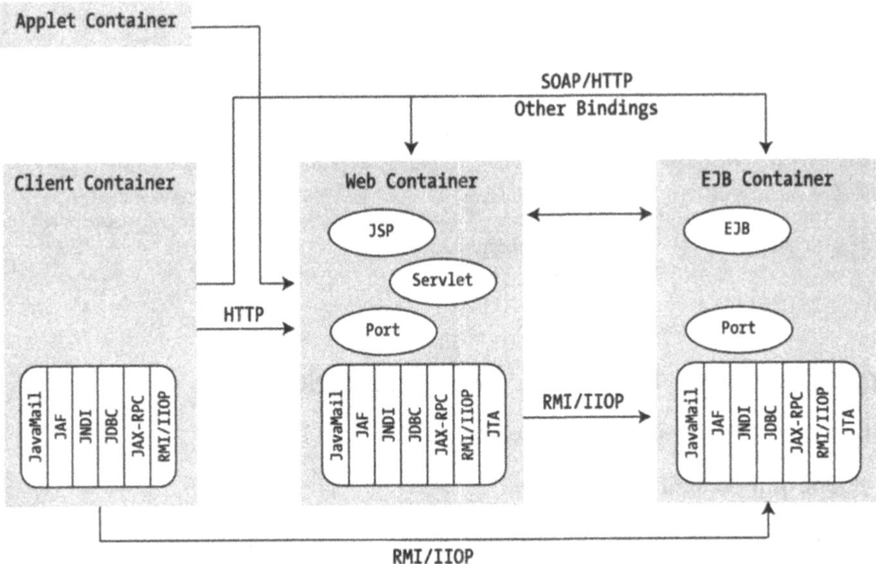

Figure 17-2. Structure of J2EE containers

J2EE applications use the following J2EE containers:

The EJB container: The EJB container provides containment and request-level interception for business logic. The EJB container allows EJBs to have access to JMS, Java Authentication and Authorization Service (JAAS), Java Transaction API (JTA), JavaMail (which uses JAF), Java API for XML Processing (JAXP), JDBC, Java API for XML-Based RPC (JAX-RPC), and the Connector architecture.

The Web container: The Web container provides interception for requests sent over Hypertext Transfer Protocol (HTTP), File Transfer Protocol (FTP), Simple Mail Transfer Protocol (SMTP), and other protocols. Most Web containers support only HTTP(S), but they could support a broader range of protocols if they so choose. The Web application container allows JSP pages and servlets to have access to the same resources as the EJB container provides.

The application client container: An application client container provides request-level interception for stand-alone Java applications. These applications run remotely, in a different Java virtual machine (JVM) from than in which the Web container and EJB container operate.

A program running in an application client container is similar to a Java program with a `main()` method. However, instead of the application being controlled by a JVM, a wrapper controls the program. This wrapper is the application client container. Application client containers are a new concept in the J2EE specification and should be provided by your application server provider.

An application client container can optimize access to a Web container and EJB container through using direct authentication, performing load balancing, allowing failover routines, providing access to server-side environment variables, and properly propagating transaction contexts.

Programs that run within an application client container have access to JAXP, JDBC, JMS, and JAAS resources on a remote application server.

The applet container: An applet container is a special type of container that provides request-level interception for Java programs running within a browser. An important point to remember is that an applet container doesn't provide access to any additional resources such as JDBC or JMS.

Applets running within an applet container are expected to make requests for resources directly to an application server (as opposed to making the request to the container and letting the container ask the application server). The EJB specification doesn't regulate how an applet should communicate with an EJB container, but the J2EE specification does. The J2EE specification requires that applets that want to directly use an EJB must use the HTTP(S) protocol and tunnel Remote Method Invocation (RMI) invocations. Many application server vendors support a form of HTTP tunneling to allow for this.

The components that can be packaged into a J2EE EAR file don't directly correlate to those components that contain containers. No basic requirements exist for what must minimally be included into an EAR file. An EAR file is composed of any number of the following components:

EJB application JAR files: An EJB application's Java archive (JAR) file contains one or more EJBs.

Web application WAR files: A Web archive (WAR) file contains a single Web application. As an EAR file can contain multiple Web applications, each Web application in an EAR file must have a unique deployment context. The deployment mechanism for EAR files allows just such a specification of different contexts.

Application client JAR files: The application client JAR file contains a single, stand-alone Java application that's intended to run within an application client container. The application client JAR file contains a specialized deployment descriptor and is composed similarly to the way an EJB JAR file is composed.

The JAR file contains the classes required to run the stand-alone client, in addition to any client libraries needed to access JDBC, JMS, JAXP, JAAS, JAX-RPC, or an EJB client.

Resource adapter RAR files: The resource adapter archive (RAR) file contains Java classes and native libraries required to implement a JCA resource adapter to an enterprise information system.

Resource adapters don't execute within a container. Rather, they're designed to execute as a bridge between an application server and an external enterprise information system.

Each of these components are developed and packaged individually apart from the J2EE EAR file and own deployment descriptor. A J2EE EAR file is a combination of one or more of these components in a unified package with a custom deployment descriptor.

Application Deployment Descriptor

As explained earlier, J2EE applications are packages of EAR files. An EAR file can contain EJB JAR files, WAR files, RAR files, application client JAR files, and any other JAR files that contain utility classes. Deployable modules such as EJBs, Web components, resource adapters, and application clients have their own module-level deployment descriptors. In addition to this, the EAR file should have its own deployment descriptor called `application.xml` in the `META-INF` directory. This file contains descriptions about the various modules available in the EAR file. Figure 17-3 shows the structure of this file.

The various elements in the EAR deployment descriptor happen as follows:

1. The `<application>` tag declares an enterprise application. The `<application>` tag can contain `<icon>`, `<display-name>`, and `<description>` tags for use by a deployment tool to provide descriptive information about the application. The content of these tags is the same as the content for the same tags in EJB, Web application, and resource adapter deployment descriptors.

2. Each J2EE module included in the enterprise application must have an equivalent `<module>` tag describing the module. EJBs are described using the `<ejb>` tag, Web applications are described using the `<web>` tag, resource adapters are described using the `<connector>` tag, and application client programs are described using the `<java>` tag. With the exception of the `<web>` tag, the content of the other tags is a relative uniform resource indicator (URI) that names the file that contains the J2EE module within the EAR file. The URI must be relative to the root of the EAR file.

3. If your enterprise application contains a Web application J2EE module, you need to provide a <web-uri> tag and a <context-root> tag. The <web-uri> tag is a relative URI that names the file that contains the J2EE module within the EAR file. This is the same type of URI that's specified for the <ejb>, <connector>, and <java> tags. The <context-root> tag specifies the name of the context under which the Web application will run. Subsequently, all requests for JSP pages and servlets for that Web application must be preceded by this Web context. For example, if you deploy a Web application with the following:

   ```
   <context-root>web1</context-root>
   ```

   then all HTTP requests for JSP pages and servlets will always be preceded with the following:

   ```
   http://host:port/web1/<AsSpecifiedInServletSpec>
   ```

   Each Web application packaged within the EAR file must have a unique <context-root> value. Two Web applications packaged in the same EAR file can't have identical <context-root> values. If there's only one Web application in the EAR file, the value of <context-root> may be an empty string.

Listing 17-1 shows the content of an application deployment descriptor.

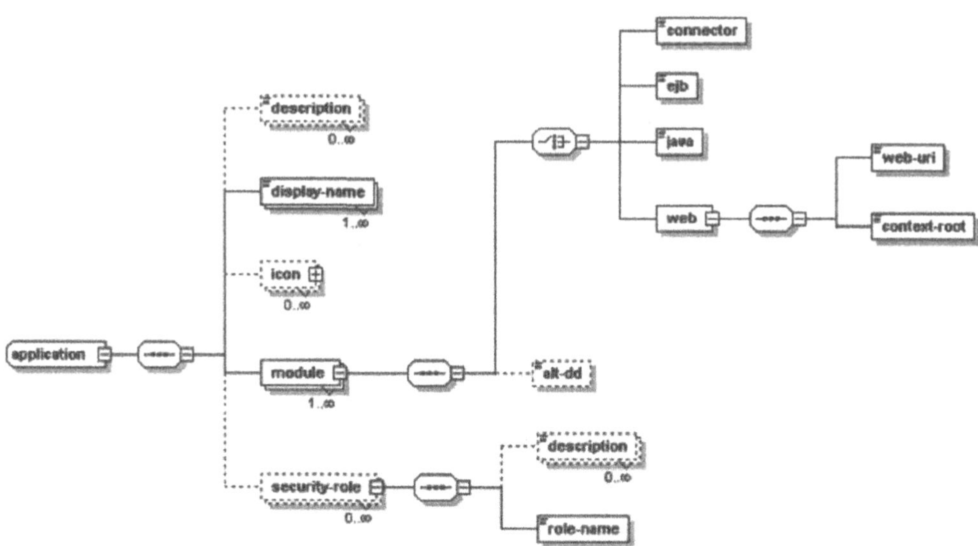

Figure 17-3. Structure of the EAR deployment descriptor

Listing 17-1. Application Deployment Descriptor

```
<?xml version="1.0" encoding="UTF-8"?>

<!DOCTYPE application PUBLIC '-//Sun Microsystems, Inc.//DTD J2EE Application
1.4//EN' 'http://java.sun.com/dtd/application_1_4.dtd'>

<application>
  <display-name>Acme Auction</display-name>
  <description>Application description</description>
  <module>
    <ejb>entities-ejb.jar</ejb>
  </module>
  <module>
    <ejb>signon-ejb.jar</ejb>
  </module>
  <module>
    <ejb>customer-ejb.jar</ejb>
  </module>
  <module>
    <ejb>offer-ejb.jar</ejb>
  </module>
   <module>
    <web>
      <web-uri>auction.war</web-uri>
      <context-root>auction</context-root>
    </web>
  </module>
  <module>
    <ejb>message-ejb.jar</ejb>
  </module>
</application>
```

The contents of the EAR file in Listing 17-1 are as follows:

```
/META-INF/application.xml
/entities-ejb.jar
/signon-ejb.jar
/customer-ejb.jar
/offer-ejb.jar
/auction.war
/message-ejb.jar
```

NOTE *In addition to the standard J2EE modules, the EAR file can contain any supporting JAR files containing utility classes that are common to the modules. The modules don't need to be stored in the root of the EAR; they can be in subfolders. You can build EAR files using deployment and configuration tools provided by the vendors. However, most of the large-scale, modern enterprise projects rely on automated version control extract, compile, build, deploy, and test cycles. These projects may use custom Ant build files driven by build managers such as Anthill or CruiseControl.*

Optional Deployment Descriptor Tags

You can use two optional deployment descriptor tags in certain scenarios: `<alt-dd>` and `<security-role>`.

`<alt-dd>` is a subtag of `<module>`. The value of this tag is a URI that points to another deployment descriptor file for the module referenced from the root of the EAR file. The file doesn't have to be named the same as it's named inside the J2EE module. For example, all EJB module deployment descriptors must be named `ejb-jar.xml`. The value of this tag can be a file named other than `ejb-jar.xml` if it's referencing an alternative deployment descriptor for an EJB module.

The deployment descriptor file will override the one contained within the J2EE module. This is a type of postassembly deployment descriptor. You can use this tag to reference an external version of the deployment descriptor that should be used if a deployer wants to use a deployment descriptor that's different from the one contained within an EJB, a Web application, a resource adapter, or an application client module. If this value isn't specified, then the deployment tool must use the values specified within the JAR, WAR, or RAR files provided in the EAR file. For example, to specify a Web application with an external, alternative deployment descriptor that's located at the root of the EAR file, you'd write the following:

```
<module>
  <web>
    <web-uri>web.war</web-uri>
    <context-root>web</context-root>
  </web>
  <alt-dd>external-web.xml</alt-dd>
</module>
```

`<security-role>` allows the deployer to specify application-level security roles that should be used for all J2EE modules contained within the EAR file. If an EAR file contains multiple EJB modules and/or multiple Web application modules, each of those modules may have its own security roles defined within it. One of the deployer's responsibilities is to ensure that the names of all security roles contained within all J2EE modules are unique and have meaning for the application as a whole. Security roles can be "pulled up" from the J2EE module level to the enterprise application level and included in this tag. If there's a duplicate security role value in one of the J2EE modules, that value can be removed if the value is provided at the enterprise application level.

This tag requires a `<role-name>` subtag to actually provide the symbolic name of the security role. An example of configuring a `<security-role>` tag is as follows:

```
<security-role>
  <description>
    This is administrator's security role
  </description>
  <role-name>Administrator</role-name>
</security-role>
```

Issues with the Ordering of Modules

The J2EE specification doesn't make any specifications for how J2EE modules contained within an EAR file should be deployed. In particular, the order in which modules must be deployed isn't explicitly outlined in the specification. This can be an issue if a component in one module needs to use another component in another module that has yet to be deployed.

Most application servers will deploy EAR files using the same approach:

1. All resource adapters contained within the EAR file will be deployed into the connector infrastructure. If multiple resource adapters are configured, they'll be deployed in the order they're listed in the `application.xml` deployment descriptor.
2. All EJB modules will be deployed. EJBs are deployed after resource adapters since EJBs may use a particular resource adapter during their initialization stage. If multiple EJB modules are configured, they will be deployed in the order they're listed in the `application.xml` deployment descriptor.
3. All Web application modules will be deployed. Web applications are deployed after EJBs and resource adapters since Web applications may use these resources during their initialization stage. If multiple Web application modules are configured, they'll be deployed in the order they're listed in the `application.xml` deployment descriptor.

Configuring a Component's Environment

As explained earlier, one of the real strengths of J2EE is how you can configure the behavior of application components without changing the component code. Altering the application behavior by changing the deployment descriptors does this. One of the key areas that's used for configuring a component's behavior is its naming environment. The naming environment allows you to make configurable properties and references available to your component that the component can access through standard Java Naming and Directory Interface (JNDI) calls.

All the J2EE Web and EJB components can access their naming environments through the JNDI context `java:comp/env`. The following snippet shows how a component can access its naming environment:

```
Context ctx = new InitialContext();
Context envCtx = (Context)ctx.lookup("java:comp/env");
```

> **NOTE** *Even though components can look up objects that are bound in their naming environment, they aren't allowed to alter objects or bind them to their naming environments. If a component tries to do so, the container will throw a JNDI* `OperationNotSupportedException`.

Component providers can use the naming environment for the following purposes:

- Looking up simple properties
- Looking up remote and local EJB references that are used by the components
- Looking up resource factory references such as URL connection factories, JDBC data sources, mail sessions, JMS connection factories, and other JCA managed connection factories
- Looking up resource environment references such as JMS destinations
- Message linking

NOTE *Even though a component provider can hard-code the real JNDI names of the object references that are looked up, it isn't a recommended approach. This is because at the time of writing the component the component provider may not have any control or knowledge over the operational environment in which the component will be deployed. J2EE deployment descriptors allow component providers to define coded names in the deployment descriptor and use those coded names for looking up references. These coded names are mapped to real JNDI names in the operational environment by the deployer using container-specific tools and deployment descriptors. During deployment the container will make the coded names available in the component's naming environment.*

Environment Entries

You can use environmental entries for defining properties that are passed to the component through its environment naming context (ENC). They're used for defining those properties that may have to be modified during deployment and hence can't be hard-coded within the component. For example, you're writing a generic EJB component that can be used by auction applications for evaluating the bids submitted by customers. Different auction organizations have different policies for charging. Hence, it wouldn't be a good idea to hard-code the percentage that's charged within the bean. The component provider can instead define an environment entry and access it through the bean's naming context. Deployers can alter the value of this entry during deployment, if they want.

You can define environment entries for both EJB and Web components using the `ejb-jar.xml` and `web.xml` files, respectively. You do this using the `env-entry` element in the deployment descriptor. Figure 17-4 shows the structure of this element.

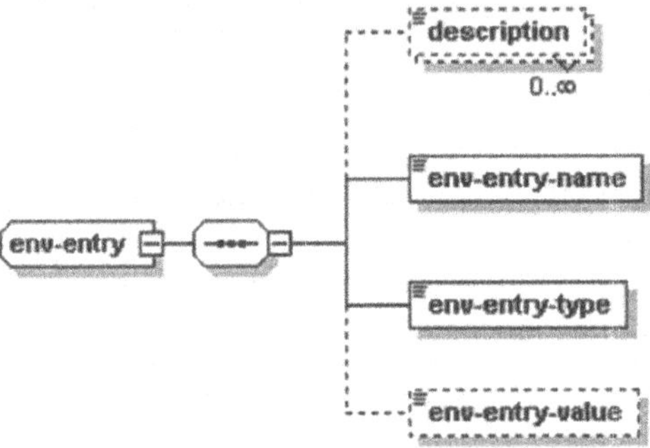

Figure 17-4. Structure of the env-entry *element*

A bean or a Web component can have any number of environment entries. For Web applications, the env-entry elements are defined as the immediate children of the root web-app element. For EJBs, these are defined at bean level as immediate children of entity, message-driven, or session elements.

- The env-entry-name element defines the coded name by which the component accesses the environment entry.
- The env-entry-type element defines the type of the entry. This is the type of the object that's returned by the JNDI lookup. The possible values are Boolean, Byte, Character, Double, Float, Integer, Long, Short, and String.
- The optional env-entry-value element defines the value for the element. The value can be defined either the component provider, application assembler, or deployer.

The following snippet shows how environment entries are defined:

```
<session>
   .....................
      <env-entry>
        <env-entry-name>interval</env-entry-name>
        <env-entry-type>java.lang.Long</env-entry-type>
        <env-entry-value>30000</env-entry-value>
      </env-entry>
   .....................
</session>
```

NOTE *The value defined using the* env-entry *element should be compatible to the type defined using* env-entry-type.

The following code shows how to access the environment entry from the component:

```
Context ctx = new InitialContext();
Context envCtx = (Context)ctx.lookup("java:comp/env");
Long auctionExpiry = (Float)envCtx.lookup("interval");
```

> **NOTE** *Environment entries are scoped local to the component. Component instances of same type can access the environment entries configured in their deployment descriptors. However, components of different types can't access them.*

EJB References

EJB references allow component developers to access the home objects of local and remote EJBs using logical names. These logical names are resolved to real EJBs either by the application assemblers or deployers. The deployers can link the EJB reference to another EJB in the same application using the standard deployment descriptor or to EJBs in a different application using container-specific deployment descriptors.

Both Web components and EJB components can use EJB references. Web components use `ejb-ref` and `ejb-local-ref` elements as immediate children of the `web-app` element to define references to remote and local EJBs, respectively. EJB components use the same elements to define EJB references; however, the references scoped for individual beans are defined as immediate children of `entity`, `message-driven`, or `session` elements. Figure 17-5 shows the structure of the `ejb-ref` and `ejb-local-ref` elements.

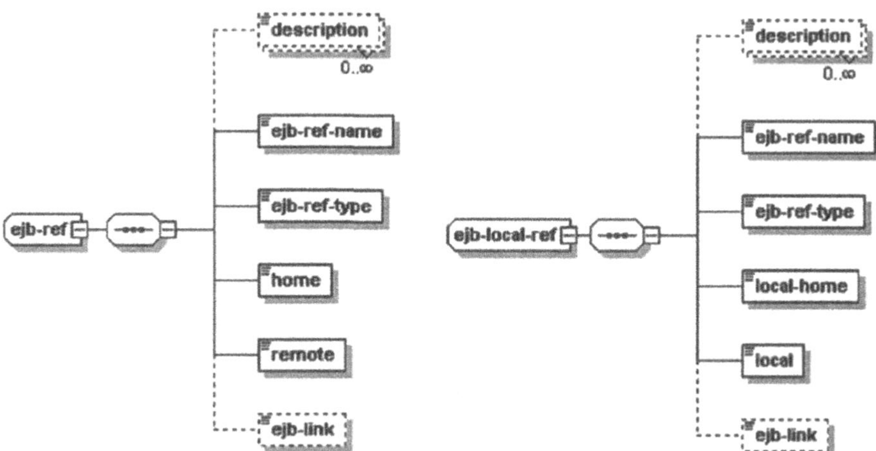

Figure 17-5. Structure of the `ejb-ref` *and* `ejb-local-ref` *elements*

The elements used for defining EJB references are as follows:

- The `ejb-ref-name` element defines the coded name the components will use to look up the referred EJB's home object.
- The `ejb-ref-type` element can be `Session` or `Entity` to identify whether the referred EJB is a session or an entity bean.
- The `home` and `local-home` elements define the fully qualified name of remote or local home interfaces, respectively.
- The `remote` and `local` elements define the fully qualified name of remote or local component interfaces, respectively.
- The `ejb-link` is optionally used to link the logical name to an EJB in the same application.

The following example shows how a session bean refers to another session bean:

```
<session>
  .....................
  <ejb-ref>
    <ejb-ref-name>ejb/offerController</ejb-ref-name>
    <ejb-ref-type>session</ejb-ref-type>
    <home>com.apress.auction.offer.client.OfferControllerHome</home>
    <remote>com.apress.auction.offer.client.OfferController</remote>
  </ejb-ref>
  .....................
</session>
```

You can look up the previous EJB by the name `java:comp/env/ejb/offerController`.

> **NOTE** *It's recommended to define EJB references under the subcontext* `ejb`.

Resolving References

The application assembler or the deployer resolves EJB references. If the referred EJB is in the same application as the referring EJB, the application assembler can resolve the reference using the `ejb-link` element (see Listing 17-2).

Listing 17-2. EJB Reference

```
<session>
  ....................
  <ejb-ref>
    <ejb-ref-name>ejb/offerController</ejb-ref-name>
    <ejb-ref-type>session</ejb-ref-type>
    <home>com.apress.auction.offer.client.OfferControllerHome</home>
    <remote>com.apress.auction.offer.client.OfferController</remote>
    <ejb-link>OfferController</ejb-link>
  </ejb-ref>
  ....................
</session>
```

Listing 17-2 links the reference to an EJB whose `ejb-name` value is `OfferController` in its deployment descriptor. The EJB should be in the same application as the referring component. If the referring component is an EJB and the referred EJB is in the same module (shares the same deployment descriptor), it's safe to assume that the EJB names are unique. However, with the previous approach, if the referring and referred EJBs are across different modules in the same application, a drawback is that you need to make sure that the EJB name is unique across all the modules in the same application. To avoid this the J2EE specification provides an alternative scheme for providing EJB links, as shown in Listing 17-3.

> **NOTE** *This isn't an issue if the referred component is local, as local components are required to be in the same application as the referring component.*

Listing 17-3. EJB Reference

```
<session>
  ....................
  <ejb-ref>
    <ejb-ref-name>ejb/courseController</ejb-ref-name>
    <ejb-ref-type>session</ejb-ref-type>
    <home>com.apress.ta.course.session.CourseControllerHome</home>
    <remote>com.apress.ta.course.session.CourseController</remote>
    <ejb-link>../offer-ejb.jar#OfferController</ejb-link>
  </ejb-ref>
  ....................
</session>
```

Listing 17-3 links the reference by specifying the relative URI of the referred EJB's JAR file in the enterprise application followed by # and the EJB name. In the previous example, the `OfferController` is assumed to be in the `offer-ejb.jar` file at the same location as the referring component.

> **NOTE** *EJB names are required to be unique within a JAR file.*

However, if the referred EJB isn't in the same application as the referring component, the deployer has the responsibility to resolve the reference using container-specific tools and deployment descriptors. For example, in the reference implementation, you do this using the `ejb-ref` element available for EJBs and Web components in the reference implementation RI–specific deployment descriptor. This element maps the coded name of the referred EJB to the actual JNDI name in the operational environment in which the referring component is deployed. Listing 17-4 shows an example.

Listing 17-4. Mapping EJB Reference in RI

```
<j2ee-ri-specific-information>
  .....................
  <enterprise-beans>
    .....................
    <ejb>
      <ejb-name>SomeOtherBean</ejb-name>
      .....................
       <ejb-ref>
         <ejb-ref-name>ejb/offer</ejb-ref-name>
         <jndi-name>OfferController</jndi-name>
       </ejb-ref>
      .....................
    </ejb>
    .....................
  </enterprise-beans>
  .....................
</j2ee-ri-specific-information>
```

In Listing 17-4 the referred bean is bound to the JNDI name `OfferController` in the operational environment.

> **NOTE** *J2EE doesn't provide a standard mechanism for defining JNDI names to which EJB home objects are bound. This is often done using container-specific deployment descriptors. Most of the containers use the EJB name to bind the home object in the JNDI namespace, if an explicit JNDI name isn't specified.*

Resource Factory References

Resource factory references serve the same purpose for defining resource factories in a component's environment as EJB references do for defining EJB home object references. Resource factories are used for creating connections to managed resources. Managed resources include JDBC connections, JMS connections, URL connections, and so on. Resource factories include JDBC data sources, JMS connection factories, URL connection factories, mail sessions, and custom JCA managed connection factories. The component developers use logical names in their code to look up resource factory references. It's the responsibility of the deployers to link these logical names to real JNDI names to which the resource factory references are bound in the operational environment.

You define resource factory references using the `resource-ref` element in the deployment descriptors for the Web and EJB components. For Web components, this element is defined as an immediate child of the `web-app` element, and for EJBs they're scoped at bean level and defined as the immediate children of `entity`, `message-driven`, and `session` elements. Figure 17-6 shows the structure of this element.

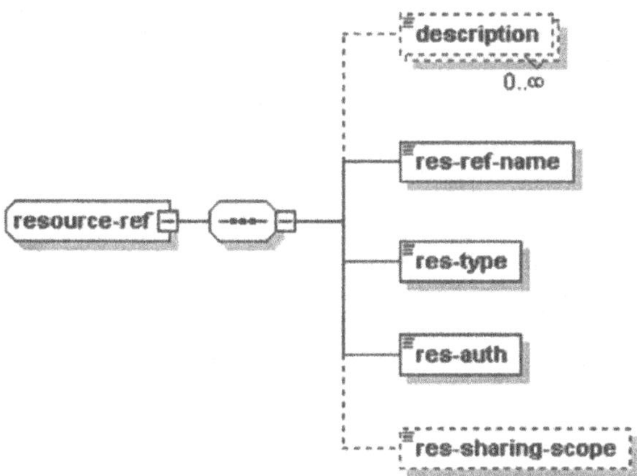

Figure 17-6. Structure of the `resource-ref` *element*

The elements used for defining resource factory references are as follows:

The `res-ref-name` defines the name by which the component looks up the resource factory from its naming environment. It's recommended to use `jdbc`, `jms`, `url`, and `mail` subcontexts for data sources, JMS connection factories, URL connection factories, and mail connection factories, respectively.

The `res-type` element defines the fully qualified class name of the connection factory.

The `res-auth` element can be either `Application` or `Container` to indicate whether the application or container performs the authentication. For example, if you're using data sources and you have set the authentication to `Container`, after looking up the data source you can call the `getConnection()` method to get the connection. However, if the authentication is set to `Application`, you should call the `getConnection(user, passwd)` method. If authentication is set to `Container`, the deployer should configure the connection factory by specifying the credentials to the resource manager in a container-specific way.

The res-sharing-scope can be either Shareable or Unshareable to indicate that the managed connections created using the resource factory can be shared with other components that use references to the same resource factory in the same transaction. Sharing resources can improve performance, and the container can implement local transaction optimizations.

The following snippet shows an example of defining resource factory references:

```
<resource-ref>
  <res-ref-name>jdbc/auctionDS</res-ref-name>
  <res-type>javax.sql.DataSource</res-ref-type>
  <res-auth>Container</res-auth>
</resource-ref>
```

You can look up the data source from the component's environment by the JNDI name java:comp/env/jdbc/auctionDS.

Resolving References

It's the responsibility of the deployer to link the logical names used by the component developers to real JNDI names of connection factories configured in the operational environment. The deployer uses container-specific deployment descriptors and tools to perform this mapping. System administrators normally configure the resource factory references. The J2EE RI, for example, uses the container-specific deployment descriptor as shown in Listing 17-5 to perform this mapping.

Listing 17-5. Resolving Refernces in J2EE RI

```
<j2ee-ri-specific-information>
  .....................
  <enterprise-beans>
    .....................
    <ejb>
      <ejb-name>OfferControllerBean</ejb-name>
      .....................
       <resource-ref>
         <res-ref-name>jdbc/auctionDS</res-ref-name>
         <jndi-name>oracle/AuctionDataSource</jndi-name>
       </resource-ref>
      .....................
    </ejb>
    .....................
  </enterprise-beans>
  .....................
</j2ee-ri-specific-information>
```

Resource Environment References

Components use resource environment references to refer to administered objects associated with the resources using logical names. Administered objects include JMS queues, topics, and so on. It's the responsibility of the system administrators to make the actual administered objects configured in the operational environments, and it's the deployers' responsibility to link the logical names used by components to the real JNDI names.

Resource environment references are defined using the `resource-env-ref` element in the deployment descriptors for the Web and EJB components. For Web components this element is defined as an immediate child of the `web-app` element, and for EJBs they're scoped at bean level and defined as the immediate children of `entity`, `message-driven`, and `session` elements. Figure 17-7 shows the structure of this element.

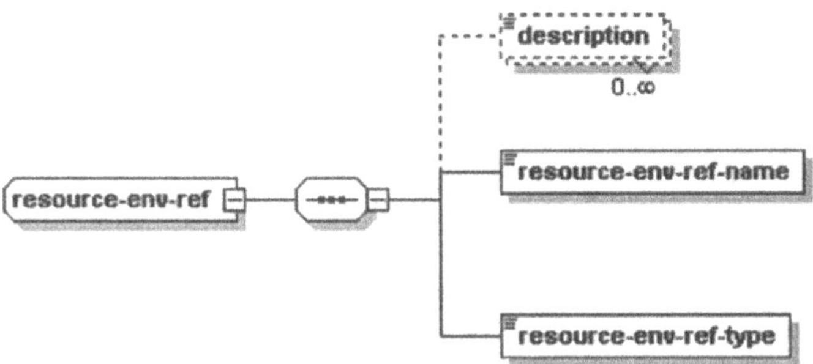

Figure 17-7. Structure of the `resource-env-ref` *element*

The elements used for defining resource environment references are as follows:

- The `res-env-ref-name` defines the name by which the component looks up the resource factory from its naming environment. It's recommended to use the `jms` subcontext for JMS destinations.
- The `res-env-ref-type` element defines the fully qualified class name of the administered object.

The following snippet shows an example of defining resource environment references:

```
<resource-env-ref>
  <res-env-ref-name>jms/bidQueue</res-env-ref-name>
  <res-env-ref-type>javax.jms.Queue</res-env-ref-type>
</resource-env-ref>
```

You can look up the queue from the component's environment by the JNDI name `java:comp/env/jms/bidQueue`.

Resolving References

It's the responsibility of the deployer to link the logical names used by the component developers to real JNDI names of the administered objects configured in the operational environment. The deployer uses container-specific deployment descriptors and tools to perform this mapping. System administrators normally configure the administered object. The J2EE RI, for example, uses the container-specific deployment descriptor as shown in Listing 17-6 to perform this mapping.

Listing 17-6. Resource Environment References in J2EE RI

```
<j2ee-ri-specific-information>
  .....................
  <enterprise-beans>
    .....................
    <ejb>
      <ejb-name>OfferControllerBean</ejb-name>
      .....................
      <resource-env-ref>
        <res-env-ref-name>jms/bidQueue</res-env-ref-name>
        <jndi-name>bidQueue</jndi-name>
      </resource-env-ref>
      .....................
    </ejb>
    .....................
  </enterprise-beans>
  .....................
</j2ee-ri-specific-information>
```

In Listing 17-6 the referred topic is bound to the JNDI name `bidQueue` in the operational environment (application server).

Message Destination Reference

Message destination references are a new feature introduced in J2EE 1.4 that allows you to link components that produce/consume messages to JMS destinations and MDBs in the same application. Chapter 12 covers message destination references in detail.

Resolving Dependencies

A J2EE server may contain multiple J2EE applications that are deployed as EAR files. Each EAR file will contain multiple modules. You may have utility JAR files that are shared across applications and shared by the modules within the applications. Classes that are shared across applications include Extensible Markup Language (XML) parsers, logging API classes, and so on. These classes are normally included in the server's static classpath so that they're visible to all the applications within the server.

The classes that are shared across the modules in an application include value objects that are exchanged between the various layers of an application, framework type classes that the classes in the various modules depend on, and so on. Even for utility classes for logging, you may want to have different versions for different applications. For example, you may want to use different log4j versions in different applications on the same server. This means the classes loaded by one application shouldn't be visible to those in another applications.

To understand how class dependencies are resolved in J2EE applications, you need a good understanding of how classloaders work in J2EE.

Classloaders in Java

Classes are loaded in Java the first time they're referenced. This could be instantiation using the `new` operator, `Class.forName(...)`, or static access to the class. The responsibility of loading a class is that of a classloader. Java uses a hierarchical delegation-based approach for classloaders. This means classloaders form a pyramid-like structure with the primordial classloader at the top. The primordial classloader is responsible for loading boot classes. This classloader will normally have the extensions classloader as a child that's responsible for loading the installed extensions. This classloader will usually have the system classloader as a child that's responsible for loading the classes in the static classpath. In a J2EE environment the system classloader will have one or more child classloaders, each responsible for loading classes specific to each application. You may even have one or more classloaders associated with a single application, depending on the classloading strategy adopted by your application server.

Classloaders are hierarchical and delegation based in the sense that whenever a classloader is asked to load a class, it checks whether it has already loaded that class. If it hasn't, it asks its parent classloader whether it has loaded it before it loads the class itself. This will go up to the parent classloader until it finds the class definition. Only when not finding the class by traversing up until the primordial classloader will a classloader load a class on its own. Classes loaded by a classloader are visible to all its descendants and not visible to its parents and siblings.

J2EE application servers maintain their own classloaders for each deployed application for a variety of purposes:

- To enable hot deployment
- To implement pass-by-reference semantics for local references
- To control visibility to classes used between applications

NOTE *It's important to understand the classloading strategy adopted by your J2EE server, because it influences heavily how you decide to package your application.*

Classloading Example

To explain the classloading intricacies, say you have the following hypothetical situation. You have an application bundled as an EAR file, with the following components:

- **Framework.jar**: A set of utility classes used by all the modules
- **Value.jar**: Value objects shared by all the layers
- **Session.jar**: Session beans that implement the use cases
- **Entity.jar**: Entity beans implemented as local references
- **Web1.war**: A Web application
- **Web2.war**: Another Web application
- **TagLibrary.jar**: Third-party tag library

Here all JAR files except `TagLibrary.jar` are dependent on `Framework.jar`. `Entity.jar` is dependent on `Framework.jar` and `Value.jar`. `Session.jar` is dependent on `Framework.jar`, `Entity.jar`, and `Value.jar`. `Web1.jar` is dependent on `Framework.jar`, `Session.jar`, `TagLibrary.jar`, and `Value.jar`. `Web2.jar` is dependent on `Framework.jar`, `Session.jar`, and `Value.jar`.

The requirements expected of the classloading mechanism are the following:

- Framework classes should be visible to `session`, `entity`, `value`, and `web` classes without duplicating the classes.
- The value classes should be visible to `session`, `entity`, `web1`, and `web2` classes without duplicating classes.
- The session classes should be visible to `web1` and `web2` classes.
- The tag library classes should be visible only to `web1` classes.
- The entity classes should be visible to `session` classes and should respect the call-by-reference semantics for local references.

Most of the modern J2EE servers provide a separate classloader for Web applications for loading classes from the `WEB-INF/lib` and `Web-INF/classes` directories of the Web application. This means the `web1` application can have the tag library JAR in its `WEB-INF/lib` directory. In a similar way, both `web1` and `web2` could have the `session` classes in their respective `WEB-INF/lib` directory. However, this would mean duplicating the classes. Similarly you need to resolve dependencies between other classes. Resolving these dependencies need a good understanding of your server's classloading mechanisms.

For example, with WebLogic 7.0, when an EJB JAR or WAR is deployed stand-alone it will get its own dynamic classloader. However, when you deploy it as an EAR, an entire hierarchy of classloaders are created depending on the contents of the EAR. For an EAR file an application classloader is responsible for loading all the EJBs in the EAR and any JAR files referenced by the manifests of those EJB JAR files. The "Understanding the Manifest Classpath" section covers manifests in detail. This means the same classloader loads all the EJBs in an EAR. This will solve the issue of pass-by-reference semantics for local references. Each Web application in the EAR gets its own classloader that's a child of the application classloader. This means classes loaded by the application classloader are visible to the Web application classes, and hence you don't need to include the session client views, value objects, and framework classes in the `WEB-INF/classes` or `WEB-INF/lib` directories of the Web applications, as shown in Figure 17-8.

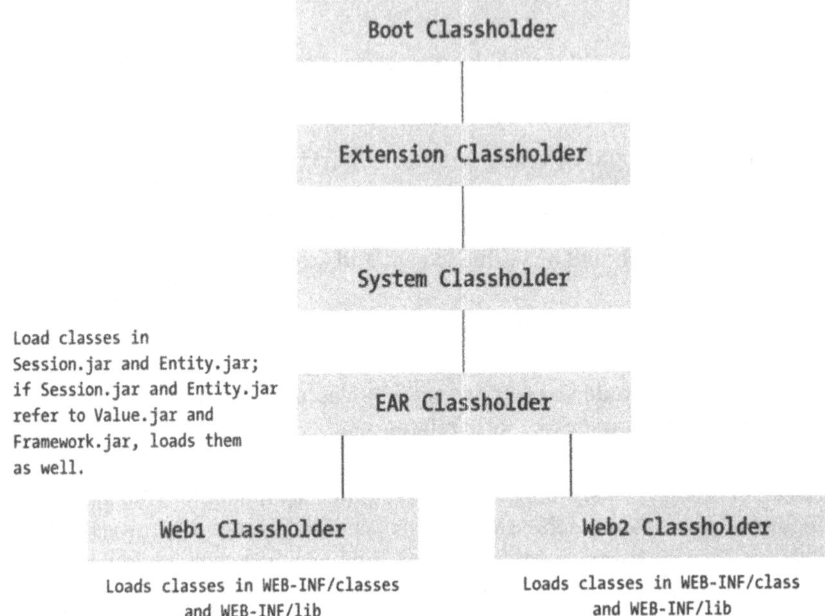

Figure 17-8. Classloading

> **NOTE** *Some ambiguity exists here. The Servlet specification requires the Web application classloader to load the classes from the* `WEB-INF/lib` *and* `WEB-INF/classes` *directories. However, the delegation-based model requires the Web classloader to consult with its parent before loading the classes itself. So what will happen if you have the same classes in the scope of Web application classloader and the parent EAR classloader or one of its ancestors? Most of the Web containers such as Tomcat or Jetty with JBoss allow you to specify this as a configuration option to set which classloader takes precedence.*

Bundled Extensions

With the release of JDK 1.3, Sun Microsystems redefined the "extension mechanism" that's the functionality necessary to support optional packages. The extension mechanism is designed to support the following:

- JAR files can declare their dependency upon other JAR files, allowing an application to consist of multiple modules.
- Classloaders are modified to search optional packages and application paths for classes.

Additionally, the J2EE 1.4 specification mandates that application servers must support the extension mechanism as defined for JAR files. This requires any deployment tool that references a JAR file be capable of loading any optional libraries defined through the extension mechanism. It also implies that if an application server or deployment tool supports runtime undeployment and redeployment of EJB applications that use libraries via the extension mechanism, then that tool or application server must also support undeployment and redeployment of any dependent libraries.

Web applications have the freedom of using the extension mechanism or the `WEB-INF\lib` directory when specifying a dependency library. As discussed earlier, how a dependency library is loaded can vary depending upon whether the library is specified using the extension mechanism or the `WEB-INF\lib` directory.

Enterprise applications need to repackage any libraries that are needed by the Web application or EJB application as part of the EAR file. Once packaged, the extension mechanism provides a standard way for Web application WAR files and EJB application JAR files to specify which dependency libraries that exist in the enterprise application EAR file are needed.

Understanding the Manifest Classpath

How does the extension mechanism work with EJB applications? A JAR file can reference a dependent JAR file by adding a `Class-Path:` attribute to the manifest file that's contained in every JAR file. The `jar` utility automatically creates a manifest file to place in a JAR file and names it `manifest.mf` by default. This file can be *edited* to include a `Class-Path:` attribute entry in addition to the other entries that already exist in the file. In fact, many EJB packaging tools that are being released by vendors are taking dependency packages into account as part of the packaging process and will automatically create an appropriate `manifest.mf` file that contains a correct `Class-Path:` attribute entry.

For example, if you create an EJB JAR file and modify the `manifest.mf` to include a `Class-Path:` attribute, the container generation utility provided by your application server vendor *must* preserve this entry when it generates a new EJB application file. With WebLogic Server, if you provide an EJB JAR utility that already contains a `Class-Path:` entry in the `manifest.mf` file, the `weblogic.ejbc` utility will preserve this entry when it generates a new EJB application with the container files.

The `Class-Path:` manifest attribute lists the relative URLs to search for utility libraries. The relative URL is always from the component that contains the `Class-Path:` entry (not the root of the EAR file). You can specify multiple URLs in a single `Class-Path:` entry, and a single manifest file can contain multiple `Class-Path:` entries. The general format for a `Class-Path:` entry is as follows:

```
Class-Path: list-of-jar-files-separated-by-spaces
```

For example, the session JAR file could have the following:

```
Class-Path: Framework.jar Value.jar
```

If you use the extension mechanism in a J2SE application, the `Class-Path:` manifest entry can reference directories, too. However, for J2EE applications that are wholly contained within JAR files, the `Class-Path:` manifest entry can reference only other JAR files. Additionally, the `Class-Path:` entry must reside on a separate line apart from other attribute entries in the same manifest file.

Installed Extensions

J2EE components can specify dependency on other JAR files using the `Extension-List` attribute in the manifest file. If the deployment tool is unable to resolve the dependency specified using this manifest attribute, it should fail the deployment of the component. For example, an EAR file can register dependency on an installed extension using the `Extension-List` manifest attribute. Once the deployment tool has resolved the dependency, it should make the installed extension available to all the components within the EAR file. This is useful for writing portable applications that require specific versions of XML parsers, regular expression packages, and so on.

The following example shows how the auction application's EAR file registers it dependency on the Acme' XML parser using the manifest attributes shown below:

```
Extension-List: acmeParser
acmeParser-Extension-Name: com/acme/xml
acmeParser-Extension-Specification-Version: 2.6
```

The contents of the manifest of the installed extension `AcmeXmlParser.jar` are as follows:

```
Extension-Name: com/acme/xml
Specification-Version: 2.6
Specification-Title: XML Parser
Specification-Vendor: Acme Corporation
Implementation-Version: build8976
```

Here the `Extension-Name` manifest attribute of the installed extension should match the name requested (in this case, `acmeParser-Extension-Name`) of the manifest attribute of the component being deployed.

Summary

In this chapter you learned how to package J2EE components. The chapter covered the various component types and the application deployment descriptors. Finally, the chapter showed how to resolve dependencies and classloading issues.

Index

Symbol

B

C

D

H

J

K

L

N

P

Q

R

U

V

X

Printed in the United States
By Bookmasters